1st Edition

Hawaii

by Jocelyn Fujii & Rick Carroll

with Jeanette Foster

Macmillan • USA

ABOUT THE AUTHORS

Kauai-born **Jocelyn Fujii,** a resident of Honolulu, is one of Hawaii's leading journalists. She has authored *Under the Hula Moon: Living in Hawaii* and *The Best of Hawaii* as well as articles for the *New York Times, National Geographic Traveler, Islands, Condé Nast Traveler, Travel Holiday,* and other national and international publications. Jocelyn has now brought her expertise to Frommer's; she covered the dining, shopping, arts, and nightlife scenes on each of the Hawaiian islands for this book.

Rick Carroll reported on accommodations, outdoor activities, and sightseeing in the islands, and contributed all of the trip-planning information and chapter introductions to this book. A former journalist with the *San Francisco Chronicle,* he bought a one-way ticket to Hawaii in 1983. He later covered Hawaii and the Pacific as a special correspondent for UPI, and received the Lowell Thomas Award from the Society of American Travel Writers for his photojournalism. The author of *Great Outdoor Adventures of Hawaii* and *Frommer's Best Beach Vacations: Hawaii* and a contributing editor to *Aloha: The Magazine of Hawaii and the Pacific,* he lives and writes at Oahu's Lanikai Beach.

A resident of the Big Island, **Jeanette Foster** is a prolific writer widely published in travel, sports, and adventure magazines. In addition to reporting on the natural world and outdoor activities for this book, she has contributed to numerous other travel guides, including *Frommer's Hawaii from $60 a Day.*

MACMILLAN TRAVEL

A Simon & Schuster Macmillan Company
1633 Broadway
New York, NY 10019

Find us online at **http://www.mgr.com/travel**
or on America Online at Keyword: **Frommer's.**

ISBN 0-02-860895-X
ISSN 1090-3180

Editor: Cheryl Farr
Thanks to Bill Goodwin, Suzanne Roe, and Tracy McNamara
Production Editor: Whitney K. Ward
Digital Cartography: Raffaele DeGennaro and Ortelius Design
Design by Michele Laseau
Maps © by Simon & Schuster, Inc.

SPECIAL SALES

Bulk purchases (10+ copies) of Frommer's Travel Guides and selected Macmillan travel guides are available to corporations, organizations, mail-order catalogs, institutions, and charities at special discounts, and can be customized to suit individual needs. For more information write to: Special Sales, 1633 Broadway, New York, NY 10019.

Manufactured in the United States of America

Contents

7   Maui, the Valley Isle   276

List of Maps

AN INVITATION TO THE READER

In researching this book, we discovered many wonderful places—hotels, restaurants, shops, and more. We're sure you'll find others. Please tell us about them, so we can share the information with your fellow travelers in upcoming editions. If you were disappointed with a recommendation, we'd love to know that, too. Please write to:

Frommer's Hawaii, 1st Edition
Macmillan Travel
1633 Broadway
New York, NY 10019

AN ADDITIONAL NOTE

Please be advised that travel information is subject to change at any time—and this is especially true of prices. We therefore suggest that you write or call ahead for confirmation when making your travel plans. The authors, editors, and publisher cannot be held responsible for the experiences of readers while traveling. Your safety is important to us, however, so we encourage you to stay alert and be aware of your surroundings. Keep a close eye on cameras, purses, and wallets, all favorite targets of thieves and pickpockets.

WHAT THE SYMBOLS MEAN

✪ Frommer's Favorites

Hotels, restaurants, attractions, and entertainment you should not miss.

ⓢ Super-Special Values

Hotels and restaurants that offer great value for your money.

The following abbreviations are used for credit cards:

AE	American Express	EU	Eurocard
CB	Carte Blanche	JCB	Japan Credit Bank
DC	Diners Club	MC	MasterCard
DISC	Discover	V	Visa
ER	enRoute		

The Best of Hawaii

Hawaii is an exceptional place. The islands brim with superlatives, from America's best beaches to world-class resorts; and there's more than enough to see and do here to keep you busy for a lifetime, let alone a short vacation. It can be bewildering to plan your trip with so many options vying for your attention. To make your task easier, we've chosen what we believe to be the very best that Hawaii has to offer—the places and experiences you won't want to miss.

1 The Best Beaches

by Rick Carroll

No doubt about it—Hawaii is where you'll find the best beaches in the United States. They come in a rainbow of sizes, textures, and colors—Hawaii's sands are black, red, green, gold, sometimes even white. Here are our favorites:

- **Lanikai Beach** (Oahu): With golden sand that's soft as talcum powder and two islands set in a turquoise lagoon, this one's simply too gorgeous to be real. Its giant saltwater pool with gentle waves is one of Hawaii's safest swimming places; the mile-long beach, on Oahu's windward coast, is also perfect for walking or catching rays. Lanikai ("heavenly sea") was recently named "best in the nation" by "Dr. Beach," marine geologist Dr. Stephen Leatherman of the University of Maryland Coastal Laboratory. You don't need a Ph.D. to see why. See Chapter 5.

- **Hapuna Beach** (Big Island): The biggest beach on the Big Island, Hapuna is broad, flat, golden, and more than a half-mile long. The island's most popular beach slopes gently into the water with a sandy bottom. Summer swells are perfect to play in, but winter waves may be too rough for most. The best place to snorkel is an almost-secret cove full of tropical fish in the lee of the black lava point nearest the Hapuna Prince Hotel. See Chapter 6.

- **Kapalua Beach** (Maui): On an island with many great beaches, Kapalua takes the prize. It's a postcard-perfect beach no matter how you look at it: Golden, palm-fringed, and sheltered by black lava points, this gorgeous beach is a marine preserve full of tropical fish, sea turtles, and delighted beachgoers. See Chapter 7.

- **Hulopoe Beach** (Lanai): Palm-fringed, gold-sand Hulopoe is a great place to swim, snorkel, or just slosh about in the waves;

even spinner dolphins love to splash in the surf here. This great sheltered marine preserve has tide pools safe enough for the kids to swim in. See Chapter 9.

- **Mahaulepu Beach** (Kauai): Mahaulepu is the best-looking unspoiled beach on Kauai, possibly in the whole state. Two miles of reddish-gold sand, it sits on the southeastern shore of the island at the foot of 1,500-foot-high Haupu Ridge, just beyond the Hyatt Regency Poipu and sugar cane fields that end in sand dunes. It's almost untouched by the 20th century—two Hawaiian boys were casting fishnets the last time I was there. A great escape from the real world. See Chapter 10.

2 The Best Travel Experiences

by Rick Carroll

Good times in Hawaii are easy to find; it's the best times you never forget. They simply happen. It's all timing and luck; some call it serendipity. You discover something you never knew existed. Or the moment finds you—a new taste, a new scent, maybe the way the light falls just so—and brings on a burst of clarity that takes you to a new level. Hawaii is full of these moments. It's as simple as coming face to face with your first green sea turtle in Kapalua Bay. Or showering under the Kalalau waterfall at sunset. Or snorkeling a virgin lagoon on private Niihau. I can only give you a hint of where to go and what to look for—the rest is up to you.

- **Stay in Historic Hotels & B&Bs:** Luxury resorts are spectacular places to kick back, but the real Hawaii lies beyond their gates. Go, explore. Seek out old hotels, historic places like Waikiki's Sheraton Moana Surfrider (Oahu, Chapter 5), Lahaina's Pioneer Inn (Maui, Chapter 7), the Big Island's Volcano House on the rim of Halemaumau crater (Chapter 6), Waimea Plantation Cottages at the foot of Waimea Canyon (Kauai, Chapter 10). Or choose one of the hundreds of new bed-and-breakfasts that have popped up on all the islands to get an idea of what life in Hawaii is really like. One of the best sources of unusual accommodations is **Hawaiian Islands Bed-and-Breakfast and Vacation Rentals** (☎ **800/ 258-7895**), which offers a free brochure with a thumbnail sketch of great places on all the major Hawaiian islands.
- **Visit the National Parks:** Hawaii's national parks are the nation's most unusual. Maui's Haleakala National Park features one of the biggest volcanic craters on earth; it's an otherworldly place that holds the secrets of past millennia. The Big Island's Hawaii Volcanoes National Park, on the other hand, holds the key to the future: At its heart is still-erupting Kilauea volcano, where you can watch nature in action, sculpting the island before your eyes. See the parks. If you have to choose just one, choose Hawaii Volcanoes; it's simply spectacular. See Chapters 6 and 7.
- **Go to the Beach:** A beach is a beach is a beach, right? Not in Hawaii. With 132 islands, shoals, and reefs in the tropical Pacific and a general coastline of 750 miles, Hawaii has beaches in all different sizes, shapes, and colors, from white to black; the variety on the seven inhabited islands is astonishing. You can go to a different beach every day for a decade and still not see them all. And there's one for everyone, whether you're looking for a scene or want to get away from it all. For the best of a spectacular bunch, see "The Best Beaches," above; also see the "Beaches" sections in the individual island chapters.
- **Take a Plunge:** If you go to Hawaii and don't go in the water, you're missing the point. Half your world's off-limits. It's the water that makes Hawaii great. Learn

to windsurf on Oahu's Kailua Bay. Ride an outrigger canoe on a Waikiki wave. Paddle a kayak up Kauai's Huleia River. Sail around the islands on a vintage steamship, like the SS *Independence*. Plunge in a waterfall pool or take a shower under a waterfall. Snorkel Hawaii's fantastic underwater world. Whatever you do in Hawaii, get wet. See "The Active Vacation Planner" in Chapter 3, and "Hitting the Water" in the individual island chapters.

- **Meet Local Folks:** If you go to Hawaii and only see people like those you see back home, you might as well stay home. Extend yourself, leave the resorts and tourist quarters, go out and make a new friend, learn about Hawaii and its people. Just smile and say "owzit?"—which means "how is it?" "It's good," is the usual response—and you'll usually make a new friend. Hawaii is remarkably cosmopolitan; every ethnic group in the world seems to be here. It's delightful to discover the varieties of food, culture, language, and customs. The best place to start meeting strangers is Oahu's Polynesian Cultural Center; see Chapter 5.

- **Take a Hike:** Lush valleys, steep canyons, hidden beaches, tropical rain forests, native birds—it's all there for anyone who sets out off the beaten track, and on foot. All it takes is a day pack, good walking shoes, and a map. Some of the best hikes are found on Oahu's new Maunawili Trail, across the foothills of the Koolau range (Chapter 5); Kauai's famous Kalalau Trail down the Na Pali coast (Chapter 10); and any of the trails across black lava fields of Hawaii Volcanoes National Park (Chapter 6). Many new guided hikes are opening up on private land; one of the best is the guided ecotour sponsored by The Ritz-Carlton, Kapalua into Kahakuloa Valley, on the northwest shore of the West Maui Mountains; see Chapter 7. Also see the Hiking sections in each island chapter.

- **Visit Museums:** Nobody ever wants to go inside a stuffy museum where the outdoors are so spectacular. But the art, history, and culture of Hawaii won't make any sense to you if you don't spend at least a few hours exploring Honolulu's Bishop Museum, Hawaii Maritime Center, Mission Houses Museum (Chapter 5), or other small museums on the outer islands chiefly devoted to the sugar plantation days, whaling, and natural history (see individual island chapters). One of the best is Kokee Natural History Museum on Kauai (Chapter 10), which serves as the gateway to the Alakai Swamp, home to endangered native birds.

3 The Best of Underwater Hawaii

by Rick Carroll

A whole different Hawaii greets anyone with a face mask, snorkel, and fins. Under the sea, you'll find millions of bright tropical fish, thick forests of coral, green sea turtles, slack-jawed moray eels, some serious-looking manta rays, and maybe—but not likely—even a shark (but don't worry, since they're ancestral relatives of Hawaiians, most sharks are friendly). It's a kaleidoscope of color and wonder.

- **Hanauma Bay** (Oahu): I know, it's too crowded, but for clear, warm water, an abundance of fish that are so friendly they'll eat right out of your hand, protection from the open ocean, a beautiful setting, and easy access, there's no place like Hanauma Bay. Just wade in waist-deep and look down to see more than 50 species of reef and inshore fish common to Hawaiian waters. Snorkelers hug the safe, shallow inner bay—it's really like swimming in an outdoor aquarium. Serious divers shoot "the slot," a passage through the reef, to gain Witch's Brew, a turbulent cove. See Chapter 5.

- **Kealakekua Bay** (Big Island): Mile-wide Kealakekua Bay, at the foot of massive U-shaped sea cliffs, is rich with marine life and snorkelers. And history: A white obelisk marks that spot where, in 1778, the great British navigator Capt. James Cook, who charted most of the Pacific, was killed by Hawaiians. The bay itself is a marine sanctuary that teems with schools of polychromatic tropical fish. See Chapter 6.
- **Kapalua Bay** (Maui): Flanked by two black lava points, this marine preserve has an abundance of tropical fish—at least 30 species inhabit the inner bay—and small widely scattered coral colonies along the flanks that make for exceptional snorkeling and underwater fish-spotting. When you come up for a breather, you'll have an impressive view of Molokai across the 8.8-mile Pailolo Channel. See Chapter 7.
- **Molokini** (Maui): Like a crescent moon that fell from the sky, the parenthetical islet of Molokini serves on its shallow concave side as a sheltering backstop against sea currents for tiny tropical fish, and on the opposite side as a deep-water cliff inhabited by spiny lobsters, moray eels, and white-tipped sharks. Neo-snorkelers report to the concave side, experienced scuba divers the other. Either way, the clear water and abundant marine life make this islet off the Makena coast one of Hawaii's most popular dive spots. See Chapter 7.
- **The "Forbidden" Isle of Niihau:** Manta rays, tiger sharks, and Hawaiian tuna loom about Lehua, the tiny island off the coast of Niihau, the private island that's been off-limits for more than a century. You can dive there now, but only in summer and only with Bubbles Below (☎ **808/822-3483),** one of Kauai's best dive operators. This 3-tank trip, for experienced divers only, is the hottest new dive in Hawaii. Divers should be comfortable in strong currents, underwater caverns, and not afraid of sharks. See Chapter 10.

4 The Best Golf Courses

by Rick Carroll

I've played 18 holes at Mauna Kea, hit a few balls at Mauna Lani, and cruised around The Challenge at Koele in a cart just to see what the fuss was all about, and I still prefer snorkeling to golf. So when it comes to this peculiar activity, I always defer to experts like my pal George Fuller, author of *Hawaii Golf: The Complete Guide* and editor of *LINKS: The Best of Golf* magazine. An inveterate golfer, Fuller awards "Best of Golf" trophies to the world's great golf courses each year, including these recent Hawaii winners:

- **Mauna Kea's Beach & Hapuna Courses** (Big Island; ☎ **808/882-7222** for Beach Course, **808/882-1111** for Hapuna Course): Out on the Kohala Coast, the Mauna Kea Beach Course is everyone's old favorite. One of the first fields of play to be carved out of the black lava back, the dramatic, always-challenging par-72, 18-hole championship course is still one of Hawaii's top three. The new Arnold Palmer/Ed Seay–designed Hapuna Course rests in the rolling foothills above Hapuna Beach Prince Hotel and provides a memorable and scenic links-style golf experience and one of the best views of this unusual coast. See Chapter 6.
- **Mauna Lani Resort Courses** (Big Island; ☎ **808/885-6655**): Longtime host of the Senior Skins game, Mauna Lani's two resort golf courses, North and South, feature a combination of oceanfront and interior lava-lined holes. Both combine wonderful scenery with strategic golf, and the Mauna Lani Bay Hotel and Bungalows offer lavish accommodations and great packages for golfers. See Chapter 6 and "The Active Vacation Planner" in Chapter 3.

- **Kapalua Resort Courses** (Maui; ☎ **808/669-8044**): Kapalua is probably the best nationally known golf resort in Hawaii, due to the Lincoln Mercury Kapalua International, played here each November. The Bay Course and the Village Course are vintage Arnold Palmer designs, while the new Plantation Course is a strong Ben Crenshaw/Bill Coore design. All are sited on Maui's windswept northwestern shore, at the rolling foothills of Puu Kukui, the summit of the West Maui Mountains. Kapalua Villas offers great packages. See Chapter 7 and "The Active Vacation Planner" in Chapter 3.
- **Wailea Resort Courses** (Maui; ☎ **808/879-2966**): On the sun-baked south shore of Maui stands Wailea Resort, *the* hot spot for golf in the islands, where three resort courses combine with a string of beachfront hotels. Golf is found at the Blue course (an Arthur Jack Snyder design) and the recently opened Emerald and Gold courses (both by Robert Trent Jones, Jr.). All three boast outstanding views of the Pacific and the mid–Hawaiian Islands. See Chapter 7.
- **The Lanai Courses** (Lanai; ☎ **808/565-GOLF**): For quality and seclusion, nothing in Hawaii can touch Lanai's two golf resort offerings. The Ted Robinson and Greg Norman–designed Experience at Koele and the Challenge at Manele, a wonderful Jack Nicklaus effort with ocean views from every hole, both rate among Hawaii's best courses. Both are tremendous fun to play, with the Experience featuring the par-4 eighth hole, which drops some 150 yards from tee to fairway, and the Challenge boasting the par-three 12th, which plays from one cliff side to another over a Pacific inlet—one of the most stunning holes in Hawaii. See Chapter 9.
- **Poipu Bay Resort Golf Course** (Kauai; ☎ **808/742-8711**): On Kauai's flat, dry south shore is a Robert Trent Jones, Jr.–designed course that skirts along dramatic cliffs above the Pacific. The 210-acre links-style course, host to the PGA Tour's Grand Slam of Golf, runs along sheer ocean cliffs and the sandy beach of Keoneloa Bay and offers azure ocean views at every hole. This course boasts some scenically spectacular holes and is a lot of fun to play. Whales, monk seals, and green sea turtles are often seen along the shore, and a flock of native Hawaiian Nene geese frequents the course's lakes. See Chapter 10.
- **Princeville Golf Club Courses** (Kauai; ☎ **808/826-5000** for Prince Course; **808/826-3580** for Makai Course): You'll find 45 of the best tropical holes of golf in the world here, ranging along green bluffs below sharp mountain peaks and offering stunning views in every direction. Two Robert Trent Jones, Jr. courses, the 27-hole Makai Course and the 18-hole Prince Course, make up the Princeville Golf Club. One of the top three courses in Hawaii, the Prince provides a round of golf few ever forget; it winds along 390 acres of scenic table land bisected by tropical jungles, waterfalls, streams, and ravines. The championship Makai Course, a favorite tournament spot since it opened in 1971, is playable for all levels of golfers. See Chapter 10.

5 The Best Views

by Rick Carroll

Hawaii's full of good-looking lookouts. Here are our favorites:

- **Diamond Head Crater** (Oahu): The view from atop this old 720-foot-tall volcano, famous the world over, stretches from green mountains to aqua sea and reveals Waikiki, nestled on the edge of Mamala Bay, as one of the world's best urban beaches. See Chapter 5.

Impressions

The camera can not do justice, also words are a vain thing. Haleakala has a message of beauty and wonder for the human soul that cannot be delivered by proxy.

—Jack London

- **Nuuanu Pali Lookout** (Oahu): Oahu's best-looking side, the Windward Coast, can be seen in its full natural glory from this gusty perch, set amid jagged jade cliffs that pierce the puffy white clouds that go scudding by. A thousand sheer feet below, the island is a carpet of green that runs to an azure Pacific dotted by tiny offshore islets. See Chapter 5.
- **Puu Ualakaa State Park** (Oahu): This city park offers an easy-to-reach spectacular urban view of Oahu. By day, you can see half the island in a single glance; by night, young lovers park and smooch as Honolulu's city lights twinkle below. See Chapter 5.
- **Mauna Kea** (Big Island): Up here on a lonely pinnacle of lava rock, sometimes under snow and ice in the middle of the tropical Pacific, it's hard to believe that you're in Hawaii. In this anomalous alpine setting stands a dozen domes loaded with big-gauge telescopes, including the mighty Keck, the world's biggest scope, which astronomers use to probe deep space. By night, the field of vision is positively galactic; by day, you gaze down on clouds poked only by the summits of nearby Mauna Loa and Haleakala. See Chapter 6.
- **Waipio Valley Lookout** (Big Island): At road's end on the northern tip of Hawaii Island is one of the state's scenic treasures: Waipio Valley. Many come to stand at the edge and stare down sheer sea cliffs, their eyes drawn along the curving coast and captivated by the waves crashing on the black-sand beach. A great place for a picnic. See Chapter 6.
- **Haleakala Summit** (Maui): On a clear day, from high atop 10,023-foot Haleakala, one of the world's biggest dormant volcanoes, you can see nearly 30 miles across Alenuihaha Channel to majestic, often snowcapped Mauna Kea on the Big Island of Hawaii. Many go right to the top to greet the dawn, but any time is good—sunset's quite extraordinary, too. See Chapter 7.
- **Kalaupapa Lookout** (Molokai): Everyone who plans to ride a mule down the world's steepest seacliffs to Father Damien's old leper colony can get a breathtaking preview by going to the edge of the Kalaupapa Lookout. If you're afraid of heights or just plain don't trust mules, this may be the only look you get at the most spectacular side of Molokai, where fluted emerald cliffs drop almost straight down to a little tongue of old lava that once was a place of exile, and the azure sea beyond. See Chapter 8.
- **Lanaihale Summit** (Lanai): Go on a clear day to the summit of 3,377-foot-high Mount Lanaihale, and you'll see five islands in a single glance: Maui, Molokai, Kahoolawe, Oahu, and the Big Island. You'll see most of Lanai as well on your way up. Take the narrow four-wheel–drive Munro Trail across the razorback spine of Lanai's ancient volcanic caldera, and drive through field and forest to the green, cool summit for this rare view. See Chapter 9.
- **Kalalau Lookout** (Kauai): It's hard to take your eyes off this grand view over the broad amphitheater valley of remote Kalalau, which can only be reached on foot or by sea; the sight of ancient mountain peaks worn to crinkled steeples and clad with vivid green foliage is simply majestic. You may have seen it on magazine covers, postcards, or in travelogues, but nothing can capture that view quite like your own naked eye. See Chapter 10.

6 The Best Luxury Hotels & Resorts

No Hawaiian king or queen ever had it this good. Great luxury resort hotels stand like temples of hedonism on the sea coasts of all the major islands. Here are the top ten:

- **Halekulani** (Oahu; ☎ **800/367-2343**): None finer in all Hawaii—and it's in Waikiki! An oasis of calm amid the buzz, this marble beach hotel is Oahu's only Five Diamond luxury resort. When price is no object, this is really the only place to stay. Even if you don't stay here, pop by for a sunset Mai Tai to hear Sonny Kamehele sing the old hapa-haole tunes of the 1930s and 1940s while a lovely hula girl dances under the old keawe tree. See Chapter 5.
- **Ihilani** (Oahu; ☎ **808/679-0079**): Far away from Waikiki yet close to the heart of Hawaii (not to mention some world-class shopping), this contemporary Mediterranean-inspired hotel and spa on Oahu's Leeward coast stands between five man-made coves and the jade greens of an 18-hole championship golf course. The rooms are bigger than any on Oahu, with private lanais and big ocean views. A fabulous spa attracts the health-and-fitness set, and shoppers delight in the nearby Waikele factory-outlet complex. See Chapter 5.
- **Kona Village** (Big Island; ☎ **808/325-5555**): This is the best place to stay in Hawaii if you seek excellent service in a vintage resort. On 82 coastal acres of palms and tropical flowers, the site of an ancient village, now stands an absolutely peaceful, eclectic Polynesian village, with thatched huts and various styles of Pacific architecture clustered by the blue Pacific. The authentic architecture and isolated setting of this oasis combine to revive wounded urban souls who swing in hammocks, splash like children in the bay, actually smile when spoken to, and move slowly with the calm and grace that comes from great leisure. Trade winds rustle the palms, gentle waves lap ashore. Why anyone ever leaves is a wonder. See Chapter 6.
- **Hapuna Beach Prince Hotel** (Big Island; ☎ **808/880-1111**): Everybody's got a favorite big fancy resort hotel; this is mine. It's the last of the big splendors, the Mauna Kea for the 21st century, a beach hotel like no other. The world's richest man, Yoshiaki Tsutsumi, spent $360 million to create this contemporary vision of luxury designed by Wimberly, Allison, Tong & Goo, the world's best resort architects, who nestled it between the Big Island's best beach and a world-class golf course. Elegant, sophisticated, and refined, it's only two years old, but it looks as if it's been there for decades. Service and food are first rate, and every room, of course, has an ocean view. See Chapter 6.
- **Four Seasons Hualalai** (Big Island; ☎ **808/325-8000**): Outdoor showers, private pools, unimpeded ocean views, excellent food, and a new 18-hole championship golf course—what more can any mortal want? At this new low-impact, high-ticket hideaway under the dormant Hualalai volcano, Four Seasons ups the ante with its residential resort of two-story bungalows clustered around five seaside swimming pools on a black lagoon. This place is pretty showy compared to the humble thatch shelters at nearby Kona Village, but it's a small fry compared to the megaresort originally planned by Japanese investors who downsized when the value of the yen turned south. If you decide to stay here forever, there are oceanfront condos for sale, too, starting at $1.2 million. See Chapter 6.
- **Kea Lani** (Maui; ☎ **808/875-4100**): This Mediterranean fantasy on Maui's sunsoaked Wailea Coast attracts celebrities who hide out in the private bungalows. The architecture is controversial, but the soaring white-domed open-air lobby seems to frame the natural beauty of Maui. Every room is a big, luxurious suite with lots

of extra amenities and wonderful surprises, like milk and cookies at bedtime. Many of the vegetables and herbs served in the open-air restaurants come from the backyard garden. And it has its own nice, albeit small, beach. See Chapter 7.

• **Four Seasons Wailea** (Maui; ☎ **808/874-8000**): This is the ultimate beach hotel for latter-day royals, with excellent cuisine; spacious rooms; gracious service; and Wailea Beach, one of Maui's best gold-sand beaches, out the front door. Every room has at least a partial ocean view from a private lanai. The luxury suites are big as some Honolulu condos, and full of marble and deluxe appointments. Since Four Seasons lured Chef George Mavrothalassitis away from the Halekulani, the hotel's cuisine has improved 150%, especially at Seaside, the outdoor bistro on Wailea Bay. See Chapter 7.

• **Ritz-Carlton, Kapalua** (Maui; ☎ **808/669-6200**): With location, style, and loads of hospitality, this is the best Ritz anywhere. On the coast below the picturesque West Maui Mountains, this breezy grand hotel overlooks the Pacific and Molokai across the channel. The natural setting, on an old coastal pinapple plantation, is a picture of tranquillity. The service is legendary, the golf courses daunting, and the nearby beaches are perfect for snorkeling, diving, and just relaxing. See Chapter 7.

• **The Lodge at Koele** (Lanai; ☎ **808/565-7300**): For old world luxury in an old pineapple plantation town, come to The Lodge. There's nothing else like it in Hawaii: an extravagant inland hotel set amid a misty grove of pines far from any beach. It's like visiting Emile DeBeque's rubber plantation house in the Hollywood film classic *South Pacific*. With giant stone fireplaces, stuffed furniture, and lavishly chintzed rooms, the decor is a bit arrogant for this red dirt island, but appealing nonetheless to big spenders seeking absolute seclusion. If sun, sand, and surf don't top your list of requirements, this sophisticated retreat is the perfect choice. And you can always catch the free shuttle down to Manele Bay for a dip with the spinner dolphins. See Chapter 9.

• **Hyatt Regency Resort and Spa** (Kauai; ☎ **808/742-1234**): This art deco beach hotel recalls Hawaii in the 1920s—before the crash—when gentlemen arrived in blue blazers and ladies in summer frocks, and they came to the islands to learn to surf and play the ukulele. Its architecture and location, on the sunny side of Kauai, make this the island's best holiday hotel. The golden beach is a bit too rough for swimming, but the saltwater swimming pool's the biggest on the island. There's an old-fashioned reading room by the sea with club chairs, billiards, and a bar well stocked with cognac and port; and Tidepools, a thatched-roof seafood restaurant, is a nice touch. Golf, horseback riding, and the shops of Koloa, a boutiqued plantation town, are nearby diversions. See Chapter 10.

7 The Best Moderately Priced Accommodations

by Rick Carroll

You heard about those $3,500-a-night Big Island bungalows and decided not to go to Hawaii this year. Who can blame you? The price of paradise seems out of this world. But you can find great affordable lodging if you know where to book. The best deals in Hawaii can be found in condos, bed-and-breakfasts, and cottages. When was the last time you spent a night in a rain forest? There are even some great regular ol' hotels near the beach that offer some terrific bargains.

• **Outrigger Coral Seas** (Oahu; ☎ **800/688-7444**): This small gem, on a lively Waikiki side street near the beach, is one of the great bargains in the tourist quarter, especially in summer, when a room goes for $60 a night. There's no ocean view, and the rooms aren't grand, but at these prices, the location—right near the Halekulani—can't be beat. My top choice in Waikiki for budget travelers. See Chapter 5.

- **John Walker's Lanikai Beach House** (Oahu; c/o Hawaiian Islands B&B and Vacation Rentals; ☎ **808/261-7895**): This vintage 1930s beach house is set on spectacular gold-sand Lanikai Beach. Staying here is like stepping back into the blue-blazer era, when everyone arrived by steamship. This classic beach house with modern amenities sleeps six, and rents for $295 a night—quite a deal. See Chapter 5.

- **Carson's Volcano Cottage** (Big Island; ☎ **808/967-7683**): Tiny tree frogs sing into the night as you snuggle under a down comforter before a crackling wood fire in this honeymoon cottage, nestled under giant tree ferns in a tropical rain forest. It's so wonderful that visitors pen sonnets of joy in the guest registry. See Chapter 6.

- **McCandless Ranch Bed & Breakfast** (Big Island; ☎ **808/328-9313**): Set between a forest and a pool at 1,100 feet on the slopes of Mauna Loa, where the nights are cool and the view is both Pacific and pastoral, is this elegant monarchy-style guest cottage for two. The grounds are a working cattle ranch and the last bastion for the nearly extinct Hawaiian crow. Perfect for birders and anybody who loves the country life. See Chapter 6.

- **Tommy Tinker's Cottage at Kealakekua Bay** (Big Island; ☎ **808/889-5584**): A dab of hot pink by the deep blue sea, this oceanfront cottage is not to be missed. It's only steps away from world-class snorkeling in a marine preserve where dolphins play. The two-bedroom, $1^1/2$-bath cottage sleeps four. At $150 a night, it's a deal just for the view. See Chapter 6.

- **Waipio Wayside Inn** (Big Island; ☎ **800/833-8849**): Jacqueline Horne renovated this 1938 Hamakua Coast sugar plantation house and transformed it into a gracious, traditional B&B. The five-room inn, full of antique wicker, hand-painted silk curtains, and Chinese rugs, is near Waipio Valley and its mile-long black-sand beach. See Chapter 6.

- **Pioneer Inn** (Maui; ☎ **800/457-5457**): This waterfront charmer is smack-dab in the middle of Lahaina, with a front-row seat on the busy harbor front and all the action on Front Street. It's been remodeled with style, and the big, airy, spacious rooms—some with private verandas—are shady and cool in the tropic heat. If you don't like big fancy resorts, this is the place to stay. See Chapter 7.

- **Kamalo Plantation Bed & Breakfast** (Molokai; ☎ **808/558-8236**): At the foot of 4,970-foot Mount Kamakou, Glenn and Akiko Foster's B&B is nestled in a 5-acre tropical garden and lime orchard (bring your own gin and tonic), just 5 minutes away from a terrific gold-sand beach. See Chapter 8.

- **Hotel Lanai** (Lanai; ☎ **800/321-4666**): Lanai's only budget lodging is a simple, down-home plantation era relic that's recently been Laura Ashley–ized. It may be too froufrou for the deer, goat, and pig hunters who check in during hunting season, but times they are a'changing, even on this little island. The Hotel Lanai is homey, funky, and fun, and, best of all, a real bargain compared to its ritzy neighbors. See Chapter 9.

- **Hanalei Colony Resort** (Kauai; ☎ **800/628-3004**): The only North Shore resort right on the beach, these old-style two-story condos attract a loyal following of devoted beach lovers. What brings them back year after year? It's the location, ambience, and the staff, always friendly and caring. The roar of the surf and scent of the reef will haunt you long after you leave this small, appealing resort. It's one of my favorite escapes. See Chapter 10.

- **Waimea Plantation Cottages** (Kauai; ☎ 808/338-1625): This vintage village of 47 turn-of-the-century sugar plantation houses, each fully restored and bearing the name of the family who once called them home, sits under a coconut palm grove at the beach on Kauai's western shore. They have a cottage that's right for just about everyone, from honeymooning couples to family reunions. See Chapter 10.

8 The Best Culinary Experiences

by Jocelyn Fujii

- **A Pacific Cafe** (Oahu; ☎ 808/593-0035): The appetizer bar is the ultimate seduction: pleasant surroundings, its own separate kitchen, one of the top menus in Hawaii, and the notion that grazing is greatness in Hawaii Regional Cuisine. Jean-Marie Josselin's menu includes black-Thai-rice nachos, garlic shrimp pizza, warm tiger-eye sushi tempura, and a host of other irresistibles. See Chapter 5.
- **Jimbo's Restaurant** (Oahu; ☎ 808/947-2211): The ultimate Japanese noodle house. A bowl of homemade udon in homemade broth comes steaming in an earthenware pot, topped with shiitake mushrooms and vegetables, with crisp shrimp tempura on the side, all for just $10.75. The atmosphere is like a modest Japanese inn straight out of *Tampopo*—noodle heaven. See Chapter 5.
- **Parc Cafe** (Oahu; ☎ 808/921-7272): Expect the best Hawaiian food Wednesdays at the Waikiki Parc hotel, where an extravagant spread of lau lau, taro au gratin, kalua pork, squid luau, and dozens of other delicacies attract lovers of the native cuisine. This is the most imaginative Hawaiian spread you can hope to encounter on Oahu: varied and impeccably prepared, and sprinkled with gourmet touches that manage not to detract from its authenticity. See Chapter 5.
- **Akasaka** (Oahu; ☎ 808/942-4466): The spicy tuna roll and sizzling tofu are among the many dishes that will have you clamoring for more. The tiny sushi bar is hidden among the shadowy night clubs of Kona Street—off the beaten track, yet always jumping with regulars. See Chapter 5.
- **Maha's Cafe** (Big Island; ☎ 808/885-0693): This cafe, in Waimea's historic Spencer Building, offers the perfect blend of Hawaiian ambiance, fresh local ingredients (everything from lamb to tomatoes), and pure charm. The fresh-fish sandwich with Waipio Valley taro and green-olive pesto are reason enough to go, but morning fans swear by the hotcakes, too. See Chapter 6.
- **Kilauea Lodge** (Big Island; ☎ 808/967-7366): The duck à l'orange and hasenpfeffer are worthy of the long drive, served in a high-beamed stone building surrounded by native ohia trees and blindingly blue hydrangeas. Dinner only. See Chapter 6.
- **Maui Tacos** (Maui; ☎ 808/665-0222): This local chain, with outposts in Napili, Kahului, and Kihei, serves fresh-fish tacos and healthy Tex-Mex fare that's tasty, quick, and cheap. No fuss, no pretensions, just Mark Elliman's great Mexican food, the best thing you'll find on paper plates. See Chapter 7.
- **Charley's Restaurant** (Maui; ☎ 808/579-9453): Fans drive miles for a bowl of Washington clams, fleshy and succulent in a lemon-butter-garlic broth. For under $10, the clams are a show-stopper, but others go for the famous hotcakes and Cajun-style fresh ono eggs Benedict, an appropriate launch to the day. See Chapter 7.

- **Kea Lani Restaurant** (Maui; ☎ **808/875-4100**): The hunter-style opakapaka with wild mushrooms, and Wagyu-style free-range steak from the Big Island served with garlic mashed potatoes are accompanied by the island's most impressive selection of organic fresh vegetables and fruit, grown on the hotel grounds. When soft jazz wafts through the Mediterranean-style dining room from the lounge next door, it's better than Casablanca. See Chapter 7.
- **Joe's Bar & Grill, Wailea** (Maui; ☎ **808/875-7767**): Julia Child holds court every night at Joe's Bar and Grill, and it's worth many trips to the loo just to hear her. Tapes of the gourmet chef run continuously in the ladies' room, and they're almost enough to detain you from the garlic mashed potatoes and gravy, the fork-tender grilled quail, and the smoked-salmon quesadilla at your table. See Chapter 7.
- **Hamura's Saimin Stand** (Kauai; ☎ **808/245-3271**): It's a cultural experience: a seat at one of three U-shaped Formica counters, a look at the kitchen that's larger than the dining area (where steam is produced in voluminous blasts from pots of broth and noodles), and finally, a bowl of the legendary noodle soup with the topping of your choice, accompanied by smoky beef teriyaki sticks. They open early, close late, and the price is definitely right. See Chapter 10.
- **Casa di Amici** (Kauai; ☎ **808/828-1555**): The risotto is substantial but not crippling, the fettuccine Alfredo is a paean to garlic, and the ambience (open-air, with trellises and fairy lights in the plants at night) changes throughout the day, but never loses its appeal. It's more than worth the long drive from south and east Kauai to the North Shore locale. See Chapter 10.

9 The Best Shopping

by Jocelyn Fujii

- **Avanti Fashion** (Oahu; 2229 Kuhio Ave., Honolulu): Avanti aloha shirts and sportswear, in authentic prints from the 1930s and 1940s reproduced on silk, elevate tropical garb from high kick to high chic. Casual, comfortable, easy-care, and light as a cloud, the silks look vintage but cost a fraction of collectibles prices. The nostalgic treasures are available at many stores statewide, but the best bets are at the Avanti retail store, a restored gingerbread house with the brightest windows on Waikiki's Kuhio Avenue; and at the new Avanti store in Waikiki Shopping Plaza, 2270 Kalakaua Ave. See Chapter 5.
- **Silk Winds** (Oahu; Kilohana Square, Kapahulu): Cricket cages and one-of-a-kind bamboo calligraphy wrist-rests are among the Asian treasures you'll find here. Mah-jongg tiles, jade and porcelain, Buddhas and beads beckon from the mysterious corners of this antiques store for everyone, from casual to serious collectors. See Chapter 5.
- **Contemporary Museum Gift Shop** (Oahu; 2411 Makiki Heights Rd., Honolulu): After you've absorbed the Diamond Head view framed by Oriental gardens, duck into the Contemporary Museum Shop on the slopes of Tantalus, where everything is art. Jon Hamblin's wire men, stars, fish, and birds romp across the wall like guardians of the gift world. The avant-garde jewelry, stationery, books, and gift items are brilliant, spirited, and functional. See Chapter 5.
- **Nohea Gallery** (Oahu; Ward Warehouse, Honolulu): This gallery offers an islandwide look at the finest crafts of Hawaii. From the simplest hair-stick to the fragile goblets and grand chests of curly koa, the works are stunning. See Chapter 5.

- **Paradise Produce Company** (Oahu; 83 N. King St., Chinatown): Spring and summer shopping at Paradise Produce Company, near Chinatown, yields a dizzying assortment: voluptuous mangoes, papayas, and a host of palate-pleasers for a special corner of the picnic basket. Local litchis—usually available in late summer and rarely sold in standard supermarkets—are worth the hunt. See Chapter 5.

- **Silver Moon Emporium** (Oahu; North Shore Marketplace, 66-250 Kamehameha Hwy., Haleiwa): This Haleiwa shop, along with its sister store, **Bella Luna** (66-037 Kamehameha Hwy.), lure a legion of fans (women, and men shopping for women) from all over the island. We drive for an hour and arrive with empty car trunks, knowing that we'll leave with a lot of cargo and a lot less cash. The owner scours little-known sources across the country and brightens Haleiwa—and our closets—with her finds in clothing, footwear, and accessories. See Chapter 5.

- **Hula Heaven** (Big Island; Kona Inn Shopping Village, Kailua-Kona): You'll turn giddy at Hula Heaven, *the* spot for collectors of Hawaiiana. Aloha shirts, hula-girl lamps, one-of-a-kind 1940s textiles, Don Blanding dinnerware, the passionate expertise of the owners—it's a lifestyle, a celebration of nostalgia. Don't miss it. See Chapter 6.

- **Waimea Booksellers** (Big Island; Opelo Plaza, Hi. 19, Waimea): This place is small but potent: new, used, and out-of-print books, window benches looking out over flower beds, an informed staff, and dozens of book review subscriptions to help you decide. Offbeat titles and mainstream hits keep broad reading tastes satisfied. See Chapter 6.

- **Sig Zane Designs** (Big Island; 122 Kamehameha Ave., Hilo): A Sig Zane fabric design is culturally meaningful, visually striking, and uniquely identifiable. There are those who wear Sig Zane shirts and muumuus, lounge on Sig Zane cushions and upholstery, sleep under Sig Zane bedspreads, and pad around home in Sig Zane slippers—and nothing else. Lauhala mats and accessories, handcrafted koa books by a third-generation Vatican book-binder, calabashes, jewelry, and the inspired line of authentic Sig Zane Hawaiian wear make Sig's shop the best stop in Hilo. See Chapter 6.

- **Ola's** (Maui; Paniolo Bldg., 1156 Makawao Ave., Makawao): With its beach-glass counters and concrete floors, Ola's sprouted suddenly in Makawao, and everybody noticed. Everything here—the lamps, vases, blown glass, strumsticks, and jewelry, even Bella's at Ola's handmade chocolates—is a work of art. See Chapter 7.

- **The Mercantile** (Maui; 3673 Baldwin Ave., Makawao): Down the block from Ola's, the Mercantile is off-the-charts stylish, too. Flaxseed eye pillows and scented neck pillows, Italian lamps, all-cotton down sofas, dinnerware, Kiehl's shampoo, and vetiver soaps from Provence—a place of pampering, extravagant and delicious. See Chapter 7.

- **Robert Hamada's Studio** (Kauai; ☎ **808/822-3229**): Wood turner Robert Hamada works in his studio at the foot of the Sleeping Giant, producing museum-quality works with unique textures and grains. His skill, his lathe, and 60 years of experience bring luminous life to the kou, milo, kauila, and native woods he logs himself. See Chapter 10.

- **Ola's** (Kauai; Hi. 560, Hanalei): Pay attention to the display spaces as well as what's displayed here. Look for Doug Britt's paintings, vanities, armoires, desks, lamps, and bookshelves scattered unobtrusively among the fine American crafts. The hand-painted candlesticks, Lundberg studio glass, one-of-a-kind tableware, and unique gift items are top-drawer. See Chapter 10.

- **Yellowfish Trading Company** (Kauai; Hanalei Center, Hanalei): In Hanalei town, surprise yourself at Yellowfish Trading Company, where vintage bark cloth and that one-of-a-kind 1940s rattan sofa are among owner Gritt Benton's short-lived pleasures. The collectibles—1940s vases, 1950s lunch boxes, 1930s lampshades, antique silk piano shawls—move quickly. See Chapter 10.
- **Kong Lung Company** (Kauai; Kilauea Rd., Kilauea): Housed in a 1942 high-ceilinged stone building that was the original plantation store, Kong Lung is the center of chic in Kilauea, a Gump's-like emporium of personal and home accessories. See Chapter 10.

10 The Best Art Galleries

by Jocelyn Fujii

- **The Contemporary Museum** (Oahu; 2411 Makiki Heights Dr., Honolulu) and **Honolulu Academy of Arts** (Oahu; 900 S. Beretania St., Honolulu): Architectural and cultural wonders, a legacy of the same kamaaina family, the Contemporary Museum and the Honolulu Academy of Arts both house peerless collections in garden settings. For Asian, American, and European masters, go to the Academy. For a look at some of this country's most significant art since 1940 (and the prettiest forest drive in Honolulu), TCM is the only game in town. See Chapter 5.
- **Volcano Art Center** (Big Island; Hawaii Volcanoes National Park): I love its creaky wood floors, the smoky scent in the air, the rolling mists, and the art. Thriving in an 1877 building, the art center offers art education, programs and performances, and wondrous works in all media, featuring the most prominent artists on the island.
- **Jovian Gallery** (Maui; 7 N. Market St., Wailuku): This is Wailuku's design atelier, owner Marcia Godinez's constantly evolving wish list of art with an edge. A settee and a teapot invite lingering among the lush canvases, sculptures, and the affordable gift items her discerning eye collects from Maui and the mainland. See Chapter 7.
- **Hui No'eau Visual Arts Center** (Maui; 2841 Baldwin Ave., Makawao): Upcountry in Makawao, in a 1917 Mediterranean manse on a 9-acre estate, this arts hui is part gallery, part exhibition space, part gift shop, classes and demonstration center, and every inch a paean to beauty. See Chapter 7.
- **Hana Coast Gallery** (Maui; Hotel Hana Maui, Hana): The long and winding road leads to the Hotel Hana-Maui, where the works in the Hana Coast Gallery reflect a deep commitment to Hawaii's cultural art. Native Hawaiian artists and the master crafts of Hawaii have a presence and integrity unlike any other gallery in the islands. See Chapter 7.

11 The Best of Hawaii After Dark

by Jocelyn Fujii

- **Cocktails at Halekulani's House Without a Key** (Oahu; ☎ 808/923-2311): The best begins at sunset at the House Without a Key, where a Mai Tai and hula show under the oldest tree in Waikiki leave even the most jaded of viewers speechless. The view of Diamond Head and the ocean, the twang of the steel guitar, and the graceful dancing of Kanoelehua Miller evoke a time when surfers on long boards were all that dotted the horizon. See Chapter 5.

- **Olomana at Hilton Hawaiian Village's Paradise Lounge** (Oahu; ☎ 808/949-4321): Olomana, featuring the 12-string guitar virtuoso and award-winning composer Haunani Apoliona with Jerry Santos and Wally Suenaga, has a big, soulful sound that can barely be contained by the Paradise Lounge, where they perform on weekends. When friends and family in the audience erupt in spontaneous hula and music, it's the best party in town. See Chapter 5.
- **The Hawaii Theatre Center** (Oahu; ☎: 808/528-0506): Butoh dancing, the Brothers Cazimero, Mel Torme, ballet and taiko drums—the Hawaii Theatre Center downtown has booked them all. The newly reopened 1922 beaux-arts landmark is the city's grandest multipurpose rental hall, as big an attraction as the show itself. Check the local papers to see what's playing; the $22-million restoration has it gleaming. See Chapter 5.
- **La Pastaria** (Maui; ☎ 808/879-9001): Kihei isn't exactly nirvana, but La Pastaria is, especially for those who love blues and jazz. This late-night magnet has a small corner stage, so you can enjoy good riffs along with your risotto. See Chapter 7.
- **Casanova** (Maui; ☎ 808/572-0220): Up-country in Makawao, Casanova is *the* hot spot for dancing, disco, blues, rock-and-roll, jazz, reggae, and contemporary Hawaiian, plus War or Los Lobos when they're visiting the islands. See Chapter 7.

12 The Best Mai Tais

by Rick Carroll

Most Mai Tais served in Hawaii today are too strong, too sweet, and, at $7 and up, too expensive. They're pale imitations of the original, by a legendary California restaurateur, the late Vic Bergeron, of Trader Vic's fame. Some taste like gasoline, others like cough syrup; they burn the throat, produce terrible headaches, and generally give Hawaii a bad name. They should be served with a Surgeon General's warning. These tacky concoctions have little in common with a real Mai Tai, and should be avoided at all costs.

The classic Mai Tai is an unforgettable cocktail, an icy Jamaican rum and fresh-lime-juice drink with a subtle hint of oranges and almonds and a sprig of fresh mint for garnish. Now, that's a Mai Tai. As long as they don't alter the basic ingredients, variations on the original theme are perfectly acceptable, and can be excellent.

Of course, where you sip a Mai Tai is almost as important as the ingredients. This tropical drink always tastes better in a thatch hut on a lagoon, with coco palms lining the shore. A great Mai Tai in, say, the Tonga Room of San Francisco's Fairmont Hotel is not the same as a great Mai Tai on Waikiki Beach. Here are the best places to the premier Hawaii Mai Tai experience:

- **Halekulani's House Without a Key** (Oahu; $7.25): The search for the perfect Mai Tai begins and ends here. It's as close to the original as you'll find in Waikiki. This sophisticated version is comprised of a fine blend of two rums, lemon and lime juice, and sweet orange curacao. A purple Vanda orchid adds a splash of color. See Chapter 5.
- **Jameson's by the Sea** (Oahu; $5): Up on Oahu's north shore, big waves may draw surfers from around the world, but Mai Tai connoisseurs pack the lanai at Jameson's at sundown to catch the wave of Mai Tais prepared by head barman Jim Bragaw. The best in Surf City. See Chapter 5.
- **New Otani Kaimana Beach Hotel** (Oahu; $5.75): Go on Aloha Friday, when the exotic sounds of Arthur Lyman waft across the golden sand, and ask veteran

bartender Clara Nakachi for a classic Mai Tai. Sit under the tree where Robert Louis Stevenson wrote poems to Princess Kaiulani. Take a sip, stare out to sea and wonder, is this not paradise? See Chapter 5.

- **Shipwreck Bar** (Kona Village, Big Island; $7): Johnno Jacko wrecked his 42-foot schooner on the reef at Kaupulehu in 1959 and stayed on in the islands to build Kona Village. The hull today serves as the Shipwreck Bar, where host Fred Duerr still serves the traditional Mai Tai, according to Trader Vic's recipe. See Chapter 6.
- **The Bay Club** (Kapalua Bay Hotel & Villas, Maui; $7.25): Maui may be the Chardonnay capital of the Hawaiian Islands (it's all those California wine-bibbers), but you also can get a great Mai Tai at the newly renovated Bay Club, overlooking Kapalua Bay, where head barman James "Kimo" Tagupa knows how to make a good one. See Chapter 7.
- **Ohia Lounge** (Kaluakoi Hotel & Golf Club, Molokai; $5): At the end of the day, after a hot, dusty trail ride on the Molokai Ranch, nothing tastes finer than a Mai Tai in the Ohia Lounge, an airy seaside bar on Hawaii's biggest white-sand beach. Mai Tais taste like they should here because hardly anything ever changes on Molokai, thank goodness. See Chapter 8.
- **Tahiti Nui** (Kuhio Hwy., Hanalei, Kauai; $5): This Hanalei hangout got smashed by Hurricane Iniki, but its world-famous Mai Tai lives on. It's Auntie Louise Marston's secret 30-year-old family recipe, imported from Tahiti. The only change over the years: no vanilla beans. The new Nui reopened on New Year's Eve—same place, same Mai Tais, the best on Kauai. See Chapter 10.

2 Getting to Know the Hawaiian Islands

If wealth is measured as in Polynesia not by what you have but how you feel, then Hawaii may be the richest spot on earth.

Indeed, there's no place quite like this handful of sun-drenched mid-Pacific islands, so remote from any continent yet visited by nearly 7 million guests a year. They come from the far corners of the globe seeking relaxation under the tropic sun, and leave feeling good inside and out.

That's the nature of Hawaii's overwhelming beauty and almost perfect climate: It makes people feel fulfilled and restored. Those who live here have an inherent sense of well-being and personal connection, which they readily share with strangers through their famous form of hospitality known as "Aloha!"

In Hawaii, aloha means hello, good-bye, and I love you. With 25 different ethnic groups living in rare harmony on the islands, it's more than a popular expression. It's also a public law. It's on bumper stickers which proclaim "Live Aloha." It makes Hawaii a gentle, kind place where a shaka sign precedes a handshake, where total strangers return your smile, and where old friends meet with a kiss.

Yes, the mythical Hawaii of South Seas literature and Hollywood films really does exist. Here you will find palm-fringed blue lagoons, Green-Mansionlike rain forests, singing waterfalls, wild rivers running through rugged canyons, and smoking yet snowcapped volcanoes soaring 2 miles into the sky.

The possibilities for adventure are endless. You can snorkel in lagoons full of tropical fish, kayak up a *Raiders of the Lost Ark* river, coast down from Maui's 2-mile-high Haleakala crater on a bicycle, hike the "Grand Canyon of the Pacific," or watch lava explode from Kilauea, the world's most active volcano. You can fly-fish for rainbow trout on Kauai, kayak along the wild side of Molokai, hang-glide over Oahu's Windward Coast, or hike in the half-light of the Big Island's rain forest.

Or you can just lounge on a beach, for the gold, red, black, and even green sands caressed by an endless surf are just as you imagined they would be. And when the sun sets, the balmy nights are laced with the perfume of tropical flowers.

Each of the six main islands is separate and distinct, larger than life and infinitely complex, as anyone who ventures here soon discovers. There's far too much to see and do on any 2-week vacation, which is why so many people return to the Aloha State year after year.

Impressions

If paradise consists solely of beauty, then these islands were the fairest that man ever invaded, for the land and sea were beautiful and the climate was congenial.

—James A. Michener, *Hawaii*

1 Hawaii Today

by Rick Carroll

Not just another pretty place in the sun, America's only island state is emerging as the cultural center and meeting place of the Pacific Rim, with an international cast of characters playing key roles.

Even busy Waikiki is cleaning up its act, replacing time-share vendors with flower lei stands, and offering authentic chant and hula in traditional costumes at sunset nightly. No longer a place of tacky T-shirts and souvenir stands, it's evolving into the shopping capital of the Pacific, where people fly in to browse European designer boutiques like Cartier, Dunhill, Ferragamo, and Ettore Bugatti. Adding to the state's international importance will be a new $214 million Hawaii Convention Center now rising at the gateway to Waikiki. Completion of the four-story, 1.1-million-square-foot center is due in late 1997, with the grand opening scheduled for July 1998.

Hawaii now has some of the world's newest and finest world-class beach resorts, contemporary palaces that would astound even the islands' hedonistic kings. Here you can dine on the freshest seafood and island-grown fruits and vegetables, be attended by your own butler, and while away lazy days in secret gardens and private pools.

And old and new are combining to create a level of style and service that only enhances Hawaii's own aloha spirit: Outside urban Honolulu, the islands are in transition from small farm towns of the rural plantation era to destinations now fully dependent on tourism for their economy.

A CULTURAL RENAISSANCE

A conch shell sounds, a young man in a bright feather cape chants as torch light flickers at sunset on the Waikiki Beach, and hula dancers begin telling their graceful centuries-old stories by hand.

It's a cultural scene out of the past come to life once again, and not just in Waikiki but throughout the islands—for Hawaii is enjoying a renaissance of hula, chant, and other aspects of its ancient culture. In fact, it's rare to visit Hawaii these days and not see the real hula danced in traditional costumes.

Once banned by New England missionaries and then almost forgotten in the rush to embrace America's consumer-based ideals, the hula is a movement of its own today. And a major event: The Merrie Monarch Festival, in honor of King David Kalakaua who repealed the missionary ban on hula, attracts an annual crowd of 20,000 to Hilo. Founded in 1970, the week-long festival features costumed men and women dancers from every Hawaiian island and from the U.S. mainland, all of whom compete in ancient and modern hula.

The biggest, longest, and most elaborate celebrations of Hawaiian culture are the Aloha Festivals, more than 500 different cultural events from August to October throughout the state. These include a reenactment of the ancient ceremony when the king was crowned and received by the royal court. The only such statewide events in the United States, the Aloha Festivals organization celebrated its 50th anniversary in 1996.

❓ Did You Know?

- The aloha shirt Montgomery Clift wore in his final scene in *From Here to Eternity* is worth $3,500 today.
- Honolulu is second only to San Francisco in restaurant spending—but the locals' favorite meat is Spam.
- There haven't been any billboards in Hawaii since 1926.
- Although capital of the 50th state, Honolulu is closer to Tokyo than to Washington, D.C.
- Strong trade winds during heavy rains cause waterfalls to go *up* the dramatic cliffs of Oahu's eastern Koolau mountains instead of down.
- Alarmed citizens thought a Russian sea captain attacked Honolulu in 1925; in fact, a 30-pound meteorite blasted to earth near Punchbowl Crater.
- It can snow in February and March on the Big Island's 13,796-foot Mauna Kea volcano, making Hawaii the only place in the world where you can ski and snorkel on the same day.
- Buffaloes imported from Wyoming roam the Hanalei River valley on Kauai. Some end up in Hanalei and Kapaa restaurants as buffalo burgers.
- Princess Abigail Kinoiki Kekaulike Kawananakoa of Honolulu may have become Queen Abigail Kawananakoa if the United States hadn't overthrown the Hawaiian monarchy in 1893.

"Our goal is to teach and share our culture," says Gloriann Akau, who manages the Big Island's Aloha Festivals. "In 1946, after the war, Hawaiians needed an identity. We were lost and needed to regroup. When we started to celebrate our culture, we began to feel proud. We have a wonderful culture that had been buried for a number of years. This brought it out again. Self esteem is more important than making a lot of money."

In 1985, as glitzy megaresorts with borrowed cultures began to appear in the islands, native Hawaiian educator, author, and *kupuna* George Kanahele started integrating Hawaiian values in hotels like the Big Island's Mauna Lani and Maui's Kaanapali Beach Hotel. (A *kupuna* is an elder with leadership qualities who requires great respect; Kanahele is a *kupuna* with a Ph.D. from Cornell.)

"You have the responsibility to preserve and enhance the Hawaiian culture, not because it's going to make money for you but because it's the right thing to do," Kanahele told the Hawaii Hotel Association. "Ultimately, the only thing unique about Hawaii is its Hawaiianess. Hawaiianess is our competitive edge."

From general managers to maids, employees at both resorts took 16 hours of Hawaiian cultural training. They held focus groups to discuss the meaning of aloha—the Hawaiian concept of unremitting love. They applied aloha to their work and their lives. Kaanapali Beach Hotel on Maui was first to instill Hawaiian ways in the hotel staff, followed by the Outrigger Hotel chain, one of the biggest in Hawaii. Many others have joined the movement.

No longer content with trying hula as a joke, visitors now learn from real *kumu hula* (hula teacher) like the Big Island's Nani Lim. Or visit a *heiau* (Hawaiian temple) with a *kupuna,* and try native Hawaii medicine from the rain forest.

THE QUESTION OF SOVEREIGNTY

The cultural renaisssance has made its way into politics, so don't be surprised if you see clenched-fist native Hawaiians taking to the streets and beaches to call for independence for their homeland.

Under the banner of sovereignty, many *kanaka maoli*—or native people, as they call themselves—are demanding restoration of rights taken away more than a century ago when the United States overthrew the Hawaiian monarchy and claimed the islands. In the past few years members of some 30 activist groups have invaded Waikiki Beach to hand out sovereignty leaflets and tell sun-worshipping tourists to "Go Home Now." Thousands recently blocked Kalakaua Avenue, Waikiki's main drag, for 2 hours on a protest march. They demonstrated before 400 delegates at a state-sponsored congress intended to promote tourism. Then-governor John Waihee, the first person with Hawaiian blood ever elected to the office, raised the Hawaiian flag instead of the Stars and Stripes over the state house at the 100-year observance of the U.S. overthrow of the Hawaiian monarchy. In a 1994 rally on Iolani Palace grounds, where the monarchy was toppled, some 500 Hawaiians known as the Ohana Council declared independence from the United States and claimed the land as their own.

Their demands for sovereignty were not lost on President Bill Clinton, who was picketed at a Democratic political fund raiser at Waikiki Beach in July 1993. Four months later, Clinton signed a law in which the U.S. Congress "apologizes to Native Hawaiians on behalf of the people of the United States for the overthrow of the Kingdom of Hawaii on January 17, 1893, with the participation of agents and citizens of the United States, and deprivation of the rights of Native Hawaiians to self-determination."

While that could be construed to mean a return to the way things were in Hawaii a century ago with kings and queens and a royal court, not even neo-nationalists are convinced that's possible. First, the Hawaiians themselves must decide if they want sovereignty, since each of the 30 identifiable sovereignty organizations, and more than 100 splinter groups, has a different view of self-determination. They range from total independence from the United States to a nation-within-a-nation similar to the status of American Indians.

In 1993, the Hawaii State Legislature created a 20-member Hawaiian Sovereignty Advisory Commission made up of native Hawaiians to "determine the will of the native Hawaiian people." The commission plans to pose the sovereignty question in a referendum open to anyone with Hawaiian blood over 18 years of age wherever they live, including those in jail or prison. There are an estimated 250,000 Hawaiians in Hawaii and elsewhere.

2 History 101

by Rick Carroll

Paddling outrigger canoes, the first ancestors of today's Hawaiians followed the stars and birds across a trackless sea to Hawaii, which they called "the land of raging fire." Those first settlers were part of the great Polynesian migration that settled the vast triangle of islands stretching from New Zealand in the southwest to Easter Island in the east to Hawaii in the north. No one is sure when they arrived in Hawaii from Tahiti and the Marquesas Islands, some 2,500 miles to the south, but a dog-bone fish hook found at the southernmost tip of the Big Island has been carbon-dated to A.D. 700.

An entire Hawaiian culture arose over the next 1,500 years. The settlers built temples, fishponds, and aqueducts to irrigate taro plantations. Sailors became farmers and fishermen. Each island was a separate kingdom. The *alii* (high ranking chiefs) created a caste system and established taboos. Violators were strangled. High priests asked the gods Lono and Ku for divine guidance. Ritual human sacrifices were common.

The "Fatal Catastrophe"   No ancient Hawaiian ever imagined a *haole* (a person with "no breath") would ever appear on "a floating island." But then one day in 1779 just such a white-skinned person sailed into Waimea Bay on Kauai, where he was welcomed as the god, Lono.

The man was 50-year-old Capt. James Cook, already famous in Britain for "discovering" much of the southern Pacific. Now on his third great voyage of exploration, Cook had set sail from Tahiti northward across uncharted waters to find the mythical Northwest Passage purportedly linking the Pacific and Atlantic oceans. On his way, Cook stumbled upon the Hawaiian Islands quite by chance. He named them the Sandwich Islands, for the Earl of Sandwich, First Lord of the Admiralty, who bankrolled the expedition.

Overnight, Stone Age Hawaii entered the age of iron. Gifts were presented and trade established: nails for freshwater, pigs, and the affections of Hawaiian women. The sailors brought syphillis, measles, and other diseases to which the Hawaiians had no natural immunity, thereby unwittingly wreaking havoc on the native population. (While on a trip to Europe in 1825, King Kamehameha II and his queen Kamamalu, died of measles in London.)

After an unsuccessful attempt to find the Northwest Passage, Cook returned to Kealakekua on the Big Island, where a fight broke out over guns. The great navigator was killed by a blow to the head. After this "fatal catastrophe," the British survivors sailed home.

Hawaii was now on the sea charts. French, Russian, American, and other traders on the fur route between Canada's Hudson Bay Company and China anchored in Hawaii to get freshwater. More trade and more disastrous liaisons ensued.

Two more sea captains left indelible marks on the islands: The first was American John Kendrick, who in 1791 filled his ship with sandalwood and sailed to China. By 1825, Hawaii's sandalwood forests were gone, enabling invasive plants to take charge. The second was Englishman George Vancouver, who in 1793 left cows and sheep, which nibbled the islands to the high-tide line. The king sent to Mexico and Spain for cowboys to round up the wild cattle, thus beginning the islands' *paniolo* tradition.

The tightly woven Hawaiian society, enforced by royalty and religious edicts, began to unravel after the death in 1819 of King Kamehameha I, who had used guns seized from a British ship to unite the islands under his rule. His successor, Queen Kaahumanu, abolished the old taboos, thus opening the door for a religion of another form.

Impressions

We continued to see birds every day . . . sometimes in greater numbers than at others: and between the latitude of 10 and 11, we saw several turtle. All these are looked up as signs of the vicinity of land; we however saw none till daybreak in the Morning of the 18th when an Island was discovered. . . .

—Capt. James Cook, *Journal* entry of Friday, Jan. 2, 1778.

Staying to Do Well   In April of 1820, god-fearing missionaries arrived from New England bent on converting the pagans. "Can these be human beings," exclaimed their leader, the Rev. Hiram Bingham, upon first glance of "the almost naked savages" whose "appearance of destitution, degradation, and barbarism" he found "appalling."

Intent on instilling their brand of rock-ribbed Christianity in the islands, the missionaries clothed the natives, banned them from dancing the hula, and nearly dismantled their ancient culture. They tried to keep the whalers and sailors out of the bawdy houses, where a flood of whiskey quenched fleet-size thirsts and where the virtue of native women was never safe.

The missionaries taught reading and writing, created the 12-letter Hawaiian alphabet, started a letter press, and began writing the islands' history, until then only an oral account in half-remembered chants.

Children of the missionaries became the islands' business leaders and politicans. They married Hawaiians and stayed on in the islands, causing one wag to remark that the missionaries "came to do good and stayed to do well."

In 1848 King Kamehameha III proclaimed the Great Mahele (division) that enabled commoners and eventually foreigners to own crown land. In two generations more than 80% of all private land was in haole hands. Sugar planters imported waves of immigrants to work the fields as contract laborers. The first Chinese came in 1952, followed by 7,000 Japanese in 1885 and the Portuguese in 1878.

King David Kalakaua was elected to the throne in 1874. This popular "Merrie Monarch" built Iolani Place in 1882, threw extravagant parties, and restored the hula and other native arts to grace. For this he was much loved. He also gave Pearl Harbor to the United States; it became the westernmost bastion of the U.S. Navy—and the bulls-eye of the infamous Japanese air raid on the sleepy Sunday morning of December 7, 1941.

In 1891, King Kalakaua visited chilly San Francisco, caught a cold, and died in the royal suite of the Sheraton Palace. His sister, Queen Liliuokalani, assumed the throne.

A Sad Farewell   On January 17, 1893, a group of American sugar planters and missionary descendants, with the support of gun-toting U.S. marines, imprisoned Queen Liliuokalani in her own palace, where she penned the sadly lyric *"Aloha Oe,"* Hawaii's song of farewell. The monarchy was dead.

A new republic was established, controlled by Sanford Dole, a powerful sugarcane planter. In 1898 Hawaii became an American territory ruled by Dole and his fellow sugarcane planters and the Big Five, a cartel which controlled banking, shipping, hardware, and every other facet of economic life in the islands.

Oahu's central Ewa Plain soon filled with row crops. The Dole family planted pineapple on their vast acreage. Planters imported more contract laborers from Puerto Rico (1900), Korea (1903), and the Philippines (1907–1931). Most of the new immigrants stayed on to establish families and become a part of the islands. Meanwhile, the native Hawaiians became a landless minority in their homeland.

For a half-century sugar was king, generously subsidized by the U.S. federal government. The sugar planters dominated the territory's economy, shaped its social fabric, and kept the islands in a colonial plantation era with bosses and field hands. But the workers eventually struck for higher wages and improved working conditions; the planters were unable to compete with cheap third world labor costs, and their market share was shrinking. Hawaii's lush fields of sugar and pineapple gradually went to seed, and the plantation era ended.

For me, its balmy airs are always blowing, its summer seas flashing in the sun, the pulsing of its surf beat is in my ears. . . . (Hawaii is) the loveliest fleet of islands anchored in any ocean.

—Mark Twain (1866)

The Tourists Arrive   Tourism proper began in the 1860s. Kilauea became the world's prime attraction for adventure travelers who rode on horseback 29 miles from Hilo to peer into the boiling hell fire of Halemaumau. The journal of missionary William Ellis, the first American to see the Kilauea volcano in 1823, inspired many to visit it. "Astonishment and awe for some moments rendered us mute and like statues we stood," he wrote. "Our eyes riveted on the abyss below . . . one vast flood of burning matter . . . rolling to and fro its fiery surge and flaming billows." In 1865, a grass version of Volcano House was built on the Halemaumau Crater rim to shelter them. It was Hawaii's first tourist hotel.

But Hawaii's tourism really got off the ground with the demise of the plantation era, and it has shaped the islands' history in ways that sugarcane and pineapples never did.

In 1901, W. C. Peacock built the elegant beaux-arts Moana Hotel on Waikiki Beach, and W. C. Weedon convinced Honolulu businessmen to bankroll his plan to advertise Hawaii in San Francisco. Travelers were going to California, and Weedon meant to persuade them to see Hawaii too. Armed with a stereopticon and tinted photos of Waikiki, Weedon sailed off in 1902 for 6 months of lecture tours to introduce "those remarkable people and the beautiful lands of Hawaii." He drew packed houses. A tourism promotion bureau was formed in 1903, financed by the port's rat-control plague tax. About 2,000 visitors came to Hawaii that year.

Steamships were Hawaii's tourism lifeline. It took 4¹/₂ days to sail from San Francisco to Honolulu. Streamers, leis, pomp, and a warm "Boat Day" welcomed each Matson Liner at downtown's Aloha Tower. Well-heeled visitors brought trunks, servants, even their Rolls, and stayed for months. Hawaii amused the idly rich with personal tours, floral parades, and shows spotlighting that naughty dance, the hula.

Beginning in 1935 and running for the next 40 years, Webley Edwards's weekly live radio show "Hawaii Calls" planted the sounds of Waikiki—surf, sliding steel guitar, sweet Hawaiian harmonies, drum beats—in the hearts of millions of listeners in America, Australia, and Canada.

In 1936, visitors could fly to Honolulu on the *Hawaii Clipper,* a seven-passenger Pan American Martin M-130 flying boat, for $360 one way. The flight took 21 hours, 33 minutes. Modern tourism was born, with five flying boats providing daily service between San Francisco and Honolulu. The 1941 visitor count was a brisk 31,846 through December 6.

Bombs Away!   On December 7, 1941, Japanese Zeros came out of the rising sun to bomb American warships based at Pearl Harbor. It was the "day of infamy" which plunged the United States into World War II and gave the nation its revenge-laced battle cry, "Remember Pearl Harbor!"

The aftermath of the attack brought immediate changes to the islands. Martial law was declared, thus stripping the Big Five cartels of their absolute power in a single day. Feared to be spies, Japanese-Americans were interned in Hawaii as well as in California. Hawaii was "blacked out" at night, Waikiki Beach was strung with barbed wire, and Aloha Tower was painted in camouflage. Only young men bound for the

Pacific came to Hawaii during the war years. Some come back to graves in a cemetery called The Punchbowl.

The postwar years saw the beginnings of Hawaii's faux culture. Harry Yee invented the Blue Hawaii cocktail and dropped in a tiny Japanese parasol. Vic Bergeron created the Mai Tai, a rum and fresh-lime-juice drink, and opened Trader Vic's, America's first theme restaurant that featured the art, decor, and food of Polynesia. Arthur Godfrey picked up a ukulele and began singing *hapa-haole* tunes on early television shows. Burt Lancaster and Deborah Kerr made love in the surf at Hanauma Bay in the 1954 movie *From Here to Eternity.* In 1955, Henry J. Kaiser built the Hilton Hawaiian Village, and the 11-story high-rise Princess Kaiulani Hotel opened on a site where the real princess once played. Hawaii greeted 109,000 visitors that year.

Statehood!   In 1959 Hawaii became the last star on the Stars and Stripes, the 50th state of the union. But that year also saw the arrival of the first jet airliners, which brought 250,000 tourists to the fledgling state. The personal touch that had defined aloha gave way to the sheer force of numbers. Waikiki's room count virtually doubled in 2 years, from 16,000 in 1969 to 31,000 units in 1971, and more followed before city fathers finally clamped a growth lid on the world's most famous resort. By 1980, the number of annual arrivals reached 4 million.

In the early 1980s, the Japanese government decided its citizens should travel overseas, and out they went. Waikiki was one of their favorite destinations, and they brought lots of yen to spend. Their effect on sales in Hawaii was phenomenal: European boutiques opened stores in Honolulu, and Duty-Free Shoppers became the main supporter of Honolulu International Airport. Japanese investors competed for the chance to own or build part of Hawaii. Hotels sold so fast and at such unbelievable prices that heads began to spin with dollar signs.

In 1986, Hawaii's visitor count passed 5 million. Two years later, it went over 6 million. Expensive fantasy megaresorts bloomed on the neighbor islands like giant artificial flowers, swelling the luxury market with ever swankier accommodations.

The highest visitor count ever recorded hit 6.9 million in 1990, but the bubble burst in early 1991 with the Gulf War and worldwide recessions. In 1992, Hurricane Iniki devastated Kauai, only now staggering back on its feet. Airfare wars sent Americans to Mexico. Over-built with luxury hotels, Hawaii slashed its room rates, enabling consumers entree to luxury digs at affordable prices—a trend that continues.

3 Life & Language

by Rick Carroll

Plantations brought so many different people to Hawaii that the state is now a rainbow of ethnic groups. No one group is a majority; everyone's a minority. Living here are Caucasians, African-Americans, American Indians, Eskimos, Aleuts, Japanese, Chinese, Filipinos, Koreans, Tahitians, Asian Indians, Vietnamese, Hawaiians, Guamanians, Samoans, Tongans, and other Asian and Pacific islanders. Add a few Canadians, Dutch, English, French, German, Irish, Italians, Portuguese, Scottish, Puerto Ricans, and Spanish.

More than a century ago, W. Somerset Maugham noted that "All these strange people live close to each other, with different languages and different thoughts; they believe in different gods and they have different values; two passions alone they share: love and hunger." More recently, noted travel journalist Jan Morris said of Hawaii's population: "Half the world's races seem to be represented and interbred here, and

Real Hawaiian Style

With 25 different ethnic groups, including the largest Asian mix in the United States, Hawaii has a real diffusion of styles and cultures. Yet out of this rich melange there emerges a distinct Hawaiian style. Sooner or later everyone, even the visitor, picks up on it and puts it into practice. It's speech, body language, local habits, and a way of life that distinguishes those who live in the islands from those who visit.

It's a mix of surfer, Hawaii hang-loose, traditional Chinese, and coastal haole. There's Aloha Friday (every Friday), pidgin ('*Eh fo'real, brah*), and the shaka greeting (stick out your pinky and thumb, pull in your three middle fingers, and shake—*hang loose, brah*).

People ask for "two scoops rice," stand in line at noon to order plate lunches, like to eat Spam, and drink Budweiser beer. They seldom honk their car horns (it's considered rude). They're at home with chopsticks. They barbecue in public beach parks and hold baby luaus for kids when they turn one year old.

They vote Democratic, check the surf report on "Good Morning Hawaii," listen to Hawaiian music on KCCN, and register their opinion on The Hawaii Poll. They worry about the high cost of housing and loss of jobs.

They wear shower sandals known as zoris outdoors but never indoors, and they often go barefoot. They specify "aloha attire" at the funeral when their *tutu* (grandmother) dies, but only morticians, lawyers, and other uptight individuals tuck their aloha shirts into their pants. Everyone else leaves them out.

Some young men wear queues—the long plait of hair hanging down their backs that their Asian grandfathers gladly shed—as a sign of ethnic pride. Some now affect the traditional Polynesian zig-zag tattoos that English sailors first saw in Tahiti in 1767.

Although women in old Hawaii went topless, young women today wear the long *muumuu* dresses introduced by the missionaries. The only bare breasts you'll see today are on nude beaches, which technically are illegal—but never mind that.

Everyone wears flowers, in their hair or around their neck. Men and women often tuck a single blossom over their ear. It's very Polynesian, and a clue to your current status with the opposite sex: Over the right ear means available, over the left means spoken for.

Make eye contact and say hello by raising your eyebrows with a smile. That's Hawaiian style. Try it—it works.

between them they have created an improbable microcosm of human society as a whole."

In combination, it's a remarkable potpourri. Nearly everyone, I have noticed, retains an element of the traditions of their homeland. Some Japanese-Americans of Hawaii, even after three and four generations removed from the homeland, are more traditional than the Japanese of Tokyo. And the same is true of many Chinese, Korean, Filipinos, and the rest of the 25 or so ethnic groups that make Hawaii a kind of living museum of various Asian and Pacific cultures.

WHAT HAOLE MEANS

When Hawaiians first saw Western visitors, they called the pale-skinned, frail men *haole* because they looked so out of breath. In Hawaiian, *ha* means breath, *ole* means an absence of what precedes it. In other words, a lifeless looking person. The longer I live in Hawaii, the more I can see what they meant.

Today, the term haole is generally a synonym for Caucasian or foreigner and is used casually without intending to cause any disrespect. Although hardly pale or breathless, I am a haole—in fact, I'm a "coast haole" since I came from San Francisco. I am often called a haole by my Hawaiian friends and do not consider it to be derogatory.

However, if uttered by an angry stranger who adds certain adjectives like stupid or dumb, the term haole can be construed as a mild racial slur, although both the adjective and noun may in fact be true.

THE HAWAIIAN LANGUAGE

Almost everyone here speaks English, so except for pronouncing place names, you should have no trouble communicating in Hawaii. Many folks in Hawaii now speak Hawaiian, for the ancient language is making a comeback. Everybody who visits Hawaii, in fact, will soon hear the words *aloha, mahalo, wahine,* and *kane.* If you just arrived, you're a *malahini.* Someone who's been here a long time is a *kamaaina.*

When you finish a job or your meal, you are *pau* (over). On Friday it's *pau hana,* work over. You put *pupus* in your mouth when you go *pau hana* (that's Hawaii's version of hors d'oeuvres.) Pupus are easier to spell—and eat.

The Hawaiian alphabet, created by the New England missionaries, has only 12 letters—the 5 regular vowels (*a, e, i, o,* and *u*) and 7 consonants (*h, k, l, m, n, p,* and *w*). The vowels are pronounced in the Roman fashion, that is, *ah, ay, ee, oh,* and *oo* (as in "too")—not *ay, ee, eye, oh,* and *you,* as in English. For example, *huhu* is pronounced "who-who." Almost all vowels are sounded separately, although some are pronounced together, as in Kalakaua: *Kah lah cow ah.*

SOME HAWAIIAN WORDS

Here are basic Hawaiian words, with their English meanings, that you will often hear in Hawaii and see throughout this book:

ali'i Hawaiian royalty

aloha greeting or farewell.

'ewa in the direction of Ewa, an Oahu town; generally meaning west ("Drive ewa 5 miles.")

hala the pandanus tree, the leaves of which are used for weaving

halau school

hale house or building

haole foreigner, Caucasian.

heiau Hawaiian temple or place of worship

holoholo to have fun, relax

ho'olaulea celebration

hui a club, assembly

hula native dance

imu underground oven lined with hot rocks, used for cooking the luau pig

kahili royal standard of red and yellow feathers

kahuna priest or expert

kalua to bake underground in the imu (as in kalua pig)

kamaaina old-timer

Kanaka maoli native Hawaiians

kane man

kapa tapa, bark cloth

kapu taboo, forbidden

keiki child

kokua help, cooperate

kumu hula teacher of Hawaii dance

kupuna an elder with leadership qualities who commands great respect; grandparent

lanai porch or veranda

lei garland

lomilomi massage

luau feast

mahalo thank you

makai a direction, toward the sea
malihini stranger, newcomer
malo loin cloth
mana spirit power
mauka direction, toward the mountains
mele song or chant
muumuu loose fitting gown or dress

nene official state bird, a goose
ohana family
ono delicious
pahu drum
pau finished, done
pali cliff
poi crushed taro root, made into a starchy paste
pupu hors d'oeuvre
wahine woman

PIDGIN: 'Eh fo'real, brah

As you get to know Hawaii, you'll reach beyond "aloha" and "mahalo" and discover words like *da kine,* a ubiquitous multipurpose term that can mean "that thing over there," or the "whatchamacallit," or "the very best," as in "when you care enough to send da kine card." Da kine is from Hawaii's other native tongue: pidgin English.

Pidgin developed as a method by sugar planters to communicate with their Chinese laborers in the 1800s. Today pidgin is spoken by people who grew up in Hawaii to talk with their peers. It's a manner of speaking that seems to endure despite efforts to suppress it.

At a local ball game, fans may shout *"Geevum!"* (Give 'em what-for). A ruffled clerk may tell her friend someone gave her "stink eye" (a dirty look). "No huhu" (don't get mad), soothes the friend. You could be invited to hear an elder "talk story" (relating myths and memories), or to enjoy local treats like "shave ice" (tropical snow cone) and "crack seed" (highly seasoned preserved fruit). Little words that correspond to Japanese "neh," show up on the ends of sentences like punctuation: "Got to be there 6am, you know. Junk, yeah? Maybe humbug, but, boss's speech, 'ats why."

Action words undergo a kind of poetic squeeze, so that each has a lot of meanings. Take the word "broke." It's immortalized in the most famous pidgin phrase of all—the motto of the 442nd Infantry Battalion, World War II's fearless band of Japanese-American heroes from Hawaii and California who risked their lives to prove their loyalty: "Go For Broke." Then there's "wen' go broke" (something got busted or torn, or simply stopped).

"Broke da mouth" (tastes really good) is the favorite pidgin phrase of Dr. Derek Bickerton, professor of linguistics at University of Hawaii, who teaches a course on Creole languages. He says Hawaiian pidgin is more than a makeshift list of singsong terms used to bridge a language gap. Over decades, a real Creole language developed with its own order and syntax, relying not only on English and Hawaiian but borrowing words and some grammar from several languages—Japanese, Chinese, Filipino, Portuguese, and the tongues of all the other ethnic groups who came to work the sugarcane fields a century ago.

Today, although the plantations are almost gone, the next generations and the new immigrants continue the pidgin tradition in their own way. However, modern pressures may be driving pidgin underground. Pure pidgin speakers these days tend to be older people in remote areas. Visitors to Waikiki will be lucky to hear the real thing at all.

A FEW MORE PIDGIN WORDS & PHRASES

'owzit!	How's it?
laters	See you later.
chance em	Go for it.

moah bettah	the best
cheeken skeen	goose bumps
Eh, fo' real, brah	It's true, brother.

4   A Taste of Hawaii

by Jocelyn Fujii

THE NEW GUARD: HAWAII REGIONAL CUISINE

A decade ago, visitors could expect to find frozen mahimahi beurre blanc with frozen or canned vegetables as the premium dish on a fine-dining menu in Hawaii. But not anymore. It's a whole new world in Hawaii's restaurant kitchens.

Today, you can expect to encounter Indonesian sates, Chinese stir-frys, Polynesian imu-baked foods, and guava-smoked meats in sophisticated presentations in the finest dining rooms in the state. If there's pasta or risotto or rack of lamb on the menu, it could be nori (seaweed) linguine with opihi (limpet sauce), or risotto with local seafood served in taro cups, or a rack of lamb in Cabernet and Hoisin sauce (fermented soybean, garlic, and spices), or with macadamia nuts and coconut.

It has been called many things: Euro-Asian; Pacific Rim; Pacific Edge; Euro-Pacific; Fusion cuisine; Hapa cuisine. By whatever name, Hawaii Regional Cuisine has evolved as Hawaii's singular cooking style, what some say is the last American regional cuisine, this country's final gastronomic, as well as geographic, frontier. This cuisine highlights the fresh seafood and produce of Hawaii's rich waters and volcanic soil, the cultural traditions of Hawaii's ethnic groups, and the skills of well-trained chefs—such as Roy Yamaguchi (Roy's on Oahu, Maui, and Kauai), Peter Merriman (Merriman's on the Big Island), and Jean-Marie Josselin (A Pacific Cafe on Kauai, Maui, and Oahu)—who broke ranks with their European predecessors to forge new ground in the 50th state.

Fresh ingredients are foremost, and farmers and fishermen work together to provide steady supplies of just-harvested seafood, seaweed, fern shoots, vine-ripened tomatoes, goat cheese, lamb, herbs, taro, gourmet lettuces, and countless harvests from land and sea that wind up in myriad forms on ever-changing menus, prepared in Asian and Western culinary styles.

Fresh fruit salsas and sauces (mango, litchi, papaya, pineapple, guava), ginger-sesame-wasabi flavorings, corn cakes with sake sauces, tamarind and fish sauces, coconut-chili accents, tropical-fruit vinaigrettes, and other local and newly arrived seasonings from Southeast Asia and the Pacific impart unique qualities to the preparations.

Here's a sampling of what you can expect to find on a Hawaii Regional menu: seared Hawaiian fish with lilikoi shrimp butter; tiger shrimp in sake-uni (sea urchin) beurre blanc; taro cakes and Pahoa corn cakes; Molokai sweet-potato vichyssoise; Ka'u orange sauce and Kahua Ranch lamb; pot stickers with ginger sauce; fern shoots from Waipio Valley; Maui onion soup and Hawaiian bouillabaisse, with fresh snapper, Kona crab, and fresh aquacultured shrimp; gourmet Waimanalo greens, picked that day. With menus that often change daily, and the unquenchable appetites that the leading chefs have for cooking on the edge, the possibilities for once-in-a-lifetime dining adventures are more available than ever in Hawaii.

PLATE LUNCHES & MORE: LOCAL FOOD

Although Hawaii Regional Cuisine has put Hawaii on the epicurean map, at the other end of the spectrum is the cuisine of the hoi polloi, the vast and endearing

Ahi, Ono & Opakapaka: A Hawaiian Seafood Primer

The fresh seafood in Hawaii has been described as the best in the world. In the pivotal book, *The New Cuisine of Hawaii* by Janice Wald Henderson, acclaimed chef Nobuyuki Matsuhisa (chef-owner of Matsuhisa in Beverly Hills and Nobu in Manhattan) wrote, "As a chef who specializes in fresh seafood, I am in awe of the quality of Hawaii's fish; it is unparalleled anywhere else in the world." Without a doubt, the islands' surrounding waters, the waters of the remote northwestern Hawaiian Islands, and a growing aquaculture industry are fertile grounds for this most important of Hawaii's food resources.

The reputable restaurants in Hawaii buy fresh fish daily at predawn auctions or from local fishermen. Some chefs even spear-fish their ingredients themselves. "Still wiggling" is the ultimate term for freshness in Hawaii. The fish can then be grilled over *kiawe* (mesquite) or prepared in innumerable ways.

Although most menus include the Western description for the fresh fish used, most often the local nomenclature is listed, turning dinner for the uninitiated into a confusing, quasi-foreign experience. To help familiarize you with the menu language of Hawaii, here's a basic glossary of Hawaiian Island fish:

Ahi: yellowfin or bigeye tuna, important for its use in sashimi and poke, at sushi bars, and in Hawaii Regional Cuisine.

Aku: skipjack tuna, heavily utilized by local families in home cooking and poke.

Ehu: red snapper, delicate and sumptuous, yet lesser known than opakapaka (see below).

Hapuupuu: grouper, a sea bass whose use is expanding from ethnic to nonethnic restaurants.

Hebi: spearfish, mildly flavored and frequently featured as the "catch of the day" in upscale restaurants.

world of "local food." By that we mean plate lunches and poke, shave ice and saimin, bento lunches and manapua; cultural hybrids all.

Reflecting a polyglot population of many styles and ethnicities, Hawaii's idiosyncratic dining scene is eminently inclusive. Consider Surfer Chic: barefoot in the sand, in a swimsuit, chowing down on a plate lunch, ordered from a lunch wagon, consisting of fried mahimahi, "two scoops rice," macaroni salad, and a few leaves of green, typically julienned cabbage. (Generally, teriyaki beef or shoyu chicken are options.) Greasy gravy is often the condiment of choice, accompanied by a soft drink in a paper cup. Like saimin—the local version of noodles in broth topped with scrambled egg, green onions, and sometimes, pork—the plate lunch is Hawaii's version of high camp.

Because this is Hawaii, at least a few licks of *poi,* the Hawaiian staple of cooked, pounded taro, and the other examples of indigenous cuisine are de rigueur, if not at a corny luau, then at least in a Hawaiian plate lunch. The native samplers include foods from before and after Western contact, such as *lau lau* (pork, chicken, or fish steamed in ti leaves), *kalua* pork (pork cooked in a Polynesian underground oven known here as an *imu*), *lomi* salmon (salted salmon with tomatoes and green onions), chicken long rice, squid *luau* (octopus cooked in coconut milk and taro tops), *poke* (cubed raw fish seasoned with onions and seaweed, and the occasional sprinkling of

Kajiki: Pacific blue marlin, also called au, with a firm flesh and high fat content that make it a plausible substitute for tuna in some raw fish dishes, and as a grilled item on menus.

Kumu: goatfish, a luxury item on Chinese and upscale menus, served en papillote or steamed whole, Oriental style, with sesame oil, scallions, ginger, and garlic.

Mahimahi: dolphin fish (the game fish, not the mammal) or dorado, a classic sweet, white-fleshed fish requiring vigilance among purists because it is often disguised as fresh when it's actually "fresh-frozen"—a big difference.

Monchong: bigscale or sickle pomfret, an exotic, tasty fish, scarce but gaining a higher profile on Hawaiian Island menus.

Nairagi: striped marlin, also called au; good as sashimi and in poke, and often substituted for ahi in raw fish products.

Onaga: ruby snapper, a luxury fish, versatile, moist, and flaky; top-of-the-line.

Ono: wahoo, firmer and drier than the snappers, often served grilled and in sandwiches.

Opah: moonfish, rich and fatty, versatile; cooked, raw, smoked, and broiled.

Opakapaka: pink snapper, light, flaky, and luxurious, suited for sashimi, poaching, sautéing, and baking; the best-known upscale fish.

Papio: jack trevally, light, firm, and flavorful, and favored in island cookery.

Shutome: broadbill swordfish, of beeflike texture and rich flavor.

Tombo: albacore tuna, with a high fat content, suitable for grilling and sautéing.

Uhu: parrot fish, most often encountered steamed, Chinese style.

Uku: gray snapper of clear, pale-pink flesh, delicately flavored and moist.

Ulua: large jack trevally, firm-fleshed and versatile.

roasted *kukui* nuts), *haupia* (creamy coconut pudding), and *kulolo* (steamed pudding of coconut, brown sugar, and taro).

Bento, another popular choice for the dine-and-dash set, is also available throughout Hawaii. The compact, boxed assortment of picnic fare usually consists of neatly arranged sections of rice, pickled vegetables, and fried chicken, beef, or pork. The bento is a derivative of the "kau kau tin" that served as the modest lunch box for Japanese immigrants who labored in the sugar and pineapple fields. Today you'll find bentos dispensed ubiquitously throughout Hawaii, from department stores like Daiei and Shirokiya (bento bonanzas) to corner delis and supermarkets.

Also from the plantations come *manapua,* a bready, doughy round with tasty fillings of sweetened pork or sweet beans. In the old days, the Chinese "manapua man" would make his rounds in the camps and villages with bamboo containers balanced on a rod over his shoulders. Today you'll find white or whole-wheat manapua containing chicken, vegetables, curry, and other savory fillings.

The daintier Chinese delicacy, dim sum, is made of translucent wrappers filled with fresh seafood, pork hash, and vegetables, served for breakfast and lunch in Chinatown restaurants. The Hong-Kong style dumplings are ordered fresh and hot from bamboo steamers from invariably brusque servers who move their carts from table to table. Much like hailing a taxi in Manhattan, you have to be quick and loud for dim sum.

TASTY TREATS: SHAVE ICE & MALASSADAS

For dessert or a snack, particularly in Haleiwa, the prevailing choice is shave ice, the Island version of a snow cone. At places like Matsumoto Store in Haleiwa and Waiola Store in McCully, particularly on hot, humid days, long lines of shave ice lovers gather for their rainbow-colored cones heaped with finely shaved ice and topped with sweet tropical syrups. The fast-melting mounds require prompt, efficient consumption and are quite the local summer ritual for sweet tooths. Aficionados order shave ice with ice cream and sweetened azuki beans plopped in the middle.

You may also encounter malassadas, the Portuguese version of a doughnut, and if you do, it's best to eat them immediately. A leftover malassada has all the appeal of a heavy, lumpen cold doughnut. When fresh and hot, however, as at school carnivals (where they attract the longest lines), or at bakeries and roadside stands (such as Agnes Portuguese Bake Shop in Kailua, Oahu, and Tex Drive Inn in Honokaa), the sugary, yeasty doughnut-without-a-hole is enjoyed by many as one of the enduring legacies of the Portuguese in Hawaii.

PINEAPPLES, PAPAYAS & OTHER FRESH ISLAND FRUITS

Lanai isn't growing pineapples commercially anymore, but low-acid, white-fleshed, wondrously sweet Hawaiian Sugarloaf pineapples are being commercially grown, on a small scale, on Kauai as well as the Big Island.

That is just one of the developments in a rapidly changing agricultural scene in Hawaii, where the litchi-like Southeast Asian rambutan, longan (Chinese dragon's-eye litchis), 80-pound Indian jackfruits, starfruit, luscious, custardy mangosteen, and the usual mangoes, papayas, guava, and *lilikoi* (passion fruit) make up the dazzling parade of fresh island fruit that ebb and flow with the seasons.

Papayas, bananas, and pineapples grow year-round, but pineapples are always sweetest, juiciest, and yellowest in the summer. While new papaya hybrids are making their way into the marketplace, the classic bests include the fleshy, firm-textured Kahuku papayas, the queen of them all; the Big Island's sweet Kapoho and Puna papayas; and the fragile, juicy, and red Sunrise papayas from Kauai. Apple bananas are smaller, firmer, and tarter than the standard, and are a local specialty among the dozens of varieties (20 types grow wild) that flourish throughout the islands.

Litchis and mangoes are long-awaited summer fruit. Mangoes begin appearing in late spring or early summer and can be found at roadside fruit stands in windward Oahu, at Chinatown markets, and at health-food stores, where the high prices may shock you. My favorite is the white pirie, rare and resiny, fiberless, and so sweet and juicy it makes the high-profile Hayden seem prosaic. White piries are difficult to find but occasionally appear, along with litchis and other coveted seasonal fruit, at the Maunakea Marketplace in Chinatown, or at Paradise Produce Company nearby.

Molokai watermelons are a summer hit and the best watermelons in the state. But Kahuku watermelons, available from stands along Oahu's north shore roadside in the summer months, give them a run for their money; the Kahukus are juicy and sweet, and the season is woefully short-lived.

In the competitive world of oranges, the Kau Gold navel oranges from southern Hawaii Island put Sunkist to shame. Grown in the volcanic soil and sunny conditions of the South Point region (the southernmost point in the United States), the oranges, a winter crop, are brown, rough, and anything but pretty. But the browner and uglier they are, the sweeter and juicier. Because the thin-skinned oranges are tree-ripened, they're fleshy and heavy with liquid, and will spoil you for life.

If you're eager to sample the newly developed crops of South American and Southeast Asian fruit with unpronounceable names that are appearing in Island cuisine, check out Frankie's Nursery in Waimanalo while you're on Oahu. It's the hot spot of exotic fruit, *the* place to sate your curiosity and your palate.

5 The Natural World: An Environmental Guide to the Islands

by Jeanette Foster

Born of violent volcanic eruptions from deep beneath the ocean's surface, the first Hawaiian islands emerged about 70 million years ago—more than 200 million years after the major continental land masses had been formed. Two thousand miles from the nearest continent, Mother Nature's fury began to carve beauty from barren rock. Untiring volcanoes spewed forth curtains of fire that cooled into stone. Severe tropical storms, some with hurricane-force winds, battered and blasted the cooling lava rock into a series of shapes. Ferocious earthquakes flattened, shattered, and reshaped the islands into precipitous valleys, jagged cliffs, and recumbent flat lands. Monstrous surf and gigantic tidal waves rearranged and polished the lands above and below the reaches of the tide.

It took millions upon millions of years for nature to chisel the familiar form of Diamond Head on Oahu, to form Maui's majestic peak of Haleakala, to create the waterfalls of Molokai's northern side, to shape the reefs of Hulopoe Bay on Lanai, and to establish the lush rain forests of the Big Island. The result is an island chain like no other on the planet—a tropical dream of a landscape, rich in unique flora and fauna, surrounded by a vibrant underwater world that will haunt your memory forever.

THE ISLAND LANDSCAPES

Hawaii is more than palm trees and white sands: Nearly every type of climate and topography in the world exists in the islands, from subarctic conditions to lava-rock beaches, from verdant rain forests to arid deserts, from fertile farming areas to swamps. Each island has its own particular climate and topography.

The Big Island   The largest island at some 4,034 square miles (and still growing), the Big Island is twice the size of all the other Hawaiian islands combined. Measuring 93 miles long by 76 miles wide, it's home to every type of climate zone existing in Hawaii. It's not uncommon for there to be 12 feet of snow on the two largest mountain peaks, 13,796-foot Mauna Kea and 13,680-foot Mauna Loa. These mountains are the tallest in the state; what's more, when measured from their true base on the ocean floor, they reach 32,000 feet, making them the tallest mountains in the world. At 4,077 feet, Kilauea Volcano has been continuously erupting since January 3, 1983; it has added more than 600 acres of new land to the Big Island since then. Just a few miles from the barely cooled barren lava lies a pristine rain forest, while on the southern end there's an arid desert. The rest of the island contains tropical terrain; white-, black-, even green-sand beaches; windswept grasslands; and productive farming and ranching areas producing tropical fruits, macadamia nuts, coffee, and ornamental flowers.

Maui   When two volcanoes—Mauna Kahalawai, a 5,277-foot ancient volcano in the West Maui Mountains, and 10,000-foot Haleakala—flowed together a million or so years ago, the event gave the "Valley Isle" of Maui a range of climates from arid desert to tropical rain forest. The 728-square-mile island is the only place in the world where you can drive from sea level to 10,000 feet in just 34 miles, passing through tropical beaches, sugar and pineapple plantations, rolling grassy hills, past the timber line, up to the lunarlike surface of the top of Haleakala. In addition to 33 miles of public beaches on the south and western shores, Maui is home to the arid dry lands of Kihei, the swampy bogs of the West Maui Mountains, the rain forest of Hana, and the desert of Kaupo.

Kahoolawe Just 7 miles southwest of Maui lies Kahoolawe, the smallest of the main Hawaiian islands. This island has a very unique topography: After years of overgrazing by ranchers, then as a U.S. Military bombing target from 1945 to 1994, the fairly flat island has lost most of its topsoil. Kahoolawe is an arid island with some beautiful white-sand beaches. Native Hawaiians, who recently reclaimed the island from the federal government, are attempting to restore, reforest, and replant the island. Access to Kahoolawe is restricted.

Lanai This small, kidney bean–shaped island—only 13 miles wide by 17 miles long—rises out of the ocean like the shell of a turtle, with cliffs on the west side that rise to a high point of 3,370 feet. Lanai slopes down to sea level on the east and south sides. The only town on the island, Lanai City, sits in the clouds at 1,600 feet. The high point of the island is covered with Norfolk pines and is usually shrouded in clouds. The arid beaches survive on minimal rainfall. One area in particular stands out: the Garden of the Gods, just 7 miles from Lanai City. Here, oddly strewn boulders lie in the amber- and ocher-colored dirt, and bizarre stone formations dot the landscape. The ancient Hawaiians formed romantic legends explaining this enigma, but modern-day scientists are still debating this mystery.

Molokai Roughly the shape of Manhattan, Molokai is 37 miles long and 10 miles wide, with a thumb protruding out of the north shore. The north shore begins on the west, with miles of white-sand beaches that fringe a desertlike landscape. The protruding thumb—the Kalaupapa Peninsula—is cut off by a fence of cliffs, some 2,000 feet tall, which lines the remainder of the north side. Molokai can be divided into two areas: the dry west end, where the high point is 1,381 feet; and the rainy, tropical east and north ends where the high point is Mount Kamakou, at 4,970 feet.

Oahu Home to Honolulu, Oahu is the third largest island in Hawaii (behind the Big Island and Maui). It's also the most urban, with a population of nearly 900,000. Oahu, which is 40 miles long by 26 miles wide, is defined by two mountain ranges: the Waianae Ridge (Mt. Kaala, at 4,050 feet, is the highest point on the island) in the west, and the jagged Koolaus in the east, which form a backdrop for Honolulu. The mountain ranges divide the island into three different environments: The windward side of the island is lush with greenery, ferns, tropical plants, and waterfalls. On the other side, the area between the Waianae Range and the ocean is drier, with sparse vegetation, little rainfall, and an arid landscape. In between the two mountain ranges lies the central Ewa Valley; it's moderate in temperature and vibrant with tropical plants, agricultural fields, and trees.

Kauai This compact island, 25 miles long by 33 miles wide with 137 miles of coastline, has Mount Waialeale, the island's highest point at nearly 5,000 feet and the earth's wettest spot, with more than 400 inches of rain annually. Just west of Mount Waialeale is the barren landscape of Waimea Canyon—dubbed "the Grand Canyon of the Pacific"—the result of the once 10,000-foot-tall Olokele shield volcano, which collapsed and formed a caldera (crater) some 3,600 feet deep and 14 miles across. Peaks and craters aren't Kauai's only distinctive landscape features, though, for miles of white-sand beaches rim most of the island, with majestic 2,700-foot cliffs—the spectacular Na Pali Coast—completing the circle. Lush tropical jungle inhabits the north side of the island while balmy, palm tree–lined beaches are located in the south.

Hawaiian Islands

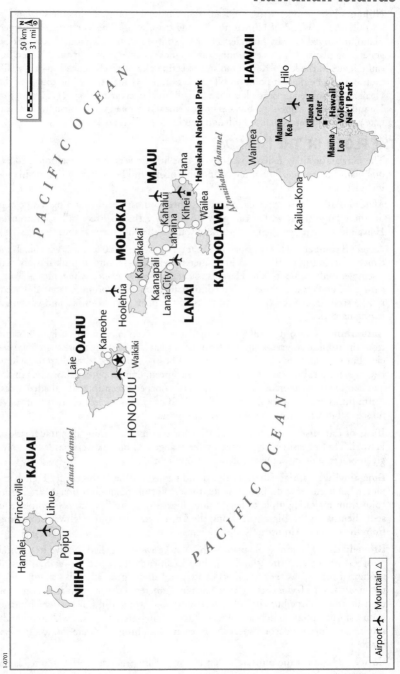

Airport ✈   Mountain △

33

Niihau   Just 17 miles across the Kaulakahi Channel from Kauai lies the small 6-by-18-mile-square island of Niihau, the "forbidden island." This is a privately owned island, inhabited only by Hawaiians living a simple life (no telephones, no electrical generating plant). It's also a working cattle ranch. Niihau is very dry and barren because it sits in the lee of Kauai; moisture-bearing clouds rarely make it past Kauai's mountains. The highest point on Niihau is only 1,281 feet, but at the center of the bleak and desolate landscape lies Lake Halalii, the largest natural lake (182 acres) in Hawaii. Niihau's white-sand beaches border emerald-colored waters offshore. You can take a day trip from Kauai to Niihau if you like; see Chapter 10.

THE FLORA OF THE ISLANDS

The Hawaii of today radiates with sweet-smelling flowers, lush vegetation, and exotic plant life. Some of the more memorable plants and flowers found in the islands include:

African Tulip Trees   Even at a long distance, you can see the flaming red flowers on these large trees, which can grow to be more than 50 feet tall. Children in Hawaii love them because the buds hold water—they use them as water pistols.

Angel's Trumpet   This is a small tree that can grow up to 20 feet tall, with an abundance of large (up to 10 inches in diameter) pendants—white or pink flowers that resemble, well, trumpets. The Hawaiians call them *nana-honua,* which means "earth gazing." The flowers, which bloom continually from early spring to late fall, have a musky scent. However, beware: All parts of the plant are poisonous and contain a strong narcotic.

Anthurium   One of Hawaii's most popular cut flowers, anthuriums originally came from the tropical Americas and the Caribbean islands. There are more than 550 species, but the most popular in Hawaii are the heart-shaped red, orange, pink, white, and even purple flowers with a tail-like spathe (green, orange, pink, red, white, purple, and combinations thereof). Look for the heart-shaped green leaves in shaded areas. Anthuriums are very prolific on the Big Island of Hawaii. These exotic plants have no scent, but will last several weeks as cut flowers.

Birds of Paradise   This native of Africa has become something of a trademark of Hawaii. They're easily recognizable by the orange and blue flowers nestled in gray-green bracts, looking somewhat like birds in flight.

Bougainvillea   Originally from Brazil and named for the 18th-century French explorer Louis Antoine de Bougainville, these colorful, tissue-thin bracts ranging in color from majestic purple to fiery orange hide tiny white flowers. A good place to spot them is on the Big Island along the Queen Kaahumanu Highway stretching from the Keahole Airport to Kailua-Kona.

Bromeliads   The pineapple plant is the best-known bromeliad. Native to tropical South America and the islands of the Caribbean, there are more than 1,400 species. "Bromes," as they are affectionately called, are generally spiky plants ranging in size from a few inches to several feet in diameter. They're popular not only for their unusual foliage but also for their strange and wonderful flowers, which range from colorful spikes to delicate blossoms resembling orchids. Used widely in landscaping and interior decor, especially in resort areas, bromeliads are found on every island.

Coffee   Hawaii is the only state that commercially produces coffee. Coffee is an evergreen shrub with shiny, waxy, dark-green, pointed leaves. The flower is a small, fragrant white blossom that develops into half-inch berries that turn bright red when ripe. Look for coffee at elevations above 1,500 feet on the Kona side of the Big Island, where it has been cultivated for more than 100 years, and on large coffee plantations on Kauai, Molokai, and Maui.

FRUIT TREES

Papaya   One of the sweetest of all tropical fruits, the pear-shaped papaya turns yellow or reddish pink when ripe. They are found at the base of the large, scalloped-shaped leaves on a pedestal-like, nonbranched tree whose trunk is hollow. Papayas ripen year-round.

Breadfruit   A large tree—over 60 feet tall—with broad, sculpted, dark-green leaves, the famous breadfruit produces a round, head-size green fruit which is a staple in diets of all Polynesians. When roasted or baked, the whitish-yellow meat tastes somewhat like a sweet potato.

Banana   Edible bananas are among the oldest of the world's food crops. By the time Europeans arrived in the islands, the Hawaiians had more than 40 different types of bananas planted. Most banana plants have long green leaves hanging from the tree, with the flower giving way to fruit in clusters.

Litchi   This evergreen tree, which can grow to well over 30 feet across, originated in China. Small flowers grow into panicles about a foot long in June and July. The round, red-skinned fruit appears shortly afterward.

Macadamia   A transplant from Australia, macadamia nuts have become a commercial crop in recent decades in Hawaii, especially on the Big Island of Hawaii and Maui. The large trees—up to 60 feet tall—bear a hard-shelled nut encased in a leathery husk, which splits open and dries when ripe.

Mango   From Indonesia and Malaysia comes the delicious mango, a fruit with peachlike flesh. Mango season usually begins in the spring and lasts through the summer, depending on the variety. The trees can grow to more than 100 feet tall. The tiny reddish-flowers give way to a green fruit that turns red-yellow when ripe. Some people enjoy unripe mangoes, either thinly sliced or in chutney, a traditional Indian preparation. The mango sap can cause a skin rash on some people.

MORE FLOWERS

Gingers   Some of the most fragrant flowers in Hawaii are white and yellow gingers, which the Hawaiians call 'awapuhi-ke'oke'o and 'awapuhi-melemele. Usually found in clumps and growing 4 to 7 feet tall in areas blessed by rain, these sweet-smelling, 3-inch-wide flowers are composed of three dainty petal-like stamens and three long, thin petals. Both white and yellow gingers are so prolific that many people assume they are native to Hawaii; actually, they were introduced in the 19th century from the Indonesia-Malaysia area. Look for white and yellow ginger from late spring to fall. If you see them on the side of the road, stop and pick a few blossoms—your car will be filled with a divine fragrance for the rest of the day. The only downside is that, once picked, they live only briefly.

Other members of the ginger family frequently seen in Hawaii (there are some 700 species) include red, shell, and torch gingers. Red ginger consists of tall, green stalks with foot-long red "flower heads." The red "petals" are actually bracts; inch-long white flowers are protected by the bracts and can be seen if you look down into the red head. Red ginger ('awapuhi-'ula'ula in Hawaiian), which does not share the heavenly smell of white ginger, will last a week or longer when cut. Look for red ginger from spring through late fall. Cool, wet mountain forests are ideal conditions for shell ginger; Hawaiians called them 'awapuhi-luheluhe, which means "drooping" ginger. Natives of India and Burma, these plants, with their pearly white, clam shell–like blossoms, bloom from spring to fall.

Perhaps the most exotic gingers are the red or pink torch gingers. Cultivated in Malaysia as seasoning (the young flower shoots are used in curries), torch ginger rises directly out of the ground; the flower stalks, which are about 5 to 8 inches in length, resemble the fire of a lighted torch. One of the few gingers that can bloom year-round, the Hawaiians called this plant *'awapuhi-ko'oko'o,* or "walking-stick" ginger.

Heliconias Some 80 species of the colorful heliconia family came to Hawaii from the Caribbean and Central and South America. The bright yellow, red, green, and orange colored bract overlap and appear to unfold like origami birds. The most obvious heliconia to spot is the lobster claw, which resembles a string of boiled crustacean pincers—the brilliant crimson bracts alternate on the stem. Another prolific heliconia is the parrot's beak. Growing to about hip height, the parrot's beak is composed of bright-orange flower bracts with black tips, not unlike the beak of a parrot. Look for parrot's beak in the spring and summer, when they bloom in profusion.

Hibiscus One variety of this year-round blossom, the yellow hibiscus, is the official state flower. The 4- to 6-inch hibiscus flowers come in a range of colors, from lily white to lipstick red. The flowers resemble crepe paper, with stamens and pistils protruding spirelike from the center. Hibiscus hedges can grow up to 15 feet tall. Once plucked, the flowers wither quickly.

Jacaranda Beginning around March and sometimes lasting until early May, these huge, lacy-leaved trees metamorphose into large clusters of spectacular lavender-blue sprays. The bell-shaped flowers drop quickly, leaving a majestic purple carpet beneath the tree.

Night-Blooming Cereus Look along rock walls for this spectacular night-blooming flower. Originally from Central America, this vinelike member of the cactus family has green scalloped edges and produces foot-long white flowers that open as darkness falls and wither as the sun rises. The plant also bears a red fruit that is edible.

Orchids To many minds, nothing says Hawaii more than orchids. The orchid family is the largest in the entire plant kingdom; orchids are found in most parts of the world. There are some species that are native to Hawaii, but they're inconspicuous in most places, so most people overlook them. The most widely grown orchid—and the major source of flowers for leis and garnish for tropical libations—are the vanda orchids. The vandas used in the commercial flower industry in Hawaii are generally lavender or white, but they grow in a rainbow of colors, shapes, and sizes. The orchids used for corsages are the large, delicate cattleya; the ones used in floral arrangements—you'll probably see them in your hotel lobby—are usually dendrobiums. When you're on the Big Island, don't pass up a chance to wander through the numerous orchid farms around Hilo.

Plumeria Also known as frangipani, this sweet-smelling, five-petal flower, found in clusters on trees, is the most popular choice of lei makers. The Singapore plumeria has five creamy-white petals, with a touch of yellow in the center. Another popular variety, ruba—with flowers from soft pink to flaming red—is also used in leis. When picking plumeria, be careful of the sap from the flower, as it is poisonous and can stain clothes.

Protea Originally from South Africa, this unusual plant comes in more than 40 different varieties. Proteas are shrubs that bloom into a range of flower types. Different species of proteas range from those resembling pincushions to a species that looks just like a bouquet of feathers. Proteas are long-lasting cut flowers; once dried, they will last for years.

OTHER TREES & PLANTS

Among the world's largest trees, **banyans** have branches that grow out and away from the trunk, forming descending roots that grow down to the ground to feed and form additional trunks, making the tree very stable during tropical storms. The banyan in the courtyard next to the old Court House in Lahaina, on Maui, is an excellent example of a spreading banyan—it covers two-thirds of an acre.

Monkeypod trees are among Hawaii's most majestic trees; they grow more than 80 feet tall and 100 feet across. Seen near older homes and in parks, the leaves of the monkeypod drop in February and March. The wood from the tree is a favorite of wood-working artisans.

One very uncommon and unusual plant—in fact seen only on the Big Island and in the Haleakala Crater on Maui—is the **silversword.** Once a year, this rare relative of the sunflower family blooms between July and September. Resembling more of a pinecone than a sunflower, the silversword in bloom is a fountain of red-petaled, daisylike flowers that turn silver soon after blooming.

Around pools, streams, and in neatly planted fields, you'll see the green heart-shaped leaves of **taro,** whose dense roots are a staple of all Polynesians. The ancient Hawaiians pounded the roots into poi. Originally from Sri Lanka, taro is not only a food crop, but is also grown as an ornamental.

One not so rare-and-unusual plant is **marijuana,** or *pakalolo*—"crazy weed" as the Hawaiians call it—which is grown throughout the islands. You probably won't see it as you drive along the roads, but if you go hiking you may glimpse the feathery green leaves with tight clusters of buds. Despite years of police effort to eradicate the plant, the illegal industry continues. Don't be tempted to pick a few buds, as the purveyors of this nefarious industry don't take kindly to poaching.

THE ISLANDS' FAUNA

When the first Polynesians arrived in Hawaii between 500 and 800 A.D., scientists say they found some 67 varieties of endemic Hawaiian birds, a third of which are now believed to be extinct. What's even more astonishing is what they didn't find—there were no reptiles, amphibians, mosquitoes, lice, or fleas, not even a cockroach.

MAMMALS

There were only two endemic mammals: the **hoary bat** and the **monk seal.** The small bat, called *ope'ape'a,* must have accidentally blown to Hawaii earlier from either North or South America. It still can be seen during its early evening forays, especially around the Kilauea Crater on the Big Island of Hawaii.

The Hawaiian monk seal, a relative of warm water seals found in the Caribbean and Mediterranean, was nearly slaughtered into extinction for its skin and oil during the 19th century. These seals have recently experienced a minor population explosion, forcing relocation of some males from their protected homes in the islets north of the main Hawaiian islands. Periodically, these endangered marine mammals turn up at various beaches throughout the state. They are protected under federal law by the Marine Mammals Protection Act. If you're fortunate enough to see a monk seal, just look; don't disturb one of Hawaii's living treasures.

The first Polynesians brought a few animals from home: dogs, pigs, and chickens (all were for eating). A stowaway on board the Polynesian sailing canoes was the rat. All four animals are still found in the Hawaiian wild today.

BIRDS

More species of native birds have become extinct in Hawaii in the last 200 years than anywhere else on the planet. Of the 67 native species, 23 are extinct, 29 are endangered, and one is threatened. Even the Hawaiian crow, **'alala,** is threatened.

The **a'eo,** or Hawaiian stilt, a 16-inch-long bird with a black head, black coat, white underside, and long pink legs, can be found in protected wetlands like the Kanaha Wild Life Sanctuary on Maui (where it shares its natural habitat with the Hawaiian coot), the Kealia Pond on Maui, and the Hanalei National Wildlife Refuge on Kauai, which is also home to the Hawaiian duck. Other areas to see protected birds are the Kipuku Puaulu (Bird Park) and the Ola'a Rain Forest, both in Hawaii Volcanoes National Park on the Big Island, and at Goat Island bird refuge off Oahu, where you can see wedge-tailed shearwaters nesting.

Another great birding venue is the 4,345-acre Kokee Wilderness Forest on Kauai. Various native birds that have been spotted include some of the 22 species of the native honey creepers whose songs fill the forest. Frequently seen are the **apapane** (a red bird with black wings and curved black bill), **i'iwi** (another red bird with black wings but with orange legs and salmon-colored bill), the **amakihi** (a plain olive-green bird with a long straight bill), and the **anianiau** (a tiny yellow bird with a thin, curved bill). Also seen in the forest is the **elepaio,** a small, gray flycatcher with an orange breast and an erect tail. A curious fellow, the elepaio comes out to investigate any unusual whistles. The most common native bird at Kokee—and the most easily seen—is the **moa,** or red jungle fowl, a chicken that was brought to Hawaii by the Polynesians.

To get a good glimpse of the seabirds that frequent Hawaii, drive to Kilauea Point on Kauai's north shore. Here, you can easily spot **red-** and **white-footed boobies, wedge-tailed shearwaters, frigate birds, red-tailed tropic birds,** and the **Laysan albatross.**

Endemic to the islands, the **nene** is Hawaii's state bird. It is being brought back from the brink of extinction through captive breeding and by strenuous protection laws. A relative of the Canadian goose, the nene stands about 2 feet high and has a black head and yellow cheek, a buff neck with deep furrows, a grayish-brown body, and clawed feet. It gets its name from its two syllable, high nasal call, "nay-nay." The approximately 500 nenes in existence can be seen in only three locations: at Haleakala National Park on Maui, at Mauna Kea State Park bird sanctuary, and on the slopes of Mauna Kea on the Big Island.

The Hawaiian short-eared owl, **pueo,** which grows to about 12- to 17-inches in size, can be seen at dawn and dusk on Kauai, Maui, and the Big Island when the black-billed, brown-and-white bird goes hunting for rodents. Pueos were highly regarded by Hawaiians; according to legend, spotting a pueo is a good omen.

OTHER LAND FAUNA

Geckos   These harmless, soft-skinned, insect-eating lizards come equipped with suction pads on their feet that enable them to climb walls and windows, so that they can reach tasty insects like mosquitoes and cockroaches. You'll see them on windows outside a lighted room at night, or hear their cheerful chirp.

Mongooses   The mongoose was a mistake in Hawaii. It was brought here in the 19th century to counteract the ever-growing rat problem. But rats are nocturnal creatures, sleeping during the day and wandering out at night. Mongooses, however, are day creatures. Instead of getting rid of the rat problem, the mongooses eat bird eggs, enhancing the deterioration of the native bird population in Hawaii.

Snakes   Thanks to strict measures to keep snakes out of the state, Hawaii has but one tiny earthwormlike snake. On the island of Guam, the brown tree snake has obliterated most of the bird population. Officials in Hawaii are well aware of this danger and are committed to preventing snakes from entering the state.

SEALIFE

Approximately 680 species of fish are known to inhabit the waters around the Hawaiian Islands. Of those, approximately 450 species stay close to the reef and inshore areas.

CORAL

The reefs surrounding Hawaii are made up of various coral and algae. The living coral grow through sunlight that feeds a specialized algae, called zooxanthellae, which in turn allows the development of the coral's calcareous skeleton. It takes thousands of years for reefs to develop. The reef attracts and supports fish and crustaceans, which use the reef for food, habitat, mating, and raising their young. Mother Nature can cause the destruction of the reef with a strong storm or large waves, but humans—through a seemingly unimportant act such as touching the coral—has proven even more destructive to the fragile reefs.

The coral most frequently seen in Hawaii are hard, rocklike formations named for their familiar shapes: antler, cauliflower, finger, plate, and razor coral. Wire coral looks just like its name—a randomly bent wire growing straight out of the reef. Some coral appear soft, such as tube coral; it can be found in the ceilings of caves. Black coral, which resemble winter-bare trees or shrubs, are found at depths of over 100 feet.

REEF FISH

Of the approximately 450 reef fish, about 27% are native to Hawaii and are found no where else on the planet. This may seem surprising for a string of isolated islands, 2,000 miles from the nearest land mass. But over the millions of years of gestation of the Hawaiian Islands, as they were born from the erupting volcanoes, ocean currents—mainly from Southeast Asia—carried the larvae of thousands of marine animals and plants to Hawaii's reef. Of those, approximately 100 species not only adapted, but thrived.

Some species are much bigger and more plentiful than their Pacific cousins, and many developed unique characteristics. Some, like the lemon or milletseed butterfly fish, are not only particular to Hawaii but also unique within their larger, worldwide family in their specialized schooling and feeding behaviors. Another surprising thing about Hawaii endemics is how common some of the native fish are: You can see the saddleback wrasse, for instance, on virtually any snorkeling excursion or dive in Hawaiian waters.

Some of the reef fish you might spot while you're underwater are:

Angel Fish   Often mistaken for butterfly fish, angel fish can be distinguished by the spine, located low on the gill plate. Angel fish are very shy; several species live in colonies close to coral for protection.

Blennys   Small, elongated fish, blennys range from 2 to 10 inches long, with the majority in the 3- to 4-inch range. Blennys are so small that they can live in tide pools; you might have a hard time spotting one.

Butterfly Fish   Some of the most colorful of the reef fish, butterfly fish are usually seen in pairs (scientists believe they mate for life) and appear to spend most of their day feeding. There are 22 species of butterfly fish, of which three (blue-stripe, lemon or milletseed, and multiband or pebbled butterfly fish) are endemic. Most butterfly fish have a dark band through the eye and a spot near the tail resembling an eye, meant to confuse their predators (the moray eel loves to lunch on butterfly fish).

Eels   Moray and conger eels are the common eels seen in Hawaii. Morays are usually docile unless provoked, or if there is food or an injured fish around. Unfortunately, some morays have been fed by divers and—being intelligent creatures—associate divers with food; thus, they can become aggressive. But most morays like to keep to themselves, hidden in their hole or crevice. While morays may look menacing, conger eels look downright happy, with big lips and pectoral fins (situated so that they look like big ears) that give them the appearance of a perpetual smiling face. Conger eels have crushing teeth so they can feed on crustaceans; in fact, since they're sloppy eaters, they usually live with shrimp and crabs who feed off the crumbs they leave.

Parrot Fish   One of the largest and most colorful of the reef fish, parrot fish can grow up to 40 inches long. Parrot fish are easy to spot—their front teeth are fused together, protruding like buck teeth and resembling a parrot's beak. These unique teeth allow them to feed by scraping algae from rocks and coral. The rocks and coral pass through the parrot fish's system, resulting in fine sand. In fact, most of the white sand found in Hawaii is parrot fish waste; one large parrot fish can produce a ton of sand a year. Hawaiian native parrot fish species include yellowbar, regal, and spectacled.

Scorpion Fish   This is a family of what scientists call "ambush predators." They hide under camouflaged exteriors and ambush their prey when they come along. Several sport a venomous dorsal spine. These fish don't have a gas bladder, so when they stop swimming, they sink—that's why you usually find them "resting" on ledges and on the ocean bottom. Although they're not aggressive, an inattentive snorkeler or diver could feel the effects of those venomous spines—so be very careful where you put your hands and feet in the water.

Surgeon Fish   Sometimes called tang, the surgeon fish get their name from the scalpel-like spines located on each side of their bodies near the base of their tails. Some surgeon fish have a rigid spine; others have the ability to fold their spine against their body until it's needed for defense purposes. Some surgeon fish, like the brightly colored yellow tang, are boldly colored. Others are adorned in more conservative shades of gray, brown, or black. The only endemic surgeon fish—and the most abundant in Hawaiian waters—is the convict tang, (*manini* in Hawaiian), a pale white fish with vertical black stripes (like a convict's uniform).

Wrasses   This is a very diverse family of fish, ranging in size from 2 to 15 inches. Several wrasses are brilliantly colored and change their colors through aging and sexual dimorphism (sex changing). Wrasses have the ability to change gender from female (when young) to male with maturation. There are several wrasses that are endemic to Hawaii: the Hawaiian cleaner, shortnose, belted, and gray (or old woman).

GAME FISH

Sportfishing lovers have a huge variety to choose from in Hawaii, from pan-sized snapper to nearly 1-ton marlin. Hawaii is known around the globe as *the* place for big game fish—marlin, swordfish, and tuna—but its waters are also great for catching other offshore fish like mahimahi, rainbow runner, and wahoo; coastal fish like barracuda and scad; bottom fish such as snappers, sea bass, and amberjack; and inshore fish like trevally, bonefish, and others.

There are six different kinds of **billfish** found in the offshore waters around the islands: Pacific blue marlin, black marlin, sailfish, broadbill swordfish, striped marlin, and shortbill spearfish. Hawaii billfish range in size from the 20-pound shortbill spearfish and striped marlin to an 1,805-pound Pacific blue marlin, the largest marlin ever caught on rod and reel anywhere in the world. **Tuna** ranges in size from small (a pound or less) mackerel tuna used as bait (Hawaiians call them *oioi*), to 250-pound yellowfin ahi tuna. Other species of tuna found in Hawaii are bigeye, albacore, kawakawa, and skipjack.

Some of the best eating fish are also found in offshore waters: **mahimahi** (also known as dolphin fish or dorado) in the 20- to 70-pound range, **rainbow runner** (*kamanu*) from 15 to 30 pounds, and **wahoo** (*ono*) from 15 to 80 pounds. Shoreline fishermen are always on the lookout for **trevally** (the state record for giant trevally is 191 lb.), **bonefish, ladyfish, threadfin, leatherfish,** and **goatfish.** Bottom fishermen pursue a range of **snappers**—red, pink, gray, and others—as well as **sea bass** (the state record is a whopping 563 lbs.) and **amberjack,** which weigh up to 100 pounds.

Reservoirs on Oahu and Kauai are home to Hawaii's many freshwater fish: **bass** (large, smallmouth, and peacock), **catfish** (channel and Chinese), **rainbow trout, bluegill sunfish, pungee,** and **oscar.** The state record for freshwater fish is the 43-pound, 13-ounce channel catfish caught in Lake Wilson on Oahu.

WHALES

The most popular visitors to Hawaii come every year around November and stay until the springtime (April or so) when they return to their summer home in Alaska. Humpback whales—some as big as a city bus and weighing many tons—migrate to the warm, protected Hawaiian waters in the winter to mate and calve.

On every island you can take whale-watching cruises that will let you observe these magnificent leviathans close up, or you can spot their signature spouts of water from shore as they expel water in the distance. Humpbacks grow to up to 45 feet long, so when they breach (propel their entire body out of the water) or even wave a fluke, you can see it for miles.

Humpbacks are among the biggest whales found in Hawaiian waters, but other whales—like pilot, sperm, false killer, melon-headed, pygmy killer, and beaked whales—can be seen year-round, especially in the calm waters off the Big Island's Kona Coast. These whales usually travel in pods of 20 to 40 animals and are very social, interacting with each other on the surface.

SHARKS

Yes, Virginia there are sharks in Hawaii, but more than likely you won't see a shark unless you specifically go looking for one. The ancient Hawaiians had great respect for sharks and believed that some sharks were reincarnated relatives who had returned to assist them.

About 40 different species of sharks inhabit the waters surrounding Hawaii, ranging from the totally harmless whale shark—at 60 feet, the world's largest fish—which has no teeth and is so docile that it frequently lets divers ride on its back, to the not-so-docile, infamous—and extremely uncommon—great white shark. The most common sharks seen in Hawaii are white-tip reef sharks, gray reef sharks (about 5 ft. long), and black-tip reef sharks (about 6 ft. long). Since records have been kept, starting in 1779, there have been only about 100 shark attacks in Hawaii, of which 40% have been fatal. The biggest number of attacks occurred after someone fell into the ocean from the shore or from a boat. In these cases, the sharks probably attacked after the person was dead.

General rules for avoiding sharks are: Don't swim at sunrise, sunset, or where the water is murky due to stream runoff—sharks may mistake you for one of their usual meals. And don't swim where there are bloody fish in the water (sharks become aggressive around blood).

HAWAII'S ECOSYSTEM PROBLEMS

Officials at Hawaii Volcanoes National Park on the Big Island saw a potential problem a few decades ago with people taking a few rocks home with them as "souvenirs." To prevent this problem from escalating, the park rangers "created" a legend that the fiery volcano goddess, Pele, did not like people taking anything (rocks, chunks of lava) from her home, and bad luck would befall anyone disobeying her wishes. There used to be a display case in the park's visitor center filled with letters from people who had taken rocks from the volcano, relating stories of all the bad luck that followed. Most of the letters begged Pele's forgiveness and instructed the rangers to please return the rock to the exact location that was its original home.

Unfortunately, Hawaii's other ecosystem problems can't be handled as easily.

Marine Life   Hawaii's beautiful and abundant marine life has attracted so many visitors that they threaten to overwhelm it. A great example of this overenthusiasm is Oahu's Hanauma Bay. Crowds flock to this beautiful bay, a marine preserve that features calm, protected swimming and snorkeling areas loaded with tropical reef fish. It was such a perfect spot that too many people flocked here, forcing government officials to limit the number of people that can enter the bay at any one time. Commercial tour operators have been restricted entirely in an effort to balance the people-to-fish ratio.

Another marine life conservation area that suffers from overuse is Molokini, a small crater off the coast of Maui. In the 1970s, residents made the area a conservation district in order to protect the unique aquariumlike atmosphere of the waters inside the arms of the crater. Unfortunately, once it was protected, everyone wanted to go there just to see what was worth special protection. Twenty years ago, one or two small 6-passenger boats made the trip once a day to Molokini; today, it is not uncommon to sight 20 or more boats, each carrying 20 to 49 passengers, moored inside the tiny crater. One tour operator has claimed that, on some days, it's so crowded that you can actually see a slick of suntan oil floating on the surface of the water.

People who fall in love with the colorful tropical fish and want to see them all the time back home are also thought to be impacting the health of Hawaii's reefs. The growth in home, office, and decor aquariums has risen dramatically in the last 20 years. As a result, more and more reef fish collectors are taking a growing number of reef fish from Hawaiian waters.

The reefs themselves have faced increasing impacts over the years. Runoff of soil and chemicals from construction, agriculture, erosion, and even heavy storms can blanket and choke a reef, which needs sunlight to survive. In addition, the intrusion of foreign elements—like breaks in sewage lines—can cause problems to Hawaii's reef. Human contact with the reef can also upset the ecosystem. Coral, the basis of the reef system, is very fragile; snorkelers and divers grabbing on to it can break off pieces which took decades to form. Feeding the fish can also upset the balance of the ecosystem (not to mention upsetting the digestive systems of the fish). One glass-bottom boat operator reported that they fed an eel for years, considering it their "pet" eel. One day the eel decided that he wanted more than just the food being offered and bit the diver's fingers. Divers and snorkelers report that in areas where the fish are fed, the fish have become more aggressive; clouds of reef fish—normally shy—surround divers, demanding food.

Flora   One of Hawaii's most fragile environments is the rain forest. Any intrusion— from a hiker carrying seeds in on their shoes to the rooting of wild boars—can upset the delicate balance in these complete ecosystems. In recent years, development has moved closer and closer to the rain forest. On the Big Island of Hawaii, people have protested the invasion of bulldozers and the drilling of geothermal wells in the Wao Kele O Puna rain forest for years, claiming that the damage done is irreparable.

Fauna   The biggest impact on the fauna in Hawaii is the decimation of native birds by feral animals, which have destroyed the bird's habitats, and by mongooses that have eaten the birds' eggs and young. Government officials are vigilant about snakes because of the potential damage tree snakes can do to the remaining birdlife.

Vog   The volcanic haze caused by gases released by the continuous eruption of the volcano on the flank of Kilauea on the Big Island, and the smoke from the fires set by the lava, has been dubbed "vog." This hazy air, which looks like smog from urban pollution, limits viewing from scenic vistas and plays havoc with photographers trying to get clear panoramic shots. Some people claim that the vog has even caused bronchial ailments.

3

Planning a Trip to Hawaii

by Rick Carroll

Hawaii looks and sounds so much like a foreign country that mainland Americans sometimes forget it's been the 50th state of the union since 1959. If you aren't careful, you could become one of those mainlanders who mistakenly begins a sentence with: "When I get back to the States . . . "

This chapter is devoted to the where, when, and how of your trip to this familiar yet different destination. Whether you plan to stay just a few days, a week, 2 weeks, or longer, there are many choices you'll need to make *before* leaving home. All this, and more, can be found in the sections that follow.

1 Visitor Information & Money

VISITOR INFORMATION

For information about traveling in Hawaii, contact the **Hawaii Visitors and Convention Bureau** (**HVCB**), Suite 801, Waikiki Business Plaza, 2270 Kalakaua Ave., Honolulu, HI 96815 (☎ **800/ GO-HAWAII** or 808/923-1811). Among other things, the bureau publishes the helpful *Accommodations and Car Rental Guide.*

The HVCB also has a U.S. mainland office at 180 Montgomery St., Suite 2360, San Francisco CA 94104 (☎ **800/353-5846**). All other HVCB offices on the mainland are now closed due to budget constraints.

If you want information about working and living in Hawaii, contact **The Chamber of Commerce of Hawaii,** 1132 Bishop St., Suite 200, Honolulu, HI 96815 (☎ **808/545-4300**).

HAWAII ON THE NET Hawaii may be the world's most remote inhabited island group, but more than 200 Internet sites now originate from the state, making it one of the most "wired" places in the country. You can preview the islands, visit or book a hotel room, get the weather report, order Kona coffee or exotic tropical flowers, check on surf conditions, see Maui's beaches, and much more. Many Hawaii bed-and-breakfasts now are on the net.

Here're some of my favorite links to Hawaii:

Hawaii Visitors Bureau: **http://www.visit.hawaii.org**
Great Outdoor Adventures of Hawaii: **http://www. cyber-hawaii.com/travel/**

Outrigger Hotels: **http://www.outrigger.com/infoweb**
NASA's Virtually Hawaii: **http://www.satlab.hawaii.edu/space/hawaii**

MONEY

Hawaii pioneered the use of automatic teller machines (ATMs) nearly 2 decades ago, and now has them everywhere except on Lanai. Elsewhere you'll find them at most banks, in supermarkets, at Long's Drugs stores, at Honolulu International Airport, and in some resorts and shopping centers like Ala Moana Center and Aloha Tower Market Place on Oahu and Whaler's Village in Kaanapali, Maui. It's actually cheaper and faster to get cash from an ATM than to fuss with traveler's checks; and credit cards are accepted just about everywhere. To find the location of the ATM nearest you, call **800/424-7787** for the Cirrus network or **800/843-7587** for the Plus system.

While the United States dollar is the coin of the realm in Hawaii, you can easily exchange most major foreign currencies (see "Money" in Chapter 4).

2 When to Go

CLIMATE

Since Hawaii lies just inside the tropical zone, it technically has only two seasons, both of them warm. There's a dry season that corresponds to summer, while the rainy season generally runs during the winter from November to March. It rains every day somewhere in the islands anytime of the year, but the rainy season can cause "gray" weather and spoil your tan. Fortunately, it seldom rains for more than 3 days straight.

The year-round temperature usually varies no more than 10°F, but it depends on where you are. The islands are like ships in that each has a leeward and a windward side. The leeward sides (the west and south) usually are hot and dry, while the windward sides (east and north) generally are cooler and moist. When you want arid, sun-baked, desertlike weather, go to leeward. When you want lush, often wet, junglelike weather, go to windward. Your best bet for total year-round sun is the Kohala Coast on the Big Island's leeward coast.

Hawaii also is full of microclimates because of its interior valleys, coastal plains, and mountain peaks. Mount Waialeale on Kauai is the wettest spot on earth, yet the Waimea Canyon just a few miles away is almost a desert. On the Big Island, Hilo is the wettest city in the nation with 180 inches of rainfall a year, while at Puako, only 50 miles away, it rains less than 6 inches a year.

If you travel into the mountains, it can change from summer to winter in a matter of hours, since it's cooler the higher up you go. In other words, if the weather doesn't suit you, go to the other side of the island—or head into the hills.

I think the best months to be in Hawaii are May and October, when the nearly perfect weather is even better—not so windy, not so humid, just right. It's off-season, kids are in school, and the tourists have thinned out. The state's "carrying capacity," as they say here, isn't maxed out. Hotels, restaurants, and attractions are not so crowded, and everyone is more relaxed. I'd say the third week in October or the third week in May are just about perfect.

On rare occasions the weather can be disastrous, like when Hurricane Iniki, the most powerful Pacific storm in history, crushed Kauai in 1992 with 225-mile-an-hour winds. Tsunamis, huge tidal waves caused by far-off earthquakes, have swept Hilo and the south shore of Oahu. But mostly, one day follows another here in glorious sunny procession, each quite like the other. You have only to decide where and how to spend them.

SEASONS

The tourist season doesn't correspond to the months when the weather's the best in Hawaii, but when it's the worst elsewhere. Since people prefer to come to Hawaii to get away from miserable winter weather, the "high" season, when prices are up and resorts are booked, is generally from mid-December through March or mid-April. The last 2 weeks of December in particular are the prime time to come to Hawaii; if you plan a holiday trip, make your reservations as early as possible, expect to travel with holiday crowds, and forget about bargain rates.

The demand is lowest in spring and fall—a paradox since these are the best seasons in Hawaii, in terms of reliably great weather and less competition for airline seats and rooms. If you're looking to save money, or just want to avoid the crowds, this is the time to go. Hotel rates tend to be lower—sometimes significantly—during this "off" season. Airfares also tend to be lower, and good packages and special deals are available; check with your travel agent or the "Travel" section of your local paper. Also see "Tips on Finding Accommodations," below.

HOLIDAYS

When Hawaii observes holidays, especially those over a long weekend, travel between the islands increases, interisland airline seats are fully booked, rental cars are at a premium, and hotels and restaurants will be busier than at other times.

Federal, state, and county government offices are closed on all **federal holidays:** January 1 (New Year's Day); third Monday in January (Martin Luther King, Jr., Day); third Monday in February (Presidents' Day, Washington's Birthday); last Monday in May (Memorial Day); July 4 (Independence Day); first Monday in September (Labor Day); second Monday in October (Columbus Day); November 11 (Veteran's Day); fourth Thursday in November (Thanksgiving Day); and December 25 (Christmas).

State and county offices also are closed on **local holidays** including Prince Kuhio Day (March 26), honoring the Birthday of Hawaii's first delegate to the U.S. Congress; King Kamehameha Day (June 11), a statewide holiday commemorating Kamehameha the Great who united the islands and ruled from 1795 to 1819; and Admission Day (third Friday in August), which honors Hawaii's being admitted as the 50th state on August 21, 1959.

Other **special days** celebrated in Hawaii by many people but which involve no closing of federal, state, and county offices are Chinese New Year (Jan or Feb), Japanese Girl's Day (Mar 3), Buddha's Birthday (Apr 8), Father Damien's Day (Apr 15), Japanese Boy's Day (May 5), Samoan Flag Day (Aug), Aloha Week (Sept or Oct), and Pearl Harbor Day (Dec 7).

HAWAII CALENDAR OF EVENTS

January

- **Morey World Body Boarding Championship,** Banzai Pipeline, North Shore, Oahu. Competition is determined by the best wave selection and maneuvers on the wave. Early January. Call 808/396-2326.
- **Hula Bowl Football All-Star Classic,** Aloha Stadium, Oahu. An annual all-star football classic featuring America's top college players. Second week in January. Call 808/947-4141.
- **Celebration of Whales,** Four Seasons Resort, Wailea, Maui. Cetacean experts host discussions, whale-watching excursions, entertainment, social functions, and art exhibits. Last weekend in January. Call 808/847-8000.

- **Women's World Body Boarding Championship,** Banzai Pipeline, North Shore, Oahu. Held in conjunction with the bodysurfing competition, this international event crowns the world champion and awards the largest purse, now more than $20,000, on the women's tour. Late January to mid-Febraury. Call 808/ 638-1149.

- **Annual Cherry Blossom Festival,** Bishop Museum, Oahu. A culture and craft fair celebrating aspects of Japanese culture. Entertainment, games, and demonstrations. January through March. Call 808/949-2255.

February

- **NFL Pro Bowl Battle of the Gridiron,** Ihilani Resort & Spa, Oahu. Kicking off the NFL Pro Bowl, a position and skills-oriented challenge between the best of the best in the National Football League. First Saturday in February. Call 808/ 521-4322.

- **Buffalo's Big Board Classic,** Makaha Beach, Oahu. Surfing, longboarding, and canoe surfing contest. First 2 weeks in February. Call 808/951-7877.

- **NFL Pro Bowl,** Aloha Stadium, Oahu. The National Football League's best pro players square off in this annual gridiron all-star game. First Sunday in February. Call 808/486-9300.

- **United Airlines Hawaiian Open,** Waialae Country Club, Oahu. A $1.2 million PGA golf event featuring some of the top pros. Second week in February. Call 808/ 526-1232.

- **The Great Aloha Run,** Oahu. Thousands run 8.25 miles from Aloha Tower to Aloha Stadium. Always held on Presidents' Day (3rd Mon in Feb). Call 808/ 528-7388.

March

- **Hawaii Challenge International Sport Kite Championship,** Kapiolani Park, Oahu. First weekend in March. Call 808/922-5483.

- **Annual Mauna Kea Ski Meet,** Big Island. Host Dick Tillson invites intrepid skiers to open competition in men and women's parallel slalom on the biggest Pacific peak. First weekend in February. Call 808/943-6643.

- **Outrigger Hotels Hawaiian Mountain Tour,** Oahu. The world's top professional mountain bikers compete for a $50,000 purse in a 4-day, 5-stage race plus Downhill Mania and Dual Slalom. Event is open to all amateur classes too. Last weekend in March. Call 808/521-4322.

- **Molokai Hawaiian Paniolo Heritage Rodeo,** Molokai Rodeo Arena, Maunaloa Molokai. Molokai's cowboys celebrate Hawaii's *paniolo* heritage. Call 808/ 552-2681 for exact schedule and details.

April

- ✪ **Merrie Monarch Hula Festival,** Hilo, Big Island. Hawaii's biggest hula festival features three nights of modern and ancient dance competition in honor of King David Kalakaua, the "merrie monarch" who revived the dance. Usually the week after Easter. Call 808/935-9168.

- **Merrie Monarch Quilt Show, Wailoa Center,** Hilo, Big Island. Quilters offer workshops, classes and display traditional quilts. First Saturday in April to end of month. Call 808/935-9168.

- **Annual Ritz-Carlton, Kapalua Celebration of the Arts,** Ritz Carlton Kapalua, Maui. Contemporary and traditional artists give hands-on lessons. Mid-April. Call 808/669-6200.

May

- **Annual Lei Day Celebration,** various locations on all islands. May Day is Lei Day in Hawaii, celebrated with lei making contests, pageantry, arts and crafts, and a concert at the Waikiki Shell. May 1. Call 808/924-8934.

✪ **Pineapple Festival,** Hulopoe Beach Park, Lanai. Some of Hawaii's best musicians participate in Lanai's liveliest event, celebrating the golden fruit with everything from fishing tournaments to pineapple cooking contests, food and craft booths, water activities, and demonstrations by well-known chefs. Call 808/565-7600 or 808/524-0722.

- **Molokai Kayak Challenge,** Molokai-to-Oahu. Kayakers race 38 grueling miles from Kaluakoi Resort on Molokai to Hawaii Kai's Koko Marina. Mid-May. Call 808/239-4123.

- **World Fire-Knife Dance Championships & Samoan Festival,** Polynesian Cultural Center, Laie, Oahu. Junior and adult fire-knife dancers from around the world converge on the Center in the most amazing performance you'll ever see. Authentic Samoan food and cultural festivities. Mid-May. Call 808/293-3333.

- **State Fair,** Aloha Stadium, Honolulu. Our annual state fair is a great state fair, with the biggest rides and shows. A good time is had by all. Last Saturday in May through mid-June. Call 808/488-3389.

- **Banana Poka Festival,** Kokee State Park, Kauai. A forest education fair with slack-key music and craft-making activities. Usually last Sunday in May. Call the Kokee Natural History Museum at 808/335-9975.

June

- **King Kamehameha Holua Race,** Big Island. Ancient Hawaiians made sleds which they called holua, to slide down grassy slopes and even Mauna Kea when it snowed. This event recalls those golden days on the slopes with skis, sleds, and snowboards. Early June. Call 808/943-6643.

- **King Kamehameha Celebration,** statewide. It's a state holiday with a massive floral parade, *hoolaulea* (party) and much more. First weekend in June. Call 808/586-0333.

- **AT&T Dragon Boat Festival,** Ala Moana Beach, Honolulu. Teams from throughout Asia race. Mid-June. Call 808/734-6900.

- **King Kamehameha Hula Competition,** at Honolulu's Neal Blaisdell Center. One of the top hula competitions with dancers from as far away as Japan. Third weekend in June. Call 808/586-0333.

- **Taste Of Honolulu,** Civic Center Grounds, Honolulu. Benefiting Easter Seals campaign, Hawaii's premier outdoor food festival features tastings from 30 restaurants. Entertainment, beer and wine tasting, cooking demos, gourmet marketplace, children's activities. End of June. Call 808/536-1015.

- **Cowhorse Classic,** Molokai Rodeo Arena, Maunaloa, Molokai. The island's cowboys celebrate Hawaii's *paniolo* heritage. Call 808/552-2681 for the exact schedules and details.

July

- **Pacific Island Taro Festival,** Windward Community College, Kaneohe, Oahu. Music, storytelling, dance, arts-and-craft fair, and farmers markets celebrate the cultures and traditions of the Pacific Islands. Usually first Saturday in July. Call 808/235-7433.

- **Hawaii Seafood Festival.** Celebrations, cooking contests, demonstrations, themed restaurant meals, and more throughout the islands. Call 808/587-2683.

- **Walter J. McFarlane Regatta and Surf Race,** Waikiki, Oahu. An outrigger canoe regatta featuring 30 events. July 4. Call 808/921-1400.

✪ **Spotting Sea Turtles,** Mauna Lani Resort & Bungalows, 68-1400 Mauna Lani Dr. (off Hi. 19). Kevin Costner paid a total of $640,000 to sleep in a $3,500-a-night bungalow here during the year he shot *Waterworld* at Kawaihae Harbor. You can see where he slept if you want, but it's more fun to watch scores of endangered green sea turtles race down to the sea each year when they're released from the historic fishponds at Mauna Lani. July 4. Call 808/885-6622.

• **Na Wahine O' Hawaii,** McCoy Pavilion, Ala Moana Park, Honolulu. This all-female competition focuses on all aspects of the performing arts. Early July. Call 808/239-4336.

• **Kapalua Wine Symposium,** Kapalua, Maui. Famous wine and food experts and oenophiles gather at Ritz Carlton and Kapalua Bay hotels for formal tastings, panel discussions, and to sample new releases. Mid-July. Call 800/527-2581.

• **Hawaii International Jazz Festival,** Sheraton Waikiki, Honolulu. Presenting evening concerts plus daily jam sessions. Scholarship giveaways, the USC jazz band, along with many popular jazz and blues artists. Mid-July. Call 808/941-9974.

• **Prince Lot Hula Festival,** Moanalua Gardens, Honolulu. Authentic ancient and modern hula, as well as demonstrations and arts and crafts. Third Sunday in July. Call 808/839-5334.

• **Kolekole Pass Half Marathon,** Oahu. One of the state's most spectacular runs, a 13.1-mile course also open to race-walkers and walkers. From Schofield Barracks to the leeward side. Simply spectacular views. Third Sunday in July. Call 808/486-8420.

• **Ukulele Festival,** Kapiolani Bandstand, Honolulu. This annual event features 400 children and special guest stars. Presented by Sheraton Hotels in Waikiki. End of July. Call 808/732-3739.

August

• **Maui Onion Festival,** Whaler's Village, Kaanapali, Maui. Everything you ever wanted to know about the sweetest onions in the world. Food, entertainment, tasting, and Maui Onion Cook-Off. First week in August. Call 808/661-3271.

• **Duke Kahanamoku Beach Doubles Volleyball Championship,** Outrigger Canoe Club, Waikiki, Oahu. Mid-August. Call 808/923-1585.

• **Hawaiian Slack-Key Guitar Festival,** Oahu. Five-hour festival held annually, each year at a different location on Oahu, presenting the best of Hawaii's slack-key guitar players. Mid-August. Call 808/239-4336

• **Annual Hawaiian International Billfish Tournament,** Kailua-Kona, Big Island. World's largest billfish tournament attracts 66 teams who compete to catch the largest fish. Third week in August. Call 808/326-7820.

September

✪ **Aloha Festivals,** various locations statewide. Parades and other events celebrate Hawaiian culture and friendliness throughout the state. Mid-September. Call 808/545-1771 or 808/885-8086 for schedule of events.

• **Mountain Bike World Cup Finals,** Oahu locations. Mountain bikers from around the globe compete in the final events of the World Cup Cross-Country and Downhill. Early September. Call 808/521-4322.

• **Waikiki Rough-Water Swim,** Oahu. A 2.4-mile swim from Sans Souci Beach to Duke Kahanamoku Beach. Labor Day. Call 808/988-7788.

• **Na Wahine O Ke Kai,** Waikiki. A women's 40.8-mile Molokai to Oahu outrigger canoe race. Finishes at Duke Kahanamoku Beach, Hilton Hawaiian Village. End of September. Call 808/262-7567.

- **Outrigger Hotels Hawaiian Oceanfest,** various Oahu locations. A 2-week celebration of ocean sports includes the Hawaiian International Ocean Challenge featuring teams of the world's best professional lifeguards; Outrigger Waikiki Kings Race, an ocean iron-man race; Diamond Head Wahine Windsurfing Classic, the only all-women professional windsurfing competition; and Diamond Head Biathlon, a run/swim event. Great competitors, serious competition, a variety of evening events, and more. Second through last week in September, winds up with Armed Forces Family Festival on last Sunday in September. Call 808/521-4322.
- **Honolulu International Triathlon,** Waikiki, Oahu. Combines a 1.5km swim, 40km bike ride, and 15km run. End of September. Call 808/737-2422.

October

- **Makihiki Festival,** Waimea Valley, Oahu. Hawaiian games, crafts, music, and food, all in a tremendous natural setting, The Hula Kahiko Competition is a major highlight. First weekend in October. Call 808/638-8511.
- **Emalani Festival,** Kokee State Park, Kauai. This festival honors Her Majesty Queen Emma, an inveterate gardener and Hawaii's first environmental queen, who made an 1871 forest trek to Kokee with 100 friends. Call 808/335-9975.
- **Hawaii International Rugby Tournament,** Kapiolani Park, Waikiki, Honolulu. Teams from around the world gather to compete in this exciting tournament. The event has a division for all players including Masters, Social, Championship, 7-side, 9-side, and touch. Second week in October. Call 808/926-5641.
- **Molokai Hoe,** Molokai to Oahu. The season's biggest canoe race, this men's 40.8-mile outrigger contest crosses the channel from Molokai to finish at Fort DeRussy Beach in Waikiki. Mid-October. Call 808/261-6615.
- **Ironman World Triathalon.** World-class athletes run (26.2 miles), swim (2.4 miles), and bike (112) around the Big Island of Hawaii. Call 808/329-0063 for information.

November

- **Hawaii International Film Festival,** various locations in Honolulu. A cinema festival with a cross-cultural spin featuring filmmakers from Asia, the Pacific Islands, and the U.S. First 2 weeks in November. Call 808/528-FILM.
- **World Invitational Hula Festival,** Waikiki Shell, Oahu. Competitors from all over the world dance for the prizes. Early to mid-November. Call 808/486-3185.
- **Annual Kona Coffee Cultural Festival,** Kailua-Kona, Big Island. Celebrates harvest of only U.S.-grown coffee with bean picking contest, lei contests, song and dance, and Miss Kona Coffee pageant. Mid- to late November. Call 808/326-7820.
- **Triple Crown Of Surfing,** North Shore, Oahu. The world's top professional surfers compete in 3 events for a total of $215,000 in prize money. Mid-November to mid-December. Call 808/377-5850.
- **Molokai Ranch Rodeo,** Molokai Rodeo Arena, Maunaloa, Molokai. The island's cowboys celebrate Hawaii's *paniolo* heritage. Call 808/552-2681 for the exact schedules and details.

December

- **Honolulu Marathon,** Honolulu. One of the largest marathons in the world with more than 30,000 competitors. Early December. Call 808/734-7200.
- **Festival Of Trees,** Honolulu. Downtown display of one-of-a-kind decorated trees, wreaths and decorations. To benefit Queen's Medical Center. First or second week of the month. Call 808/547-4780.

- **Aloha Bowl,** Aloha Stadium, Oahu. The winner of the PAC 10 will play the winner of the Big 12 in this nationally-televised collegiate football classic. Christmas Day. Call 808/947-4141.
- **Rainbow Classic,** University of Hawaii, Manoa Valley, Oahu. Eight of the best NCAA basketball teams compete at the Special Events Arena. Week after Christmas. Call 808/956-6501.
- **First Night,** downtown Honolulu. Hawaii's largest festival of arts and entertainment. For 12 hours, 40 city blocks become a showcase for 1,500 musicians, dancers, actors, jugglers, magicians, and mimes. Alcohol-free. December 31. Call 808/532-3131.

3 Tips on Finding Accommodations

It's no secret that Hawaii is one of the most expensive places in the world. It's in the middle of the Pacific Ocean, after all, which means that everything arrives by air or sea. That's why a box of breakfast cereal costs $7 in the local supermarkets. And because land is finite in the islands, it's expensive (the average Honolulu house is worth nearly $400,000). All this means it costs a lot to build and maintain a hotel or resort.

A vacation in Hawaii doesn't have to cost a fortune, though. True, the Aloha State has the world's greatest collection of super-expensive luxury resorts. The seaside Presidential Suite at Oahu's Ihilani Resort & Spa, for example, goes for $5,000 a night. These are swell places for an iced tea—at $3 a glass—but if you're looking for a deal, you might want to choose a place that's a few blocks from the beach. You also might want to stay at home during the holidays and visit Hawaii during the "off" season if you're looking for the best deal (see "Seasons" in "When to Go," above).

Hawaii has scores of hotels with reasonable rates (the average cost of a hotel room here is about $143 a night). There are thousands of condos and scores of small hotels on all the islands. You'll find a complete list in the free *Accommodations and Car Rental Guide* distributed by the Hawaii Visitors Bureau (see "Visitor Information & Money," above). You can also call the **Hawaii Reservation Service** (☎ **800/ 895-0012**), which handles accommodations in all price ranges and on all islands.

TRY BARGAINING

The rates quoted in this book are known in the hotel industry as "rack" or "published" rates; that is, the maximum a property charges for a room. Hotels pay travel agents as much as 30% of these rack rates for sending clients their way. If business is slow, some hotels may give you the benefit of at least part of this commission if you book directly instead of going through an airline or travel agent. Most also have *kamaaina* or "local" rates for islanders, which they may extend to visitors during slow periods. It never hurts to ask politely for a discounted or local rate; there are also a host of special rates available for the military, seniors, members of the travel industry, families, corporate travelers, and long-term stays. Lots of condos and hotels throw in a car rental or other plum to sweeten the rate.

BED-AND-BREAKFAST & VACATION RENTAL SERVICES

With more than 500 such establishments on all the islands, Hawaii is a real hotbed of bed-and-breakfasts. Rates start at $50 a night, with an average of $70 a night—a bargain compared to the cost of a hotel room in Waikiki.

A Hawaii-style B&B may be a small, private room or a 1,200-square-foot apartment. There's a cottage on a lagoon on Molokai for $65 a night—palm trees and hammock included. Or, how about a $55-a-night cottage with a hot tub in a wild orchid plantation with a view of bubbling Kilauea volcano? And when was the last time you slept in a rain forest?

Only Oahu is opposed to B&Bs. The city and county of Honolulu "grand-fathered" in existing B&Bs a few years ago, allowing them to continue to operate as is, but it has refused to permit more. Meanwhile, there are plenty of units to choose from for a pleasant and inexpensive way to enjoy Hawaii in a real residential neighborhood instead of a resort.

One way to find the right B&B or rental condominium for you is through a reservations service. **Hawaiian Islands Bed-and-Breakfast & Vacation Rentals,** 572 Kailua, Rd., Suite 201 Kailua, HI 96734 (☎ 808/261-7895 or 800/258-7895), lists more than 500 accommodations from $50-a-night B&B accommodations to $1,000-a-night beach estates on all islands. It also offers discount air and rental-car packages. Call or write for a free brochure listing the top 50 lodgings in Hawaii.

Bed-and-Breakfast Honolulu, 3242 Kaohinani Dr., Honolulu, HI 96817 (☎ 808/595-7533 or 800/288-4666), is a "hands-on" agency which books "homestay" units and studios on six islands, including Molokai and Lanai.

At **Hawaii's Best Bed & Breakfasts,** P.O. Box 563, Kamuela, HI 96743 (☎ 808/885-4550 or 800/262-9912; fax 808/885-0559), Barbara and Sarah Campbell personally select traditional homestays, cottages, and inns on all islands based on hospitality, distinctive charm, and attention to detail.

At **My Island,** P.O. Box 100, Volcano, HI, 96785 (☎ 808/967-7110; fax 808/967-7719), Gordon and Joann Morse specialize in Big Island properties designed to acquaint the adventure traveler with the various climates, atmosphere, and lifestyles of the biggest tropical island in the Pacific.

4 The Active Vacation Planner

"Most people have no idea how awesome Hawaii really is," says naturalist Rob Pacheco, who daily leads people into the Big Island's rain forest to see native birds or down to its volcano coast, where lava meets the sea. "They think it's only a place to sit on the beach."

Indeed, when I thought about Hawaii years ago, I always pictured tourist couples in matching aloha shirts sipping Mai Tais at a $500-a-night beach hotel with man-made waterfalls. Or a kind of tropical paradise where people surfed all day, then ate luau pig while someone played ukulele and sang "Tiny Bubbles." I pictured old sailors with blurry tattoos trying to remember Pearl Harbor, descendants of Boston missionaries riding around in BMWs, and bleached blonde pot-smoking surfers from Malibu. Anyone who went there either was on their honeymoon, a grand prize winner on a TV game show, or in the Navy en route to the South China Sea. Not my kind of place. Then one cold, foggy April day in San Francisco my wife, Marcie, won a fellowship to study Japanese history and culture at University of Hawaii's Asian and Pacific Studies Center. I quit the Fog City to join her in the sun-blessed tropics. "What will you do after you get a tan?" a pal asked. I wondered that myself.

I set out, wide-eyed, to discover the real Hawaii. I paddled a kayak to desert islands, splashed in waterfalls, sailed around the Big Island on a sloop, and hiked inside Haleakala crater, a hole big enough to swallow New York City. I ventured into Ola'a rain forest to see rare native birds and strange insects like the Happy Face Spider. I saw night rainbows on Maui and watched red-hot lava boil into the Pacific. The real Hawaii captivated me, and from my experiences I wrote *Great Outdoor Adventures of Hawaii,* the first adventure guide to the islands. After 15 years here, I still haven't done or seen it all, and I work at playing in the great outdoors. (What can I say? It's my job.)

When you come to Hawaii, you can sit on the beach and relax with other nice tourists—a perfectly fine thing to do (I've done plenty of it myself)—or you can have some of the greatest adventures on earth.

PREPARING FOR YOUR ACTIVE VACATION

If you've been to Hawaii before or are a seasoned traveler in the tropics, you may want to skip this section or review it just in case you've forgotten how easy it's to prepare for an active vacation in the Hawaiian Islands.

What to Pack & What to Rent   Bring t-shirts, shorts, tennis shoes, boat shoes, rubber water shoes, and several pairs of good socks if you're hiking. The tropical sun poses the greatest threat to anyone who ventures into the great outdoors; bring a pair or two of sunglasses, plenty of strong sunscreen, a light hat (like a baseball cap or a sun visor), a windbreaker or light jacket (if you're planning to hike above 3,000 feet in elevation), a rain poncho, and a canteen or water bottle—you'll easily dehydrate on the trail in the tropic heat, so figure on carrying two liters of water per day on any hike. Campers should bring water purification tablets or devices. See also "Staying Safe & Healthy," below.

If you have your own snorkel gear or other water-sports equipment, by all means bring it if you can. However, if you don't have it, or just don't feel like carrying it, don't fret; everything you'll need is available for rent in the islands. We've discussed all kinds of places to rent or buy gear in each island chapter.

If you're planning on traveling to multiple islands and would like to rent gear on one island and keep it with you for your whole trip, try **Snorkel Bob's, Inc.,** with locations on Oahu, Maui, the Big Island of Hawaii, and Kauai. Snorkel Bob lets you rent snorkels, masks, fins, boogie boards, life jackets, and wet suits on any one island and return it on another. The basic set of snorkel gear is $2.50 a day, or $14 a week—a deal. The best gear is $6.50 a day, or $29 a week; if you need a prescription mask, it's $9 a day, or $39 a week. You can find Snorkel Bob's on Oahu at 702 Kapahulu Ave. (☎ **808/735-7944**); on Maui at 1651 Lahaina Luna Rd., Lahaina (☎ **808/611-4231**) and at Napili Village Hotel, 5425 Lower Honapiilani Hwy., Napili (☎ **808/669-9603**); on the Big Island at 75-5744 Alii Dr., Kailua-Kona (☎ **808/329-0770**); and on Kauai at 4480 Ahukini Rd., Lihue (☎ **808/245-9433**) and 3236 Poipu Rd., Poipu (☎ **808/742-2206**).

Doing It Yourself vs. Using an Outfitter   There are two ways to go: Plan all the details before you go and schlep your gear 2,500 miles across the Pacific, or go with an outfitter or a guide and let them worry about the details.

Experienced outdoors enthusiasts may follow their nose to coastal campgrounds or even trek to the 13,796-foot-high summit of Mauna Loa on their own, but in Hawaii it's often preferable to go with a local guide, who knows the local conditions at both sea level and summit peaks, and knows the land and its flora and fauna in detail. And many forests and valleys in the interior of the islands are either on private property or in wilderness preserves that are accessible only on guided tours.

And these folks work hard at presenting Hawaii in a new, natural way. Naturalist Rob Pacheco of Hawaii Forest and Trail leads treks into Big Island rain forests. Chino and Micco Godinez of Kayak Kauai Outfitters lead guided kayak tours up Kauai's Hanalei River and down the Na Pali coast. Eric Enos plants taro on Oahu's Waianae coast and invites visitors to learn about Hawaii's legendary staple. Ralph Blancato takes visitors on what can only be called environmental cruises around the

Big Island on the sloop *Maile*. And Stan Butler, host of the annual Whales Alive! conference on Maui, helps to save the whales and introduces visitors to them.

See "Ecotours" below and the individual island chapters for local outfitters and tour guide operators.

Ecotours Hawaii is emerging as one of the world's prime destinations for eco-travelers. And you may not even need to leave your hotel to participate: Many island resorts now offer ecological tours. Kapalua Bay Resort, which sits between a marine preserve and the West Maui rain forest, takes guests on guided tours into the Puu Kukui forest. The Big Island's Royal Waikoloan Hotel, near the King's Trail and ancient petroglyph fields in Hawaii, is ideally sited for exploring the historic Kohala Coast; and the Mauna Lani's green sea turtle project, which raises hatchlings and returns them to the sea on the Big Island's Kohala Coast, is an excellent example of eco-tourism in action.

The Nature Conservancy of Hawaii (☎ **808/537-4508** on Oahu; **808/5721-7849** on Maui; **808/553-5236** or 808/524-0779, on Molokai) and the Hawaii Chapter of the **Sierra Club,** P.O. Box 2577, Honolulu, HI 96803 (☎ **808/538-6616**) both offer guided hikes on preserves and special places during the year, as well as one-day to week-long work trips to restore habitats and trails and root out invasive plants like banana poka, New Zealand flax, non-native gorse, and wild ginger. It might not sound like a dream vacation to everyone, but volunteers often see the "real" Hawaii—wilderness areas ordinarily off-limits. At Oahu's **Cultural Learning Center at Kaala,** Eric Enos grows taro in the ancient ponds of Waianae Valley, where special groups can learn and share traditional values of resource management by working in the ancient ponds. By reservation only; call **808/696-7241.**

Local ecotourism opportunities are discussed in each island chapter. For more information, contact the **Hawaii Ecotourism Association,** c/o the University of Hawaii Sea Grant Extension Service, 1000 Pope Rd., MSB 226, Honolulu, HI 96822 (☎ **808/956-2866;** fax 808/956-2858; e-mail: **http://planet-hawaii.com/hea**).

Staying Safe & Healthy While some Hawaii-bound adventurers may fret about shark bites, the most common cause of injury in the islands is sunburn. The islands lie south of the Tropic of Cancer, only about 1,400 miles north of the equator in the tropical zone. So the sun is extremely harsh, and only intermittent clouds and trade winds keep the islands from stifling temperatures. Wear plenty of sunscreen with a high SPF, and wear a hat and sunglasses. If you do get a burn, apply aloe vera liberally; it's Hawaii's favorite local remedy to ease the pain.

You can drink the water. In fact Oahu's water, naturally purified by 30 years of filtering though volcanic rock of the Koolau Mountains before it comes out of the tap, is regularly judged America's best-tasting water in blind tastings. Water on outer islands is not quite as good, but at least it's not chlorinated and fluoridated. However, if you go camping, you must treat all water from waterfalls and streams; it can be contaminated by wild pigs, goats, and cattle.

Hikers should let someone know when they're going, where they're heading, and when they plan to return. Too many hikers are lost in Hawaii because they don't let others know the basic facts. Check weather conditions with the **National Weather Service** (☎ **808/973-4381**) before you go. Hike with a pal, never alone. Wear hiking boots, a sun hat, and clothes to protect from sun and scratches. Take water. Stay on the trail. Watch your step. It's easy to slip off precipitous trails and into steep canyons, with often disastrous and fatal results. Incapacitated hikers are often plucked to safety by Fire and Rescue squads, who must use helicopters to gain access to remote sites. Many experienced hikers and boaters today often pack a cellular phone in case of emergency. Just call 911.

Outdoor Etiquette   Act locally, think globally, and carry out what you carry in. Observe *kapu* and no trespassing signs. Don't climb on ancient Hawaiian heiau and temples, or carry home rocks that belong to Madame Pele. Some say it's just a silly superstition or coincidence, but each year the U.S. Park Service gets boxes of lava rocks in the return mail sent back to Hawaii by visitors who've experienced unusually bad luck.

ACTIVITIES A TO Z
BIRDING

Hawaii's tropical birds are found nowhere else on earth. There are curved-bill honeycreepers, black-winged red birds, and the rare o'o, whose yellow feathers Hawaiians once plucked to make royal capes.

When you go birding, take *A Field Guide to the Birds of Hawaii and the Tropical Pacific* by H. Douglas Pratt, Phillip L. Bruner, and Delwyn G. Berett (Princeton University Press, 1987). It belongs in the hands of every birder who comes to Hawaii. For binoculars, most birders prefer a Leitz 10 x 40, easily adjustable and clear from 10 feet to infinity; they're powerful but expensive, about $800. If you go birding with a local guide, they'll usually provide a good pair for you to use.

Kauai and Molokai, in particular, are great places to go birding in Hawaii. On Kauai, large colonies of seabirds nest at Kilauea National Wildlife Preserve and along the Na Pali coast. The lush rain forest of Molokai's Kamakou Preserve is home to the Molokai Thrush and Molokai Creeper, which live only on this 30-mile-long island. For details on birding on those islands and the others, including where to go, what birds you'll see, and which outfitters will take you, see "Birding" in the individual island chapters.

BOATING

Almost every type of nautical experience is possible in the islands. You can go to sea on old-fashioned Polynesian outrigger canoes, high-tech kayaks, fast-moving catamarans, inflatable rubber Zodiacs, smooth moving SWATH vessels that promise not to make you seasick, gaff-rigged schooners, America's Cup racing sloops, Kona charter fishing boats, ferries, booze cruise barges, snorkel and dive boats, submarines, even an interisland cruise ship. There are details on all of these seafaring experiences throughout the individual island chapters.

No matter which vessel you choose, be sure to see the Hawaiian islands from offshore, from the water. The main harbors are Kewalo Basin, Oahu; Honokohau, Kailua-Kona, and Kawaihae on the Big Island of Hawaii; Lahaina and Maaalea, Maui; Nawiliwili and Port Allen, Kauai; and Kaunakakai, Molokai.

Cruising the Islands   For those who'd like to take a sea cruise through the Hawaiian archipelago, there are two excellent ways to go: Skipper Ralph Blancato cruises around the islands on the sloop *Maile* (☎ 800/726-SAIL), which leaves out of Kawaihae Harbor on Kohala Coast; see "Sailing: Seeing the Big Island by Sloop" in the Big Island chapter for more details.

You can also take a weekly interisland cruise aboard the vintage SS steamship *Independence,* which departs from Honolulu's Aloha Tower every Saturday night. For details and reservations, contact **American Hawaii Cruises,** 2 N. Riverside Plaza, Chicago, IL 60606 (☎ **800/474-9934**).

BODY BOARDING (BOOGIE BOARDING) & BODYSURFING

Bodysurfing—riding the waves without a board, becoming one with the rolling water—is a way of life in Hawaii. Some bodysurfers just rely on their outstretched hands (or hands at their sides) to ride the waves; others use hand boards (flat, paddlelike gloves). For additional maneuverability, try a boogie- or body board (also known as belly boards or paipo boards). These 3-foot-long vehicles, which support the upper part of your body, are easy to carry and very maneuverable in the water. Both bodysurfing and body boarding require a pair of open-heeled swim fins to help propel you through the water. Both kinds of wave riding are very popular in the islands because the equipment is inexpensive, easy to carry, and both sports can be practiced in the small, gentle waves. See the individual island chapters for details on where to rent boards and where to go.

CAMPING

Hawaii's year-round balmy, tropical climate makes camping a breeze. Forget your fleece anoraks and goose-down mummy bags, but bring your mosquito net and rain poncho. It's always warm and dry somewhere on each of the islands any day of the year. However, there is a wet season (some call it winter), and a dry season, which corresponds to the mainland's summer, but tropical campers should always be ready for rain. It rains every day somewhere in the islands, and mosquitoes are abundant when the air is still. Carry a good mosquito repellent and be prepared to deal with contaminated water (purify by boiling, filtration, or iodine tablets) and the tropical sun (protect yourself with sunscreen, a hat, and a long-sleeved shirt).

Otherwise, camping is ideal in the islands, with many established campgrounds at beach parks, including Kauai's Anini Beach, Oahu's Malaekahana Beach, Maui's Waianapanapa Beach, and the Big Island's Hapuna Beach. Campgrounds also are open in the interior at Maui's Haleakala National Park and Hawaii Volcanoes National Park on the Big Island of Hawaii. Camping also is permitted at Kalalau Beach on Kauai's Na Pali Coast and in the cool uplands of Kokee State Park. Remote beach camps accessible by kayak may soon open on Molokai's West End. See "Beaches" and "Camping" in the individual island chapters for the best places to camp in the islands.

The **Hawaiian Trail and Mountain Club,** P.O. Box 2238, Honolulu, HI 96804, offers an information packet on hiking and camping throughout the Hawaiian Islands. Send $1.25 and a legal-size, self-addressed, stamped envelope for information. Another good source of information is the *Hiking/Camping Information Packet,* available from **Hawaii Geographic Maps and Books,** 49 S. Hotel Street, Suite 218, Honolulu, HI 96813 (☎ **808/538-3952**), for $7 (postage included).

DEEP-SEA FISHING

The largest blue marlin ever captured on rod and reel anywhere on the planet was landed on a charter boat operated by Capt. Cornelius Choy off Oahu. The monster weighed in at 1,805 pounds!

Big-game fishing at its best is found on the Big Island of Hawaii at Kailua-Kona, where the deep blue water offshore yields trophy marlins year-round, but especially in August—that's usually when the trophy-winners are hauled in. You can also try for sailfish, swordfish, various tunas, rainbow runner, wahoo, barracuda, trevally, bonefish, and various snappers, groupers, and other bottom fish. Each island offers deep-sea boat charters for good-eating fish like tuna, mahimahi, and opakapaka, and visiting anglers need no license. Freshwater fishing also is available in stocked streams and ponds, but the seasons are brief and conditions so crowded that the experience borders on mayhem.

Charter fishing boats range both in size from small 24-foot open skiffs to luxurious 50-foot-plus yachts, and in price, from a low of less than $50 per person to "share" a boat with other anglers to more than $800 a day to book an entire luxury sportfishing yacht on an exclusive basis. See the individual island chapters for details.

GOLF

Nowhere else on earth can you tee off to whale spouts, putt under rainbows, or play around a live volcano. If it all sounds like paradise, be forewarned: Each course features hellish natural hazards like razor-sharp lava, gusty trade winds, an occasional wild pig, and the tropical heat. And it's very expensive. Still, golfers flock here from around the world, and love every minute of it. See the individual island chapters for details on the top courses.

Golf Packages   A few resorts now offer golf packages—room, car, and greens fees for one inclusive rate. On Maui, try **Kapalua Villas** (☎ **800/545-0018**), which offers the "Golfer's Holiday" for a great escape: Seven nights in a one-bedroom villa by the sea with rental car and daily golf on three championship courses, plus Kapalua logo visor and golf balls, from $994 per person, double occupancy. There's also the "Par Five": 5 days of golf with one-bedroom villa and rental car, from $768 person. Or try "The Eagle," a one-bedroom villa for 3 days of golf, from $324 per person. All packages include cart, club storage, and cleaning. The villas overlook Kapalua Bay, a marine preserve full of tropical fish, with a gold-sand beach that's consistently rated as one of Hawaii's top ten.

Cruising Hawaii's Top Golf Courses

If you look at the Hawaiian Islands as a chain of golf courses in the middle of the Pacific Ocean, you begin to see the challenge they pose. There are 80 spectacular courses on six inhabited islands—courses with exotic names like Hapuna, Ihilani, Koolau, and Mauna Lani, set like jewels in black lava beds, on turquoise lagoons, near erupting volcanoes, at the edge of lush rain forests, and deep in jungle valleys.

Hawaii is truly a golfer's paradise. Of course, there's one major handicap—that big blue ocean between you and the islands poses a time and distance problem. It's impossible to play all of Hawaii's great courses, unless you move there and take up golf full time (some do just that). There's an easier way, though, to sample the best island courses. It's a golf cruise known as "The Floating Greens of Hawaii." I sailed on the inaugural golf cruise 3 years ago and must admit it was a great adventure. On the 7-night cruise, we played 7 championship courses on four islands.

Tee times are all arranged in advance at the course of the day by the cruise's golf coordinator; all you do is go ashore and tee off on the fabulous course of the day, which may be one of Kauai's fabulous Princeville courses, the Big Island's fabled Mauna Kea course, a Grand Wailea course on Maui's top resort coast, or one of Hawaii's many other championship greens. Fares range from $1,345 per person for a budget cabin to $3,150 per person for a superior suite, which includes onboard meals, activities, and entertainment. Golfers pay individual greens fees, which range from $90 to $145 per person for 18 holes and include cart and greens fees. Rental clubs are available at most courses for an additional charge. For more information and reservations, contact **American Hawaii Cruises,** 2 N. Riverside Plaza, Chicago, IL 60606 (☎ **800/474-9934**).

With two spectacular championship 18-hole courses, you'll need at least 3 days to gain a true sense of the game as it's played at the **Mauna Lani Bay Hotel & Bungalows** (☎ **800/367-2323**) on the Big Island of Hawaii's Kohala Coast. Carved from ancient lava flows, the courses feature two striking ocean holes that challenge pros and amateurs alike, who try to beat the records of Arnold Palmer, Jack Nicklaus, Lee Trevino, and Raymond Floyd. The 1996 Mauna Lani Golf Package, based on a 3-night minimum, begins at $335 a night for one player, $375 for two, and includes a garden-view room, welcome amenity, and golf certificate.

Tee time on Lanai means unlimited golf at two stunning courses: The Experience at Koele and the Challenge at Manele. The Jack Nicklaus–designed Challenge is a target-style course carved from lava cliffs by the sea; the Experience is a Greg Norman/Ted Robinson course with a signature hole that plays into a ravine from 250 feet above the fairway. A 3-night stay at either **The Lodge at Koele** or the **Manele Bay Hotel** (☎ **800/321-4666**), based on the 1996 Tee Time golf package, ranges from $1,194 to $1,590 double occupancy, and includes unlimited golf on either course, complimentary range-balls daily, a $50 gift certificate, a Lanai golf amenity, and a poster of either course. Rates for nongolfing spouses are also available. Additional nights start at $378.

HIKING

Hiking in Hawaii is a breathtaking experience full of drama, extraordinary vistas, and great outdoor encounters. Hawaii has hundreds of miles of hiking trails, and the reward at the end of the trail may be a hidden beach, a private waterfall, an Eden-like valley, or a stunning view. However, mountain climbers are, sadly, out of luck: Hawaii's volcanic cliffs are too steep and too brittle to scale.

Hawaiian Trail and Mountain Club, P.O. Box 2238, Honolulu, HI 96804, offers an information packet on hiking and camping in Hawaii. To receive a copy, send $1.25 and a self-addressed, stamped legal-size envelope. **Hawaii Geographic Maps and Books,** 49 S. Hotel St., Suite 218, Honolulu, HI 96813 (☎ **808/538-3952**), offers a *Hiking/Camping Information Packet* for $7. **The Nature Conservancy of Hawaii** (☎ **808/537-4508** on Oahu; **808/5721-7849** on Maui; **808/553-5236** or 808/524-0779 on Molokai) and the Hawaii Chapter of the **Sierra Club,** P.O. Box 2577, Honolulu, HI 96803 (☎ **808/538-6616**) both offer guided hikes on preserves and special places during the year. Also see the individual island chapters for complete details on the best hikes for all ability levels.

HORSEBACK RIDING

One of the best ways to really see Hawaii is on horseback; almost all the islands offer riding opportunities. You can ride into Maui's Haleakala Crater, along Kauai's Mahaulephu Beach, into Oahu's remote windward valleys on Kualoa Ranch, or gallop across the wide-open spaces of the Big Island's Parker Ranch, one of the biggest privately owned ranches in the United States. Some of the most fun you can have on a horse is at the Malihini Rodeo on Molokai, where you enter the actual rodeo arena and compete in rodeo events like pole bending and barrel racing, and then try your hand at herding cattle. See the individual island chapters for details. Be sure to bring a pair of long jeans and close-toed shoes to wear on your ride.

HUNTING

In season, Lanai offers hunters good opportunities for hunting Axis deer, pheasants, wild turkeys, quail, and francolins. On Molokai, you can hunt year-round with rifle or bow and arrow for oryx, Indian blackbuck, Greater Kudu, and Barbary sheep with an experienced guide. And third-generation pig hunter Bobby Caires will take you out hunting natural enemy number one, the destructive wild pig, on Maui. See the individual island chapters for details.

All hunters must have a license; to obtain one, you must have proof of having attended a hunter's education class, and you must apply for an exemption if the course was in another state. For exemptions contact: Enforcement, **State Division of Forestry and Wildlife,** 1151 Punchbowl, Room 311, Honolulu, HI 96813 (☎ **808/587-0166**). After obtaining either proof of a hunter's education class or obtaining an exemption for a class given in another state, you must apply for a hunting license. Licenses are $95 a year for non-Hawaii residents. Apply to the **State Division of Forestry and Wildlife,** 1151 Punchbowl, Room 325, Honolulu, HI 96813.

KAYAKING

Hawaii is one of the world's most popular destinations for ocean kayaking. Beginners can paddle across a tropical lagoon to two uninhabited islets off Lanikai Beach on Oahu, while more experienced kayakers can take on Kauai's awesome Na Pali coast. Experts time their kayak expeditions in summer to take advantage of the usually flat conditions on the north shore of Molokai, where the sea cliffs are the steepest on Earth, and the remote valleys can only be reached sea. See "Hitting the Water" in the individual island chapters for local outfitters and tour guides.

SCUBA DIVING

In 1840, when Mr. Dibble dove to inspect the hull of the USS *Porpoise,* whose copper bottom "he found somewhat out of repair," he could hardly imagine his pioneering underwater adventure in Hawaii would be followed by thousands of pleasure seekers.

Some people come to the islands solely to take the plunge in the tropical Pacific and explore the underwater world. You can see the great variety of tropical fish (more than 150 species) and rare and unusual coral, explore sea caves, and swim with sea turtles and monk seals in the clear tropical water of Hawaii, one of the world's top-ten dive destinations.

If you go to Hawaii to dive, go early in the morning. Trade winds rough up the seas in the afternoon, especially on Maui, so most dive operators schedule early morning dives that end at noon, and take the rest of the day off.

If you're not certified, take classes before you come to Kauai so you don't "waste" time learning and can dive right in. Unsure about scuba diving? Take an introductory dive; most operators offer no-experience-necessary dives, ranging from $40 to $95. You can learn from this glimpse into the sea world if diving is for you.

Over the years, many dive shops have come and gone in Hawaii. When you go diving in Hawaii, go with a reputable dive master like **Ed Robinson Diving Adventures** on Maui (☎ **800/635-1273**), **Aaron's Dive Shops** on Oahu (☎ **808/262-2333**), and **Bubbles Below Scuba Charters** on Kauai (☎ **808/822-3483**). Other reliable firms are discussed in the individual island chapters.

Impressions

Thousands have daily lined the wharves to witness the carpenter, Mr. Dibble, in his novel suit of India-rubber with a glass helmet disappear beneath the surface of the water . . . .

—1840 Honolulu newspaper article

If you dive on your own, order the *Dive Hawaii Guide,* which describes 44 locations on a chart created by Dive Hawaii, a nonprofit outfit at the University of Hawaii Sea Grant Extension Service. Send $2 to **UH/SGES,** attention: Ray Tabata, 100 Pope Rd., MSB 226, Honolulu, HI 96844.

SNORKELING

Snorkeling is the main attraction in Hawaii and anyone can do it. To enjoy the Hawaii's underwater world, all you need is a mask, snorkel, fins, and some basic swimming skills. It's like a dream, floating over underwater worlds through colorful clouds of tropical fish. In many places, all you have to do is wade into the water and look down.

If you've never snorkeled before, most resorts and excursion boats offer snorkeling equipment and lessons. However, you won't really need lessons; it's plenty easy to figure out for yourself, especially once you're at the beach—everybody around you will be doing it.

While everyone heads for Oahu's Hanauma Bay—the perfect spot for first-timers—other favorite snorkel spots like Ke'e Lagoon on Kauai, Kealakekua Bay on the Big Island, Hulopoe Bay on Lanai, and Kapalua Bay on Maui. Although snorkeling is excellent on all the islands, Maui probably offers some of the best snorkel spots because of its abundant small bays and pocket beaches.

If you don't have your own, you can rent gear from dozens of dive shops and activity booths, discussed in the individual island chapters. The best deals, though, are at **Snorkel Bob's;** not only do you get mask, fins, and snorkel for $15 a week, but you get a net bag, a snorkel map, fish food (although it's really not cool to feed the fish in the wild; you never know what might show up for lunch), no-fog goop for your mask (although spitting in it works just as well), and a fish identification card. Prices go up for prescription masks and high-end gear. For **Snorkel Bob's** locations throughout the islands, see "What to Pack and What to Rent," above.

Always snorkel with a buddy. Look up every once in a while to see where you are, how far offshore you are, and if there's any boat traffic. Don't touch anything; not only can you damage coral, but camouflaged fish and shells with poisonous spines may surprise you. Always check with a dive shop or lifeguards or others on the beach about the area in which you plan to snorkel: Are there any dangerous conditions you should know about? What are the current surf, tide, and weather conditions?

SNUBA

If you want to go beyond snorkeling but you're not quite ready for scuba, try Snuba, one of the most popular new ways to enjoy the underwater world. It's just like scuba, but your oxygen tank floats on the surface instead of being strapped to your back. The only problem is that you can't go further than the length of your hose, usually 20 to 25 feet. (That's probably as far as most folks want to go the first time, anyway.) It's actually easier than snorkeling, because the water is calmer beneath the surface. After 15 minutes of instruction, anyone can be in the water enjoying the marine life, says Lynn Ekstrom of Big Island Snuba. For local snuba operators, see the individual island chapters.

WHALE WATCHING

The best time to see the whales in Hawaii is between January and April from any island, but especially Maui, Kauai, and Oahu. Just look out to sea. Each island also offers a variety of whale-watching cruises, which will bring you up close and personal with the mammoth mammals; see the individual island chapters.

Off Maui's Old Lahaina Road, where New England whalers stood at anchor, whales now play without fear. To 100 fathoms, the waters around Maui, Molokai, and Lanai are designated an official humpback whale national marine sanctuary. The shallow, warm, sheltered waters, especially those on the leeward side of the islands, are the principal breeding, calving, and nursing area for the endangered North Pacific Humpback Whale. Other marine mammals found in these waters include the highly endangered Hawaiian monk seal, sperm and pilot whales, and a variety of dolphins. Three species of sea turtles also frequent the waters, and several seabird nesting areas are found on offshore rocks and isolated cliff areas. The sanctuary's goal is to protect humpback whales and their habitat and interpret the relationship of humpback whales to the Hawaiian Islands. Contact the **Hawaiian Island Humpback Whale National Marine Sanctuary,** 300 Ala Moana Blvd., Room 5350, Honolulu, HI 96850 (☎ **808/541-3184;** fax 808/541-3450) for free whale-watching brochures.

WINDSURFING

Maui is Hawaii's top windsurfing destination. World-class windsurfers head for Hookipa Beach, where the wind roars through the isthmus of Maui and creates some of the best windsurfing in the world. Funky Paia, a derelict sugar town saved from extinction by surfers, is the world capital of big-wave board sailing. Along the Hana Highway, there are lookouts where you can watch the pros flip off 10-foot waves and gain "hang time" in the air. Others, especially beginners, set their sails for Oahu's Kailua Bay, home of world champ windsurfer Robbie Naish, or Kauai's Anini Beach, where gentle onshore breezes make learning this sport a snap. See the individual island chapters for outfitters and local instructors.

5 Getting Married in Hawaii

Whatever your dreams and your budget, Hawaii is a great place for a wedding. Not only does the whole place exude romance and beauty, but after the ceremony, you're already on your honeymoon. And members of your wedding party will be delighted, since you have given them the perfect excuse for their own island vacation.

Just being in these spectacular islands takes the pressures down a notch or two and promotes a feeling of celebration. Many couples who were married long ago come to Hawaii to renew their vows, enjoy a second honeymoon, and rediscover the loving spirit that brought them together the first time.

Couples can get married, or remarried, in historic Hawaiian churches, on the beach, under a waterfall in a rain forest, on horseback in a pasture with an ocean view, in a lush tropical garden, on a sailboat, on a lava flow, under a volcano, with Diamond Head as a backdrop, on a deserted islet, underwater with a school of brilliant-colored fish for witnesses, barefoot on the beach at sunset and draped in fragrant leis, or in full regalia on formal parade from chapel to luxury hotel.

It happens every day of the year in the islands, where more than 20,000 marriages are performed annually, mostly on Oahu. Nearly half (44.6%) of couples married here are from somewhere else. This booming business has spawned more than 70 companies that can help you organize a long-distance event and stage an unforgettable wedding Hawaiian-style or your-style. That's not counting dozens of hotels with wedding coordinators, plenty of catering expertise indoors and outdoors and all the extras at hand, for guests or nonguests, as well as package prices for weddings and/or honeymoons that can include champagne, cake, flowers, private meals, music, and other special touches.

Weddings seem to gravitate naturally toward resort areas where the sunsets are famous—Waikiki, Maui's Wailea, Makena and Kaanapali resorts, Kauai's Princeville, Poipu and Kalapaki, Big Island's Kona-Kohala coast. But dawn in Hawaii, with its dramatic skies and occasional green flash at sunrise, is hard to beat at nonresort areas like Oahu's Lanikai Beach with its two offshore islets, or Hilo's bayfront gardens and parks.

HOTEL WEDDINGS

Some hotels have wedding facilities on their property, like the chapel decorated with Hawaiian scenes in stained-glass art at the **Grand Wailea Resort Hotel & Spa** in Wailea, or the octagonal pavilion chapel over the lagoon near the Kauai Marriott at **Kauai Lagoons Resort. Hilton Hawaiian Village** in Waikiki has a brand new "rainbow chapel," complete with stained glass, marble floors, reception area, and photo studio.

Many hotels offer picturesque beachfront and garden locations for staging ceremonies. At **Kea Lani Hotel, Suites & Villas** at Wailea, Maui, guests can partake of a free group-style vow renewal ceremony weekly at sunset, with guitar, scenery, minister, and commemorative certificate. Flash your certificate at the hotel restaurant and they'll serve two glasses of complimentary champagne with dinner. The offer is meant to encourage spontaneous "I Still Do's."

In Waikiki, you could fancy yourselves heirs to the Hawaiian throne at the beachfront Grand Salon of the **Sheraton Moana Surfrider Hotel,** a sparkling Victorian setting opening onto broad verandas surrounding a courtyard and a huge banyan tree by the sea. Fall in love forever at the Rudolph Valentino–like **Royal Hawaiian Hotel,** where the seaside gardens, lawns and ancient coconut groves have a timeless grace, or perhaps the Hau Terrace at the **Halekulani,** where the silhouette of Diamond Head backs your photo opportunities and a wedding party can spill out onto breezy terraces overlooking the sea.

The **Four Seasons Maui Resort** is happy to help plan weddings and sets a romantic table for two in a private sea-cliff garden for newlyweds and other intimates. **Westin Maui at Kaanapali Beach Resort** features a gazebo setting or the amphitheaterlike dining room filled with man-made waterfalls and real flamingoes, plus two Directors of Romance to help you plan.

Hyatt Regency Kauai will stage a Hawaiian wedding, complete with conch-blowing herald and choice of Hawaiian *holoku* gowns, a Victorian-style gown with handmade train. At **Princeville Hotel,** also on Kauai, the dramatic view of Hanalei Bay and the famous "Bali Hai" mountain on the Na Pali Coast from the pool and beach will make your wedding photos memorable (the bay and mountains provided the backdrop for the movie *South Pacific,* after all).

It's hard to imagine a more romantic spot than **Kona Village Resort** on the Big Island. Everyone can help you celebrate at the Friday night luau. Many a lasting marriage began on the sunset tees of the venerable Mauna Kea Beach Golf Course, followed by outdoor celebrations at the **Mauna Kea Beach Hotel.**

Okay, so you're not computer software magnate Bill Gates, who rented the entire island of Lanai for his wedding bash. A good, less expensive choice is the **Keauhou Beach Hotel** on the Big Island's Kona Coast, where ceremonies are conducted on the scenic oceanfront grounds, beside the quaint historic cottage on a pond where King Kalakaua once lived. Catering and lodging at the moderately priced hotel are located just steps across the lawn.

See "Accommodations" in the individual island chapters for the addresses and phone numbers of these hotels.

OTHER ROMANTIC SETTINGS

Hawaii has attractive, romantic, wedding settings other than at its hotels. Consider the following:

Kilohana, Lihue, Kauai   Once the sweet home of sugar planters, this handsomely restored plantation estate is now a collection of boutiques and galleries with interior and outdoor party areas, 35 acres of gardens, lawns, polo grounds, and a century-old wedding coach drawn by huge Clydesdale horses. Call **808/245-9593.**

Haiku Gardens, Windward Oahu   This lush jungle garden setting in a bowl-shaped grotto at the foot of the mystical Koolau Mountains has a gazebo, lily ponds, and the adjacent open-air Charthouse Restaurant with Old-Hawaii decor, overlooking the gardens. Call **808/247-6671.**

Aboard a Luxury Catamaran   A 2-hour sail aboard a choice of large sailboats off the Kohala Coast, Big Island, staged by **Ocean Sports Waikoloa** (☎ **808/885-5555**).

By Helicopter to a Secret Maui Spot   **Sunshine Helicopters** (☎ **800/544-2520**) will fly you to a remote spot on Maui. The wedding package includes leis, minister, witnesses, and video.

Historic Hawaiian Churches   Picturesque churches are sprinkled in communities throughout the state, from stately **Kawaiahao Church** in downtown Honolulu, built in 1821 of coral blocks carved from a nearby reef, to charming **Church of the Holy Ghost** in up-country Maui, an octagonal Catholic structure with koa wood interiors and views from windows on all sides. Hanalei's little green **Waioli Huiia Church** has sheltered weddings since missionary days. In the South Kona District, the famous "painted church" is the tiny **St. Benedict's** in Honaunau, a white New England missionary church with trompe l'oeil paintings inside to make it look like a big cathedral. If you like, the ceremony can be conducted in Hawaiian.

WEDDING PLANNERS

Wedding planners charge anywhere from around $450 up to a small fortune to arrange a wedding, usually outdoors, from a small private affair to a formal ceremony in a tropical setting. **Paradise Weddings Hawaii** in Waikoloa on the Big Island (☎ **800/428-5844**) comes recommended, as does **A Wedding Made in Paradise** in Kihei, Maui (☎ **800/453-3440**); **Royal Hawaiian Weddings** in Puunene, Maui (☎ **800/639-1866**); **Coconut Coast Weddings & Honeymoons** of Hanalei, Kauai (☎ **800/585-5595**); and **Aloha Wedding Planners** in Honolulu (☎ **800/288-8309**). Consult the Hawaii Visitors and Convention Bureau (see "Visitor Information & Money," above) or any island phone book for more wedding coordinators.

THE PAPERWORK

To obtain a Hawaii marriage license, you need to appear in person at the **State Department of Health, Marriage Licensing Office,** 1250 Punchbowl St., Honolulu, HI 96813 (☎ **808/586-4544** or 808/586-4545), or before a marriage licensing agent on the neighbor islands. Ask the Honolulu office to send a free copy of "Getting Married," a wedding information packet which includes a list of neighbor-island agents. Your hotel or wedding coordinator can also help.

A marriage license costs $25 in cash and is good for 30 days before the ceremony. No waiting period is required, but both partners must be 18 years of age or older to be married without parental consent. You won't need your birth certificates, but bring a driver's license, passport, or other form of picture identification. Hawaii marriage licenses also require the names of each partner's parents and birthplace. Brides no longer have to undergo a premarital rubella screening.

If either partner has been married before, he or she must state the date, county, and state or country in which the divorce was final.

6 Tips for Travelers with Special Needs

FOR TRAVELERS WITH DISABILITIES

Travelers with disabilities are made to feel very welcome in Hawaii. There are more than 2,000 ramped curbs in Oahu alone, hotels are usually equipped with wheelchair-accessible rooms, and tour companies provide many special services. The **Commission on Persons with Disabilities,** 919 Ala Moana Blvd., Honolulu, HI 96814 (☎ **808/586-8121**), and the **Hawaii Center for Independent Living,** 677 Ala Moana Blvd., Suite 118, Honolulu, HI 96813 (☎ **808/537-1941**) can provide information and send you a copy of the *Aloha Guide to Accessibility* ($3).

HandiCabs of the Pacific, P.O. Box 22428, Honolulu, HI 96823 (☎ **808/524-3866**) provides wheelchair taxi service and a variety of wheelchair-accommodated activities, including sightseeing tours, luaus, and cruises.

FOR SENIORS

Discounts for seniors are available at almost all the major attractions in the islands, and occasionally at hotels and restaurants. When making hotel reservations, always ask. Members of the **American Association of Retired Persons (AARP),** 601 E St. NW, Washington, D.C. 20049 (☎ **202/434-2277** or 800/424-3410) are usually eligible for such discounts; they also put together organized tour packages at moderate rates through the AARP Travel Service. The **National Council of Senior Citizens,** 925 15th St. NW, Washington, D.C. 20005 (☎ **202/347-8800**) also offers travel discounts to seniors.

If you're planning to visit Hawaii's national parks—Haleakala National Park on Maui and Hawaii Volcanoes National Park on the Big Island—you can save sightseeing dollars if you're 62 or older by picking up a **Golden Age Passport** from any national park, recreation area, or monument. This lifetime pass has a one-time fee of $10 and provides free admission to the parks, plus 50% savings on camping and recreation fees. You can pick one up at the park entrance.

7 Getting There & Getting Around

ARRIVING IN THE ISLANDS

Occasionally you can get to Hawaii on a cruise ship, but today the overwhelming majority of visitors arrive by plane. All major American and many international carriers fly to Honolulu International Airport.

United Airlines (☎ 800/225-5825) offers the most frequent service from the U.S. mainland, but **American Airlines** (☎ 800/433-7300), **Continental Airlines** (☎ 800/231-0856), **Delta Airlines** (☎ 800/221-1212), **Northwest Airlines** (☎ 800/225-2525), and **Trans World Airlines** (☎ 800/221-2000) all have regular flights from both the East and West coasts. In addition to flying to Honolulu, United flies nonstop from Los Angeles and San Francisco to Kailua-Kona on the Big Island and Kahului, Maui; and American flies a "through flight" from Dallas or Los Angeles to Kahului, Maui, with a stopover, but no plane change, in Honolulu.

Based in Honolulu, **Hawaiian Airlines** (☎ 808/537-5100 or 800/367-5320) offers nonstop service on wide-body DC-10s from San Francisco, Seattle, Los Angeles, Portland, and Las Vegas. Hawaiian works with Fly AAway, the tour unit of

And Fragrant Flowers Fill the Airport: The Welcoming Lei

When you arrive in Hawaii, the air is fragrant with flowers. Sweet scents are everywhere, a profusion of perfumes from gardens, street trees, and fields—and around your neck in a welcoming flower lei.

A tradition born in the Pacific and cherished by all who love Hawaii, the lei is a necklace of fresh, fragrant flowers. It's given to honor guests and to celebrate birthdays, weddings, graduations, triumphs, and farewells. Bus drivers tuck fragrant blossoms behind their ears or onto their dashboards. Musicians hang leis from their microphones. The dance isn't really hula without leis, and no woman is fully dressed for evening unless she's wearing flowers.

Lei making is a tropical art form. All are fashioned by hand in a variety of traditional patterns. Some leis are sewn of hundreds of tiny blooms or shells, or bits of ferns and leaves. Some last only a few hours. The memory is forever.

Every island has its own special flower lei. On Oahu, they use the *ilima,* a small orange flower. On Kauai, it's the *mokihana,* a fragrant green vine and berry. Big Islanders prefer the *lehua,* a large delicate red puff. Maui likes the *lokelani,* a small rose. And Molokai prefers the *kukui,* the white blossom of a candlenut tree. Lanai's lei is made of *kaunaoa,* a bright yellow moss, while Niihau utilizes its abundant seashells to make leis once prized by royalty and now worth a small fortune.

So pick up a lei when you arrive at the airport, and feel the spirit of Aloha. Welcome to Hawaii!

American Airlines. For information about its package tours, phone **Hawaiian Airlines Vacations** at 800/353-5393, or ask your travel agent.

Airlines serving Hawaii from other countries include **Air New Zealand** (☎ 800/262-1234), **Canadian Airlines International** (☎ 800/426-7000), **China Airlines** (☎ 800/227-5118), **Garuda Indonesian** (☎ 800/231-0856), **Japan Airlines** (☎ 800/525-3663), **Korean Airlines** (☎ 800/223-1155 on the East Coast, 800/421-8200 on the West Coast), **Philippine Airlines** (☎ 800/435-9725), and **Qantas** (☎ 800/227-4500). *But note:* You can fly to Hawaii on one of these foreign carriers *only* if you are continuing on with them to—or returning with them from—an overseas destination.

For details on navigating Honolulu International Airport, see "Arriving" under "Orientation" in Chapter 5.

Agricultural Screening at the Airports   At Honolulu International and the neighbor-island airports, baggage and passengers bound for the mainland and other countries must be screened by agricultural officials before boarding. This takes a little time, but isn't a problem unless you happen to be carrying a football-sized local avocado home to Aunt Emma. Officials will confiscate fresh avocados, bananas, mangoes, and many other kinds of local produce in the name of fruit-fly control. Pineapples, coconuts, and papayas inspected and certified for export, boxed flowers, leis, and processed foods (macadamia nuts, coffee, jams, dried fruit, and the like) will pass. Call federal or state agricultural officials before leaving for the airport if you're not sure about your trophy.

INTERISLAND FLIGHTS

Don't expect to jump a ferry between any of the Hawaiian islands. Today everyone island-hops by plane. In fact, almost every 20 minutes of every day from just before sunrise to long after sunset (usually around 10pm), a jet plane takes off or lands at Honolulu International Airport on the interisland shuttle service. If you miss a flight, don't worry, they are like buses—another one will be along real soon.

There's a big waste of jet fuel with these 20-minute flights, but the sheer volume of traffic requires jets to whisk visitors to and from the neighbor islands.

My personal favorites are the twin-engine De Haviland Twin Otters, the most airworthy propeller-driven planes ever built. They may take a little longer, but they fly lower and enable you to see and appreciate the beauty of the islands as you travel between them. And they don't burn up all those millions of gallons of jet fuel imported to Hawaii by steam ship.

Hawaiian Airlines (☎ 800/367-5320 or 808/835-3700), Hawaii's oldest interisland airline, has carried more than 100 million passengers around the state. It's one of the world's safest airlines, never having had a fatal incident since it started flying in 1929. Its popular **Hawaiian Airline Pass** starts at $169 for a 5-day pass, which enables you to make unlimited flights between the islands. Other versions cost $189 for 8 days, $229 for 10 days, and $269 for 2 weeks. It's a good deal.

Aloha Airlines (☎ 800/367-5250 or 808/484-1111) is the state's largest provider of air transport service. It offers 275 regularly scheduled daily flights throughout Hawaii and enjoys one of the lowest complaint records in the airline industry. Aloha's sister company, **Aloha IslandAir** (☎ 800/323-3345 or 808/484-2222), operates eight deHavilland Twin Otter turboprop aircraft and serves Hawaii's small interisland airports in West Maui, Princeville, Hana, Waimea and Kaunakakai.

Mahalo Air (☎ 800/277-8333 or 808/833-5555), the youngest carrier here, usually charges the lowest fares for round-trips to all islands except Lanai in its 50-seat turboprop Fokker aircraft. If you are in no hurry and can travel midweek, Mahalo is the thrifty alternative. Exteriors of their eye-catching planes feature renditions of Hawaii's endangered species like the nene goose, Hawaiian owl, green sea turtle, and humpback whale.

For details on making interisland connections at Honolulu International Airport, see "Arriving" under "Orientation" in Chapter 5.

CAR RENTALS

All major rental car agencies are represented at Honolulu International Airport and most neighbor-island airports, including **Alamo** (☎ 800/327-9633), **Avis** (☎ 800/ 321-3712), **Budget** (☎ 800/935-6878), **Enterprise** (☎ 800/325-8007), **Hertz** (☎ 800/654-3011), **National** (☎ 800/227-7368), **Payless** (☎ 800/729-5377), **Sears** (☎ 800/527-0770), and **Thrifty** (☎ 800/367-2277). It's almost always cheaper to rent a car at the airport than in Waikiki or through your hotel.

If you're going to visit multiple islands, it's usually easiest—and cheapest—to book with one company and carry your contract through on each island for your entire stay; you just drop off your car on the island you're leaving, and there will be one waiting for you on the next island with the same company. By booking your cars this way, as one interisland rental, you can usually take advantage of weekly rates that you'd be excluded from if you treated each rental separately. Inquire about interisland rental arrangements when booking.

Rental cars are usually at a premium on Kauai, Molokai, and Lanai, and may be sold-out on the neighbor islands on holiday weekends; be sure to book well ahead.

To rent a car in Hawaii, you must be at least 25 years of age and have a valid driver's license and a credit card. Your valid home-state license will be recognized here.

Insurance   Hawaii is a no-fault automobile state, which means that if you don't have collison damage insurance, you are required to pay for all damages before you leave the state, whether the accident was your fault or not. Your personal car insurance may provide rental-car coverage; read your policy or call your insurer before you leave home. Bring your identification card if you decline the optional insurance, which usually costs about $12 a day. Obtain the name of your company's local claim representative before you go. Some credit card companies also provide collision damage insurance for their customers; ask yours before you rent.

Driving Rules   Hawaii has a mandatory seat belt law; if you're caught not buckled up, you'll get a $20 ticket. Infants must be strapped in car seats. Pedestrians always have the right of way, even if they are not in the crosswalk. You can turn right on red from the right lane after a full and complete stop.

Gasoline stations are difficult to find on Oahu outside of Honolulu and on the neighbor islands, so keep your tank full. If you break down, call your car rental agency for emergency road service.

Road Maps   The fold-out map at the back of this book should get you around all the islands well.

The best and most detailed island maps are by Honolulu-based cartographer James A. Bier and are published by University of Hawaii Press. Updated periodically, they include a detailed network of island roads, large-scale insets of towns, historical and contemporary points of interest, parks, beaches, and hiking trails. They cost about $3 each, or about $15 for a complete set. If you can't find them in a bookstore near you, write to **University of Hawaii Press,** 2840 Kolowalu St., Honolulu, HI 96822.

If you seek topographical maps of the Hawaiian Islands, go to **Hawaii Geographic Society,** 49 S. Hotel St., Honolulu, HI 95813, or write to them at P.O. Box 1698 Honolulu, HI, 96806 (☎ **808/546-3952;** fax 808/536-5999). Old road maps and sea charts are available at **Tusitala Bookshop,** 116 Hekili St., Kailua, HI 96734 (☎ **808/262-6343**).

FAST FACTS: The Hawaiian Islands

American Express   For 24-hour traveler's check refunds and purchase information, call 800/221-7282. For local offices, see "Fast Facts" sections in the individual island chapters.

Area Code   All of the Hawaiian Islands are in the 808 area code.

Business Hours   Most offices open at 8am and close by 5pm. The morning commute usually runs from 6 to 8am, while the evening rush is from 4 to 6pm. Many people work at two or three jobs and drive their children to and from private schools, which creates extra traffic. Bank hours are Monday to Thursday from 8:30am to 3pm, Fridays from 8:30am to 6pm. Some banks open on Saturdays. Shopping centers open Monday to Friday from 10am to 9pm, Saturdays from 10am to 5:30pm, and Sundays from noon to 5 or 6pm.

Driving Rules   See "Getting There & Getting Around," above.

Electricity   Like the rest of the United States, Hawaii's electric power is 110 volts, 60 cycles.

Emergencies   Dial 911 for police, fire, or ambulance.

Legal Aid   Call the Legal Aid Society of Hawaii, 1108 Nuuanu Ave., Honolulu HI 96817 (☎ 808/536-4302).

Liquor Laws   The legal drinking age in Hawaii is 21.

Newspapers   *The Honolulu Advertiser* and the *Honolulu Star Bulletin* are circulated statewide. Other newspapers on Oahu include the *Honolulu Weekly* and *Pacific Business News*. Neighbor-island newspapers are published daily on Maui (*Maui News*), Kauai (*Garden Island* and *Kauai Times*), and the Big Island (*West Hawaii Today*); Molokai has two weeklies.

Radio & TV   Honolulu has a score of radio stations that broadcast in English, Hawaiian, Japanese, and Filipino. The most popular are KCCN (1420 AM), which features Hawaiian music; KHPR (88.1 FM), the National Public Radio station; KGU (760 AM), for news and talk radio; KUMU (94.7 FM), for easy listening; and KSSK (590 AM), the pop-music station.

All major Hawaiian islands are equipped with cable TV and receive major mainland network broadcast programs, which local stations delay by several hours so they will appear as "prime time" in Hawaii's time zone. This includes sports events, so fans who wish to follow their teams "live" should seek out establishments with satellite dishes. CNN is the prime source of 24-hour news.

Safety   Although Hawaii is generally a safe tourist destination, visitors have been crime victims, so stay alert. The most common crime against tourists is rental car break-ins. Never carry large amounts of cash in Waikiki and other tourist zones. Stay in well-lighted areas after dark. Don't hike on deserted trails alone.

Smoking   It's against the law to smoke in public buildings, including the airports. Hotels have nonsmoking rooms available, restaurants have nonsmoking sections, and car rental agencies have nonsmoking cars. Most bed-and-breakfasts prohibit smoking inside their buildings.

Taxes   Hawaii's sales tax is 4.17%. Hotel occupancy tax is 6%. Taxes of 10.17% are added to every hotel bill.

Telephone   Hawaii's telephone system operates like any other state's. Long distance calls may be directly dialed to the islands from the U.S. mainland and from most foreign countries. The international country code is 1, the same as for the rest of the United States and for Canada. Local calls costs 25¢ at a pay phone (if you can find one). Interisland calls are billed at the same rate as long distance. Hotels add a surcharge on local, interisland, mainland, and international calls.

Time   Hawaii standard time is in effect year-round (there is no daylight saving time here). Hawaii is 2 hours behind Pacific standard time and 5 hours behind Eastern standard time. In other words, when it's noon in Hawaii, it's 2pm in California and 5pm in New York during standard time on the mainland. When daylight saving time is in effect on the mainland, Hawaii is 3 hours behind the West Coast and 6 hours behind the East Coat. That is, when it's noon in Hawaii, it's 3pm in California and 6pm in New York during daylight saving time on the mainland.

Hawaii is east of the international date line, putting it in the same day as the U.S. mainland and Canada, and a day behind Australia, New Zealand, and Asia.

For Foreign Visitors 4

Although American fads and fashions have spread across Europe and other parts of the world so that the United States may seem like familiar territory before your arrival, there are still many peculiarities and uniquely American situations that any foreign visitor will encounter, even in this island state that differs in a few respects from the U.S. mainland.

1 Preparing for Your Trip

ENTRY REQUIREMENTS

Immigration laws are a hot political issue in the United States these days, and the following requirements may have changed somewhat by the time you plan your trip. Check at any U.S. embassy or consulate for current information and requirements.

Document Regulations   Canadian citizens may enter the United States without visas; they need only proof of residence.

The U.S. State Department has a **Visa Waiver Pilot Program** allowing citizens of certain countries to enter the United States without a visa for stays of up to 90 days. At press time these included Andorra, Austria, Belgium, Brunei, Denmark, Finland, France, Germany, Iceland, Ireland, Italy, Japan, Liechtenstein, Luxembourg, Monaco, the Netherlands, New Zealand, Norway, San Marino, Spain, Sweden, Switzerland, and the United Kingdom. Citizens of these countries need only a valid passport and a round-trip air or cruise ticket in their possession upon arrival. If they first enter the United States, they may then visit Mexico, Canada, Bermuda, and/ or the Caribbean islands and return to the United States without needing a visa. Further information is available from any U.S. embassy or consulate.

Citizens of all other countries including Australia must have (1) a valid **passport** with an expiration date at least 6 months later than the scheduled end of their visit to the United States; and (2) a **tourist visa** which may be obtained without charge from the nearest U.S. consulate.

To obtain a visa, the traveler must submit a completed application form (either in person or by mail) with a $1^1/_2$-inch-square photo, and they must demonstrate binding ties to a residence abroad. Usually you can obtain a visa at once or within 24 hours, but it may take longer during the summer rush from June to August. If you cannot go in person, contact the nearest U.S. embassy or consulate for directions on applying by mail. Your travel agent or airline office may also be able to provide you with visa applications and instructions. The U.S. consulate or embassy that issues your visa will determine whether you will be issued a multiple- or-single-entry visa and any restrictions regarding the length of your stay.

Foreign **driver's licenses** are recognized in Hawaii, although you may want to get an international driver's license if your home license is not written in English.

Medical Requirements   No inoculations are needed to enter the United States unless you are coming from, or have stopped over in, areas known to be suffering from epidemics, particularly cholera or yellow fever.

If you have a disease requiring treatment with medications containing narcotics or drugs requiring a syringe, carry a valid signed prescription from your physician to allay any suspicions that you are smuggling drugs.

Customs Requirements   Every adult visitor may bring in free of duty: 1 liter of wine or hard liquor; 200 cigarettes or 100 cigars (but no cigars from Cuba) or 3 pounds of smoking tobacco; $100 worth of gifts. These exemptions are offered to travelers who spend at least 72 hours in the United States and who have not claimed them within the preceding 6 months. It is altogether forbidden to bring into the country foodstuffs (particularly cheese, fruit, cooked meats, and canned goods) and plants (vegetables, seeds, tropical plants, and so on). Foreign tourists may bring in or take out up to $10,000 in U.S. or foreign currency with no formalities; larger sums must be declared to customs on entering or leaving.

In addition, you cannot bring fresh fruits and vegetables into Hawaii, even if you're coming from the U.S. mainland and have no need to clear customs. Every passenger is asked shortly before landing to sign a certificate declaring that he or she does not have fresh fruits and vegetables in their possession. The form also asks questions for the Hawaii Visitors Bureau about your visit, such as how long you plan to stay, which island or islands you will visit, and how many times you have been to Hawaii.

Insurance   There is no nationwide health system in the United States, and although Hawaii has one of the least expensive health insurance schemes in the country, the cost of medical care still is extremely high. Accordingly, we strongly advise every traveler to secure health insurance coverage before setting out.

You may want to take out a comprehensive travel policy that covers (for a relatively low premium) sickness or injury costs (medical, surgical, and hospital); loss or theft of your baggage; trip-cancellation costs; guarantee of bail in case you are arrested; costs of accident, repatriation, or death. Such packages (for example, "Europe Assistance" in Europe) are sold by automobile clubs at attractive rates, as well as by insurance companies and travel agencies.

MONEY

Currency   The American monetary system has a decimal base: one U.S. **dollar** ($1) = 100 **cents** (100¢). Dollar bills commonly come in $1 ("a buck"), $5, $10, $20, $50, and $100 denominations (the last two are not welcome when paying for small purchases and are not accepted in taxis or at subway ticket booths).

There are six denominations of coins: 1¢ (one cent or a "penny"), 5¢ (five cents or a "nickel"), 10¢ (ten cents or a "dime"), 25¢ (twenty-five cents or a "quarter"), 50¢ (fifty cents or a "half-dollar"), and the rare $1 piece.

Exchanging Currency   Unlike most other states, in which exchanging foreign currency for U.S. dollars can be a pain, you can easily change most currencies in

Hawaii. All major banks on Oahu provide this service. In downtown Honolulu, you also can get reliable currency service at **Thomas Cook Currency,** 1000 Bishop St., Bishop Trust Building, Ground Level, facing King Street (☎ **808/523-1321**). In Waikiki, go to **A1 Foreign Exchange,** which has offices in the Royal Hawaiian Shopping Center, 2259 Kalakaua Ave., and in the Hyatt Regency Waikiki Tower, 2424 Kalakaua Ave. (☎ **808/922-3327**); or to **Monyx International,** 307 Royal Hawaiian Ave. (☎ **808/923-6626**).

Traveler's Checks   It's actually cheaper and faster to get cash at an automatic teller machine (ATM) than to fuss with traveler's checks. As noted in "Visitor Information & Money" in Chapter 3, Hawaii has ATMs almost everywhere except on Lanai. If you do bring them, traveler's checks denominated in U.S. dollars are readily accepted at most hotels, motels, restaurants, and large stores. But the best place to change traveler's checks is at a bank. Do not bring traveler's checks denominated in any currency other than U.S. dollars.

Credit Cards   The method of payment most widely used is the credit card: Visa (BarclayCard in Britain), MasterCard (EuroCard in Europe, Access in Britain, Chargex in Canada), American Express, Diners Club, Discover, and Carte Blanche. You can save yourself trouble by using "plastic money" rather than cash or traveler's checks in most hotels, motels, restaurants, and retail stores (a growing number of food and liquor stores now accept credit cards). You must have a credit card to rent a car in Hawaii.

SAFETY

General   While tourist areas are generally safe, crime is on the increase everywhere in the United States, and Hawaii—especially Waikiki—is no exception. Visitors should always stay alert. It's wise to ask the island tourist office if you're in doubt about which neighborhoods are safe. Avoid deserted areas, especially at night. Don't go into any city park at night unless there's an event that attracts crowds—for example, the Waikiki Shell concerts in Kapiolani Park. Generally speaking, you can feel safe in areas where there are many people and many open establishments.

Avoid carrying valuables with you on the street, and don't display expensive cameras or electronic equipment. Hold onto your pocketbook, and place your billfold in an inside pocket. In theaters, restaurants, and other public places, keep your possessions in sight.

Remember also that hotels are open to the public, and in a large hotel, security may not be able to screen everyone entering. Always lock your room door—don't assume that once inside your hotel you are automatically safe and no longer need to be aware of your surroundings.

Driving   Safety while driving is particularly important. Question your rental agency about personal safety, or ask for a brochure of traveler safety tips when you pick up your car. Obtain written directions or a map with the route marked in red from the agency showing how to get to your destination.

Recently more crime has involved burglary of tourist rental cars in hotel parking structures and at beach parking lots. Park in well-lighted, well-traveled areas if possible. If you leave your rental car unlocked and empty of your valuables, you are probably safer than locking your car with valuables in plain view. Never leave any packages or valuables in sight. If someone attempts to rob you or steal your car, do *not* try to resist the thief/carjacker—report the incident to the police department immediately.

2 Getting to & Around the United States

Travelers from overseas can take advantage of the **APEX** (**Advance Purchase Excursion**) fares offered by all major U.S. and European carriers. Aside from these, attractive values are offered by **Icelandair** on flights from Luxembourg to New York and by **Virgin Atlantic Airways** from London to New York/Newark. You can then catch a connecting domestic flight to Honolulu. Advance purchase fares are available to travelers from Australia via **Qantas Airways,** which runs daily flights from Sydney to Honolulu (plus additional flights 4 days a week); they are also available for travelers from New Zealand via **Air New Zealand,** which runs 40 flights per week from Auckland.

Some large American airlines (for example, TWA, American Airlines, Northwest, United, and Delta) offer travelers on their transatlantic or transpacific flights special discount tickets under the name **Visit USA,** allowing travel between any U.S. destinations at reduced rates. They are not on sale in the United States, and must, therefore, be purchased before you leave your foreign point of departure. This system is the best, easiest, and fastest way to see the United States at low cost. You should obtain information well in advance from your travel agent or the office of the airline concerned, since the conditions attached to these discount tickets can be changed without advance notice.

The visitor arriving by air should cultivate patience and resignation before setting foot on U.S. soil. Getting through immigration control may take as long as 2 hours on some days, especially summer weekends. Add the time it takes to clear customs and you'll see that you should make very generous allowance for delay in planning connections between international and domestic flights—an average of 2 to 3 hours at least.

For further information about travel to Hawaii, see "Getting There & Getting Around" in Chapter 3.

FAST FACTS: For the Foreign Traveler

Automobile Organizations   Auto clubs will supply maps, suggested routes, guidebooks, accident and bail-bond insurance, and emergency road service. The major auto club in the United States, with 955 offices nationwide, is the **American Automobile Association** (AAA; often called "triple A"). Members of some foreign auto clubs have reciprocal arrangements with the AAA and enjoy its services at no charge. If you belong to an auto club, inquire about AAA reciprocity before you leave. The AAA can provide you with an **International Driving Permit** validating your foreign license. You may be able to join the AAA even if you are not a member of a reciprocal club. To inquire, call 800/336-4357. In Hawaii, the local office of the AAA is at 590 Queen St., Honolulu (☎ 808/528-2600). In addition, some automobile rental agencies now provide these services, so you should inquire about their availability when you rent your car.

Automobile Rentals   See "Getting There & Getting Around" in Chapter 3.

Business Hours   See "Fast Facts: The Hawaiian Islands" in Chapter 3.

Climate   See "When to Go" in Chapter 3.

Currency & Currency Exchange   See "Preparing for Your Trip," above.

Electricity   Hawaii, like the U.S mainland and Canada, uses 110–120 volts, 60 cycles, compared to 220–240 volts, 50 cycles, as in most of Europe and in other areas of the world including Australia and New Zealaned. In addition to a 100-volt transformer, small appliances of non-American manufacture, such as hairdryers or shavers, will require a plug adapter, with two flat, parallel pins.

Embassies & Consulates   All embassies are located in the national capital, Washington, D.C. Some consulates are located in major cities, and most nations have a mission to the United Nations in New York City.

Listed here are the embassies and some consulates of the major English-speaking countries. Travelers from other countries can obtain telephone numbers for their embassies and consulates by calling directory informaton for Washington, D.C. (☎ 202/555-1212).

The embassy of **Australia** is at 1601 Massachusetts Ave. NW, Washington, D.C. 20036 (☎ 202/797-3000). There is also an Australian consulate in Hawaii at 1000 Bishop St., Penthouse Suite, Honolulu, HI 96813 (☎ 808/524-5050).

The embassy of **Canada** is at 501 Pennsylvania Ave. NW, Washington, D.C. 20001 (☎ 202/682-1740). Canadian consulates are also at 1251 Avenue of the Americas, New York, NY 10020 (☎ 212/768-2400), and in Los Angeles, San Francisco, and Seattle.

The embassy of the **Republic of Ireland** is at 2234 Massachusetts Ave. NW, Washington, D.C. 20008 (☎ 202/462-3939). Irish consulates are in Boston, New York, and San Francisco.

The embassy of **New Zealand** is at 37 Observatory Circle NW, Washington, D.C. 20008 (☎ 202/328-4800). The only New Zealand consulate in the United States is in Los Angeles.

The embassy of the **United Kingdom** is at 3100 Massachusetts Ave. NW, Washington, D.C. 20008 (☎ 202/462-1340). British consulates are at 845 Third Ave., New York, NY 10022 (☎ 212/745-0200), and in Los Angeles.

The embassy of **Japan** is at 2520 Massachusetts Ave. NW, Washington, D.C. 20008 (☎ 202/939-6700). The consulate general of Japan is located at 1742 Nuuanu Ave., Honolulu, HI 96817 (☎ 808/536-2226). There are several other consulates, including one in New York at 299 Park Ave., New York, NY 10171 (☎ 212/371-8222).

Emergencies   Call **911** to report a fire, call the police, or get an ambulance. If you encounter traveler's problems, check the local directory to find an office of the **Traveler's Aid Society,** a nationwide, nonprofit, social-service organization geared to helping travelers in difficult straits. Their services might include reuniting families separated while traveling, providing food and/or shelter to people stranded without cash, or even emotional counseling. If you're in trouble, seek them out.

Gasoline (Petrol)   One U.S. gallon equals 3.8 liters, while 1.2 U.S. gallons equals one Imperial gallon. You'll notice there are several grades (and price levels) of gasoline available at most gas stations. And you'll also notice that their names change from company to company. The ones with the highest octane are the most expensive, but most rental cars take the least expensive "regular" gas with an octane rating of 87.

Holidays   See "When to Go" in Chapter 3.

Languages   English is the official language. Major Hawaii hotels may have multilingual employees, and most Honolulu and Waikiki shops have multilingual staff who speak English, Japanese, Korean, and several dialects of the Phillipines. Unless your language is very obscure, they can usually supply a translator on request. See "Life & Language" in Chapter 2 for information about the Hawaiian language and the local version of pidgin.

Legal Aid The ordinary tourist will probably never become involved with the American legal system. If your are pulled over for a minor infraction (for example, driving faster than the speed limit), never attempt to pay the fine directly to a police officer; you may wind up arrested on the much more serious charge of attempted bribery. Pay fines by mail, or directly into the hands of the clerk of the court. If accused of a more serious offense, it's wise to say and do nothing before consulting a lawyer (you have a right to both remain silent and to consult an attorney under the U.S. Constitution). Under U.S. law, an arrested person is allowed one telephone call to a party of his or her choice. Call your embassy or consulate.

Mail If you want your mail to follow you on your vacation and you aren't sure of your address, your mail can be sent to you, in your name, c/o **General Delivery** at the main post office of the city or region where you expect to be. The addressee must pick it up in person and produce proof of identity (driver's license, passport, etc.).

Generally to be found at intersections, mailboxes are blue with a blue-and-white eagle logo and carry the inscription "U.S. Postal Service." If your mail is addressed to a U.S. destination, don't forget to add the five-figure postal code, or zip code, after the two-letter abbreviation of the state to which the mail is addressed. The abbreviation for Hawaii is HI.

International air mail rates are 60¢ for letters and 20¢ for postcards. All domestic first-class mail goes from Hawaii to the U.S. mainland by air, so don't bother paying the extra amount to send a letter back to your grandmother in Michigan.

Newspapers/Magazines National newspapers include the *New York Times,* (often available at hotels in a condensed fax edition), *USA Today,* and the *Wall Street Journal.* These are available in major hotels, as are major West Coast newspapers like the *San Francisco Chronicle* and the *Los Angeles Times.* National news weeklies include *Newsweek, Time,* and *U.S. News and World Report. The Honolulu Advertiser* and the *Honolulu Star-Bulletin* are the major local newspapers on Oahu and throughout the islands; the *Maui News* serves Maui; *Garden Island* and *Kauai Times* serve Kauai; and *West Hawaii Today* serves the Big Island of Hawaii. Molokai has two weekly newspapers.

Radio & Television The United States has five coast-to-coast television networks—ABC, CBS, NBC, Fox, and the Public Broadcasting System (PBS). These networks and the cable network CNN play a major part in American life. In Honolulu, televiewers have a choice of about a dozen TV channels, most of them transmitting 24 hours a day, not counting the pay-TV channels showing recent movies or sports events. All options are usually indicated on your hotel TV set. You'll also find a wide choice of local radio stations, each broadcasting particular kinds of talk shows and/or music—classical, country, jazz, pop, gospel—punctuated by news broadcasts and frequent commercials. For more information, see "Fast Facts: The Hawaiian Islands" in Chapter 3.

Safety See "Safety" under "Preparing for Your Trip," above.

Taxes The United States has no VAT (Value-Added Tax) or other indirect taxes at a national level. Every state, and each city in it, has the right to levy its own local tax on all purchases, including hotel and restaurant checks, airline tickets, and so on. In Hawaii, sales tax is 4.17%; there's also a 6% hotel room tax, so the total tax on your hotel bill will be 10.17%.

Telephone & Fax The telephone system in the United States is run by private corporations, so rates, particularly for long-distance service and operator-assisted calls, can vary widely—especially on calls made from public telephones. Local calls made from public phones in Hawaii cost 25¢.

Generally, hotel surcharges on long-distance and local calls are astronomical. You are usually better off using a **public pay telephone,** which you will find clearly marked in most public buildings and private establishments as well as on the street. Outside Honolulu, public telephones are more difficult to find in Hawaii. Stores and gas stations are your best bet.

Most **long-distance and international calls** can be dialed directly from any phone. For calls to Canada and to other parts of the United States, dial 1 followed by the area code and the seven-digit number. For international calls, dial 011 followed by the country code, city code, and the telephone number of the person you wish to call.

In Hawaii, interisland phone calls are considered long-distance and often are as costly as calling the U.S. mainland.

For **reversed-charge or collect calls,** and for **person-to-person calls,** dial 0 (zero, *not* the letter "O") followed by the area code and number you want; an operator will then come on the line, and you should specify that you are calling collect, or person-to-person, or both. If your operator-assisted call is international, ask for the overseas operator.

Note that all phone numbers with the area code 800 are toll-free.

For local **directory assistance** ("information"), dial 411; for **long-distance information,** dial 1, then the appropriate area code and 555-1212.

Fax facilities are widely available, and can be found in most hotels and many other establishments. Try Mailboxes Etc. or any photocopying shop.

Telephone Directory   There are two kinds of telephone directories in the United States. The general directory is the so-called **White Pages,** in which private and business subscribers are listed in alphabetical order. The inside front cover lists the emergency number for police, fire, and ambulance, and other vital numbers (like the Coast Guard, poison-control center, crime-victims hot line, and so on). The first few pages are devoted to community-service numbers, including a guide to long-distance and international calling, complete with country codes and area codes.

The second directory, printed on yellow paper (hence its name, *Yellow Pages*), lists all local services, businesses, and industries by type of activity, with an index at the back. The listings cover not only such obvious items as automobile repairs by make of car, or drugstores (pharmacies), often by geographical location, but also restaurants by type of cuisine and geographical location, bookstores by special subject and/or language, places of worship by religious denomination, and other information that the tourist might otherwise not readily find. The *Yellow Pages* also include city plans or detailed maps, often showing postal zip codes and public transportation routes.

Time   See "Fast Facts: The Hawaiian Islands" in Chapter 3.

Tipping   It's part of the American way of life to tip, on the principle that you must expect to pay for any service you get. Many personnel receive little direct salary and must depend on tips for their income. In fact, the U.S. federal government imposes income taxes on service personnel based on an estimate of how much they should have earned in tips relative to their employer's total receipts. In other words, they may have to pay taxes on a tip you didn't give them!

Here are some rules of thumb:

In **hotels,** tip bellhops at least $1 per piece ($2–$3 if you have a lot of luggage) and tip the chamber staff $1 per day. Tip the doorman or concierge only if he or she has provided you with some specific service (for example, calling a cab for you or obtaining difficult-to-get theater tickets).

In **restaurants, bars, and nightclubs,** tip service staff 15% to 20% of the check, tip bartenders 10% to 15%, tip checkroom attendants $1 per garment, and tip valet-parking attendants $1 per vehicle. Tip the doorman only if he has provided you with some specific service (such as calling a cab for you). Tipping is not expected in cafeterias and fast-food restaurants.

Tip **cab drivers** 15% of the fare.

As for **other service personnel,** tip redcaps at airports or railroad stations at least 50¢ per piece ($2 to $3 if you have a lot of luggage) and tip hairdressers and barbers 15% to 20%.

Tipping ushers at movies and theaters and gas-station attendants is not expected.

Toilets   Foreign visitors often complain that public toilets are hard to find in most U.S. cities. True, there are none on the streets, but the visitor can usually find one in a bar, restaurant, hotel, museum, department store, or service station—and it will probably be clean (although the last-mentioned sometimes leaves much to be desired). Note, however, a growing practice in some restaurants and bars of displaying a notice that "toilets are for the use of patrons only." You can ignore this sign, or better yet, avoid arguments by paying for a cup of coffee or soft drink, which will qualify you as a patron. The cleanliness of toilets at railroad stations and bus depots may be more open to question, and some public places are equipped with pay toilets, which require you to insert one or more coins into a slot on the door before it will open.

Oahu, the Gathering Place   5

A wise Hawaiian *kupuna* once told me that the islands are like children—that each is special yet different, that each is to be loved for its individual qualities. One thing's for sure: You will never find another island like Oahu, the commercial and population center of Hawaii.

It's astounding to spend hours flying across the barren blue of the Pacific and then to suddenly see below you the whites and pastels of Honolulu, the most remote big city on earth, a 26-mile-long metropolis of some 850,000 souls living in the middle of nowhere. Once on its streets, you'll find bright city lights, five-star restaurants, nearly all-night nightclubs, world-class shopping, great art and architecture, and grand old hotels.

Nine out of ten visitors to Hawaii—some 5 million a year—stop on Oahu, and most of them end up along the canyonlike streets of Waikiki, Honolulu's famous hotel district and its most densely populated neighborhood. Some days it seems like the entire world is sunning itself on Waikiki's famous beach.

Beyond Waikiki, Honolulu is clean and easy to enjoy. Founded by King Kamehameha in 1850, "reformed" by Boston missionaries, and once dominated by the "Big Five" cartels, the coming of age is just in time for the 21st century. The old port town is reshaping its waterfront, altering its skyline, building a convention center, opening new world-class hotels, and all the while trying to preserve its historic roots and revive its Polynesian heritage.

Out in the country, Oahu can be as down-home as a slack-key guitar. That's where you'll find a big blue sky, perfect waves, empty beaches, rainbows and waterfalls, sweet tropical flowers, and fiery Pacific sunsets. In fact, nowhere else within 60 minutes of a major American city can you snorkel in a crystal-clear lagoon, climb an old volcano, surf monster waves, fish for record marlin, kayak to a desert isle, picnic on a sandbar, soar in a glider over tide pools, skin dive over a sunken airplane, bicycle through a rain forest, golf a championship course, or sail into the setting sun.

And weatherwise, no other Hawaiian island has it as nice as Oahu. The Big Island is hotter, Kauai is wetter, Maui has more wind, Molokai and Lanai are drier. But Oahu enjoys a kind of perpetual late spring, with light trade winds and 82°F days almost year round. In fact, the climate is supposed to be the best on the planet. Once you have that, the rest is easy.

1 Orientation

by Rick Carroll

ARRIVING

Honolulu is your gateway to the Hawaiian Islands; chances are, no matter which islands you're visiting, you'll come to Oahu first. **Honolulu International Airport** sits on the south shore of Oahu, west of downtown Honolulu and Waikiki near Pearl Harbor. All major American and many international carriers fly to Honolulu from the mainland; see "Getting There & Getting Around" in Chapter 3 for a list of carriers and their toll-free numbers.

LANDING AT HONOLULU INTERNATIONAL AIRPORT

Landing at Honolulu is like arriving in a foreign country full of strangers from every corner of the world. On any given day, it's probably the most cosmopolitan spot in the Pacific.

While the airport is large and constantly expanding, the layout is quite simple and easy to grasp. You can walk or take the **Wiki-Wiki Bus,** a free airport shuttle, from your arrival gate to the main terminal and Baggage Claim, on the ground level. After collecting your bags, unless you're getting on an interisland flight immediately, exit to the palm-lined street, where uniformed attendants flag down taxis, Waikiki shuttles, and rental car vans; they can also direct you to TheBUS (for transportation information, see below).

Passengers connecting to neighbor island flights will need to take the Wiki-Wiki shuttle, either to the large Inter-Island Terminal serving Aloha and Hawaiian Airlines, or the more distant Commuter Terminal, which serves the smaller airlines like Mahalo and Aloha IslandAir. (For details on interisland flights, see "Getting There & Getting Around" in Chapter 3).

Tips to Make Life Easier   When departing the islands or making interisland connections, allow yourself plenty of time—at least 45 minutes for interisland flights, more than an hour's lead for mainland flights, around two for international. Like most major airports, Honolulu sprawls over a huge area—larger than you want to sprint around in the tropic heat. The Wiki-Wiki Bus links the various terminals and connects distant gates with baggage areas, but it's not automated and therefore only somewhat more "wiki-wiki" than walking. Allow time to fit the island-style schedule.

GETTING TO & FROM THE AIRPORT

By Rental Car   All major rental companies have cars available at Honolulu International Airport (see "Getting Around," below). Rental agency vans will pick you up curbside outside baggage claim and take you to their off-site lot.

By Taxi   Taxis are abundant at the airport; an attendant will be happy to flag one down for you. Taxi fare from Honolulu International to downtown Honolulu is about $16, to Waikiki about $23. If you need to call a taxi, see "Getting Around," below, for a list of cab companies.

By Airport Shuttle   Shuttle vans operate 24 hours a day every day of the year between the airport and all 350 hotels and condos in Waikiki. **Trans-Hawaiian Services** (☎ **808/566-7000**) serves the airport with passenger vans every 20 to 30 minutes, depending on traffic; it's $7 one-way to Waikiki, $12 round-trip. No reservation is necessary; you can pick it up at street level outside Baggage Claim. Look for attendants in red shirts that say "shuttle vehicle." You can board with two pieces of luggage and a carry-on at no extra charge; surfboards and bicycles are prohibited for safety reasons. Backpacks are okay. Tips are welcome. For advance purchase of group or family tickets, contact Norman Brown at the number above. Do book ahead for hotel pickup for a departing flight.

By TheBUS   Bus nos. 10 and 20 (Waikiki Beach and Hotels) runs from the airport to downtown Honolulu and Waikiki. The first bus from Waikiki to the airport is at 4:50am on weekdays and 5:25am on weekends; the last bus departs the airport for Waikiki at 11:45pm on weekdays, 11:15pm on weekends. There are two bus stops on the main terminal's upper level; a third is on the second level of the Inter-Island terminal.

You can board TheBUS with a carry-on or small suitcase as long as it fits under the seat and doesn't disrupt other passengers; otherwise, you'll have to take a shuttle or taxi. The approximate travel time to Waikiki is an hour. The one-way fare is $1, 50¢ for students, exact change only. For information on routes and schedules, call **TheBUS** at **808/848-4444.**

VISITOR INFORMATION

The **Hawaii Visitors and Convention Bureau,** 2270 Kalakaua Ave., 7th floor, Honolulu, HI 96815 (☎ **808/923-1811**), supplies free brochures, maps, accommodation guides, and *Islands of Aloha,* the official HVCB magazine. **Waikiki Oahu Visitors Association,** 1001 Bishop St., Pauahi Tower, Suite 47, Honolulu, HI 96813 (☎ **808/524-0722** or 800/OAHU-678) distributes a free 64-page visitors booklet.

THE REGIONS IN BRIEF
HONOLULU

America's 11th largest city looks like any other big metropolitan center with tall buildings. In fact, some cynics refer to it as "Los Angeles West." But within Honolulu's metes and bounds you'll find rain forests, deep canyons, valleys and waterfalls, a nearly mile-high mountain range, coral reefs, and gold-sand beaches. The city proper—where most of Honolulu's 850,000 residents live—is approximately 12 miles wide and 26 miles long, running east-west roughly between Diamond Head and Pearl Harbor (you'll see Pearl Harbor from the left side of your airplane on your final approach into Honolulu International). It folds over seven hills laced by seven streams that run to Mamala Bay.

Up close, Honolulu becomes exceedingly complex: Downtown, street vendors sell papayas from a truck on skyscraper-lined concrete canyons, where professional women wear muumuus and carry briefcases. Joggers and BMWs rush by a lacy palace where champions of liberty stole the kingdom. Burly bus drivers sport fragrant white ginger flowers on their dashboards, Methodist churches look like Asian temples, businessmen wear aloha shirts to billion-dollar meetings. Doctors and dope dealers share surfing spots, and the entire social spectrum spreads mats edge to edge on a lawn to hear folksy Hawaiian music and watch hula under the stars. Tokyo teenagers sun on the beach in bikinis while their older Hawaiian cousins carry parasols for shade, and waiters, if asked, will stand and recite their 14 cultural antecedents in a tradition as old as Polynesia. What under the tropical sun is this place? The third world's American capital, mankind's hope for the future, or just the stuff between the airport and the beach at Waikiki? Watch out while you find out; some cities tug at your heart, but Honolulu is a whole love affair.

Waikiki   When King Kalakaua played in Waikiki, it was "a hamlet of plain cottages . . . its excitements caused by the activity of insect tribes and the occasional fall of a coconut." The Merrie Monarch, who gave his name to Waikiki's main street, would love the scene today. It's where all the action is. Waikiki is an urban beach backed by 175 high-rise hotels with more than 33,000 guest rooms, all in a 1.5-square-mile beach zone. The beach district boasts 279 drinking establishments, 240 restaurants, 90 hotels, and four churches. Waikiki is honeymooners and sun seekers, bikinis and bare buns, a round-the-clock beach party every day of the year. And it's all because of a thin crescent of imported sand.

Some say Waikiki is past its prime and that everybody goes to Maui now. If it's fallen out of popularity, you couldn't prove it by me. Waikiki is the very incarnation of Yogi Berra's comment about Toots Shor's famous New York restaurant: "Nobody goes there anymore. It's too crowded."

Downtown   Now a tiny cluster of high rise offices west of Waikiki, downtown Honolulu is the financial, business, and government center of Hawaii. Fort Street runs inland from the iconic 1926-vintage Aloha Tower, once the tallest building on Oahu.

The history of Hawaii can be read architecturally downtown, where Italianate Monarchy–style buildings stand next to New England Mission Houses and the 1920s buildings of the "Big Five" cartel. There's a Carnegie-built Mediterranean library, a Spanish-style City Hall, a Julia Morgan YWCA, and a State Capitol designed by John Carl Warnecke that looks like a volcano. And there's the gingerbread palace that became a prison for Hawaii's last queen.

Chinatown Historic District   In Chinatown, on the edge of downtown, you can buy thousand-year-old duck eggs or fresh flower leis, find an ancient potion, get a $3 haircut, play pool in a 1930s bar, get treated by an acupuncturist, buy fresh Chinese *manapua,* eat Vietnamese *pho,* or browse Oahu Market, where 17 vendors sell fish, ducks, spices, fresh fruits, and vegetables under a tin roof. Founded in 1860 by Chinese immigrants, it's the oldest Chinatown in America and still one of Honolulu's liveliest neighborhoods. A quaint village of tin-roofed sheds, brightly painted shops, and often crowded streets, this historic 15-block district is a nonstop pageant of people, sights, sounds, smells, and tastes—not all Chinese, now that Southeast Asians, including many Vietnamese, share the old storefronts. Go on Saturday morning when everyone shops in Chinatown for fresh goods like ginger root, fern fronds, and hogsheads.

Ala Moana   A great beach as well as a famous shopping center, Ala Moana is the retail and transportation heart of Honolulu, a place where you can both shop and suntan in one afternoon. All bus routes lead to the open air Ala Moana Shopping Center, a modern mall across the street from Ala Moana Beach. This 50-acre, 200-shop emporium attracts 56 million customers a year. People fly up here from Tahiti just to buy their Christmas gifts. Every European designer from Armani to Vuitton has a shop here, and Neiman-Marcus will open here in 1998. It's Honolulu's answer to Beverly Hills' Rodeo Drive.

Manoa Valley   First inhabited by white settlers, the Moana Valley above Waikiki still has vintage *kamaaina* homes, one of Hawaii's premiere botanical gardens in the Lyon Arboretum, ever-gushing Manoa Falls, and the 320-acre campus of the University of Hawaii, where 50,000 students hit the books when they're not on the beach and where scholars develop solutions to third world problems at the East-West Center, a major Pacific Rim think tank.

Oahu

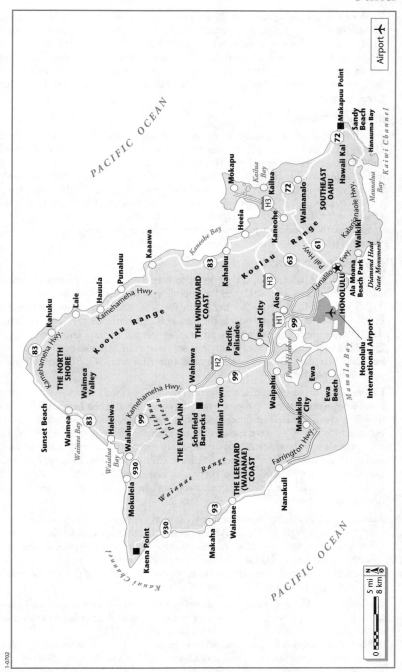

To the East: Kahala   Except for the grandiose estates of world-class millionaires and the newly opened Mandarin Oriental Hotel (with Hoku's, its outstanding new beachfront restaurant), there's not much out this way that's of interest to visitors. The Vegas-like temples that displaces the grand old homes that formerly stood here have turned the once-elegant district into a ghostly version of its former self. In between the gated mansions, you can find narrow sand alleys to the thin, gnarly beach that fronts the estates.

SOUTHEAST OAHU

Beyond Kahala lies East Honolulu and the suburban bedroom communities of Aina Haina, Niu Valley, Kuliouou, Hawaii Kai, Portlock, and Kalama Valley, all linked by Kalanianaole Highway and each chockablock with homes, condos, fast-food joints, and shopping malls. It looks like southern California on a good day. The only reasons you're likely to find yourself out here are dinner at Roy's, the original and still-outstanding Hawaii Regional restaurant, in Hawaii Kai; if you're bound for Hanauma Bay for some snorkeling, or heading to Sandy Beach to watch daredevil surfers risk their necks; or just looking to enjoy the natural splendor of the lovely coastline, which might include a hike to Makapuu Lighthouse.

THE WINDWARD COAST

For years, travel writers (hoping no doubt to keep a great secret) portrayed Oahu's northeastern side as wet, windy, and unappealing to tourists. Well, the secret's out. The Windward Coast looks like the South Pacific of the travel posters: green and lush, backed by the awesome cliffs of the Koolau Range, with plenty of sun, cool trade winds, and miles of empty coral-sand beaches fronted by bays and reefs. This is Oahu's natural state, a place of beauty not yet violated by high-rise hotels. There are no hotels here, but plenty of beach cottages (some for rent) and B&Bs in little villages on big beaches.

Kailua   The biggest little beach town in Hawaii, Kailua sits at the foot of the sheer green Koolau mountains, on a great bay with two of Hawaii's best beaches. The town itself is a low-rise cluster of time-worn shops and homes. Instead of hotels, Kailua became the bed-and-breakfast capital of Hawaii, an affordable alternative to Waikiki, with rooms and vacation rentals from $60-a-day and up. It's a funky little town full of fun restaurants like Buzz's (where President Clinton ate when he came to town); the publike Kailua Beach Grill, and Brent's, an authentic New York–style deli. With the prevailing trade winds whipping up a cooling breeze, Kailua attracts windsurfers from around the world.

Kaneohe   Helter-skelter suburbia sprawls around the edges of Kaneohe, one of the most scenic bays in all the Pacific. After you clear the trafficky maze of Kaneohe, you return to Oahu's more natural state. This great bay beckons you to get out on it, and you can depart from Heeia Boat Harbor on snorkel or fishing charters and visit Ahu a Laka a, the sandbar that appears and disappears in the middle of the bay. From out there, you'll get a panoramic view of the Koolau Range.

Kualoa/Laie   The upper northeast shore is one of the most sacred spots on Oahu, an early Hawaiian landing spot where even kings dipped their sails, the cliffs hold ancient burial sites, and ghosts still march in the night.

Sheer cliffs stab this sea coast fringed by coral reef. Old fishponds are tucked along the two-lane coast road that weaves around beautiful Kahana Bay and by empty gold sand beaches in towns with too many vowels, like Kaaawa. Thousands "explore" the South Pacific at the Polynesian Cultural Center, in Laie, a Mormon settlement with its own Tabernacle Choir of sweet Samoan harmony.

THE NORTH SHORE

Only 28 miles from downtown Honolulu, the little beach town of Haleiwa seems like a separate paradise; once some people get the roar of the surf in their head, they never leave. They come to see the big waves, eat shave ice, go deep-sea fishing, visit the island's biggest *heiau*, explore Oahu's Waimea Canyon, shop in artsy Haleiwa town, and stay in a beachfront cottage within a splash of the roaring surf.

CENTRAL OAHU: THE EWA PLAIN

Flanked by the Koolau and Waianae mountain ranges, the hot, sun-baked Ewa Plain runs up and down the center of Oahu. Once covered with the sandalwood forests hacked down for the China trade, and later the sugarcane and pineapple backbone of Hawaii, Ewa today sports a new crop: suburban houses stretching to the sea. But let your eye wander west to the Waianae Range and Mount Kaala, at 4,020 feet, the highest summit on Oahu. Up there in the misty rain forest, native birds thrive in the hummocky bog.

Hawaiian chiefs once fought on the Ewa Plain for supremacy of Oahu. In 1928 the U.S. Army pitched a tent camp on the plain. It became Schofield Barracks, which author James Jones called "the most beautiful army post in the world." Hollywood filmed Jones's *From Here to Eternity* here, thus launching crooner Frank Sinatra on his comeback.

LEEWARD OAHU: THE WAIANAE COAST

The west coast of Oahu is a hot and dry place of naturally spectacular beauty—big beaches, steep cliffs, and wildness. You'll find virtually no tourist services out here; the funky west coast villages of Nanakuli, Waianae, and Makaha are the last stands of native Hawaiians. This side of Oahu is seldom visited except by surfers bound for Yokohama Bay and anyone else who wants to see needle-nose Kaena Point (the island's westernmost outpost) and a coastal wilderness park under a 768-foot peak named for the endangered Hawaiian owl.

2 Getting Around

by Rick Carroll

BY CAR

All of the major car-rental firms have agencies on Oahu, at the airport and in Waikiki, including **Alamo** (☎ 800/327-9633); **Avis** (☎ 800/321-3712), **Budget** (☎ 800/935-6878); **Enterprise** (☎ 800/325-8007); **Hertz** (☎ 800/654-3011); **National** (☎ 800/227-7368); **Payless** (☎ 800/729-5377); **Sears** (☎ 800/527-0770); and **Thrifty** (☎ 800/367-2277).

Oahu residents own 600,000 registered vehicles, but they have only 1,500 miles of mostly two-lane roads. That's 400 cars for every mile, a fact which becomes abundantly clear during morning and evening rush hours. You can avoid the gridlock by driving between 9am and 3pm or after 6pm.

BY BUS

One of the best deals anywhere, **TheBUS** (☎ **808/848-4444,** or 808/296-1818 for recorded information) goes around the whole island for $1. In fact, more than 260,000 people daily use the system's 68 lines and 4,000 bus stops. TheBUS goes almost everywhere almost all the time. The most popular route is no. 8, which shuttles people between Waikiki and Ala Moana Center every 10 minutes or so (the ride is 15 to 20 min.); the no. 19 (Airport/Hickam), no. 20 (Airport/Halawa Gate),

TheBUS

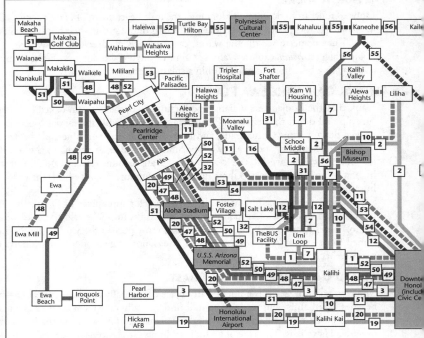

Common Bus Routes:

Ala Moana Shopping Center: Take bus #8 & #58 ALA MOANA CENTER, #19 & #20 AIRPORT or #47 WAIPAHU. Return #8 WAIKIKI or #19 WAIKIKI, or across Ala Moana Blvd. #20 & #47.

Bishop Museum: Take #2 SCHOOL STREET get off at Kapalama St., cross School St., walk down Bernice St. Return to School St. and take #2 WAIKIKI.

Byodo-In Temple: Take bus #2 to Hotel-Alakea St. (TRF) to #55 KANEOHE-KAHALUU. Get off at Valley of the Temple cemetery. Also #19 & #20 AIRPORT to King-Alakea St., (TRF) on Alakea St. to #55 KANEOHE-KAHALUU.

Circle Island: Take a Bus to ALA MOANA CENTER (TRF) to #52 WAHIAWA CIRCLE ISLAND or #55 KENEOHE CIRCLE ISLAND. This is a four-hour bus ride.

Chinatown or Downtown: Take any #2 bus going out of Waikiki, to Hotel St. Return take #2 WAIKIKI on Hotel St., or #19, #20, #47 WAIKIKI on King St.

Contemporary Museum & Punchbowl (National Cemetery of the Pacific): Take #2 bus (TRF) at Alapai St. to #15 MAKIKI-PACIFIC HGTS. Return, take #15 and get off at King St., area (TRF) #2 WAIKIKI.

Diamond Head Crater: #22 or #58 HAWAII KAI-SEA LIFE PARK to the crater. Take a flashlight. Return to the same area and take #22 WAIKIKI or #58 ALA MOANA.

Dole Plantation: Take bus to ALA MOANA CENTER (TRF) to #52 WAHIAWA CIRCLE ISLAND.

Foster Botanic Gardens: Take #2 bus to Hotel-Riviera St. Walk to Vineyard Blvd. Return to Hotel St. Take #2 WAIKIKI, or take #4 NUUANU and get off at Nuuanu-Vineyard. Cross Nuuanu Ave. and walk one block to the gardens.

Hawaii Maritime Center: Take #19-#20 AIRPORT, #47 WAIPAHU and get off at Alakea–Ala Moana. Cross the Street to the Aloha Tower.

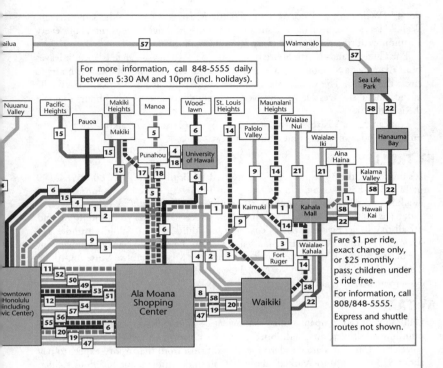

Honolulu Zoo: Take any bus on Kuhio Ave. going DIAMOND HEAD direction to Kapahulu Ave.

Iolani Palace: also **State Capitol, Honolulu Hale, Kawaihao Church, Mission Houses, Queen's Hospital, King Kamehameha Statue, State Judiciary Bldg.,** take any #2 bus and get off at Punchbowl and Beretania St. Walk to King St. Return #2 WAIKIKI on King St.

Kahala Mall: #22 or #58 HAWAII KAI–SEA LIFE PARK to Kilauea Ave. Return #22 WAIKIKI or #58 ALA MOANA CENTER.

Kodak Hula Show: (Tues-Thurs 10ᴀᴍ.) Free. Take #8, #19, #20, #47 WAIKIKI or #2 KAPIOLANI PARK to Kapiolani Park. Walk to the Waikiki Shell.

Pearl Harbor (Arizona Memorial): Open Daily 8ᴀᴍ to 3ᴘᴍ. Free. Take #20 AIRPORT or #47 WAIPAHU. Get off across from Memorial, or take a bus to Ala Moana Center (TRF) to #49, #50 or #52.

Polynesian Cultural Center: Take a bus to ALA MOANA CENTER (TRF) to #55 KANEOHE CIRCLE ISLAND. Bus ride takes two hours one way. PCC opens at 12:30ᴘᴍ. Closed on Sundays.

Queen Emma's Summer Home: Take #4 NUUANU and it will take you there, or board a bus to ALA MOANA CENTER (TRF) to #55 KANEOHE, #56-#57 KAILUA.

Sea Life Park: #22-#58 HAWAII KAI-SEA LIFE PARK. #22 will stop at Hanauma Bay enroute to the park.

University of Hawaii: Take #4 NUUANU. The bus will go to the University enroute to Nuuanu.

Waimea Falls Park: Take a bus to ALA MOANA CENTER (TRF) to #52 WAHIAWA CIRCLE ISLAND or #55 KANEOHE CIRCLE ISLAND.

no. 47 (Waipahu), and no. 58 (Waikiki/Ala Moana) also cover the same stretch. Waikiki service begins daily at 5am and runs until midnight; buses run about every 15 minutes during the day and every 30 minutes in the evening.

The Circle Island–North Shore route is no. 52 (Wahiawa/Circle Island); it leaves from Ala Moana Shopping Center every 30 minutes, and takes about $4^1/2$ hours to circle the island. The Circle Island–South Shore route is no. 55 (Kaneohe/Circle Island) and also leaves Ala Moana every half-hour and takes about 3 hours to circle the island.

You can buy a **Visitors Pass** for $10 at any ABC store in Waikiki. It's good for unlimited rides anywhere on Oahu for 4 days.

BY TROLLEY

It's fun to ride the 34-seat, open air, motorized **Waikiki Trolley** (☎ **808/596-2199** or 800/824-8804), which looks like a San Francisco cable car. It loops around Waikiki and downtown Honolulu, stopping every 40 minutes at 12 key places. A 1-day pass at $17 for adults, $5 for children under 12, allows you to jump on and off all day long. Five-day passes cost $30 for adults, $10 for children under 12. Major stops are at Hilton Hawaiian Village, Iolani Palace, Wo Fat's in Chinatown, the State Capitol, King Kamehameha's Statue, the Mission House Museum, Aloha Tower, Honolulu Academy of Arts, Hawaii Maritime Museum, Ward Centre, Fisherman's Wharf, and Restaurant Row.

BY TAXI

Oahu's major cab companies offer islandwide, 24-hour radio-dispatched service, with multilingual drivers, air-conditioned cars, limos, vans, and vehicles equipped with wheelchair lifts. Fares are standard for all taxi firms; from the airport, expect to pay about $23 (plus tip) to Waikiki, about $16.50 to downtown, about $35 to Kailua, about $35 to Hawaii Kai, and about $75 to the North Shore. Try **Aloha State Cab** (☎ 808/847-3566); **Charley's Taxi & Tours** (☎ 808/531-1333); **City Taxi** (☎ 808/524-2121); **Royal Taxi & Tour** (☎ 808/944-5513); **Sida Taxi & Tours** (☎ 808/836-0011); **Star Taxi** (☎ 808/942-7827); or **TheCab** (☎ 808/422-2222). **Coast Taxi** (☎ 808/261-3755) serves Windward Oahu; **Hawaii Kai Hui/Koko Head Taxi** (☎ 808/396-6633) serves East Honolulu/Southeast Oahu.

FAST FACTS: Oahu

American Express   The Honolulu office is at 1440 Kapiolani Blvd., Suite 104 (☎ 808/946-7741).

Dentists   If you need dental attention while you're on Oahu, contact the Hawaii Dental Association (☎ 808/536-2135).

Doctors   Doctors on Call has offices at the Hyatt Regency Waikiki, Diamond Head Tower, 4th floor (☎ 808/971-8001); Hawaiian Regent Hotel, 2nd floor (☎ 808/923-3666); Hilton Hawaiian Village, Rainbow Bazaar (☎ 808/923-5252); Outrigger Waikiki (☎ 808/971-6000); and the Royal Hawaiian Medical Center, Royal Hawaiian Hotel (☎ 808/923-4499).

Emergencies   Call 911 for police, fire, and ambulance.

Hospitals   Hospitals offering 24-hour emergency care include Queens Medical Center, 1301 Punchbowl St. (☎ 808/538-9011); Kaiser Permanente Medical Center, Honolulu Clinic, 1010 Pensacola St. (☎ 808/593-2950); Kuakini Medical Center, 347 Kuakini St. (☎ 808/536-2236); Straub Clinic and Hospital,

888 S. King St. (☎ 808/522-4000); Moanalua Medical Center, 3288 Moanalua Rd. (☎ 808/834-5333); Kapiolani Medical Center for Women and Children, 1319 Punahou St. (☎ 808/973-8511); and Kapiolani Medical Center at Pali Momi, 98-1079 Moanalua Rd. (☎ 808/486-6000). In Central Oahu is Wahiawa General Hospital, 128 Lehua St. (☎ 808/621-8411). On the windward side is Castle Medical Center, 640 Ulukahiki St., Kailua (☎ 808/263-5500).

Newspapers The *Honolulu Advertiser* and *Honolulu Star-Bulletin* are Oahu's daily papers. *Midweek, Pacific Business News,* and *Honolulu Weekly* are weekly papers. *Honolulu Weekly,* available free at restaurants, clubs, shops, bookstores, and newspaper racks around Oahu, is the best source for what's going on around town. It features discriminating restaurant reviews and an informed critique of the nightclub scene, plus a weekly Calendar of Events that lists concerts, theater and dance performances, gallery and museum shows, workshops, children's events, hikes and walks, and often neighbor island events, too.

Poison Control Center At 1319 Punahou St. (☎ 808/941-4411).

Post Office To find the location nearest you, call 808/423-3990. In downtown Honolulu, there's a branch office at 335 Merchant St.; in Waikiki, at Ala Moana Shopping Center and 330 Saratoga Ave.

Weather Reports For National Weather Service recorded forecasts for Honolulu, call 808/973-4380; for elsewhere on the island, call 808/973-4381. For marine reports, call 808/973-4382. For surf reports, call 808/973-4383; for coastal wind reports, call 808/973-6114.

3 Accommodations

by Rick Carroll

Oahu has 32,000 "visitor units," ranging from North Shore surfer digs to palatial world-class hotels. Most of them are in densely built Waikiki Beach. You can spend as much as $5,000 a night for a presidential suite, but overall, the price of admission is still a bargain, since Waikiki hotel rooms start at $85 a night. Please note that taxes of 10.17% are added to every hotel bill.

Bed-and-Breakfasts An affordable alternative to hotels and resorts are Oahu's 200 bed-and-breakfasts. In fact, Windward Oahu is the bed and breakfast capital of Hawaii, with scores of beachfront rooms, apartments, and cottages. Prices start at $55 per night for a room and go up to $1,000 for a Lanikai beachfront estate.

The City and County of Honolulu are offically on record opposing vacation rentals in residential neighborhoods, and the local Department of Land Utilization is trying to eliminate them altogether by raising fees, creating new requirements, and refusing to permit new operators to enter the hospitality business. Most of the original units have been "grandfathered" under variances and granted licenses, however, and the total numbers actually are increasing, especially on the North Shore and windward side. Many of the operators require payments to be made in cash to avoid hassles with city hall.

See "Tips on Finding Accommodations" in Chapter 3 for agencies through which you can find and reserve B&B accommodations on Oahu.

Vacation Rentals The 20-story luxury ✪ **Colony Surf** condominium-hotel, 2895 Kalakaua Ave., Honolulu, HI 96815 (☎ and fax **808/593-1800**) recently went bankrupt, but it may reopen in 1997. In the meantime, the savvy who prefer this swanky address at the foot of Diamond Head can rent one of 50 privately owned, remodeled condos for a 2-week-minimum stay through rental agent Lynn Aila (telephone and fax numbers above). Most of these have a sunset ocean view, and all have kitchens. You'll have to pay by cash or check, but at $100 a day, they're a real deal on this "gold coast" of $1 million pads.

WAIKIKI
ON THE BEACH

✪ **Halekulani.** 2199 Kalia Rd., Honolulu, HI 96815. ☎ **808/923-2311** or 800/367-2343. Fax 808/926-8004. 456 rms, 44 suites. A/C TV MINIBAR TEL. $275–$440 double, from $595 suite. Packages available. AE, DC, JCB, MC, V. Valet parking $10.

This hotel first rose in 1907 as bungalows by the sea but is today a world-class resort that lives up to its Hawaiian name: "House Befitting Heaven." In fact, this graceful example of old-style Hawaii architecture deserves its reputation as Waikiki's top hotel. It has only a thin sliver of beach, but it has a wonderful pool—with a signature orchid mosaic—set in a lawn full of sun lounges. Interior courtyards lend a green calm that's always a welcome retreat from the busy street scene outside.

In tiered towers, the 456 handsome rooms are the biggest and best appointed in Waikiki. Each has a memorable view of Diamond Head and the sea.

Dining/Entertainment: The dining facilities here are in a class by themselves. La Mer is the finest seaside dining room in Hawaii; the oceanside, indoor-outdoor Orchids Dining Room specializes in Pacific cuisine (see "Dining," below, for reviews of both restaurants). The House Without a Key—an outdoor patio set with tables and chairs for enjoying live, old-fashioned Hawaiian music and hula from late afternoon on—is a popular first-night venue for visitors to the islands.

Services: Guests are greeted with a lei and personally escorted to to their rooms, where registration is conducted in private. There's twice-daily maid service including nightly turndown, complimentary daily newspapers, in-room safes, free local phone calls, secretarial services, valet service, multilingual concierge, in-house laundry and dry cleaning, free safe-deposit boxes, 24-hour room service, and night butler service.

Facilities: Beach, pool, 7 upscale shops, hair salon, conference facilities, fitness room with Ergo bike, treadmills, and trainer.

Hilton Hawaiian Village. 2005 Kalia Rd., Honolulu, HI 96815. ☎ **808/949-4321** or 800/ HILTONS. Fax 808/947-7898. 2,542 rms, 365 suites. A/C MINIBAR TV TEL. $165–$335 double, from $305 suite. Packages available. AE, DC, DISC, JCB, MC, V. Self-parking $9, valet parking $12.

Hawaii's largest resort is a fanciful modern re-creation of a Hawaiian village. The 20 acres includes hundreds of coconut trees; South African penguins, scarlet macaws, and plumed cockatiels; at 10,000 square feet, Waikiki's largest swimming pool; a dinner theater starring Charo; and Waikiki Beach right in the front yard. There's an extensive shopping village of some 100 stores, not to mention 22 restaurants and lounges, including one right on the sand. Perhaps its most memorable feature is a man-made lagoon near the beach. Also on the premises is a large and well-used complex of convention facilities—but it only seems like you need a "Hello" badge to stay here, for gardens, trees, pools, and lagoons with exotic wildlife ranging from parrots to penguins help soften the effects of mass tourism. With curving bricked walkways and lots of separate buildings, it's easy to get lost here (the resort is so big it even has its own post office).

Even the rooms are dazzling—extravagant by Waikiki standards, big and beautifully furnished with wicker and rattan, framed art, fresh flowers, and enough marble

Waikiki Accommodations

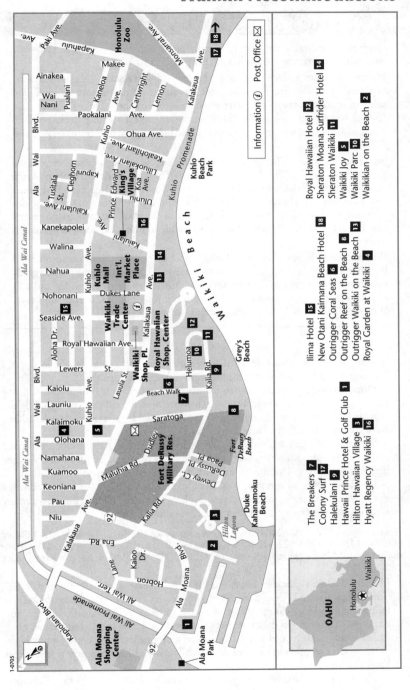

Information ⓘ   Post Office ✉

The Breakers **7**
Colony Surf **17**
Halekulani **9**
Hawaii Prince Hotel & Golf Club **1**
Hilton Hawaiian Village **3**
Hyatt Regency Waikiki **16**

Ilima Hotel **15**
New Otani Kaimana Beach Hotel **18**
Outrigger Coral Seas **6**
Outrigger Reef on the Beach **8**
Outrigger Waikiki on the Beach **13**
Royal Garden at Waikiki **4**

Royal Hawaiian Hotel **12**
Sheraton Moana Surfrider Hotel **14**
Sheraton Waikiki **11**
Waikiki Joy **5**
Waikiki Parc **10**
Waikikian on the Beach **2**

OAHU

Honolulu

Waikiki

👪 Family-Friendly Resorts

Oahu is, in general, a very family-friendly place; but the resorts listed below are particularly welcoming to families traveling with kids.

Hilton Hawaiian Village (Waikiki)   Hawaii's biggest resort hotel boasts 20 acres of gardens, pools, waterfalls, a man-made lagoon, rare birds and exotic wildlife, and submarine rides from a great beach named for legendary surfer Duke Kahanamoku. If that's not enough to keep the kids occupied, the resort's Young Explorers Club offers nature walks, lagoon fishing, and guided field trips to the Honolulu Zoo and Waikiki Aquarium.

Sheraton Waikiki   The Keiki Aloha Sunshine Club is free to guests between the ages of 5 and 12. The club meets daily from 9am to 5pm, and 6:30 to 9pm. *Keikis* enjoy arts and crafts like hula and lei making; go kite-flying in Kapiolani Park; learn to surf, snorkel, and boogie board at Waikiki; and take field trips to the Honolulu Zoo and Waikiki Aquarium. Pint-sized guests at Waikiki's other Sheraton resorts (the Royal Hawaiian, Sheraton Moana Surfrider, and Princess Kapiolani) are also welcome.

Ihilani Resort & Spa (Leeward Oahu)   If Oahu is a giant sandbox surrounded by water, then the Ihilani is the perfect sand castle. It sits on five man-made gold-sand lagoons that are safe even for small kids. Inside, there's a vast video and CD library, a kids' computer room, and a playroom full of books, puzzles, and toys. Why didn't anybody build a hotel like this when we were kids?

to make you worry about depleted Italian quarries. VIP guests delight in the Alii Tower, an upscale hotel-within-a-hotel with ultraluxurious suites.

Dining/Entertainment: Leading the many restaurants here is the award-winning Bali by the Sea (see "Dining," below). There are five cocktail lounges including the beachfront Tropics Bar. Entertainment is highlighted by a salute to Hawaii's King Kalakaua of yore with fireworks every Friday night.

Services: Valet parking, multilingual concierge, American Express office, car rental desks, free safe-deposit boxes, year-round children's program, laundry and dry cleaning, Rainbow Tower Executive Club with personal butler service.

Facilities: Three swimming pools, including two-tiered 10,000-square-foot Super Pool, Waikiki's largest; fitness center; 36-hole mini golf course; business center; shopping arcade; beauty and barber shops; wedding chapel.

Hyatt Regency Waikiki. 2424 Kalakaua Ave., Honolulu, HI 96815, ☎ **808/923-1234** or 800/233-1234. Fax 808/922-9404. 1,230 rms, 26 suites. A/C TV MINIBAR TEL. $190–$380 double, from $475 suite. Packages available. AE, DC, DISC, JCB, MC, V. Self-parking $8, valet parking $10.

Literally Waikiki's splashiest hotel, this Hyatt has a three-story indoor waterfall providing tropical sound effects between two 40-story octagon towers. The ground-floor lobby is a city-block–long atrium of shops, gardens, sidewalk cafe, lounge, and attractive walkways. Up the escalators you'll find the actual lobby, restaurants, pool, and sundeck—and marvel at the huge metal sculpture dangling between two high-rise towers. The portion of Waikiki Beach known as Kuhio Beach is just across Kalakaua Avenue.

The rooms are some of the largest and freshest in Waikiki thanks to the completion of the first phase of a $10 million renovation, which included Waikiki's first politically correct low-flush toilets, new carpets and textiles in elegant blues and golds, 22 new wheelchair-accessible rooms, and a new fitness center. The view from the upper-floor rooms is awesome.

The renovation also brought the resort the wholly incongruous Texas Rock 'N Roll Sushi Bar, featuring Ninja bartenders and country-and-western music with karaoke sing-a-long. The menu features such epicurean delights as the Saddlesore Beef Fajita Roll and Chubby Checker Pie. Thankfully, other less trendy dining establishments abound, such as Musashi, serving Japanese; Ciao Mein, with a combination Chinese/Italian menu; and a traditional steak house. There's also a Japanese-style dance club featuring 1950s rock-and-roll. Free performances of hula and old-time Hawaiian music are presented daily.

✪ **New Otani Kaimana Beach Hotel.** 2863 Kalakaua Ave., Honolulu, HI 96815, ☎ **808/923-1555** or 800/356-8264. Fax 808/922-9404. 125 rms, 30 suites. A/C TV MINIBAR TEL. $99–$225 double, $170–$590 suite. AE, DC, DISC, JCB, MC, V. Valet parking $6.

Location, size, and service combine in this small beachfront hotel that long ago was discovered by artists, musicians, writers, and other travelers who like to be near but not in Waikiki's 24-hour beach party. Kaimana is the Hawaiian word for "diamond," and this 125-room gem is a sophisticated tropical hideaway on Sans Souci Beach, at the foot of Diamond Head across Kapiolani Park from Waikiki. Sans Souci Beach is quiet and less crowded than Waikiki because it's used primarily by local residents. You can snorkel here over an offshore barrier reef which creates a quiet lagoon for swimming. The Hau Tree Lanai is one of Honolulu's favorite beachside restaurants and scene of countless romantic liaisons, while the other dining option here is Miyako, a traditional Japanese tatami-mat restaurant with kimono-clad hostesses (see "Dining," below, for reviews of both outlets). The regular rooms are small, but the corner suites have notable views, of the park, Diamond Head, Waikiki and the sea. Book a junior suite facing the sea and you'll have the best oceanfront digs in Waikiki for the money. Everything in this small inn of contentment is a delight—including the price.

Outrigger Reef on the Beach. 2169 Kalia Rd., Honolulu, HI 96815. ☎ **808/923-3111** or 800/688-7444. Fax 808/924-4957. 885 rms, 47 suites. A/C TV TEL. $95–$115 double, from $140 suite. Packages available. AE, CB, DC, DISC, ER, JCB, MC, V. Parking $7.

Next door to Halekulani, the deluxe Reef fronts a nice sweep of beach. Recently renovated throughout its three high-rise towers, the hotel was modified to include more units with handicap access and connecting rooms with small refrigerators and coffeemakers for families. A fitness center was added. The Shorebird, a beachfront open-air restaurant where patrons can barbecue their own steak, chicken, or fish on huge grills, was also spiffed-up and now serves three meals a day.

Outrigger Waikiki on the Beach. 2335 Kalakaua Ave., Honolulu, HI 96815. ☎ **808/923-0711** or 800/688-7444. Fax 808/921-9749. 530 rms, 32 suites. A/C TV TEL. $160–$305 double, $445–$690 suite. Packages available. AE, DC, DISC, ER, JCB, MC, V. Parking $7.

On the beach between the Royal Hawaiian and the Sheraton Moana Surfrider, this high-rise Outrigger provides the same access to sun, surf, and sand as its luxury neighbors, but at far lower rates. Of course, there's no glamorous history, but the rooms are perfectly comfortable, and there's a lanai, pool, health club, shops, and a choice of restaurants and bars. These include Duke's, an informal gathering spot for meals, drinks, and live Hawaiian music; it features memorabilia celebrating the late Duke Kahanamoku, Hawaii's most famous surfer. The hotel is midstream in the shopping district—next door to the Royal Hawaiian Shopping Center and across Kalakaua Avenue from the International Marketplace.

⭐ **Royal Hawaiian Hotel.** 2259 Kalakaua Ave., Honolulu, HI 96815. ☎ **808/923-7311** or 800/325-3535. Fax 808/924-7098. 527 rms, 58 suites. A/C TV MINIBAR TEL. $275–$475, from $425 suite. Package rates available. AE, DC, JCB, MC, V. Self-parking $9, valet parking $13.

In the days of steamship travel, perhaps the only Waikiki hotel that could eclipse the Moana was this exotic neighbor built in 1927, a Valentino movie-set come to life in radiant flamingo pink (if you ever get lost in Waikiki, just look for the Pink Palace at midbeach). The turrets and curlicues of this romantic Moorish fantasy have been lovingly maintained ever since, and today it's Sheraton's most luxurious property on Oahu. The old glamour is expressed in octagonal suite drawing rooms, custom-made floral wool carpets, koa wood doors carved with the Hawaiian royal seal, and other flourishes, yet the hotel also offers modern touches like modular phone jacks for laptop computers. The Royal's more modern oceanfront tower rises beside the historic hotel, surrounded by cool leafy gardens of royal palms and dwarfed by high-rise neighbors.

   Dining/Entertainment: The open-air Surf Room serves breakfast, lunch, and dinner on an oceanside terrace. The Mai Tai Bar is an open-air beachside cocktail lounge with Hawaiian music nightly (they claim this is the "home" of the Mai Tai cocktail, but that's an overstatement: the drink they serve here bears scant relation to the original). There's a luau every Monday on the ocean lawn.

   Services: Flower lei greeting, freshly baked banana bread on arrival, nightly turndown service available, in-room dining available 24 hours, multilingual concierge, complimentary morning newspaper, laundry and dry cleaning, valet parking, 24-hour bell service.

   Facilities: Freshwater pool, barber shop, beauty salon, hospitality suite for early arrivals and late departures, 20 gift and specialty shops in lobby and garden arcade, banquet and conference facilities.

⭐ **Sheraton Moana Surfrider Hotel.** 2365 Kalakaua Ave., Honolulu, HI 96815. ☎ **808/922-3111** or 800/325-3535. Fax 808/923-0308. 790 rms, 45 suites. A/C TV MINIBAR TEL. $210–$350 double; from $650 suite. Packages available. AE, CB, DC, ER, JCB, MC, V. Self-parking $9, valet parking $15.

The "First Lady of Waikiki" is a registered national landmark proud of her history as the hotel that really launched tourism in Hawaii nearly 100 years ago. The white-washed beaux-arts Moana sports a striking Victorian edifice, but you must specify the Historic Banyan Wing if you want to stay among the historic ambiance, since the hotel also includes the adjoining concrete high-rise tower formerly known as the Surfrider. Restored in an extensive 1989 renovation that won a presidential award for excellence, rooms in the Moana's historic wing aren't large by today's standards, but they are furnished with 19th-century period pieces like antique koa wood armoires and four-poster beds with early Hawaiiana etchings of flowers, giving them an inimitable Victorian charm that persists despite modern intrusions like a black-box bedside electronic console. Rooms in the 1950s-era, recently renovated Surfrider tower have balconies and share lobbies and public areas with the Moana, including the famous seaside Banyan Court, dominated by a huge tree.

   For those who "collect" historic hotel experiences, the Moana is more than a room with a view of the past. It's an attraction all its own. Even if you don't stay here, come look at the history exhibits or have a sunset cocktail while enjoying live old-style Hawaiian music on the veranda.

   Dining/Entertainment: The Ship's Tavern offers continental fare with tableside preparation of old favorites like Moana classic clam chowder, hot spinach salad, and cherries Jubilee; the Beachside Cafe serves breakfast, lunch, and dinner indoors and on a lanai; the Banyan Veranda offers Sunday brunch with Hawaiian entertainment;

and W. C. Peacock & Co. Ltd. offers seafood and *kiawe*-grilled steaks. A Hawaiian singer and musicians appear throughout the day and evening in The Banyan Court.

Services: Flower lei greeting, 24-hour room service, daily newspaper, multilingual concierge, daily maid service, nightly turndown, dry cleaning, laundry service, baby-sitting; in-room movies, free summer children's program, video checkout.

Facilities: Beach, pool, tour desk, rental car desk, beauty salon, shopping arcade, banquet and conference facilities. Guests can use fitness center at Sheraton Waikiki and business center at the Royal Hawaiian Hotel.

Sheraton Waikiki. 2255 Kalakaua Ave., Honolulu, HI 96815. ☎ **808/922-4422** or 800/ 325-3535. Fax 808/923-8785. 1,852 rms, 130 suites. A/C TV MINIBAR TEL. $195–$365 double; from $500 suite. Packages available. AE, CB, DC, ER, JCB, MC, V. Parking $9.

Built in the curvilinear shape of a wave to maximize ocean views, the 31-story Sheraton Waikiki has the state's largest ballroom and caters to the meetings trade as well as individuals. It's a happening kind of place—always busy along the open-air lobby which extends from street to beach and on the mezzanine, where groups meet. Two types of rooms, *mauka* (facing the mountains) and *makai* (facing the ocean), are available. Spring for a makai room; they offer panoramic views from Diamond Head to Honolulu Harbor.

High atop the 30-story tower is the 1950s-style swellegant Hanohano Room, which has the best sunset view of Diamond Head, hands down; but the food leaves a bit to be desired. Take the glass elevator up for a sundown MaiTai, then head out to Alan Wong's for dinner. Nightclubs (including the Hanohano Room), a fitness center, lots of shops, and children's programs and activities are available to guests, including free performances of hula and Hawaiian music, free weekly history walks through the neighborhood, and Hawaiian crafts.

☉ Waikiki Parc. 2233 Helumoa Rd., Honolulu, HI 96815. ☎ **808/921-7272** or 800/ 422-0450. Fax 808/923-1336. 298 rms. A/C MINIBAR TV TEL. $170–$255 double. Extra person $30. Children 14 and under free in parents' room. Inquire about room packages. AE, CB, DC, JCB, MC, V. Valet parking $9.

Just when you thought there wasn't space in Waikiki for one more room—let alone an entire hotel—the Waikiki Parc has gone and done it. They've conjured up some space and opened a 22-story luxury hotel 100 yards from the beach at Waikiki and directly across from the Halekulani. In fact, this hotel has been dubbed the "Halekulani, Jr.," since it is managed by the same corporation and is similar to its parent hotel in its elegant simplicity, personalized service, and sophisticated style.

But the difference here is in the prices: This hotel was designed to combine luxury with affordability, and prices are considerably lower than those at the Halekulani. Rooms are all the same, beautifully done in blue and white, with ceramic tile floors and inlaid carpeting, conversation areas, armoires, custom rattan furniture, adjust-able white shutter doors on the lanai or view balcony, business desks in most rooms, and either a king-size or two twin beds. There are two phones in each room, an AM/FM radio, an in-room safe, data ports, a fax modem, and guest voicemail. Eight rooms are equipped for wheelchairs.

Dining/Entertainment: Waikiki Parc has two excellent restaurants: Parc Cafe, with its garden-terrace atmosphere, serves fabulous buffet-style meals, featuring island specialties (see complete review in "Dining," below); and Kacho, one of Hawaii's few Kyoto-style restaurants, a charming oasis for true devotees of sushi and Japanese seafood dishes.

Services: Concierge desk, daily maid service, secretarial and other business services, wheelchair accessibility to public areas, room service.

Facilities: Freshwater pool on the eighth-floor recreation deck, a great stretch of Waikiki beach nearby.

Waikikian on the Beach. 1811 Ala Moana Blvd., Honolulu, HI 96815. ☎ **808/949-5331** or 800/92-ASTON. 132 rms and suites. A/C TV TEL. $63–$97 double, $115–$135 suite, $160– $180 penthouse. AE CB, DC, JCB, MC V. Parking $5.

The days are numbered for this Waikiki landmark, known as "Hawaii's most beautiful hotel" when it opened in the late 1950s. James Michener wrote *Hawaii* here, and Prince Charles booked a suite in his Honolulu polo-playing days. This 132-room low-rise hotel on a lagoon still attracts a loyal following, but it has already been threatened with demolition once by Japanese landlords, and the end appears in sight. Bulldozers already have scrapped the lobby, a soaring arched-roof hut built to resemble a Polynesian spirit house, and the original Garden Wing with its funky rooms may be next. Meanwhile, lift a Mai Tai at the nostalgic Papeete Bar, or enjoy a poolside lunch in an authentic Tahitian Lanai thatched hut, but don't count on this great old place being here much longer.

NEAR THE BEACH

❸ **The Breakers.** 250 Beach Walk, Honolulu, HI 96815. ☎ **808/923-3181** or 800/426-0494. Fax 808/923-7174. 64 rooms, 15 suites. $91–$97 double, $120–$146 suite. AE, DC, MC V. Free parking.

A little gem in the midst of high-rise Waikiki, The Breakers is full of old-fashioned Hawaiian aloha, and it's only a few steps to the beach at Waikiki. This two-story hotel has a friendly staff and a loyal following, with more than 70% returning for another stay. It's set in six buildings around a tropical garden and pool, and it captures the tropical ambiance with wooden jalousies and shoji doors. Slightly oversize rooms have a lanai and kitchen. The Breaker's Bar & Grille is poolside with cocktails and heavy pupus.

Hawaii Prince Hotel & Golf Club. 100 Holomoana St., Honolulu, HI 96815. ☎ **808/ 956-1111** or 800/321-6248. Fax 808/946-0811. 521 rms, 57 suites. A/C TV MINIBAR TEL. $220–$350 double, from $450 suite. Packages available. AE, DC, DISC, JCB, MC, V. Self-parking $8, valet parking $12.

Waikiki's newest hotel, this establishment with lots of marble throughout is a world-class city hotel that happens to be near the beach (it overlooks Ala Moana Beach Park and Magic Island). It may not have its own beach, but every room has an ocean view. It doesn't sell drinks with a Japanese parasols speared to pineapple wedges, nor does it even have a coffee shop, but it does serve English tea in the lobby every afternoon with fresh-baked scones and Devonshire cream (with or without currants).

Hawaii's fastest elevators shoot up twin towers of flamed limestone sheathed in rose-tinted floor-to-ceiling windows and separated by a 60-foot-wide Italian marble lobby that frames a mast-high view of sloops at Ala Wai Yacht Harbor. Although the rooms don't have lanais, their windows open wide to embrace the trade winds.

The Prince is the only Waikiki hotel with its own golf club, a 27-hole championship course designed by Arnold Palmer but located in west Oahu where there is room for links. The hotel shuttle gets golfers to and from the tees.

Dining/Entertainment: Four restaurants include Prince Court, a bastion of excellent Hawaii Regional Cuisine (see "Dining," below). Hakone and Takanawa offers Japanese cuisine. The Promenade Deck has poolside dining and cocktails. In the lobby, the Marine Front lounge offers continental breakfast and afternoon coffee and tea.

Services: Hot towels on check-in; complimentary fruit juice; room service until midnight; VCRs; turndown service; full service salon; multilingual concierge; free shuttle to Waikiki attractions, Ala Moana Shopping Center, and nearby beaches.

Facilities: Pool, whirlpool, business center, fitness room, free shuttle to and from golf course and two tennis courts, banquet facilities.

Ilima Hotel. 445 Nohonani St., Honolulu, HI 96815. ☎ **808/923-1877.** Fax 808/524-8371. 74 studios, 24 suites. $77–$99 double, $105–$159 suite. AE, CB, DC, DISC, JCB, MC, V. Free parking.

One of Hawaii's small, well-located condominium hotels, the 17-story light pink Ilima Hotel (named for Hawaii's orange ilima flower used for royal leis) is two blocks to Waikiki Beach, near the International Marketplace and the Royal Hawaiian Shopping Center. There's no ocean view here, just a lot of value for the money. A tasteful koa-wood lobby greets guests with paintings by Hawaiian artists. There's a 24-hour front desk, daily maid service, free local phone calls, and a full kitchen in every unit. Built in 1968, the Ilima recently underwent renovation. Sergio's Italian restaurant is on the first floor.

☉ Outrigger Coral Seas. 250 Lewers Rd., Honolulu, HI 96815. ☎ **808/923-3881** or 800/ 688-7444. 885 rms, 47 suites. A/C TV TEL. $60–$75 double, $125 suite. Packages available. AE, CB, DC, DISC, ER, JCB, MC, V. Parking $7.

At the heart of Waikiki on a busy little street of shops that dead-ends at the Halekulani, this small, clean hotel is one of the great bargains here, especially in summer when a room goes for $60 a night. The rooms don't have ocean views and aren't grand, but the location, near the Halekulani, can't be beat at this price. This is the top choice in Waikiki for budget travelers. If you get a room overlooking Lewers Street, you can sit on your semiprivate lanai and watch the incredible parade of humanity go by. Okay, Lewers Street is noisy, but it's also the best free show in town.

☉ Royal Garden at Waikiki. 440 Olohana St., Honolulu, HI 96815. ☎ **808/943-0202** or 800/367-5666. Fax 808/946-8777. 230 rms, 19 suites. A/C TV TEL. $120–$500 double, $295–$500 suite. Rates include continental breakfast and free shopper shuttle. AE, DC, DISC, JCB, MC, V. Valet parking $7.

Tucked off on a quiet side street in Waikiki, all this little gem lacks is the beach, and that's a bit of a hike. The lobby is filled with European marble and chandeliers. The rooms have VCRs, minikitchens with small refrigerator and wet bar, robes and slippers, and marble baths. A Euro-Asian restaurant with a sunny yellow decor is called Cascada, perhaps for the waterfall in the swimming pool just outside (see "Dining," below). There's a great Japanese sushi bar, Shizu, on the fourth floor. Laundry machines are located on each floor.

Waikiki Joy. 320 Lewers St., Honolulu, HI 96815. ☎ **808/923-2300,** or 800/733-5569. Fax 808/924-4010. 52 rms, 42 suites. A/C TV TEL. $140–$150 double, $165–$175 club suite, $225–$240 executive suite. Extra person $15. Rates include continental breakfast and are often lower at certain periods of the year; call to inquire about property specials. AE, DC, MC, V. Valet parking $10.

This is one hotel that truly deserves its name. It's a hidden jewel, an oasis right in the heart of busy Waikiki, offering not only outstanding personal service but also a Bose entertainment system and Jacuzzi in every room. The Italian marble-accented open-air lobby and the tropical veranda, with swimming pool, sauna, and furnished deck, set the scene for the beautifully decorated guests rooms.

Rooms are located either in the hotel tower or in the all-suite tower. The hotel rooms, decorated in soft pastels, have a marble entry, a refrigerator, a safe, and a lanai wide enough for you to sit and enjoy the views. The suites are even more luxurious: Club suites have either a king-size bed or two double beds, a refrigerator, microwave, coffee maker, and wet bar. Executive suites have two double beds and a kitchen with a microwave and full refrigerator. The more expensive executive king suites add a separate living room and bedroom. Every room comes with voice mail, as well as fax and modem hookups.

Cappucino's, the hotel's Mediterranian-style cafe, features specialty coffees, petite sandwiches, and desserts. Guests can also enjoy a free hour of private karaoke fun (for up to nine people) in the hotel's state-of-the-art GS Studio. And there's a free continental breakfast at the Tropical Veranda every morning.

HONOLULU BEYOND WAIKIKI
DOWNTOWN

Executive Centre Hotel. 1088 Bishop St., Honolulu, HI 96813. ☎ **808/539-3000** or 800/ 949-EXEC. Fax 808/523-1088. 116 suites. A/C TV TEL. $105–$150 suite. Rates include continental breakfast. Monthly rates available. AE, DC, DISC, JCB, MC, V. Parking $10.

This glossy 40-story high-rise is the only downtown hotel, smack dab in the middle of Bishop Street. You can walk to meetings, explore the Capitol District or nearby Chinatown and Aloha Tower Marketplace. It's a long hike (or a 10 minute drive) to the nearest beach. It has a mix of residential and hotel units, all on the top 10 floors so they enjoy panoramic views of Punchbowl, Honolulu Harbor, and the Ewa Plain. There's Centre Court restaurant in the lobby, and every unit has a kitchen. Also on premises are a pool and hot tub, coin-operated laundrys, a 24-hour fitness center, full-service business center, and conference facilities.

MANOA VALLEY

Manoa Valley Inn. 2001 Vancouver Dr., Honolulu, HI 96822. ☎ **808/947-6019** or 800/ 535-0085. Fax 808/946-6168. 8 rms, 1 suite, 1 cottage. A/C. $99–$190 double. Rates include continental breakfast and evening wine and cheese. AE, DC, JCB, MC, V. Free parking.

It's off the tourist trail completely and far from the beach and Waikiki, but that doesn't stop travelers from heading to this historic 1915 eclectic Carpenter Gothic home on a quiet residential street near the University of Hawaii campus. Saved from demolition by Rick Ralston, the Red Adair of historic renovation in Hawaii, this seven-room Manoa landmark is on the National Register of Historic Places. It offers guests a taste of lifestyles of the rich in early Honolulu. Built by Iowa timber baron Milton Moore, who shipped the lumber from the Northwest, the house served as Benjamin Dillingham's home, then became the residence of John Guild, who embezzled a small fortune from Alexander & Baldwin and died in prison.

Waikiki's 2 miles away, but those who prefer to avoid resorts find it refreshing. Rooms have old-fashioned decor, and a genteel manner pervades the place. Guests regularly gather in the parlor to listen to the Victrola or play the nickelodeon.

EAST OF HONOLULU & WAIKIKI: KAHALA

Kahala Mandarin Oriental Hotel. (formerly the Kahala Hilton) 5000 Kahala Ave., Honolulu, HI 96816-5498. ☎ **808/734-2211** or 800/367-2525. Fax 808/737-2478. 370 rms, 29 suites. A/C TV MINIBAR TEL. $260–$560 double, from $600 suite. AE, CB, DC, DISC, JCB, MC, V. Parking $12.

The only hotel in a suburban residential district, about 5 miles from Waikiki, now looks like a four-star bed-and-breakfast. Ex–Hong-Kong hotelier Seamus McManus hopes to "recapture the glamour that was here" and attract a new generation of young, well-heeled guests to what was the Kahala Hilton. At $260 a night for a basic room, he's got his work cut out for him.

If they'd scraped this old dog and started over it could have been the grand hotel for the new millennium; but the new Hong Kong owners, who gave the old Hilton a $72 million face-lift (which included important safety stuff like up-to-code wiring), didn't go far enough to hide its tired old sun-bleached neo-Brutalist bones. Decorators even kept the lobby's beach-glass chandeliers, which look like Janis Joplin's estate jewelry.

The Los Angeles architects did clean up the crowded reception desk area, pitch the roof with green slate, paint the exterior a sea-foam green, move the Plumeria restaurant closer to the ocean, and shut down windowless Maile Room, the former black hole of Honolulu restaurants. New rooms are as ritzy as a Ritz-Carlton, with wooden four-poster beds, grass cloth walls, and nostalgic prints of old Honolulu. But the Humboldt penguins are gone (one grew old and surly, I was told), the captive dolphins are back (isn't it time to let them go?), and the Murphy beds are gone from the suites. Gone too is Danny ("Ambassador of Aloha") Kaleikini, who sang for his supper longer than Don Ho, and the Kit Samson Orchestra, Honolulu's last band with a steady gig.

Views from the rooms are still wonderful, whether to mountains or sea; but if they'd done it right, it would have been something to write home about. Instead, it's just another rich old lady with a face-lift.

Dining/Entertainment: Hoku's is the new star of the Honolulu restaurant scene; see "Dining," below, for details. Plumeria Beach Cafe, serves breakfast, lunch, and dinner in a casual open-air setting. Poolside Snack Bar serves to-die-for sandwiches at lunch only. There's live Hawaiian music and a jazz piano bar just off the lobby at Hoku's.

Services: Welcome tropical-fruit drink greeting, 24-room service, valet and self parking, nightly turndown, free electronic eye-level safe, full minibar, 27-inch TV with Nintendo, two telephone lines, fax/modem computer link, umbrellas in room, free laundry soap, free scuba lessons in pool.

Facilities: Beach; swimming pool; gardens with man-made waterfall, lagoons, and islet; separate men's and women's fitness centers with steam rooms, dry saunas, outdoor Jacuzzis, Stairmasters, treadmills, weight rooms; Kahala Keiki Club for children; business center; shopping arcade; banquet and meeting facilities.

THE WINDWARD COAST

Pat O'Malley of **Pat's Kailua Beach Properties** (☎ 808/261-1653 or 808/262-4128; fax 808/262-8275 or 808/261-0893) offers more than 25 houses and cottages near Kailua Beach, from a million-dollar estate right on the water to cottages on or close to the beach that served as staff quarters for the area estates. Studio or one-bedroom cottages go for about $60 to $100; two-bedroom cottages go for about $80 to $100; superb beach homes go for about $325 a night. Each unit is different, but all are fully furnished and include cooking and dining utensils, bedding and towels, telephone and TV. Call Pat for information and reservations; be sure to ask about deposit requirements.

✪ **John Walker's Beach House.** 826 Mokulua Dr., Lanikai Beach, HI 96734. ☎ **808/261-7895** or 800/258-7895. Fax 808/262-2181. 1 cottage (sleeps up to six). $295. AE, VISA, MC. Three-night, four-person minimum. Free parking.

On Oahu's most scenic gold-sand beach, this gracious and nostalgic 1924 beach house was built by an adventurous Scotsman who served as royal contractor to Queen Liluokalani. He also helped build the Bishop Museum and Honolulu Hale (City Hall). His story is told through pictures in the entry hall of this old three-bedroom house that's full of nice touches—hardwood floors, pandanus mats, high ceilings, ceiling fans, and a great room with a dazzling view of Lanikai Beach and two islets in the turquoise lagoon. This is a fully equipped, restored beach hideaway with modern amenities. The inviting sun-washed lanai is exactly three giant steps to the beach.

THE NORTH SHORE

Ke Iki Hale. 59-579 Ke Iki Rd., Haleiwa, HI 96712. ☎ **808/638-8229** or 800/377-4030. 6 units, 1 cottage. $85–$131 one-bedroom unit (sleeps two or three), $156–$173 two-bedroom unit (sleeps up to six), $151 cottage (sleeps up to three). AE, MC, V. Two-night minimum stay required. Free parking.

This collection of rustic one- and two-bedroom duplex cottages (one stands by itself) is snuggled on a stretch of beach between two legendary surf spots—Waimea Bay, where the winter waves can tower 30 feet or more, and the Banzai Pipeline, where experts shoot the perfect wave tubes. Needless to say, swimming is for flat, summer seas only. But there is a large lava reef nearby with tide pools to explore, and on the other side, Shark's Cove, a relatively protected snorkeling area. The North Shore doesn't have many places for visitors to stay—this is a good choice for people who enjoy the beach. Kitchens, barbecues, hammocks, and laundries provide some of the comforts of home.

Turtle Bay Hilton Golf & Tennis Resort. 57-091 Kamehameha Hwy., Kahuku, HI 96731. ☎ **808/293-8811** or 800-HILTONS. 485 rms, 6 suites. $180–$330 double, from $400 suite. AE, DC, DISC, JCB, MC, V. Parking $3.

If location's the key to a hotel's success, this Turtle Bay Hilton should be booked 100% year-round. It sits on fabulous Kuilima Point, surrounded by 5 miles of secluded coves and beaches, and spectacular ocean and mountain views. Big waves come in Kawela Bay just a short distance offshore from the Hilton's reefy vantage point. And this 485-room hotel is the only resort on the North Shore, so why don't I like it? Sadly neglected, the place smells musty and damp, the public areas look rusty and worn; it obviously needs an ton of money to bring it back. Where is Baron Hilton when Hawaii needs him? Built in the days when Hilton thought casino gambling would come to Hawaii, this beach hotel has seen better days, but it's sure got a great location. For details on the golf club, see "Golf & Other Outdoor Activites," below.

LEEWARD OAHU

✪ **Ihilani Resort & Spa.** 92-1001 Olani St., Kapolei, HI 96707. ☎ **808/679-0079** or 800/626-4446. Fax 808/679-0080. 387 rms, 42 suites. A/C TV MINIBAR TEL. $275–$550 double, from $800 suite. AC, CB, DC, JCB, MC, V. Free parking.

On Oahu's dry western coast, a 25-minute drive west of Honolulu International Airport, the luxurious Ihilani rises in lonely splendor by the sea at Ko Olina Resort. It's a great escape, popular with rich Honolulu folks, who say it's like driving to a neighbor-island resort.

The hotel, Ko Olina Golf Course, and some deluxe residential condos have this resort to themselves—at least until the economy improves enough to build other planned hotels. This 15-story hotel, built in 1993, is an architectural hybrid, combining some of the best elements of Hawaii's beach hotels in one structure with inner gardens and terraces and big views of Oahu's natural coastline toward Yokohama Beach. Four man-made lagoons were scooped from the lava reef and made into beaches, one of which fronts the hotel.

The resort has Oahu's best full-service spa, which pipes in seawater for some of its treatments. The 35,000-square-foot facility has Swiss showers, Grand Jets, Vichy Showers, Roman Pools, and herbal wraps of chamomile, sassafras, or peppermint. Facilities include a lap pool, Jacuzzis, cardiovascular room, aerobic classes, and cafe.

Ihilani's standard guest rooms are among the biggest in the islands, and each has a lanai with a Queen Mary teak deck lounge. Most rooms have ocean and lagoon views. The rooms feature marble baths, teak furnishing, large screen television, and high-tech appointments including a computerized phone with instructions in six languages on how to operate room gadgets. CD players are standard.

Ihilani really makes you feel like you are far away in a special place, so this is a good choice if you don't mind being a long way from the bright lights of Waikiki and Honolulu.

Dining/Entertainment: Azul, the signature bistro, offers gourmet Pacific regional cuisine. Ushio-tei has casual Japanese cuisine and a sushi bar open for dinner only. Naupaka Terrace features casual, open-air dining for breakfast, lunch, and dinner, plus nightly Hawaiian music. The Poolside Grill provides daily snacks and sandwiches. The Hokulea Bar features a jazz pianist daily from 5pm to midnight.

Services: Valet, 24-hour room service, multilingual concierge, activities and tour desk, in-house movie and CD library, licensed child-care, year-round Keiki Beachcomber's Club for children.

Facilities: Secluded gold-sand beaches on four man-made lagoons, two pools, full service health spa (see above for details), championship tennis courts with Kramer sports surface, Ted Robinson–designed 18-hole Ko Olina championship golf course, shopping arcade, meeting facilities.

4 Dining

by Jocelyn Fujii

Oahu's dining scene falls into several categories: Waikiki restaurants, chef-owned glamour restaurants, neighborhood eateries, fast-food joints, ethnic restaurants, and restaurants and food courts in shopping malls.

Chefs once trained and celebrated in Hawaii's top resorts are moving into their own spheres beyond hotel properties and walk-in traffic, creating their own destinations and loyal clienteles who are willing to find them in unexpected neighborhoods and urban niches. Chefs such as Alan Wong, Jean-Marie Josselin, Sam Choy, and Roy Yamaguchi are worth renting a car to find, but so are the plate-lunch palaces for casual dining on the run.

The recommendations below will lead you to the few noteworthy hotel dining rooms, neighborhood hangouts worth finding, ethnic winners, and isolated marvels in all corners of the island.

Chain Restaurants   It's hard to spend more than $5 at the ⊙ **Ba-le Sandwich Shops,** whose French and Vietnamese specialties such as pho (the noodle soup that's a national ritual in Vietnam), croissants as good as the espresso, and wonderful taro/tapioca desserts have won an islandwide following. Hard work, low prices, and delectable offerings have made them a roaring success. Recommended: shrimp rolls in translucent rice paper, tofu sandwiches, seafood pho, lemongrass sandwich. Branches are in Ala Moana Center (☎ **808/944-4752**); at 333 Ward Ave. (☎ **808/591-0935**); in Kahala Mall, 4211 Waialae Ave. (☎ **808/735-6889**); in Manoa Marketplace, 2855 E. Manoa Rd. (☎ **808/988-1407**); and in Chinatown at 150 N. King St. (☎ **808/521-3973**).

With branches in Waikiki, Kaimuki, Kailua, Kaneohe, Wahiawa, and Kaneohe, the high-profile **Boston's North End Pizza Bakery** chain has an enthusiastic following among pizza lovers, and not just because it boasts "Hawaii's largest slice." Boston's reasonable prices and hefty sizes (19 in. and 3 lb.!) add extra value, and fans swear by the sauces and toppings. The Waikiki branch is at 2145 Kuhio Ave. (☎ **808/922-7992**).

The streets of Waikiki are lined with famous fast-food joints from Denny's to McDonald's, from Burger King to Jack in the Box. Oahu also has most of the familiar sit-down chain restaurants and pubs. In Waikiki, the local **Hard Rock Cafe** resides at 1837 Kapiolani Blvd. (☎ **808/955-7383**), while **Planet Hollywood Honolulu** is nearby at 2155 Kalakaua Ave. (☎ **808/924-7877**). On downtown's Restaurant Row, beef eaters can chow down at **Ruth's Chris Steak House,** 500 Ala Moana Blvd. (☎ **808/599-3860**). In Kahala Mall, you can taste the intriguing toppings offered by the local branch of **California Pizza Kitchen,** 4211 Waialae Ave. (☎ **808/ 737-9446**). On the North Shore, the **Chart House Haleiwa,** 66-011 Kamehameha Hwy. (☎ **808/637-8005**), has a fine view of the harbor from outdoor tables to complement its fresh fish and prime rib.

Food Courts   Several shopping centers have food courts where you can grab a quick and cheap meal on the run. The largest is the Makai Court in **Ala Moana Shopping Center,** at Ala Moana Blvd. and Atkinson Dr. (☎ **808/946-2811**). There are 17 different types of cookery in this busy, noisy complex on the ground floor of the rambling mall. Our favorites: Tsuruya Noodles (the Tenzaru is excellent), Sbarro's pizza, Poi Bowl (Hawaiian plates), and the Thirst Aid Station with its smoothies and fresh fruit juices. Korean, Italian, Thai, Chinese, and other ethnic foods, as well as health foods, are also available. Open Monday to Saturday from 9:30am to 9pm, Sunday from 10am to 5pm.

WAIKIKI

Very Expensive

✪ **La Mer.** In the Halekulani, 2199 Kalia Rd. ☎ **808/923-2311.** Reservations recommended. Main courses $34–$41; prix fixe $85–$105. AE, CB, DC, JCB, MC, V. Daily 6–10pm. Jackets required for men. NEOCLASSIC FRENCH.

Honolulu's most elegant, sumptuous, and expensive dining takes place in this second-floor, open-sided oceanside room with views of Diamond Head and the sunset between palm fronds. Southern French influences meld seamlessly with the fresh island ingredients that La Mer has always celebrated. The impressive offerings of Michelin-award–winning chef Yves Garnier include a flawless foie gras steeped in sauternes and layered with black truffles; sea scallops in white wine with a dab of caviar, a triumph of delicate flavors; the bouillabaisse, a La Mer signature now served out of puff pastry; a thyme-marinated rack of lamb that is redolent with garlic. Lovers of seafood will find it hard to choose between the *onaga* fillet, cooked crisp on the skin, and the Hawaiian salt-crusted version, a La Mer signature. Both are sublime, as are the Gallic splendors of the cheese tray, served with walnut bread. Desserts, including the Symphony of La Mer (almond tart, crème brûlée, mousse of three chocolates) are not to be ignored. Frightfully expensive though it is, La Mer is in a class of its own in Honolulu.

Miyako Japanese Restaurant. In New Otani Kaimana Beach Hotel, 2863 Kalakaua Ave. ☎ **808/923-4739.** Reservations recommended. Main courses $30–$40. AE, DC, DISC, JCB, MC, V. Daily 6pm to closing. JAPANESE.

Ikebana arrangements accent the dining room, and servers in gorgeous kimonos bustle to bring you brisk, courteous service. The food presentation is flawless: lacquer trays, precious sake cups, esthetically arranged morsels reminiscent of imperial dining in Kyoto. Offerings include make-your-own hand sushi rolls (temaki) from a tray of vegetables, mountain yam, crab, king clam, sashimi, nori, and salmon roe; pre-arranged kaiseki dinners ($60); and several combinations of tempura, sashimi, shrimp, fresh lobster, soup, and pickled vegetables. This is a pretty room on the second floor of the hotel, with the Waikiki skyline glittering in the distance.

Nicholas Nickolas. In Ala Moana Hotel, 410 Atkinson Dr. ☎ **808/955-4466.** Reservations recommended. Main courses $19–$42. AE, CB, DC, DISC, MC, V. Daily 5:30–11:30pm. AMERICAN/CONTINENTAL/SEAFOOD.

Take the express elevator at the Ala Moana Hotel to the 36th floor, where the circular dining room reveals the city in its mountain-to-sea splendor. The menu is spare and to the point, strong on appetizers and seafood: crab cakes (a best seller), the signature Cajun-seared ahi, and a terrific Greek salad. The four pasta selections are a bit pricey at $19 to $28, we think. Blackened onaga has always been a house specialty, seared in Cajun spices and baked. The baked mahimahi is another Nicholas Nickolas classic, as well as the lemon-caper butter opakapaka. You'll dine at tables along the edge of the dining room, or at cozy booths along the interior, and when dinner's over, the dancing begins with live music Sunday to Thursday from 9:30pm, Friday and Saturday from 10pm. Ask about the appetizer menu, available daily from 5pm to 2:30pm. There's a dress code in effect for men here: collared shirt, slacks, and shoes.

Nick's Fishmarket. In Waikiki Gateway Hotel, 2070 Kalakaua Ave. ☎ **808/955-6333.** Reservations recommended. Main courses $20–$55. AE, CB, DC, DISC, JCB, MC, V. Sun–Thurs 5:30–10pm, cafe menu 5:30pm–midnight; Fri–Sat 5:30–11pm, cafe menu 5:30pm–1am. SEAFOOD.

With its extensive menu and lobster specialties, Nick's will always be the restaurant for seafood lovers with upscale tastes. Call it old-fashioned; it still has a following among celebrities and others who are used to the clubby, macho ambiance and may even find it refreshing in these days of bustling open kitchens and noisy, lively dining rooms. The menu is an awesome flexing of Neptunian muscle. Appetizers include a cold platter, Dungeness crab, salmon cakes, and an ounce of Beluga caviar (the latter at a hefty $120). The entrees include chicken, rack of lamb that has a large following, and a few obligatory pasta dishes. The fresh fish selection reeks of authority: several kinds of ahi, mahimahi, broadbill swordfish, ono, salmon, and snappers—whatever is fresh on the auction block. But the true bonanza is the luxury lobster: whether it's slipper, rock, spiny, or Maine, the selection is the best we've seen. The chef's specials change weekly.

Orchids. In the Halekulani, 2199 Kalia Rd. ☎ **808/923-2311.** Reservations recommended. Main courses $25–$39; prix fixe $43 and $52. AE, DB, DC, JCB, MC, V. Daily 7:30–11am, 11:30am–2pm, and 6–10pm. REGIONAL AMERICAN.

The stunning oceanside ambiance of this Honolulu landmark hasn't changed, but its menu has. Prices have gone up, and the offerings are no longer Pacific Rim, or Pacific Edge, or Euro-anything. It's now a house of sophisticated American grill and rotisserie specialties. So, while viewing Diamond Head over crisp, blindingly white linens, or over flickering candlelight, you can sample veal chops with wild mushrooms, New York steak in Pinot Noir sauce, and an attractive roster of roasted meats: duckling with wild rice and a honey ginger glaze, New Zealand venison with polenta and poached pears, rack of lamb Provençale, and herb-crusted rib-eye steak. Thankfully, some of the lighter fare we love and remember remains, such as the Dungeness crab-cake appetizers, seared ahi, Peking duck salad, and goat cheese wontons in ginger broth with scallops. Highlighting the seafood dishes is the onaga steamed Oriental-style, a local favorite that the Halekulani has always offered with a flourish.

Prince Court. In Hawaii Prince Hotel, 100 Holomoana St. ☎ **808/956-1111.** Reservations recommended. Main courses $18–$38; prix fixe $44.50. AE, CB, JCB, MC, V. Daily 6–10:30am and 6–9:30pm, Mon–Fri 11:30am–2pm, Sun brunch 11am–1pm. HAWAII REGIONAL.

The gorgeous view of the boat harbor is an asset any time of the day or night, particularly at sunset, or on Friday nights when fireworks light up the skies from Waikiki shores. For $34, diners can sample a lavish seafood buffet Friday and Saturday nights, or order off an à la carte menu appealing to both seafood and steak lovers. For a proponent of Hawaii Regional Cuisine, Prince Court offers stunningly simple grilled and roasted meats: rack of lamb, prime rib of beef, and a perfectly done, buttery-tender New York steak with fresh shiitake mushrooms and fresh rosemary. Lighter fare includes a melt-in-your-mouth ahi carpaccio with a tapenade and drizzle of olive oil, crab-crusted opakapaka, and a small selection of salads highlighting locally grown produce.

Expensive

Acqua. In Hawaiian Regent Hotel, 2552 Kalakaua Ave. ☎ **808/924-0123.** Reservations recommended. Main courses $10–$34. Prix fixe $25. AE, DC, DISC, JCB, MC, V. Sun–Thurs 6–9:30pm, Fri–Sat 6–10:30pm. MEDITERRANEAN/PACIFIC.

The trendy Acqua serves simple fare with cross-cultural touches, everything from smoked chicken quesadilla to ahi/octopus poke to a very rich roasted chicken risotto. The specialty, rack of lamb, is graciously offered in a half-size, but the full order is still considered a bit steep at $34 despite its imaginative pistachio nut crust and rosemary Merlot sauce. The dining is casual, around an open kitchen, and the Thursday-through-Saturday evening live entertainment has featured some prominent names in island music.

Bali by the Sea. In Hilton Hawaiian Village, 2005 Kalia Rd. ☎ **808/941-2254.** Reservations recommended. Main courses $25–$30. AE, DC, JCB, MC, V. Mon–Fri 7am–10am and 11am–2pm, Mon–Sat 6–10pm. CONTINENTAL/PACIFIC RIM.

Bali by the Sea is one of Waikiki's most memorable oceanfront dining rooms—pale and full of light, with a white grand piano at the entrance and sweeping views of the ocean. Some diners call it stuffy; others, supremely elegant. The menu includes lunchtime offerings that score high on the culinary scale: taro and crab cakes with green papaya salad; Black Angus beef burger with gourmet cheeses and teriyaki mayonnaise; Scottish smoked salmon clubhouse sandwich; and, for extravagant lunchers without time or waistline considerations, macadamia-nut herb-crusted lamb and a number of seafood and pasta dishes. Dinner inches upward in scale and extravagance, with the herb-crusted lamb still popular, and the Kaiwi opakapaka (with shiitake and tobiko) the prevailing choice among seafood lovers. The substantial, sophisticated appetizer menu with the likes of fresh coriander-flavored lobster tartar, escargots strudel, and eggplant Napoleon make the Bali a plausible choice for glamorous grazers as well.

Caffelatte. 339 Saratoga Rd. ☎ **808/924-1414.** Reservations recommended. Prix fixe $35. MC, V. Wed–Mon 6:30pm to closing. NORTHERN ITALIAN.

Owner/chef Laura Magni makes everything from scratch and to order; you wouldn't catch her near a microwave oven. As a result, you won't find a better bruschetta, pasta carbonara, marinara, or risotto in Honolulu. Because of her generations-old recipes and long hours of simmering soups and sauces, the menu is built on solidly good, uncompromising basics. The prix-fixe–only dinner consists of appetizer or salad, soup (usually fish, lentil, or vegetable, and always good), and the entree, which could be a porcini risotto, or homemade ravioli, or any of the five veal selections (for an additional $5). While fans swear by the food quality, complaints have mounted lately about the lack of parking and the inflexibility of the prix fixe format, not to mention the price, which could end up being a bit steep for pasta in a dining room this casual.

Waikiki Dining

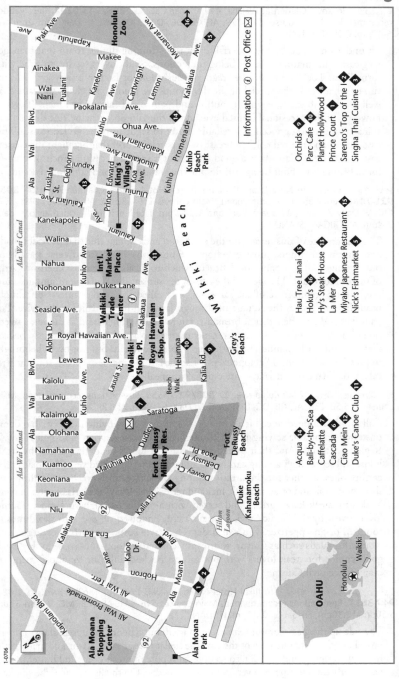

Information *i* Post Office ⊠

Orchids **9**
Parc Cafe **10**
Planet Hollywood **8**
Prince Court **1**
Sarento's Top of the I **2**
Singha Thai Cuisine **3**

Hau Tree Lanai **15**
Hoku's **16**
Hy's Steak House **13**
La Mer **14**
Miyako Japanese Restaurant **15**
Nick's Fishmarket **5**

Acqua **14**
Bali-by-the-Sea **4**
Caffelatte **7**
Cascada **6**
Ciao Mein **12**
Duke's Canoe Club **11**

OAHU

Honolulu ★
Waikiki

Cascada. In Royal Garden at Waikiki, 440 Olohana St. ☎ **808/943-0202.** Reservations recommended. Main courses $17–$29. AE, CB, DC, DISC, JCB, MC. V. Daily 11am–2pm and 6–10pm. CONTINENTAL.

Sit under umbrellas by the waterfall or in this stunning dining room that manages to gleam with marble without being pretentious. Soup lovers, waste no time with formalities: Tuck right into the cream of mushroom or French onion soup au gratin, or whatever is the special of the day. Soups are among the chef's specialties, as well as the crab cakes, eggplant soufflé, and pan-seared salmon at lunch. (Beware, however, of the occasional bruised avocado in the salmon fettucine.) At dinner, the spinach and ricotta gnocchi is a reliable starter to segue into the grilled sea scallops, osso bucco, and roasted chicken breast (with porcini sauce) that highlight the elegant roster of entrees. Cascada is a good choice for a special-occasion lunch or dinner, formal enough without being stiff despite the grand hotel lobby that precedes it.

Hau Tree Lanai. In New Otani Kaimana Beach Hotel, 2863 Kalakaua Ave. ☎ **808/921-7066.** Reservations recommended. Main courses $19–$32.50. AE, CB, DC, DISC, JCB, MC, V. Daily 7–11am, 11:30am–2pm and 5:30–9pm; late lunch in the open-air bar, daily 2–4pm. AMERICAN/ISLAND.

The centerpiece of this terrace on the sand is an ancient hau tree that provides shade and charm for diners, most of whom are busy observing the diverse parade of beachgoing bodies at Sans Souci Beach, which to locals is the most cherished strip of urban Honolulu. The view of the ocean, the sunset, the Waianae mountains, and the historic architecture of the saltwater pool called the Natatorium is blindingly beautiful and carries the restaurant through lapses in food quality and service. Poi pancakes and eggs Benedict at breakfast, sandwiches at lunch, and at dinner, a selection of fresh moonfish, red snapper, Oriental-style opakapaka, and meats (osso bucco, filet mignon, garlic lemon chicken) offer a diverse enough, but not overwhelmingly impressive, selection. The appetizers—fish tartar, Vietnamese spring rolls, grilled calamari, Thai chicken satay—are especially appealing.

Hy's Steak House. 2440 Kuhio Ave. ☎ **808/922-5555.** Reservations recommended. Main courses $15.50–$36. AE, CB, DC, DISC, MC, V. Daily 6–10pm. AMERICAN.

Call it old-fashioned or call it a survivor, but there's no denying that Hy's has demonstrated admirable staying power through nouvelle, vegetarian, and light Hawaii Regional Cuisine. And their prices have escalated too. This dark and clubby steak house still scores high among carnivores and even offers a grilled vegetable platter for carniphobes, a relief for the arteries among the chateaubriand, beef Wellington, shrimp scampi, and other fruits de mer and terre. "The Only" is its classic best, a New York strip steak kiawe-grilled and served with a mysterious signature sauce. Garlic lovers swear by the Garlic Steak Diane, a richly endowed rib eye with sliced mushrooms. For an appetizer, you can order Thai-style scallops, buttery escargots, or wonderful salads such as Caesar, warm spinach, and seafood-and-avocado. Hy's is a great choice for steak lovers with bottomless pocketbooks, or for those tiring of Hawaii Regional Cuisine.

Sarento's Top of the I. In Ilikai Hotel Nikko Waikiki, 1777 Ala Moana Blvd. ☎ **808/949-3811.** Reservations recommended. Main courses $16–$41. AE, JCB, MC, V. Sun–Thurs 5:30pm–10:30pm, Fri–Sat 5:30–11pm. ITALIAN.

The ride up the glass elevator is an event in itself, but Sarento's is not all show. Diners rave about the romantic view of the city, the stellar Caesar salad, a frutti de mare that's rich but engaging, and the sautéed scallops with porcini mushrooms and butter. Pizza, particularly the shrimp pesto version, is also a success. On the lighter side, the smoked salmon Italiano is a safe bet with a judicious sprinkling of olive oil and cracked pepper, as is the crisp cold appetizer platter of salmon, bruschetta, artichokes, and roasted peppers.

Moderate

Canoes. In Ilikai Hotel Nikko Waikiki, 1777 Ala Moana Blvd. ☎ **808/949-3811.** Reservations recommended. Main courses $11–$33. AE, DISC, MC, V. Daily 6am–2pm and 5:30–10pm. Fri–Sun buffet, with last seating at 9:30pm. CONTINENTAL/SEAFOOD.

Weekend dinner buffets and a Friday Hawaiian lunch buffet are the current offerings at the Ilikai's informal alfresco dining room. With its lomi salmon, poi, kalua pig, lau lau, chicken long rice, barbecued fish, and haupia cake, the Hawaiian spread offers a chance for visitors to sample what is usually laid out at a luau, minus the beachfront location and fire-dancing. On Saturday the buffet is strictly seafood, and on Sunday, family fare (less-than-imaginative roast beef, ham, mahimahi with Maui onions, fried chicken) take over the dining room. The well-intentioned à la carte menu is all over the cultural map in its attempts to please everyone: ramen, Waimanalo greens, fish-, cheese-, and chicken burgers, a Hawaiian plate, grilled chicken and shrimp, and the standard seafood and steak entrees. Save room for the Bubbie's ice cream and deep-fried Hawaiian coconut pudding, two local favorites.

Ciao Mein. In Hyatt Regency Waikiki, 2424 Kalakaua Ave. ☎ **808/923-2426.** Reservations recommended. Main courses $6–$20; prix fixe $24–$33; Sun brunch $23. AE, CB, DC, DISC, JCB, MC, V. Daily 6–10pm, Sun brunch 10am–2pm. ITALIAN/CHINESE.

The cross-cultural connection seemed gimmicky at first, but Ciao Mein has managed to pull it off in a large, pleasing dining room with efficient service, surprisingly good Chinese food (especially for a hotel restaurant), and award-winning menu items that make this a haven for noodle lovers. The honey-walnut shrimp, with snap peas and honey-glazed walnuts, is worth every penny of its $18.25 price. The crispy fried noodles with chicken and lobster is hailed by fans and equalled in aplomb by the bell-pepper-and-sausage penne. And few Honolulu festival-goers will forget the spicy wok-fried eggplant that won accolades and helped put Ciao Mein on Honolulu's culinary map.

☻ Hawaii Seafood Paradise. 1830 Ala Moana Blvd. ☎ **808/946-4514.** Reservations recommended. Main courses $7–$32. AE, JCB, DC, MC, V. Daily 6:30am–3am. CHINESE/SEAFOOD.

You can dine as simply or as lavishly as you choose in this quirky, unpretentious restaurant that serves nine kinds of roast duck (Peking-style and smoked tea duck are winners); a peerless shrimp fried rice; many selections of chicken, noodles, and seafood; an impressive selection of abalone and clam dishes; and "hotpot" casseroles with everything from lamb to lobster and fish. Chinese-food aficionados swear by the food here, and we agree. A few of the best items on the menu are written in Chinese with no English translation, so don't be afraid to ask questions. There are Thai selections as well, among them the spicy, delectable Tom Yum soup with prawns, a hint of coconut, and lemongrass—rich but irresistible. Highly recommended: the Peking-style duck, with skin that is crisp, translucent, and sweet.

☻ Parc Cafe. In the Waikiki Parc Hotel, 2233 Helumoa Rd. ☎ **808/921-7272.** Reservations recommended. Buffets $11.50–$22.50. Open Mon–Sat 7–10am and 11:30am–2pm, Sun 7–9:30am and 11am–2pm; daily 5:30–9:30pm. BUFFETS/BRUNCH.

The Halekulani's sister hotel may not be on the beach, but it's made a name for itself as Honolulu's top spot for buffets, with food and prices so good it has won over even the most dedicated buffet bashers. Regulars flock to the dining room for the Wednesday and Friday Hawaiian buffet, which at $15.50 is the finest such spread around: lau lau, lomi salmon, kalua pig, steamed fresh catch, mashed Molokai potatoes, Kauai taro au gratin, and dozens of salads. Chafing dishes notwithstanding, this is gourmet fare using fresh, fine ingredients. A carving station serves up rotisserie duck and prime rib. The seafood soup is reliably good, and the squid luau, with coconut milk, taro tops, and a brilliant smattering of tomatoes, is arguably the best in Hawaii. Otherwise there are breakfast and luncheon buffets (the latter featuring salads, sandwiches, pasta, and rotisserie chicken). The seafood dinner nightly is a roaring success: sashimi, poke, and oysters on the half shell; crab legs and fresh catch; made-to-order pastas; charbroiled eggplant; tofu, watercress, and Peking duck salad; and many other selections, including smashing desserts.

Singha Thai Cuisine. 1910 Ala Moana Blvd., ☎ **808/941-2898.** Reservations recommended. Main courses $7–$22. CB, DC, DISC, JCB, MC, V. Mon–Fri 11am–11pm. THAI.

Classical Thai dancers, imaginative combination dinners, and the use of local organic ingredients are among the special touches of this Thai restaurant at the Ala Moana end of Waikiki. Complete dinners for two to five cover many tastes and are an ideal way for the uninitiated to sample this cuisine, as well as the elements of Hawaii Regional Cuisine that have had considerable influence on the chef. Some highlights on a diverse menu: local fresh catch with Thai chili and light black-bean sauce; red, green, yellow, and vegetarian curries; spicy Thai eggplant; ginseng chicken soup; and many seafood dishes. Unusual for a Thai restaurant is such extensive use of fresh fish (mahimahi, ono, ahi, opakapaka, onaga, and uku) in traditional Thai preparations. Curry puffs (shrimp, pork, and vegetables in puff pastry), chicken and shrimp sate, fresh ahi tempura (very Japanese), blackened ahi summer rolls (very Hawaii Regional), and naked squid salad are among the many curiosities of the menu that have received acceptance.

Inexpensive

🔴 **Cha Cha Cha.** 342 Seaside Ave. ☎ **808/395-7797.** Complete dinners $7–$9. MC, V. Daily 7:30am–midnight. MEXICAN/CARIBBEAN.

Nothing wimpy about the flavors here; the lime, coconut, and Caribbean spices make Cha Cha more than plain ole Mex, adding zing to the fresh fish and shrimp ceviche, the jerk-chicken breast, and the shrimp and fish stew in lime broth. We love the vegetarian black-bean burritos, red chili tortilla shells, toe-curling salsas, and spinach tortillas, but you may want to start the day with the more traditional huevos rancheros. The temperatures rise from there, with red chilies, jalapenos, and savory Caribbean spices perking up the pork, chicken, and beef dishes. Finally, jump-start the sweet tooth with coconut custard, Jamaican rum flan, and piña-colada ice cream pie—extraordinary desserts all.

There's another branch with the same prices in Hawaii Kai Town Centre. It's open Sunday to Thursday from 11am to 9pm, Friday and Saturday from 11am to 10pm.

HONOLULU BEYOND WAIKIKI
ALOHA TOWER MARKETPLACE

Gordon Biersch Brewery Restaurant. In Aloha Tower Marketplace, 1 Aloha Tower Dr. ☎ **808/599-4877.** Reservations recommended. Main courses $8–$20. AE, DISC, JCB, MC, V. Sun–Wed 11am–10pm, Thurs–Sat 11am–11pm. PACIFIC-ASIAN.

The three German-style lagers brewed on the premises would be enough of a draw, but chef Kelly Degala's cooking is the reason non–beer-drinkers love this place too. The lanai bar and brewery bar, open until 1 am, are the brightest spot in the Aloha Tower Marketplace, always teeming with downtown types who think that suds are swell as they nosh on pizza, baby-back ribs, and any number of American classics with Degala's deft cross-cultural touches. Other standouts include the sautéed tiger prawns on linguine and the thick, moist, and generously garlicked fries—as famous as the beer and indubitably the best in the Pacific.

DOWNTOWN

⑤ **Legend Seafood Restaurant.** In Chinese Cultural Plaza, 100 N. Beretania St. ☎ **808/ 532-1868.** Reservations recommended. Most items under $15. AE, DC, MC, V. Mon–Fri 10:30am–2pm, Sat–Sun 8am–2pm, daily 5:30–10pm. DIM SUM/SEAFOOD.

It's like dining in Hong Kong here, with a Chinese-speaking clientele poring over Chinese newspapers, and the clatter of chopsticks punctuating conversations. Excellent dim sum comes in bamboo steamers that parade by in carts. Although you must often wave madly to catch the server's eye, and then point to what you want, the system doesn't seem to deter diners from returning. Among our favorites: deep-fried taro puffs and prawn dumplings, shrimp dim sum, vegetable dumplings, and the open-faced seafood with shiitake, scallop, and a tofu product called aburage. Dim sum is only served at lunch, but at dinner the seafood shines.

Yanagi Sushi. 762 Kapiolani Blvd. ☎ **808/597-1525.** Reservations recommended. Main courses $8–$33, complete dinners $11.50–$18.50. AE, CB, DC, JCB, MC, V. Daily 11am–2pm, Mon–Sat 5:30pm–2am, Sun 5:30–10pm. JAPANESE.

We love the late-night hours, the sushi bar with its fresh ingredients and well-trained chefs, and the extensive choices in the combination lunches and dinners. But we also love the à la carte Japanese menu, which covers everything from chazuke (rice with tea, salmon, seaweed, and other condiments; a comfort food) to shabu shabu and other steaming earthenware-pot dishes. Complete dinners offer choices of sashimi, shrimp tempura, broiled salmon, New York steak, and other possibilities. Nearly 20 different types of sashimi, consistently crisp tempura, and one of the town's finer spicy ahi hand-rolled sushis make Yanagi worth remembering. There are tables at the sushi bar, in an adjoining dining room, and in two small private rooms.

ALA MOANA

Expensive

◐ **A Pacific Cafe Oahu.** At Ward Centre, 1200 Ala Moana Blvd. ☎ **808/593-0035.** Reservations recommended. Main courses $19–$26. AE, DC, DISC, MC, V. Mon–Fri 11:30am–2pm, daily 5:30–10pm; appetizer bar Fri–Sat 5:30–11pm. PACIFIC RIM/FRENCH/MEDITERRANEAN.

With this, his first Oahu restaurant, noted chef Jean-Marie Josselin has sealed his fate as the brightest star in Hawaii's culinary galaxy. This is his fourth Hawaii restaurant and his flagship, following 6 years of international accolades at A Pacific Cafe on Kauai and, more recently, A Pacific Cafe on Maui and The Beach House in Poipu, Kauai. Honolulu diners who have waited patiently for a Josselin outpost of their own are stunningly rewarded in this temple of creativity. Curved walls; the colors of coral, ocean, reef, and sand; and avant-garde sea-glass lighting create a unique environment that's a match for Josselin's crisp, vibrant cuisine. The ambiance is informal, elegant, and inviting.

The appetizer bar has its own kitchen and invites lingering over the long list of appetizers for which the famed chef is known. Musts: warm tiger-eye ahi sushi tempura, a Josselin signature, in a crisp, thin skin with an eye-opening hot mustard; wood-fired garlic shrimp pizza topped with Caesar salad and cheese, a triumph of tastes and textures; warm potato salad, the best of the comfort foods; and what many agree is Josselin's most successful appetizer, nachos of black Thai rice (instead of beans), seasoned with a tropical chipotle sauce and blackened ahi. The appetizers are so seductive that it's tough to make the leap to the main courses; we recommend the pan-seared salmon with baby lentils and any of the fresh fish dishes that are seared

Honolulu Area Dining

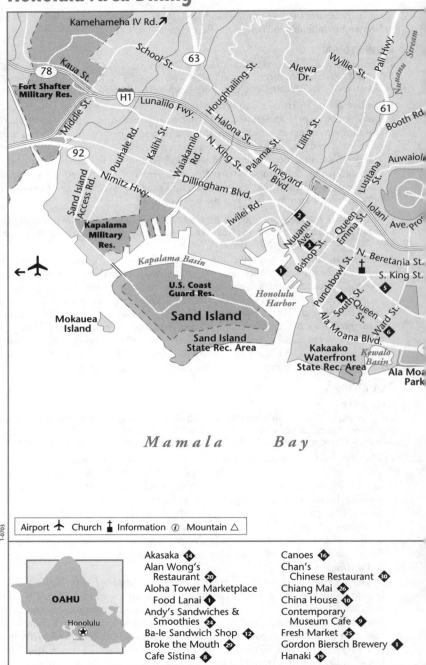

Airport ✈ Church ⌖ Information ⓘ Mountain △

Akasaka ⑭
Alan Wong's
  Restaurant ⑳
Aloha Tower Marketplace
  Food Lanai ❶
Andy's Sandwiches &
  Smoothies ㉔
Ba-le Sandwich Shop ⑫
Broke the Mouth ㉙
Cafe Sistina ⑧

Canoes ⑯
Chan's
  Chinese Restaurant ㉚
Chiang Mai ㉖
China House ⑩
Contemporary
  Museum Cafe ⑨
Fresh Market ㉕
Gordon Biersch Brewery ❶
Hanaki ⑲

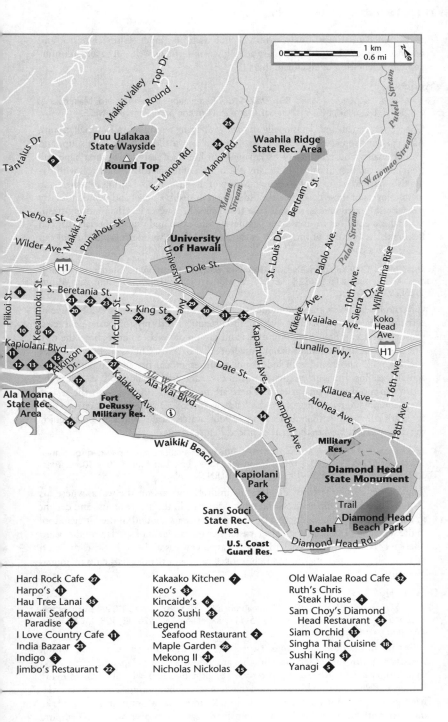

Hard Rock Cafe ⬥27
Harpo's ⬥11
Hau Tree Lanai ⬥35
Hawaii Seafood
  Paradise ⬥17
I Love Country Cafe ⬥11
India Bazaar ⬥23
Indigo ⬥3
Jimbo's Restaurant ⬥22

Kakaako Kitchen ⬥7
Keo's ⬥33
Kincaide's ⬥6
Kozo Sushi ⬥23
Legend
  Seafood Restaurant ⬥2
Maple Garden ⬥28
Mekong II ⬥21
Nicholas Nickolas ⬥15

Old Waialae Road Cafe ⬥42
Ruth's Chris
  Steak House ⬥4
Sam Choy's Diamond
  Head Restaurant ⬥34
Siam Orchid ⬥13
Singha Thai Cuisine ⬥18
Sushi King ⬥31
Yanagi ⬥5

and cradled in sumptuous seasonings such as lime-ginger, Chinese pesto, and Moroccan spices. Lunch options are achingly wonderful as well. All in all, an unforgettable celebration of epicurean joy.

Moderate

✪ Akasaka. 1646B Kona St. ☎ **808/942-4466.** Reservations recommended. Main courses $10–$19. AE, DC, DISC, MC, V. Mon–Sat 11am–2:30pm and 5pm–2am. JAPANESE.

Cozy, busy, casual, and occasionally smoky, with a tiny tatami room for small groups, Akasaka wins top scores for sushi, sizzling tofu and scallops, miso-clam soup, and overall quality and integrity of its Japanese cuisine. The zesty, spicy tuna hand-roll (temaki) is the best in town, and many claim the California roll, scallop roll with flying fish roe, and hamachi also occupy the top of the sushi heap. During soft-shell crab season, lovers of these delicacies can order them in sushi, a novel and wonderful tasty treat. Fresh ingredients at the sushi bar (the hamachi is never less than buttery-fresh) make this a good bet for topnotch Japanese, with lunch and dinner specials that can help take the bite out of the bill. À la carte sushi here is wonderful, but the bill can sneak up on you.

China House. 1349 Kapiolani Blvd. ☎ **808/949-6622.** Reservations recommended for large parties. Main courses $6.50–$28. AE, MC, V. Mon–Fri 10am–10pm, Sat–Sun, 9am–10pm. CHINESE.

Cavernous and noisy and synonymous with dim sum, China House is a beehive of activity: servers pushing carts with bamboo steamers and trays of exotic delicacies, brusque service, much craning of necks and raising of voices to hear above the din. But this is one of Honolulu's major purveyors of the dainty Chinese delectables, with a selection (37 choices!) that includes some surprises: mochi-rice chicken pouch, spinach-and-scallop dim sum, pan-fried turnip cake, and fresh scallop roll, as well as the more commonly known varieties. There are more than 100 items on the rest of the menu, including some that we think are overpriced. On a menu that charges $28 for shark's-fin soup with crabmeat and $20 for sautéed scallops in a taro nest, enjoy the dim sum but beware the market-priced items.

Cafe Sistina. 1314 S. King St. ☎ **808/596-0061.** Reservations recommended for dinner. Main courses $12–$13. AE, DC, MC, V. Mon–Fri 11am–2pm, Sun–Mon 5:30–9:30pm, Tues–Thurs 5:30–10pm, Fri–Sat 5:30–10:30pm. NORTHERN ITALIAN.

Chef/owner Sergio Mitrotti displays his multiple talents on the walls, where his Sistine Chapel work-in-progress and pope's portraits in the alcove amuse and delight in a an otherwise industrially stylized room. His talents abound in the kitchen, too, in the steaming platters of homemade pasta. The extensive list of specials on the board offer great possibilities (roasted red peppers, asparagus pasta), but otherwise, the frutti de mare, linguine puttanesca, and rich smoked salmon-artichoke fettucine are touted by regulars.

Inexpensive

✪ Hanaki. Sam Sung Plaza #101, 655 Keeaumoku St. ☎ **808/955-1347.** Reservations recommended for groups. Main courses $5.25–$14; Kaiseki $17.50–$20. AE, JCB, MC, V. Daily 11am–2pm, 5–10pm. JAPANESE.

Nabeyaki and noodles are Hanaki's specialties. Small and newly renovated, with a pleasantly quirky mix of Japanese noodles and oddities such as Japanese bacon maki (hamburger steak with bacon, in teriyaki or ponzu sauce), Hanaki crosses many barriers in delivering simple, good food that is anything but boring. The reckless order fried gyoza (dumplings); we love the shiitake mushroom udon and the shiitake donburi, with the tasty black mushrooms and eggs served over hot rice. Tempura udon (with shrimp and vegetables esthetically arranged over the thick, steaming noodles) and the teishoku (combination) dinners of three or four choices are so elegant you'll forget you're in a modest eatery without tablecloths.

Harpo's Restaurant. In Ala Moana Plaza, 451 Piikoi St. ☎ **808/591-0040.** Reservations not accepted. Pizzas $18.50–$28 for large; pasta $6.50–$9.95. MC, V. Daily 10:30am–10pm. PIZZA.

This is for those who love thick-crust pan pizzas that can feed a family without breaking the bank. Two of the six Oahu locations (this one and the one at 477 Kapahulu Ave.) have tables and a full menu of sandwiches, pasta, and pizza, including at least 14 varieties of toppings for the individual, medium, and large pizzas. Among them: Thai chicken, grilled eggplant, artichoke pesto, the Gourmet (everything from their homemade Italian sausage to pepperoni and olives), and prosciutto tomato. Pizza by the slice goes for $1.85; a hunger-buster for diners in a rush.

⑤ I ♥ Country Cafe. In Ala Moana Plaza, 451 Piikoi St. ☎ **808/596-8108.** Main courses $5–$8.50. MC, V. Mon–Sat 10:30am–9pm, Sun 10:30am–8pm. INTERNATIONAL.

Give yourself time to peruse the lengthy list of specials posted on the menu board, as well as the prodigious printed menu. Stand in line at the counter, place your order and pay, and find a Formica-top table or wait about 10 minutes for your take-out order to appear in a Styrofoam plate heaping with salad and other accompaniments. This place is a beehive, with a mind-boggling selection that includes shredded, moist roast turkey that may be better than grandma's; nine types of cheese steaks, including vegetarian tofu; garlic mahimahi; spinach-stuffed ravioli; Cajun meat loaf; Thai curries; shoyu chicken; vegetarian or eggplant lasagna; and a long list of other choices spanning many cultures and tastes. The health-conscious menu appeals equally to bodybuilders and hedonists, because the cooking is as wholesome as it is flavorful. Favorites include the lasagna, roast turkey, oven-roasted chicken Dijon, and the Cajun-style ahi.

Kakaako Kitchen. 1216 Waimanu St. ☎ **808/596-7488.** Main courses $5.75–$8.50. Mon–Sat 6:30am–2pm. No credit cards. GOURMET PLATE LUNCHES.

Island-style chicken linguine is the headliner in this industrialesque kitchen near Ala Moana Center, where the owners of 3660 On the Rise, a popular Kaimuki restaurant (see below), have turned their attentions to elevating the local tradition called a plate lunch. Vegetarian specials, homemade veggie burgers, home-style pot roast, shrimp curry, fresh catch, mahimahi sandwich on taro roll, burgers, ahi steak, and "mixed plate" with two entrees are becoming the lunch of choice among office workers in the Ala Moana–Kakaako area. At breakfast, omelets, scones, and fried rice fly out of the open kitchen. Although much of the business is takeout, there are tables for casual dining in a high-ceilinged, warehouselike room.

Kincaide's. In Ward Warehouse, 1050 Ala Moana Blvd. ☎ **808/591-2005.** Reservations recommended. Main courses $9–$30. AE, DC, JCB, MC, V. Daily 11:15am–10pm (later for pupus). SEAFOOD.

Kincaide's is always winning surveys for one thing or another—best place for a business lunch, best seafood restaurant—and manages to please those who aren't looking for haute cuisine. Brisk service, a pleasant view of Honolulu Harbor, and a wide-ranging seafood menu keep the large dining room full. The warm San Francisco sourdough bread is another big plus. Great fresh fish sandwiches, seafood chowders and French onion soups, kiawe-grilled salmon with thyme butter, fresh mahimahi with key-lime butter, herbed chicken breast, and garlic prawns are among Kincaide's highlights. If you're longing for an Asian twist, ask about the bamboo-steamed fresh fish, with shiitake mushrooms, fresh seaweed, and ginger-soy sauce. It's a not-too-rich dish that bodes well for dessert, the original burnt creme that Honolulu diners still clamor for, rich and custardy with a glazed sugar topping.

Siam Orchid. 1514 Kona St. ☎ **808/955-6161.** Reservations recommended. Main courses $6.25–$13.50. AE, JCB, DC, DISC, MC. V. Mon–Sat 11am–2pm, daily 5:30–9:30pm. THAI.

Come here for great Thai food with no gimmicks. Tucked away on a side street bordering the Ala Moana Center, Siam Orchid is an old Honolulu favorite with great lunch specials and consistently high quality. Consider the tasty-beyond-belief Tom Yum spicy shrimp soup, the assertively flavored Thai garlic shrimp, or the panang vegetable curry and tofu, one of a dozen great offerings for vegetarians. Noodle lovers may consider the Pad Thai fried noodles with shrimp, while curry lovers will be pleased with the extensive selection of chicken, beef, pork, shrimp, and vegetable in the peanut-curry panang sauce or in traditional red, green, and yellow versions.

MANOA VALLEY/MOILIILI/MAKIKI
Expensive
✪ **Alan Wong's Restaurant.** 1857 S. King St., 5th Floor. ☎ **808/949-2526.** Reservations recommended. Main courses $15–$20. AE, MC, V. Daily 5–10pm. HAWAII REGIONAL.

Renowned for his innovative flavors at the Mauna Lani Bay Hotel's CanoeHouse on the Big Island, Alan Wong achieved instant success when he chucked the resort world for a neighborhood in Honolulu that is neither glamorous nor particularly convenient. A brilliant chef with staying power who has influenced the direction of regional cuisine, he owns what is arguably Honolulu's busiest restaurant, a 90-seat room with a glassed-in terrace and open kitchen, accented with stylish and imposing floral arrangements, minimalist avant-garde lighting, and curly-koa wall panels. Vertical cuisine is the trend here. Many of the dishes come in high-rise towers of multiple layers and colors, such as the crab-and-chicken lumpia (a Filipino crepe) with three sauces, and his famous ahi cake with layers of grilled eggplant, Maui onion, seared ahi, and Big Island goat cheese with lemongrass sauce. The wild mushroom risotto with basil oil, grilled vegetables, and salmon coulis also appears in a column. Despite this overworked motif, the flavors shine with Asian lemongrass, sweet-sour, garlic, wasabi, and other assertive ingredients deftly melded with the fresh seafood and produce of the islands. The California roll is a triumph, made with salmon roe, wasabi, and Kona lobster instead of rice, served warm. But don't get attached, because the menu changes daily.

Moderate
Sushi King. 2700 S. King St. ☎ **808/947-2836.** Reservations recommended. Main courses $9.50–$22. AE, JCB, MC, V. Wed–Mon 11:30am–2pm and 5:30pm–2am; Tues 5:30–10pm. JAPANESE.

Brusque service sure doesn't deter diners from arriving in throngs for the lunch specials here, and they are highly recommended. This is the king of excellent jumbo platters, with soup, pickles, California roll sushi, and your choice of chicken teriyaki, beef teriyaki, shrimp and vegetable tempura, and calamari and vegetable tempura—for an unbelievable $6.50. Other combination lunches offer a head-turning assortment of choices: sashimi, tempura, butterfish, fried oysters, soba noodles, udon noodles, and more than a dozen selections. Pick two for $9, with soup, pickles, and rice—a top value. Otherwise, the à la carte menu holds its own with noodles, donburi (steamed rice with tempura and other toppings), and sushi from the always-full sushi bar. The lunch specials are continued as early-bird specials daily from 5:30 to 6:30pm. With or without the specials, this is the typical neighborhood restaurant whose stern ways are usually forgiven by diners who appreciate the value and the food quality. A smile now and then would be welcome, though.

Inexpensive

Andy's Sandwiches & Smoothies. 2904 E. Manoa Rd., opposite Manoa Marketplace. ☎ **808/988-6161.** Most items under $5. MC, V. Mon–Thurs 7am–6pm, Fri 7am–5pm, Sun 7am–12:30pm. HEALTH FOOD.

It started as a health food restaurant, expanded into a juice bar, and today is a neighborhood fixture for fresh baked bread, healthy breakfasts and lunches (its mango muffins are famous), and homemade vegetarian fare. Andy's is a roadside stop that always carries fresh papayas, sandwiches, and healthy snacks for folks on the run.

❾ Broke the Mouth. Puck's Alley, 1023 University Ave., Moiliili. ☎ **808/955-5599.** Plate lunches $4–$6. Mon 9am–8pm, Tues–Sat 9am–9pm. HEALTH FOOD/PLATE LUNCHES.

Big Island farmer Tip Davis successfully cloned his Hilo plate-lunch stand into two Honolulu locations, to rave reviews by busy diners who continue to embrace his taro/sweet potato salad and tofu manapua. Everything is healthy, vegetarian, and inexpensive. Best bets: Mamo plate lunch, with greens, pesto pasta, or Hawaiian potato salad; the meatless hot dog and a slice of taro/coconut pudding, for $5; the salad of taro, sweet potato, and veggies with macadamia nut dressing, and the sweet potato/basil pesto manapua.

The other branch is downtown at 1148 Bishop St. (☎ **808/524-0355**). It's open Monday to Friday from 7am to 5:30pm, Saturday from 10am to 2pm. Both are the health foodie's fast-food fantasy, no-muss, no-fuss, and painless to waistline and pocketbook.

❾ Chan's Chinese Restaurant. 2600 S. King St. ☎ **808/949-1188.** Reservations recommended for large groups. Main courses $6–$13.50. AE, MC, V. Sun–Thurs 10:30am–midnight. CANTONESE/NORTHERN CHINESE.

Chan's is the quintessential, modest neighborhood eatery that opens early and closes late, doesn't over-salt its food, and serves noodles, seafood, and dim sum that would hold its own in Hong Kong. (We have learned to ignore the decor; no one comes here for style.) The dim sum arrives in bamboo steamers in wrappers so translucent you can clearly see the fillings. The clams in black-bean sauce are succulent, drenched in the savory sauce, peppered with fresh scallions, in a perfectly seasoned composition that is not over-salted. You can order everything from roast duck to elegant taro nest dishes with five different fillings that please vegetarians, beef eaters, and seafood lovers. We heartily recommend the spinach garlic and the boneless chicken with black-bean sauce and fine, soft noodles—a triumph.

Chiang Mai. 2239 S. King St. ☎ **808/941-1151.** Reservations suggested for dinner. Main courses $6.50–$11. AE, DISC, MC, V. Mon–Fri 11am–2pm, daily 5:30–10pm. THAI.

One of Honolulu's early Thai restaurants, Chiang Mai has managed to maintain its popularity despite fierce competition, and we know why. Diners line up outside the tiny restaurant for sticky rice in bamboo steamers that accompany excellent curries, the signature Cornish game hen in lemongrass and spices, and wonderful green papaya salad marinated in tamarind sauce. Consistently good quality is maintained in a small kitchen that miraculously produces 80 menu items, including seven types of curry (fresh fish curry is excellent) and 25 vegetarian items. This is a palate- and people-pleasing restaurant that is inviting in its modesty.

Contemporary Museum Cafe. In The Contemporary Museum, 2411 Makiki Heights Dr. ☎ **808/523-3362.** Reservations recommended. Main courses $8–$11. MC, V. Tues–Sat 11am–3pm (coffee and desserts 2–3pm), Sun noon–2pm (coffee and desserts only). PACIFIC RIM/MEDITERRANEAN.

The surroundings are an integral part of the dining experience, because this tiny lunchtime cafe is part of an art museum nestled on the slopes of Tantalus, amid carefully cultivated Oriental gardens, a breathtaking view of Diamond Head, and priceless contemporary art displayed indoors and outdoors. The cafe's menu is limited to sandwiches, soups, salads, and appetizers, so it's best to keep your expectations in check. What is offered, however, does the job well, and chances are you won't leave disappointed, especially if you crown the meal with the flourless chocolate cake. But first, consider the grilled eggplant sandwich, or the baked Brie and Indonesian mushrooms, or the oven-roasted turkey breast sandwich. The ubiquitous garden burger is given a taste twist with a homemade barbecue sauce, and the house-smoked mahi-mahi with Caesar dressing and a tower of greens is the choice for fish lovers.

☉ Diem. 2633 S. King St. ☎ **808/941-8657.** Reservations recommended for dinner. Main courses $6–$10. AE, DISC, JCB, MC, V. Daily 10am–10pm. VIETNAMESE.

We love Diem for its Royal Seafood Noodle Soup, the best pho in town, its roll-up appetizers (fish, shrimp, beef, seafood); its spicy fried rice, vegetarian or with shrimp or chicken; and its lemongrass fish, chicken, seafood, and vegetarian dishes. Crispy fish and curries also score high on this menu of simple delights, which caters as much to tofu-loving vegetarians as to beef and pork enthusiasts. The tiny eatery in the university area has earned its following by word of mouth, and spreads the taste treats with a thriving catering business.

Fresh Market. 2972 E. Manoa Rd. ☎ **808/988-5919.** Most items under $8.50. No credit cards. Mon–Fri 7am–5pm, Sat–Sun 7am–4pm. HEALTH FOOD.

What began as Manoa's brightest corner produce stand is now the tiniest of cafes, with a small coffee bar, a good selection of local produce, limited health foods, and a small deli for takeout or dining at one of the few tables in the house. Manoa residents swear by the breakfasts here (pancakes made with purple Okinawan sweet potato), and the lunch specials, notably the smoked turkey and ahi frittata with hearty country fries, are worth a trip to Manoa Valley. Hot vegetarian chili and soup are always available in large pots in the corner, and they're good.

India Bazaar. Old Stadium Square, 2320 S. King St. ☎ **808/949-4840.** Main courses 5.75–$6.75. No credit cards. Mon–Sat 11am–9pm, Sun 11am–7pm. INDIAN.

Spicy curries, crispy papadams, moist chapatis, and the full range of Indian delicacies are served from a counter where you point and choose. The vegetables are usually overcooked in the Indian fashion. A handful of tables are scattered about a room filled with the scent of spices; one wall is lined with exotic chutneys and Indian condiments for home cooking. The vegetarian thali is a favorite: the spiced Indian rice comes with your choice of three vegetable curries, and there are many good choices. Lentil, cauliflower, eggplant, tofu/peas, potato, spinach/lentil, garbanzo beans, okra, and other selections beckon. Chicken tandoori (with two vegetable curries) and shrimp thali appeal to nonvegetarians.

☉ Jimbo's Restaurant. 1936 S. King St. ☎ **808/947-2211.** Reservations not accepted. Main courses $4.50–$11. CB, JCB, MC, V. Wed–Mon 11am–3pm; Wed–Thurs and Sun–Mon 5–10pm, Fri–Sat 5–11pm. JAPANESE.

Jimbo's is tiny, fewer than a dozen tables, and there is such demand for its sublime fare that you may have to wait for a seating. It's worth it. A must for any noodle lover, Jimbo's serves homemade udon noodles in a flawless homemade broth, then tops the works with shrimp tempura, chicken, egg-and-vegetable, seaweed, roasted mochi, and a variety of accompaniments of your choice. The Zouni, with chicken, vegetables, and mochi rice roasted to a toasty flavor, is one of life's great pleasures. Cold noodles, stir-fried noodles, donburi steamed rice dishes with assorted toppings, Japanese-style curries, and combination dinners served on trays are among the many delights that keep diners returning. The earthenware pot of noodles, shiitake mushrooms, vegetables, and udon, with a platter of tempura on the side, is the top-of-the-line combo, a designer dish at an affordable price.

Kozo Sushi. 2334 S. King St. ☎ **808/973-5666.** Most items under $3.50; party plates $15–$24. No credit cards. Mon–Sat 9am–7pm, Sun 9am–6pm. SUSHI.

Into the pricey, floating world of expensive sushi houses came Kozo—fast, affordable, take-out sushi that isn't Kyoto quality, but is respectable and extremely popular. Kozo's combination platters are ubiquitous at pot luck functions and large gatherings, but individual sushi can also be ordered: California roll, unagi roll, salmon and shrimp, and dozens of other choices, including the newest addition, the odd hybrid called BLT maki. There are four other locations in Honolulu.

Maple Garden. 909 Isenberg St. ☎ **808/941-6641.** Main courses $5–$28. AE, JCB, MC, V. Daily 11am–2pm and 5:30–10:30pm. SZECHUAN.

Aside from the Peking duck at $28, which must be ordered a day in advance and which has earned its reputation for greatness, there are many specialties for which Maple Garden is known. The Chinaman's Hat, a version of mu shui pork, is a good choice, as well as the braised scallops with Chinese mushroooms and the scallops with hot garlic sauce. Fiery palates usually enjoy the diced chicken with chili or the prawns in chili sauce; the more subdued can try the vegetarian selections (sautéed spinach or crispy string beans), or any of the dozens of seafood entrees—everything from sea cucumbers to lobster with black-bean sauce and braised salmon. A visual feast adorns the dining room walls, covered with noted artist John Young's original drawings, sketches, and murals.

Old Waialae Road Cafe. 2820 S. King St. ☎ **808/951-7779.** Reservations not accepted. Main courses $5–$8. No credit cards. Mon–Fri 11am–9pm, Sat–Sun 8am–9pm. LOCAL/PLATE LUNCH.

Two enterprising women resurrected a fading pillar in the plate lunch world and infused it with new ideas and a gourmet touch without losing any of its "local" quality. There are a few tables outdoors, but mostly it's a gourmet take-out stand that serves an ahi plate, kimchee burgers, a sliced chicken breast pasta with Waimanalo gourmet greens, and a familiar list of local favorites. Items from the old menu board inside, a holdover from the old Ted's Drive-In, are still offered, but there's an excellent Hawaiian plate lunch now, spinach lasagna with polenta, garlic bread, and greens, and an impressive selection of daily changing specials. Weekend breakfasts are gaining a following, everything from huevos rancheros and banana French toast to a handsome tofu scramble with Maui onions and many vegetables. Along with Kakaako Kitchen, Old Waialae Road Cafe takes the modest plate lunch to new levels of wholesomeness, style, and imagination.

KAIMUKI/KAPAHULU
Expensive
3660 On the Rise. 3660 Waialae Ave. ☎ **808/737-1177.** Reservations required. Main courses $17.50–$24.50. AE, DC, MC, V. Tues–Thurs 5:30–9:30pm, Fri–Sat 5:30–10pm, Sun 5:30–9pm. EUROPEAN/ISLAND.

This is a busy, noisy restaurant with a menu that has retained only tried-and-true favorites, ranging from the basics like roasted chicken and an excellent rack of lamb to exotic touches such as ti-leaf–wrapped seafood in a tomato-butter sauce. Our favorites: the ahi katsu, wrapped in nori and deep-fried rare, an excellent appetizer; Caesar salad; and the opakapaka simmered in Chinese black-bean broth. Like all Hawaii eateries, though, the place is getting pricier.

Baci Due. 3196 Waialae Ave. ☎ **808/735-5899.** Reservations recommended. Main courses $10–$28. AE, DISC, MC, V. Mon–Fri 11:30am–2pm, daily 6–10:30pm. ITALIAN.

An old, split-level wooden house makes a fine setting for this trattoria, with cozy booths, sensitive lighting, and a menu of fresh-made pasta, four kinds of risotto (saffron/Parmesan, porcini, seafood, and vegetarian), and one of the largest veal selections in town, six choices at last count, with the herb-marinated veal chop the most popular. The ravioli is made fresh daily, and the garlic bread, served with roasted whole garlic that spreads like butter, is an old favorite that goes well with the charcoaled shrimp chilled in lime juice.

Keo's. 625 Kapahulu Ave. ☎ **808/737-8240.** Reservations recommended. Main courses $8–$15; set dinners for 2 to 10 people, $22 per person. AE, JCB, DC, DISC, MC, V. Daily 5–10pm. THAI.

One of Honolulu's celebrity haunts, Keo's is the grandfather of Thai eateries in Hawaii. The herbs, vegetables, fruits, and many of the spices used here are grown without pesticides on a North Shore farm, and the large banana stalks and dangling heliconias bring a strong dose of sophisticated country into this popular urban eatery. Orchids are everywhere. Service is brisk, the mango daiquiris are legendary, and the Evil Jungle Prince, eggplant with basil and tofu, and luxurious selection of curries make Keo's a longtime Honolulu favorite. You can choose medium or hot on the curries (caution: hot is incendiary). The green curry with seafood, panang curry with kaffir lime leaves and fresh lemongrass, and green papaya salad are among Keo's best items, but don't forget the shrimp or vegetarian fried rice, a moist explosion of tastes with tomato, onion, cucumber, and garlic.

✪ Sam Choy's Diamond Head Restaurant. 449 Kapahulu Ave. ☎ **808/732-8645.** Reservations required. Main courses $19–$30. AE, MC, V. Mon–Thurs 5:30–9:30pm, Fri–Sun 5–9:30pm. HAWAII REGIONAL.

You'll know you're in the right place if you see a parade of exiting diners clutching their Styrofoam bundles, for leftovers are de rigueur at any Sam Choy's operation, where the servings are almost embarrassingly gargantuan. But the food is as big-bodied and big-hearted as the servings. Choy has won over a sizable chunk of Hawaii's dining population, so successfully that you must often book weeks in advance. It's noisy, informal, and full of hearty diners. The master of poke, Choy serves several of the best versions ever invented, among them a white fish (ono, opakapaka) drizzled with hot oil and topped with chopped herbs and condiments. The ti-leaf steamed seafood laulau is a signature dish, though we miss the traditional taro greens on top. Heartily recommended are the Brie wontons, the teriyaki-style rib-eye steak, the no-fat steamed fish with ginger and shiitake mushrooms, and his Kapakahi mashed potatoes—the best. The entrees are served with salad and soup, which doubles the generosity and makes each meal more than most single diners can consume.

Moderate

Azteca. 3617 Waialae Ave. ☎ **808/735-2492.** Most items under $10. AE, MC, V. Mon–Tues 11am–9:30pm, Fri–Sat 11am–10pm, Sun 5–9:30pm. MEXICAN.

Recently reopened after a prolonged closure, Azteca is one-third its original size and still has customer loyalty going for it. Diners who frequented the old eatery with its memorably regrettable decor, blaring Mexican music, and frothy pitchers of margaritas are returning for the fresh cilantro-laden salsa, tasty huevos rancheros, and enchiladas, chimichangas, and homemade tamales that established it in the '80s as a Mexican staple.

Beau Soleil. 3184 Waialae Ave. ☎ **808/732-0967.** Reservations recommended. Prix fixe, $20–$27. AE, DC, DISC, MC, V. Mon–Thurs 6–9pm, Fri–Sat 6–10pm. CONTEMPORARY MEDITERRANEAN.

The ambiance scores high (cobalt vases on the table, painted pink exterior, window boxes, and innlike atmosphere), and the food, though not riveting, is pleasant and affordable. There are three nightly specials and no printed menu, but they make a sincere effort to please vegetarians and fish lovers as well as carnivores. Neighborhood diners come to this charmingly appointed restaurant for eggplant terrine or fresh swordfish with couscous pilaf.

Inexpensive

Ⓢ **Cafe Laufer.** 3565 Waialae Ave. ☎ **808/735-7717.** Most items under $7. AE, MC. V. Sun–Mon and Wed–Thurs 8am–10pm, Fri–Sat 8am–11pm. COFFEE SHOP.

Unlike many Honolulu coffee shops, which lean toward the bohemian, this small, airy, and cheerful cafe has frilly decor and sublime pastries, from apple scones and linzer tortes to fruit flans, decadent chocolate mousses, and carrot cakes to accompany the lattes and espresso. Lunch fans drop in for simple soups and deli sandwiches on fresh-baked breads, or biscotti for their coffee break, or a hearty loaf of seven-grain for breaking bread tomorrow. Don't miss the soufflés; they're the real thing.

Hale Vietnam. 1140 12th Ave. ☎ **808/735-7581.** Reservations recommended for groups. Main courses $4.50–$16. DISC, MC, V. Daily 11am–10pm. VIETNAMESE.

Duck into this house of pho and brave the no-frills service for the steaming noodle soups that are the house specialty. The stock is simmered and skimmed for many hours and is accompanied with noodles beef, chicken, and a platter of bean sprouts and fresh herbs. Test the green chilis before diving in; it's hard to know if they're the ones that can scorch and disable you. Although we love the chicken soup and shrimp vermicelli as well as the seafood pho and imperial rolls, caution is advised because this restaurant, like most other Vietnamese eateries, uses MSG.

Hee Hing Restaurant. 449 Kapahulu Ave. ☎ **808/735-5544** or 808/734-8474. Reservations required for parties of five or more. Main courses $5–$22. AE, DISC, MC, V. Mon–Thurs, Sun 10:30am–9:30pm, Fri–Sat 10:30am–10:30pm. CANTONESE.

Cavernous and noisy like most popular Chinese restaurants, Hee Hing is a local institution that draws multigeneration local families around large tables for retirement and anniversary parties. Lazy Susans rotate relentlessly with their weighty cargoes of drunken prawns, boneless crisp duck, crackling chicken, 15 types of rice soup, and fresh Dungeness crab in black-bean sauce. There are hundreds of choices here. Complete multicourse, family-style dinners can be prearranged affordably and generously. For lunch, Hee Hing's Hong Kong–style dim sum is a local legend. Best of all, Hee Hing's cookery is fine, tasty, and free of MSG.

Java Java Cafe. 760 Kapahulu Ave. ☎ **808/732-2670.** Most items under $6. No credit cards. Mon–Thurs 8am–midnight, Fri–Sat 8am–1am, Sun 10am–10pm. COFFEE HOUSE.

Quite the Kapahulu hangout, Java Java is the classic coffee house where students reading Nietzsche and aspiring playwrights mingle over coffee, drinks, salads, and sandwiches. The coffees outnumber all other items on the menu. Sandwiches (garden burgers, cumin chicken salad, tuna), bagels, Belgian waffles, salads (tuna/tomato, Greek, cumin/chicken), and fresh fruit smoothies appeal to diners from early morning to the wee hours. Italian cream sodas are a hit, and the milky Thai tea competes with the Zombie, mochaccino, iced chocolate mint latte, and dozens of specialty and iced coffees that are sipped by javanistas who seem oblivious to the uncomfortable chairs.

S Wahoo Kitchen. 3046A Monsarrat Ave. ☎ **808/732-5594.** Main courses $6.50–$11. No credit cards. Mon–Sat 11am–2pm, 5:30pm–9pm. JAPANESE/LOCAL.

Industrial chic is the mood here; you'll feel you're dining in a garage with style, particularly when you hit the rest room and find yourself standing on gravel. The shedlike atmosphere sets the tone for a charmingly oddball and affordable dining experience. The food, especially the seafood at these prices, is a bonus. A menu board announces the constantly changing specials: garlic ahi, Cajun swordfish, chicken katsu curry, ahi sukiyaki, seared ahi, ahi poke, and a parade of fresh fish and chicken dishes cooked in Japanese- or island-style. The combination dinner, a choice of two entrees with rice and all the accompaniments is the best value in town, at a stunning $11. The brisk take-out business may make this appear to be a glorified plate-lunch stand, but it's really a cult phenomenon, a totally hip restaurant with food and ambiance unique enough to impress a date. The Wahoo Kitchen does not sell alcoholic beverages, so bring your own.

EAST OF HONOLULU & WAIKIKI
KAHALA

Hoku's. In Kahala Mandarin Oriental Hotel, 5000 Kahala Ave. ☎ **808/739-8777.** Reservations recommended. Main courses $18–$65. AE, CB, DC, DISC, JCB, MC, V. Daily 11:30am–2pm and 5:30–10pm. PACIFIC/EUROPEAN.

The eagerly anticipated fine dining room of the revamped Kahala Hilton, now the Kahala Mandarin, has received mixed reviews in its so-far brief period of reclamation. Some diners claim it's overrated and suffers from an identity crisis; others exclaim that this is the finest cuisine they've encountered in years. Indisputable, however, is the beauty of the room, every table with an ocean view and the bamboo floor glistening underfoot. Booths and an open kitchen make this a more casual room than you may expect. Reflecting its cross-cultural influences, the kitchen is equipped with a *kiawe* grill, an Indian tandoori oven for its chicken and naan bread, and Szechuan woks for the prawn, lobster, tofu, and other stir-fried specialties. Is there an identity crisis here? We think so. You'll find everything from Scottish smoked salmon to kalua pig wontons to pizza and ahi spring rolls at lunch, and an expanded menu at dinner. The deep-fried whole fresh fish comes in a black-bean sauce with wok-fried vegetables, while the pepper-crusted rare tuna delights the senses with the piquancy of daikon radish and a ginger-sesame vinaigrette. Traditionalists can stick to the rack of lamb, roasted chicken (much too big a serving), and the grilled rib-eye steak with mashed potatoes and Maui onions.

S Olive Tree Cafe. 4614 Kilauea Ave., next to Kahala Mall. ☎ **808/737-0303.** Reservations not accepted. Main courses $5–$8. No credit cards. Mon–Fri 5–10pm, Sat 11am–11pm, Sun 11am–10pm. GREEK/MEDITERRANEAN.

The legions of Olive Tree fans are continually amazed at the delectables streaming out of the tiny open kitchen at bargain prices. With umbrellas over tables on the sidewalk, a few seats indoors, and the best Greek food in Hawaii, this informal cafe is one of the top values in town. The tabouli salad is generously greened with herbs and mint, perfectly balanced in flavor and texture. The falafel, hummous, and taramasalata—a pink caviar spread with pita—are a pleasurable launch to a meal that will only ascend. Lamb, boneless and skinless chicken, and fresh fish souvlakis (kebabs with a mint-cucumber-yogurt sauce) are consistently excellent, as is the spanakopita, perfectly crisped and buttered and layered with spinach and cheeses. Located next door to Kahala Mall (where you can buy your own libations), Olive Tree is BYOB, which means a large group can dine like sultans for a song.

⭐ **Kahala Moon Cafe.** 4614 Kilauea Ave. ☎ **808/732-7777.** Reservations recommended. Main courses $15–$24. AE, MC, V. Tues–Fri 11am–2pm and 5:30–9:30pm; Fri–Sat 5:30–10pm; Sun 5:30–9:30pm. HAWAII REGIONAL.

Stylish without being pretentious, with designer flowers in behemoth pots accenting the windowless room, Kahala Moon gets our vote as a top choice for lunch and one of the top values for a special-occasion dinner. It isn't cheap by any means, but many other restaurants of this ilk charge far more for far less culinary enjoyment. We love the sake-steamed clams and lemon-herb–crusted crab cakes. Add the whole-leaf Caesar salad, another favorite, and you have a light and satisfying meal. But wait! There's too much else to stop there. At dinner, the grilled lamb chops with caramelized onions, roasted potatoes, and sherry-coriander-lemon butter are among Honolulu's finest, and the sautéed salmon with wild mushroom stuffing is a salmon-lover's dream. Save room for the mango bread pudding or lemongrass crème brûlée, ambrosia to the final spoonful.

HAWAII KAI

⭐ **Roy's Restaurant.** 6600 Kalanianaole Hwy. ☎ **808/396-7697.** Reservations recommended. Main courses $9–$25. AE, JCB, MC, V. Daily 5:30–9:15pm. EUROPEAN/ASIAN.

He built in Hawaii Kai, and diners came—in droves. Roy Yamaguchi's flagship Hawaii restaurant was the first of what is now a chain of 10 throughout Hawaii and the Pacific. The formula—open kitchen, fresh ingredients, ethnic touches, and a good dose of nostalgia mingling with European techniques and traditions—is smashingly successful. The menu changes nightly, but you can generally count on individual pizzas; a varied appetizer menu (summer rolls, blackened ahi, hibachi-style salmon); a small pasta selection; and entrees such as lemongrass roasted chicken, garlic mustard short ribs, mustard-crusted lamb shanks, and several types of fresh catch prepared at least five different ways. The scallion seared opakapaka and the teppanyaki-style mahimahi are reliably good. Roy's is also renowned for its high-decibel–style of dining, so full and so noisy you'll have to join in the fracas to be heard. But the food quality, service, timing, and eclectic, well-priced wine list are impressive.

THE WINDWARD COAST

Assaggio Italian Restaurant. 354 Ulunui St., Kailua. ☎ **808/261-2772.** Reservations recommended. Main courses $8–$18. AE, DC, DISC, MC, V. Mon–Fri 11:30am–2:30pm, daily 5–10pm. ITALIAN.

You may not want to make the half-hour trip over the Pali for dinner here, but it's nice to know about Assaggio if you happen to visit the Windward Coast. Affordable prices, attentive service, and some winning items have won Assaggio loyal fans throughout the years. The best-selling homemade hot antipasto has jumbo shrimp, fresh clams, mussels, and calamari in a sauce of cayenne pepper, white wine, and garlic. You can choose linguine, fettucine, or ziti with 10 different sauces in small or regular portions, or any of nine chicken pastas (the chicken Assaggio, with garlic, peppers, and mushrooms, is especially flavorful). Especially impressive is the extensive list of seafood pastas in various combinations, including the plainly wonderful garlic/olive oil sauté. The homemade tiramisu and zabaglione are local legends worth every calorie.

There's another branch in Hawaii Kai at 7192 Kalanianaole Hwy. (☎ **808/ 396-0756**).

Brent's Restaurant & Delicatessen. 629-A Kailua Rd. ☎ **808/262-8588.** Most items under $15. MC, V. Tues–Sun 7am–9pm. KOSHER DELI.

Finally, a kosher deli with real cheese blintzes, cream cheese and shrimp omelets, and some spirited cultural digressions, such as pesto poached eggs and an artichoke-laced frittata. And bagels galore, with baked salmon, sturgeon-and-cream cheese, or any number of accompaniments to compete with the New York–style pastrami and hot corned-beef sandwiches on Brent's abundant menu.

Harry's Cafe. 629 Kailua Rd. ☎ **808/261-2120.** Main courses $7–$12.95. MC, V. Mon–Sat 11am–3pm and 5:30–9pm. MEDITERRANEAN.

Nostalgia reigns in Tim Owens's tribute to his father, the late Harry Owens, who composed more than 300 songs, among them the 1938 Oscar winner "Sweet Leilani," written for his daughter. The entrance to Harry's Cafe is lined with Harry Owens's music sheets and memorabilia, and the motif and mood of the place are what I call Hawaiian Deco. At lunch, the sandwiches and salads are a good bet: shrimp cobb, Greek salad, avocado-and-bacon sandwich, the broiled mushroom-cheese sandwich. For dinner, the St. Tropez is not to be missed—chopped artichoke hearts baked with cheese and served with bread and vegetables, a meal in itself for just $7.50. There are ample choices for vegetarians and light grazing; for more substantial pleasures, consider the shrimp angelica (sautéed in garlic butter with pasta, artichoke hearts, and capers), a steal for under $10, or the Shrimp Scorpio, poached in a light tomato sauce with Ouzo, cognac, and feta cheese.

San Francisco Sourdough Pizza. 407 Uluniu St. ☎ **808/263-3287.** Pizzas $10–19. CB, DC, DISC, MC, V. Mon–Thurs 11am–9pm, Fri–Sat 11am–10pm, Sun 4–9pm. PIZZA.

So this isn't the Bay Area, but there's a great sourdough here after all: the pizza crust at this Kailua hot spot of gumball machines, San Francisco posters, and pizzas with names like The Ghirardelli, The Tourist Special, and the 49er. The Specialty Chicken has a smoky barbecue sauce and five different cheeses; the Jason's Special is for garlic lovers, a potent pie of sourdough, garlic, onions, and fresh tomatoes. Television sets, live music, and specials with real-life associations ("Seinfeld" on Thursday nights, for example) make this a cordial, spirited atmosphere in which to enjoy theme pizza and beer.

Solana. 30 Aulike St. ☎ **808/263-1227.** Reservations required. Main courses $12–$20. AE, MC, V. Mon–Fri 7am–1pm, Sun–Thurs 5:30–9:30pm, Fri–Sat 5:30–10:30pm. MEDITERRANEAN.

Kailua's newest destination offers an impressive sampling of Mediterranean fare and the cuisines of sunny climates: salmon in grape leaves and Chianti sauce; polenta with ratatouille; grilled lamb chops marinated in tomato, oregano, and Chianti sauce; osso bucco on couscous; no-nonsense crab cakes; and a host of seafood and meat selections in zesty tapenades, pestos, and sauces of peppers and pignolas. In this bastion of Hawaii Regional Cuisine, a restaurant like Solana, with its lusty, intense flavors and bustling creativity, is most welcome. The instant popularity of this newcomer, however, has spawned some complaints of rude service; we hope the raves don't go to Solana's head.

THE NORTH SHORE

⑤ **Ahi's Restaurant.** Old Mill Rd., Kahuku. ☎ **808/293-5650.** Reservations not accepted. Main courses $8.25–$11.25. No credit cards. Tues–Sat 11am–9pm. SEAFOOD/ISLAND.

The bad news is that Ahi's—a 1950s Army barracks with concrete floors, an old jukebox, tables indoors and outdoors, coconuts dangling in the yard, and the nicest folks you'll ever find in a North Shore restaurant—burned down recently. The good news is that they plan to reopen as soon as a new location can be found. If chef Byron Logan went free-diving that day, you could expect some great fresh catch, and if you were lucky, brother Bulla would be running the store. Owner Ahi Logan, a respected leader in the Hawaiian community, also served up some sautéed chicken that was so tender some folks mistook it for opakapaka. The fresh aquacultured clams from a neighboring farm, fed on microalgae, were the sweetest, most succulent clams to hit the palate, prepared sautéed or steamed. The shrimp sampler was another winner, prepared four ways, each one better than the next. Ahi's was a long drive from Honolulu, but townies made a special trip, and will continue to do so when this North Shore favorite reopens. Call to see if Ahi's is back in business by the time you're on Oahu.

⑤ Cafe Haleiwa. 66-460 Kamehameha Hwy., Haleiwa. ☎ **808/637-5516.** Reservations not accepted. Main courses $5.50–$10.50. AE, MC, V. Mon–Sat 7am–3pm, Sun 7am–2pm. MEXICAN/LOCAL.

Haleiwa's legendary breakfast joint is a big hit with surfers, urban gentry with weekend country homes, reclusive artists, and anyone who loves mahimahi plate lunches and homemade Mexican food. It's one of those wake-up-and-hit-the-beach kind of places serving generous burritos and omelets with names like Off the Wall, Off the Lip, and Breakfast in a Barrel. Surf pictures line the walls, and the ambiance is Formica-style casual. You can order a mahimahi plate lunch with home fries, rice, or beans. Spicy chicken tacos; fish tacos with grilled mahi, tomatoes, lime, and cilantro; and burritos, tostadas, and combination plates will make it hard for you to stick to a veggie or chicken sandwich. But they serve those too—tuna salad, mahimahi, burgers, steak sandwiches—made with individual attention and grilled onions on request. Our favorite breakfast is the truly epic huevos rancheros, smothered with cheese and salsa.

Coffee Gallery. In North Shore Marketplace, 66-250 Kamehameha Hwy., Haleiwa. ☎ **808/ 637-5355.** Reservations not accepted. Most items under $6. AE, DISC, MC, V. Mon–Fri 6am– 9pm, Sat–Sun 7am–9pm. COFFEE HOUSE/VEGETARIAN.

On the other side of town from Kua Aina (see below) and its meat-lover's cuisine, this indoor-outdoor coffee house has carved a firm niche in the hearts of Haleiwa's health-conscious diners, vegetarians, and coffee lovers. The lemon squares here are famous (its recipe was printed, by popular request, in the local newspaper), and the granola is made with premium Big Island honey. There are tofu burritos with fresh spinach and roasted garlic tomato sauce, bagels galore, salads and pastas, and a spicy three-bean vegetarian chili served with renetless cheddar cheese. The vegan soup is served with fresh baked whole-wheat French bread. Spinach pesto, vegetarian enchiladas, tempeh and garden burgers, hummous platters, and many pages of healthy enticements make this one of Haleiwa's heavenly stops, as inexpensive as it is thoughtful.

Jameson's by the Sea. 62-540 Kamehameha Hwy., Haleiwa. ☎ **808/637-4336.** Reservations recommended. Main courses $13–$39 in upstairs dining room; downstairs lunch menu $7–$12. AE, DC, DISC, JCB, MC, V. Downstairs, daily 11am–5pm; pub menu Mon–Tues 5–9pm, Sat–Sun 11am–9pm. Upstairs, Wed–Sun 5–9pm. SEAFOOD.

The roadside watering hole across the street from the ocean is a place to duck in for cocktails, sashimi, and salmon pâté, or for other hot and cold appetizers, salads, and sandwiches throughout the day. Jameson's vegetarian and curried chicken salads are also recommended. Eternally popular are the grilled crab and shrimp sandwich (pardon the mayonnaise) on sourdough bread, as well as the fresh fish sandwich of the day, grilled plain and simple. Upstairs, the dining room opens its doors 5 nights a week for the usual surf-and-turf choices: fresh opakapaka, ulua (Hawaiian jack fish), and mahimahi; scallops in lemon butter and capers; and lobster tail, New York steak, and filet mignon. Jameson's and the nearby Chart House (see "Chain Restaurants," above) are similarly cast as North Shore standbys that have stuck to their generic formulas, without apology, for years.

🟢 **Kua Aina.** 66-214 Kamehameha Hwy., Haleiwa. ☎ **808/637-6067.** Most items under $6. No credit cards. Daily 11am–8pm. AMERICAN.

Because there's always a line outside this famous sandwich shop and never enough tables inside or on the porch, many diners pick up their burgers and head for the beach. Kua Aina's thin and spindly french fries are renowned islandwide and are the perfect accompaniment to its legendary burgers. Fat, moist, and homemade, the burgers can be ordered with avocado, bacon, and many other accompaniments in addition to its tower of sprouts and greens. Also highly recommended are the roast beef and mahimahi sandwiches, tried-and-true and totally satisfying.

North Shore Pizza Company. In North Shore Marketplace, 66-250 Kamehameha Hwy., Haleiwa. ☎ **808/637-2782.** Main courses and pizzas $6–$20. AE, MC, V. Mon–Fri 4–9pm, Fri 4–10pm, Sat–Sun 11am–10pm. PIZZA.

The same folks who opened trendy Portofino and who introduced Zorro's Pizza to Hawaii also make and deliver (free) the pizzas, calzones, focaccia sandwiches, and pastas from a small but dynamic menu fashioned by chefs from Milan and Florence. The 16-inch New York–style pizzas are named after North Shore surf spots and are topped with fresh island produce such as Maui onions, North Shore basil, Portuguese sausage, and, for pizza heretics, Hawaiian pineapple. The Kaena Point, with barbecue chicken, Maui onions, fresh tomatoes, and cilantro, is a nontraditional good bet. Healthy eaters will notice the Healthy Italian, a calzone with grilled zucchini, eggplant, peppers, mushrooms, onions, and marinara sauce. A mouthful to be sure, but it's the real thing. A small pasta selection with Mediterranean touches is a bonus.

Paradise Found Cafe. 66-443 Kamehameha Hwy., Haleiwa. ☎ **808/637-4540.** Most items under $5. No credit cards. Mon–Sat 9am–6pm, Sun 10am–6pm. VEGETARIAN.

We love Haleiwa for its vegetarian choices, and this is one of them. A tiny cafe behind the Celestial Natural foods, Paradise Found takes looking for, but it's a totally charming way to begin a North Shore sojourn. You can buy a bowl of vegetarian chili and rice for $3, and for a dollar more, a hummous dip with pita and cucumber. It's as good as the baba ganouj, the veggie burgers (with cheese and avocado, a winner), and any of the fresh fruit smoothies that have fueled many a beach-lover's day. The mix of Mexican favorites (quesadilla with chili and avocado) and Middle-Eastern samplings is a solid success at this tiny corner of the health food store, barely more than a take-out counter.

Portofino. In North Shore Marketplace, 66-250 Kamehameha Hwy., Haleiwa. ☎ **808/637-7678.** Reservations recommended. Main courses $6.25–$13. AE, MC, V. Sun–Thurs 11am–10pm, Fri–Sat 11am–11pm. NORTHERN ITALIAN.

The North Shore's newest and most attractive restaurant has terra-cotta tile floors, columns and arches, and hand-painted murals that bring a splendid scene of Portofino into the airy room. Although the decibel level can get high, it's a cordial environment in which to enjoy the aromas and creations emanating from the wood-burning oven and open kitchen. Chefs from Italy have devised a menu of homemade pastas, focaccia, calzones, sandwiches, and 9-inch pizzas, as well as everyday comforts such as rosemary chicken and a classic meatloaf served with roasted-garlic mashed potatoes. So far, the execution has fallen short of expectations, but North Shore diners are hoping they're just temporary growing pains.

Impressions

If anyone desires such old-fashioned things as lovely scenery, quiet, pure air, clear seawater, good food, and heavenly sunsets hung out before his eyes over the Pacific and the distant hills of Waianae, I recommend him cordially to the Sans Souci.
> —Robert Louis Stevenson (1889)

5 Beaches

by Rick Carroll, with Jeanette Foster

With 50 miles of sandy beaches, Oahu is Hawaii's premier beach playground.

BEACHES ALONG THE WAIKIKI COAST
ALA MOANA BEACH PARK

Quite possibly America's best urban beach, gold sand Ala Moana ("by the sea") stretches for more than a mile along Honolulu's coast between downtown and Waikiki on sunny Mamala Bay. This 76-acre midtown beach park, with spreading lawns shaded by banyans and palms, is one of the island's most popular playgrounds. It has a man-made beach, created in the 1930s by filling a coral reef with Waianae coast sand. It has its own lagoon, yacht harbor, tennis courts, music pavilion, bathhouses, and picnic tables, and enough wide-open green spaces to accommodate its 4 million visitors a year. The water's calm almost year-round, protected by black lava rocks set offshore. There's a large parking lot as well as metered street parking.

WAIKIKI BEACH

No beach anywhere is so widely known or so universally sought after than this narrow, 1 1/2-mile-long crescent of imported sand (from Molokai) at the foot of a string of high-rise hotels. Home to the world's longest-running beach party, Waikiki attracts nearly 5 million visitors a year from every corner of the planet. First-timers are always amazed to discover how small Waikiki Beach actually is, but there's always a place for them under the tropical sun here.

Waikiki is actually a string of beaches that extends between Sans Souci State Recreational Area near Diamond Head to the east, and Duke Kahanamoku Beach, in front of the Hilton Hawaiian Village, to the west. Kuhio Beach, next to the Sheraton Moana Surfrider, is one of my favorites, because it's the first unobstructed view of the beach and Malama Bay you get from Kalakaua Avenue, Waikiki's main drag. It's also the quickest way to actually get on the beach: You can search for the beach access alleyways (they're squeezed between the main hotels), but Kuhio offers direct and easy access. Other top spots include the stretch in front of the Royal Hawaiian Hotel, which is canted so it catches the rays perfectly; and Sans Souci, the small, popular beach in front of the New Otani Kaimana Beach Hotel that's locally known as "Dig Me" Beach because of all the gorgeous bods who strut their stuff here.

Waikiki is fabulous for swimming, board and bodysurfing, outrigger canoeing, diving, sailing, snorkeling, and pole fishing. Every imaginable type of marine equipment is available for rent nearby. The best place to park is at Kapiolani Park, near Sans Souci. Facilities include showers, lifeguards, rest rooms, grills, picnic tables, and pavilions at the Queen's Surf end of the beach (at Kapiolani Park, between the zoo and the aquarium).

⭐ Frommer's Favorite Oahu Experiences

Snorkeling Hanauma Bay. I know, it's too crowded—but for clear, warm water and an abundance of fish that are so friendly they'll eat out of your hand, there's no place like Hanauma Bay. The best thing about this underwater park is that anyone can join the fun: Just wade in and look down to see the kaleidoscope of fish that call Hawaii's waters home. Go early to avoid the crush.

Climbing Diamond Head. The hike to the summit of this 760-foot-high volcanic crater takes about 45 minutes, but the reward is a breathtaking 360° view—with Waikiki, Honolulu, and the Pacific Ocean at your feet. This one's for everyone, especially kids.

Watching the North Shore Waves. Humongus. Totally awesome. No other words describe the monster winter waves of Oahu's north shore. You've seen it on TV, in the opening shot of *Hawaii Five-0*: blue-green water in a perfect tube. But see it in person for full effect: It snarls out of the Pacific like a tsunami and roars like a 50-foot-high freight train before smashing almost at your feet in foam. The surfers who take them on will keep you spellbound for hours.

Exploring Oahu's Rain Forests. In the misty sun beams, colorful birds flit among giant ferns and hanging vines, and towering tropical trees form a thick canopy that shelters all below in cool shadows. This emerald world is a true Eden. For the full experience, try Manoa Falls Trail, a walk of about a mile that ends at a freshwater pool and waterfall.

Wearing an Aloha Shirt. Aloha shirts are one of the best things about tropical Honolulu. They're light, colorful, and fun. You don't have to button them or tuck them in. Some think only tourists wear them; it's not true. In Honolulu, the aloha-shirt capital of the world, men wear bright floral-print shirts to work every day. Invitations to many of Honolulu's exclusive social engagements specify "aloha attire." Funeral notices in Honolulu even suggest aloha attire for those who attend, as well as the recently departed.

Drinks and Dinner at the Halekulani. Put on your linen and silk, pin a flower in your hair, and *hele on* (that's Hawaiian for go) to this classic resort for an evening you won't forget. Arrive before sunset so you get the full effect of Waikiki's smashing version of day's end: a changing palette of oranges, yellows, pinks, and deep red reflecting off Diamond Head and across the calm sea of evening. Sip a Mai Tai on the outdoor terrace as soft Hawaiian music plays and a woman dances a graceful hula, then move on to dinner at Orchids or La Mer, the Halekulani's two fabulous restaurants. Be sure to ask for an oceanfront table when you reserve.

✪ HANAUMA BAY

Oahu's most popular snorkeling spot is this volcanic crater with a broken sea wall; its small, curved, 2,000-foot gold-sand beach is packed elbow-to-elbow with people year-round. The bay's shallow shoreline water and abundant marine life are the main attractions, but this good-looking beach is also popular for sunbathing and people watching.

Serious divers shoot "the slot" (a passage through the reef) to gain Witch's Brew, a turbulent cove, then brave strong currents in 70-foot depths at the bay mouth to see coral gardens, turtles, and—that's right—sharks. (Divers: Beware the Molokai Express, a strong current that can put you in Kaunakaki, li'dat!) Snorkelers hug the

Beaches & Outdoor Activities on Oahu

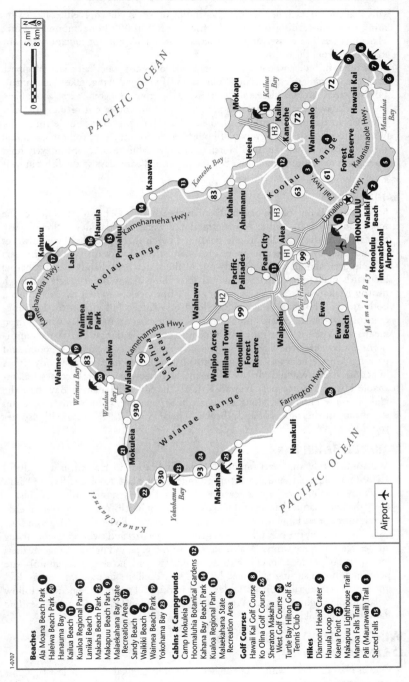

N
5 mi
8 km

PACIFIC OCEAN

Mokapu
Kailua Bay
Kaneohe Bay
Mamalua Bay
Koolau Range
Forest Reserve
Kalanianaole Hwy.
Hawaii Kai
Waimanalo
Kaneohe
Kailua
Heeia
Kahaluu
Ahuimanu
Aiea
HONOLULU
Honolulu International Airport
Waikiki Beach
Mamala Bay
Pearl Harbor
Pearl City
Waipahu
Ewa
Ewa Beach
Pacific Palisades
Wahiawa
Waipio Acres
Mililani Town
Honouliuli Forest Reserve
Lunalilo Frwy.
Pali Hwy.
Kaaawa
Hauula
Laie
Kahuku
Kamehameha Hwy.
Koolau Punaluu Range
Waimea Falls Park
Waialua
Haleiwa
Waimea
Waimea Bay
Waialua Bay
Mokuleia
Kaena Channel
Yokohama Bay
Makaha
Waianae
Nanakuli
Waianae Range
Lehileau Plateau
Farrington Hwy.
PACIFIC OCEAN

Airport ✈

Beaches
Ala Moana Beach Park **1**
Haleiwa Beach Park **20**
Hanauma Bay **6**
Kailua Beach **11**
Kualoa Regional Park **13**
Lanikai Beach **10**
Makaha Beach Park **25**
Makapuu Beach Park **9**
Malaekahana Bay State Recreation Area **17**
Sandy Beach **7**
Waikiki Beach **2**
Waimea Beach Park **19**
Yokohama Bay **23**

Cabins & Campgrounds
Camp Mokuleia **21**
Hoomaluhia Botanical Gardens **12**
Kahana Bay Beach Park **14**
Kualoa Regional Park **13**
Malaekahana State Recreation Area **18**

Golf Courses
Hawaii Kai Golf Course **8**
Ko Olina Golf Course **26**
Sheraton Makaha West Golf Course **24**
Turtle Bay Hilton Golf & Tennis Club **18**

Hikes
Diamond Head Crater **5**
Hauula Loop **16**
Kaena Point **22**
Makapuu Lighthouse Trail **9**
Manoa Falls Trail **4**
Pali (Maunawili) Trail **3**
Sacred Falls **15**

1-0707

safe, shallow (10 ft.) inner bay that, depending on when you go, is either like swimming in a fish-feeding frenzy or bathing with 300,000 honeymooners. Since Hanauma Bay is a conservation district, you may look but not touch or take any marine life from the ocean here.

Facilities include parking, rest rooms, a pavilion, grass volleyball court, lifeguard, barbecue, picnic tables, and food concession. If you're driving, take Kalanianaole Highway to Koko Head Regional Park. Avoid the crowds by going early, about 8am, on a weekday morning; once the parking lot's full, you're out of luck. Or take TheBUS to escape the parking problem: The Hanauma Bay Shuttle runs from Waikiki to Hanauma Bay every half-hour from 8:45am to 1pm; you can catch it at the Ala Moana Hotel, the Ilikai Hotel, or at any city bus stop. It returns every hour from noon to 4:30pm. Hanauma Bay is closed on Wednesdays so the fish can have a day off.

SANDY BEACH

Sandy Beach is one of the best bodysurfing beaches on Oahu; it's also one of the most dangerous. It's better to just stand and watch the daredevils literally risk their necks at this 1,200-foot-long gold sand beach that's pounded by wild waves and haunted by a dangerous shore break and strong backwash. Weak swimmers and children should definitely stay out of the water here. Sandy Beach's heroic lifeguards make more rescues in a year than those at any other beach (although nearby Makapuu is almost as chancy). Visitors, easily fooled by experienced bodysurfers who make wave-riding look easy, often fall victim to the bone-crunching waves. Lifeguards post flags to alert beachgoers to the day's surf: Green means safe, yellow caution, and red indicates very dangerous water conditions; always check the flags before you dive in. Facilities include rest rooms and parking. Go weekdays to avoid the crowds, weekends to catch the bodysurfers in action. From Waikiki, drive east on the H-1 freeway, which becomes Kalanianaole Hwy.; proceed past Hawaii Kai, up the hill to Hanauma Bay, past the Halona Blow Hole, and along the coast. The next big, gold, sandy beach you see ahead on the right is Sandy Beach. TheBUS no. 22 (Kuhio) will also get you there.

MAKAPUU BEACH PARK

Makapuu Beach, the most famous bodysurfing beach in Hawaii, is a beautiful 1,000-foot-long gold-sand beach cupped in the stark black Koolau cliffs on Oahu's easternmost point. Even if you never venture into the water, it's worth a visit just to enjoy the great natural beauty of this classic Hawaiian beach. You've probably already seen it in countless Hollywood TV shows, from "Hawaii Five-O" to "Magnum P.I."

In the summer, the ocean here is as gentle as a Jacuzzi and swimming and diving are perfect, but come winter, Makapuu is hit with big, pounding waves that are ideal for expert bodysurfers. Small boards—3 feet or less with no skeg (bottom fin)—are permitted; board surfing is banned by state law. Facilities include rest rooms, lifeguard, barbecue grills, picnic tables, and parking. To get to Makapuu, follow Kalanianaole Highway toward Waimanalo, or take TheBUS no. 57 or 58 (Sea Life Park) from Waikiki.

WINDWARD COAST BEACHES
✪ LANIKAI BEACH

One of Hawaii's best swimming beaches, gold sand Lanikai's crystal-clear lagoon is like a giant saltwater swimming pool that you're lucky enough to be able to share with the resident tropical fish and sea turtles. Too gorgeous to be real, this is one of

Hawaii's postcard-perfect beaches: It's a mile-long and thin in places, due to misplaced residential sea walls, but the sand's as soft as talcum powder. Prevailing onshore trade winds make this an excellent beach for sailing and windsurfing. Kayakers often paddle out to the two tiny offshore Mokulua islands, which are seabird sanctuaries.

Because Lanikai is in a residential neighborhood, it's less crowded than other Oahu beaches; it's the perfect place to enjoy a quiet day at the beach. Sun worshippers should arrive in the morning, though, as the Koolau Range blocks the afternoon rays. There are no facilities, just off-street parking. From Waikiki, take the H-1 to the Pali Highway (Hi. 61) through the Nuuanu Pali Tunnel to Kailua, where the Pali Highway becomes Kailua Road as it proceeds through town. At Kalaheo Avenue, turn right and follow the coast about 2 miles to Kailua Beach Park; just past it, turn left at a T intersection and drive uphill on Aalapapa Drive, a one-way street that loops back as Mokulua Drive. Park on Mokulua Drive and walk down any of the eight public access lanes to the shore. Or take TheBUS no. 56 or 57 (Kailua), then transfer to the shuttle bus.

KAILUA BEACH

Windward Oahu's premier beach is a 2-mile-long, wide golden strand with dunes, palm trees, panoramic views, and offshore islets. The swimming is excellent, and the azure waters are usually decorated with bright sails; this is Oahu's premier windsurfing beach. It's also a favorite spot to sail catamarans, bodysurf the gentle waves, or paddle a kayak. Water conditions are quite safe, especially at the mouth of Kaelepulu Stream, where toddlers play in the freshwater shallows at the middle of the beach park. The tiny offshore islands of Moku Manu, Popoia, and Mokolea are home to seabirds. The water's usually about 78°F, the views are spectacular, and the setting, at the foot of the sheer, green Koolaus, is idyllic. Best of all, the crowds haven't found it yet.

The 35-acre beach park is intersected by a freshwater stream, and watched over by lifeguards. Facilities include picnic tables, barbecue facilities, rest rooms, a volleyball court, a public boat ramp, and free parking; Buzz's, an open-air beachside cafe, is also at hand. Kailua's new bike path weaves through the park, and windsurf and kayak rentals are available. To get here, take Pali Highway (Hi. 61) to Kailua, drive through town, turn right on Kalaheo Avenue, and go a mile until you see the beach on your left. Or take TheBUS no. 56 or 57 (Kailua) into Kailua, then take the no. 70 shuttle.

KUALOA REGIONAL PARK

One of Hawaii's most scenic beach parks is this 150-acre coco palm–fringed peninsula on Kaneohe Bay's north shore, at the foot of the spiky Koolau Ridge. The biggest beach park on the windward side, it has a broad, grassy lawn and a long, narrow white-sand beach ideal for swimming, walking, beachcombing, kite flying, or just enjoying the natural beauty of this once-sacred Hawaiian shore, listed on the National Register of Historical Places. The waters are shallow and safe for swimming year-round. Offshore is Mokolii, the picturesque islet otherwise known as Chinaman's Hat. At low tide, you can swim or wade out to the island, which has a small sandy beach and is a bird preserve—so don't spook the red-footed boobies. Lifeguards are on duty. The park is located on Kamehameha Highway (Hi. 83) in Kualoa; TheBUS no. 55 (Circle Island) will get you there.

THE NORTH SHORE
MALAEKAHANA BAY STATE RECREATION AREA

This almost mile-long white-sand crescent lives up to just about everyone's image of the perfect Hawaii beach. It's excellent for swimming. On any weekday, you may be the only one here; but should some net fisherman—or kindred soul—intrude upon your delicious privacy, you can swim out to Goat Island (or wade across at low tide) and play Robinson Crusoe. (The islet is a sanctuary for seabirds and turtles, so no chase 'em, brah.) Facilities include rest rooms, barbecue grills, picnic tables, outdoor showers, and parking. To get there, take Kamehameha Highway (Hi. 83) 2 miles north of the Polynesian Cultural Center; as you enter the main gate, you'll come upon the wooded beach park.

WAIMEA BEACH PARK

This deep, sandy bowl has gentle summer waves that are excellent for swimming, snorkeling, and bodysurfing. To one side of the bay is a huge rock that local kids like to climb up and dive off. In this placid scene, the only clue of what's to come in winter are those evacuation whistles on poles beside the road. But what a difference a season makes: Winter waves pound the narrow bay, sometimes rising 50 feet high. When the surf's really up, very strong currents and shore breaks sweep the bay—and it seems like everyone on Oahu drives out to Waimea to get a look at the monster waves and those who ride them. Go on weekdays when this popular beach is less crowded; on the other hand, the weekends are great if you're looking for the surf crowd. Facilities include lifeguards, rest rooms, showers, parking, and nearby restaurants and shops in Haleiwa town. The beach is located on Kahemameha Highway (Hi. 83); from Waikiki, you can take TheBUS no. 52 (Circle Island).

LEEWARD OAHU/THE WAIANAE COAST
MAKAHA BEACH PARK

When surf's up here, it's spectacular: Monstrous waves pound the beach. This is the original home of Hawaii's big-wave surfing championship; surfers today know it as the home of Buffalo's Big Board Surf Classic, where surfers ride the waves on 10-foot long wooden boards, in the old Hawaiian style of surfing. Nearly a mile-long, this half-moon gold-sand beach is tucked between Lahilahi Point, a 231-foot rock locals call Black Rock, and Kepuhi Point, a toe of the Waianae mountain range. Summer is the best time to hit this beach; the waves are small, the sand abundant, and the water safe for swimming. Children hug the shore on the north side of the beach, near the lifeguard stand, while surfers dodge the rocks and divers seek an offshore channel full of big fish. A caveat: This is a "local" beach; you are welcome, of course, but you can expect "stink eye" (mild approbation) if you misbehave and act too *haole*—if you know what I mean. Facilities include rest rooms, lifeguard, and parking. To get here, you can take TheBUS no. 51 (Makaha).

YOKOHAMA BAY

Where Farrington Highway (Hi. 93) ends, the wilderness of Kaena Point State Park begins. It's a remote 853-acre coastline park of empty beaches, sand dunes, cliffs, and deep blue water. This is the last sandy stretch of shore on the northwest coast of Oahu. Some call it Keawalua Beach or Puau Beach, but everybody here calls it Yokohama, after the Japanese immigrants who came from that port city to work the cane fields, and fished along this shoreline. When the surf's calm—mainly in summer—this is a good area for snorkeling, diving, swimming, shore fishing, and picnicking. When surf's up, board and bodysurfers are out in droves; don't go in the water then unless you're an expert. There are no lifeguards or facilities, except at the park entrance, where there's a rest room and lifeguard stand.

6 Hitting the Water

by Rick Carroll, with Jeanette Foster

BODY BOARDING (BOOGIE BOARDING) & BODYSURFING

An excellent beach to learn bodysurfing is Kailua, while the best for experts are Makapuu and Sandy beaches. You can rent boogie boards for as little at $13 a day from **Surf & Sea,** 62-595 Kamehameha Hwy., Haleiwa (☎ **808/637-9887**), **Aloha Beach Service,** Sheraton Moana Surfrider Hotel, 2365 Kalakaua Ave., Waikiki (☎ **808/922-3111**), and at all **Local Motion** locations: 1714 Kapiolani Blvd., Honolulu (☎ **808/955-7873**), Koko Marina Shopping Center (☎ **808/396-7873**), Windward Mall, Kaneohe (☎ **808/263-7873**) and Pearl Kai Center, Aiea (☎ **808/486-7873**). These outfitters will rent you the fins you need as well.

DEEP-SEA FISHING

Kewalo Basin, located between the Honolulu International Airport and Waikiki, is the main location for charter fishing boats on Oahu. Top sportfishing boats from Kewalo Basin include the *Brooke Kay* (☎ **808/396-8257**), the *Fish Hawk* (☎ **808/596-8338**), **Kono Fishing Charters** (☎ **808/536-7472**) and *Mary I* Sportfishing (☎ **808/596-2998**). From Waikiki, take Kalakaua *ewa* (west) beyond Ala Moana Shopping Center; Kewalo Basin is on the left, across from Ward Centre. Look for charter boats all in a row in their slips; on lucky days, the captains display the catch of the day in the afternoon. You can also take TheBUS no. 19 or 20 (Airport).

OCEAN KAYAKING

A wonderful adventure is to rent a kayak, arrive at Lanikai Beach just as the sun is appearing, and paddle across the emerald lagoon to the pyramid-shaped islands off the beach called Mokulua—it's an experience you won't forget. First-timers also should go to **Waimea Falls Park,** 59-864 Kamehameha Hwy. (☎ **808/638-8511**), on the North Shore, for kayak lessons and equipment, at a cost of $15 per person. The kayaking takes place along the Waimea River and paddles out to the golden sands of Waimea Bay, where you can rest or swim.

Kayak equipment rental starts at $10 an hour or $37 for a day; try **Prime Time Sports,** Fort DeRussy Beach, Waikiki (☎ **808/949-8952**); or in Kailua, **Karel Tresnak,** 789 Kailua Rd., Kailua (☎ **808/261-8424**).

SAILING

From a 2-hour sunset sail to a day-long adventure on the waves, Oahu offers a variety of sailing activities, including sailing lessons—picture yourself at the helm! **Honolulu Sailing Co.,** 47-335 Lulani, Kaneohe (☎ **808/239-3900**), has been in the business for nearly 2 decades, providing everything from weddings at sea to honeymoon cruises, sailing/snorkeling sails, private lessons, and exclusive charters. The fleet ranges from 36- to 70-foot yachts. Charters start at $50 per person and lessons start at $125 per person per day.

SEA CRUISES

A funny thing happens to people when they come to Hawaii: Maybe it's the salt air, the warm tropical nights, or the blue Hawaiian moonlight, but otherwise rational people who have never set foot on a boat in their life suddenly want to go out to sea. You can go to sea on a "booze cruise" with a thousand loud, rum-soaked strangers, or you can sail on one of three special yachts: one for landlubbers and two for more experienced sailors.

NAVATEK I

You've never been on a boat, you don't want to be on a boat, you are being dragged aboard a boat to see the sunset you can see perfectly well from your hotel lanai. Why are you boarding this weird-looking boat? It guarantees that you'll be "seasick-free," that's why. The 140-foot long *Navatek I* isn't even called a boat; it's actually a SWATH (Small Waterplane Area Twin Hull) vessel. That means the ship's superstructure—the part you ride on—rests on twin torpedolike hulls that cut through the water so you don't bob like a cork and spill your Mai Tai. It's the smoothest ride on Mamala Bay. Dinner cruises leave Pier 6 (across from the Hawaii Maritime Museum) 7 nights a week at 5:30pm, and last until 8pm; they're $155 for adults, $115 for kids 12 and under. Lunch cruises are offered daily from noon to 2pm at $45 for adults, $26.50 for kids. Call **Hawaiian Cruises Ltd.** (☎ **808/848-6360** or 800/852-4183) to reserve.

LEAHI

You're a sailor and you want the real thing. Come fly aboard the *Leahi,* the green-sailed, aluminum-hulled 45-foot racing catamaran skippered by George Howland Parsons III, an ex–Pearl Harbor submariner and great-grandson of a New Bedford whaler who called on Lahaina in the late 1700s. Parsons's sleek 48-passenger catamaran is the best choice for authentic experience and price. One-hour sightseeing tours sail five times daily; it's $12 for adults, $6 for kids 7 to 14; those under 6 ride free. The sunset sail is $22 adults, including open bar; $16 for no-alcohol passengers; $12 for children. You board the *Leahi* on the beach in front of the Sheraton Waikiki; call **808/922-5665** to reserve.

CAPTAIN BOB'S ADVENTURE CRUISES

See the majestic Windward Coast the way it should be seen—from a boat. Captain Bob will take you on a 4-hour, lazy-day sail of Kaneohe Bay aboard his 42-foot catamaran, which skims across the almost-always calm water above the shallow coral reef, lands at Ahu o Laka, a disappearing sandbar, and takes you past two small islands and to snorkel spots full of tropical fish and, sometimes, turtles. The color of the water alone is worth the price. It's $69 for adults, $59 kids 13 to 17, $49 for those 12 and under. A shuttle will pick you up at your Waikiki hotel at 9:30am and return you there at about 4pm. Call **Captain Bob's Adventure Cruises** at **808/942-5077.**

SCUBA DIVING

Oahu is a wonderful place to scuba dive, especially for those interested in wreck diving. One of the more famous wrecks in Hawaii is the *Mahi,* a 185-foot former mine sweeper easily accessible just south of Waianae. Abundant marine life makes this a great place to shoot photos—schools of lemon butterfly fish and taape are so comfortable with divers and photographers that they practically pose. Eagle rays, green sea turtles, manta rays, and white-tipped sharks occasionally cruise by, and eels peer from the wreck.

For non–wreck-diving, one of the best dive spots in the summer is Kahuna Canyon. In Hawaiian, Kahuna translates as priest, wise man, or sorcerer; this massive amphitheater, located near Mokuleia, is a perfect example of something a sorcerer might conjure up: Walls rising from the ocean floor create the illusion of an underwater Grand Canyon. Inside the amphitheater, crabs, octopi, slippers, and spiny lobsters abound (be aware that taking them in the summer is illegal), and giant trevally, parrot fish, and unicorn fish congregate. Outside the amphitheater, an occasional shark can be seen in the distance.

Oahu's best dives on Oahu are offshore, so book a two-tank dive from a dive boat. **Atlantis Reef Divers,** 1085 Ala Moana Blvd. (☎ **808/973-1310**) offers two-tank dive trips starting at $74. Free hotel pickup is available in the Waikiki area; Atlantis also will videotape your dive. On the other side of the island, try **Ocean Concepts Scuba,** 94-547 Ukee St., Waipahu (☎ **808/677-7975**); they'll take you diving in local lava caves, volcanic ledges, and the Mahi wreck. Prices range from $45 to $220, depending on the number of dives you do.

Hawaii's oldest and largest dive shop is **Aaron's Dive Shop,** 602 Kailua Rd., Kailua (☎ **808/262-2333**). Aaron's offers boat and beach dive excursions off the coast of Oahu. The boat dive is $90 per person; it includes two tanks and all gear and transportation from the Kailua shop or their Pearl City location. The beach dive off the North Shore in summer and Waianae Coast in winter is $60 per person, including all gear and transportation.

SNORKELING

Some of the best snorkeling in Oahu is at the underwater park at Hanauma Bay. It's crowded and sometimes it seems there are more people than fish, but Hanauma has clear, warm, protected waters and an abundance of friendly reef fish—including Moorish idols, scores of butterfly fish, damsel fish, and wrasses—and it's easy to get there. Hanauma Bay has two reefs, an inner and an outer—the first for novices, the other for experts. The inner reef is calm and shallow (less than 10 ft.); in some places you can just wade and put your face in the water. Go early; it's packed by 10am. For details on getting there, see "Beaches," above.

The braver snorkelers among us may want to head to Shark's Cove, on the North Shore just off Kamehameha Highway, between Haleiwa and Pupukea. Sounds risky, I know, but I've never seen nor heard of any sharks in this cove, and in summer this big, lava-edged pool is one of Oahu's best snorkel spots. Waves splash over the natural lava grotto and cascade like waterfalls into the pool full of tropical fish. There are deep-sea caves to explore to the right of the cove.

Snorkel rentals are available at most dive shops and beach activity centers, including **Aloha Dive Shop,** Koko Marine Shopping Center (☎ **808/395-5922**), the closest dive shop to the underwater park at Hanauma Bay; **Snorkel Bob's,** also on the way to Hanauma Bay at 700 Kapahulu Ave., Honolulu (☎ **808/735-7944**); and **Haleiwa Surf Center,** 66-167 Haleiwa Rd., Haleiwa (☎ **808/637-5051**), which also teaches snorkeling and offers guided snorkeling tours.

SURFING

In the summertime, when the water's warm and there's a soft breeze in the air, the south swell comes up. It's surf season in Waikiki, the best place to learn how to surf on Oahu. To learn to surf, go early to **Aloha Beach Service,** next to the Sheraton Moana Surfrider Hotel in Waikiki (☎ **808/922-3111**). The beach boys offer

---

Impressions

The boldness and address with which we saw them perform these difficult and dangerous maneuvers was altogether astonishing . . .
—Capt. James Cook's observations of Hawaiian surfers

surfing lessons for $25 an hour and board rentals are $8 for 1 hour and $12 for 2 hours. You must know how to swim.

More experienced surfers should drop in on any surf shop around Oahu, or call the **Surf News Network Surfline** at **808/596-SURF** or 808/836-1952 to get the latest surf conditions. A good surfing spot for advanced surfers is The Cliffs, at the base of Diamond Head. The 4- to 6-feet waves churn here, allowing high-performance surfing. And the view of Diamond Head is great, which helps to make this place ideal for surfers.

If you're in Hawaii in the winter and want to see the serious surfers catch the really big waves, bring your binoculars and grab a front-row seat on the beach near Kalalua Point. To get there from Waikiki, take the H-1 toward the North Shore, veering off at H-2, which becomes Kamehameha Highway (Hi. 83). Keep going to the funky surf town of Haleiwa and drive by Waimea Bay to the big waves on your left, just past Pupukea Beach Park.

WHALE WATCHING

The *Navatek II,* the so-called "no seasick" boat (see "Sea Cruises," above), is the only tourist vessel that ventures into the often choppy waters off Koko Head, where the whales cruise to and from Maui. In whale season (roughly January to April), whale-watching cruises depart from Pier 6, on the Diamond Head side of Aloha Tower Marketplace at 8:30am, and return at 11am. The cost is $39 adults, $24 kids 2 to 11. Call **Hawaiian Cruises Ltd.** (☎ **808/848-6360** or 800/852-4183) to reserve.

WINDSURFING

Windward Oahu's Kailua Beach Park is the home of champion and pioneer windsurfer Robbie Naish; it's also the best place to learn. The oldest and most established windsurfing business in Hawaii is **Naish Windsurfing Hawaii,** 156-C Hamakua Dr., Kailua (☎ **808/261-3539**). The company offers everything: sales, rentals, instruction, repair, and free advice on where to go when the wind and waves are happening. Lessons start at $37.50 and equipment rental is $25 for a half-day and $30 for a full day. Or, you can just venture out to the North Shore to watch the windsurfers dance over the waves.

7 Nature Hikes

by Rick Carroll, with Jeanette Foster

Everyone thinks Oahu is just one big urban island, so they're always surprised to discover that the great outdoors is less than an hour away from downtown Honolulu. The island's 33 major trails take you across razor-thin ridge backs, or deep into waterfall valleys. Check out Stuart Ball's *The Hikers Guide to Oahu* (Honolulu: University of Hawaii Press, 1993) before you go. For a free Oahu Recreation Map, listing all 33 trails, write to the **Deptartment of Land and Natural Resources,** 1151 Punchbowl St., Room 130, Honolulu, HI 96813 (☎ **808/587-0300**). They'll also send you free topographic trail maps on request and issue camping permits. Another good source of information is the Hiking/Camping Information Packet from **Hawaii Geographic Maps and Books,** 49 S. Hotel Street, Suite 218, Honolulu, HI 96813 (☎ **808/538-3952**), for a cost of $7, (postage included).

The **Hawaiian Trail and Mountain Club,** P.O. Box 2238, Honolulu, HI 96804, offers regularly scheduled hikes on Oahu. You bring your own lunch and drinking water; you'll meet up with the club at the Iolani Palace to join them on a hike. They also have an information packet on hiking and camping in Hawaii, as well as a schedule of all upcoming hikes; send $1.25, plus a legal-sized, self-addressed, stamped envelope to the address above.

The **Sierra Club,** 1111 Bishop Street, Honolulu, HI 96813 (☎ **808/538-6616**), also offers regularly scheduled hikes on which they welcome visitors. The **Hawaii Nature Center** (☎ **808/955-0100**) is another organization that offers organized hikes, as well as "Sunday Adventures" for children.

DIAMOND HEAD CRATER

Everyone can make this easy walk to the summit of Hawaii's most famous landmark. Kids love the top of the 760-foot volcanic cone, where they have 360° views of Oahu up the leeward coast from Waikiki. The 1.4-mile round-trip will take about an hour.

Diamond Head was created by a volcanic explosion about a half-million years ago. The Hawaiians called the crater Leahi (meaning the brow of the ahi, or tuna, referring to the shape of the crater). Diamond Head was considered a sacred spot; King Kamehameha offered human sacrifices at a heiau (temple) on the western slope. It wasn't until the 19th century that Mount Leahi got its current name. A group of sailors found what they thought were diamonds in the crater; it turned out they really only found worthless calcite crystals, but the Diamond Head moniker stuck.

Before you begin your adventure hiking to the top of the crater, gather a flashlight (you walk through several dark tunnels), binoculars (for better viewing at the top), water, and your camera. Go early, before the noonday sun starts beating down. Start your hike to the summit of Diamond Head at Monsarrat and 18th avenues on the crater's inland (or mauka) side. To get thre, take TheBUS no. 58 from the Ala Moana Shopping Center or drive to the intersection of Diamond Head Road and 18th Avenue. Follow the road through the tunnel (which is closed 6pm–6am) and park in the lot. The trailhead starts in the parking lot and proceeds along a paved walkway (with handrails) as it climbs up the slope. You'll pass old World War I and II pillboxes, gun emplacements, and tunnels built as part of the Pacific defense network. Several steps take you up to the top observation post on Point Leahi. The views are indescribable.

MANOA FALLS TRAIL

This easy, eight-tenths of a mile (one-way) hike is terrific for families; it takes less than an hour to reach idyllic Manoa Falls. The trailhead, marked by a footbridge, is at the end of Manoa Road, past Lyon Arboretum. The often-muddy trail follows Waihi Stream and meanders through the forest reserve past guava, mountain apple, and wild ginger. The forest is moist and humid and inhabited by giant blood-thirsty mosquitoes, so bring repellent.

PALI (MAUNAWILI) TRAIL

For a million-dollar view of the Windward Coast, take this easy 11-mile (one-way) foothill trail. The trailhead is about 6 miles from downtown Honolulu, on the windward side of the Nuuanu Pali Tunnel, at the scenic lookout just beyond the hairpin turn of the Pali Highway (Hi. 61); just as you begin the turn, look for the SCENIC OVERLOOK sign, slow down, and pull off the highway into the parking lot. The mostly flat, well-marked, easy-to-moderate trail goes through the forest on the lower slopes of the 3,000-foot Koolau Mountain range and ends up in the backyard of the coastal Hawaiian village of Waimanalo. Go halfway to get the view and return to your car, or have someone meet you in 'Nalo.

MAKAPUU LIGHTHOUSE TRAIL

You've seen this famous old lighthouse on episodes of "Magnum P.I." and "Hawaii Five-O." No longer manned by the Coast Guard (it's fully automated now), the lighthouse is the goal of hikers who challenge a precipitous cliff trail to gain an airy perch over the Windward Coast, Manana (Rabbit) Island, and the azure Pacific. It's about a 45-minute, 1-mile hike from Kalanianaole Highway, along a paved road that begins across from Hawaii Kai Executive Golf Course and winds around the 646-foot-high sea bluff to the lighthouse lookout.

To get to the trailhead from Waikiki, take Kalanianaole Highway (Hi. 72) past Hanauma Bay and Sandy Beach to Makapuu Head, the southeastern tip of the island. Look for a sign that says NO VEHICLES ALLOWED on a gate to the right, a few hundred yards past the entrance to the golf course. The trail isn't marked, but it's fairly obvious: Just follow the abandoned road that leads gradually uphill to a trail that wraps around Makapuu Point. It's a little precarious, but anyone in reasonably good shape can handle it. Blow Hole Alert: When the south swell is running, usually in summer, there are a couple of blow holes on the south side of Makapuu Head that put the famous Halona Blow Hole to shame.

HAUULA LOOP

For one of the best views of the coast and the ocean, follow the Hauula Loop Trail on the windward side of the island. It's an easy, 2½-mile loop on a well-maintained path that passes through a whispering ironwood forest and a grove of tall Norfolk pines. The trip takes about 3 hours and gains some 600 feet in elevation.

To get to the trail, take TheBUS no. 55 (Circle Island) or take Hi. 83 to Hauula Beach Park. Turn toward the mountains on Hauula Homestead Road; when the road forks to the left at Maakua Road, park on the road. Walk along Maakua Road to the wide, grassy trail that begins the hike into the mountains. The climb is fairly steep for about 300 yards, but continues on to easier-on-the-calves switchbacks as you go up the ridge. Look down as you climb: You'll spot wildflowers and mushrooms among the matted needles. The trail continues up, crossing Waipilopilo Gulch, where you'll see several forms of native plant life. Eventually you reach the top of the ridge, where the views are spectacular.

The Division of Forestry does permit camping along the trail, but it's difficult to find a place to pitch a tent on the steep slopes and in the dense forest growth. There are a few places along the ridge wide enough for a tent. Contact the **Division of Forestry and Wildlife,** 1151 Punchbowl St., Honolulu, HI 96813 (☎ **808/587-0166**) for information on camping permits.

SACRED FALLS

It's easy to see why this place was given the name "Sacred": Clear, cold water, originating from the top of the Koolau Mountains, descends down the Kaluanui Stream and cascades over Sacred Falls into a deep, boulder-strewn pool. The hike to this awe-inspiring waterfall passes under guava and mountain apple trees and through a fern-filled narrow canyon that parallels the stream bed.

A few words of warning before you grab your walking shoes and hiking boots: Do not attempt this hike in wet weather. In fact, the State Parks Division closes the falls if there is a danger of flash floods. This is no idle warning—in 1987, five hikers attempting to reach the falls died in three separate incidents while the normally babbling stream was flooded; in October 1993, a Boy Scout troop had to be rescued by helicopter during a flash flood. And go in a group—there have recently been a few muggings along the 2.2-mile trail.

The best time to take this hike is in the morning, when the light is good. Be prepared with rain gear and insect repellent. The easy 4.4-mile round-trip will take about 2 to 3 hours. To get to the trail, drive north on the Kamehameha Highway (Hi. 83) to the turnoff for Sacred Falls State Park, or take TheBUS no. 20 (Circle Island). The trail begins at the parking lot and heads for the mountains, paralleling the Kaluanui Stream. About a mile into the trail is a grassy area with emergency warning equipment inside a cyclone fence; the trailhead is to the left of the fence. The beginning is a bit rough—the trail is muddy and passes under tangled branches and through a tunnel of Christmas berry. About a half-mile beyond the trailhead, you'll cross the Kaluanui Stream; if the water is high or muddy, don't cross—you could become trapped in the canyon during a flash flood. As you continue up the trail, the canyon becomes increasingly narrow, with steep walls on either side. Be on the lookout for falling rocks. At the end of the trail are the majestic falls and an extremely cold pool, home to spidery Malaysian prawns.

KAENA POINT

At the very western tip of Oahu lie the dry, barren lands of Kaena Point State Park, 853 acres consisting of a remote, wild coastline of jagged sea cliffs, deep gulches, sand dunes, endangered plant life, and a wind- and surf-battered coastline. Kaena means "red-hot" or "glowing" in Hawaiian; the name refers to the brilliant sunsets visible from the point.

Kaena is steeped in numerous legends. A popular one concerns the demigod Maui: Maui had a famous hook that he used to raise islands from the sea. He decided that he wanted to bring the islands of Oahu and Kauai closer together, so one day he threw his hook across the Kauai Channel and snagged the island of Kauai (which actually is visible from Kaena Point on clear days). Using all his might, Maui was only able to pull loose a huge boulder, which fell into the waters very close to the present lighthouse at Kaena. The rock is still called Pohaku o Kauai (the rock from Kauai). Like Black Rock in Kaanapali on Maui, Kaena is thought of as the point on Oahu from which souls depart.

To hike out to the departing place, take the clearly marked trail from the parking lot of the Makua-Kaena Point State Park. The moderate, 5-mile round-trip hike to the point will take a couple of hours. The trail along the cliff passes tide pools abundant in marine life and rugged protrusions of lava reaching out to the turbulent sea; seabirds circle overhead. There are no sandy beaches and the water is nearly always turbulent. During the winter months, when a big north swell is running, the waves at Kaena are the biggest in the state, averaging heights of 30 to 40 feet. Even when the water appears calm, offshore currents are powerful, so don't plan to swim. Go early in the morning to see the school of porpoises that frequent the area just offshore.

To get to the trailhead from Honolulu or Waikiki, take the H-1 freeway west to its end; continue on Hi. 93 past Makaha and follow Hi. 930 to the end of the road. There's no bus service.

8 Camping & Wilderness Cabins

by Rick Carroll, with Jeanette Foster

If you don't plan to bring your own camping gear, you can rent or buy it at **Omar the Tent Man,** 650A Kakoi St. (☎ **808/836-8785**), **The Bike Shop,** at 1149 S. King St. (☎ **808/595-0588**) or Windward City Shopping Center (☎ **808/ 235-8722**).

The best places to camp on Oahu are listed below. TheBUS's Circle Island route can get you to or near all these sites, but since you're not allowed to bring gear on board, you're going to have to drive (or take a cab).

HOOMALUHIA BOTANICAL GARDENS

This windward campground, outside Kaneohe, is almost a secret place and a real treasure. It's hard to believe that you're just a half-hour from downtown Honolulu.

Hoomaluhia, or "peace and tranquillity," accurately describes this 400-acre botanical garden at the foot of the jagged Koolaus. In this lush tropical setting, gardens are devoted to the plants specific to tropical America, native Hawaii, Polynesia, India, Sri Lanka, and Africa. A 32-acre lake sits in the middle of the scenic park (no swimming or boating is allowed, though), and there are numerous hiking trails. The visitor's center offers guided walks to demonstrations of ancient Hawaiian plant use.

Facilities for this tent-camp area include rest rooms, cold showers, dish washing stations, picnic tables, grills, and water. A public phone is available at the visitor's center, and shopping and gas are available in Kaneohe, a mile away.

Permits are free, but stays are limited to 5 nights (the park's closed Tues and Wed). For information, contact **Hoomaluhia Botanical Gardens,** 45-680 Luluku Rd., Kaneohe, HI 96744 (☎ **808/233-7323**). The gate is locked at 4pm and doesn't open again until 9am, so you're locked in for the night.

KUALOA REGIONAL PARK

Located on a peninsula on Kaneohe Bay, this park has a spectacular setting. The gold-sand beach is excellent for snorkeling, and fishing can be rewarding (see "Beaches," above, for details). There are two campgrounds: One is in a wooded area with palm trees, ironwoods, kamani, monkeypods, and a sandy beach that's mainly reserved for groups but has a few sites for families. The other campground is on the main beach; it has fewer shade trees and a great view of Mokolii Island. Facilities at both sites include rest rooms, showers, picnic tables, drinking fountains, and a public phone. The group campground also has sinks for dish washing, a volleyball court, and a kitchen building. Gas and groceries are available in Kaaawa, 2¹/₂ miles away.

In the summer, the group site is nearly always full. Permits are free, but limited to 5 days (no camping on Wed and Thurs). Contact the **Honolulu Department of Parks and Recreation,** 650 S. King St., Honolulu, HI 96713 (☎ **808/523-4525**), or any satellite city hall. Two nearest Kualoa are in Hauula at 54-316 Kamehameha Hwy. (☎ **808/293-8551**), or Kaneohe at 46-018 Kamehameha Hwy. (☎ **808/ 235-4571**).

KAHANA BAY BEACH PARK

Under Tahiti-like cliffs, with a beautiful, gold-sand crescent beach framed by piney-needle casuarina trees, Kahana Bay Beach Park is a place of serene beauty. You can swim, bodysurf, fish, hike, and picnic, or just sit and listen to the trade winds whistle through the beach pines.

Tent and vehicle camping only is allowed at this oceanside oasis. Facilities include rest rooms, picnic tables, drinking water, public phones, and a boat-launching ramp. Do note that the rest rooms are located at the north end of the beach, far away from the camping area, and there are no showers. There's no fee for camping, but you must get a permit. Reservations are taken no earlier than two Fridays before the date requested. Applicants must appear in person to get a permit at any satellite city hall or at the **Honolulu Department of Parks and Recreation,** 650 S. King St., Honolulu 96813 (☎ **808/523-4525**). Permits are limited to 5 days; no camping is allowed on Wednesdays and Thursdays.

To get there from Waikiki, take the H-1 west to the Likelike Highway (Hi. 63). Continue north on the Likelike, through the Wilson Tunnel, turning left on Hi. 83; Kahana Bay is 13 miles down the road on the right.

MALAEKAHANA BAY STATE RECREATION AREA

One of the most beautiful beach camping areas in the state, with a mile-long gold-sand beach (see "Beaches," above, for details) is on Oahu's Windward Coast. There are two areas for tent camping. Facilities include picnic tables, rest rooms, showers, sinks, drinking water, and a phone. Permits are free, but limited to 5 nights and may be obtained at any state parks office, including the **State Parks Division,** P.O. Box 621, Honolulu, HI 96809 (☎ **808/587-0300**).

For your safety, the park gate is closed between 6:45pm and 7am; vehicles cannot enter or exit. Groceries and gas are available in Laie and Kahuku, less than a mile away.

CAMP MOKULEIA

A quiet, isolated beach on Oahu's north shore, 4 miles from Kaena Point, is the centerpiece of a 9-acre campground that's a great getaway. Camping is available on the beach or in a grassy, wooded area. Activities include swimming, surfing, shore fishing, and beachcombing.

Facilities include tent camping, cabins, and lodge accommodations. The tent-camping site has portable chemical toilets, a water spigot, and outdoor showers; there are no picnic tables or barbecue grills, so come prepared. The cabins sleep up to 18 people in bunk beds. Lodge facilities include rooms with or without private bath. The cabins are $125 per night for the 14-bed cabin and $160 per night for the 18-bed cabin. Rooms at the lodge are $45 to $50 for a shared bath and $55 to $60 for a private bath. Tent camping is $5 per person, per night. Many groups use the camp, but there's a real sense of privacy. Reservations are required; contact **Camp Mokuleia,** 68-729 Farrington Hwy., Waialua, HI 96791 (☎ **808/ 637-6241**).

To get there from Waikiki, take the H-1 to the H-2 exit. Stay on H-2 until the end. Where the road forks, bear left to Waialua (Hwy. 803), which turns into Hi. 930 to Kaena Point. Look for the green fence on the right, where a small sign at the driveway reads CAMP MOKULEIA, EPISCOPAL CHURCH OF HAWAII.

9   Golf & Other Outdoor Activities

by Rick Carroll, with Jeanette Foster

BICYCLING

Island Triathlon and Bike, 569 Kapahulu Ave. (☎ **808/732-7227**), has mountain bike rentals complete with lock, pump, repair kit, and helmet for $25 the first day and $10 for each additional day. They're also in the know about upcoming bicycle events or interesting bike rides you can enjoy on your own. If you'd like some company while you bike, contact the **Hawaii Bicycle League,** P.O. Box 4403, Honolulu, HI 96812 (☎ **808/735-5756**). Not only will they fix you up with someone to ride with, but they can also provide you with a schedule of upcoming rides, races, and outings.

GOLF

These are the best of Oahu's 35 courses. Cart costs are included in all greens fees.

KO OLINA GOLF COURSE

Golf Digest named this 6,867-yard, par-72 course one of "America's Top 75 Resort Courses" in 1992. The Ted Robinson–designed course has rolling fairways and elevated tee and water features. The signature hole—the 12th, a par-3—has an elevated tee that sits on a rock garden, with a waterfall cascading just a few feet away from the tee into a landscaped garden. Wait until you see the 18th hole; you'll see and hear water all around you—seven pools begin on the right side of the fairway and slope down to a lake, and a waterfall is on your left off the elevated green. You'll have no choice but to play the left and approach the green over the water. There's a dress code for the course: Men are asked to wear shirts with a collar. Facilities include a driving range, locker rooms, Jacuzzi/steam rooms, and a restaurant/bar. Lessons and twilight rates are available. Greens fees are $165. This course is crowded all the time, so book in advance by calling **808/676-5300.**

HAWAII KAI GOLF COURSE

This par-72, 6,350-yard course is between Sandy Beach and Makapuu Point in East Oahu. It's a moderately challenging course with scenic vistas, and the greens fees are easy on the pocketbook—$80; rates for the par-3 course are a mere $37. Lockers are available. Call **808/395-2358** for tee times.

TURTLE BAY HILTON GOLF & TENNIS CLUB

Chose either the George Fazio–designed 9-hole course—this is the only course he designed in Hawaii—or the 18-hole Links at Kuilima, designed by Arnold Palmer and Ed Seay—*Golf Digest* rated it the fourth best new resort course in 1994. Turtle Bay used to be labeled a "wind tunnel;" it still is one, but the casuarina (ironwood) trees have matured and dampened the wind somewhat. But Palmer-Seay never meant for golfers to get off too easy; this is a challenging course. The front 9 holes, with rolling terrain, only a few trees, and lots of wind, play like a British Isles course. The back 9 holes have narrower, tree-lined fairways and water. The course circles Punahoolapa Marsh, a protected wetland for endangered Hawaiian waterfowl. Facilities include pro shop, driving range, putting and chipping green, and snack bar. Greens fees are $99 for the Links at Kuilima and $55 for 18 holes on the 9-hole course. Twilight rates are available. Weekdays are best for tee times; call **808/293-8574.**

SHERATON MAKAHA GOLF CLUB

Some 45 miles west of Honolulu is this challenging golf course, surrounded by swaying palm trees, neon bright bougainvillea, even strutting peacocks. Designed by William Bell, the par-72, 7,091-yard course meanders toward the ocean before turning and heading into the Makaha Valley. With the Waianae range rising in the background, the beauty of the course might make it difficult to keep your mind on the game if it weren't for the challenges of it: eight water hazards, 107 bunkers, and frequent and brisk winds. Facilities include a pro shop, bag storage, and a snack shop. This course is packed on weekends, so it's best to try weekdays. Greens fees are $80 for guests of Waikiki's Sheraton resorts (Sheraton Moana Surfrider, Royal Hawaiian, Sheraton Waikiki, and Princess Kaiulani) and $160 for nonguests. Twilight rates are available. Call **808/695-9544.**

HORSEBACK RIDING

Up into the valley of kings, riders on horseback go deep into Oahu's interior, which only a lucky few have ever seen. Scenes of the Hollywood movie *Jurassic Park* were filmed in this natural place of beauty. Take a ride on **Kualoa Ranch,** 49-560

Kamehameha Hwy., Kaneohe (☎ **808/237-8515** or 800/231-7321), a 4,000-acre working cattle ranch that John Morgan, a scion of a sugar planter, turned into an outdoor playground. The ranch offers a number of different tours through their 4,000-acre ranch, starting at $45. They require that you wear long pants and closed-toe shoes.

Or you can gallop on the beach at the **Turtle Bay Hilton Golf and Tennis Resort,** 57-091 Kamehameha Hwy., Kahuku (☎ **808/293-8811**), where 1-hour tours start at $32. If you've dreamed of learning how to ride, the **Hilltop Equestrian Center,** 41-430 Waikupanaha St., Waimanalo (☎ **808/259-8463**), will be happy to teach you. They offer lessons in either British or Western style from British Horse Society–accredited instructors for $35.

TENNIS

Oahu has 181 free public tennis courts. To get a complete list of all facilities, as well as any upcoming tournaments, contact the **Department of Parks and Recreation,** 650 S. King St., Honolulu 96813 (☎ **808/523-4182**). The courts are available on a first-come first-served basis; playing time is limited to 45 minutes.

If you're staying in Waikiki, the **Ilikai Sports Center** at the Ilikai Hotel, 1777 Ala Moana Blvd. (☎ **808/949-3811**), has six courts, equipment rental, lessons, and repair service. Courts are $7.50 per person per hour. If you're on the other side of the island, the **Turtle Bay Hilton Golf and Tennis Resort,** 57-091 Kamehameha Hwy., Kahuku (☎ **808/293-8811**, ext. 24), has ten courts, four of which are lighted for night play. You must make reservations for the night courts in advance, as they are very popular. Court rates are $12 for the entire day. Equipment rental and lessons are available. The "Thursday Night Mixer" is a very popular activity where both resort guests and nonguests, including local residents, participate in a clinic from 5 to 7pm for $9 per person.

10 Orientation & Adventure Tours

by Rick Carroll

WALKING TOURS

Waikiki   One Saturday morning a month, Glen Grant and his story-telling guides of **Journey to Old Waikiki** (☎ **808/943-0371**) lead 2-hour history walks. Much of what they "show" you doesn't exist anymore, so they need to be quite skilled— and you need a little imagination—to get the picture. Guides appear in turn-of-the-century togs and tell it like it was in lively anecdotes of King Kalakaua, Prince Kuhio, Robert Louis Stevenson, and Mark Twain. The tour ends with a 30-minute multimedia show at the International Marketplace. Tours start at Duke Kahanamoku's statue and are $7 for adults, $5 for children 5 to 12; call for schedule and reservations.

Downtown Honolulu   The **Mission Houses Museum** offers walking tours of historic downtown buildings on Thursday mornings. Tours start at 9am at the museum, last until 12:30pm, and include the regular Mission Houses tour (see "Attractions In & Around Honolulu & Waikiki," below); $7 adults, $4 college students, $3 kids 4 to 18. Reserve a day ahead in person or by phone (☎ **808/531-0481**).

Chinatown Historic District   Two guided tours of Chinatown are offered once a week. The **Chinese Chamber of Commerce** (☎ **808/533-3181**) leads a 3-hour walking tour on Tuesdays at 9:30am. The tour leaves from 42 N. King St. and costs $5 per person; call to reserve.

The **Hawaii Heritage Center** (☎ **808/521-2749**) conducts walking tours every Friday at 9:30am that focus on the history and culture of Chinatown. Tours begin at the Ramsay Gallery, 1128 Smith St.; the cost is $4 per person.

SUBMARINE DIVES

Here's your chance to play Jules Verne and experience the underwater world in the comfort of a submarine. It'll take you on a 2-hour ride 60 feet below the surface. A mask, snorkel, and some fins will do you even better—and much cheaper—but this is a good way to go if the snorkel route isn't for you. The entire trip is narrated, and professional divers feed the tropical fish just outside the sub so you can get a better look at them. Subs leave from Hilton Hawaiian Village Pier. The cost is $85 for adults, $39 for kids 12 and younger; call **Atlantis Submarines** at **808/973-9811** or 800/548-6262 to reserve.

GUIDED ECOTOURS

Darren Akau's a local boy who was chosen as Hawaii's tour guide of the year in 1989, then set out on his own to show visitors Hawaii his way. A day with Darren is a rare chance to explore the "real" Hawaii. He takes groups of eight or more on guided, active day-long outings, such as a hike to Manoa Falls for a splash in the waterfall pool, a beach picnic, and boogie boarding at very local Waimanalo Beach. Along the way, Darren discusses island ways and local customs, flora and fauna, history and culture, language and food, and more.

The day starts at 9am, and usually ends at about 4:30pm. The cost is $75 for adults and $64 for kids, which includes lunch, and hotel pickup and return. You should be in fairly good shape and be able to hike at least a half-mile in a rain forest and at ease in gentle-to-moderate waves. Reservations are required at least a day in advance; call **Darren Akau's Hideaway Tours** (☎ **808/259-9165**).

11 Attractions in & Around Honolulu & Waikiki

by Rick Carroll

HISTORIC HONOLULU

For just about as long as we can remember, the Eastman Kodak Company has been hosting the **Kodak Hula Show** at the Waikiki Band Shell at Kapiolani Park. It's really more '50s nostalgia than ancient culture, but it's a good bit of fun any way you slice it. Shows are at 10am every Tuesday, Wednesday, and Thursday; they last until 11:15 am. Admission is free. For more information, call **808/627-3300.**

✪ **Bishop Museum.** 1525 Bernice St. ☎ **808/847-3511** or 808/848-4129. $8 adults, $7 children 6–17 and seniors. Daily 9am–5pm.

This forbidding, four-story Romanesque lava rock structure (it looks like something out of a Charles Addams cartoon) holds safe the world's greatest collection of natural and cultural artifacts from Hawaii and the Pacific. The museum was founded by a Hawaiian princess, Bernice Pauahi, who collected priceless artifacts and in her will instructed her husband, Charles Reed Bishop, to establish a Hawaiian museum "to enrich and delight" the people of Hawaii. The museum is now world-renowned, and home to Dr. Yoshihiko Sinoto, the last in a proud line of adventuring archaeologists who explored more of the Pacific than Captain Cook, and traced Hawaii's history and culture through its fish hooks.

The Bishop is jam-packed with more than 20 million acquisitions—there are 12 million insect specimens alone—from ceremonial spears to calabashes to old photos of topless hula dancers. A visit here will give you a good basis for understanding Hawaiian life and culture. You'll see the great feathered capes of kings, the last grass shack in Hawaii, preindustrial Polynesian art, even the skeleton of a 50-foot sperm whale. There are seashells, koa-wood bowls, nose flutes, and Dr. Sinoto's major collection of fish hooks. For a taste of what you'll see at the Bishop, take a look at their web page: **http://www.bishop.hawaii.org/.**

In addition to the collections, the planetarium explores Pacific skies, shows you the stars the Polynesians followed across the Pacific to Hawaii. A hula *halau* performs weekdays, and various Hawaiian crafts like lei making, feather working, and quilting are demonstrated. Call for schedules. And Hawaii's best-known entertainers, The Brothers Cazimero, perform in the museum's Hawaiian Hall on Sunday, Wednesday, and Thursday nights; at press time, however, they were planning a change of venue, so be sure to call ahead. See "Oahu After Dark," below, for details.

Hawaii Maritime Center. Pier 7 (near Aloha Tower), Honolulu Harbor. ☎ **808/536-6373.** Admission $7.50 adults, $4.50 children 6–17. Daily 8:30am–5pm.

From the ancient journey of Polynesian voyagers to the nostalgic days of the *Lurline,* which once brought tourists from San Francisco on 4-day cruises, the story of Hawaii's rich maritime heritage is told with artifacts and exhibits at the Hawaii Maritime Center's Kalakaua Boat House, patterned after His Majesty King David Kalakaua's own canoe house.

Outside, the *Hokulea,* a double-hulled sailing canoe that in 1976 re-enacted the Polynesian voyage of discovery, is moored next to the *Falls of Clyde,* a four-masted schooner that once ran tea from China to the West Coast. Inside, the more than 30 exhibits include Matson cruise ships, which brought the first tourists to Waikiki; flying boats that delivered the mail; and the skeleton of a Pacific humpback whale that beached on Kahoolawe. The museum's open-air harborfront restaurant is a popular downtown lunch spot with its view of passing tugboats, sampans, and cargo and cruise ships.

Iolani Palace. King and Richards streets. ☎ **808/522-0832.** Admission $6 adults, $1 children 5–13. Guided tours conducted Wed–Sat 9am–2:15pm. Call ahead to reserve. You must be booked on a guided tour to enter the palace; children under 5 not permitted.

This royal palace was built by King David Kalakaua, who spared no expense. The 4-year project, completed in 1882, cost $360,000—and nearly bankrupted the Hawaiian kingdom. The four-story Italian Renaissance palace, complete with Corinthian columns imported from San Francisco, was the first electrified building in Honolulu (it had electricity before the White House and Buckingham Palace). Royals lived here for 11 years, until Queen Liliuokalani was deposed, and the Hawaiian monarchy fell forever, in a January 17, 1893, palace coup led by U.S. Marines at the demand of sugar planters and missionary descendants.

Cherished by latter-day royalists, the 10-room palace stands as a flamboyant architectural statement of the monarchy period. (Iolani, often identified as the only royal palace on American soil, actually shares that distinction with the Big Island's Hulihee Palace, which also served as royal house.) Open to the public since 1970, Iolani Palace attracts 100,000 visitors a year in groups of 20, who must don denim booties to scoot across the royal floors. The 45-minute tour is well worth your time. Some areas are unfurnished, but the State Dining Room, Throne Room, King's Library, and Privy Council Chamber are complete. The two-story staircase is the largest koa wood case on earth.

Kawaiahao Church. 957 Punchbowl St. ☎ **808/522-1333.** Free admission (small donations appreciated). Mon–Sat 8am–4pm; Sun services 10:30am.

In 1842, Kawaiahao Church stood at last, the crowning achievement of missionaries and Hawaiians working together for the first time on a common project. Designed by Rev. Hiram Bingham and supervised by Kamehameha III, who ordered his people to help build it, the project took 5 years. Workers quarried 14,000-thousand-pound coral blocks from the offshore reefs and cut timber in the forests for the beams.

The proud stone church, complete with bell tower and colonial colonnade, was the first permanent Western house of worship in the islands. It became the church of the Hawaiian royalty and remains in use today by Hawaiians who conduct services in the Hawaiian language (which probably sets old Rev. Bingham spinning in his grave). Some fine portraits of Hawaiian royalty hang inside. Hawaiian-language services are conducted on Sundays at 10:30am.

Mission Houses Museum. 553 S. King St. ☎ **808/531-0481.** Admission $5 adults, $4 seniors, $1 children. Tues–Sat 9am–4pm, Sun noon–4pm.

A 14-square-foot New England wood-frame salt box shipped round the Horn served as home to the Calvinist missionary Hiram Bingham. The Boston prefab, now dwarfed now by Honolulu's modern 44-story high rises, stands at South King and Kawaiahao streets as part of the Mission Homes Museum complex. The museum, a collection of mission-era homes restored and refurnished to reflect the daily life and work of American missionaries, includes the 1831 two-story Chamberlain House, built of coral blocks and lumber from salvaged ships and the 1835 Adobe Schoolhouse designed by missionary Amos Starr Cooke in the style of a California hacienda.

Walking tours of historic downtown buildings are offered on Thursday mornings. For details, see "Orientation & Adventure Tours," above.

Oahu Cemetery. 2162 Nuuanu Ave., north of Judd St. ☎ **808/538-1538.** Free admission. Daily 7am–6pm.

Not the oldest cemetery nor even the biggest, this 150-year-old, 35-acre cemetery is a burying place in America's rural, monumental tradition—more a garden than a Golgotha. It holds the earthly remains of Honolulu's "Who's Who" of days gone by. Here lies Honolulu history: advisors to kings, sugar barons and sea captains, musicians and missionaries, all buried in a reclaimed taro patch on the outskirts of the mud-and–grass-thatch village they helped transform into the city of Honolulu. Under shade trees beside old carriage trails are Damons, Judds, and Thurstons, the missionaries who stayed on in the islands; and patriarchs of Hawaii's first foreign families, whose names now appear on buildings and street signs: Blaisdell, Dudoit, Farrington, Magoon, Stangewald, Wilder. Here, too, lies Alexander Joy Cartwright, Jr., who some consider to be the real father of baseball; he chaired the committee that adopted the rules of play in 1845 and set base paths at 90 feet, and he umpired in the first official game in 1846. A few grave markers give sketchy details of death: a British sea captain spilled from his horse; a nine-year-old girl drowned off Kauai; a Boston missionary, the victim of consumption; an Army private killed while looking for a leper in Kalalau. It's all there, carved in stone, old obituaries and grim reminders of timeless mortality.

Queen Emma Summer Palace. 2913 Pali Hwy. ☎ **808/595-3167.** Admission $4 adults, $3 seniors, $1 children. Daily 9am–4pm.

Queen Emma had a summer palace in the once-secluded uplands of Nuuanu Valley, now split with a six-lane highway full of 60 m.p.h. cars that oddly sound like surf as they zip by. This simple, six-room New England–style house, built in 1847, holds an interesting blend of Victorian furniture and hallmarks of Hawaiian royalty, including feather cloaks and kahili, those bushy totems that mark the presence of *alii*. Other royal treasures include a canoe-shaped cradle for Queen Emma's baby, Prince Albert, who died at the age of 4. (Kauai's Princeville Resort is named for the little prince.)

Royal Mausoleum. 2261 Nuuanu Ave. ☎ **808/536-7602.** Free admission. Mon–Fri 8am–4:30pm.

In the cool uplands of Nuuanu, on a 3.7-acre patch of sacred land dedicated in 1865—and never surrendered to America—stands the Royal Mausoleum, the final resting place of King Kalakaua, Queen Kapiolani, and 16 other Hawaiian royals. Only the Hawaiian flag flies over this grave remnant of the kingdom.

JUST BEYOND PEARL HARBOR

Hawaii's Plantation Village. 59-788 Kamehameha Hwy., Waipahu. ☎ **808/677-0110.** Admission $5 adults, $3 seniors and children 5–17. Mon–Sat 9am–3pm, Sun 10am–3pm.

This symbolic cornerstone of Hawaii's multiethnic society offers a glimpse back in time when sugar planters from America shaped the land, economy, and culture of territorial Hawaii. From 1852, when the first contract laborers arrived here from China, until 1947, when the plantation era ended, more than 400,000 men, women, and children from China, Japan, Portugal, Puerto Rico, Korea, and the Philippines came to work the sugarcane fields. It stands as a collective monument to these brave immigrants, who brought their food, culture, language, art, and architecture to Hawaii, making it a cosmopolitan place.

The $2.7 million, 50-acre village was developed from old blueprints, photos, and oral histories. It includes 30 faithfully restored Filipino camp houses, Chinese and Japanese temples, the Plantation Store, and even a sumo wrestling ring.

WARTIME HONOLULU

✪ **USS *Arizona* Memorial at Pearl Harbor.** Pearl Harbor. ☎ **808/422-0561.** Daily 7:30am–5pm (shuttles run 8am–3pm). Free admission. Children under 12 must be accompanied by adults.

On December 7, 1941, while moored in Pearl Harbor, the USS *Arizona* was bombed in a Japanese air raid. The 608-foot battleship sank in 9 minutes without firing a shot, taking 1,177 sailors and Marines to a fiery death—and plunging the United States into World War II.

Nobody who visits the memorial will ever forget. The deck of the ship lies under 6 feet of water. Oil still oozes slowly up from the Arizona's engine room to stain the calm blue water of Pearl Harbor; some say the ship still weeps for its lost crew. The memorial is a stark white 184-foot rectangle that spans the sunken hull of the ship; it was designed by the late Alfred Pries, a German architect interned on Sand Island during the war. It contains the ship's bell, recovered from the wreckage, and a shrine room with the names of the dead carved in stone.

Today, free U.S. Navy launches take visitors to the *Arizona*. Try to arrive early at the visitor's center, operated jointly by the National Park Service and the U.S. Navy, to avoid the huge crowds; waits of 1 to 3 hours are common. No reservations are taken. While you're waiting for the shuttle to take you out to the ship—you'll be issued a number and time of departure, which you must pick up yourself—you can explore the arresting museum, with personal mementoes, photographs, and historical documents. A 20-minute film precedes your trip to the ship. Allow at least 4 hours to visit the memorial. Shirts and shoes are required; no swimsuits or flip-flops (shorts are okay). Wheelchairs are gladly accommodated.

To get there, drive west on H-1 past the airport; take the USS *Arizona* Memorial exit, and follow the green-and-white signs; there's ample free parking. You can take TheBUS no. 20 from Waikiki, but the ride takes more than an hour. A better bet

Tour of Duty

We are bound for Pearl Harbor in Honolulu's early-morning commute when the radio announcer suddenly interrupts: *"The Japanese have attacked Pearl Harbor."* Even now, a half-century later, the bulletin is arresting.

"Now, hear this," says Jim Wetmore, the lieutenant-looking chap in a World War II pilot's outfit at the wheel of our tour van, as he pops another cassette in the tape deck. *"This is CBS in America, calling Honolulu,"* intones a New York announcer on that fateful day in 1941. *"Come in, Honolulu. . . ."*

There's a silence as big as the Pacific as we roll down the highway. We're on a tour of duty, back into Hawaii's khaki past, on a Hawaii military base tour that's so historically accurate and information-packed that it's almost like being there that Sunday morning. All it takes is a little imagination.

Conducted with a "you are there" flourish by well-informed guides, this new 8-hour tour in 15-passenger vans began operating 6 days a week on January 21, 1996, after Pearl Harbor's 50th anniversary revived national interest. Along the route, you'll see the bullet holes at Hickam Air Field, cruise Pearl Harbor to Battleship Row, pay your respects to the 1,177 men lost aboard the battleship USS *Arizona,* board a heroic World War II submarine credited with 44 enemy "kills," see a B-17 bomber and P-40 Mustang, eat lunch at Schofield Barracks Officers Club, trace the history of Hawaii's 25th Infantry ("Tropic Lighting") Division, and visit graves of "unknown" heroes at the National Memorial Cemetery of the Pacific; all the while, your soundtrack is the Big Band music of the 1940s and such historic sound bites as President Roosevelt's war speech (*"We have suffered a severe setback in Hawaii"*).

"Our biggest surprise is that so many young people go on the tour," said tour director Glen Tomlinson. "We thought it would only attract veterans." Our two-van group on this journey back in time is no exception. We are a Norman Rockwell portrait of Americans young and old, from coast-to-coast. Two men are veterans, of Korea and Vietnam. Ahead of us lie the ghosts of Pearl Harbor.

A melancholy pervades the USS *Arizona* Memorial, which serves as an eternal tomb for the 1,177 sailors and Marines trapped below when the battleship sank in 9 minutes on December 7, 1941. The only sound is the soft whirr of video cameras recording names of victims carved in tombstone.

On this gray day, the memorial smells like a gas station. A rivulet of 1941-vintage bunker oil gushes out of the broken battleship's hull, slicking the blue-green water. A steel plate has rusted through, perhaps. On days when oil flows heavily, people say the ship weeps.

A few visitors turn the *Arizona* into a wishing well by tossing pennies over the side. The copper coins tumble, flashing back glints of light before settling on the hull. Strange behavior—but people aren't sure how to behave at this funereal attraction. Nobody talks as we head for shore in the thin drizzle.

On Pearl Harbor's near shore, the USS *Bowfin* submarine offers the only bright ray against the Arizona's gloom. Nicknamed the "Pearl Harbor Avenger," this sub

is the **Arizona Memorial Shuttle Bus,** which operates from Waikiki daily between 6:50am and 1pm; it's $3 ($6 round-trip) for the 40-minute nonstop ride. Reservations required; call **808/839-0911.**

USS *Bowfin* Submarine Museum & Park. Next to Arizona Memorial, Pearl Harbor. ☎ **808/423-1342.** Admission $8 adults, $6 active duty military. $3 children 4–12. Daily 8am–5pm.

got to war a year late—it was launched December 7, 1942—but her valiant crew wasted no time, sinking 44 ships on nine South Pacific patrols.

Aboard the sub, we tiptoe around torpedoes and slip into the gleaming engine room; we squeeze through narrow passageways into crew quarters so squared away that it looks as if all 80 men just went ashore for liberty. We try to imagine ourselves down here, under the sea, and are reminded that 3,505 submariners died aboard 52 U.S. subs in World War II. We scramble up the open hatch, glad to be free, and climb back into the van.

Driving down Freedom Avenue—in 1941 the main runway of Hickam Air Field—we pass a B-17 bomber outside 1940s-era hangars with big blue stars symbolizing the U.S. Army Air Corps. Our destination is Hale Makai barracks, shot up by Japanese Zero pilots, who killed 35 airmen at breakfast that Sunday. The barracks is a Pacific Air Force headquarters, a base museum, and a National Historic Monument.

"If you walk around the building, you can see bullet holes on all sides," says Air Force Sgt. Gail Ornong, our official escort. Up close, the stucco walls look like Swiss cheese. "We didn't get a plane up that day," Sergeant Ornong says. "Not a plane." Some craters are so big and deep that they can swallow your fist. One commander ordered the holes filled, but veterans protested. These scars will not heal.

Our next stop is Schofield Barracks. In his 1951 best-selling novel *From Here to Eternity,* James Jones called this "the most beautiful army post the U.S. has or ever had." With broad, palm-lined boulevards and art deco buildings, it still is. It looks just as it did in 1941—an enigma to those who believe the Japanese bombed Schofield. Our guide knows better. "Not a single bomb fell here," Jim says over hula burgers at the Schofield Officers Club. But in the film version of the novel— filmed on location, starring Montgomery Clift, Frank Sinatra, Burt Lancaster, and Deborah Kerr—that myth became gospel truth. Other Hollywood embellishments also live on: The World War II P-40 inside Wheeler Field's main gate is a replica built in 1966 for *Tora! Tora! Tora!*

Late in the afternoon, after a few moments of reflection at the National Memorial Cemetery of the Pacific, we are coming down the old volcanic crater called Punchbowl, leaving behind the 35,000 simple graves of American service personnel killed in the Pacific in World War II and the Korean and Vietnam wars. We are coming down the mountain road counterclockwise, spiraling back to real time. As we re-enter Honolulu, Jim plays "The Star Spangled Banner"—the jazzy Whitney Houston version. "I tried to find Kate Smith's version," he says, apologetically. The national anthem ends and we ride in silence to Waikiki. You could tell the veterans wanted to hear Kate Smith.

The **Home of The Brave Hawaii Military Base Tour** departs from Waikiki daily at 6am, and returns at 1:30pm. It's $69 for adults, $59 for kids, and includes a stop at Wheeler Army Air Base in addition to those mentioned above; hotel pickup and drop-off are also included. Call **808/396-8112** to reserve.

Next to the *Arizona* Memorial Visitor Center is the USS *Bowfin,* a World War II submarine launched a year after the attack on Pearl Harbor. You can go below deck of this famous submarine—nicknamed the "Pearl Harbor Avenger" for its successful retaliatory attacks on the Japanese—and see how the 80-man crew lived during wartime. And the *Bowfin* Museum has an impressive collection of

Honolulu Attractions

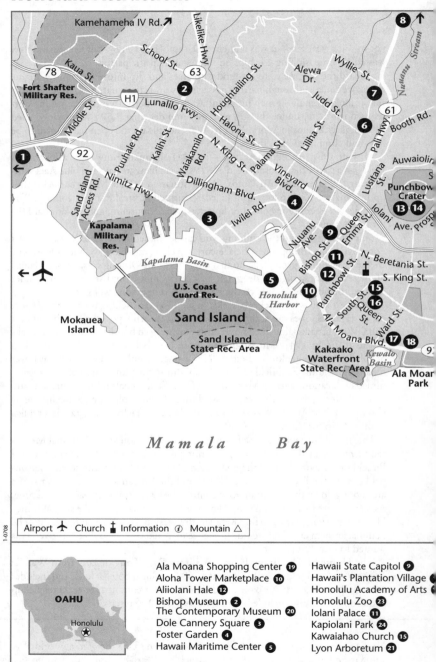

Airport ✈ Church ☩ Information ⓘ Mountain △

1-0708

OAHU

Honolulu ★

Ala Moana Shopping Center ⑲
Aloha Tower Marketplace ⑩
Aliiolani Hale ⑫
Bishop Museum ②
The Contemporary Museum ⑳
Dole Cannery Square ③
Foster Garden ④
Hawaii Maritime Center ⑤

Hawaii State Capitol ⑨
Hawaii's Plantation Village
Honolulu Academy of Arts
Honolulu Zoo ㉓
Iolani Palace ⑪
Kapiolani Park ㉔
Kawaiahao Church ⑮
Lyon Arboretum ㉑

146

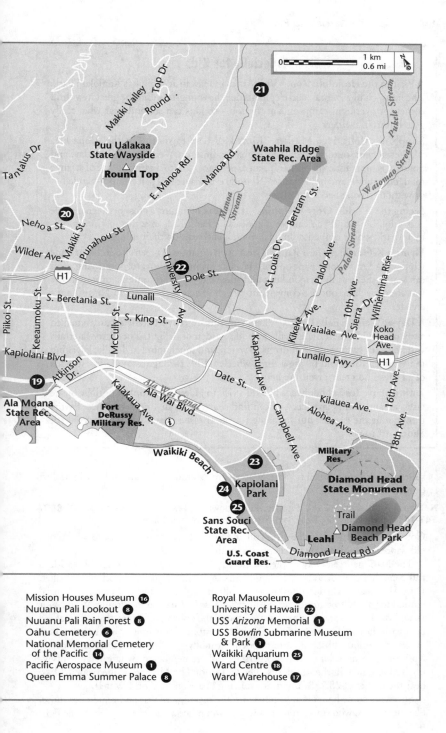

0 | 1 km
0.6 mi

21

Makiki Valley
Top Dr
Round

Puu Ualakaa
State Wayside
△ Round Top

Waahila Ridge
State Rec. Area

Tantalus Dr

E. Manoa Rd.

Manoa Rd.

Manoa Stream

Bertram St.

Pukele Stream

Waiomao Stream

Nehoa St.

20

Wilder Ave.

Makiki St.

Punahou St.

University Ave.

Dole St.

St. Louis Dr.

Palolo Ave.

Palolo Stream

Wilhelmina Rise

H1

22

S. Beretania St.

Lunalil

Kilkee Ave.

Waialae Ave.

10th Ave.

Sierra Dr.

Koko
Head
Ave.

Piikoi St.

Keeaumoku St.

McCully St.

S. King St.

Kapahulu Ave.

Lunalilo Fwy.

H1

16th Ave.

Kapiolani Blvd.

Atkinson Dr.

19

Ala Moana
State Rec.
Area

Kalakaua Ave.

Ala Wai Canal
Ala Wai Blvd.

Date St.

Campbell Ave.

Kilauea Ave.

Alohea Ave.

18th Ave.

Fort
DeRussy
Military Res.
ⓘ

Waikiki Beach

23

Military
Res.

Diamond Head
State Monument

24

Kapiolani
Park

25

Sans Souci
State Rec.
Area

Trail

Leahi

△ Diamond Head
Beach Park

U.S. Coast
Guard Res.

Diamond Head Rd.

Mission Houses Museum ⑯
Nuuanu Pali Lookout ⑧
Nuuanu Pali Rain Forest ⑧
Oahu Cemetery ⑥
National Memorial Cemetery
  of the Pacific ⑭
Pacific Aerospace Museum ❶
Queen Emma Summer Palace ⑧

Royal Mausoleum ❼
University of Hawaii ㉒
USS *Arizona* Memorial ❶
USS B*owfin* Submarine Museum
  & Park ❶
Waikiki Aquarium ㉕
Ward Centre ⑱
Ward Warehouse ⑰

147

Especially for Kids

A Visit to the Honolulu Zoo   Visit Africa in Hawaii at Waikiki's Kapiolani Park. The lions, giraffes, zebras, and elephants delight youngsters. But the great new thrill comes for overnight camp-outs at the zoo—so kids can see and hear what really goes bump in the dark.

Shopping Aloha Flea Market   Most kids hate to shop. But the Aloha Flea Market, a giant outdoor bazaar at Aloha Stadium on Wednesday, Saturday, and Sunday, is more than shopping: It's an experience akin to a carnival, full of strange food, odd goods, and bold barkers. Nobody ever leaves this place empty-handed—or without having had lots of fun.

Seeing the World's Only Wolphin   It's a freak of nature, a cross between a whale and a dolphin—and you can see it at Sea Life Park. Kids love this marine amusement park, where trained dolphins, whales, and seals do their thing.

Flying a Kite at Kapiolani Park   Great open expanses of green and constant trade winds make this urban park one of Hawaii's prime locations for kite-flying. You can watch the pros fly dragon kites and stake kite-fighting contests, or join in the fun after checking out the convenient kite shop across the street in New Otani's arcade.

A Day at Waimea Falls Park   What many think is only a botanical garden tucked away on the North Shore is really a child's garden of delight. There are waterfalls and pools for swimming, cliff divers to watch, and much more to do, like kayaking the Waimea River and taking a three-wheeled ATV through a jungly forest. Kids of all ages find great adventure here.

Eating Shave Ice at Haleiwa   No kid's visit to Hawaii is complete until he or she tastes an authentic shave ice. You can find shave ice in all kinds of tropical flavors throughout the islands, but for some reason, it tastes better in this funky North Shore surf town.

submarine-related artifacts. The Waterfront Memorial honors submariners lost during World War II.

National Cemetery of the Pacific. Punchbowl Crater, 2177 Puowaina Dr. ☎ **808/ 541-1434.** Free admission. Daily 8am–5:30pm; Mar–Sept to 6:30pm.

Go in the morning when the air is still and listen. Except for the occasional sob of a sad widow, the Punchbowl is silent as a tomb.

The National Cemetery of the Pacific, as it's officially known, is an ash-and-lava tuff cone that exploded about 150,000 years ago—like Diamond Head, only smaller. Early Hawaiians called it Puowaina, or "hill of sacrifice." The old crater is a burial ground for 35,000 victims of three American wars in Asia and the Pacific: World War II, and the Korean and Vietnam wars. Among the graves you'll find many unmarked ones with the date December 7, 1941 carved in stone. Some forever will be unknown; others are famous, like war correspondent Ernie Pyle, killed by a Japanese sniper in April of 1945 on Okinawa; still others are only remembered by family and surviving buddies, now in their mid-70s. The Courts of The Missing, white stone tablets, bear the names of 28,788 Americans missing in action in World War II.

Survivors come here often to reflect on the meaning of war and remember those, like themselves, who stood in harm's way to win peace a half-century ago. Some fight back tears, remembering lost buddies, lost missions, and the sacrifice of all who died in "the last good war."

FISH, FLORA & FAUNA

Foster Garden. 50 N. Vineyard Blvd., at Pali Hwy. ☎ **808/522-7066** or 808/531-1939. Admission $5 adults, $1 children 6–12. Mon–Fri 9am–4pm; guided tours at 1pm.

A leafy oasis amid the high-rises of downtown Honolulu, this 14-acre garden on the north side of Chinatown was born in 1853 with a single tree planted by German physician and botanist William Hillenbrand. Today, it's the showcase of 24 native Hawaiian trees and the last stand of several rare trees, including an East African whose white flowers only bloom at night. There are orchids galore, plus all kinds of spices and herbs.

Honolulu Zoo. 151 Kapahulu Ave., at entrance to Kapiolani Park. ☎ **808/971-7171.** Admission $6 adults, $4 children 6–12. Daily 9am–4:30pm.

Nobody comes to Hawaii to see an Indian elephant, or African lions and zebras. Right? Wrong. This 43-acre municipal zoo in Waikiki attracts visitors in droves, who come to see the new African Savannah, a 10-acre wild preserve exhibit with more than 40 uncapped African critters roaming around in the open. The zoo, which now offers night walks—when the nocturnal beasties are out—also has a rare Hawaiian nene goose, a Hawaiian pig, and Mouflon sheep. (Only the goose, an evolved version of the Canadian honker, is considered to be truly Hawaiian; the others are imported from Polynesia, India, and elsewhere.)

Lyon Arboretum. 3860 Manoa Rd. ☎ **808/988-7378.** $1 donation requested. Mon–Sat 9am–4:30pm.

Six-story-tall breadfruit trees . . . yellow orchids no bigger than a bus token . . . ferns with fuzzy buds as big as a human head: Lyon Arboretum is 125 budding acres of botanical wonders. A whole different world opens up to you along the self-guided 20-minute hike through Lyon Arboretum to Inspiration Point. You'll pass more than 5,000 exotic tropical plants full of birdsong in this cultivated rain forest (a research facility that's part of the University of Hawaii) at the head of Manoa Valley.

Guided tours for serious plant lovers are offered one or two Saturdays a month. Led by a resident botanist, the tour may take up to 3 hours and focus on one species. Call **808/988-3177** for tour schedule and reservations.

✪ Waikiki Aquarium. 2777 Kalakaua Ave. ☎ **808/923-9741.** Admission $6 adults, $4 seniors and students, $2.50 children 13–17. Daily 9am–5pm.

Behold the chambered Nautilus, nature's submarine and inspiration for Jules Verne's *20,000 Leagues Under the Sea:* You may see this tropical cephalopod mollusk with its many-chambered spiral shell any day of the week at the Waikiki Aquarium.

This tropical aquarium Diamond Head of Waikiki is worth a peek if only to see the only living Chambered Nautilus born in captivity. Its natural habitat is the deep waters of Micronesia; but Bruce Carlson, director of the aquarium, succeeded not only in trapping the pearly shell in 1,500 feet of water by dangling chunks of raw tuna, but also managed to breed this ancient relative of the octopus. The aquarium was also the first to successfully display the cuttlefish and Hawaii's own mahimahi.

There are plenty of other fish as well in this small but first-class aquarium, located on a live coral reef. Owned and operated by the University of Hawaii, the aquarium, after a $3 million upgrade, now features a Hawaiian reef habitat with sharks, eels, a touch tank, and habitats for the endangered Hawaiian monk seal and green sea turtle.

IN NEARBY EAST OAHU

Sea Life Park. On Kalanianaole Hwy., at Makapuu Point. ☎ **808/259-7933.** Admission $19.95 adults, $10.95 seniors 65 and over, $8.95 chidren 6–12, $3.95 children 4–5, children under 4 free. Daily 9:30am–5pm, Fri to 10pm.

I cheered *Free Willy*, and think all trained dolphin shows should be scrapped and the critters let go, but it appears I'm in the minority here. This 62-acre ocean theme park is one of Oahu's main attractions. It features orca whales from Puget Sound, Atlantic bottle-nosed dolphins, California sea lions, and penguins going through their hoops to the delight of children. There's a Hawaiian Reef Tank full of tropical fish (many of which swim for free at Hanauma Bay), a "touch" pool where you can grab a real sea cucumber (commonly found in tide pools), and a Bird Sanctuary where you can see birds like the red-footed booby and Frigate bird that usually fly overhead. There's also an incongruous whaling museum that tells how New England whalers harpooned whales and made scrimshaw out of their bones. The chief curiosity, though, is the world's only "wolphin"—a cross between a false killer whale and an Atlantic bottle-nosed dolphin. On site, marine biologists from the National Marine Life Fisheries operate a recovery center for endangered marine life; during your visit, you'll be able to see restored Hawaiian monk seals and seabirds.

OTHER NATURAL WONDERS & SPECTACULAR VIEWS

Nuuanu Valley Rain Forest. Take Old Nuuanu Pali Rd. exit off Pali Hwy. (Hi. 61).

It's not the same as a peaceful nature walk, but if time is short and hiking isn't your thing, Honolulu has a rain forest you can drive through. It's only a few minutes from downtown Honolulu in verdant Nuuanu Valley, where it rains nearly 300 inches a year. And it's easy to reach: As the Pali Highway leaves residential Nuuanu and begins its climb though the forest, the last stoplight is the Nuuanu Pali Road turnoff; turn right for a jungly detour of about 2 miles under a thick canopy strung with liana vines, past giant golden bamboo that creaks in the wind, Norfolk pines, and wild shell ginger. The road rises and the vegetation clears as you drive, blinking in the bright light of day, past a small mountain reservoir.

Soon the road rejoins the Pali Highway. Kailua is to the right; Honolulu is to the left—but it can be a hair-raising turn. Instead, turn right, go a half-mile to the **Nuuanu Pali Lookout,** stop for the best panoramic look at Oahu's Windward side, and return to the town-bound highway on the other side.

✪ **Nuuanu Pali Lookout.** Near the summit of Pali Hwy. (Hi. 61); take Nuuanu Pali Lookout turnoff.

Sometimes gale-force winds howl through the mountain pass at this 1,186-foot high perch guarded by 3,000-foot peaks, so hold on to your hat—and small children. But if you walk up from the parking lot to the precipice, you'll be rewarded with a view that'll blow you away. At the edge, the dizzying panorama of Oahu's windward side is breathtaking: Clouds low enough to pinch scoot by on trade winds; pinnacles of the *pali* (cliffs), green with ferns, often disappear in the mist. From on high, the tropical palette of green and blue runs down to the sea.

ON THE WAY TO WINDWARD OAHU

✪ **Puu Ualakaa State Park.** At the end of Round Hill Dr. Daily 7am–6:45pm (to 7:45pm in summer).

The best sunset view of Honolulu is from a 1,048-foot-high hill named for sweet potatoes. Actually, the poetic Hawaiian name means "rolling sweet potato hill," which is how early planters used gravity to harvest their crop. The panorama from on high

---

Factoid

Amelia Earhart was the first woman to fly solo from Hawaii to the U.S. mainland in 1935. A plaque on Diamond Head Road memorializes her 12-hour, 50-minute flight from Honolulu to Oakland, California.

---

is sweeping and majestic. On a clear day, which is almost always, you can see from Diamond Head to the Waianae range, almost the length of Oahu. At night, several scenic overlooks provide romantic spots for young lovers, who like to smooch under the stars with the city lights at their feet. It's a top-of-the-world experience—the view, that is. To get there from Waikiki, take Ala Wai Boulevard to McCully Street, turn right, and drive *mauka* beyond the H-1 on-ramps to Wilder Street; turn left and go to Makiki Street, turn right and continue onward and upward about 3 miles.

MORE MUSEUMS

Aliiolani Hale. 417 S. King St. ☎ **808/539-4999.** Free admission. Tues–Thurs 10am–3pm; by appointment only Mon and Fri.

Don't be surprised if this place looks familiar; you probably saw it on "Magnum P.I." or "Hawaii Five-O." Hollywood always uses it as the Honolulu Police Station, although the made-for-TV movie *Blood and Orchids* correctly used it as the courthouse where Clarence Darrow defended the perpetrators in the famed Massie case in 1931. This gingerbread Italianate, designed by Australian Thomas Rowe in Renaissance Revival–style, was built in 1874 and originally intended to be a palace. Instead, Aliiolani Hale ("House of the heavenly chiefs" in Hawaiian) became the Parliament-Government Office Building and later, the Judiciary Building.

Aliiolani Hale operates a **Judiciary History Center,** open from 10am to 3pm Tuesday, Wednesday, and Thursday. There's a free guided tour, a video presentation, a restored historic courtroom, and exhibits tracing Hawaii's transition from ancient Hawaiian law to modern Western law.

✪ **The Contemporary Museum.** 2411 Makiki Heights Dr. ☎ **808/526-0232.** Admission $5 adults, $3 seniors and students, children 12 and under free. Tues–Sat 10am–4pm, Sun noon–4pm; docent-led tours at 1:30pm.

Gaze on works by Hockney, Warhol, and other contemporary masters of the past 40 years in this converted 1925 home, set on a wooded 3-acre estate. It's a pleasant escape from Waikiki—and there's a contemporary cafe that serves modern lunches, too. To get there, take Mott-Smith Drive to Makiki Heights Drive and follow signs to the entrance. The no. 15 bus from downtown Honolulu goes by the museum.

Honolulu Academy of Arts. 900 S. Beretania St. ☎ **808/532-8701.** Admission $4 adults, $2 students, military, and seniors; children free. Tues–Sat 10am–4:30pm, Sun 1pm–5pm.

Hawaii's best art collection—including ancient Chinese jades, 14th-century Italian oils, and Japanese scrolls—is exhibited in intimate galleries of a graceful 1927 building, overlooking serene courtyards. While both Hawaiian Island and Western masters, including Picasso and van Gogh, are represented, the real glory is the Asian collection. The museum also has permanent American, European, and Pacific (with works from Hawaii, the South Pacific, Micronesia, and Papua New Guinea) collections.

Pacific Aerospace Museum. In the Central Waiting Lobby, Honolulu International Airport, 300 Rodgers Blvd. ☎ **808/839-0767.** Admission $3 adults; $2.50 children 13–17, seniors, military, and students; $1 children 12 and under. Sun–Tues 9am–6pm, Wed–Thurs 9am–7pm, Fri 9am–9pm, Sat 9am–10pm.

While waiting for your flight to depart, check out the history of flight in the Pacific at this $3.8 million shrine to flying. You can trace elapsed time and distance of all direct flights from Honolulu on a 6-foot globe using fiber optics; watch old film clips of NASA astronauts splashing down in Hawaiian waters after landing on the moon; see models of early planes and flying boats (including a life-size replica of the Flight Deck of the space shuttle *Challenger*), and hear the heroic stories of the aviators who pioneered sky routes to the islands and beyond.

ARCHITECTURAL HIGHLIGHTS
DOWNTOWN HONOLULU

Some plug-ugly new buildings violate Honolulu's skyline, such as the controversial First Hawaiian Bank, a New York monolith that replaced a 1925 neoclassical revival masterpiece, and Darth Vader–like structures clad in black glass, but around the edges of downtown you can find some still-surviving, delightful examples of the architecture of a more sensitive era.

Start at the **Aloha Tower,** at Pier 9 at Honolulu Harbor (Ala Moana Blvd. and Nuuanu Ave.), a perpendicular point of interest erected in 1926 to welcome all to Hawaii's shores. The clock in the art deco tower is still going strong, and now a cluster of waterfront restaurants and shops known as the **Aloha Tower Marketplace** greet the newly arrived. You can ride the elevator to the 10th floor observation deck of the tower for a bird's-eye view of busy Honolulu Harbor.

Head mauka up Bishop Street, the financial center of Honolulu, to see the 1929 **Dillingham Transportation Building,** a surviving pioneer just like its neighbor, the eclectic 1929 **Alexander and Baldwin Building,** which blended Hawaiian and oriental features. Also on Bishop Street is the graceful 1930s **C. Brewer Building** and Hawaii's first skyscraper, the 1901 six-story **Stangenwald Building,** an early Italian Renaissance structure by C. W. Dickey, often called the father of Hawaiian architecture. Dickey's double-hipped, green tile–roofed **U.S. Immigration Center** on Ala Moana Boulevard between Punchbowl and South streets (across from the Restaurant Row movie complex), is an excellent example of his work. It inspired the architecture of the modern Aloha Tower Marketplace (see above).

In the Capitol District, the campuslike civic center in the heart of the city bordered buy Beretania, Punchbowl, Queen, and Alakea streets, John Carl Warnecke's **State Capitol** (1969), an open-air, volcanolike structure surrounded by a lagoon that appears to rise above the water like an island, stands next to Hawaii's ginger-bread **Iolani Palace** (1882) a perfect representation of Hawaii's monarchy period, is one of two excellent examples of that grandiose era open to the public; the other is **Aliiolani Hale** (1874; see "More Museums," above). Also of note here are the **Coronation Bandstand** (1883); **Washington Place** (1847), the oldest continuously occupied building in Honolulu, now serving as the governor's mansion; **St. Andrew's Cathedral** (1902); **Hawaii State Library** (1913); and the **Federal** (1922) and **Territorial** (1926) **buildings.** Nearby are **Kawaiahao Church** (1842) and the **Mission Houses** (1821); see "Historic Honolulu," above.

Other Honolulu highlights include Julia Morgan's **YWCA** (1927), at 1040 Richards St. (between King and Hotel streets), which the architect built during a break from building Hearst Castle in San Simeon, California; the **Yokohama Specie Bank** (1909), 36 Merchant St. (at Bethel St.), in Chinatown; and the **Honolulu Academy of Arts** (1927), a Hawaiian grass house done in a Mediterranean style by a New York architect (see "More Museums," above).

WAIKIKI: 1950S REDUX

In the 1950s, America gave the world tail fins, ducktails, and Marilyn Monroe. Streamline made headlines. Life became "cool" and "modern." The future, everyone said, was now, and Waikiki was the place to be.

Buckminster Fuller, a pear-shaped professor from Carbondale, Illinois, came to Honolulu in 1957, bolted tetrahedrons together to create a self-supporting hemispherical structure, and called it the **Geodesic Dome** (at Ala Moana Blvd. and Kalia Rd.). It was the first public dome in America. Erected in 36 hours, the futuristic-looking, 2,000-seat dome opened February 17, 1957 with a nationally televised gala, featuring the Broadway hit *South Pacific.* For the last decade, it served as the home of Don Ho (who now sings "Tiny Bubbles" at the Waikiki Beachside). Skeptics said it would collapse in the first strong wind, but it's still going strong (despite a few leaks).

With torch lights, brass roof, lava-rock walls, and the stark styling of the 1950s, **Canlis Restaurant** (2100 Kalakaua Ave.), was one swanky tropical nightclub and restaurant, complete with an indoor waterfall and the first fern bar in the world. Everyone who was anyone went there until the early 1980s, when it closed. Recently acquired by the Honolulu Police Department, it's now a Waikiki substation, specializing in investigations. It's the best-looking cop shop anywhere, even if they did turn off the waterfalls. Old-timers who return to Waikiki often stroll in thinking Canlis is open for business again. It is, but not for dinner.

UNIVERSITY OF HAWAII

In misty, rainbow-streaked Manoa Valley, students ponder marine biology, tropic agriculture and medicine, geophysics, astronomy, linguistics, and Asia-Pacific Studies; the Travel Industry Management school is considered the nation's best. Established in 1909, the university is an architectural mishmash with works by some great architects, including I. M. Pei, who designed the **East-West Center,** a congressionally funded Pacific Rim think tank established by Lyndon B. Johnson in 1960 to daily disprove Rudyard Kipling, who said "East is east and West is west and never the twain shall meet." Free campus tours are offered at 1:30pm on Wednesdays; they start at Friends Lounge, on the garden level of Jefferson Hall, 2444 Dole St. Call **808/956-8111.**

12 Beyond Honolulu: Exploring the Island

by Rick Carroll

The moment always arrives—usually after 2 or 3 days at the beach, snorkeling in the warm blue-green waters of Hanauma Bay, enjoying sundown Mai Tais, listening to the mellifluous tones of Sonny Kamahele and The Sunset Serenaders at the Halekulani—when a certain curiosity kicks in about the rest of Oahu, largely unknown to most visitors. It's time to find the rental car in the hotel garage and set out around the island.

OAHU'S SOUTHEAST COAST

Some head immediately to the North Shore, but I suggest you go south because you can get out of town faster. Once you clear suburban Hawaii Kai and Kalanianaole Highway (Hi. 72) heads uphill to Hanauma Bay, you're on one of the last unspoiled coasts on Oahu. It's a great little getaway, especially if you spin around the south coast and loop back to town on the Pali Highway (Hi. 61). All in all, it's my favorite island drive.

Around Koko Head, Oahu looks like Arizona-by-the-sea, an arid moonscape with prickly cacti on shore and, in winter, spouting whales cavorting in the water. Some call it the south shore, others Sandy's after the mile-long beach here, but Hawaiians call it Ka Iwi, which means "the bone"—no doubt because of all the bone-cracking shore break along this popular body-boarding coastline. The beaches here are long, wide, and popular with local daredevils.

This open, scenic coast is the best place on Oahu to watch sea, shore, and even land birds. It's also a good whale-watching spot in season, and the night sky is ideal for amateur astronomers to watch meteors, comets, and stars.

The jagged lava coast itself spouts sea foam at the **Halona Blowhole.** Look out to sea from Halona over Sandy Beach and out across the 26-mile gulf to neighboring Molokai, and the faint triangular shadow of Lanai on the far horizon. **Sandy Beach** (see "Beaches," above) is Oahu's most dangerous beach; it's the only one with an ambulance always standing by to whisk injured body boarders to the hospital. Body boarders just love it.

The coast looks raw and empty along this stretch, but the road weaves past old Hawaiian fishponds and past the famous formation known as **Pele's Chair,** just off Kalanianaole Highway above Queen's Beach. From a distance, the lava rock outcropping looks like a mighty throne; it's believed to be the fire goddess's last resting place on Oahu before she flew off to continue her work on other islands.

Ahead lies 647-foot-high **Makapuu Point,** with a lighthouse that once signaled safe passage for arriving steamship passengers from San Francisco. The automated light now brightens Oahu's south coast for passing tankers, fishing boats, and sailors. You can take a short hike up here for a spectacular vista; see "Nature Hikes," above.

If you're with the kids, you may want to spend the day at **Sea Life Park,** a marine amusement park; see "Fish, Flora & Fauna" under "Attractions In & Around Honolulu & Waikiki," above.

Turn the corner at Makapuu and you're on Oahu's windward side, where cooling trade winds propel windsurfers across turquoise bays and the waves at **Makapuu Beach** are perfect for bodysurfing.

Ahead, the coastal vista is a profusion of fluted green mountains and strange peaks, edged by golden beaches and the blue, blue Pacific. The 3,000-foot-high sheer green Koolau mountains plunge almost straight down, presenting an irresistible jumping-off spot for hang-glider pilots, who catch the thermals on hours-long rides.

Winding down the coast, Kamehameha Highway (Hi. 72) leads through rural **Waimanalo,** a country beach town of nurseries and stables, fresh fruit stands, and some of the island's best conch and triton shell specimens at roadside stands. **Waimanalo Beach,** nearly 4 miles long, is Oahu's longest and the most popular for bodysurfing. Take a swim here or head on to **Kailua Beach,** one of Hawaii's best beaches (see "Beaches," above).

Hang around for sunset, and you'll inevitably find yourself next to Oahu's best salad bar at **Buzz's Original Steak House,** on the outskirts of Lanikai. They also serve a lobster Caesar Salad that's quite tasty.

If you're in a hurry to get back to Waikiki, turn left at Castle Junction and head over the Pali Highway (Hi. 61), which becomes Bishop Street in Honolulu and ends at Ala Moana. Turn left for Waikiki; it's the second beach on the right.

DRIVING THE WINDWARD COAST

From the **Nuuanu Pali Lookout,** near the summit of Pali Highway (Hi. 61), you get the first hint of the other side of Oahu, a region so green and lovely that it could be an island sibling of Tahiti or Moorea. With many beaches and bays, the scenic 30-mile Windward Coast parallels the corduroy-ridged, nearly perpendicular cliffs of the Koolau Range, which separates the windward side of the island from Honolulu and the rest of Oahu.

From the Pali Highway, to the right is **Kailua,** Hawaii's biggest beach town, with more than 50,000 residents and two special beaches, **Kailua** and **Lanikai,** begging for visitors. Funky little Kailua is lined with $1 million houses next to tar-paper shacks, antique shops, and bed-and-breakfasts. Although the Pali Highway (Hi. 61) proceeds directly to the coast, it undergoes two name changes, becoming first Kalanianaole Highway—from the intersection of Kamehameha Highway (Hi. 83)— and then Kailua Road as it heads into Kailua town. Kailua Road ends at the T-intersection at Kalaheo Drive, which follows the coast in a northerly and souther-ly direction. Turn right on South Kalaheo Drive to get to Kailua Beach Park and Lanikai Beach. No signs point the way, but you can't miss them.

If you spend a day at the beach here, stick around for sunset, when the sun sinks behind the Koolau range and tints the clouds pink and orange. After a hard day at the beach you work up an appetite and Kailua has several great, inexpensive restau-rants (see "Dining," above). And don't forget to stop by the Agnes Portuguese Bake Shop, **A Panadaria,** which makes and sells Hawaii's best malassadas. Don't go snor-keling after eating two or three of these weighty treats, or you'll sink to the bottom.

As you descend on the serpentine Pali Highway beneath often gushing waterfalls, you'll see the nearly 1,000-foot spike of **Olomana,** the bold pinnacle that always re-minds me of that mountain in *Close Encounters,* and beyond, the Hawaiian village of **Waimanalo.** If you want to skip the beaches this time, turn left on North Kalaheo Drive, which becomes Kaneohe Bay Drive as it skirts Kaneohe Bay and leads back to Kamehameha Highway, which then passes through **Kaneohe.** The suburban maze of Kaneohe is one giant strip mall of retail excess that mars one of the Pacific's most pic-turesque bays. After clearing this obstacle, the place begins to look like Hawaii again.

Incredibly scenic **Kaneohe Bay** is spiked with islets, and lined with gold-sand beach parks like **Kualoa,** a favorite picnic spot (see "Beaches," above). The bay has a barrier reef and four tiny islets, one of which is known as Moku o loe, or Coco-nut Island. Don't be surprised if it looks familiar—it appeared in "Gilligan's Island." It's now the United States' only tropical marine research laboratory on a coral reef.

Little poly-vowelled beach towns like **Kaaawa, Hauula, Punaluu,** and **Kahaluu** pop up along the coast, offering passersby shell shops and art galleries to explore. Famed hula photographer Kim Taylor Reese lives on this coast; his gallery is often open during the week. There are also working cattle ranches, fisherman's wharfs, and roadside fruit and flower stands vending ice cold coconuts (to drink) and tree-ripened mangoes, papayas, and apple bananas.

At **Heeia State Park** (☎ 808/247-3156) is **Heeia Fishpond,** which ancient Hawaiians built by enclosing natural bays with rocks to trap fish on the incoming tide. Heeia Fishpond is now being restored. The 88-acre fishpond, made of lava rock, had four watchtowers to observe fish movement and several sluice gates along the 5,000-foot long wall, is now in the process of being restored.

If I could be anywhere at this very moment, I'd choose to be on **Heeia Pier,** which juts onto Kaneohe Bay. You can take a snorkel cruise here, or paddle a kayak out to a sandbar in the middle of the bay for an incredible view of Oahu that most people, even those who live here, never see. Before you go, stop in and see Ernie Choy at the **Deli on Heeia Kea Pier** (☎ 808/235-2192). Since 1979, Ernie Choy has served fishermen, sailors, and kayakers the beach town's best sandwiches, plate lunches, and loco mocos.

Everyone calls it Chinaman's Hat, but the tiny island off the eastern shore of Kualoa Regional Park is really **Mokolii.** It's a sacred *puu honua,* or place of refuge, like the restored Puu Honua Honaunau on the Big Island of Hawaii. Excavations have unearthed evidence that this area was the home of ancient alii. Early Hawaiians believed the island of Mokolii (or "fin of the lizard"), is all that remains of a *mo'o,* or lizard, slain by Pele's sister, Hiiaka, and hurled into the sea. At low tide, you can swim out to the island, but keep watch on the changing tide, which can sweep you out to sea. The islet has a small sandy beach and is a bird preserve, so don't spook the red-footed boobies.

Farther along, on the east side Kahana Bay by Kamehameha Highway is **Huilua Fishpond.** This National Historic Landmark is one of Windward Oahu's most beautiful fishponds and the easiest to see. Once fed by a freshwater spring and refreshed by the ocean, this pond proved ideal for raising mullet and milk fish.

Sugar, once the sole industry of this region, is gone. But **Kahuku,** the former sugar plantation town, has new life as a small aquaculture community with prawn and clam farms that supply restaurants, like **Ahi's,** which hopefully has reopened by the time you make the drive (see "Dining," above). Then continue on to the North Shore.

ATTRACTIONS ALONG THE WAY

Hoomaluhia Botanical Gardens. 45-680 Luluku Rd., Kaneohe. ☎ **808/233-7323.** Free admission. Daily 9am–4pm.

This 400-acre botanical garden at the foot of the steepled Koolau mountains is the perfect place for a *mauka* picnic. Its name means "a peaceful refuge." That's exactly what the Army Corps of Engineers created—quite by accident, I'm sure—when they created a flood control project here, which resulted in a 32-acre freshwater lake and the garden. Just unfold a beach mat, lay back and watch the clouds race across the rippled cliffs of the majestic Koolau range. It's one of few public places on Oahu that provides a close-up view of the steepled cliffs. The park has hiking trails, and—best of all—the island's only free inland campground (see "Camping," above). Guided nature hikes start at 10am Saturdays and 1pm Sunday from the visitor center.

Valley of the Temples. 47-200 Kahekili Hwy., Kaneohe. ☎ **808/239-8811.** Admission $2 adults, $1 children under 12. Daily 9am–5pm.

The people of Honolulu bury their pets and their grandparents in this graveyard. For 4 years awhile back, Ferdinand Marcos, the exiled Filipino dictator, was also here; he occupied a temporary mausoleum until the Philippines relented and let him be buried in his native land. Marcos is gone now, but dogs and cats and a lot of local folks remain. In a cleft of the pali, the graveyard is stalked by wild peacocks and about 700 curious people a day, who pay to see the 9-foot meditation Buddha, 2 acres of ponds full of more than 10,000 Japanese Koi carp, and a replica of Japan's 900-year-old Byodo-in Temple of Equality. The original, made of wood, stands in Uji, on the outskirts of Kyoto; the Hawaiian version, made of concrete, was erected in 1968 to commemorate the 100th anniversary arrival of the first Japanese immigrants to Hawaii. It's not the same as seeing the original, but it's worth a detour. A 3-ton brass temple bell brings good luck to those who can ring it—although the gongs do jar the Zen-like serenity of this little bit of Japan.

Senator Fong's Plantation & Gardens. 47-285 Pulama Rd., Kaneohe. ☎ **808/239-6775.** Admission $8.50 adults, $5 children 5–12. Hour-long tours daily from 10:30am; last tour 3pm.

Senator Hiram Fong, the first Chinese-American elected to the U.S. Senate, served 17 years before retiring to tropical gardening years ago. Now you can ride an open-air tram through five gardens named for the American presidents he served. His

Eastern Oahu & the Windward Coast

Halona Blowhole ❶
Heeia Pier ⑮
Heeia State Park/
  Heeia Fishpond ⑯
Hoomaluhia Botanical Garden ⑫
Huilua Fishpond ⑱
Kailua Beach ❾
Kualoa Beach Park ⑰
Lanikai Beach ❽
Makapuu Beach ❺
Makapuu Point ❹
Nuuanu Pali Lookout ⑩
Pele's Chair ❸
Polynesian Cultural Center ⑲
Sandy Beach ❷
Sea Life Park ❻
Senator Fong's Plantation
  & Gardens ⑭
Ulupo Heiau ⑪
Valley of the Temples ⑬
Waimanalo Beach ❼

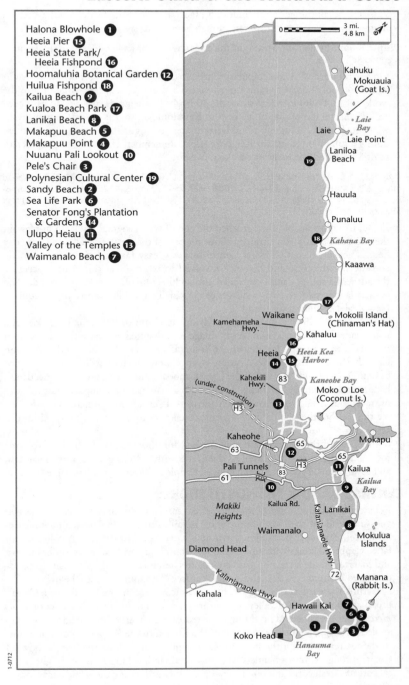

0   3 mi.
     4.8 km

Kahuku
Mokuauia
(Goat Is.)

Laie Bay

Laie
Laie Point
Laniloa
Beach

⑲

Hauula

Punaluu

⑱ *Kahana Bay*

Kaaawa

⑰

Waikane ○ Mokolii Island
(Chinaman's Hat)
Kamehameha
Hwy.
Kahaluu

Heeia ⑯
⑭ ⑮ *Heeia Kea Harbor*

Kahekili
Hwy.   83

⑬   *Kaneohe Bay*
Moko O Loe
(Coconut Is.)

(under construction)
H3

Kaheohe   65   Mokapu

63   ⑫
H3   65

Pali Tunnels   ⑪ Kailua
61   83
⑩   ❾ *Kailua Bay*

Kailua Rd.
Makiki Heights   Lanikai

Waimanalo   ❽ Mokulua
Islands

Diamond Head

Kalanianaole Hwy.   72   Manana
(Rabbit Is.)
Kahala

Kalanianaole Hwy.   ❼
Hawaii Kai   ❻ ❺
❶   ❷ ❸ ❹
Koko Head ■

Hanauma Bay

1-0712

157

725-acre botanical garden includes 75 plants and flowers. It's definitely worth an hour—if you haven't already seen enough botanics to last a lifetime.

Ulupo Heiau. Behind the YMCA on the Kaneohe side of Kailua Rd. (Hi. 61), at end of Manuoo Rd., Kailua.

On a street lined with contemporary Christian churches, out of sight behind a YMCA gym and pool is one of Oahu's most sacred ancient sites, where some believe the world began. Built of stacked rocks, the 30-by-40-foot temple is believed to have been an agricultural temple, since it's next to Kawainui Marsh, the largest body of fresh-water in Hawaii. Its name roughly translates to "night inspiration," so go there during a full moon to get the full, eerie effect. Remember, Hawaii's heiau are sacred, so don't walk on the rocks or dare to move one.

Polynesian Cultural Center. 55-370 Kamehameha Hwy., Laie. ☎ **808/293-3333.** Waikiki office, 2255 Kuhio Ave., Suite 1601. ☎ **808/923-2911.** Mon–Sat 12:30pm–9:30pm. Admission $44 adults, $27 children 5–11; luau $57 adults, $37 children; Ambassador VIP (deluxe) tour $92 adults, $61 children.

If you, like most people, have reached the end of your geographical leash in Hawaii, then you can satisfy you curiosity about the rest of the far Pacific all in a single day here. The Polynesian Cultural Center makes it easy (and relatively inexpensive, considering the time and distance involved to see the real thing) to experience the authentic songs, dance, costumes, and architecture of seven Pacific islands. The 42-acre lagoon park re-creates villages of Hawaii, Tonga, Fiji, Samoa, the Marquises, New Zealand, and Easter Island.

You "travel" through this kind of "living" museum of Polynesia by canoe on a man-made freshwater lagoon. Each village is "inhabited" by native students from Polynesia, who attend Hawaii's Bright Young University. Operated by the Mormon Church, the park also features a variety of stage shows, including "Manna! The Spirit of Our People," and "Pageant of the Long Canoes," which celebrate the music, dance, history and culture of Polynesia. There's also a luau every evening. It's not my idea of travel, but it's perfect for armchair travelers. I suggest you go here once, then go see the real South Pacific. Since a visit can take up to 8 hours, it's a good idea to arrive before 2pm.

Just beyond the center is a replica of the Mormon Tabernacle, built of volcanic rock and concrete in the form of a Greek cross with reflecting pools, formal gardens, and royal palms. It was the first Mormon temple built outside of Salt Lake City.

CENTRAL OAHU & THE NORTH SHORE

Rent a bright shiny convertible—the perfect car for Oahu since you can tan as you go—and head for the North Shore and Hawaii's surf city: **Haleiwa,** a quaint turn-of-the-century sugar plantation town designated as a historic site. A collection of faded clapboard stores with a picturesque harbor, it has evolved into a surfer outpost and major roadside attraction with art galleries, restaurants, and shops that sell hand-decorated clothing, jewelry, and sports gear (see "Shopping A to Z," below).

Getting there is half the fun. You have a choice: cruise up the H-2 through Oahu's broad and fertile central valley, past Pearl Harbor and Schofield Barracks of *From Here to Eternity* fame and on through the red-earthed heart of the island where pine-apple and sugarcane fields stretch from the Koolau to the Waianae mountains, un-til the sea reappears on the horizon. Or meander north along the lush Windward Coast, through country hamlets with roadside stands selling mangos, bright tropi-cal pareaus, fresh corn, and pond-raised prawns (see "Driving the Windward Coast," above).

Central Oahu & the Leeward Coast

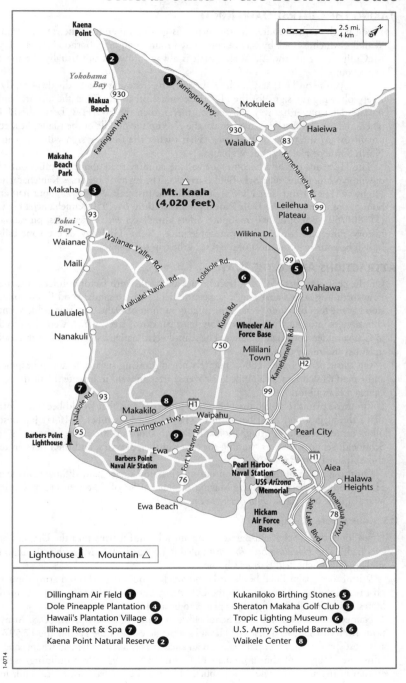

0 _____ 2.5 mi.
4 km

Kaena Point

Yokohama Bay

Makua Beach

930

Farrington Hwy.

Mokuleia

Haieiwa

930

Waialua

83

Makaha Beach Park

Makaha

Mt. Kaala
(4,020 feet)

Leilehua Plateau

99

Kamehameha Rd

Pokai Bay

Waianae

Waianae Valley Rd.

Wilikina Dr.

99

Wahiawa

Maili

Kolekole Rd.

Lualualei Naval Rd.

Lualualei

Nanakuli

Kunia Rd.

Wheeler Air Force Base

750

Mililani Town

Kamehameha Rd.

H2

Malakole Rd.

93

Makakilo

Farrington Hwy.

H1

Waipahu

99

Pearl City

Barbers Point Lighthouse

95

Ewa

Fort Weaver Rd.

Barbers Point Naval Air Station

76

Pearl Harbor Naval Station

USS Arizona Memorial

H1

Aiea

Halawa Heights

Ewa Beach

Hickam Air Force Base

Salt Lake Blvd

Moanalua Frwy.

78

Lighthouse 🗼 Mountain △

Dillingham Air Field **1**
Dole Pineapple Plantation **4**
Hawaii's Plantation Village **9**
Ilihani Resort & Spa **7**
Kaena Point Natural Reserve **2**

Kukaniloko Birthing Stones **5**
Sheraton Makaha Golf Club **3**
Tropic Lighting Museum **6**
U.S. Army Schofield Barracks **6**
Waikele Center **8**

1-0714

TAKING THE CENTRAL OAHU ROUTE

If you go the central route, the tough part is getting on and off the freeway from Waikiki, which is done by way of convoluted routing on neighborhood streets. Try McCully Street off the Ala Wai, which is always crowded but usually the most direct route.

Once you're on H-1, stay to the right side; the freeway tends to divide abruptly. Keep following the signs for the H-1 (it separates off to Hi. 78 at the airport, and reunites later on; either way will get you there), then the H-1/H-2. Leave the H-1 where the two "interstates" divide; take the H-2 up the middle of the island, headed north toward the town of Wahiawa. That's what the freeway sign will say—not North Shore or Haleiwa, but Wahiawa.

The H-2 runs out and becomes a two-lane country road about 18 miles out of downtown Honolulu, near **Schofield Barracks.** The highway becomes Kamehameha Highway (Hi. 99 and later Hi. 83) at **Wahiawa.** Just past Wahiawa, about half an hour out of Honolulu, the **Dole Pineapple Plantation,** 64-1550 Kamehameha Hwy. (☎ **808/621-8408;** daily 9am–6pm), offers a rest stop with pineapples, pineapple history, pineapple trinkets, and pineapple juice. "Kam" Highway, as everyone calls it, will be your road for most of the rest of the trip to Haleiwa.

ATTRACTIONS ALONG THE WAY

On the central plains of Oahu, tract homes and malls with factory outlet stores are now spreading across abandoned sugarcane fields, where sandalwood forests once stood at the foot of Mount Kaala, the mighty summit of Oahu. Hawaiian chiefs sent commoners into thick sandalwood forests to cut down trees, which were then sold to China traders for small fortunes. The scantily-clad natives caught cold in the cool uplands, and many died.

On those plains in the 1800s, planters began growing sugarcane and pineapple, and a man named James Campbell discovered artesian wells to irrigate the fields that changed Hawaii forever.

On those plains in 1908, the U.S. army pitched a tent that would become a fort that's the biggest and most beautiful in Hawaii. On December 7, 1941, Japanese pilots came screaming through Kolekole Pass to shoot up the art deco barracks at Schofield, sending soldiers running for cover in their skivvies, and then flew on to sink ships at Pearl Harbor.

On those plains in the 1950s, an out-of-work pop singer named Sinatra made a Hollywood comeback portraying Maggio, a soldier at Schofield on the eve of World War II in the film classic *From Here to Eternity.*

U.S. Army Schofield Barracks.

James Jones called Schofield Barracks "the most beautiful army post the U.S. has or ever had." The *Honolulu Star Bulletin* called it a country club. More than 1 million soldiers called Schofield Barracks home.

With broad, palm-lined boulevards and art deco buildings, this old army calvary post is still the largest operated by the U.S. Army outside of the continental United States. And it's still one of the best places to be a soldier.

Named for Lt. Gen. John M. Schofield, commanding general of the U.S. Army from 1888 to 1895, who first saw Hawaii's strategic value in the Pacific, the 17,597-acre post sprawls across central Oahu on an ancient Hawaiian battlefield where chieftains once fought for the supremacy of Oahu. In the 1930s, the buildings were erected in the art deco style then popular. The red-tile–roofed post office, built in 1939, reflects Hawaii's version of the Mediterranean style.

The North Shore

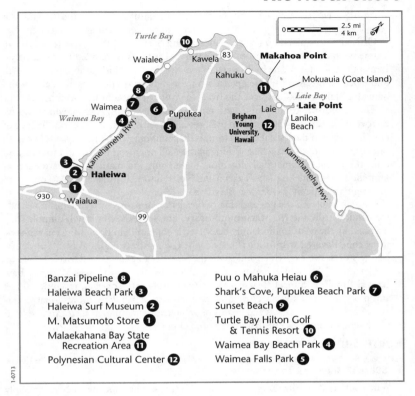

Banzai Pipeline **8**
Haleiwa Beach Park **3**
Haleiwa Surf Museum **2**
M. Matsumoto Store **1**
Malaekahana Bay State
  Recreation Area **11**
Polynesian Cultural Center **12**

Puu o Mahuka Heiau **6**
Shark's Cove, Pupukea Beach Park **7**
Sunset Beach **9**
Turtle Bay Hilton Golf
  & Tennis Resort **10**
Waimea Bay Beach Park **4**
Waimea Falls Park **5**

The history of Schofield Barracks and the 215th Infantry Division is told in the small **Tropic Lightning Museum,** Schofield Barracks (☎ **808/655-0438;** free admission; Tues–Sat 10am–4pm). Artifacts range from relics of the War of 1812 to a replica of Vietnam's infamous Cu Chi tunnels.

Kukaniloko. Off Kamehameha Hwy. between Wahiawa and Haleiwa, opposite the road to Whitmore Village.

Two rows of 18 lava rocks once flanked a central birthing stone, where women of ancient Hawaii gave birth to potential alii. The rocks, according to Hawaiian belief, held the power to ease the labor pains of childbirth. Birth rituals involved 48 chiefs who pounded drums to announce the arrival of newborns likely to become chiefs. Children born here were taken to the now destroyed Holonopahu Heiau in the pineapple field, where chiefs ceremoniously cut the umbilical cord.

Used by Oahu's alii for generations of births, the *pohaku* (or rocks), many in bowl-like shapes, now lie strewn in a coconut grove in a pineapple field at this, the most sacred site in central Oahu. Some think it also may have served as an ancient astronomy site, sort of a Hawaiian Stonehenge. Petroglyphs of human forms and circles appear on some of the stones.

HALEIWA

Only 28 miles from Waikiki is Haleiwa, the funky ex–sugar-plantation town that's the world capital of big-wave surfing. This beach town really comes alive in winter, when big waves rise up, light rain falls, and temperatures dip into the 70s; then, it seems, every surfer in the world is here to see and be seen, surfing the big swells.

Officially designated a Historic Cultural and Scenic District, Haleiwa thrives in a time warp recalling the turn of the century, when it was founded by sugar baron Benjamin Dillingham; he built a 30-mile railroad to link his Honolulu and North Shore plantations in 1899. He opened a Victorian hotel overlooking Kaiaka Bay and named it Haleiwa, or "house of the Iwa," the tropical seabird often seen here.

The turn-of-the-century hotel and railroad are gone, but Haleiwa, which was rediscovered in the late 1960s by hippies, resonates with rare rustic charm. Tofu, not taro, is a staple in the local diet. Arts and crafts, boutiques and burger stands line both sides of the town; there's a busy fishing harbor full of charter boats and captains who hunt the Kauai Channel daily for tuna, mahimahi, and marlin. The bartenders at Jameson's make the best Mai Tais on the North Shore; it's the classic, according to the original recipe by Trader Vic Bergeron.

Once in Haleiwa, the hot and thirsty traveler reports directly to the nearest shave-ice stand, usually the **M. Matsumoto Store.** For 40 years, this small, humble shop operated by the Matsumoto family has served a popular rendition of the Hawaii-style snow cone flavored with tropical tastes. The cooling treat is also available at neighboring stores, some of which still shave the ice with a hand-crank device.

Just down the road are some of the fabled shrines of surfing—**Waimea Bay, Banzai Pipeline, Sunset Beach**—where the world's largest waves, reaching 20 feet and more, rise up between November and January. They draw professional surfers as well as reckless daredevils and hoards of onlookers, who jump in their cars and head north when word goes out that "surf's up." Don't forget your binoculars.

NORTH SHORE ATTRACTIONS

Haleiwa Surf Museum. North Shore Marketplace. 66-250 Kamehameha Hwy., Haleiwa. ☎ **808/637-3406.** Free admission. Daily 9:30am–6:30pm.

When surfers aren't hanging ten at Sunset Beach or the Pipeline, they're probably hanging out at John E. Moore's nifty little museum, which celebrates the sport of Hawaiian kings. Even if you've never set foot on a surfboard, you'll want to visit Oahu's only surf museum to trace the sport. His collection of memorabilia includes vintage surfboards (a 1915 redwood longboard owned by North Shore surfer Jerry Kermode is a treasure), classic 1950s surf-meet posters, 1960s surf music album covers, old beach movie posters starring Frankie Avalon and Sandra Dee, the early black-and-white photos by legendary surf photog LeRoy Grannis, and a killer 1950 Ford Woody that every surfer I know once had and wishes he kept.

✪ **Waimea Falls Park.** 59-864 Kamehameha Hwy., Haleiwa, HI 96712. ☎ **808/638-8511,** 808/942-5700, or 800/767-8046. Admission $19.95 adults, $9.95 children 6–12. Daily 10am–5:30pm.

If you only have 1 day to spend on Oahu and want to see an ancient hula, sniff tropical flowers, go kayaking along the shore or hiking to archaeological sites and a waterfall, and play the games of ancient Hawaii (spear-throwing, lawn bowling), there's only one place to be: Waimea Falls Park. This is the perfect family place—it takes a whole family to do everything. You can explore remnants of the old Hawaiian settlements in a scenic 1,800-acre river valley that's full of tropical blooms. Or watch authentic demonstrations of the ancient (*kahiko*) hula by the park's own *halau* (school), and see cliff divers swan-dive into a pool fed by a 45-foot waterfall. Everyone is invited to explore the valley. You can ride a mountain bike, paddle a kayak, or run the Elehaha River on an all-terrain vehicle into the jungle—my favorite adventure here.

Puu o Mahuka Heiau. One mile past Waimea Bay; take Pupukea Rd. mauka off Kamehameha Hwy. and drive seven-tenths of a mile up a switchback road.

Go around sundown to feel the mana of this sacred Hawaiian place, the largest sacrificial temple on Oahu, associated with the great kahuna Kaopulupulu, who sought peace between Oahu and Kauai. The prescient *kuhuna* predicted that the island would be overrun by strangers from a distant land. In 1794, three of Capt. George Vancouver's men of the *Daedalus* were sacrificed here. In 1819, the year before New England missionaries landed in Hawaii, King Kamehameha II ordered all idols at the heiau to be destroyed.

A National Historical Landmark, this 18th-century heiau, known as the "hill of escape," sits on a 5-acre, 300-foot bluff overlooking Waimea Bay and 25 miles of Oahu's wave-lashed north coast—all the way to Kaena Point, where the Waianae Range ends in a spirit leap to the other world. The heiau appears as a huge rectangle of rocks twice as big as a football field (170 by 575 ft.), with an altar often covered by the flower and fruit offerings left by native Hawaiians. With the rise of the Hawaiian sovereignty movement, simple graven images have begun to reappear on this site.

13 Shopping A to Z

by Jocelyn Fujii

In this land of the alluring outdoors, few people like to admit that shopping is a major temptation. With bodysurfing, hiking on volcanoes, and other invigorating, exotic adventures beckoning, spending time in a shopping mall seems so, well, bourgeois. Truth be known, the proliferation of topnotch made-in-Hawaii products, the vitality of the local crafts scene, and the unquenchable thirst for mementos of the islands lend a new respectability to shopping here. And Oahu (Maui, too) is a haven for mall mavens. From T-shirts to Versace, posh European to down-home local, avant-garde to unspeakably tacky, Oahu's offerings are wide-ranging indeed. But shopping on this island is slightly schizophrenic. You must sometimes wade through oceans of schlock to arrive at the mother lode. Nestled amid the Louis Vuitton, Chanel, and Ettore Bugatti boutiques on Waikiki's Kalakaua Avenue are plenty of tacky booths hawking air-brushed T-shirts, gold by the inch, and tasteless aloha shirts.

The section that follows is not about finding cheap souvenirs or tony items from designer fashion chains. You can find these on your own. Rather, we offer a guide to finding those special treasures that lie somewhere in between.

SHOPPING IN & AROUND HONOLULU & WAIKIKI
ALOHA WEAR

One of Hawaii's lasting afflictions is the penchant tourists have for wearing loud, matching aloha shirts and muumuus. We applaud such visitors' good intentions (to act local), but they are not Hawaiian. No local resident would be caught dead in such a get-up. Muumuus and aloha shirts are wonderful, but the real thing is what island folks wear on Aloha Friday (every Friday), to the Brothers Cazimero Lei Day Concert (every May 1st), or to work (where allowed). It's what they wear at home and to special parties where the invitation reads "Aloha Attire."

Our favorite aloha wear designer is **Avanti,** who makes a stunning line of silk shirts and dresses in authentic 1930s to 1950s fabric patterns. The shirts are the ne plus ultra of aloha shirts, with all the qualities of a vintage silkie without the high price or the web-thin fragility of authentic antique shirts. For about $60, you can find a stylish shirt that is wearable long after you leave Hawaii. Women's dresses, high-collared tea timers from the 1930s, pant sets, and many other styles are the epitome of comfort and nostalgic good looks. The line is distributed in better boutiques and department stores throughout Hawaii. In Waikiki, the major retail outlets for the designs are **Avanti Fashion** (2229 Kuhio Ave., ☎ 808/926-6886), housed in a distinctive old gingerbread house, and the new Avanti location in Waikiki Shopping Plaza (2270 Kalakaua Ave.; ☎ 808/926-6886).

Also noteworthy is the extensive line of aloha shirts and dresses by **Kahala Sportswear.** Kahala has faithfully reproduced, with astounding success, the linoleum-block prints of noted Big Island artist Avi Kiriaty. Designs include Mandarin-style dresses, tank dresses, and distinctive aloha shirts bearing scenes of fishing, canoeing, farming, and other idyllic Polynesian pursuits. Kahala is sold in department stores (from Liberty House to Nordstrom), surf shops, and stylish boutiques throughout Hawaii and the mainland.

For the most culturally correct aloha wear, check out the aloha shirts, dresses, and pareus of **Sig Zane Design** (see "Shops & Galleries" in Chapter 6, "Hawaii: The Big Island"), available on Oahu at **Martin & MacArthur** (☎ 808/524-6066) in Aloha Tower Marketplace. Zane, an accomplished hula dancer married to one of Hawaii's most revered hula masters, has an unmistakable visual style and profound knowledge of Hawaiian culture that bring depth and meaning to his boldly styled renditions of the ti plant, ohia, kukui, ieie, koa, kaunaoa, and other prominent Hawaiian flora. Each Sig Zane pareu and aloha shirt, in pure cotton, tells a story. No wonder it's the garb of the cultural connoisseurs, who also buy fabrics by the yard to bring the rain forest into their homes.

Another name to watch for is **Tutuvi,** whose T-shirts, dresses, and pareus are distinctive for their brilliant color combinations and witty juxtaposition of design motifs. Tutuvi designs, as well as a wide selection of attractive aloha shirts, T-shirts, and other Hawaii-themed fashions, can be found at **Tahiti Imports** (☎ 808/941-4539) in Ala Moana Center, or by appointment at **Tutuvi,** 2850 S. King St. (☎ 808/947-5950).

If you love the vintage look, but are not so wild about vintage price tags, the kamaaina label of **Tori Richard** has come out with an attractive line called Pau Hana, a series of retro prints and styles for women. Another source for attractive aloha shirts and muumuus in traditional and contemporary styles is **Reyn's,** with stores in Ala Moana Center, Kahala Mall, and the Sheraton Waikiki. The reverse-print aloha shirt, the uniform of downtown boardrooms, was popularized by Reyn's, which has also jumped aboard the vintage-look bandwagon with its old-Hawaii cotton fabric prints, some of them in two-color pareu patterns.

Well-known muumuu labels in Hawaii include **Mamo Howell,** who has boutiques in Kahala Mall and Ward Warehouse; **Princess Kaiulani** and **Bete** for the dressier muus, sold along with many other lines at Liberty House and other department stores; and **Sun Babies** for casual styles, also found at Liberty House. **Hilo Hattie's** (☎ 808/537-2926) offers daily shuttle service from Waikiki to its sprawling retail outlet on Nimitz Highway in Iwilei. The silk aloha shirts are cheap ($29.99), but we can't vouch for the quality. You'll also find macadamia nuts, Hawaii coffees, jewelry, aloha wear, and other Hawaii souvenirs, as well as live Hawaiian entertainment and free Kona coffee samples.

ANTIQUES & COLLECTIBLES

Antiques hunting on Oahu is usually an eclectic endeavor, a treasure hunt for Asian, European, Hawaiian, and South Pacific antiquities.

Aloha Antiques and Collectables. 926 Maunakea St. ☎ **808/536-6187.**

You may find a priceless Lalique antique among the tchotchkes that fill every square inch of this dizzying shop. But you'll have to look hard, because there are so many items they literally spill out onto the sidewalk. Upstairs, downstairs, in adjoining rooms, around corners—the place defies inventory. Jewelry, vintage aloha shirts, vases, silver, ephemera, and countless eclectic items make up this mind-boggling collection of junk, treasures, and nostalgia.

Aloha Flea Market. Aloha Stadium. ☎ **808/486-1529.**

Our advice is to go as early as possible, take a hat, and wear sunscreen. It gets very hot in this neck of the woods, and with more than 1,000 vendors sprawling across the stadium floor, it can be exhausting as well. You'll find the more interesting individuals and estates offering vintage treasures interspersed among produce stands and tacky stalls with cheap sunglasses and T-shirts. You never know when that extra-special 1940s tablecloth, Matson liner menu, John Kelly print, vintage silkie aloha shirt, or Roseville pottery vase will appear. These treasures are snatched up quickly by flea market habitués, so serious collectors had best go early. Admission is 50¢ per person. Open Wednesday, Saturday, and Sunday from 6am to 3pm.

Anchor House Antiques. 471 Kapahulu Ave. ☎ **808/732-3884.**

This highly eclectic collection of Hawaiian, Oriental, and European pieces, located here for 26 years, sprawls over thousands of square feet. You'll find wooden calabashes, camphor chests, paintings, Hawaiian artifacts, and trinkets, priced from $10 to $2,000.

Antique Alley. 1347 Kapiolani Blvd. ☎ **808/941-8551.**

Antique Alley is chockablock with the passionate collections of several vendors under one roof. The showcases include estate jewelry, antique silver, Hawaiian bottles, collectible toys, pottery, Depression glass, linens, plantation photos and ephemera, and a wide selection of nostalgic items from Hawaii and across America. Salt-and-pepper shakers, Pillsbury dough-boy statuettes, old phones, radios, ivory, china, and cameras spill out across the narrow shop. At the rear is a small, attractive selection of Soiree clothing, made by Julie Lauster out of antique kimonos and obis.

Antique House. 2259 Kalakaua Ave., the Royal Hawaiian Hotel. ☎ **808/923-5101.**

Small but tasteful, the low-profile Antique House is hidden below the lobby level of this illustrious hotel. Come here for small items: Oriental antiques, Chinese and Japanese porcelains, and a stunning selection of snuff bottles, bronzes, vases, and china.

Garakuta-Do. 580 N. Nimitz Hwy., across from Gentry Pacific Center. ☎ **808/524-7755.**

If it's Japanese antiques you're after, it's worth driving to the industrial harbor area to view the late-Edo period (1800s through early 1900s) antiques collected and sold by cheerful owner Wataru Harada. A wide selection of gorgeous tansus, mingei folk art, Japanese screens, scrolls, Imari plates, bronze sculptures, kimono, obi, and stone objects fill the sprawling space.

✪ Kilohana Square. 1016 Kapahulu Ave., Kapahulu.

If there is any one destination that we would recommend for antiques, it would be this tiny square in Kapahulu. Kilohana's five antiques shops cover a rich range of Oriental art, Japanese and European antiques, and high-quality collectibles. Many of the shops have loyal clients across the country who know they can find authentic goods, particularly Asian antiques, here. Our favorites are **T. Fujii Japanese Antiques** (☎ **808/732-7860**), a long-standing icon in Hawaii's antiques world and an

.impeccable source for Ukiyoe prints, scrolls, obis, Imari porcelain, tansus, tea ceremony bowls, and screens, as well as contemporary ceramics from Mashiko and Kasama, with prices from $25 to $18,000; **Miko Oriental Art Gallery** (☎ 808/735-4503), a large repository of Chinese, Japanese, Korean, and Southeast Asian ceramics, bronzes, and furniture, ranging in price froom $50 to $22,000; **Silk Winds** (☎ 808/735-6599), a tasteful collection of Asian antiques, everything from beads and jewelry to cricket cages, jade sculptures, and porcelain; and **Carriage House Antiques** (☎ 808/737-2622), whose owner is an expert in antique silver and European porcelain. Each shop has its own hours; call to be sure they're open.

۞ Robyn Buntin. 848 S. Beretania St. ☎ **808/523-5913.**

The gracious and authoritative Robyn Buntin is an expert in netsuke and a highly esteemed resource in Oriental art. Located not far from the Honolulu Academy of Arts, the 2,500-square-foot space, as much a gallery as an antiques store, radiates a tasteful serenity. The offerings include jade, netsuke, scholar's table items, Buddhist sculpture, Japanese prints, contemporary Chinese, Japanese, and Korean pictorial (graphic) art, and a large and magnificent collection of Hawaiiana. Some pieces are 5,000 years old, while many others are hot off the press from Tokyo, Seoul, and Beijing. Buntin represents five Japanese contemporary print artists, an artist from Seoul, and a handful of Hawaiian artists. The brilliant selection of netsuke and Japanese carving is complemented with Hawaiian works by John Kelly, Isami Doi, Avi Kiriaty, Guy Buffet, Mark Kadota, and others. Few people know that John Kelly's legacy includes Oriental works; they're here, along with rare etchings and prints that move swiftly to waiting collectors. Also known for his meticulous craftsmanship and taste in framing, Buntin has a framing operation in downtown Honolulu.

BOOKSTORES

Specialty booksellers include **Pacific Book House** (435 Atkinson Drive, ☎ 808/942-2242), which is tops in Hawaiiana, antiques and rare prints, book restoration, and rare and out-of-print books; **Rainbow Books and Records** (1010 University Ave., ☎ 808/955-7994), a little weird, but notable for its selection of textbooks, popular fiction, records, and Hawaii-themed books, secondhand and reduced; the **Book Cellar** (222 Merchant St., ☎ 808/523-3772), a downtown niche spilling over with used, rare, and collectible books focusing on Hawaii and the Pacific. **Tusitala Bookshop** (116 Hekili St., Kailua, ☎ 808/262-6343) also offers a strong selection of used, rare, and out-of-print books on Hawaii and the South Pacific.

CONSIGNMENT SHOPS

Honolulu has its quota of budget-saving Goodwill and Salvation Army stores, but it's **The Ultimate You** (851 Pohukaina St., ☎ 808/591-8388) that really thrills the woman with confidence enough to wear another person's cast-offs with neither apology nor announcement. This is a resale boutique, not a vintage or secondhand store, so the clothes are current and not always cheap, but always 50% to 90% off retail. The joy is in the hunt here, as you peruse the selection of perfectly good clothes (all 3 years old or less, and freshly laundered or cleaned). This means designer suits and dresses, often new or barely worn, from such famous names as Escada, Chanel, Prada, Gianfranco Ferre, Donna Karan, and Ann Taylor. You'll also find scads of separates, cashmere sweaters, dresses, shoes, scarves, and purses of equal (or greater) beauty and lesser renown. **Consignment Closet** (2970 E. Manoa Rd., ☎ 808/988-7442) is cheaper (much) and funkier, with a smaller yet very honorable selection of shoes, dresses, and separates. Almost-new Kikit silk blouses for $10 and $20, blazers for $15 and up, and a wall lined with dresses make this a worthy stop.

EDIBLES

In addition to the stores listed below, we also recommend **Executive Chef** in the Ward Warehouse and **Islands' Best** in the Ala Moana Center.

Asian Grocery. 1319 S. Beretania St. ☎ **808/531-8371.**

The influx of newcomers from Southeast Asia has spawned new sources of exotic food products. Asian Grocery supplies many of Honolulu's Thai and Vietnamese eateries with authentic spices, rices, noodles, produce, sauces, herbs, and adventurous ingredients for their native cookery. Browse among the shallots, kaffir lime leaves, tamarind and fish pastes, red and green chiles, fresh basil, curry sauces, chutneys, lotus leaves, gingko nuts, jasmine and basmati rices, and shelf upon shelf of medium-to-hot chili sauces.

Daiei. 801 Kaheka St. ☎ **808/973-4800.**

Stands offering take-out sushi, Korean food, pizza, Chinese food, flowers, Mrs. Fields cookies, and other items for self and home rim this huge emporium. Inside you'll find household products, electronics, cosmetics, a pharmacy, and inexpensive clothing, but it is the prepared foods and produce that excel. When Ka'u navel oranges, macadamia nuts, Kona coffee, Chinese taro, and other Hawaii products are on sale, savvy locals arrive in droves to take advantage of the high quality and good value.

Farmers Market. ☎ **808/597-1800.**

The stunningly successful Hilo Farmers Market has arrived in Honolulu, with many of its fresh flowers, produce, and food booths straight from Big Island farmers and producers. The Farmers Market is aesthetically, spiritually, gastronomically, and economically fulfilling, with good buys and varied selection, including fresh aquacultured seaweed from Oahu's north shore, a hearty ingredient in even the finest restaurants; ready-to-harvest herbs in pots, $1 per pot; Mark Twain Bakery guava and banana breads; fresh oyster mushrooms and savory Indian spices; lau lau and pickled vegetables from Hilo; and dewey-fresh greens and cut flowers. The booths change every weekend, but you can always count on fresh-cut anthuriums of all colors (at a fraction of florists' prices) and a full range of local produce and fruit in season, from papayas to mangoes to rambutan. Call the number listed above for the current location. Open Saturday from 6am to noon.

Honolulu Chocolate Co. At Ward Centre. ☎ **808/591-2997.** 2908 E. Manoa Rd. ☎ 808/988-4999. 500 Ala Moana Blvd., Restaurant Row. ☎ 808/528-4033.

Life's greatest pleasures are dispensed here with abandon: expensive gourmet chocolates made in Honolulu, chocolate-covered macadamia nuts, Italian and Hawaiian biscotti, boulder-sized turtles (caramel and pecans covered with chocolate), truffles, chocolate-covered coffee beans, jumbo apricots dipped in white and dark chocolate. There are cheese and chocolate cakes, tinned biscuits, European candies, and sweets in a million disguises.

✪ Mauna Kea Marketplace Food Court. 121 N. Hotel St., Chinatown. ☎ **808/524-3409.**

Hungry patrons line up in front of the no-nonsense food booths that offer Vietnamese noodle soup, pizza, Japanese food, Chinese plate lunches, and a dozen other types of quick, authentic, inexpensive ethnic cuisine. The best seafood fried rice comes from the woks of Malee Thai/Vietnamese Cuisine at the mauka end of the marketplace—generous, perfectly flavored, endowed with morsels of fish, squid, and shrimp. Walk the few steps down to the produce stalls (pungent odors, pig heads and feet on counters: not for the squeamish) and join in the spirit of discovery. Fish counters and produce stalls vend everything from fresh ahi and whole snappers to mangoes in season, Kapoho papayas, Southeast Asian durian (in season), yams and taro, seaweed, shellfish, and greens of every shape and size.

Paradise Produce Co. 83 N. King St., Chinatown. ☎ **808/533-2125.**

Neat rows of mangoes, top-quality papayas, and reasonably priced and very fresh produce make this a paradise for food lovers. When asparagus is plentiful, it will be very inexpensive here, and very fresh. When mangoes are in season, you'll find Yee's Orchard Haydens set apart from the less desirable Mexican mangoes, and, if you're lucky, a stash of ambrosial Piries that will sell out quickly. Chinese taro, bok choy, basil, litchis in season, local eggplant, and dozens of types of fruit and vegetables are offered up fresh, neat, and colorful.

People's Open Markets. Various sites around town. ☎ **808/522-7099.**

Truck farmers from all over the island bring their produce to Oahu's neighborhoods in regularly sheduled, city-sponsored open markets. Among the tables of ong choy, choi sum, won bok, Okinawan spinach, opal basil, papayas, mangoes, and litchis in season, you'll find homemade banana bread, Chinese pomelo (like large grapefruit), fresh fiddleheads (fern shoots) when available, and colorful, bountiful harvests from land and sea. The offerings change by the week and the season, but you will always find a satisfying sampling of Island-grown, inexpensive, freshly gathered greens. Call the number above to find the open market nearest you.

✪ R. Field Wine Co. 1200 Ala Moana Blvd., Ward Centre. ☎ **808/596-9463.**

Oenophile, gourmet, and cigar aficionado Richard Field combines all his interests in this ultrachic shop of culinary pleasures. His sophisticated selection includes exclusive, limited, hard-to-find vintages; the classic malts of Scotland; organic vine-ripened tomatoes; salmon mousse; poha and ohelo berry preserves; plum pudding; designer vinegars; Kulana "organic" beef; Langenstein estate Kona coffee; estate-grown, super-luxe Hawaiian Vintage Chocolate, grown on the Big Island; Petrossian caviar; Waimanalo baby greens; gourmet cheeses, and, of course, cigars. R. Field is synonymous with fine dining, good living, and healthful choices, and prices, though expensive, are not out of this world. Regular wine and cigar tastings, annual culinary festivals, a radio program, and ongoing efforts to expand and elevate his customers' dining experiences make this an epicurean center of Hawaii—not quite Dean & DeLuca, but growing.

Shirokiya. At Ala Moana Shopping Center. ☎ **808/941-9111.**

Shirokiya's upstairs food department is renowned throughout Honolulu. Food samples hot off the grill or oven are offered from the counters: fish, mochi, pickled vegetables, and black beans fill the air with briny, smoky scents. A separate take-out food department sells sushi, udon and noodle soups, and many varieties of boxed bento lunches. Tables are available, or you can order the food to go.

✪ Strawberry Connection of Hawaii. 1931 Kahai St., Kalihi. ☎ **808/842-0278.**

If you love food enough to search for it in the bowels of industrial Honolulu, give this place a try. Foodies in the know swear by Strawberry Connection, the most stunning showcase of Hawaii food products in the state (aside from culinary festivals and annual fairs). Shopping here is an adventure. If you don't bring a jacket, they'll loan you one: The walk-in chill rooms are *cold,* and you have to enter them to pick the best portobello or shiitake mushrooms, flawless asparagus spears, plump strawberries, Waimanalo gourmet greens, and stacks of designer produce from all the Hawaiian islands. Sections of prepared foods (preserves, sauces, dressings, seasonings, rice, pasta, cheeses, chocolates, Sierra bean soups, cholesterol-free New York flatbread, frozen and freeze-dried vegetarian meals) appear in front of and inside the retail space. Friendly service, good prices, and regular culinary classes and demonstrations are part of the deal.

Bakeries

The **Saint-Germain** bakeries in Shirokiya at Ala Moana Shopping Center (☎ 808/955-1711), near Times Supermarket (11296 S. Beretania St., ☎ 808/593-8711), and at Pearlridge Center (☎ 808/488-4967) bake the best French breads, baguettes, country loaves, and oddball delicacies, such as mini mushroom and spinach pizzas in Danish-type shapes and dough, in town. How good are the breads? Many of the fine restaurants in Honolulu serve their French loaves at candlelit tables. In Ward Warehouse, **Mary Catherine's** (☎ 808/591-8525), the darling of the gourmet bakeries, still turns out sinful cakes, fruit tarts, and cookies despite its smaller, more modest, less European space—and prices that are nothing to sneeze at. In Kaimuki, old-timers still line up at **Bea's Pies & Deli** (1117 12th Ave., ☎ 808/734-4024), which often runs out of pies by noon. Across the Pali in Kailua town, **Agnes Portuguese Bake Shop** (35 Kainehe St., ☎ 808/262-5367) is the favorite of the malassada mavens. These sugary Portuguese dumplings, like doughnuts without holes, fly out of the bakery along with the corn bread, Portuguese bean soup, fresh Portuguese sausage, carrot cake, scones, cookies, and potato breads that infuse the neighborhood with irresistible aromas (also see Cafe Laufer, p. 117).

Fish Markets

Safeway on Beretania Street has an exceptional fish counter with fresh choices and a staff that takes pride in their deftness with prepared foods.(If you're curious, don't be shy about asking for a taste.) **Foodland** on Beretania Street also offers good buys on live lobster and Dungeness crab, fresh ahi and aku poke, ahi sashimi and steaks, and a wide variety of fresh fish and shellfish, including whole snappers and oysters when available.

Tamashiro Market. 802 N. King St., Kalihi. ☎ **808/841-8047.**

You'll think you're in a Fellini movie amid the tanks of live lobsters and crabs, and the dizzying array of counters glistening with fresh slabs of ahi, opakapaka whole and in fillets, onaga, and ehu. Point and ask if you don't know what you're looking at, and one of the many fish cutters will explain, then clean and fillet your selection. Good service and the most extensive selection in Honolulu make Tamashiro the grandfather of fish markets and the ace-in-the-hole for home chefs with bouillabaisse or paella in mind. Also a magnet for shoppers is the separate counter of seaweed salads, prepared poke, lau lau, lomi salmon, Filipino and Puerto Rican ti-wrapped steamed rice, Japanese pickles, fresh produce, and dozens of other ethnic foods.

Yama's Fish Market. 2203 Young St., Moiliili. ☎ **808/941-9994.**

Neighbor islanders have been known to drive directly from the airport to Yama's for a plate lunch, Honolulu's best. Robust Hawaiian plates with pork or chicken lau lau (20 combinations!), baked ahi, chili, beef stew, shoyu chicken, and dozens of other varieties stream out to those who line up at the counter and to offices who order by the dozen. But Yama's is also known for its inexpensive fresh fish (fresh mahimahi is always less expensive here than in the supermarkets), tasty poke (ahi, aku, Hawaiian-style, Oriental-style, with seaweed), lomi salmon, and many varieties of prepared seafood. Chilled beer, boiled peanuts, and fresh ahi they'll slice into sashimi are popular for local-style pot luck dinners, sunset beach parties, and festive *pau hana* (end of work) gatherings.

Health Food

Kokua Market, 2643 S. King St., Moiliili (☎ 808/941-1922), is Honolulu's best source of healthy grinds in all categories but vitamin supplements. Voluminous, leafy organic vegetables; an excellent variety of cheeses; pastas and bulk grains; sandwiches, salads, and prepared foods; and a solid selection of organic wines elevate Kokua to a special place in the hearts of health-minded shoppers. Ample parking is offered behind and *makai* (toward the beach) of the store. **Down to Earth** (2525 S. King St., Moiliili, ☎ 808/947-7678), located a few blocks away, is another respectable source of organic vegetables and bulk foods, with a strong department in supplements and herbs. Down to Earth also offers many varieties of honey, nonalcoholic beer, teas, and household products. We think **Eco-Foods Hawaii** (1541 S. Beretania St., ☎ 808/ 955-6168), a co-op, has the best prices and a wide and user-friendly selection of health-food supplements to complement its McDougall breads, frozen vegetarian foods, and healthy snacks. **Huckleberry Farms** (1613 Nuuanu Ave., Nuuanu, ☎ 808/524-7960) across town has a serviceable selection of produce, vitamins, cosmetics, and books, with a small selection of prepared vegetarian foods.

FLOWERS & LEIS

For a special-occasion, top-of-the-line, designer bouquet or lei, you can't do better than Michael Miyashiro of **Rain Forest Plantes et Fleurs** (1550 Rycroft St., near Ala Moana Center, ☎ 808/942-1550). He is a nature-loving, ecologically aware, and highly gifted lei maker—pricey, but worth it. His nontraditional leis include one-of-a-kind garlands made from maʻo flowers (Hawaiian cotton) entwined with pikake, pakalana with a new twist, a New Guinea blossom brand-new to the islands, or strands of regal ilima. He custom designs the lei for the person and the occasion, and the personalized attention shows.

The other primary sources for flowers and leis are the shops lining the streets of Moiliili and Chinatown. Moiliili favorites include **Rudy's Flowers** (2722 S. King St., ☎ 808/944-8844), a local institution with the best prices on roses, Micronesian ginger leis (they can go as low as $8.50 here while others sell them for $15), and a variety of cut blooms. Across the street, **Flowers for a Friend** (2739 S. King St., ☎ 808/955-4227) has a limited lei selection but occasionally has good prices on cut flowers. In Chinatown, lei vendors line Beretania and Maunakea streets, and the fragrances of their wares mix with the earthy scents of incense and ethnic foods. Our top picks in Chinatown are **Lita's Leis** (59 N. Beretania St., ☎ 808/521-9065), which has fresh puakenikeni, gardenias that last, and a supply of fresh and reasonable leis; **Sweetheart's Leis** (69 N. Beretania St., ☎ 808/537-3011), with a worthy selection of the classics at fair prices; **Lin's Lei Shop** (1017 A Maunakea St., ☎ 808/537-4112), with creatively-fashioned, unusual leis (Kauai mokihana in season, Hilo maile, stefanotis, baby roses); and **Cindy's Lei Shoppe** (1034 Maunakea St., ☎ 808/536-6538), a household word with terrific sources for unusual materials such as Kauai maile, the occasional colvillea or other special bloom, and the everyday favorites such as plumeria and pikake, at reasonable prices.

HAWAIIANA/GIFT ITEMS

Our top recommendations in this category are the **Academy Shop** at the Honolulu Academy of Arts (900 S. Beretania St., ☎ 808/523-8703) and the **Contemporary Museum Gift Shop** (2411 Makiki Heights Rd., ☎ 808/523-3447), two of the finest shopping stops on Oahu and worth a special trip whether or not you're in a museum mood. As the retail operations of Hawaii's two finest art museums, each is stocked with the best in books, cards, and ethnic and contemporary gift items. The

Academy Shop offers art books, jewelry, basketry, beadwork, ikats, saris, ethnic fabrics from all over the world, posters and books, native crafts, and fiber vessels and accessories. The Contemporary Museum shop focuses on contemporary arts and crafts, such as avant-garde jewelry, cards and stationery, books, and gift items made by artists from Hawaii and across the country.

Other good sources for quality gift items are the **Little Hawaiian Craft Shop** (in the Royal Hawaiian Shopping Center) and **Martin and MacArthur** (in the Aloha Tower Marketplace).

Following Sea. 4211 Waialae Ave. ☎ **808/734-4425.**

The buyers scour the country for the best representations of fine American craftsmanship in everything from candles and bath products to sculpture, fiber art, jewelry, ceramics, glassware, and functional and nonfunctional works of wood. Hawaii is well represented in the collection, with handsome hand-turned bowls made of native and introduced woods, jewelry, ceramics, handmade paper and hand-bound books, and a stunning selection of koa boxes. Bread boards, koa mirrors, hair sticks, chopsticks of fine woods, and Hawaii-inspired jewelry in gold and silver are among the offerings of local artists.

Hula Supply Center. 2346 S. King St., Moiliili. ☎ **808/941-5379.**

Hawaiiana meets kitsch in this shop's marvelous selection of Day-Glo cellophane skirts, bamboo nose flutes, T-shirts, hula drums, shell leis, feathered rattle gourds, lauhala accessories, fiber mats, and an assortment of pareu fabrics. Although hula dancers shop here for their dance accoutrements, it's not all serious shopping. This is fertile ground for finding souvenirs and memorabilia of Hawaii.

✪ **Native Books & Beautiful Things.** 222 Merchant St., Downtown. ☎ **808/599-5511.**

Come here to be enveloped in a love of things Hawaiian. You'll find the best selection of Hawaii-themed books here, as well as contemporary and Hawaiian clothing, handmade koa journals, leis made of wiliwili, Hawaii-themed home accessories, lauhala handbags and accessories, jams and jellies, and a spate of quality gift items. Favorites include the cotton tablecloths and napkins by Skinny Dip, hand-painted in cheerful flower motifs, and the retro and vintage clothing sold in the same booth. Some of Hawaii's finest artists in everything from photography to lei making have their works available here on a regular basis.

✪ **Nohea Gallery.** At Ward Warehouse. ☎ **808/596-0074.** Also at Kahala Mandarin Oriental Hawaii, 5000 Kahala Ave., ☎ 808/737-8688.

One of Hawaii's finest showcases for contemporary Hawaiian Island art, Nohea celebrates the islands with thoughtful, topnotch selections in all media, from pit-fired raku and finely turned wood vessels to jewelry, glassware, fabrics (including Hawaiian-quilt cushions), and furniture. Ninety percent of the works are by Hawaii artists. Handcrafted koa rockers by Marcus Castaing and Mike Riley; raku teapots by Gail Bakutis; koa calabashes by Jack Straka; low-fired ceramics by Vicky Chock; pareus by Tutuvi; glass by Kurt McVay; and gleaming koa accessories, from hair sticks to jewelry boxes, grace the pleasing showrooms. Holualoa artist Wilfred Yamazawa has his handblown glass pieces here, and Fabienne Blanc's extraordinary watercolors are much coveted among the two-dimensional works. The new location in the Kahala Mandarin is small but satisfying; the flagship store in Ward Warehouse has a much larger selection.

Quilts Hawaii. 2338 S. King St. ☎ **808/942-3195.**

Handmade Hawaiian quilts drape the shop from top to bottom, in traditional Hawaiian and contemporary patterns. Hawaiian-quilt cushions (much more affordable than full-sized quilts, which run, understandably, in the thousands of dollars) and quilt-sewing kits can also be found here. You can also custom-order the larger works.

Shop Pacifica. 1335 Kalihi St. (in the Bishop Museum). ☎ **808/848-4158.**

Local crafts, lauhala and Cook Island woven coconut, Hawaiian music tapes and CDs, pareus, and a stunning selection of Hawaii-themed books anchor the museum's gift shop selection. Hawaiian quilt cushion kits, jewelry, glassware, seed and Niihau shell leis, silk-screened dish towels, cookbooks, and a multitude of other gift possiblities will keep you occupied between stargazing in the planetarium and pondering the shells, insects, and antiquities of this esteemed historical museum.

SHOPPING CENTERS
Ala Moana Center. 1450 Ala Moana Center. ☎ **808/946-2811.**

Ala Moana Center, a teeming megalopolis of consumerism, also has airline ticket counters (in **Sears**), a foreign exchange service (**Thomas Cook,** street level), a dry cleaners (**Al Phillips,** street level), a Honolulu Satellite City Hall (street level), a U. S. Post Office (street level), several optical companies (including 1-hour service by **LensCrafters**), the **Foodland Supermarket,** a pharmacy, and several services for quick photo processing. Its 200 shops and restaurants sprawl over several blocks, catering to every imaginable need, from over-the-top upscale (**Tiffany, Dior, Chanel, Armani, Versace**), to mainland chains such as **The Gap, The Body Shop, Williams-Sonoma,** and **J. C. Penney.** Departments stores such as **Liberty House** and the endlessly entertaining **Shirokiya** sell fashion and household needs, and **Longs Drugs** has everything from film, sunscreen, and cosmetics to terrific sales on macadamia nuts. One of the best stops for Hawaiian gifts is **Islands' Best,** a small, wonderful street-level store that spills over with Hawaiian-made foodstuffs, ceramics, fragrances, and more. **Splash! Hawaii** is a good source for women's swimwear; for men's swimwear, try **Liberty House, Town & Country Surf,** or the terminally hip **Hawaiian Island Creations.** Lovers of Polynesian wear and pareus should not miss **Tahiti Imports** (see Aloha Wear, above). Open Monday through Saturday from 9:30am to 9pm, Sunday from 10am to 5pm. You can get there on the Ala Moana Shuttle Bus, running daily every 15 minutes from eight spots in Waikiki; or take TheBUS no. 8 (Ala Moana Center), no. 19 (Airport or Airport/Hickam AFB), or no. 20 (Airport/Halawa Gate). The Waikiki Trolley also stops at Ala Moana from various Waikiki locales; an all-day pass costs $15.

Aloha Tower Marketplace. 1 Aloha Tower Dr., on the waterfront between piers 8 and 11, Honolulu Harbor. ☎ **808/528-5700.**

Despite valet parking and trolley stops, parking is a discouraging aspect of shopping at Aloha Tower. Once you get to the new harborfront complex, however, a sense of nostalgia, of what it must have been like in the "Boat Days" of the 1920s to 1940s, will inevitably take over. Sleek ocean liners still tie up across the harbor, and the refurbished Aloha Tower stands high over the complex, as it did in the days when it was the tallest structure in Honolulu. Dining and shopping diversions abound. Places we love include **Martin & MacArthur,** for its Sig Zane clothing, kupee shell and wiliwili leis, and kamaaina-style accents and furnishings; **Magic Attic,** for its spirited hand-painted furniture, paintings, sculptures, palm frond masks, animal mailboxes, clothing, vintage beaded purses, and fun and funky gift items from $5 and up; and topnotch fragrance maven **Caswell Massey,** even though it is a chain store. Open Sunday through Thursday from 9am to 9pm, Friday and Saturday from 9am to 10pm. Various Honolulu trolleys stop at the Marketplace, but if you want a direct ride from Waikiki, take the $2 Aloha Tower Marketplace Express, which continues on to Hilo Hattie's in Iwilei.

Dole Cannery Square. 650 Iwilei Rd. ☎ **808/548-6600.**

There are some signs of life here—a few people at **Subway** and **McDonald's**—but mostly it's a smattering of boutiques amid a lot of empty space waiting to be filled. The **Sunglass Hut, Dockers** and **Levi's** stores, and **Sbarro** pizza are here, but it's an out-of-the-way place for so few offerings.

Kahala Mall. 4211 Waialae Ave. ☎ **808/732-7736.**

Chic, manageable, unfrenzied, Kahala Mall is home to some of Honolulu's best shops. Located past Kaimuki, in the posh neighborhood of Kahala, the Kahala Mall has everything from **Liberty House** (smaller and more limited than Ala Moana, but complete enough for basic needs) to chain stores such as **Banana Republic, The Body Shop,** and **The Gap.** One of the town's more popular coffee counters, **Espresso Bravissimo,** is here along with some 90 other restaurants and specialty shops. Some of our favorites include **Riches,** a tiny kiosk with a big, bold selection of jewelry; **Rafael,** for sleek, chic women's wear; **The Compleat Kitchen,** a salvation for culinary needs; and **Eyewear Hawaii,** for sunglasses from dawn to dusk. Look also for the **Liberty House Men's Store** at the mauka corner of the mall, under a separate roof from the main store. Our picks for the mall's best and brightest are **Corner Loft,** ablaze with gorgeous estate jewelry, glass, and dazzling collectibles; **Paradizzio,** for accessories for the home; and the **Following Sea** (see "Hawaiiana/Gift Items," above), a gallery of fine crafts and gift items from Hawaii and across the mainland. Open Monday through Saturday from 10am to 9pm, Sunday from 10am to 5pm.

Royal Hawaiian Shopping Center. 2201 Kalakaua Ave. ☎ **808/922-0588.**

This three-block shopping complex in the heart of Waikiki occupies 6.5 acres and, if you let it, it could absorb your entire Hawaii budget. Upscale is the operative word here. Although there are drugstores, lei stands, many restaurants, and food kiosks, the most conspicuous stores are the European designer boutiques (**Chanel, Loewe, Celine, Cartier, Hermès, Versace, Prada, Van Cleef & Arpels**) that cater largely to visitors from Japan. One of our favorites stops is the **Little Hawaiian Craft Shop** (☎ **808/926-2662**), which features a fabulous collection of Niihau shell leis, museum replicas of Hawaiian artifacts, and works by Hawaii artists, as well as South Pacific tapa, fiber bags and handicrafts, and Papua New Guinea shields and masks. **Beretania Florist,** located in the hut under the large banyan tree, will ship cut tropical flowers (anthuriums, bromeliads, orchids, gingers) anywhere in the United States. A favorite fashion stop is **McInerny Galleria,** a cluster of boutiques under one roof, with such big names as **DKNY, Ralph Lauren, Coach,** and **Armani.** Open Monday through Saturday from 9am to 10pm, Sunday from 9am to 9pm.

Waikele Center. Waikele. ☎ **808/676-5858.**

Waikele is synonymous with discount shopping. Bargains are to be had on everything from perfumes, luggage, and hardware, to sporting goods, fashions, china, and footwear. This teeming complex of 75 shops, anchored by **Borders Books and Music, Eagle Hardware & Garden,** and **K-Mart,** attracts busloads of Japanese tourists as well as carloads of value-conscious shoppers eager to purchase Geoffrey Beene, Donna Karan, Saks Fifth Ave., Anne Klein, Max Studio, Mikasa, Levi's, and dozens of other name brands at a fraction of retail. Open Monday through Friday from 9am to 9pm,

Sunday from 10am to 6pm. To get there by car, take H-1 West toward Waianae and turn off at exit 7. To get there on TheBUS, take the no. 2 from Waikiki and transfer at King and Beretania streets to the no. 48, which drops you off directly in front of the center.

Ward Centre. 1200 Ala Moana Blvd. ☎ **808/591-8411.**

Although it has a high turnover and a changeable profile, Ward Centre, formerly a yuppie haven, is still a standout for several reasons, mostly gastronomic. It holds a concentration of good restaurants, including **Mocha Java** (coffee bar and health food), **Keo's Thai Cuisine,** and dining mecca **Pacific Cafe Oahu** (see "Dining," above), as well as gift shops and galleries, including the very attractive **Art à la Carte.**

Ward Warehouse. 1050 Ala Moana Blvd. ☎ **808/591-8411.**

Older than its sister property, Ward Centre, and endowed with an endearing patina and rustic quality that are very un-mallish, Ward Warehouse has more shopping possibilities than its dining-oriented relative down the block. Recommended stops in the low-rise brown wooden structure include **Executive Chef,** for gourmet Hawaii food items; **Pomegranates in the Sun,** for creative, colorful sportswear; **Out of Africa,** for pottery, beads, and interior accents; **East of Sun, West of Moon,** for its sensuous array of fragrances, linens, music, bath products, bedspreads, candles, and accessories for body, home, and spirit; **Mamo Howell,** for distinctive aloha wear; **Private World,** for delicate sachets, linens, and fragrances; and **Cinnamon Girl,** for lively sportswear. For T-shirts and swimwear check out the **Town & Country Surf Shop,** and for an excellent selection of sunglasses, knapsacks and footwear to take you from the beach to the ridgetops don't miss **Thongs 'N Things.** Another favorite shop is the **Nohea Gallery** (See "Hawaiiana/Gift Items," above), one of the finest sources in the state for quality Hawaii-made arts and crafts.

SOUVENIRS

Finally, for cost-conscious souvenir hunting that's quirky enough to be fun, try **Woolworth** (There! We've said it) on Kalakaua Avenue in Waikiki (☎ **808/ 971-2455**). It's a phantasmagoria of inexpensive aloha shirts, T-shirts, books, Hawaiian music tapes and CDs, macadamia nuts and chocolates, jams and jellies and made-in-Hawaii food products, and countless gifts and souvenirs to go. Some inexpensive silk and cotton aloha shirts can be found on the first floor, but don't ignore the second floor with its music and mac nuts, all at low or competitive prices. Aloha wear and gifts to go can also be found at Duty-Free Shoppers on Royal Hawaiian Avenue, a side street between Kalakaua and Kuhio avenues.

SURF & SPORTS

The surf-and-sports shops scattered throughout Honolulu are a highly competitive lot, with each trying to capture your interest (and dollars). At **Honsport** (Pearlridge, ☎ **808/487-1517** or 808/488-7442, and in Windward Mall, ☎ **808/247-8733**) you'll find good values in athletic wear and accessories, sports shoes, weights, and workout equipment. The always-friendly prices are even better during the stores' well-known sales. The top sources for sports gear and accessories in town are **McCully Bicycle & Sporting Goods** (2124 S. King St., McCully, ☎ **808/955-6329**), with everything from bicycles and fishing gear to athletic shoes and accessories, and a stunning selection of sunglasses, and **The Bike Shop** (1149 S. King St., near Piikoi St., ☎ **808/531-7071**), excellent for cycling and camping equipment for all levels. **The Sports Authority** (333 Ward Ave., ☎ **808/596-0166,** and at Waikele Center, ☎ **808/677-9933**) is a megaoutlet offering clothing, cycles, accessories, and equipment at a discount.

Surf shops, centers of fashion as well as definers of daring, include **Local Motion** (1714 Kapiolani Blvd., ☎ **808/955-7873,** and other locations in Waikele, Windward Mall, and Koko Marina) and **Hawaiian Island Creations** (Ala Moana Shopping Center, ☎ **808/941-4491**). Local Motion is the icon of surfers and skateboarders, both professionals and wanna-bes. The shop offers surfboards, T-shirts, aloha shirts, dresses and casual wear, skateboards, boogie boards, and every imaginable accessory for life in the sun. Its competitor, Hawaiian Island Creations, is another super-cool surf shop offering sunglasses, sun lotions, surf wear, bicycles, and accessories galore.

VINTAGE CLOTHING

It costs big bucks to wear old clothes if they're in good shape and have a past—$600 to $1,000, say, for a vintage silkie in perfect condition. Take a peek in **Bailey's Antiques and Aloha Shirts** (517 Kapahulu Ave., ☎ **808/734-7628**) and check out vintage finds from the tatty to the sublime: old lamps, cushions, movie costumes, vintage jewelry, salt and pepper shakers, figurines, fur stoles, hats, and a dizzying selection of clothing for serious collectors and neophytes. A vintage rayon Chinese-style muu with pointed long sleeves, called a "pake muu," or any vintage schmatte in perfect condition could fetch $600 and up, but you may be able to turn up some cheaper options. Prices begin below $20 and a lucky hunter could find a velvet dress or sarong skirt for under $50. Also in Kapahulu, **Coconut Bay** (3114 Monsarrat Ave., ☎ **808/737-2699**) is a neighborhood hit with its unique Hawaiian wear and Southeast Asian imports. Its clothing *looks* vintage, and pulls it off with panache. Quilts, clothing, retro Hawaiian wear, and scads of men's shirts, not to mention a coffee shop next door, have gained this Kapahulu newcomer a lot of fans.

SHOPPING AROUND THE ISLAND
WINDWARD OAHU
Kailua

Longs Drugs and **Liberty House,** located side-by-side on Kailua Road in the heart of this windward Oahu community, form the shopping nexus of the neighborhood—the one-stop convenience stores that no Kailua resident can live without. Except for food, these two stores provide all the basic needs, from film and cosmetics and household products to apparel and gift items. For maps, books, and food for thought, the **Honolulu Book Shop** in the Kailua Shopping Center provides great books and good service.

Heritage Antiques & Gifts. 767 Kailua Rd. ☎ **808/261-8700.**

In its 20th year, Heritage is a Kailua landmark known for its large selection of Tiffany-style lamps ($200–$2,000), many of which are hand-carted back to the mainland. The shop's mind-boggling selection also includes European, Asian, local, American, and Pacific Island collectibles. It's fun, the people are friendly, and the selection is diverse enough to appeal to the casual as well as serious collector. Glassware, china, furniture, and estate, costume, and fine jewelry are among the crowd-pleasers here. Heritage has its own jeweler who custom-designs, repairs, and resurrects jewelry, while a stable of wood craftsmen turn out custom-made koa rockers and hutches to complement the antique furniture selection.

Kaneohe

Windward Mall, 46-056 Kamehameha Hwy. (☎ **808/235-1143**), is basically a suburban mall serving windwardites. Its more than 100 stores and services include health stores, department stores (**Liberty House, Sears, J.C. Penney**), **Honsport** sporting

Oahu's Vibrant Art Scene

Passionate art lovers find solace and serenity in Hawaii's two top cultural resources, the **Contemporary Museum** (at Spalding Estate, 2411 Makiki Heights Dr., ☎ 808/526-0232) and the **Honolulu Academy of Arts** (900 S. Beretania St., ☎ 808/532-8701). The vastly differing collections are housed in two of Hawaii's most memorable settings, both the legacy of one woman, Mrs. Charles Montague Cooke, who built the Alice Cooke Spalding house in 1925 and named it after her daughter. Two years later, Cooke founded the Academy, which remains a beacon in the arts to this day. The Alice Cooke Spalding house became the Contemporary Museum in 1988. One shudders to think what Hawaii's art world would have been without these two kamaaina legacies.

The Honolulu Academy of Arts claims one of the finest Asian art collections in the country, as well as an acclaimed collection of American and European masters and prehistoric works that include Mayan, Greek, and Hawaiian art. Special exhibitions and annual events have received international recognition. The Moorish structure is a paragon of graciousness, with curved, tiled roof lines, open courtyards and lily ponds, and wide hallways leading to sensitively organized galleries. The Academy's setting, art collections, Garden Cafe, gift shop, and theatre make this a must for any resident or visitor. Open Tuesday through Saturday from 10am to 4:30pm, Sunday from 1 to 5pm. Admission is $5 per adult, with discounts for seniors and military personnel; members free.

Located up on the slopes of Tantalus, one of Honolulu's most prestigious residential communities, the Contemporary Museum, established in 1988, is renowned for several features: its $3^{1}/_{2}$ acres of Oriental gardens with reflecting pools, sun-drenched terraces, views of Diamond Head, and stone benches for quiet contemplation; the Cades Pavilion, housing David Hockney's *L'Enfant et les Sortileges,* an environmental installation of his sets and costumes for Ravel's 1925 opera; its excellent cafe and gift shop; and six galleries representing significant work and artists of the last 4 decades. Equally prominent is the presence of contemporary Hawaii artists in the museum's programs and exhibitions. Open Tuesday through Saturday from 10am to 4pm, Sunday from noon to 4pm. A 1-day membership for adults is $5; senior and students, $3; members and children free. The third Thursday of each month is free. Ask about their daily docent-led tours.

Galleries   Longevity matters in Hawaii's art world. Like restaurants, galleries come and go in Chinatown, where well-meaning efforts to revitalize the area have moved in fits and spurts, especially in recent years. Two exceptions are the **Ramsay Galleries** in the striking brick Tan Sing Building (1128 Smith St., ☎ 808/537-2787), celebrating its 150th exhibition and 15th year in 1996, and the **Pegge Hopper Gallery** (1164 Nuuanu Ave., ☎ 808/524-1160). Both are housed in historic Chinatown buildings that have been renovated and transformed into stunning showplaces for their and other artists' work. Nationally known quill-and-ink artist Ramsay, who has drawn everything from the Plaza in New York to most of

goods, airline counters, surf shops, **The Hobby Company** craft shop, **LensCrafters,** and dozens of other retail businesses spread out over windward Oahu's largest shopping complex. The star of the mall is gift-and-craft gallery **Kauila Maxwell** (see

Honolulu's historic buildings, maintains a vital monthly show schedule featuring her own work as well as one-person shows of her fellow Hawaii artists. The finest names in contemporary crafts and art have appeared here, in media ranging from photography to sculpture to glass, painting, prints, and, yes, computer art. When Ramsay's work is exhibited, each drawing is displayed with a magnifying glass to invite intimate viewing of the rich details.

Pegge Hopper's widely collected paintings of Hawaiian women with broad, strong features, shown in simple lines and colors in relaxed poses, are displayed in her attractive two-story gallery. One of Hawaii's most popular artists, Hopperpainted eight murals depicting fashionable people from the 1920s for the newly reopened Hawaii Theatre, downtown Honolulu's newest performing arts venue.

The darling of Hawaii's ceramics world, Gail Bakutis, gathered 11 other artists in varied media and formed **Art à la Carte** in Ward Centre (1200 Ala Moana Blvd., ☎ **808/597-8034**). The gallery celebrated its tenth anniversary in 1996. Wandering around the gallery is an exercise in restraint, because there are many pieces worth coveting, including works in ceramics, paper, clay, scratch board, oils, acrylics, watercolors, collage, woodblock, lithographs, and fresh and dried flowers. The fragility of the botanical medium complements the sturdiness of Bakutis's award-winning raku- and pit-fired ceramics and adds to the range of choices at Art à la Carte. You can browse among the two-dimensional fine art, select greeting cards to go with them, and order table-length floral runners, made of haku-lei–style (plaited or wound) flowers, seeds, and vines, which the gallery will ship to the mainland. The tropical blooms are also sold in lauhala baskets and in some of Bakutis's pottery—a gift nonpareil, for yourself or a deserving friend.

Hawaii's most unusual gallery is perched on the slopes of Punchbowl. It is the **Tennent Art Foundation Gallery** (203 Prospect St., ☎ **808/531-1987**), devoted to the *oeuvre* of internationally esteemed artist Madge Tennent, whose work hangs in the National Museum of Women with the work of Georgia O'Keeffe. In its dozens of Tennent originals, the gallery traces the artist's development. Tennent's much-imitated style depicts Polynesians throughout the 1920s to the 1940s in bold, modernist strokes that left an indelible influence on Hawaii art. The gallery is open only limited hours or by appointment.

In windward Oahu, flush against the lush Koolau Mountains, the garden idyll of **Hart Tagami and Powell Gallery and Gardens** (Kahaluu, ☎ **808/239-8146;** please call before going) turns out to be the most memorable Oahu stop for many visitors. The gallery, showcasing works by local artists, including Hiroshi Tagami and Michael Powell, both well known for their inspired paintings of Hawaii, is itself a work of art, a place of simple majesty where art and nature converge. The paintings, hand-turned bowls of native woods, ceramics, and sculptures by the best of Hawaii's artists are arranged in a serene environment surrounded by lush gardens. Tagami, an inveterate gardener, planted every tree himself, and has introduced several magnificent botanical species to Hawaii.

below). A small food court serves pizza, Chinese food, tacos, and other morsels for the dine-and-dash set. Open Monday through Saturday from 9:30am to 9pm, Sunday from 10am to 5pm.

Kauila Maxwell. 46-056 Kamehameha Hwy. ☎ **808/235-8383.**

The shop specializes in serious, top-quality Hawaiian crafts and gift items and in educating shoppers on their value and cultural significance. Everything is made in Hawaii, from the tools, paddles, adzes, and other reproductions of traditional implements to the extensive selection of calabash bowls in koa, milo, kamani, mango, Norfolk pine, and other gleaming woods. The 1,000-square-foot shop also specializes in Niihau shell leis, made by a couple from Niihau and beautifully displayed in the shop with generous educational literature. You can pay $30 for a pair of Niihau shell earrings or up to $5,000 for a lei. Jewelry, locally made tropical perfumes (plumeria, gardenia, orchid), rare kou wood sculptures, koa jewelry boxes, and a few pieces of Liliuokalani-style koa rockers round out the selection.

Shopping the North Shore: Haleiwa

Haleiwa means serious shopping for the growing cadre of townies who drive an hour each way just to stock up on wine and clothes at its stores of growing renown. (I know; I'm one of them.) I always bring a cooler, in case I find that Bordeaux I can't live without, or for storing the picnic lunch that I'll inevitably assemble along the way. It's not a good idea to store valuables in the car or trunk, so I always cross my fingers that my North Shore stash (wine from Fujioka's, clothes and accessories from Silver Moon and Bella Luna) will make it home with me intact, because if not, I would turn right around and start over again. Here are our Haleiwa highlights:

Art, Gifts & Crafts

Haleiwa's seven galleries display a combination of marine art, watercolors, sculpture, and a multitude of crafts trying to masquerade, unsuccessfully, as fine art. This is the town for gifts, crafts, fashions, and surf stuff rather than fine art, despite some price tags (Wyland, for example) in the hundreds of thousands of dollars. The **Art Plantation** (66-521 Kamehameha Hwy., ☎ 808/637-2343), located in a historic wooden storefront, is a pleasing showcase of the wide-ranging crafts of more than 4 dozen artisians. Potter Bob McWilliams, screen-printer Janet Holaday (who screens cheerful tropical fish and flowers on white cotton tablecloths and napkins—affordable and gorgeous), and wood turner Jerry Kermode are the standouts whose works occupy a large part of the Art Plantation space. The nearby **Kaala Art** (66-4556 Kamehameha Highway, ☎ 808/637-7065) has scaled down its Thai and Indonesian fabrics and clothing (pareus to die for) to focus on acrylics, prints, silk screens, and other mostly new-agey works by local artists.

The two locations of **Global Creations** (66-079 Kamehameha Hwy., ☎ 808/637-1505), across the street from each other, offer clothing (hemp is cheap, sturdy, and attractive here), shoes, caps, backpacks, and other accessories for top to toe. Also offered are international imports for the home, including high-quality Balinese bamboo furniture and lamps as well as colorful Yucatan hammocks and gifts and crafts by local potters, painters, and designers.

At the high end of the gallery scene, the indomitable **Wyland,** a North Shore resident who made a name throughout Hawaii and other locales with his large "whaling walls," has his largest Hawaii gallery at 66-150 Kamehameha Hwy. (☎ 808/637-7498). The eponymous **Thomas Deir Galleries** (66-208 Kamehameha Highway, ☎ 808/637-7431) displays the artist's marine paintings and hand-painted tiles along with the works of 14 other artists, most of them from the islands. Pottery, oils, acrylics, and sculptures in themes ranging from seascapes to goddesses to strong Hawaiian women go for from $30 to $250,000.

Edibles

Haleiwa is best known for its roadside shave-ice stands: the famous **M. Matsumoto,** with the perennial queue snaking along Kamehameha Highway, and nearby **Aoki's.** Shave ice is the popular Island version of a snow cone, a heap of shaved ice topped with your choice of syrups, such as strawberry, rainbow, root beer, vanilla, or passion fruit. Aficionados order it with a scoop of ice cream and sweetened black azuki beans nestled in the middle.

For food-and-wine shopping, our mightiest accolade goes to **Fujioka Super Market** (66-190 Kamehameha Hwy., ☎ **808/637-4520**). Oenophiles and tony wine clubs from town shop here for the best prices on California reds, coveted Italian reds, and a growing selection of Cabernets, Merlots, and French vintages that are thoughtfully selected and unbelievably priced. So popular is this store that it makes once-weekly deliveries to corporate clients in town. Fresh produce and no-cholesterol, vegetarian health foods, in addition to the standards, fill the aisles of this third-generation store.

Tiny, funky **Celestial Natural Foods** (66-443 Kamehameha Hwy., ☎ **808/637-6729**) is the health foodies' Grand Central for everything from wooden spine-massagers to health supplements, produce, cosmetics, and bulk foods.

Fashion

Although Haleiwa used to be an incense-infused surfer outpost in which zoris and tank tops were the regional uniform and the Beach Boys and Ravi Shankar the music of the day, today it's one of the top shopping destinations for those with unconventional tastes. Specialty shops abound here. Top-drawer **Silver Moon Emporium** (North Shore Marketplace, 66-250 Kamehameha Hwy., ☎ **808/637-0458**) in its new larger location is still an islandwide phenomenon with the terrific finds of buyer/owner Lucie Talbot-Holu. Exquisite clothing and handbags, reasonably priced footwear, hats straight out of *Vogue,* jewelry, scarves, and a full gamut of other treasures pepper the attractive boutique. Down the road, at its original location amid banana trees and picnic tables in the shade of a towering monkeypod tree, Silver Moon's sister store, **Bella Luna** (66-037 Kamehameha Hwy., ☎ **808/637-5040**) still captures our hearts with its Victorian dresses, drop-dead–gorgeous French Connection dresses, and affordable Italian footwear. **Oogenesis Boutique** (66-249 Kamehameha Hwy., ☎ **808/637-4580**) located in the southern part of Haleiwa, features a storefront lined with vintage-looking dresses that flutter prettily in the North Shore breeze.

Highlights of the new and growing North Shore Marketplace include **Great Pacific Patagonia** (☎ **808/637-1245**) for nationally renowned, high-quality surf, swim, hiking, kayaking, and all-around adventure wear. Also in the Marketplace, **Jungle Gems** (☎ **808/637-6609**) is the mother lode of gemstones, geodes, crystals, silver, and beadwork.

Among all these Haleiwa newcomers, the perennial favorite remains **H. Miura Store and Tailor Shop** (66-057 Kamehameha Hwy., ☎ **808/637-4845**). You can custom-order swim trunks, an aloha shirt, or a muumuu from the bolts of Polynesian-printed fabrics that line the store, from tapa designs to two-color pareu prints. They will sew, ship, and remember you years later when you return. It's the most versatile tailor shop we've ever seen, with coconut-shell bikini tops, fake hula skirts, aloha shirts, and heaps of cheap and glorious tchotchkes lining the aisles.

Surf Shops

Haleiwa's ubiquitous surf shops are the best on earth, surfers say. At the top of the heap is **Northshore Boardriders Club** (66-250 Kamehameha Hwy., North Shore

Marketplace, ☎ 808/637-5026), the mecca of the board-riding elite, with sleek, fast, elegant, and top-of-the-line boards designed by North Shore legend Barry Kanaiaupuni. Also popular is the funkier **Surf & Sea Surf Sail & Dive Shop** (62-595 Kamehameha Hwy., ☎ 808/637-9887), a flamboyant roadside structure just over the bridge, with old wood floors, fans blowing, and a tangle of surf and swim wear, T-shirts, surfboards, boogie boards, fins, watches, sunglasses, and countless other miscellany. You can also rent surf and snorkel equipment there. Also popular is **Tropical Rush** (62-620-A Kamehameha Hwy., ☎ 808/637-8886) with its huge inventory of surf and swim gear, much of it for rent: longboards and Perfect Line surfboards, Reef Brazil shoes and slippers, swimwear for men and women, T-shirts, visors, sunglasses, and scads of cool gear. An added feature is the shop's surf report line for the up-to-the-minute lowdown on wave action, **808/638-7874.**

14 Oahu After Dark

by Jocelyn Fujii

IT BEGINS WITH SUNSET . . .

In Hawaii, nightlife begins at sunset, when revelers begin planning their technicolor venue to launch the evening's festivities. Waikiki's beachfront bars offer many possibilities, from the Royal Hawaiian Hotel's **Mai Tai Bar,** a few feet from the sand, to the ever-enchanting **House Without a Key** at the Halekulani, where the breathtaking **Kanoelehua Miller** dances hula to the riffs of Hawaiian steel-pedal guitar under a century-old kiawe tree. With the sunset and ocean glowing behind her and Diamond Head visible in the distance, the scene is straight out of Somerset Maugham—romantic, evocative, nostalgic. It doesn't hurt, either, that the Halekulani happens to make the best Mai Tais in the world. Halekulani has after-dinner bliss covered, too, with light jazz by the mellifluous **Loretta Ables Trio** and elegant libations by the glass at **Lewers Lounge,** at the foot of the stairs leading to La Mer.

The **Aloha Tower Marketplace** has its own version of sunset from Honolulu Harbor. No swaying palm trees at your fingertips here, but you'll see tugboats and cruise ships from the open-air **Pier Bar** and from various venues throughout the marketplace offering live entertainment during happy hour and beyond. Some of Hawaii's top entertainers appear at the Pier Bar, **Gordon Biersch Brewery,** and the **Atrium Center Court** in an ongoing program of foot-stomping good times. Sunday is jazz day at the Pier Bar, Friday Hawaiian music day, and Saturday the dance music rocks and rolls like the swells of Honolulu Harbor. At Gordon Biersch Brewery and Restaurant, diners swing to jazz on Wednesdays, contemporary Hawaiian on Thursday, and a lively mix on weekends, including reggae or alternative music on Sunday. (The **Entertainment and Event Hotline,** ☎ 808/566-2339, tells you what's happening daily at the Marketplace.) Names to watch for, here and throughout Honolululu, include **Mojo Hand,** unbeatable blues and dance music for those too hip for the Clyde Pound Orchestra and too sophisticated for a warehouse rave; **Willie K.,** versatile beyond words, a virtuoso Hawaiian falsetto who belts out blues and rock and many other genres; **Henry Kapono,** Hawaiian music; **Rolando Sanchez & Salsa Hawaii;** and **Nueva Vida,** Honolulu's darling of rhythm-and-blues and jazz. Nueva Vida gives two different presentations: Nueva Vida Big Thang, rhythm-and-blues and dance music; and Nueva Vida Jazz Thang. Hula dancing, guitar concerts, jazz nights, and special events such as Cinco de Mayo parties, magic shows, Sunday afternoon jazz jam sessions, and Tower Thursday "sunset specials" make Aloha Tower Marketplace a major entertainment venue from sunset well into the night.

HAWAIIAN MUSIC

Oahu has several key spots for Hawaiian music. Most prominent was the lavish program at the **Bishop Museum** called "Hawaii from the Heart," by the **Brothers Cazimero,** one of Hawaii's most talented duos (Robert on bass, Roland on 12-string guitar). At press time, the Brothers, alas, are planning to leave the Bishop Museum and re-enter Waikiki, so ask your hotel concierge or check the local dailies for their current venue. Wherever they are, their soaring voices resonate, and when complemented with their haunting harmonies and the primal beat of the hula drums, many layers of Hawaiian culture are revealed.

Waikiki is also peppered with casual, lively nightspots into which you can saunter spontaneously for some consummate entertainment, which often includes impromptu hula and spirited music from the family and friends of the performers. Foremost among these venues is the Hilton Hawaiian Village's ✪ **Paradise Lounge,** which (despite its pillars) serves as a large living room for the full-bodied music of **Haunani Apoliona, Jerry Santos,** and **Wally Suenaga,** known as Olomana. A venerated songwriter and 12-string guitar player, Apoliona is a musical icon in Hawaii, and when singing in harmony with Santos, makes goose-bump music that stays with you. They play on Friday and Saturday, from 8pm to midnight, no cover charge. At **Duke's Canoe Club** at the Outrigger Waikiki Hotel, it's always three deep at the beachside bar when the sun is setting and the fabulous **Moe Keale** is playing with his trio. **Del Beazley, Brother Noland, Ledward Kaapana, Henry Kapono,** and other top names in Hawaiian entertainment appear at Duke's, where extra-special entertainment is a given. Usually the entertainment is from 4 to 6pm on Friday, Saturday, and Sunday evenings, but call **808/923-0711** to see if there's anything cooking later in the evening. Nearby, the Sheraton Moana Surfrider offers a regular program of Hawaiian music in the **Banyan Veranda** that surrounds an islet-sized canopy of banyan tree and roots where Robert Louis Stevenson loved to linger. (*Hint:* drinks, though not as elegantly presented, cost much less from the ground-level bar than from the elegant veranda with the high-backed chairs, and you still get to enjoy the music.) At the Outrigger Prince Kuhio, the **Cupid's Lounge** piano bar is home to the venerable **Mahi Beamer,** a foremost Hawaiian composer, pianist, and descendant of the famed musical dynasty of Helen Desha Beamer.

Our best advice for lovers of Hawaiian music is to scan the local dailies or the *Honolulu Weekly* to see if and where the following Hawaiian entertainers are appearing: **Ho'okena,** a symphonically rich quintet featuring **Manu Boyd,** one of the most prolific songwriters and chanters in Hawaii; **Hapa,** an award-winning contemporary Hawaii duo; **Keali'i Reichel,** premier chanter, dancer, and award-winning recording artist, voted "Male Vocalist of the Year" in the 1996 Na Hoku Hanohano Awards; **Robbie Kahakalau,** "Female Vocalist of the Year" in the same awards; and slack-key guitar master **Raymond Kane.** Consider the gods beneficent if you happen to be here when the hula halau of **Frank Kawaikapuokalani Hewett** is holding its annual fund-raiser in windward Oahu. It's a rousing, inspired, family effort for a good cause, and it always features the best in ancient and contemporary Hawaiian music. For the best in ancient and modern hula, it's a good idea to check the dailies for halau fund-raisers, which are always authentic, enriching, and local to the core.

Showroom acts that have gained a following are led by the tireless, 65-year-old **Don Ho,** who still sings "Tiny Bubbles" and who reportedly is experiencing a second wind in his **Waikiki Beachcomber Hana Hou** showroom nightly except Monday. Across Kalakaua Avenue in the **Outrigger Waikiki on the Beach,** the

Society of Seven's nightclub act (a blend of skits, Broadway hits, popular music, and costumed musical acts) is into its 26th year, no small feat for performers.

THE CLASSICS

You can also drape yourself in Donna Karan and high-step it to the opera, theater, or symphony for quality entertainment in a healthy performing arts scene. Aloha-shirt–to-Armani is what we call the night scene in Honolulu, mostly casual but with ample opportunity to dress up if you dare to part with your flip-flops. The May 1996 opening of the ✪ **Hawaii Theatre** (1130 Bethel St., downtown, ☎ **808/528-0506**) following a 4-year, $22-million renovation introduced a glittering new venue for Hawaii's performing arts. The neoclassical beaux-arts landmark features a 1922 dome, 1,400 plush seats, a hydraulically elevated organ, a mezzanine lobby with two full bars, Corinthian columns, and gilt galore. Breathtaking murals, including a restored proscenium centerpiece lauded as Lionel Walden's "greatest creation," create an atmosphere that will no doubt make the theatre a leading multipurpose center for the performing arts. This glitterai's rental hall is so new there's not much in the way of a schedule yet, but stay tuned.

The **Honolulu Symphony Orchestra** has booked some shows at the new theatre, but it's unclear what will happen next season. Meanwhile, opera lovers, the highly successful **Hawaii Opera Theatre,** in its 36th season (past hits have included *La Bohème, Carmen, Turandot, Rigoletto*), still draws fans to the **Neal Blaisdell Concert Hall** (as do many of the performances of Hawaii's four ballet companies: **Hawaii Ballet Theatre, Ballet Hawaii, Hawaii State Ballet,** and **Honolulu Dance Theatre**). Contemporary performances by **Dances We Dance** and the **Iona Pear Dance Company,** a strikingly creative Butoh group, are worth tracking down if you love the avant-garde.

FILM

A quick check in both dailies and the *Honolulu Weekly* will tell you what's playing where in the world of feature films. The **Movie Museum** (3566 Harding Ave., ☎ **808/735-8771**) has special screenings of vintage films and also rents a collection of hard-to-find, esoteric, and classic films, while the **Honolulu Academy of Arts Theatre** (900 S. Beretania St., ☎ **808/532-8768**) is the film-as-art center of Honolulu, offering special screenings, guest appearances and cultural performances, as well as noteworthy programs in the visual arts.

BLUES

The best news for blues fans is the growing network of dyed-in-the-wool blues lovers here who have their own newsletter, blues festivals, club gigs, and the indomitable leadership of Louie Wolfenson of the **Maui Blues Association** (P.O. Box 1211, Puunene, Maui, HI 96784, ☎ **808/242-7318**), the primary source for information on blues activities throughout the state. The blues are alive and well in Hawaii, with quality acts both local and from the mainland drawing enthusiastic crowds in even the funkiest of surroundings. **Junior Wells, Willie & Lobo, War,** and surprise appearances by the likes of **Bonnie Raitt** are among the past successes of this genre of big-time licks. Oahu venues have included **Anna Bannanas** (2440 S. Beretania St., ☎ **808/946-5190**) and **Door 52** in Kailua (52 Oneawa St., ☎ **808/261-8561**), formerly Fast Eddie's, soon to reopen after renovations as a full-service nightclub with a disco and live acts.

JAZZ

Yes, folks, there is a Jazz Hawaii Big Band and a jazz scene that keeps the saxophones and pianos in tune and Hawaii's gifted musicians accessible. **Jazz Hawaii** (☎ 808/737-6554) has an updated list of who's playing where. Big names and regular venues include **Duc's Bistro** (1188 Maunakea St., Chinatown, ☎ 808/531-6325), where the silky-smooth chords of **Azure McCall** deliver everything from "Paradise Cafe" to "Stormy Weather," from 8 to 10pm on Thursday and until midnight on Friday and Saturday; **Alana Waikiki Hotel's Cafe Picasso** (1956 Ala Moana Blvd., ☎ 808/941-7275), where **Jimmy Borges** and **Betty Loo Taylor** cling to the classics; **Coconuts** (Ilikai Hotel Nikko Waikiki, 1777 Ala Moana Blvd., ☎ 808/949-3811), with live jazz nightly; and the perennially tasteful **Lewers Lounge** in the Halekulani (2199 Kalia Rd., ☎ 808/923-2311).

ALTERNATIVE CLUBS

Anna Bannanas (see "Blues," above) still packs them in, even with the dreaded breakup of the beloved **Pagan Babies,** who are known to have generated the most perspiration on the most enthusiastic dance floor in Honolulu through their years-long venue there. **The Jungle** (311 Lewers, Waikiki, ☎ 808/922-7808) is the hot scene for alternative music these days, a disco with occasional live entertainment, open from 10pm to 4am. You can be as cheesy as you want here, and no one will notice. The **Wave Waikiki** (1877 Kalakaua Ave., Waikiki, ☎ 808/941-0421) is rough around the edges but still popular, serving up alternative music to the heavily body-pierced crowd on the same stage that Grace Jones once spat from. And **The Groove** (1130 N. Nimitz Hwy., Kalihi, behind New Eagle Cafe, ☎ 808/528-0353) is the authentic rave-dance party, a fashion show for self-conscious Kate Moss look-alikes and good dancers who groove to the music of bands with unpronounceable names. Oh yes—**Hard Rock Cafe** (1837 Kapiolani Blvd., Waikiki, ☎ 808/955-7383), the bastion of decibels run amok, has recently joined the alternative music arena with live music on Friday and Saturday nights.

DISCOS

Maharaja (2255 Kuhio Ave., 7th floor, Waikiki Trade Center, ☎ 808/922-3030) is the mirrored wonder of the disco world, the chicest of them all (and snobby, too), with dinner and dancing on a state-of-the-art floor and peerless sound and light systems. Dress up and be seen. But it's **Nicholas Nickolas** (410 Atkinson Dr., Ala Moana Hotel, ☎ 808/955-4466) that has the best view. From the 36th floor of the hotel (take the express elevator) watch the Honolulu city lights wrap around the room and cha-cha-cha to the vertigo! Live music and dancing nightly, and an appetizer menu nightly from 5pm. Downstairs in the lobby of the same hotel, **Rumours Nightclub** (☎ 808/955-4811) is the disco of choice for those who remember that Paul McCartney was a Beatle before Wings. A spacious dance floor, good sound system, and top-40 music draw a mix of generations, but Friday night is the Big Chill featuring hits from the late sixties, seventies, and eighties. Across town in Waikiki, the sister restaurant of Nicholas Nickolas, **Nick's Fishmarket** (2070 Kalakaua Ave., Waikiki Gateway Hotel, ☎ 808/955-6333), is another sophisticated spot, with live entertainment nightly in its cozy lounge—mild jazz or top-40 contemporary hits. At Restaurant Row, **Studebaker's** (500 Ala Moana Blvd., ☎ 808/526-9888) is a retro disco with a 16-foot all-you-can-eat buffet.

. . . AND MORE

It's true that Elvis and Marilyn didn't die. They're still wowing fans through their impersonators, having achieved entertainment immortality with skillful makeup and voice coaches. Watch Prince, Whitney Houston, Marilyn Monroe, Michael Jackson, Elvis, the Blues Brothers, and other entertainment icons at the **Legends in Concert** show at the **Royal Hawaiian Shopping Center** in Waikiki (☎ 808/971-1405). Cocktail shows and dinner shows are featured 7 nights a week ($33 for cocktails, $72 for dinner show). Finally, for late-night schmoozing, with a theater complex nearby, the Restaurant Row's **Row Bar** (500 Ala Moana Blvd., Restaurant Row, ☎ 808/ 528-2345) always seems to be full, smoky, and somewhat, if impersonally, convivial, except after the theaters have emptied from an Oliver Stone movie.

LUAU!

Regrettably, there's no commercial luau on this island that comes close to Maui's Old Lahaina Luau, or Hawaii Island's legendary Kona Village luau. The two major luaus on Oahu are **Germaine's** (☎ 808/941-3338) and **Paradise Cove Luau** (☎ 808/973-LUAU), both located about a 40-minute drive away from Waikiki on the leeward coast. Bus pickups and drop-offs in Waikiki are part of the deal. Athough Germaine's tries awfully hard and is a much smaller and more intimate affair, Paradise Cove (itself a mixed bag, with 600–800 guests a night) is a more complete experience. The small thatched village makes it more of a Hawaiian theme park, with Hawaiian games, hukilau net throwing and gathering, craft demonstrations, and a beautiful shoreline looking out over what is usually a storybook sunset. O'Brian Eselu's hula halau has been entertaining luau goers here for years. Tahitian dance, ancient and modern hula, white-knuckle fire dancing, and robust entertainment make this a fun-filled evening for those who don't expect an intimate gathering, and who are spirited enough to join in with the corny audience participation. The food is safe, though not breathtaking. Hawaiian kalua pig, lomi salmon, poi, and coconut pudding and cake are provided, but for the less adventurous, there is always a spread of teriyaki chicken, mahimahi, pasta salad, potato salad, and banana bread. Paradise Cove costs $47.50 for adults and $27.50 for children 6 to 12 years old. For $10 more, the Royal Alii Service will ensure table service instead of the usual buffet, pitchers of Mai Tais and Blue Hawaii cocktails on the table, and seating close to the stage.

Hawaii: The Big Island

The Big Island of Hawaii—the island that lends its good name to the entire 1,500-mile-long Hawaiian archipelago—is like no other place on earth. Simply put, it's spectacular.

This is where Mother Nature pulled out all stops. The island looks like the inside of a barbecue pit on one side, and a legendary Green Mansion jungle on the other. The Big Island has it all: fiery volcanoes and sparkling waterfalls, black lava deserts and snowcapped mountain peaks, tropical rain forests and alpine meadows, a glacial lake and miles of beaches—with a rainbow of black, green, and golden sands. The Big Island has a diversity of terrain and climate unmatched in any one place. A 50-mile drive will take you from snowy winter to sultry summer, passing through spring or fall along the way.

The island can only be described in superlatives. It's the largest island in the Pacific (4,038 sq. miles), the youngest (800,000 years), and the least populated (with 30 people per sq. mile). It has the nation's wettest city, the southernmost point in the United States, the world's biggest telescope, the ocean's biggest trophy marlin, and America's greatest collection of tropical luxury resorts. It has the highest peaks in the Pacific, the most volcanoes of any Hawaiian island, and the newest land on Earth.

Five volcanoes—one still erupting—have created a continental island that's as big as Connecticut, and it's growing bigger daily. At its heart is snowcapped Mauna Kea, the world's tallest sea mountain, complete with its own glacial lake. Mauna Kea's nearest neighbor is Mauna Loa (or "Long Mountain"), creator of one-sixth of the island; it's the largest volcano on earth, rising 30,000 feet out of the ocean floor (of course, you can only see the 13,679 feet that are above sea level). Erupting Kilauea makes the Big Island bigger every day—you can stand just a few feet away and watch it do its work. And just 23 miles offshore, Loihi, a junior volcano about to debut in 50,000 years or so, is bubbling up 3,000 feet below the sea. But the first volcano you'll see when you land at Keahole Airport, a ribbon of tarmac set in a rumpled lava bed, is nearby Hualalai, whose peak is lost in a mist called "vog"—a hazy smog of volcanic gases.

Old as time yet new as this morning's volcanic eruption, the Big Island of Hawaii is also the fount of all things Hawaiian: It's where the islands first burst out of the sea, where the first settlers landed

---

Factoid

Kilauea volcano can fill a stadium the size of the Houston Astrodome with lava in a week.

---

their voyaging canoes, and where the King Kamehameha the Great ascended to power, uniting the island kingdom.

The Big Island's beauty, vastness, and grandeur is unsurpassed. It's often misunderstood, however, mostly because it refuses to fit the stereotype of a tropical island. This is the least explored island in the Hawaiian chain—but if you're looking to get away from it all, that might be the best thing of all about it. Maybe it's the volcano that keeps the tourists away, but it shouldn't. Where else can you witness fiery creation and swim with dolphins, ponder the stars from the world's tallest mountain and catch a record blue marlin, downhill ski and surf the waves in a single day? You can do all this, and much more, on only one island in the world—the Big Island of Hawaii. Those who come here find a place unlike any other—and an unequaled world of adventure.

1 Orientation

by Rick Carroll

Most people arrive on the Big Island at Keahole International Airport, on the island's west coast, and discover there are only two ways to go: clockwise or counterclockwise. Nobody knows why, but most Americans go clockwise and Europeans go counterclockwise, while most Japanese prefer to fly into Hilo International Airport, on the eastern side of the island, and set out around the island clockwise. Whichever way you go, all you need to know is that from Keahole, Kilauea volcano is counterclockwise, and the ritzy Kohala Coast resorts are clockwise. (If you land in Hilo, of course, the volcano is clockwise and Kohala is counterclockwise.)

If you think you can "do" the Big Island in a day, forget it. You need about 3 days just to do Hawaii Volcanoes National Park justice. Plan on spending a week on the Big Island if you hope to catch more than a glimpse of the island through the window of a speeding rental car.

ARRIVING

The Big Island has two major airports for jet traffic between the islands: **Keahole International Airport** (that's the official name, but everybody calls it "the Kona Airport"), on the island's west coast, is the island's main port of entry; you can also fly into **Hilo International Airport** on the other side of the island.

The Kora Airport receives direct overseas flights from Japan, as well as direct mainland flights from Los Angeles and San Francisco. Otherwise, you'll have to pick up an interisland flight in Honolulu. **Aloha Airlines** (☎ 800/367-5250) and **Hawaiian Airlines** (☎ 800/367-5320) offer jet service to both Big Island airports; **Mahalo Airlines** (☎ 800/462-4256) flies twin engines into Kona Airport.

VISITOR INFORMATION

The **Hawaii Visitors and Convention Bureau** has two offices on the Big Island: one at 250 Keawe St., Hilo, HI 96720 (☎ **808/961-5797;** fax 808/961-2126), and on the other side of the island at 75-5719 W. Alii Dr., Kailua-Kona, HI 96740 (☎ **808/**

329-7787; fax 808/326-7563). The **Kohala Coast Resort Association** is at 69-275 Waikoloa Beach Dr., Kamuela HI 96743 (☎ **808/885-4915;** fax 808/885-1044).

The Big Island's best free tourist publication is the *Beach and Activity Guide,* published by Alakai Publishing Co., P.O. Box 3380, Kailua-Kona, HI 96745 (☎ **808/334-0344**). It has lots of useful information as well as discount coupons for food, film, Kona coffee, souvenirs, and excursions.

THE REGIONS IN BRIEF
THE KONA COAST

One Hawaiian word everyone seems to know is Kona, probably because it's synonymous with great coffee and big fish—both of which are found in abundance along this 70-mile-long stretch of black lava–covered coast.

Kona is a state of mind more than a distinct place. A collection of tiny communities devoted to farming and fishing along the sunbaked leeward side of the island, the Kona Coast has an amazingly diverse geography and climate for such a compact area. The oceanfront town of **Kailua-Kona,** a quaint fishing village that now caters more to tourists than boat captains, is its commercial center; sooner or later, everyone meets on Kailua-Kona's Alii Drive, a 2-mile retail strip of shops and restaurants that's fun to cruise on foot or car, especially on Saturday night. The lands of Kona range from stark, black, dry coastal desert to cool, cloudy up-country so fertile that it seems anything could grow there: glossy green coffee, macadamia nuts, tropical fruit, and a riotous profusion of flowers cover the jagged steep slopes. Among the coffee, you'll find the funky, artsy village of **Holualoa.** Higher yet in elevation are native forests of giant trees filled with tiny, colorful birds, some perilously close to extinction.

The serrated Kona Coast is indented with five bays, including Kealakekua, a marine-life preserve that's the island's best diving spot and the place where Capt. James Cook met his demise; and Honaunau, where a national historic park recalls the savage days of old Hawaii.

Kona means "leeward side" in Hawaiian—and that means full-on summer sun every day of the year. It's the island's affordable vacation spot. An ample selection of midpriced condo units, peppered with a few older hotels and B&Bs, line a shoreline that's mostly rocky lava reef, interrupted by an occasional pocket beach. You'll also find two world-class resorts here: the incomparable Kona Village, and Hawaii's newest luxury retreat, the Four Seasons at Hualalai.

THE KOHALA COAST

Fringes of palms and flowers, brilliant blankets of emerald green, and an occasional flash of white building are your only clues from the road that this black lava coast north of Kona is more than bleak and barren. And, oh, is it! Down by the sea, pleasure domes rise like palaces no Hawaiian king ever imagined. This is where the Lear jet set escapes to play in world-class beachfront hotels set like jewels in the golden sand. But you don't have to chant your genealogy or your net worth in order to visit the Waikoloa, Mauna Lani, and Mauna Kea resorts; the fabulous beaches and abundant historic sites are open to the public, with parking and other facilities provided by the resorts, including restaurants, golf courses, and shopping. And some terrific bargains are available right now, so don't write these resorts off as an accommodations option just yet.

Some people check in and never leave the Kohala Coast until it's time to go home. Great golf, great food, great architecture, great place.

NORTH KOHALA

Seven sugar mills once shipped from three harbors on this knob of land at the north-ernmost reaches of the island, which at one time produced enough sugar to sweeten all the coffee in San Francisco. **Hawi,** the region's hub and home to the Kohala Sugar Co., was a flourishing sugar town. It even had its own railroad, a narrow-gauge train that hauled cane down to Mahukona, on North Kohala's lee coast.

Today, Hawi's quaint, three-block-long strip of sun-faded false-front buildings and 1920s vintage shops lives on as a minor tourist stop in one of Hawaii's most scenic rural regions. The small cosmopolitan community of 10 diverse ethnic groups, in-cluding Chinese, Japanese, Puerto Rican, Korean, and Filipino laborers, is slowly shrinking as the old timers die out. Hawi isn't a ghost town yet, but don't hold your breath.

This region is most famous for being the birthplace of King Kamehameha the Great; a statue commemorates the royal site. This region is also home to the islands' most sacred site, the 1,500-year-old Mookini Heiau.

WAIMEA (KAMUELA)

This old up-country cow town on the northern road between the coasts is in the throes of becoming Martha Stewart–ized. This is lovely country: rolling green pastures, big wide-open spaces dotted by *pu'u* (hills), and real Marlboro-smoking cow-pokes who ride mammoth Parker Ranch, Hawaii's largest working ranch. It's also headquarters for the Keck Telescope, the largest and most powerful in the world, bringing world-class, starry-eyed astronomers to town. The nightlife here is far out, in the galactic sense; bring your own telescope. Waimea is home to several B&Bs, and Merriman's Restaurant is a popular foodie outpost at Opelo Plaza.

THE HAMAKUA COAST

This emerald coast, a 52-mile stretch from Honokaa to Hilo on the island's wind-ward northeast side, was once planted in sugar cane; it now blooms with flowers, macadamia nuts, papayas, and marijuana, or *pakalolo* (still Hawaii's number one cash crop). Resort-free and virtually beachless, the Hamakua Coast's major destinations are spectacular Waipio Valley, a picture-perfect valley with impossibly steep sides, taro patches, a green riot of wild plants, and a winding stream leading to a broad black-sand beach; the historic plantation town of **Honokaa** (making a comeback as the B&B capital on the coastal trail); and **Hilo,** a quaint port city under the volcanoes (see below). Akaka Falls and Laupahoehoe Beach are also worth seeking out.

Elsewhere along the coast, communities are reeling in the wake of the sugar plan-tation shutdown, and the cane in the fields is going to seed. Valleys draining Mauna Kea's slopes meet the sea every few miles; they're so choked with foliage that they look like an Indonesian jungle.

HILO

When the sun shines in Hilo, it's one of the most beautiful tropical cities in the Pacific. Being here is an entirely different kind of island experience: Hawaii's larg-est city after Honolulu is a quaint, misty, flower-filled city of Victorian houses over-looking a half-moon bay, with a restored historic downtown and a clear view of Mauna Loa's often snowcapped peak. Hilo catches everyone's eye until it rains—and when it rains in Hilo, it pours.

Hilo is America's wettest town, with 128 inches of rain annually. (Only five cit-ies receive even half as much rain as Hilo does annually; the closest are Mobile and

The Big Island

Alenuihaha Channel

PACIFIC OCEAN

Hawi
Kapaau
NORTH KOHALA
Kukuihaele
Waipio
Honokaa
Paauilo
THE HAMAKUA COAST
Kawaihae
THE KOHALA COAST
WAIMEA (Kamuela)
Anaehoomalu
Waikoloa
Hakalau
Honomu
Mauna Kea △
Paihaaloa
Hilo Forest Reserve
Hilo Bay
Kailua-Kona
Hualalai △
HILO (see area map)
Lave Tree State Park
THE KONA COAST
Kealakekua
Captain Cook
Keeau
Kapoho
Pahoa
Issac Hale Park
Mackenzie State Park
THE PUNA REGION
Honaunau
Kealia
Hawaii Volcanoes National Park
Mauna Loa △
Volcano Village
Kilauea △
HAWAII VOLCANOES NATIONAL PARK (see area map)
Chain of Craters Rd.
(Road closed due to lava flow)
South Kona Forest Reserve
Kau Desert
Pahala
Manuka State Park
Punaluu
Mamalahoa Hwy.
Naalehu
SOUTH POINT
Ka Lae

Kohala Mountains
Saddle Rd.
Mamalahoa Hwy.
Queen Kaahumanu Hwy.
Waikoloa Rd.
Saddle Rd.
Stainback Hwy.
Hawaii Belt Rd.
S. Point Rd.

250
270
190
200
130
132
137

0   16 km
     10 mi

N

Airport ✈   Mountain △

PACIFIC OCEAN

1-0730

Akaka Falls 22
Captain Cook's Monument 2
Ellison S. Onizuka Space Center 8
Hawaii Tropical Botanical Garden 24
Hilton Waikoloa Village 10
Honokohau Harbor 7
Hulihee Palace 5
Katsu Goto Memorial 20
Kaupulehu Petroglyphs 9
King's Trail Petroglyphs, Royal Waikoloan 11
Kona Historical Society Museum 3
Kona Pier 6
Lapakahi State Historical Park 14

Laupahoehoe Beach Park & Memorial 21
Mark Twain Square & Tree 25
Mokuaikaua Church 4
Mookini Luakini 15
Onizuka Visitor Center 23
The Original King Kamehameha Statue 16
Parker Ranch 19
Pololu Valley Lookout 17
Puako Petroglyph Archaeological District 12
Puuhonua O Honaunau National Historical Park 1
Puukohola Heiau National Historic Site 13
Waipio Valley 18

What Honolulu attempts to be, Hilo is without effort.

—Isabella Bird (1890)

Pritchard in Alabama, which both receive about 64^1/$_2$ inches.) It's ideal for ferns, orchids, and anthuriums, but less desirable for sun seekers on holiday. Yet there's lots to see and do in Hilo, so grab your umbrella. The rain is warm (the temperature seldom dips below 70°), and there's usually a rainbow afterward.

Hilo's oversized airport and hotels are remnants of a dream: The city wanted to be Hawaii's major port of entry. That didn't happen, but the facilities here are excellent. Hilo is Hawaii's best bargain for budget travelers. It has plenty of hotel rooms—most of the year, that is. Hilo's magic moment comes in spring, the week after Easter, when hula *halau* (schools) arrive from throughout the islands and elsewhere for the annual Merrie Monarch Festival hula competition (see "Calendar of Events" in Chapter 3). This is a full-on Hawaiian spectacle and a wonderful cultural event to enjoy, especially if you love hula enough to watch for hours. Plan ahead if you want to go: Tickets are very hard to get, and the hotels are usually booked solid.

Hilo is also the gateway to Hawaii Volcanoes National Park and the greatest show on earth; it's just an hour's drive up-slope.

THE PUNA REGION

Lava, and lots of it, characterizes the Puna Region, on the Big Island's remote eastern shore. Lava covers almost everything, both ancient sites and latter-day villages, with alacrity: In 1963, lava ran down to Cape Kumukahi and oozed around the lighthouse, which still looks startled; it destroyed the village of Kalapana in 1990. Since it overran Chain of Craters Road in 1988, there's only one way in and out of Puna: Hi. 130. Land not buried by lava is planted in red and green anthuriums, golden sunrise papayas, and marijuana. The illegal leaf growers add an edgy element to this barren and otherwise benign region known for its lack of aloha. Be cool in Puna, or else.

HAWAII VOLCANOES NATIONAL PARK & VOLCANO VILLAGE

The sleepy village of Volcano sits in a rain forest on the edge of America's most exciting national park, where a live volcano called Kilauea erupts daily. Ideally, you should plan to spend 3 days at the park, exploring the trails, watching the volcano, visiting the rain forest, and just enjoying this most unusual, spectacular place. Bring your sweats or jackets (honest!); it's cooler up here, especially at night.

If you plan to dally in the park—and you should—Volcano has some great places to stay. Several terrifically cozy B&Bs, some with fireplaces, hide under tree ferns in this cool, misty hamlet. The tiny highland (at 4,000 ft.) community, first settled by Japanese immigrants, is now inhabited by artists, soul-searchers, and others who like the crisp air of Hawaii's high country. It has just enough civilization to sustain a good life: a few stores, a gas station, and a golf course.

SOUTH POINT

This is the Plymouth Rock of Hawaii, where the first Polynesians arrived in seagoing canoes, probably from the Marquesas Islands or Tahiti, around A.D. 500. You'll feel like you're at the end of world on this lonely windswept place, the southernmost point of the United States (a geographic claim that belonged to Key West, Florida until 1959, when Hawaii became the 50th state). Hawaii ends in a sharp black-lava point. Bold 500-foot cliffs stand against the blue sea to the west and shelter the old fishing village of Waiahukini, which was born in A.D. 750 and lasted until the 1860s. Ancient canoe moorings, shelter caves, and *heiau* (temples) poke through wind-blown *pili* grass. The east coast curves inland to reveal a lonely green-sand beach, a world-famous anomaly that's accessible only by foot or four-wheel drive. For most, the only reason to venture down to the southern tip is to say you did, or to experience the empty vista of land's end.

Everything in the two wide spots in the road called **Naalehu** and **Waiohinu** that pass for towns at South Point claims to be the southernmost this or that. Except for a monkeypod tree planted by Mark Twain in 1866, there's not much else to crow about. There is, thankfully, a gas station, a couple of eateries and a fruit stand, a picture-postcard 19th-century church, and a B&B run by an Alaskan couple with a cockatoo. These end-of-the-world towns are just about as far removed from the real world as you can get.

2 Getting Around

by Rick Carroll

You need a rental car to see the Big Island. The only time you don't need a car here is if you plan to check into a Kohala Coast resort and remain there until your flight home; in that case, a hotel shuttle van will probably be available to pick you up at Keahole Airport.

DRIVING AROUND THE BIG ISLAND

Rental cars are available at both major airports and at Kohala Coast resort hotels: **Alamo** (☎ 800/327-9633); **Avis** (☎ 800/321-3712); **Budget** (☎ 800/527-0700); **Dollar** (☎ 800/800-4000); **Hertz** (☎ 800/654-3011); **National** (☎ 800/ 227-7368); and **Payless** (☎ 800/729-5377).

There are more than 480 miles of paved road on the Big Island, but only two main highways. The one main highway that circles the island is called the Hawaii Belt Road. On the Kona side of the island you have two choices: the scenic "upper" road, Mamalahoa Highway (Hi. 190), or the speedier "lower" road, Queen Kaahumanu Highway (Hi. 19). The road that links east to west is called the Saddle Road (Hi. 200), because it crosses the "saddle" between Mauna Kea and Mauna Loa. Saddle Road is the one rental car agencies ask you to avoid, because it's rough and narrow and the weather conditions can be a handful for motorists.

OTHER TRANSPORTATION OPTIONS

TAXIS   Taxis are readily available at both Keahole and Hilo airports. In Hilo, call **A-1 Bob's Taxi.** In Kona, call **Kona Airport Taxi** (☎ 808/329-7779).

BUSES   This is the cheapest way to see the Big Island, but you've got to be flexible. The **Hele-On Bus** is a commuter bus service based in Hilo that goes almost everywhere 7 days a week, including Waimea, Kailua-Kona, South Kohala, and Volcano, with regular stops along the way. Eighteen Greyhound-sized buses run between 3:45am and 7pm daily. You can board with backpacks, and there's storage for bicycles and other gear. The most popular route, from Hilo to Volano, is $1.50—the best transit deal on the island. The 140-mile route from Hilo to Captain Cook, on the Kona Coast, is $6. Call **808/961-8343** for routes and schedules.

FAST FACTS: The Big Island

American Express   American Express has two offices on the Kohala Coast: at the Hilton Waikoloa Village (☎ 808/885-7958), and at The Orchid at Mauna Lani (☎ 808/885-6600). To report lost or stolen traveler's checks, call 800/221-7282.

Dentists   In an emergency, contact Dr. Craig C. Kimura at Kamuela Office Center (☎ 808/885-5947).

Doctors   Hilo Medical Center is at 1190 Waianuenue Ave., Hilo (☎ 808/969-4111. Kaiser Permanente's Kona Clinic is at 75-184 Hualalalai Rd., Kailua-Kona (☎ 808/327-2900).

Emergencies   For ambulance, fire, and rescue, call 808/961-6022, or dial 911. The Poison Control Center's hot line is ☎ 800/362-3585.

Hospitals   Hilo Hospital, 1190 Waianuenue Ave. (☎ 808/969-4111), and Kona Hospital in Kealakekua (☎ 808/322-9311) both have 24-hour urgent-care facilities.

Police   Dial 911, or call the Hawaii Police Department at 808/935-3111 for assistance anywhere on the island.

Post Office   In Hilo, at 1299 Kekuanaoa Ave. (☎ 808/933-7090); in Kona, at 74-5577 Palani Rd. (☎ 808/329-1927); in Waimea, at Lindsey Rd., off Hi. 19 (☎ 808/885-4026).

Weather   For conditions in and around Kailua-Kona, call 808/935-8555; for the rest of the Big Island, call 808/961-5581. For marine forecasts, call 808/935-9883.

3   Accommodations

by Rick Carroll

The Big Island, quite naturally, has the biggest, widest variety of lodging possibilities—world-class luxury resorts, affordable condos, vacation rentals, and unique bed-and-breakfasts—ranging from $30 per night for a B&B homestay on a macadamia-nut farm to a lavish bungalow overlooking Hapuna Beach for $5,000 a night (but it comes with its own chef, butler, and swimming pool on a semiprivate cove). You can stay in a tree house, in a rain forest, on a working cattle ranch, by the sea, on a black-lava tide pool, at the edge of a still-steaming volcano, by a waterfall stream, at a Buddhist retreat, or beside a black-sand beach. They even have motels here.

The rates listed below are rack rates, but you can usually do better, particularly at the big hotels; see "Tips on Finding Accommodations" in Chapter 3. Hawaii adds 10.17% in taxes to all hotel bills. Parking is free unless otherwise noted.

ON THE KONA COAST

Aston Royal Sea Cliff Resort. 75-6040 Alii Dr., Kailua-Kona, HI 96740. ☎ **808/329-8021** or 800/922-7866. Fax 808/326-1887. 148 studios, one- and two-bedroom apts, and villas. A/C TV TEL. Winter $160–$505; Apr–Christmas $145–$455. AE, CB, DC, DISC, JCB, MC, V.

These architecturally striking five-story white buildings of this resort condo complex 2 miles from Kailua-Kona are stepped back from the ocean for maximum views and privacy. Atrium gardens and hanging bougainvillea soften the structures. For the price of a moderate hotel room, you'll get a spacious unit furnished in tropical rattan with a large, sunny lanai and a full kitchen. Tennis courts, pools, spas, sauna, and barbecue facilities are available, as well as hotel-like services such as voice mail, a small store, and an activity desk. The downside is that there's no ocean swimming here, but the waves are near enough to lull you to sleep.

☼ Four Seasons Resort Hualalai at Historic Kaupulehu. P.O. Box 1119, Kailua-Kona, HI 96745. ☎ **808/325-8000** or 800/332-3443. Fax 808/325-8100. 243 rms, 31 suites. A/C TV MINIBAR TEL. $450–$6,000 double. AE, DC, JCB. MC, V.

New to Hawaii's hotel scene in September 1996, the Four Seasons is setting a new standard for modern luxury-hotel construction in Hawaii, with low-rise clusters of oceanfront villas nestled between the sea and the greens of a new, private Jack Nicklaus–designed golf course, all tucked inside a (shades of L.A.) gated seaside community. This place is pretty showy compared to the humble thatch shelters at neighboring Kona Village, but it's a small fry compared to the megaresort originally planned by Japanese investors until the yen shrank, forcing the downsize. Thank God, or Buddha. Instead, it's a low-impact—no concrete corridors, no massive central building—hotel that looks more like a two-story townhouse project, clustered around five seaside swimming pools (one carved out of black lava rock).

The rooms are furnished in Pacific tropical style: beige walls, raffia rugs over clay-colored slate, and Madge Tennent etchings over rattan and bamboo settees. The bathrooms have private gardens, so you can shower naked under the tropic sun.

Dining/Entertainment: Pacific Rim cuisine will be featured in a restaurant with dazzling sea views, and at the more casual poolside bar and grill, where there'll also be authentic Hawaiian music nightly.

Services: 24-hour room service, complimentary valet, same-day laundry, 1-hour pressing, twice-daily maid service, multilingual concierge, free shoe-shine.

Facilities: Sports club and spa, 18-hole Jack Nicklaus golf course (reserved for guests and residents), Hawaiian history and cultural interpretive center, daily "Kids for All Seasons" program, three swimming pools, eight tennis courts, conference facilities, open lava-rock amphitheater for special events.

Kanaloa at Kona. 78-261 Manukai St., Kailua-Kona, HI 96740. ☎ **808/322-9625** or 800/688-7444. Fax 808/322-3618. 166 condo units. A/C, TV, TEL. $175–$210 one-bedroom apt (sleeps up to four); $205–$245 two-bedroom apt (sleeps up to six); $245–$265 three-bedroom apt (sleeps up to eight). AE, CB, DC, DISC, JCB, MC, V.

These big, comfortable, well-managed, and spacious vacation condos border the rocky coast beside Keauhou Bay, 6 miles south of Kailua-Kona. It's hard to get excited about condos, but these are exceptional, and ideal for families. They have all the comforts of home, and some that home never had, such as the huge bathrooms with spas, dressing rooms, and bidets. Spacious lanais, tropical decor, and lots of appliances make for free and easy living. Guests get discounted rates at the two 18-hole golf courses at a nearby country club; tennis, water sports, pools, and playgrounds are all at hand. And it's easy to stock up on supplies: there's a supermarket at the new mall just up the hill.

Keauhou Beach Hotel. 78-6740 Alii Dr., Kailua-Kona, HI 96740. ☎ **808/322-3441** or 800/367-6025. Fax 808/944-2974. 318 rms, 6 suites. A/C TV TEL. $98–$170 double; $240–$415 suite. AE, DC, JCB, MC, V.

This very Hawaiian place is the pride of the Kona Coast. The hotel is set on lush, well-maintained, historic royal grounds complete with temple ruins. And, 5 miles south of Kailua-Kona, it's adjacent to the best swimming and snorkeling beach in the area, Kahaluu. The hotel itself, an older six-story building, is actually anchored in a vast shallow tide pool of lava reef. You can see exotic tropical fish from the lanais of the ocean-facing rooms. Some of the rooms, however, are slipping—torn bedspreads, stained carpets—so insist on a renovated room, preferably on the south side of the building for the best views of the tide pools and the Pacific. Kuakini Terrace, the hotel's full-service, open-air dining room, serves satisfying themed buffets nightly (see "Dining," below).

King Kamehameha's Kona Beach Hotel. 75-5660 Palani Rd., Kailua-Kona, HI 96740. ☎ **808/329-2911** or 800/367-6060. Fax 808/922-8061. 455 rms, 7 suites. A/C TV TEL. $110–$195 single or double; $300–$500 suites. AE, CB, DC, DISC, JCB, MC, V.

The King Kam, named for the ruler who once lived here, is the biggest hotel in Kailua-Kona, the only one with a beach to call its own, and the guardian of what is probably the most historic site in Hawaii. It's also convenient to downtown Kailua-Kona and the town pier, where record Pacific blue marlin are weighed in every afternoon. It's nothing fancy—a standard hotel in need of a little TLC—but it's well located. Rooms are ordinary but clean, just like a Holiday Inn, but with views of an ancient Banyan tree, the Kona Pier, or sparkling Kailua Bay. There's a Liberty House department store and other shops on the premises, as well as a poolside bar and a snack bar. The small, gold-sand beach is right out the front door.

✪ **Kona Village Resort.** P.O. Box 1299, Kailua-Kona, HI 96745. ☎ **808/325-5555** or 800/367-5290. Fax 808/325-5124. 125 hale (bungalows). Full American Plan (includes all meals, tennis, water sports, walking tours, airport transfers, welcome lei, and Friday night luau) $395–$680 double. Additional person charges range from $25 for infants to $160 for those 13 and older. Packages available. AE, DC, JCB, MC, V.

In all of Hawaii, there's only one Kona Village. For more than 30 years, those seeking the great escape crossed the black lava fields to seek refuge at this exclusive haven by the sea. A blissful languor settles in as you surrender to the gentle staff and peaceful, low-key atmosphere. Maybe it's the spirit of the ancients who once lived here. Maybe it's the luxe summer-camp setup: thatched-roof island–style bungalows with no air-conditioning and no TVs, a central dining house, and phones only at the office. The resort resembles an eclectic Polynesian village, with proudly tended palms and tropicals, historic sites, and beaches on a secluded cove. Its magic frees children of all ages (except in couples-only September) to relax and play on 82 acres by the sea, behind a lava barrier that keeps the world at bay. The bungalows all have a bedroom, bathroom, and lanai. Standard equipment includes a grind-and-perk coffeemaker; some units have outdoor hot tubs and an extra anteroom with single bed.

Kona Village is my favorite resort in the islands, bar none. The only thing wrong with it, besides the fact that you can't stay forever, is that it's acquired a ritzy new next-door neighbor with big plans to sell townhouses to new millionaires—diminishing the delicious, remote sense of place that Kona Village has enjoyed until now.

Dining/Entertainment: The menus for breakfast and dinner, served in the communal dining room, depend on what's fresh in the islands that day. A second restaurant features more formal dining. Lunch is served on the terrace alfresco: a healthy, tempting buffet of veggies and salads, sashimi, burgers, fish, grill-to-order steaks, and a help-yourself bin of freshly baked oatmeal cookies. During holidays and summer, kids can eat at an early kids-only dinner, followed by supervised activities. Something live happens nightly, whether it's dancing to a Hawaiian trio at the Bora Bora Bar, a Paniolo Cookout, or the Friday-night luau, the island's best (see "Luaus & Other Local Fun: The Big Island After Dark," below).

Facilities: Beach, water sports, tennis, two pools, petroglyph field, outdoor cocktail lounges.

◆ **McCandless Ranch Bed & Breakfast.** P.O. Box 500, Honaunau (20 miles south of Kailua-Kona), HI 96726. ☎ **808/328-9313.** Fax 808/328-8671. 2 double units. $95 ranch-house room, $125 cottage. Rates include full breakfast. No credit cards.

Far from the crowds and well off the tourist trail—but definitely worth the drive—the McCandless Ranch is a 17,000-acre working cattle spread owned by a prominent old-time Hawaii family. It's a real ranch, but don't expect rustic. Cynnie and Ray Salley's two units are lavishly furnished in monarchy era (Victorian)–style with lots of rare koa wood; you'll feel like a 19th-century royal in for a visit. The cottage, beyond the pool from the ranch house, is a Hawaiian-style residence with kitchen and living room outdoors, under a roof, and the other rooms inside. The bath opens onto a hillside garden. The ranch house overlooks miles of Kona coastline far below.

This B&B offers an attraction no other in Hawaii can claim: a high country ohia forest that's the last refuge of the endangered Hawaiian crow; currently, the count is down to 12. Avid birders will want to beat a path here to see them and the facility where hatched crows are prepared for release into the wilds (see also "Birding," below).

◆ **Tommy Tinker's Cottage at Kealakekua Bay.** P.O. Box 599, Kapaau, HI 96755. ☎ **808/889-5584.** 1 two-bedroom cottage. TV. $800–$1,000 per week for two–six persons. No credit cards.

For a half-hour beyond Kailua-Kona, the road meanders through coffee country and wild avocados, finally arriving at Kealakekua Bay (of "Little Grass Shack" fame). The bay with the musical name and its underwater sights draws snorkelers on day cruises and dolphin lovers hoping for a swim with a friendly spinner. If you'd like to stay for more than a day, it would be hard to imagine a more appealing spot than this trim oceanfront cottage directly above the surf. Its sea-facing window-wall folds away to a broad, railed lanai with steps down to a small yard and the sea. The interior is open and airy and comfortably furnished, with a full kitchen, two bedrooms, and two baths. And there's plenty to do right nearby: Good swimming beaches line the coast here, and you can rent a kayak and paddle out to the monument to Captain Cook. Four miles to the south, the Place of Refuge National Historical Park is a fascinating spot to learn about local history and culture.

UP-COUNTRY KONA

Hale Maluhia Country Inn. 76-770 Hualalai Rd., Kailua-Kona, HI 96740. ☎ **808/329-5773** or 800/559-6627. Fax 808/326-5487. 2 cottages, 4 rms. $55–$85 double (2 with wheelchair access); $115–$135 cottage (sleeps up to six); $500 entire inn (sleeps up to 18). AE, DISC, MC, V.

In true Swiss Family Robinson tradition, owner/builder Ken Smith kept hammering under huge shady trees until he created his dream compound: an eight-bedroom brown-shingle and lava rock inn with a rippling waterfall, a stream, and a koi pond, all sited in the crook of a hairpin turn on the slopeside road between Kailua-Kona and Holualoa. When there's traffic, you know it. But everything possible has been done to create an otherwise green idyll and homey retreat. Rooms are a jumble of furnishings and decor—comfortable enough, but a bit dark under the shady trees. The best is probably the Banyan Cottage, with a sunset view from the porch swing, private Jacuzzi, kitchenette, koa wood details, and beamed ceiling. Ken goes to great effort to make you feel at home; amenities include private lanais, video and book library, and bountiful breakfasts served on the lanai.

Holualoa Inn. P.O. Box 222, Holualoa, HI 96725. ☎ **808/324-1121** or 800/392-1812. Fax 808/322-2472. 4 rms (with plans to expand to 10). $125–$165 double (including breakfast); $15 extra for third person. 15% discount for 7 nights or more. AE, MC, V.

If you've dreamed of sampling the lifestyle of a wealthy missionary scion, or if you simply enjoy beautiful surroundings, try this B&B. Its quiet, secluded setting—40 pastoral acres just off the main drag of the artsy village of Holualoa, on the slope above Kailua-Kona—provides stunning panoramic views of the entire coast. Owned by a *kamaaina* (old-line) family, this contemporary Hawaiian home built of golden woods has four private suites and window-walls that roll back to embrace the gardens and views. Cows graze on the bucolic pastures below the pool, and the coffee plantation on the property is the source of the morning brew. The tasty breakfasts consist of hand-picked mangoes and freshly baked muffins, or some variation on the theme. No cooking facilities are available, children aren't encouraged here, and smoking is *kapu*. It's a short drive down the hill to busy Kailua-Kona, and about 20 minutes to the beach, but the pool has a stunning view of Kailua-Kona and the sparkling Pacific below.

Pomaikai (Lucky) Farm Bed & Breakfast. 83-5465 Mamalahoa Hwy., Captain Cook, HI 96704. ☎ **808/328-2112** or 800/325-6427. 3 rms (4th under way). $35 double, $50 barn room. Discounts for students, seniors, and longer stays. No credit cards.

Come share ex-Californian Nita Isherwood's century-old 4-acre farm, overflowing with macadamia nut trees, coffee, tropical fruits, avocados as big as footballs, and even *jaboticaba*, an exotic fruit that makes a zingy jam and local wine. Two low-priced rooms with private baths are located at the front of the up-country Kona home, near the highway. The best room in the house is in the old coffee barn, updated into rustic private guest quarters for two. Breakfast includes fresh fruits, coffee from the farm, and homemade jams and breads. A barbecue grill available. An especially affordable perch from which to explore the South Kona Coast. You're welcome to eat as many fresh Mac nuts as you can crack.

THE KOHALA COAST

Some of the resorts along the Big Island's gold coast are phenomenal enough to warrant their own visitor centers and tours. Each has two hotels, two high-ranked golf courses, beaches, shopping, tennis facilities, and a number of plushy condos available for vacation rental.

Don't let the rack rates listed below scare you off. You can often do *much* better, particularly in the off-season. Since the Kohala Coast resorts had Hawaii's lowest occupancy rates in the last year, they're now offering some deep discounts.

✪ **Hapuna Beach Prince Hotel**. At Mauna Kea. 62-100 Kaunaoa Dr., Kamuela, HI 96743. ☎ **808/880-1111** or 800/882-6060. Fax 808/880-3200. 350 rooms, 37 suites. A/C MINIBAR TV TEL. $325–$900 double. AE, DC, JCB, MC, V.

The last of the grand beach hotels (at least for now), the $360 million Hapuna Prince is the Mauna Kea for the next century (see below). It's a contemporary statement of luxury nestled between the Big Island's best beach and a world-class golf course. Everybody's got a favorite big fancy hotel, and this is mine. In all the islands, nothing compares with Hapuna.

When you enter the soaring, open-air lobby, the view of Hapuna Beach and the sea beyond is framed like a real-life mural. Other than that, the fine materials—natural slate and wood—and the building's artistic form are decor enough. The rooms and suites are comfortable, all attuned to that fabulous view and the ocean breezes. And the service is friendly and caring, with an unassuming confidence that springs from Percy Higashi's own low-key, hands-on managerial approach. Some complain about the long walk from the lobby to their rooms, but after dinner in Hapuna Court, a short hike is almost a necessity.

Dining/Entertainment: The food is uniformly excellent throughout the five restaurants (see review of Coast Grille in "Dining," below), including the sushi bar (where there's a wide variety of sakes to sample) and oyster bar. One of the best desserts we've ever had, a fresh peach cobbler, is served at the pool bar. In the evening, there's always a local trio singing Hawaiian songs in the open-air, beachfront Reef Lounge.

Services: Full luxury treatment, 24-hour room service, valet.

Facilities: Health and fitness club, 18-hole Arnold Palmer and Ed Seay–designed championship links-style golf course (reserved for guests and residents), tennis pavilion with four Omni courts, pool, Jacuzzis, specialty boutiques, ballroom, conference facilities.

Mauna Kea Beach Hotel. 62-100 Mauna Kea Beach Dr., Kohala Coast, HI 96743. ☎ **808/882-7222** or 800/882-6060. Fax 808/880-3112. 310 rooms, 10 suites. A/C MINIBAR TEL. $280–$1,050 double. AE, DC, JCB, MC, V.

The father of Hawaii's fine resort hotels, Laurance S. Rockefeller, was sailing around Hawaii ("looking for a place to swim," as he tells it) when he spotted the perfect crescent of gold sand and dropped anchor. In 1965, he built the Mauna Kea on it.

After a year-long restorative shutdown, the grand dame is now back in business, with a fresh look after a barely discernible facelift. The swimming's still great, and the food's a whole lot better. Trouble is, over the years, all the new luxury hotels have eclipsed the Mauna Kea in architectural style (its 1960s New Brutalist style is heavy and dated), size of rooms (they're minuscule compared to those at the Hapuna), and amenities (no TVs—they're available on request if you're desperate—VCRs, or even full-length dressing mirrors). Still, no other hotel has been able to claim the loyalty of its old-money guests, who keep returning to savor the relaxed clubby ambiance, remote setting, superlative beach, world-class golf course, and old Hawaii ways—the next generation is welcome to find themselves a new and better beach hotel somewhere else. It's the difference between Alan Greenspan and Bill Gates, if you get my drift.

Dining/Entertainment: Jackets are required for dinner at the Provençal-inspired Batik Room (see complete review in "Dining," below). Breakfast and more casual Mediterranean/Italian dinners at the open-air Pavilion, and lavish lunch buffets at The Terrace. All three have live music. Drinks and light fare are served at the beachside Hau Tree Gazebo, which hosts Saturday clambakes. The Tuesday night luau features outstanding Hawaiian music and hula by Nani Lim and her award-winning dancers.

Services: Concierge, room service, dry cleaning, twice-a-day towel service, and turndown treats. Coffee mugs in room so you can trot down to the free coffee-and-pastry bar in the morning and bring fresh coffee and goodies back to your room.

Facilities: Pool, spa, 13-court oceanside tennis complex, golf at two top-ranked, award-winning championship courses—Robert Trent Jones, Sr.'s famous Mauna Kea course and the Arnold Palmer–designed Hapuna course, fitness center, water sports, horseback riding on Parker Ranch, guided art tours, shops, beauty salon, free movies, free children's summer program.

Mauna Lani Bay Hotel & Bungalows. 68-1400 Mauna Lani Dr., Kohala Coast, HI 96743. ☎ **808/885-6622** or 800/367-2323. Fax 808/885-4556. 350 rms and suites; one-, two-, and three-bedroom ocean villas. A/C MINIBAR TV TEL. $260–$465 double; $795 suite; $395–$630 villas (3-day minimum). AE, CB, DC, DISC, JCB, MC, V.

Sandy beaches and lava tide pools are the focus of this tranquil seaside resort, where gracious hospitality is dispensed in a setting that's exceptional for its historic features.

The guest rooms, each with a lanai, are arranged in a mid-rise arrow-shaped building, to capture maximum ocean views, around interior atrium gardens and pools, where endangered baby sea turtles are raised for a Fourth of July "Independence Day" release to the sea. Louvered doors open onto rooms done in natural tones and teak accents. The bungalows are posh two-bedroom, 4,000-square-foot enclaves with private pool and spa.

The hotel is weathering, like beachfront properties do; the hardwood floors creak in some rooms and there's rust around the edges, but the deferred maintenance of this 10-year-old resort probably won't be noticed by most. The beautiful beach pulls your eye away from such minor details. And a shoreline trail leads across the whole 3,200-acre resort, giving you an intimate glimpse into the ancient past, when people lived in lava caves and tended the large complex of spring-fed and tidal fishponds.

Dining/Entertainment: The CanoeHouse lost master chef Alan Wong to Honolulu (where he opened his signature restaurant), but it's still one of the most appealing beachside restaurants on the coast. The Gallery, at the Francis I'i Brown Golf Course Clubhouse, is also an epicurean heaven, where island ingredients are prepared with understated excellence. (For reviews of both, see "Dining," below.)

Services: 24-hour room service, nightly turndown, twice-daily towels.

Facilities: Two celebrated Francis I'i Brown 18-hole championship golf courses, conference rooms, shops, tennis complex, spa, pool.

The Orchid at Mauna Lani. (Formerly Ritz-Carlton, Mauna Lani). 1 N. Kaniku Dr., Kohala Coast, HI 96743. ☎ **808/885-2000** or 800/782-9488. Fax 808/885-8886. 539 rms, 52 suites (incl. 36 rms and 8 suites on club levels). A/C MINIBAR TV TEL. $285–$2,800. AE, CB, DC, DISC, JCB, MC, V.

At press time, Ritz-Carlton was relinquishing management of this large, palatial hotel to ITT Sheraton. Sheraton is planning some cosmetic changes to make the resort look and feel more "Hawaiian" and less Laguna Beach–like.

Dining/Entertainment: Chef Roy Basilio presides over all of the hotel's fine restaurants, including the the poolside restaurant and the more formal Grill for dinner, where a Hawaii Regional menu is featured.

Services: 24-hour room service, twice-daily towels, nightly turndown.

Facilities: The hotel has classy conference facilities, two celebrated Francis I'i Brown golf courses, a tennis complex, pools, shops, fitness center, and a fine swimming cove. On its north side, the Puako petroglyph field can be reached by way of a trail through a thorny keawe forest.

Royal Waikoloan. 69-275 Waikoloa Beach Rd., Kamuela, HI 96743. ☎ **808/885-6789** or 800/688-7444. Fax 808/885/7852. 545 rms, 10 suites. A/C MINIBAR TV TEL. Winter $135–$750 double. Off-season $120–$750. Rates are all-inclusive. AE, DC, DISC, JCB, MC, V.

Here's the bargain of the Kohala Coast: An all-inclusive resort with food and drink included in the rate! Older and more basic than its neighbors, the comfortable Waikoloan has a breathtaking movie-set beach lined with palms and a huge historic fishpond in the back yard, plus a significant petroglyph field and golf course in the front yard. Rooms are small, and some have the lingering odor of smokers, but you can always get fresh air out on the lanai. The property also includes a beachfront picnic area suitable for hukilau and other parties. Waikoloa golf, tennis, shopping, water sports, and other amenities are all at your fingertips.

Dining/Entertainment: The open-air Petroglyph Bar is a great sunset-viewing perch.

Facilities: Golf at adjacent Waikoloa Beach course, designed by Robert Trent Jones, Jr., and the Tom Weiskopf–designed Kings course; 6 tennis courts; historic petroglyph fields and fishponds; pool; oceanfront cabanas; health club; conference rooms.

Hilton Waikoloa Village. 69-425 Waikoloa Beach Dr., Kamuela, HI 96743. ☎ **808/ 885-1234** or 800/445-8667. Fax 808/885-2900. 1,238 rms, 56 suites. A/C MINIBAR TV TEL. Winter $210–$1,455 double or suite. Off-season $280 and up. AE, CB, DC, DISC, JCB, MC, V.

This is where you belong if you're bringing the kids on holiday in the islands. This isn't just another beach hotel (it actually has no real beach)—it's a fantasy world all its own, perfect for families, honeymooners, and everyone who loves Las Vegas and Disneyland. Its high-rise towers are connected by silver-bullet trams, boats, and museumlike walkways lined with Asian/Pacific reproductions. The 62 acres feature tropical gardens, cascading waterfalls, exotic wildlife, exaggerated architecture, a 175-foot waterslide twisting into a 1-acre pool, hidden grottos, and man-made lagoons—and the biggest hit of all, the Dolphin Lagoon, where you (if you're lucky enough to be selected by lottery) can pay to swim with real dolphins. There's also an extensive spa and fitness center, a mini shopping center, a fabulous children's program, plenty of bars and restaurants, and a wide range of activities available. You're bound to be entertained here. To top it all off, the rooms and facilities are luxurious, and the rates have dropped under current management.

Dining/Entertainment: Award-winning Donatoni's Italian Restaurant is perfect for that special evening; line up with the kids at the Palm Terrace for the family buffet. For everyday casual dining, my favorite is Hang Ten, the open-air cafe by the dolphin lagoon. There's evening entertainment galore, including a Friday night luau. There's also a sports bar, so you can check out the home team from afar.

Services: 24-hour room service.

Facilities: 20 boutique shops; 25,000-square-foot spa with cardio machines and weights; indoor and outdoor function space; 3 huge swimming pools; 8 tennis courts; 2 championship 18-hole golf courses by Robert Trent Jones, Jr. and Tom Weiskopf; American Express Travel desk; Avis Rent-a-Car desk.

WAIMEA

Waimea Gardens Cottages. P.O. Box 563, Kamuela, HI 96743. ☎ **808/885-4550** or 800/ 262-9912. Fax 808/885-0559. 2 cottages (sleep up to three). TV TEL. $115 double (including continental breakfast); $15 extra for third person. 3-night minimum. DISC.

This cozy cottage, by a stream in the cool Waimea ranch lands, has two separate one-bedroom units: one with a fireplace and kitchenette, the other with a full kitchen. Both have hardwood floors, antiques, French doors that open onto a brick patio, and lots of country charm. Hosts Barbara and Charlie Campbell live on the 1 1/2-acre property. Barbara also runs a B&B booking service, Hawaii's Best Bed & Breakfasts.

The Frank Lloyd Wright Home Hawaii. P.O. Box 563, Kamuela, HI 96743 ☎ **808/ 885-4550** or 800/262-9912. Fax 808/885-0559. Four-bedroom house (sleeps up to eight). TV TEL. $500 night, $3,000 week. 2-night minimum. Available for groups, retreats, and seminars. No credit cards.

Situated on a spectacular promontory, in plain view of three of the Big Island's five volcanoes, stands this unique vacation rental, a faithful execution of plans originally designed 40 years ago by Frank Lloyd Wright for a Pennsylvania family. The house exemplifies his principles of organic architecture: a passive-solar semicircle with an earth berm, a cylindrical stairwell, and four bedrooms on a mezzanine. The master suite includes a hot tub and fireplace. The home features his signature red concrete floor and built-in custom furnishings. It's Hawaii's second Wright-designed structure (the other is Waikapu Valley Country Club on Maui).

Jenny's Country Cottage. P.O. Box 563, Kamuela, HI, 96743 ☎ **808/885-4550** or 800/ 262-9912. Fax 808/885-0559. One-bedroom cottage (sleeps up to four). TV TEL. $85 double for 2 nights or more; add $10 for 1-night stay. Continental breakfast included. No credit cards.

This nearly century-old restored cottage, on a 4-acre farm with goats and a taro patch about 2 miles outside Waimea, has cheerful country appeal with hardwood floors and lace curtains, as well as a four-poster and other furniture made of rare koa wood; there's also a full kitchen. The host family lives on the property, as it has for generations. Children are welcome.

THE HAMAKUA COAST

✪ Waipio Wayside B&B Inn. P.O. Box 840, Honokaa, HI 96727. ☎ **808/775-0275** or 800/ 833-8849. 5 rms. $60–$100 double (including breakfast). DC, MC, V.

Jackie Horne's 1930s plantation home is a really enjoyable place to stay. The comfortable house, done in old Hawaii style, abounds with thoughtful touches, such as the help-yourself tea and cookies bar with 26 different kinds of tea. A sunny lanai deck with hammocks overlooks a yard that blooms with trees and orchids (there's also a gazebo). The large guest room behind the kitchen is the most private, and opens onto the deck. The Library Room has an ocean view, hundreds of books, and a skylight in the shower. Some rooms share a bath. Jackie's friendly hospitality and excellent breakfasts, prepared by the gourmet cook herself and served on her custom mango-wood table, really round out the experience.

Waipio Wayside is on Hi. 240, just beyond the 3-mile marker as you head toward Waipio Valley; look on the right for a long white picket fence and sign.

Hale Kukui. P.O. Box 5044, Kukuihaele, HI 96727. ☎/Fax **808/775-7130** or 800/444-7130. 1 studio and 1 two-bedroom apt in one cottage (can be combined into 1 three-bedroom unit). $85 studio, $100 apt, $175 cottage. Continental breakfast included on 1st day only. No credit cards.

The draw of this remote cottage is its tropical bird's-eye view into the mouth of Waipio Valley, with haunting sea cliffs and waves crashing along miles of coastline— simply mesmerizing. Architect-hosts William and Sarah McCowatt created an otherworldly environment in this clever structure (which expands or contracts to suit guest's needs) near their home, surrounding it with lush gardens and tropical flowers. The units have a kitchenette and a lanai with the fabulous view, which can include rare glimpses of native birds and whales calving in winter. To get to Hale Kukui, take Hi. 240 almost to its end, make a hairpin right turn, continue a short distance, and look for a sign on the left; it's just outside Waipio Overlook.

Tom Araki's Waipio Hotel. In Waipio Valley. c/o Sueno Araki, 25 Malama Place, Hilo, HI 96720. ☎ **808/775-0368.** 8 rms. $15 per person. No credit cards.

Make your reservations early—like right now—if you want to stay in lush Waipio Valley, off the grid by a taro patch, with a real character for a host. Tom Araki is in his eighties and can be either totally charming or amazingly gruff. If he likes the cut of your jib, you're in—otherwise, you'll be knocking on the door of the Honokaa Club. To smooth your entry into this old way of life, bring along a bottle of sake to share (maybe even a whole one for your host). A hotel in name only, this simply decorated old valley house has eight rooms with shared baths. From Waipio Valley Lookout, go down the four-wheel-drive–only road to the valley floor, cross over the stream, and look for Araki's Waipio Hotel on the right. Bring your own food.

Waipio Treehouse. In Waipio Valley. P.O. Box 5086, Honokaa, HI 96727. ☎ **808/775-7160.** 1 treehouse, 1 cottage. $175 per day (2-day minimum). MC, V.

Way back in the valley and 30 feet up a monkeypod tree that sits by a waterfall, you'll find the perfect getaway, a place where your childhood dreams come to life. Linda Beech's treehouse has electricity, running water, and 360° views. You may be nagged by things that go bump and crawl around in the night—this is, after all, the jungle—but life is short and this *is* Hawaii's only inhabitable treehouse. The screened room has two beds, a double and a single, plus a refrigerator and hot plate. The *hale* (cottage) has a kitchen and a bedroom. The rates include round-trip shuttle from Waipio Lookout at road's end.

Luana Ola Bed & Breakfast Cottages. P.O. Box 430, Honokaa, HI 96727. ☎/fax **808/775-7727** or 800/357-7727. 2 studio cottages (each sleeps up to four; 1 cottage wheelchair accessible). TV TEL. $75 double (including continental breakfast). No credit cards.

These cottages are hard to find, but you'll be delighted once you do. They're tiny treasures off the tourist trail, at the end of a cul-de-sac in Honokaa town. The tin-roofed plantation-style cottages are newly built in a romantic 1940s style and furnished in rattan and wicker. The 180° views take in cane fields, the Hamakua Coast, the turquoise waters of the Pacific, the island of Maui across the channel, and some terrific sunsets. Check out the hut housing the laundry facilities—even it has a great view. Your genial hosts, Tim and Jeannie Mann (who live right nearby) provide breakfast every morning. The town, within walking distance, is worth exploring for its Hawaiian craft shopping and genuine, unspoiled old Hawaiian feeling.

From Honokaa's main street, go makai (toward the sea) on Maile Street; take the second left, and go one block to the cottages.

Hotel Honokaa Club. P.O. Box 247, Honokaa, HI 96727. ☎/fax **808/775-0678** or 800/808-0678. 14 rms, 6 hostel beds (shared room or private). $15–$20 hostel; $45–$50 private rm. MC, V.

This funky and humble old place has been sheltering guests—mostly sugarland workers—for nearly 100 years. The sugar mills have since closed, but the Honokaa Club refuses to die, attracting bicyclists, adventure travelers, and anyone traveling on a tight budget. The 1950s-style cafe serves three meals a day—nothing fancy, but tasty and cheap, featuring a salad bar with crispy hydroponic leaf lettuce grown by local high-school kids. Some private rooms have ocean views, but don't expect much beyond a screened room and a cot. It's a good place to stay in a pinch—the price sure is right.

HILO

🟢 **Dolphin Bay Hotel.** 333 Iliahi St., Hilo, HI 96720. ☎ **808/935-1466.** Fax 808/935-1523. 18 studio, one-, and two-bedroom apts. TV TEL. $50–$85. MC, V.

This two-story motel-like building, on a rise four blocks from downtown, is a clean, family-run property that offers good value in a quiet, Edenlike garden setting: Ripe starfruit hang from the trees, flowers abound, and there's a jungly trail by a stream. The tidy concrete-block apartments are small and often breezeless, but they're equipped with ceiling fans and jalousie windows. Rooms are brightly painted in tropical yellow and outfitted with rattan furniture and Hawaiian prints. There are no phones in the rooms, but there's one in the lobby. Children are welcome, and you're welcome to all the papaya and banana you can eat.

Hilo Hawaiian Hotel. 71 Banyan Dr., Hilo, HI 96720. ☎ **808/935-9361** or 800/367-5004. Fax 808/961-9642. 285 rms and suites. A/C TV TEL. $99–$315. Rates include free rental car or 6th night free, with some date restrictions. AE, DISC, MC, V.

Overlooking Coconut Island on picturesque Hilo Bay, this eight-story waterfront crescent, built in 1974, features comfortable, renovated (1993) rooms. Ask for one with an ocean view. This hotel and its neighbors share a gracious setting on Banyan Drive, which curves away from the roads of town into a park and is lined with shady, giant banyan trees planted by visiting celebrities, primarily in the 1930s. A pool, shops, and banquet facilities are available, as well as a restaurant and lounge.

If it's a clear day, cross the little bridge over to the island for a great view of the city and its towering volcano backdrop.

Hawaii Naniloa Hotel. 93 Banyan Dr., Hilo, HI 96720. ☎ **808/969-3333** or 800/367-5360. Fax 808/969-6622. 325 rooms and 11 suites. A/C TV TEL. $100–$240. Rates include airport shuttle. AE, JCB, MC, V.

This nine-story hotel on Hilo Bay dates from 1929, but it had a major renovation in 1991 and there are ongoing upgrades. Hilo's biggest hotel has nice rooms with lanais and enjoys a quiet, leafy Banyan Drive setting with the ocean just across the road. There are restaurants and lounges, pools, a spa, and shops. Popular with Asian tour groups, it's a generally characterless place to stay, but, in terms of comfort and amenities, one of the best that Hilo has to offer.

Wild Ginger Inn Bed & Breakfast. 100 Puueo St., Hilo, HI 96720. ☎ **808/935-5556** or 800/882-1887. 23 rooms. $39–$64 double (including continental breakfast). Weekly rates and extended-stay discounts. No credit cards.

The place has a lot of tropical charm, and the price is right. (We have, however, received some reports of a slippage in maintenance recently; please be aware, and write us with your reports.) Fat banana bunches—products of the fertile garden around which this hot-pink and turquoise-green ex-motel curls—hang in the open-air lobby for you to enjoy. One large, nice one-bedroom apartment is available; the rest are smaller, simple rooms, many with a view of the jungle stream and bamboo grove. The busy coast highway below may be a problem for sensitive sleepers; ask for a room away from the road.

HAWAII VOLCANOES NATIONAL PARK & VOLCANO VILLAGE

Volcano House. P.O. Box 53, Hawaii Volcanoes National Park, HI 96718. ☎ **808/967-7321.** Fax 808/967-8249. 42 rms. TEL. $79–$105 double. AE, DC, DISC, JCB, MC, V.

Location, location, location: This old hotel's got it—and that's about all. On the edge of Halemaumau's bubbling crater, this mountain lodge, which evolved out of a grass lean-to in 1865, is Hawaii's oldest visitor accommodation. While its edgy view of the crater is still an awesome sight, the hotel has seen better days. The improved rooms have native koa wood furniture, but service is inconsistent, and the lobby and public rooms look forlorn. This historic hotel deserves better. A novel treat: rooms are heated with volcanic steam. Drawbacks: The lodge is a major tour-bus lunch stop. The food is edible but forgettable; you may want to stop for ohelo berry pie and coffee (or something stronger) at Uncle George's Lounge and bring it back to enjoy in front of the eerie crater.

Kilauea Lodge. One block off Hi. 11 on Volcano Rd. P.O. Box 116, Volcano, HI 96785. ☎ **808/967-7366.** Fax 808/967-7367. 11 rms, 2 cottages. $95–$135 per night double; $15 per extra person. Full breakfast included. MC, V.

This crowded and popular roadside lodge, built in 1938 as a YMCA camp, is operated by Albert Jeyte, an ex-Hollywood makeup artist for *Magnum P.I.* who stayed on in the islands to play host. The pleasant overnight lodging offers fireplaces in a number of rooms and a wood stove in the one-bedroom cottage. There's also a 1929 two-bedroom cottage with a fireplace and a full kitchen just a block down the street. Breakfast is served to guests only at the restaurant, which is open to the public for dinner (see "Dining," below).

☻ **Carson's Volcano Cottage.** Mauna Loa Estates, 501 Sixth St.; P.O. Box 5030, Volcano, HI 96785. ☎ **808/967-7683** or 800/845-5282. 3 rms, 1 private cottage, 5 vacation rental homes. $75–$135 double; $15 per extra person. Homes $75–$165. Continental breakfast included. AE, DISC, MC, V.

The search for a storybook cottage ends here at Volcano. The 1925 tin-roofed cabin (it's a roar in a torrential downpour), under giant tree ferns in the rain forest, is just around the corner from the national park. It has a potbelly stove, a kitchenette, and two big, comfortable double feather beds; a hot tub's tucked under the ferns. Hosts Tom and Brenda Carson serve a hearty breakfast in your room and leave you to you own amusement. They have other well-appointed accommodations nearby, but for true romance in the rain forest, ask for the cottage.

The Log Cabin at Hale Ohia. c/o Cynthia R. Rubinstein, 1123 11th Ave., Suite 404, Honolulu, HI 96816. ☎ **808/262-7249.** Fax 808/262-3440. 1 cabin (sleeps up to four). $125 double. No credit cards.

Here's an old log cabin for the young at heart, Hale Ohia is a 95-year-old notched ohia log cabin set in a forest of native tree ferns, wild ginger, and virgin cedars. One of the first homes built in Volcano—it served as a cowboy hangout and a speakeasy before becoming a one-of-a-kind historic hideaway—it's fully equipped with all the modern conveniences, including a wood-burning fireplace (vital in Hawaii's high country), full kitchen and bath, TV and VCR, and phone. Rustic and romantic, it sleeps up to four on the second floor (two in a master bedroom and two in an antechamber), up a double spiral staircase with ohia handrails.

SOUTH POINT

Becky's Bed & Breakfast at Naalehu. P.O. Box 673, Naalehu, HI 96772. ☎/Fax **808/929-9690.** 3 rms. TV. $60–65 double. Continental breakfast included. No credit cards.

I wouldn't go all the way to South Point *just* to stay at Becky's, but if you're exploring the Big Island's south coast, your evening respite at this charming 1937 restored doctor's home can be a pleasant one. Three years ago, Becky and Chuck McLinn traded Alaska glaciers for volcanoes and the chance to welcome guests to Naalehu, a sleepy country town that happens to be the southernmost town in the United States. The rooms are fresh and comfy, and the McLinns are right friendly country folks. Becky's is 64 miles south of Hilo and 56 miles south of Kailua-Kona on Hi. 11—a perfect midway point for bicyclists on island circle treks.

4 Dining

by Jocelyn Fujii

The Big Island of Hawaii has produced its share of star chefs. Peter Merriman (the visionary behind the eponymous Merriman's in Waimea), Sam Choy (the Kona chef who prepares local food with a gourmet twist), and Alan Wong (who put the Mauna Lani's CanoeHouse on the national culinary map before heading to Honolulu to open his own place) are among the hugely talented artists who have honed and shaped Hawaii Regional Cuisine, giving it culinary muscle and a credibility that has outlasted the critics and naysayers of a decade ago.

Since then, Big Island dining has made its mark as an authentic island attraction in itself. From local-style diners to pricey dining rooms with hushed tones and budget-breaking menus, you'll find spirited cuisine anchored in the island's fertile volcanic soil and the labor of its tireless farmers, fishermen, and chefs. Every time I visit Hawaii, I sing praises to the kitchen gods as I make plans for the next day's hike, a necessary antidote to the typical day's excesses.

The haute cuisine of the island—and to some degree, the state—is concentrated in the Kohala Coast resorts, where Mauna Lani Bay Hotel and Bungalows, Mauna Kea Beach Hotel, and the new Hapuna Beach Prince Hotel claim their share of the action for deep pockets and special-occasion tastes.

Kailua-Kona, to the south, is teeming with restaurants for all pocketbooks; although most of them are touristy and many overpriced, there are some top-notch restaurants (Palm Cafe, Edward's at the Kanaloa) along the shoreline. Kona has everything from outstanding Mexican (Poquito Mas) to sublime pizzas (Bianelli's) to traditional French (La Bourgogne), and fresh fish is as ubiquitous as the ocean view.

Waimea, also known as Kamuela, is a thriving up-country hotspot, a haven for yuppies and retirees who know a good place when they see one. This is the village for serious foodies (Merriman's), discerning palates too busy to cook (Ann Sutherland's largely microwaveable Mean Cuisine), and health-conscious folks with a penchant for a Hawaiian spirit in food and ambiance (Maha's Cafe).

Expect bakeries, neighborhood diners, and one tropical-chic restaurant (Bamboo) in Honokaa on the Hamakua Coast, and watch for some big changes (and larger malassadas!) at Tex Drive-Inn and Restaurant. In Hilo, you'll find pockets of trendiness among the precious old Japanese and ethnic restaurants, providing honest, tasty, and affordable meals in unpretentious surroundings. Your finest meal between Kona and Hilo on the southern route (that's a lot of miles!) will undoubtedly be at Kilauea Lodge, where the roaring fireplace and crisp air match the excellent continental cuisine. If you need a pasta stop in between, Paolo's in Pahoa may surprise you.

In the listings below, reservations are not required unless otherwise noted.

THE KONA COAST
IN & AROUND KAILUA-KONA

Basil's Pizzeria. 75-5705 Alii Dr. ☎ **808/326-7836.** Individual pizzas $5.95–$7.95; main courses $7.95–$14.95. MC, V. Daily 11am–10pm. PIZZA/ITALIAN.

The recently expanded pizzeria now seats 100 in two dining rooms, so they're serving up a lot of pizza—and word is spreading that it's good. The rooms are redolent with the smells of cheeses, garlic, sizzling sauces, and fresh organic herbs (a big plus). Shrimp pesto and the original barbecue chicken pizzas are longstanding favorites, and so is the artichokes-olive-capers version, a sort of Greek-Italian hybrid.

Bianelli's Pizza. Pines Plaza, 75-240 Nani Kailua Dr. ☎ **808/326-4800.** Reservations recommended for dinner. Pizzas $7.95–$21.95; main courses $7.45–$18.95. CB, DC, DISC, MC, V. Open Mon–Fri 11am–10pm, Sat–Sun 5–10pm. PIZZA/ITALIAN.

Local farmers tout Bianelli's as a pioneer in the use of fresh organic herbs and produce, tastefully assembled on handmade crusts with long-simmering sauces from old family recipes. This is Kona's best pizza, made with wholesome ingredients and cheeses and no sacrifice in flavor. Everything is fresh: the herbs—straight from the farmers—the handmade dough, the homemade pasta, the organic lettuces and produce. The full bar features an international beer selection, including the local Kona Brew. Favorite combinations include the Mexican (tangy with jalapenos), Gorgonzola (with garlic and whole peeled tomatoes), the Greek, and the sensational Ricotta—dripping with garlic, Parmesan, and ricotta, yet 40% less fatty than most pizzas. The house specialty is the Buffala, with scads of garlic and buffalo milk mozzarella. With three pasta specials every day, it isn't easy to choose. Come with an appetite to this warm and lively scene, and you'll leave happy.

Chart House. Waterfront Row, 75-5770 Alii Dr. ☎ **808/329-2451.** Reservations recommended. Main courses $16.50–$26.95 (seafood at market price). AE, DC, DISC, MC, V. Daily 5–9:30pm. STEAK/SEAFOOD.

The Chart House formula—baked potato, salad bar, steaks, prime rib, and seafood—endures in this open-air restaurant on Kailua Bay. It's far from epicurean fare, and the restaurant has been eclipsed by the lighter offerings of the new Pacific Rim eateries that pepper the state, but those who seek more familiarity than creativity—and a filet mignon for less than $26 with salad bar and rice—still find their way to the Chart House. What the main course doesn't do, the dessert does: The famous mud pie (Kona coffee ice cream, a chocolate wafer crust, fudge, almonds, and whipped cream) is $6.95.

Edward's at the Kanaloa. The Kanaloa at Kona. 78-261 Manukai St. ☎ **808/322-1003.** Reservations recommended. Main courses $16.50–$30. AE, DC, MC, V. Daily 8am–2pm, 5–9pm; bar open 8am–9pm. MEDITERRANEAN.

If you're willing to drive the 10 extra minutes south from Kona to Keauhou, this stellar spot, located on a breathtaking point at the ocean, will make your day. It's a real find. Chef/owner Edward Fray's restaurant (the dining room for the Kanaloa condominiums) is an oasis without walls, where you can look for whales and dolphins and take in the ocean breeze over an excellent ragout of mushrooms, or salmon or shrimp with angel-hair pasta and a pomegranate glaze. Formerly Edward's at the Terrace, the petite and pleasing restaurant combines an unparalleled location with the culinary gifts of the man who was selected the 1995 "Chef of the Year" of the Hawaii chapter of the Culinary Federation of America. The macadamia nut–banana waffle ($7.95 with fresh-squeezed orange juice) is a hit at breakfast. At lunch, the cold lobster salad on a bed of angel-hair pasta with red roasted pepper and papaya goes for $15.95 with a glass of wine. At dinner, Fray is known for his brilliance with fresh fish and anything with mushrooms or grain. A romantic spot that will also please your palate.

Fisherman's Landing at Shipwreck Point. Kona Inn Shopping Village. 75-5739 Alii Dr. ☎ **808/326-2555.** Reservations recommended. Main courses $11–$27. AE, DC, DISC, JCB, MC, V. Daily 5:30–9pm. SEAFOOD.

The bubbling of the fountains and waterfalls competes with the lapping of the surf at this cavernous, open-air, 300-seat oceanfront restaurant. The split-level dining room is part coffee shop, part restaurant. If you can get past the lack of intimacy and the Disneyesque touches, there are $3.50 Mai Tais at sunset, fresh ahi for under $15 (with vegetables, rice, and freshly baked bread), and a tossed salad for $2 to enjoy. If you'd like a local touch, ask about the Molokai-style opakapaka, sautéed, steamed in wine, and finished with ginger and green onions, Chinese style. Seating is first-come-first-served on the terrace, and although the view is noteworthy, it's a touristy place.

Huggo's. 75-5828 Kahakai Rd. ☎ **808/329-1493.** Reservations requested. Main courses $19.95–$36.95. CB, DC, DISC, MC, V. Daily 5:30–10pm. STEAK/SEAFOOD.

Kudos to Huggo's! This old-timer seaside restaurant, in one of Kona's most prized locations, has made waves with a new chef, Mark Painter, an upgraded menu, competitive prices, a decent wine list, and a strong commitment to local organic produce. The fresh fish is a Huggo's signature, as is the coral-strewn beach with tide pools just beyond the wooden deck. At lunch, the choices range from pizza and prime rib sandwiches to hot dogs and a fresh catch, with a kid's menu of sophisticated sandwich and seafood choices. You may find it difficult choosing from among the evening's offerings: ono with rock shrimp and garlic basic aioli; pan-charred ahi with Hawaiian green-onion pesto; a seafood pesto over linguine; Kona paella; and much more from land and sea. The basics—fresh salads (including a garlic-rich Caesar), ahi poke, chowders, scampi, prime rib—are solidly satisfying thanks to the fresh ingredients.

Jolly Roger. Waterfront Row. 75-5776 Alii Dr. ☎ **808/329-1344.** Main courses $9.95–$20. AE, DC, DISC, MC, V. Daily 6:30am–10pm. AMERICAN/SEAFOOD.

This open-air restaurant in one of Kona's most attractive locations is Kona's only breakfast-to-after-hours spot, with sweeping views from four lanais and a menu for wide-ranging tastes. One of several eateries in Waterfront Row, Jolly Roger is popular for breakfast, where you can watch the sky lighten over steak and eggs, a noteworthy eggs Benedict, or macadamia nut waffles. The usual sandwiches and salads, steak, scampi, and pasta are among the lunch and dinner offerings. Be sure to ask about the specials: the barbecued ribs, chicken Polynesian, and teriyaki steak are usually a good value, and the view counts for a lot. On Friday and Saturday evenings, live entertainment and dancing make this one of Kona's late-night hot spots.

Kona Galley. In the Kona Seaside Shopping Mall, 75-5663 Palani Rd. (opposite King Kamehameha's Kona Beach Hotel). ☎ **808/329-5550.** Reservations recommended. Main courses $9.95–$32.95. AE, MC, V. Mon–Sat 11:30am–9pm; Sun 5–9pm. SEAFOOD.

Kona Galley's view takes in the lively, upbeat ocean activities that take place day and night offshore from Kailua Pier. The open-air lanai looks out over the picturesque scene of canoe clubs paddling vigorously and ocean liners and boats coming and going, with strings of lights delineating them against the dark night sky. The restaurant offers everything from pizza (11 different types) to the very popular Chicken Puna, a value at less than $10. The curried chicken breast, presented in a tasty assemblage of papaya, bay shrimp, and rice pilaf, is a standout. It'll compete for your attention with the shrimp in lilikoi and basil sauce, and the peppercorn chicken. Think big: The restaurant serves up to 300 dinners a night.

Kona Inn Restaurant. Kona Inn Shopping Village. 75-5744 Alii Dr. ☎ **808/329-4455.** Reservations recommended at dinner. Main courses $12.95–$18.95. Cafe Grill menu daily 11:30am–midnight; dinner menu daily 5:30–10pm. AMERICAN/SEAFOOD.

In terms of ambiance, Kona Inn stands out even in a string of waterfront restaurants. Its large, open terrace and panoramic view of the Kailua-Kona shoreline are its most attractive feature, especially for sunset cocktails and appetizers. With waves lapping a few feet from your table, you may be more likely to overlook a less-than-perfect sashimi or an overpriced sandwich. The ubiquitous "Kona cuisine" of seafood, sandwiches, and salads dominates the Cafe Grill menu; the more upscale dinner menu is heavier on pricier fresh catches, chicken, and steaks.

Kona Ranch House. Hi. 11, at the corner of Kuakini and Palani. ☎ **808/329-7061.** Reservations recommended for dinner. Paniolo Room, complete meal $8.95–$14.95. Plantation Lanai, complete meal $10.95–$22.95. CB, DISC, MC, V. Daily 6:30am–9pm. AMERICAN.

Two entirely different menus and atmospheres give you a choice between family-style dining and something more intimate, quiet, and pricey. For 15 years, Kona Ranch House has welcomed families to the Paniolo Room with children's menus and generous platters of steak, shrimp, pork, ribs, and chicken. There's breakfast, too, with hefty *paniolo*-style favorites that include eggs Benedict, and its crab counterpart with tomatoes and onions, for $8.95. The family-style dining includes stews, spaghetti, and broiled fish for less than $11, plus sandwiches. In the wicker-accented Plantation Lanai, ranch house favorites—complete steak, seafood, and prime rib dinners for less than $20—are big sellers and still a value, especially when accompanied by the cornbread, baked beans, and mashed potatoes that are as comforting as the friendly service.

Kuakini Terrace. Keauhou Beach Hotel. 76-6740 Alii Dr. ☎ **808/322-3441.** Reservations recommended for dinner. Chinese buffet for children, $7.95; for adults, $13.95. AE, DC, MC, V. Daily 6:30am–9pm. SEAFOOD/CHINESE/HAWAIIAN BUFFETS.

As the full-service hotel dining room, the Terrace starts with breakfast, progresses to lunchtime standards that include sandwiches and chicken Parmesan, and spreads out a buffet for evening that's popular among value-conscious diners. The Chinese buffet runs Monday and Tuesday, the Hawaiian buffet Wednesday and Thursday, and the seafood buffet on Friday, Saturday, and Sunday. The Makai Bar, once a popular gathering spot for jazz lovers, is no more; the open-air terrace has become a no-nonsense dining room that stresses value above all else. Hawaiian entertainment livens up the place on Wednesday, Friday, and Saturday nights.

La Bourgogne. 3 miles south of Kailua-Kona on Hi. 11. ☎ **808/329-6711.** Reservations recommended. Main courses $15.95–$28.50. AE, CB, D, DISC, MC, V. Mon–Sat 6–10pm. CLASSIC FRENCH.

This cozy French inn has extra appeal—even an almost defiant quality—in the open-air, relentlessly sun-drenched land of "Kona cuisine," where fresh catch is the hamburger of the day. A Kona institution, La Bourgogne has stuck to its Gallic roots in the face of mounting pressure to shed butter, sweetbreads, and venison for opakapaka and Waimea greens. So if you have a yen for uncompromising French fare, from very buttery escargots to rib-eye steak in Roquefort or tenderloin of venison with a currant-pomegranate glaze, head for this nondescript facade with provincial decor and a classic French kitchen. Menu highlights: wilted spinach salad, rack of lamb with garlic-rosemary butter, and that fruit-glazed venison. Dessert? With chocolate-lilikoi cheesecake and cherries jubilee beckoning, it's best to kiss moderation good-bye.

Ocean View Inn. 75-5683 Alii Dr. ☎ **808/329-9998.** Main courses $7.50–$10.75. No credit cards. Tues–Sun 6:30am–2:45pm, 5:15–9pm. AMERICAN/CHINESE/HAWAIIAN.

As far as we know, this is the only restaurant in town serving Hawaiian food, which is reason enough to go there. The local color is another reason, the quality of food less so. But you can't beat the prices, and Ocean View Inn is as much a Kona fixture as the sunsets that curl around Kailua Pier across the street. Give it a go if you feel like trading your gourmet standards for serviceable food in a casual and endearing atmosphere dripping with local color. Stew-and-rice, roast pork, a vegetarian selection, and local staples such as shoyu chicken and broiled ahi appear on a menu with dozens of Chinese dishes. A refreshing change, definitely, from the more touristy waterfront eateries, but don't expect epicurean fare.

✪ **Palm Cafe.** 75-5819 Alii Dr. ☎ **808/329-7765.** Reservations recommended. Main courses $19–$26. AE, DC, DISC, JCB, MC, V. Daily 5:30–10pm. PACIFIC RIM.

Ask 10 residents what the best restaurant in Kona is, and most of them, if not all, will point to Palm Cafe. It's a completely satisfying dining experience. The stylish, casual, elegant surroundings—open-air, literally a stone's throw from the ocean—match the fresh and brilliantly prepared island cuisine. From salads (such as marinated salmon with fresh organic Kona field greens) a seared-ahi appetizer on leeks, and a Jicama stir-fry to the main dishes and mixed-plate combinations, the Palm Cafe's cuisine is sophisticated without being pretentious. Signature dishes include Hunan-style lamb chops with Puna goat cheese and marinated roasted sweet peppers, tender and flawlessly seasoned; and the Marinated Mahimahi Malia, served on a rich concoction of lobster sauce and coconut cream on noodle crisps. Waimea strawberries, sunrise tomatoes, and other sumptuous Big Island produce are delivered several times a week.

Poquito Mas. Kona Coast Shopping Center, 74-5588 Palani Rd. ☎ **808/329-3528.** Most items under $5. No credit cards. Daily 11am–8pm. MEXICAN.

The tostadas, burritos, and hefty dinner plates pouring out of this tiny take-out stand have earned their place in the hearts of Mexican food lovers. Quick service at the counter, lively and assertive flavors, and a serious devotion to authenticity make Poquito Mas a recommended stop for a satisfying, no-frills meal. Excellent fresh fish tacos, warmly cradled in the restaurant's own "Baja ranchera" (a tasty onion-cilantro) sauce, are a steal at $3.50 for two "minis." Choose from charbroiled steak, chicken, pork, or vegetarian fillings in the generous burritos, or order shrimp or fish on any of the selections. The tables outside of the cubicle-sized operation are always filled with happy diners who seem oblivious to the adjacent parking lot.

Quinn's Almost by the Sea. 75-5655A Palani Rd. ☎ **808/329-3822.** Main courses $7–$19. MC, V. Daily 11am–2am. STEAK/SEAFOOD.

This is a great place to bring friends straight from the airport, as part of their decompression process, because it's pleasant without being overwhelming, and the food has been reliable for a decade and a half. The casual alfresco dining is inviting for families or couples, with a garden lanai that takes advantage of the balmy Kona weather. At the northern gateway to town, Quinn's covers all the bases: steaks, seafood, and vegetarian fare. From the pier across the street comes fresh fish, prepared several ways and served with salad, vegetables, and potatoes or rice. Fresh ahi sandwiches are among the lunchtime values. Some habitués arrive weekly for the seafood staples, vegetarian dishes, and roast-beef sandwiches.

Sam Choy's Restaurant. Kaloko Light Industrial Park, 73-5576 Kauhola St. ☎ **808/326-1545.** Reservations recommended for dinner. Main courses at dinner $17.95–$30. No credit cards. Mon–Sat 6am–2pm, Wed–Sat 5–9pm. HAWAII REGIONAL.

Jovial chef-owner Sam Choy hit upon a smashing formula: informal environs, humongous servings, and high-volume local food with a gourmet twist. These ingredients have turned a nondescript industrial area into a dining mecca that teems with diners from up and down the Kona-Kohala coastline. Their lunchtime favorites: fried poke, fried noodles, saimin, bentos made to order, burgers, and raw poke *musubi* (rice ball). Sam's legendary dinners include top-of-the-line fresh opakapaka, oriental lamb chops with shiitake-vegetable pasta, and seafood laulau, his signature dish of fresh fish with julienned vegetables and seaweed, wrapped and steamed in a pouch of ti leaves. (Many of us miss the mounds of spinachlike taro tops that mark traditional Hawaiian laulau, however.) Choy's other classics include an old-fashioned rib-eye steak with sautéed onions, fried chicken, and roast pork loin with unforgettable mashed potatoes. Comfort food abounds here, but keep in mind that the servings, invariably too big for mere mortals, can astonish the uninitiated.

Sibu Cafe. Banyan Court, 74-5695 Alii Dr. ☎ **808/329-1112.** Most items under $12. No credit cards. Daily 11:30–3pm, 5–9pm. INDONESIAN.

Affordable curries, homemade condiments, and a very popular grilled Balinese chicken are some of the items that have made this a popular eatery since its 1982 opening. Equally attractive are the Indonesian decor, courtyard dining, and excellent satays (traditional grilled skewers of vegetables, seafood, and meats), a Sibu signature. The daily specials, with their savory, authentic seasonings, are like a culinary tour of Southeast Asia. The combination plates have a huge following, and vegetarians are

Kona Coffee Mania!

Coffee houses are a conspicuously burgeoning area of Big Island dining. Many of them are pretty touristy, though: I often wince at the plethora of T-shirts and mugs that make up the visual merchandising of the coffee world. Still, the home of Kona coffee is *the* island for coffee lovers, and it's a wide open field for the dozens of vendors competing for your loyalty and dollar. Kona coffee co-ops, offering steaming cups of fresh brew or coffee by the bag to go, are simply everywhere.

The real activity, though, is concentrated in the north and south Kona districts, where coffee remains a viable industry. Here are some names to watch for: **Bong Brothers** (Hi. 11; ☎ 808/328-9289) and **Rooster Farms** (☎ 808/328-9173) both in Honaunau, have excellent reputations for the quality of their coffee beans. The **Kahauloa Coffee Company** recently opened a deli, the **Coffee Shack** (Hi. 11. Captain Cook; ☎ 808/328-9555), for honest, healthy, affordable food served on a lanai kissed by cool mauka breezes, with a view that sweeps down to Kealakekua Bay. Stop for a final boost before the long drive down and around the south end of the island. South Kona also has the **Royal Aloha Coffee Mill** (☎ 808/328-9851) the largest coffee cooperative around, with 300 farmers; both Royal Aloha and Kahauloa are weighty presences in the coffee world. **Bad Ass Coffee Co.** has franchises in Kainaliu, Kawaihae, Honokaa (see listing below), and two locations in Kailua-Kona, all selling its 100% Kona as well as coffees from Molokai and Kauai.

In Holualoa, up-country from Kailua-Kona, the **Holualoa Kona Coffee Company** purveys organic Kona: unsprayed, hand-picked, sun-dried, and carefully, precisely roasted. Also in this up-country village, the **Holuakoa Cafe** (Hi. 180; ☎ 808/322-2233) is famous for its irrepressible espresso, made by owner Meggi Worbach, who buys green beans, roasts them, grinds them, and makes and serves the coffee. She's famous for her high-octane espressos. Her caffeine mecca also serves light, reasonable fare: curried vegetables in puff pastry, spanakopita, and homemade cakes and pastries, all under $2.95.

In Waimea, the **Waimea Coffee Company** (Parker Square, Hi. 19.; ☎ 808/885-4472), a deli/coffee house/retail operation, is a whirl of activity. You wouldn't come here for a power lunch or a gourmet tasting, but this place is fine for a bite. Coffee is heady stuff here: pure Kona from Rooster Farms, pure organic from Sakamoto Estate, pure water-processed decaf. The homemade quiches, sandwiches, and pasta specials are wholesome and affordable, drawing a lively lunchtime crowd. If, by the time you reach Hilo, you're still reaching for that mug, a good bet is **Bears' Coffee** (106 Keawe St.; ☎ 808/935-0708), the quintessential sidewalk coffee house. In this world of fleeting pleasures, Bears' has been one of Hilo's stalwarts, that has weathered storms and sunny days, good times and bad. Habitués of this sidewalk cafe love to start their day here, with the coffee of the day and specialties such as soufléed eggs, cooked light and fluffy in the espresso machine and served in a croissant. It's a great lunchtime spot as well.

pampered: A selection of vegetable curries and stir-frys is always on the menu. Top off your order with the homemade three-jalapeno, red-chili, or spicy coconut condiment (or all three), and you'll see why Sibu is a Kona staple. Wine and beer are available; there's no white sugar or MSG on the premises.

⊙ **Under the Palm.** 75-5819 Alii Dr. ☎ **808/329-7366.** Most items under $8.25. AE, DC, DISC, JCB, MC, V. Daily 7am–11pm. AMERICAN/PACIFIC RIM.

The ever-popular Palm Cafe, Kona's culinary star, opened this casual eatery downstairs, with a different menu, bistro-style dining on a brick deck under an umbrella, and lighter, more reasonably priced fare. It aims to please, and is enormously successful. Gourmet pizzas, fresh local greens and fish, a full bar, an espresso machine, and good cooking are the simple pleasures here. The Palm Beni, a house version of eggs Benedict with a chutney hollandaise and skillet home fries, is a budget-friendly $6.95. At lunch, a smoked-turkey club sandwich on sourdough goes for $7.25, the wok stir-fry of Asian vegetables with yaki soba noodles for $5.25 ($6.25 with tofu, $6.95 with chicken), and linguine with artichoke hearts, olives, and pancetta for $8.25. The total package includes friendly service and a view of Kailua Bay. No one's complaining.

THE SOUTH KONA COAST: KAINALIU/CAPTAIN COOK

Aloha Cafe. Hi. 11, Kainaliu. ☎ **808/322-3383.** Reservations recommended for large parties. Most items under $7. MC, V. Mon–Sat 8am–9pm, Sun 9am–2pm. AMERICAN/VEGETARIAN.

This roadside oasis dispenses healthy food with many special touches. Place your order at the counter and grab a seat on the veranda that wraps around the old Aloha Theatre. The view sweeps down the coffee fields to the shoreline, and the air, if it's not a voggy day, is splendidly crisp and gentle. Expect heroic burgers and omelets, a "broke-your-mouth" breakfast burrito, fresh-squeezed orange juice daily, fresh fruit smoothies, and carrot cake of the gods. Vegetarians can tuck into the garden burgers, tempeh sandwiches, vegetable soup, and the ever-popular salads. Sandwiches, from fresh fish to tofu-avocado, are heaped with vegetables on tasty whole-wheat buns, generous in every way.

⑤ **Manago Hotel Restaurant.** Manago Hotel. Hi. 11, Captain Cook. ☎ **808/323-2642.** Reservations recommended for dinner. Main courses $6.50–$10.75. DISC, MC, V. Daily 7–9am and 11am–2pm, Tues–Thurs 5–7:30pm, Fri–Sun 5–7pm. AMERICAN.

The dining room of the decades-old H. Manago Hotel is a local legend, greatly loved for its unpretentious, tasty food at family prices. At breakfast, $4 buys you eggs, bacon, papaya, rice, and coffee. At lunch or dinner, you can dine handsomely on local favorites: a 12-ounce T-bone, fried ahi, opelu, or the house specialty, pork chops, for $10.75 and less. Manago T-shirts announce "the best pork chops in town": The restaurant serves 1,300 pounds monthly. When the akule or opelu are running, count on a rush by habitués. It's nothing fancy, mind you, and there's a lot of frying going on in the big kitchen, but there would be riots if anything changed after 80 years.

Teshima's. Hi. 11, Honalo. ☎ **808/322-9140.** Reservations recommended for large parties. Complete dinners $11.25 and under. No credit cards. Daily 6:30am–1:30pm, 5–9:15pm. JAPANESE/AMERICAN.

Shizuko Teshima is still cooking at 89 years old, and has a following among those who have made her miso soup and sukiyaki a part of their day. The early-morning crowd starts gathering while it's still dark for omelets or Japanese breakfast (soup, rice, and fish). As the day progresses, the orders pour in for shrimp tempura and sukiyaki, and by dinner, Number 3 teishoku trays—miso soup, sashimi, sukiyaki, shrimp, pickles, and other delights—are streaming out of the kitchen; at $11.25, it's a steal. Original art hangs on the walls of the elongated dining room. This is local-style all the way.

Wakefield Gardens & Restaurant. No. 1 Rodeo Rd., Honaunau. ☎ **808/328-9930.** Main courses $5.95–$6.95. No credit cards. Daily 11am–3pm. AMERICAN.

Part of a 5-acre garden and macadamia nut orchard, this restaurant serves basic lunch fare: sandwiches, soups, and mind-altering desserts. Arlene Wakefield serves home-roasted turkey and home-baked ham, a papaya boat stuffed with fresh-herbed tuna (featured in *Gourmet* magazine), homemade soups, burgers, and salads. They all lead up to dessert, in which macadamia nuts figure prominently. Key lime pie, coconut cream, triple-chocolate, macadamia-nut mousse, and the "Mystery Macadamia Nut" pie, made without a recipe after Wakefield dreamed about it, make up the glittering finale.

THE KOHALA COAST

✪ **Batik Room.** Mauna Kea Beach Hotel, Kawaihae. ☎ **808/882-7222.** Reservations and jackets required. Prix fixe $65 and $75. AE, DC, JCB, MC, V. Daily 6–10pm. CLASSICAL EUROPEAN/PROVENÇAL.

Some of the Mauna Kea staff retain a proclivity for grumpiness, but if you can get past them to make your reservation, the Batik is a truly elegant gastronomic experience. The vaunted reopening of the posh Mauna Kea promised great leaps in cuisine; so far, Executive Chef Goran Streng has delivered. This fine-dining shrine is a room of hushed tones and great restraint, with dark-wood ceilings, sedate (and loyal) guests, and sensitive lighting. The solidly sublime menu is a first-class flight through the upper registers of taste. The artichoke salad, its heart cradled in a mandala of petals, comes in a flawless warm vinaigrette with greens, avocados, and crimson tomatoes—succulent produce that's a Big Island signature. The medaillons of salmon, lightly basted in olive oil and a ginger-scallion sauce reduced in white wine, appear as three islands between oysters, gently cooked in extremely low heat with the oven door left open. Atop each medaillon sits a slice of leek with a petite mound of Sevruga caviar—a stroke of genius. Loyalists may go for the herb-crusted rack of lamb, chateaubriand in Burgundy sauce, and the mild curries that were Batik favorites in prerenovation days.

⑤ **Cafe Pesto.** Kawaihae Shopping Center. ☎ **808/882-1071.** Main courses $6.95–$16.95. AE, DISC, DC, MC, V. Mon–Fri 11am–9pm, Fri–Sat 11am–10pm. PIZZA/ITALIAN.

The first rave we ever heard about Cafe Pesto was years ago, from a visiting New York food editor who was among the first to stumble upon its organic greens, sizzling sauces, and world-class dressings. We're happy to report that Cafe Pesto still elicits adoration (and salivation) from devotees who drive many miles for its gourmet pizzas, calzones, and fresh organic greens grown from Kealakekua to Kamuela. Lobsters from the aquaculture farms on Keahole Point (south on the coastline), shiitake mushroms from a few miles mauka, and fresh fish, shrimp, and crab adorn the herb-infused Italian pies. Popular tastes still favor the classic pepperoni, but the more adventurous opt eagerly for the Santa Fe chicken pasta, marinated chicken breast with chipotle, sweet roasted peppers, diced tomatoes, and cilantro cream. Herb garlic Gorgonzola dressing, herb garlic vinaigrette, and curry pasta salads are among the other scene stealers. There's also a worthy beer selection.

✪ **CanoeHouse.** Mauna Lani Bay Hotel and Bungalows. ☎ **808/885-6622.** Reservations recommended. Main courses $25–$36.30. AE, CB, DC, DISC, JCB, MC, V. Daily 5:30–9pm. HAWAII REGIONAL.

A wailing arose when Chef Alan Wong departed for Honolulu, but . . . voila! David Abella, formerly of Roy's Restaurants and fresh from the Felix at the Peninsula Hotel Hong Kong, appeared at CanoeHouse to add his brand of culinary cachet to one of the most pleasing settings in Hawaii. You can dine under the stars, with the Kohala Coast waves lapping a few feet away, or in an open-air dining room with a koa canoe hanging above. Abella's penchant for Asian cooking, strengthened during his tenure in Hong Kong, is becoming apparent. Seared fresh ahi (a CanoeHouse signature), marinated rack of lamb, nori-wrapped ahi, a sashimi-poke appetizer with white vinaigrette, sake aioli, crispy ogo (seaweed), and other stand-outs are presented with a balance of European sophistication and assertive Asian flavors. Look for accents of chili pepper, wasabi, coconut, lemongrass, miso, smoked cabernet sauces, and curry melding seamlessly with the streamlined menu's salads, fish, filet mignon, and roasted chicken. The gratinee of bananas, an ambrosial marriage of custard, Kahlua, macadamia nuts, strawberries, and banana, topped with caramelized sugar like a crème brûlée, is a triumph.

Coast Grille. Hapuna Beach Prince Hotel. ☎ **808/880-1111.** Reservations recommended. Main courses $16–$35. AE, DC, DISC, JCB, MC, V. Daily 6–9pm. STEAK/SEAFOOD/OYSTER BAR.

You'll work up an appetite on the 3-minute walk from the main lobby to the open-air Grille, with its sweeping view of the sunset and the incomparable waves of Hapuna Beach lit up at night. Wicker furniture, a curved split-level dining room with banquettes lining the curve, and an imaginative menu combine to make this a pleasant, though not dazzling, dining experience. You'll find Asian touches aplenty, such as Oriental marinades and Thai hot-and-sour sauces on the seafood, and a memorable polenta clam chowder with succulent, tender clams and a hint of smokiness—highly recommended. Adventurous palates often dive into the Oriental clambake with Keahole lobster, Manila clams, sweet shrimp (amaebi), and lotus root. I chose the snapper in ti leaves, served on a bed of stir-fried vegetables with a hint of coconut and sesame, and left wishing I had ordered the special of the evening instead: The trio of Hawaiian fish—peppered opakapaka, blackened mahimahi with tropical fruit salsa, and sautéed ono with a yellow bell pepper coulis—streamed by my table and appeared to please many diners.

The Gallery Restaurant. At Mauna Lani Resort's Golf Clubhouse. ☎ **808/885-7777.** Reservations recommended. Main courses $22–$36. AE, DC, MC, V. Daily 11:15am–3:15pm, Tues–Sat 6–9pm. SEAFOOD/AMERICAN/ITALIAN.

A few of Hawaii's finest chefs have gotten their start at the Mauna Lani's Gallery, recently relocated to the Francis I'i Brown Golf Course clubhouse. While hotel guests are streaming to the CanoeHouse, golfers and resort residents have their own epicurean haven, an open-air dining room serving six-peppered ahi, macadamia-crusted mahimahi, lobster wonton raviolis, and a smashing selection of steaks, pastas, and lamb grown on the Kahua Ranch in the Kohala Mountains up north. In its ungrandiose, concise way, The Gallery celebrates the excellence of island ingredients. You can order your fresh fish grilled with a five-spice butter sauce, sautéed with fresh-lemon-caper butter, and in other preparations. Appetizers, ranging from porcini mushroom polenta to shrimp phyllo and ahi carpaccio, highlight a menu that satisfies a wide range of desires in just one page.

The Terrace. Mauna Kea Beach Hotel, Kawaihae. ☎ **808/882-7222.** Reservations recommended. Luncheon buffet $24. AE, DC, JCB, MC, V. Daily 11am–2pm. BUFFET LUNCH.

The Mauna Kea introduced the concept of the lavish luncheon buffet decades ago, only to see its culinary reputation fizzle before the hotel closed for renovations. Two months reopened at the time of this writing, the hotel has reinstituted its buffet in the open-air Terrace, a comfortable, unimposing setting that is the most casual of the hotel's three dining rooms. The choices: an attractive salad bar of Waimea greens, shrimp salad, artichokes, shrimp cocktail, snow crab legs, and many other selections; and an island of fresh fish, pasta, vegetables, teriyaki chicken, pork, potatoes, and other meats. The lunch is satisfying but not extraordinary, more a comfortable alternative than something you'd write home about.

WAIMEA

Ann Sutherland's Mean Cuisine. Opelo Plaza, Hi. 19. ☎ **808/885-6325.** Main courses $4–$13. MC, V. Mon–Sat 6am–8pm, Sun 8am–2pm. AMERICAN ECLECTIC.

Ann Sutherland has proven that busy people can eat well, too. Streaming out of this busy kitchen/bakery (the kitchen looks bigger than the dining room) are 100 loaves of bread a day, 120 pastries, cakes, and pies, and a host of take-out, microwaveable meals that are—surprise!—as good as mom's home cooking. Take it home or sit in the modest dining room with the faux-marble tables. Choices include sandwiches, soups, salads, and 12 specials a day, ranging from lamb stew to spinach crepes and eggplant burgers. Curries, a Thai chicken salad, roast turkey with mashed potatoes and gravy, beef stroganoff, vegetable enchiladas, and fresh fish every day make this a stop you won't regret. The fresh mahimahi with capers is better than what you'll get at many fancy restaurants.

Edelweiss. Kawaihae Rd. ☎ **808/885-6800.** Complete dinners $15.50–$21.50. MC, V. Tues–Sat 11:30am–1:30pm, 5–9pm. GERMAN.

Diners with a hankering for Wiener schnitzel, bratwurst, sauerkraut, black forest cake, and richly adorned fowl and meats are known to drive all the way from Kona and Hilo for the traditional German offerings at this chaletlike bistro. The upscale ranch burgers and chicken aux champignons may require siesta time after lunch, but they do have a following. In the evening, complete dinners include choices such as sautéed veal, rack of lamb, roast pork, roast duck, and other continental classics. Although heavy on the meats and sauces and certainly not a magnet for vegetarians or fat-burning enthusiasts, Edelweiss has anchored itself firmly in the hearts of Hawaii islanders. "We do not believe in all these changes," sniffs chef-owner Hans Peter Hager. "When you enjoy something, you come back for it." The menu has barely changed in his 13 years in Waimea, and the tables are always full, so who's arguing?

Island Bistro. Hi. 19. ☎ **808/885-1222.** Reservations recommended for dinner. Main courses $10–$14 for half sizes, $17–$23 full size. MC, V. Mon–Fri 11:30am–2pm, daily 5:30–9:30pm. HAWAII REGIONAL/ITALIAN.

It's definitely a bistro, with gay window boxes outside, colorful paintings and table-cloths, and a reasonable menu. But it's not affiliated with Merriman's down the street, as the owner may have you believe, and in fact has annoyed Merriman's loyalists (and there are many!) because of its derivative nature and name-dropping. That said, we admit that the food is good. The sesame-Caesar salad with seared shrimp is a value at $7.50 ($4.75 for the half-size), and the grilled salmon on a bed of couscous is an honorable dish for $9.95. Garlic lovers will revel in the shrimp pasta, a tasty paean to the stinking rose; in the evening, herb-roasted leg of lamb appeals to up-country paniolo tastes.

☺ Maha's Cafe. Spencer House, Hi. 19. ☎ **808/885-0693.** Main courses $5.50–$10.50. DC, DISC, MC, V. Mon–Sat 9am–6pm, Sun 10am–5pm. COFFEE HOUSE/SANDWICHES.

The smallest kitchen on the island—the size of a closet, literally—serves the island's best sandwiches in a tiny, wood-floored room of Waimea's first frame house, built in 1852. What a find! Harriet-Ann Namahaokalani Schutte, who cut her culinary teeth in a large Hawaiian family before making her mark at Mauna Lani Resort's Knickers, dispenses hotcakes and granola for breakfast, delectable sandwiches at lunch, finger sandwiches and homemade scones (with lilikoi butter!) at teatime, and cookies all day long. The menu reads like a map of the island: smoked ahi sandwich with lilikoi salsa; fresh roasted turkey with mushroom stuffing and squaw bread; fresh fish sandwich with Waipio taro and Kahua greens; veggie sandwich with local greens, Kahua lettuce, and Kohala sunflower sprouts; vine-ripened tomatoes with locally made feta cheese, on bread made from Waimea sweet corn. Lunch has never been grander, served at cozy wooden tables on lauhala mats and enlivened with a sublime pesto, tangy with a hint of green olive. At the other end of the room is Cook's Discoveries, but that's another story (see "Shops & Galleries," below).

✪ **Merriman's.** Opelu Plaza, Hi. 19. ☎ **808/885-6822.** Reservations recommended. Main courses $11.95–$23.95 (market price for ranch lamb or ahi). AE, MC, V. Mon–Fri 11:30am–1:30pm, daily 5:30–9pm. HAWAII REGIONAL.

Foodies the world over know Merriman's as one of Hawaii's top palate-pleasers. The brilliant, unassuming Peter Merriman has won national accolades for pioneering the use of fresh local products long before it became fashionable. His menu, in fact, is a culinary jaunt around the island: Organically grown greens, juicy, vine-ripened Lokelani tomatoes harvested around the corner, lamb from the Kohala mountains, corn from Pahoa, and fish straight off the hook are among the ingredients that appear on his East-West menu. But it's his imaginative and respectful preparations that make them sizzle: sesame-crusted fresh catch with spicy lilikoi sauce; wok-charred ahi, a Merriman's original; Puna goat cheese pâté; Cajun-grilled steak with Jack Daniels sauce on shiitake and Maui-onion noodles. The simple pleasures of a roasted chicken take on otherworldly dimensions in his mango-tamarind or lemongrass-garlic sauces. Curries, gado-gado, and Szechuan sauces make his vegetables and noodles an occasion. Although Merriman has moved to Maui to look after the Hula Grill, he maintains a strong presence in Waimea with his weekly trips, and his longtime chef, Sandy Barr, hasn't missed a Merriman's beat.

NORTH KOHALA

Bamboo. Hi. 270, Hawi. ☎ **808/889-5555.** Reservations recommended. Main courses $5.95–$18.50. MC, V. Tues–Sat 11am–2pm, 6–9pm; Sun brunch 11am–2pm. PACIFIC RIM.

Serving fresh fish and Asian specialties in a turn-of-the-century building, Hawi's self-professed "tropical saloon" is the best thing on the island's northern coastline. The exotic interior is a tribute to nostalgia, with high wicker chairs from Waikiki's historic Moana Hotel, works by local artists, and old Matson line menus accenting the walls. The fare, Island favorites in sophisticated presentations, is a match for all this style: imu-smoked pork with cabbage, chicken satay in mint-chili sauce, nori-shrimp udon (noodles) with fresh vegetables and coconut sauce, and tequila-drenched prawns are among the offerings. Produce from nearby gardens and fish fresh off the chef's own hook are among the signs of the good life. At Sunday brunch, diners gather for eggs Bamboo (eggs Benedict with a lilikoi-hollandaise sauce) and the famous passion-fruit margaritas. Melodious Hawaiian music wafts through the Bamboo from 7pm to closing on weekends. Next door is a gallery of furniture and arts and crafts, some very good and most locally made.

Don's Family Deli. Kapaau, in front of King Kamehameha Statue. ☎ **808/889-5822.** Most items under $5. No credit cards. Mon–Fri 8am–6pm, Sat–Sun 9am–5pm. DELI/ITALIAN.

This is a refreshment stop for travelers, nothing fancy, just a deli and corner storefront that opened in 1985 and proved it has staying power. Don Rich's quiches, lasagnas, enchiladas, sandwiches, mesquite chicken, and famous fruit smoothies—passion-guava with papaya and frozen banana—are served across the counter so you can seat yourself at the tables that face the square where the Kamehameha Statue stands. Lox and bagels, giant hero sandwiches, and homemade crullers harken back to the owners' New York roots.

ICE CREAM

Tropical Dreams. Hi. 270, Kapaau. ☎ **808/889-0077.**

Louis and Debby Ann Bleier were escaping from Manhattan when they stumbled upon remote North Kohala and bought 4¹/₂ acres of fruit and macadamia nut trees. They moved into the old Sakamoto Building and started making ice cream and gourmet macadamia-nut butters in flavors such as creme mac butter, crunchy mac butter, ambrosia, and Kona coffee—and that's just the butters. If you've tasted the ice cream at Merriman's, Cafe Pesto, Palm Cafe, Bamboo, Sam Choy's, and any of the Kohala Coast restaurants (except those at the Mauna Lani Bay), you've tasted Tropical Dreams. At their retail store close to the King Kamehameha statue, the apricot floral, pikake sorbet, poha (gooseberry) sorbet, white chocolate mango, passion creme, mango cheesecake, and more than other 100 flavors are flying out the door. They use healthy ingredients, no additives or preservatives.

If you're not heading for Kapaau, call the factory in Kawaihae (☎ **808/882-1891**) to find out which restaurants and stores around the islands serve Tropical Dreams.

THE HAMAKUA COAST

Bad Ass Macadamia Nut Co. Lower Lehua, Honokaa. ☎ **808/775-7743.** AE, MC, V. Daily 7am–9pm. COFFEE HOUSE.

It's more retail store than coffee house, and it's touristy, but the picnic tables under the macadamia nut trees possess a certain charm. Bad Ass sells Kona coffee, chocolate-covered macadamia nuts from the surrounding plantation, a few deli items, and the usual T-shirts, mugs, coffee bags, hats, and souvenirs (Bad Ass fanny packs are among the more irreverent items). Coffee is sold by the bag or pound, and it's pricey: from $7 to $29 a pound (for the organic variety). The so-called "Island" coffee is grown on Kauai and Molokai.

Jolene's Kau Kau Korner. At Mamane St. and Lehua, Honokaa. ☎ **808/775-9498.** Main courses $8–$20. MC, V. Mon–Fri 10am–8pm, Sat 10am–3pm. AMERICAN/LOCAL.

The poi, made from Waipio Valley taro, is reason enough to go to Jolene's. It's homey and friendly, with eight tables and windows that look out into a scene much like an old Western town, but with cars. The Hawaiian plate—laulau, Waipio Valley poi, lomi salmon, and raw fish, all for $7.95—harder to find than you'd think on this island, has a firm niche in local lunch plans. Dinner specialties, including the plate lunch–style "mixed plate," could be mahimahi, grilled chicken, or Korean-style kal bi. The splurge item of Jolene's, the $20 steak and lobster, is as fancy as you can get here.

Mamane Street Bakery. Mamane St., Honokaa. ☎ **808/775-9478.** Most items under $3. No credit cards. Mon–Fri 7am–5:30pm, Sat 7am–5pm. BAKERY/COFFEE SHOP.

Honokaa's gourmet bake shop serves Kona coffee in many forms and accompanying pastries. Mamane Street Bakery also wholesales breads and pastries to several prominent eateries around the island (its burger buns are well known). Portuguese sweet bread and honey-nut muffins are the big sellers in this easygoing, informal coffee house with lower-than-coffee-house prices: Breads sell for $2.25 to $2.95, but most pastries are under $1.25. Adjoining the coffee shop is a tiny gift shop proffering local art, pottery, and greeting cards. Very Honokaa: no marble, wing tips, or pretense.

Tex Drive-Inn & Restaurant. Hi. 19, Honokaa. ☎ **808/775-0598.** Reservations recommended for large parties. Main courses $5.50–$7.25. AE, DC, JCB, MC, V. Daily 5:30am–8:30pm. AMERICAN/LOCAL ETHNIC.

When Ada Lamme bought the old Tex, she made significant changes, including improving upon an ages-old recipe for Portuguese *malassadas*, a doughy, yeasty doughnut without a hole; Tex now sells 4,500 of these sugar-rolled morsels a month at 65¢ apiece. The menu here appeals to local tastes: kalua pork with cabbage, Korean chicken, hamburgers (a big seller, on buns by Manane Street Bakery), plate lunches with teriyaki meats, and ethnic specialties. Filipino specials are served on Monday, Japanese specials on Wednesday, and Hawaiian plates on Fridays and Saturdays. Many changes are planned for this roadside attraction, including a large new retail store–coffee bar that will carry Hawaiian crafts, local coffees, and, in a nod to her native Holland and Honokaa's large Portuguese community, European chocolates, Dutch wooden shoes, and fine pottery from Portugal.

What's Shakin'. 27-999 Old Mamalahoa Hwy. (on the 4-mile scenic drive), Pepeekeo. ☎ **808/964-3080.** Most items under $5.95; smoothies $2.95–$3.95. No credit cards. Daily 10am–5:30pm. HEALTH FOOD.

Look for the cheerful plantation-style wooden house in yellow and white, with a green roof, 2 miles north of the Hawaii Tropical Botanical Garden. This is where many of the bananas and papayas from Patsy and Tim Withers's 20-acre farm end up: in fresh-fruit smoothies with names like Papaya Paradise, an ambrosial blend of pineapple, coconut, papayas, and bananas. When mangoes are in season, they'll have mango smoothies too. If you're in the mood for something more substantial, try the Blue Hawaii blue-corn tamale with homemade salsa, a garden burger, or the teriyaki-ginger tempeh burger (made with the best tempeh in the world, by Lean Green Foods of Hilo). Every plate arrives with fresh fruit and a fresh green salad topped with Patsy's Oriental sesame dressing. You can sit outdoors in the garden, where bunches of bananas hang for the taking. The gift shop sells cards and preinspected tropical plants ready to be flown home. Patsy is understandably proud of the charming vintage touches: the old Hawaii pictures, porcelain hula girls, and kitschy accents.

HILO

🟠 **Broke the Mouth.** 93 Mamo St. ☎ **808/934-7670.** Plate lunches $3.50–$5.50. MC, V. Tues–Sat 7am–2pm. ORGANIC/VEGETARIAN.

Farmer Tip Davis has found a way to promote local agriculture and provide healthful, inexpensive food. Barely more than a take-out counter with a few outdoor tables, Broke the Mouth serves wholesome versions of local favorites. Vegetarians who had long given up *manapua* (sweet buns traditionally filled with sweetened pork) can now enjoy them in whole wheat buns with sweet potato basil, or Szechuan eggplant, or taro tops and cheese. (We'd be happy to pay more for less skimpy fillings, however.) There's also a selection of fresh baked goods like ginger buns with banana instead of sugar and ohelo berries instead of raisins, and fresh fruit turnovers filled with coconut and lime or banana with white pineapple. The salsas, dressings, and sauces change with the seasons: starfruit with sweet potato and mint marigold, fresh tomato and dill, the jalapeno-sage-basil–infused Hinges of Hell; the MacGado sauce, a house specialty, uses macadamia nuts instead of peanuts. The salads consist of everything but prosaic iceberg or Romaine. Instead you'll find mounds of basil, herbs, kale, chard, edible flowers, Okinawan spinach, sorrel, and other vitamin-packed greens. Instead of eggs or dairy, starchy taro is whipped up with fresh herbs and seasonings into a high-fiber, low-calorie mayonnaise that could give Best Foods a run for its money.

⭐ **Cafe Pesto Hilo Bay.** S. Hata Building, 308 Kam Ave. ☎ **808/969-6640.** Pizzas $6.95–$16.95. AE, DISC, MC, V. Daily 11am–9pm, Fri–Sat 11am–10pm. PIZZA/ITALIAN.

The only wood-fired Italian brick oven on the island burns many bushels of ohia and kiawe wood to turn out its toothsome pizzas, topped with fresh organic herbs and island-grown produce. The high-ceilinged 1912 room, with windows looking out over Hilo's bayfront, is filled with seductive aromas. It's difficult to resist the wild mushroom–artichoke pizza or the chipotle and tomato-drenched Santa Fe, but go with the Four Seasons—dripping with prosciutto, bell peppers, and mushrooms, it won't disappoint. Other personal favorites are the Milolii, a crab-shrimp-mushroom sandwich with basil pesto, the smoked salmon pizza with Gorgonzola, and the flash-seared poke salad on a bed of organic greens with tamarind dressing—gourmet all the way.

Dick's Coffee House. Prince Kuhio Plaza, 111 E. Puainako St. ☎ **808/959-4401.** Most items under $10. MC, V. Daily 7am–9pm. AMERICAN/LOCAL.

Pennants still adorn the walls at Dick's new location, and the fish-and-eggs breakfast remains a local fixture. Regulars huddle over steaming cups of coffee discussing the previous night's game or local politics while the kitchen sends out endless streams of pancakes, omelets, grilled fish, teriyaki steak, and other favorites. This is a diner with a local touch: gravy, rice, pies, shoyu chicken, and brusque, efficient waitresses. Everything is inexpensive, from the specials, which could be roast pork or corned beef and cabbage, to the grilled fish and clubhouse sandwiches. This isn't titillating gourmet fare, but there are no pretensions otherwise.

Don's Grill. 485 Hinano St. ☎ **808/935-9099.** Reservations for groups of 6 or more. Main courses $6.50–$11.95. AE, MC, V. Tues–Thurs 10:30am–9pm, Fri 10:30am–10pm, Sat–Sun 10am–9pm. AMERICAN/LOCAL.

The house specialty at this high-volume, high-decibel family dining room is a generous platter of moist, flavorful rotisserie chicken, served with soup or salad, vegetables, and rice, french fries, or mashed potatoes. Other inexpensive local favorites include fresh trout from the local fishery, shoyu chicken, roast turkey, lasagna, chili, and saimin. Located close to the Kanakaole Tennis Stadium, Don's is a haven for families coming to and from sports events and concerts, or simply enjoying a night of home-cooked favorites with no cleaning up to do.

Esarn-Thai Kitchen. 804 Kilauea Ave. ☎ **808/935-0296.** Reservations recommended for dinner. Most items under $8.95; lunch buffet $3.35–$5.25. Mon–Fri 10:30am–8:30pm, Sun noon–8pm. No credit cards. THAI.

The no-fuss, quick-and-easy, inexpensive buffet is the Esarn trademark. This tiny eatery serves spicy, authentic curries redolent with lemongrass, coconut milk, kaffir lime, spices, and fresh vegetables. Take-out lunch plates are a big seller, too; they're a deal at $4.50. Choose from among vegetarian, seafood, and other daily specials; the regional specialty called larb (a beef salad fragrant with lemongrass and kaffir lime); noodle soups; and several spicy stir-frys.

Fiascos. Waiakea Square, 200 Kanoelehua Ave. ☎ **808/935-7666.** Reservations recommended on weekends. Main courses $6.95–$18.95. AE, DC, DISC, MC, V. Sun–Thurs 11am–10pm, Fri–Sat 11am–11pm. AMERICAN/MEXICAN/ECLECTIC.

All the makings of fantastic fajitas arrive on sizzling cast-iron platters so you build your own at the table. Although best-known for this Mexican dish, Fiascos also offers a huge selection of soups and salads at its $8.95 soup-and-salad bar. There are also four different soups daily, fresh fish sandwiches, bountiful salads, pastas, burgers, steaks, seafood, fried chicken, smoked chicken breast with sesame dressing—something for everyone, even fried ice cream for dessert. The upstairs room is one of Hilo's few after-dark spots, with live music and dancing.

Harrington's. 135 Kalanianaole. ☎ **808/961-4966.** Reservations recommended. Main courses $16–$32.95. DISC, MC, V. Mon–Sat 5:30–10pm, Sun 5:30–9pm. SEAFOOD/STEAK.

The house specialty, thinly sliced Slavic steak swimming in butter and garlic, is part of the old-fashioned steak-and-seafood formula that makes the Harrington's experience a predictable one. The meunière-style fresh catch, sautéed in white white and topped with a lightly browned lemon-butter sauce, is popular, but it's no turf for the calorie-conscious. The menu is full of unapologetically rich cream sauces, cheese stuffings, and conscience-busting preparations. The same-old, same-old menu is offset by the tranquil beauty of Reeds Pond (also known as Ice Pond), one of Hilo's visual wonders. With the open-air restaurant perched on the pond's shore, the ambiance eclipses the menu.

Ken's House of Pancakes. 1730 Kamehameha Ave. ☎ **808/935-8711.** Most items under $9.50. AE, DC, DISC, MC, V. Daily 24 hours. AMERICAN.

You never know whom you'll bump into at Ken's after an important convention, concert, or the Merrie Monarch hula festival. The only 24-hour coffee shop in Hilo, Ken's fulfills basic dining needs with an unchanging efficiency and simplicity. Omelettes, pancakes, sandwiches, tripe stew, oxtail soup—what they call a "poi dog menu"—stream out of the busy kitchen. The affordable selections include fried chicken, steak, grilled fish, and hamburgers with salad and all the accompaniments. Most popular is the Mauna Kea hamburger, big as a mountain and topped with a pineapple, with the whole works between sweet bread buns—very local, very Hilo.

Lehua's Bay City Bar & Grill. 90 Kamehameha Ave. ☎ **808/935-8055.** Reservations recommended for dinner. Main courses $8.95–$23.95. AE, DISC, MC, V. Daily 11am–9pm. PACIFIC RIM.

Several features keep people returning to this downtown Hilo landmark: the clam chowder and Big Island greens at the soup-and-salad bar, the best Cajun ahi sandwich in town, an unforgettable Thai coconut shrimp, and vegetarian pastas that are anything but standard. From paniolo ribs to quesadillas to skewered teriyaki chicken, the menu is a medley of cultural influences. At $7.95, the soup-and-salad bar is a top value (at dinner it's a dollar more). The hefty Bay City burgers range from teriyaki chicken ($6.95) to a gardenesque veggie burger for $7.50, with a fresh-catch dinner at a refreshing $16.95, including sourdough bread, vegetables, and pesto linguine. The split-level dining room occupies a strategic corner of Hilo's bayfront, with large windows, a dance floor, and a busy, chic bar with live entertainment, usually the blues, twice a month on Friday or Saturday nights.

Ⓢ Miyo's. Waiakea Villas, 400 Hualani St. ☎ **808/935-2273.** Combination dinner $7.50–$10.50. No credit cards. Tues–Sat 11am–2pm, 5:30–8:30pm. JAPANESE.

Home-cooked, healthy Japanese food is Miyo's legacy, served in an open-air room on Wailoa Pond, where an idyll of curving footpaths and greenery fills the horizon. Sliding shoji doors bordering the dining area are left open so you can take in the view and gaze at Mauna Kea on a clear day. This is clearly the environment of someone to whom cooking and dining are a meditation. Although sesame chicken (deep fried boneless with a spine-tingling sesame sauce) is a best-seller, the entire menu is appealing. For vegetarians, there are constantly changing veggie specials, vegetable tempura, vegetarian shabu shabu (cooked in a chafing dish at your table, then dipped in a special sauce), and noodle and seaweed dishes. There are also mouthwatering selections of sashimi, beef teriyaki, fried oysters, many different types of tempura, ahi donburi (seasoned and steamed in a bowl of rice), sukiyaki, and generous combination dinners. The daily fresh fish takes many forms, and all dishes are served with rice, soup, and pickled vegetables. With its floating mushrooms and delicate flavor, the miso soup is a wonder. The ahi tempura plate, at $6.50, is one of Hilo's stellar buys.

Nihon Restaurant & Cultural Center. Liliuokalani Gardens, 123 Lihiwai St. ☎ **808/ 969-1133.** Reservations recommended. Main courses $8.95–$19.95. DC, DISC, MC, V. JAPANESE.

The room offers a beautiful view of Hilo Bay on one side and the soothing green sprawl of Liliuokalani Gardens on the other. This is a magnificent part of Hilo that's often overlooked because it's away from the central business district. The reasonably priced menu features steak-and-seafood combination dinners and sushi selections, including the innovative poke and lomi salmon hand rolls, ranging from $3.95 per order to $30.95 for an array of 4 dozen pieces. In the "Businessman's Lunch," you make two choices from among butterfish, tempura, sashimi, chicken, and other morsels, and they come with sushi, potato salad, soup, and vegetables, all for $9.95. This isn't inexpensive dining, but the return on your dollar is high, with a presentation that matches the serenity of the room and its stunning view of the bay.

Pescatore. 235 Keawe St. ☎ **808/969-9090.** Reservations recommended for dinner. Main courses $15.95–$28.95. CB, DC, MC, V. Daily 11am–2pm, Sun–Thurs 5:30–9pm, Fri–Sat 5:30–10pm. SOUTHERN ITALIAN.

This is a special-occasion restaurant, dressier and pricer than the regular spate of casual neighborhood cafes and mom-and-pop diners. It's ornate, especially for Hilo, with gilded frames on antique paintings, chairs of vintage velvet, koa walls, and a tile floor—very Francis Ford Coppola. The fresh catch is offered five ways, from reduced-cream and Parmesan to capers and wine. Chicken, veal, and fish marsala, a rich and garlicky scampi Alfredo, carpaccio, and the Fra Diavolo, a spicy seafood marinara, are the headliners on a long and satisfying menu. At lunch, pasta marinara is simple but satisfying, and rivals the $7.95 chicken Parmesan as one of the values of the day.

Restaurant Fuji. Hilo Hotel, 142 Kinoole. ☎ **808/961-3733.** Reservations recommended. Main courses $7.75–$18.87. AE, DC, JCB, MC, V. Tues–Sun 11am–1:45pm, 5–8:45pm. JAPANESE.

If you'd like to see what Hilo was like generations ago, drive to the Hilo Hotel. It's enveloped in foliage, lava rock walls, and a quiet, nostalgic simplicity—the old-timer's Hilo. You can dine indoors or in the courtyard between the dining room and the pool, in spacious surroundings that become infused with the scents of beef, seafood, and vegetables sizzling away on teppanyaki grills. Inexpensive donburi (rice steamed in individual containers with beef, chicken, and egg toppings) is one of many standouts. Although the *teishoku*—a dainty succession of vegetables and fish, chicken, or beef, esthetically presented on trays—is a specialty, it won't be easy to choose from among the teriyaki, tempura, grilled fish, and marinated, barbecued steak (*wafu*).

Restaurant Miwa. Hilo Shopping Center, 1261 Kilauea Ave. ☎ **808/961-4454.** Reservations recommended. Main courses $8–$35. AE, CB, DC, MC, V. Mon–Sat 11am–1pm, Sun 5–9pm. JAPANESE.

Duck around a corner of the shopping center and discover sensational seafood in this quintessential neighborhood sushi bar. A self-contained slice of Japan in an otherwise unremarkable shopping mall, it'll envelop you like a surprise. Kona crab (unavailable June through Aug), shabu shabu (you cook your own ingredients in an earthenware pot), teppankayi, tempura, fresh catch, and a full sushi selection are among the offerings. The top-of-the-line dinner, the $35 steak-and-crab combination, is a tasty splurge you can enjoy without dressing up. Some items, such as the fresh catch, may be ordered American-style. The *haupia* (coconut pudding)–cream cheese pie is a Miwa signature.

Reuben's Mexican Restaurant. 336 Kamehameha Ave. ☎ **808/961-2552.** Most items under $9.50. MC, V. Mon–Fri 11am–9pm, Sat noon–9pm. MEXICAN.

Reuben's is Hilo's south-of-the-border outpost, with serapes, sombreros, Mexican doilies, and rainbow colors everywhere you look. The juxtaposition of Hilo Bay outside and the dark, funky, margarita-infused atmosphere inside makes for a flamboyantly campy dining experience. The tacos, enchiladas, and hefty combination plates are authentic, as are the famous Reuben's margaritas, served in frothy, bountiful pitcherfuls that grease the wheels of conviviality. The free-flowing margaritas are a good match for the moist, tasty tortillas, cilantro-laden salsa, and chili rellenos, a Reuben's specialty. Habitués chuckle over the mustard-orange bathrooms but sing praises over the simple pleasures of rice, beans, and "plain, good old Mexican food."

Roussels. 60 Keawe St. ☎ **808/935-5111.** Reservations recommended. Main courses $13.45–$22. AE, DC, MC, V. Daily 5–10pm. CAJUN.

Butter, butter, butter! Rich cream sauces and pools of garlic-butter make this a conditional treat. With its high ceilings, polished wood floors, and dramatic columns and arches (from its past lives as a bank and a welfare office), Roussels is the perfect atmosphere for Big Easy fare. But the food can be unconscionably rich, and the soups occasionally oversalted. The two items Roussels immortalized a decade ago, blackened opakapaka and blackened sashimi, remain menu classics. Along with the Cajun prime rib, the shrimp-oyster gumbo, and an old favorite, the trout amandine, they're considered Roussels' reliable bests.

Royal Siam Thai Restaurant. 70 Mamo St. ☎ **808/961-6100.** Main courses $4.95–$8.95. AE, DC, MC, V. Mon–Sat 11am–2pm, 5–8:30pm. THAI.

One of Hilo's most popular neighborhood restaurants, Royal Siam serves consistently good Thai curries in a simple room with no pretensions. Fresh herbs and vegetables from the owner's gardens add an extra zip to the platters of noodles, soups, curries, and specialties that pour out of the kitchen in clouds of spicy fragrance. The Buddha Rama, a wildly popular concoction of spinach, chicken, and peanut sauce, is a scene stealer on a menu of stars. The Thai garlic chicken, in sweet basil with garlic and coconut milk, is equally superb.

Seaside Restaurant. 1790 Kalanianaole Hwy. ☎ **808/935-8825.** Reservations required. Main courses $10.50–$20. DC, MC, V. Tues–Sun 5–8:30pm. AMERICAN/LOCAL.

How fresh are the trout, catfish, mullet, golden perch, and *aholehole,* the silvery mountain bass devoured passionately by Island fish lovers? Fished out of the pond shortly before you arrive, that's how fresh. The restaurant has large windows overlooking the glassy ponds that spawned your dinner, so you can't be sentimental. Colin Nakagawa, whose grandparents opened the restaurant in 1946, keeps up the family tradition by raising the fish and cooking them in two unadorned styles: steamed in ti leaves with lemon juice and onions, or fried. Chicken, served teriyaki style and fried, and various cuts of steak, including calamari, are also available. The fried aholehole, which often runs out, has been known to lure diners on the next plane from Honolulu. You must call ahead, so your order can be fished from the ponds and whisked from kitchen to table.

Shibata Lunch Shop. 413 Kilauea Ave. ☎ **808/961-2434.** Most items under $5.20. No credit cards. Mon–Sat 7am–2pm, Fri 5:30–8pm. AMERICAN/LOCAL.

If Hilo is plate-lunch heaven, Shibata's is the town hall. Lunchtimers squeeze into this 14-table restaurant to peruse the day's selection on hot trays: nori chicken, chicken long rice, beef stew, roast pork, mahimahi, and nostalgic diner fare such as baked chicken with gravy served with rice, salad, and vegetables. Half-orders are available, usually for less than $3. Regulars say the baked chicken and teriyaki beef are standouts. A brisk take-out business keeps the place jumping.

Ting Hao. Puainako Town Center. ☎ **808/959-6288.** Reservations recommended for dinner. Main courses $6.50–$10.95. AE, DC, DISC, MC, V. Mon–Fri 10am–2:30pm, daily 4:30–9pm. Naniloa Hotel location: ☎ **808/935-8888.** Reservations required. AE, MC, V. Wed–Mon 11am–2pm, 5–9pm. MANDARIN.

Garlic lovers throughout Hawaii know about Ting Hao's eggplant, skinned and swimming in large chunks of savory garlic whose aroma fills the large room. A big plus: no MSG in the hundreds of Cantonese, Mandarin, and Szechuan menu items. Specialties include kung pao shrimp and chicken, shrimp with lobster sauce, kung pao cuttlefish, and light and delicate egg drop soup. While vegetarians love Ting Hao for its wide-ranging selection (the spicy tofu is superb), nonvegetarians love to tuck into the mu shu pork with fungus and eggs, served rolled up in a crepe. Ting Hao gained so many customers that it opened a slightly smaller restaurant in the Naniloa Hotel on Banyan Drive in Hilo. Specializing in seafood, the new restaurant serves lobster, crab, and more upscale dishes, and reservations are required.

ICE CREAM

Hilo Homemade Ice Cream. 1477 Kalanianaole Ave. (Keaukaha area of Hilo). ☎ **808/959-5959.**

Fresh, creamy homemade ice cream made in paradise flavors by a Zen practitioner and former preschool teacher who believes that ice cream is a happy business: That's Hilo Homemade. You won't meet a nicer person than Fred Stoeber, who got so busy scooping ice cream that he had to stop doing puppet shows for children under the nearby tree. Young Hilo ginger is used for the ginger ice cream, a best-seller; other winners include mango, lilikoi (passion fruit) sherbet, local banana, green tea, Kona coffee, macadamia nut, coconut-creme, banana-poha (gooseberry), and many others. There are takers from the store's 10am opening; some loyalists come daily or several times weekly for the same flavor.

THE PUNA REGION

The Godmother. Old Government Rd., at the Kalapana end of Pahoa. ☎ **808/965-0055.** Reservations recommended. Main courses $7.75–$15.95. AE, MC, V. Daily 11am–4pm, 4:30–9pm. ITALIAN.

Funky and laid back—you'll still see tie-dyes and catch a whiff of patchouli now and then—Pahoa is the commercial hub of east Hawaii, a mix of old West and new East. You can rent videos, buy health foods, watch movies in the oldest continuously running movie theater in Hawaii, and start your day with home fries and Italian eggs Benedict, red with marinara, at Godmother's. Alfresco dining and New York Little Italy–style family recipes are Godmother's offerings: lasagna with homemade noodles, old-fashioned Italian meat balls, and the imposing Godmother New York steak. For lighter fare, the chicken Caesar salad is a good bet among the oodles of noodles and long-simmering sauces.

Keaau Cafe. Keaau Shopping Center. ☎ **808/966-6758.** Main courses $5.75–$8.50. No credit cards. Mon–Sat 9:30am–9pm. KOREAN/JAPANESE.

Local food with a Korean twist, Japanese food with a local twist, and the Korean staples—kal bi (marinated, barbecued spare ribs), man doo (Korean dumplings), and barbecued chicken—are served in this tiny corner of the Keaau Shopping Center, with only 10 tables. The inexpensive, unremarkable plate lunches of steak, chicken katsu, and shrimp tempura, as well as the Korean specials, go more briskly in take-out.

Keaau Junction. Keaau Shopping Center. ☎ **808/966-7525.** Main courses $5–$11. MC, V. Mon–Sat 11am–9pm. MEXICAN/AMERICAN.

Keaau Junction sprouted out of the ashes of Mama Lani's, which burned down, taking with it the only real restaurant in Keaau and the home of east Hawaii's best passion fruit margaritas. Open since 1994, the Junction has retained some of the Mama Lani's raves in a dining room remodeled to look like an Old West Saloon. It is busy! The East-West Chili Relleno is ingenious, wrapped in the same rice wrapper used in spring rolls and lumpia, lightly toasted and oven-baked instead of breaded with cornmeal and fried. An old favorite, the Kilauea (a fancy name for nachos), still reigns as a hot seller, along with fresh fish when available (mahimahi at $9.95), a winner with beans and rice. Vegetarians can take heart: The tempeh and avocado burritos are more than satisfying, and may convert even the hardiest of carnivores. None of which, of course, would be complete without those legendary lilikoi margaritas.

Luquin's. Old Government Rd., Pahoa. ☎ **808/965-9990.** Main courses $6–$10. AE, DISC, MC, V. Daily 11am–9pm. MEXICAN.

Mexican food lovers throng to Luquin's for the fresh fish straight off the boat from Pohoiki in easternmost Hawaii. If it's a good fishing day, you'll find ahi tacos, or fresh catch with enchiladas, beans, and rice. The 17 different combination plates cover all bases, from steak and shrimp to chili rellenos, beef tacos, and tostadas, all reasonably priced, generously served, and cooked according to family recipes from south of the border. "Real Mexican," say aficionados, who return time and again for the fresh ahi tacos.

Naung Mai. Old Government Rd., Pahoa. ☎ **808/965-8186.** Reservations recommended. Main courses $9–$10. No credit cards. Daily 4:30–8:30pm, Tues and Sat 2–8:30pm. THAI.

Like the rest of Pahoa, this is a funky, tiny, hole in the wall, serving vociferous curries and assertive flavors from all corners of Thailand. The Pad Thai noodles are a good bet, and you can hardly go wrong with any of the five different curries. If you like egg rolls, try the shrimp version (or beef or chicken), wrapped with onions, lettuce, and sweet-and-sour sauce, deep fried and crispy. So far it's BYOB, like many small mom-and-pops, but that could change any day.

Paolo's Bistro. Old Government Rd., Pahoa. ☎ **808/965-7033.** Reservations recommended. Main courses $6.95–$14.95. MC, V. Tues–Sun 5:30–9pm. TUSCAN.

Paolo Bucchioni makes his own melt-in-your-mouth mozarella, which, when paired with the fresh local organic baby greens, olives, and relishes, makes a handsome lunch salad for $6. He also makes his own pasta, such as black-squid-ink raviolis stuffed with ahi, or black fettucine with calamari, and composes a culinary symphony every night. The ahi piccata comes in a savory lemon-caper sauce. Open only 2 years, the bistro has banked its reputation on freshness—of produce, cheeses, pasta, and homemade everything. A former Pacific Rim chef at Kona's legendary Palm Cafe, Bucchioni clearly enjoys his nightly solo performance, and he delivers like a virtuoso. The cozy dining room in front and gazebo in the back add to the appeal of this very busy, justifiably popular eatery. Paolo's working on a liquor license, but for now it's BYOB.

VOLCANO VILLAGE & HAWAII VOLCANOES NATIONAL PARK

✪ **Kilauea Lodge.** Hi. 11 (Volcano Village exit). ☎ **808/967-7366.** Reservations recommended. Main courses $14.75–$28.50. MC, V. Daily 5:30–9pm. CONTINENTAL.

There are those of us who would cross the Tundra to dine at the Kilauea Lodge, to enter its manorial driveway between the lava rock pillars, duck from the cold into the warmth of the high-ceilinged room, and sink into the sofa in front of the roaring 1938 fireplace, a spectacular Lodge martini in hand. A cross between chalet-cozy and volcano-rugged, with excellent European cooking by owner Albert Jeyte, the Lodge is the finest culinary act on the big volcano. You'll find everything from pasta primavera to rack of lamb to a splendid duck à l'orange, lean and roasted to perfection. The daily specials always include a fresh fish, occasionally venison, and, rabbit fans, a hasenpfeffer famous throughout Hawaii. If the paupiettes of beef is on the menu, word is that it's excellent: thin slices of prime rib wrapped around a beef-mushroom-cheese mixture, lightly battered and fried, and served with a Dijon mustard sauce. All dinners come with soup, a loaf of warm, freshly baked bread, and salad.

Volcano Golf & Country Club. Hi. 11, at 30-mile marker. ☎ **808/967-8228.** Reservations recommended. Dinners $15.50–$19.50. AE, DC, MC, V. Daily 7–10am, 10:30am–2:30pm, Fri–Sat 5:30–8:30pm. AMERICAN/LOCAL.

It's one of two eateries in the Volcano area, so if the Kilauea Lodge is closed, you don't have much of a choice but to head to this golf course clubhouse unless you're prepared for a long drive. Thankfully, the food ranges from okay to good, and, in hamburgers and tuna sandwiches, even great. The room looks out over a fairway, which isn't as clichéd as it sounds, especially when the mists are rolling in and the greens and grays assume an eye-popping intensity. In the typically cool Volcano air, local favorites such as chili, saimin, and Hawaiian stew with rice become especially comforting. Specials include prime rib, teriyaki beef or chicken, Chinese stir-frys, and a corned beef and cabbage that is better than it sounds. Lunch specials, at $8 with soup or salad, are anything but skimpy.

SOUTH POINT

South Point Bar & Restaurant. Hi. 11, mile marker 76. ☎ **808/929-9343.** Main courses $10.95–$15.95. No credit cards. Mon–Sat noon–8pm, Sun 8am–2pm. Bar open Mon–Thurs 11am–10pm, Fri 11am–1am; Sat 11am–10pm. AMERICAN.

It used to be a biker stop, but new owners Sandy Hiscox and Char Avery are trying hard to change that. Their 40-seat diner, the only full-service restaurant between Captain Cook and Volcano, has full ocean views and an avowedly surf-and-turf menu, although fresh fish isn't always available. So you're left with eggplant lasagna and other vegetarian specials; hefty (1-lb. rib eye and 8-oz. top sirloin) steak-and-shrimp combinations; chili rellenos; calamari steak; and specials that change nightly. Lunchtime choices are slimmer, with standard sandwiches, burgers, and garden burgers. Gourmet food this is not. The Sunday breakfast is a cook-out, which sensibly takes advantage of the sweeping ocean view.

Naalehu Fruit Stand. Hi. 11, Naalehu. ☎ **808/929-9099.** Most items under $10. No credit cards. Mon–Thurs 9am–6:30pm, Fri–Sat 9am–7pm, Sun 9am–5pm. AMERICAN/PIZZA.

This little roadside attraction is a bright spot on the long southern route, the liveliest nook in Naalehu. You can buy sandwiches, pizza, fresh salads, and baked goods—their best-loved item—and then nosh away at one of the few tables on the front porch. Big Island macadamia nuts, fresh local papayas, bananas, and the glorious Kau navel oranges are reliably good here, but it's the pastries that shine. The 2-pound fruit-bread loaves, led by the Ghirardelli chocolate-zucchini and the carrot–macadamia-nut, have a following that grows by the day. They're so popular that Naalehu Fruit Stand has begun wholesaling them at Sure-Save markets on the island. Even more seductive, and perilous, is the macadamia-nut pie, whole nuts in a sugary brown base that puts pecan pie to shame. This is the real pie; save the pizza for later.

Mark Twain Square. Hi. 11, Waiohinu. ☎ **808/929-7550.** Most items under $4.25. AE, MC, V. Mon–Fri 8:30am–6pm, Sat 8:30am–5pm. AMERICAN/LOCAL.

This is a charming stop in a charming, remote village whose most distinctive feature is the row of monkeypod trees that Mark Twain planted. Two of those trees remain, and you can have lunch under one of them. Imagine dining on chicken long rice or tuna melt on homemade sweet bread on a shaded veranda in the lap of history. Friendly service and homemade breads (banana, guava, sweet bread), spiced with Kona coffee or a trendy hot drink called Mokba (a kind of nineties hot-chocolate with vanilla), add to the appeal. You'll find everything from nachos and chef's salads to roast pork and ethnic specials that change by the day. In the adjoining gift shop, side by side with the obligatory Mark Twain T-shirts and souvenirs, you'll find a selection of Big Island crafts, from Naalehu candles to mango-mac nut jams, dolls made in Hilo, and coconut soap concocted in North Kohala.

5 Beaches

by Rick Carroll, with Jeanette Foster

Too young geologically to have many great beaches, the Big Island instead has a odd collection of unusual ones: brand-new black-sand beaches, green-sand beaches, salt-and-pepper beaches, even a rare white-sand beach.

KONA COAST BEACHES
KONA COAST STATE PARK

You'll glimpse this beach as your plane makes its final approach to Keahole Airport. It's about 2 miles north on Queen Kaahumanu Highway; turn left at a sign pointing improbably down a bumpy road. What you'll find at the end is a long, curving beach with a big cove on Mahaiula Bay. Since it's a state park, the beach is open daily from 8am to 8pm (the closing is strictly enforced, and there's no overnight camping). The cove is excellent for swimming, and there's great snorkeling and diving offshore. The big winter waves attract big wave surfers. Facilities include picnic tables and barbecue pits; you'll have to bring your own drinking water.

KAHALUU BEACH PARK

Early Hawaiians built grass houses and a stone *heiau* on this shore and called it *kahalu'u* ("the diving place"). It's still the most popular beach on the Kona Coast; these reef-protected lagoons attract 1,000 people a day almost year-round. Kahaluu, next to the Keauhou Beach Hotel 5½ miles south of Kailua-Kona, is the best all-around beach on Alii Drive, with coconut trees lining a narrow salt-and-pepper–sand shore that gently slopes to turquoise pools fringed by a protective lava-rock breakwater. The schools of brilliantly colored tropical fish that weave in and out of the well-established reef make this a great place to snorkel. This is a great place for children and beginning snorkelers to get their fins wet; the water is so shallow that you can literally stand up if you feel uncomfortable. Be careful in winter, though: The placid

Beaches & Outdoor Activities on the Big Island

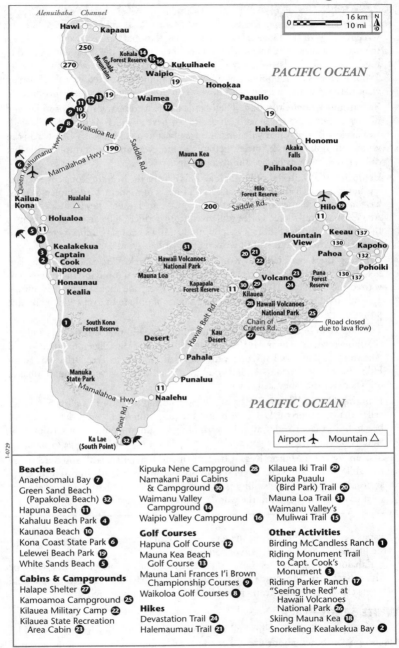

Beaches
Anaehoomalu Bay **7**
Green Sand Beach
(Papakolea Beach) **32**
Hapuna Beach **11**
Kahaluu Beach Park **4**
Kaunaoa Beach **10**
Kona Coast State Park **6**
Lelewei Beach Park **19**
White Sands Beach **5**

Cabins & Campgrounds
Halape Shelter **27**
Kamoamoa Campground **25**
Kilauea Military Camp **22**
Kilauea State Recreation
Area Cabin **23**

Kipuka Nene Campground **28**
Namakani Paui Cabins
& Campground **30**
Waimanu Valley
Campground **14**
Waipio Valley Campground **16**

Golf Courses
Hapuna Golf Course **12**
Mauna Kea Beach
Golf Course **13**
Mauna Lani Frances I'i Brown
Championship Courses **9**
Waikoloa Golf Courses **8**

Hikes
Devastation Trail **24**
Halemaumau Trail **21**

Kilauea Iki Trail **29**
Kipuka Puaulu
(Bird Park) Trail **20**
Mauna Loa Trail **31**
Waimanu Valley's
Muliwai Trail **15**

Other Activities
Birding McCandless Ranch **1**
Riding Monument Trail
to Capt. Cook's
Monument **3**
Riding Parker Ranch **17**
"Seeing the Red" at
Hawaii Volcanoes
National Park **26**
Skiing Mauna Kea **18**
Snorkeling Kealakekua Bay **2**

⭐ Frommer's Favorite Big Island Experiences

Creeping Up to the Ooze. Hawaii Volcanoes National Park is a work in progress thanks to Kilauea volcano, which pours red-hot lava into the sea and adds land to the already big Big Island every day. Since the explosive fountaining stopped in 1986, Kilauea's been bubbling and oozing in a mild-mannered way that lets you walk right up to the creeping lava flow for an up-close-and-personal encounter.

Swimming Kealakekua Bay. The islands have lots of extraordinary snorkel and dive sites, but none are so easily accessible or have as much to offer as mile-wide Kealakekua Bay, an uncrowded marine preserve on the south Kona Coast. You can swim with dolphins, sea turtles, octopuses, and every species of tropical fish that calls Hawaii's waters home. Simply dazzling.

Exploring the Galleries of Holualoa. This may be the heart of Kona coffee country, but it's the soul of the Hawaiian arts-and-crafts movement. Little Holualoa must have more galleries per square foot than any place in Hawaii. They include the Kona Arts Center, a tin-roofed coffee mill saved from extinction by an artists' collective; the serenely beautiful Studio 7 gallery; and Kimura's Lauhala Shop, where Tsuruyo Kimura and her friends still sit weaving fine lauhala goods.

Crossing the Lava Fields to Kona Coast State Park. The road across the lava fields of Kona seems too surreal for words: It looks like a thousand bulldozers pulverized the tarmac of 10,000 airport runways. Everyone should drive this bumpy 1.7-mile road to an oasislike beach at least once, if only to marvel at the incredible power of a single volcano.

Touring Hilo in a Sampan. There's nothing more fun than cruising around this charming town in an open-air 1940s sedan with a chatty Hawaiian tour guide, who'll take you past Rainbow Falls, under the cool glade of Banyan Tree Drive, and along Hilo's historic waterfront. And, if you buy a $7 all-day pass, you can jump on and off whenever the fancy strikes you.

Hanging Out in Waipio Valley. Pack a picnic and head for this gorgeously lush valley that time forgot. Delve deep into the jungle on foot, comb the black-sand beach, or just laze the day away by a babbling stream, the tail-end of a 1,000-foot waterfall. No matter how you see Waipio Valley, it's an unforgettable experience.

Stargazing from Mauna Kea. A beach mat and binoculars is all you need to see the Milky Way from here. Every star and planet shines brightly in this ultra-clean atmosphere, where the visibility is so keen that 11 nations have set up telescopes (two of them the biggest in the world), to probe deep space.

---

waters become turbulent and there's a rip current when high surf rolls in; look for the lifeguard signs warning you of conditions.

Kahaluu isn't the biggest beach on the island, but it's one of the best equipped, with off-road parking, beach gear rentals, a covered pavilion, and a food concession. It gets crowded, so come early to stake out a beach blanket–sized spot.

WHITE SANDS BEACH

As you cruise Alii Drive, blink and you'll miss White Sands Beach. This small, white-sand pocket beach about 4½ miles south of Kailua-Kona—very unusual on this lava-rock coast—is sometimes called Disappearing Beach because it does just that, especially at high tide or during storms. It disappeared completely when Hurricane Iniki hit 3 years ago, but is now back in place. (At least it was there the last time we

The Kona Coast

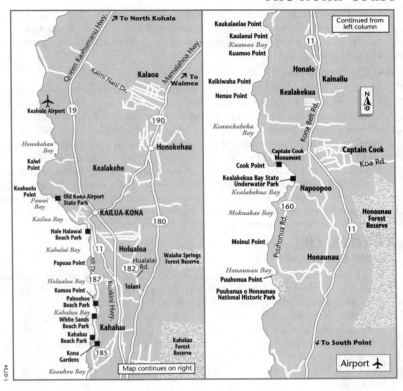

looked.) Locals use the elementary waves here to teach their children how to surf and boogie board. On calm days, the water's excellent for swimming and snorkeling. In winter, the waves swell to expert level, attracting surfers and spectators. Facilities include rest rooms, showers, lifeguard, and a small parking lot.

KOHALA COAST BEACHES

KAUNAOA BEACH

For 25 years, this gold-sand beach at the foot of Mauna Kea Beach Hotel has been the top vacation spot of America's corporate chiefs. Everyone calls it Mauna Kea Beach, but its real name is Hawaiian for "native dodder," a lacy yellow-orange vine that once thrived on the shore. A coconut grove sweeps around this golden crescent, where the water is calm and protected by two black lava points. The sandy bottom slopes gently into the bay, which often fills not only with schools of tropical fish but green sea turtles and manta rays, especially at night, when the hotel lights flood the shore. Swimming is excellent year-round, except in rare winter storms. Snorkelers prefer the rocky points, where fish thrive in the surge. Facilities include rest rooms, showers, and ample parking, but there's no lifeguard.

✪ HAPUNA BEACH

Just off Queen Kaahumanu Highway, south of the Hapuna Beach Prince Hotel, lies this crescent of gold sand—big, wide, and a half-mile long. In summer, when the beach is widest, the ocean calmest, and the crowds biggest, this is the island's best beach for swimming, snorkeling, and bodysurfing. But beware Hapuna in winter, when its thundering waves, strong rip currents, and lack of lifeguards can be dangerous. Facilities include A-frame cabins for camping, pavilions, rest rooms, showers, and plenty of parking.

ANAEHOOMALU BAY

Big Island makes up for its dearth of beaches with a few spectacular ones, like Anaehoomalu, or A-Bay, as the locals call it. This popular, peppered gold-sand beach, fringed by a grove of palms and backed by royal fish ponds still full of mullet, is one of Hawaii's most beautiful. It fronts the Royal Waikoloan Hotel (the only affordable hotel on this coast) and is enjoyed by guests and locals alike. The beach slopes gently from shallow to deep water; swimming, snorkeling, diving, kayaking, and windsurfing are all excellent here. Equipment rental and snorkeling, scuba, and windsurfing instructions are available at the north end of the beach. At the far edge of the bay is a rare-turtle cleaning station, where snorkelers and divers can watch endangered green sea turtles line up, waiting their turn to have small fish clean them. There are rest rooms, showers, picnic tables, and plenty of parking.

A HILO BEACH
LELEIWI BEACH PARK

Hilo's beaches may be few, but Leleiwi is one of Hawaii's most beautiful. This unusual cove of palm-fringed black-lava tide pools fed by freshwater springs and rippled by gentle waves is a photographer's delight—and the perfect place to take a plunge. In winter, big waves can splash these ponds, but the shallow pools are generally free of currents and ideal for families with children, especially in the protected inlets at the center of the park. Leleiwi often attracts endangered sea turtles seeking safe haven in this natural refuge, making this one of Hawaii's most popular snorkel spots. The beach is 4 miles out of town on Kalanianaole Avenue; facilities include rest rooms, showers, lifeguards, picnic pavilions, paved walkways, and the Richardson Ocean Center, a marine-life facility.

AT SOUTH POINT
GREEN SAND BEACH (PAPAKOLEA BEACH)

Hawaii's famous green-sand beach is located at the base of Puu o Mahana, an old cinder cone spilling into the sea. It's difficult to reach, the open bay is often rough, there are no facilities, no fresh water, no shade from the relentless sun, and howling winds scour the point. Despite its glaring defects, the unusual emerald-green sands attract thousands each year, who follow a well-worn four-wheel-drive–only road for $2^1/_2$ miles to the top of a cliff, which you have to climb down to reach the beach (the south end offers the safest path). Its claim to fame is crushed olivine, a green semi-precious mineral found in eruptive rocks and meteorites; Green Sand Beach isn't the only beach with olivine crystals, but it's the one that gets all the ink. If the surf's up, just check out the beach from the cliff's edge; if the water's calm, it's generally safe to swim and dive.

6 Hitting the Water

by Rick Carroll, with Jeanette Foster

The Big Island is big on water sports. Its waters are warm, clear, and usually calm year-round, especially on the leeward Kona-Kohala Coast. Underwater coral formations and dramatic drop-offs attract a kaleidoscope of marine life, making for great snorkeling, diving, and fishing, especially on the Kona side, where the seas are small, the wind is light, and it's summerlike year-round. Local afternoon breezes make sailing and windsurfing exciting. In winter, you can see humpback whales from shore or boat, and winter waves keep body- and boardsurfers happy.

For details on the activities listed below, see "The Active Vacation Planner" in Chapter 3.

BODY BOARDING (BOOGIE BOARDING) & BODYSURFING

On the Kona side of the island, the best beaches for body boarding and bodysurfing are Hapuna, White Sands, and Kona Coast State Park. On the east side, try Leleiwi, Isaac Hale, and Punaluu. You can rent boogie boards and fins from **Snorkel Bob's,** in the parking lot near Huggo's Restaurant, 75-5831 Kahakai Rd., Kailua-Kona (☎ **808/329-0770**), for $29 a week. No one offers formal boogie boarding lessons, but the staff at Snorkel Bob's can give you pointers and tell you where waves appropriate for beginners are rolling in.

DEEP-SEA FISHING: THE HUNT FOR GRANDERS

The big silver fish exploded out of the sea like a rocket, flashing and thrashing and fighting the line. It's an ono (also known as wahoo), one of Hawaii's great sport fishes to catch—and to eat. We had just wet a line outside Honokohau Harbor, where big Pacific billfish, tuna, ono, mahimahi, and great big blue marlin roam in deep cold water off the famed Kona Coast—the marlin capital of the world.

If you want to catch fish, it doesn't get any better than Kona. Old angler Ed Sheehan used to say that fishing was "a chosen boredom electrified by intense excitement"; there's no better way to describe a day on a Kona fishing boat. It can be all or nothing, but you seldom come away empty-handed. A guy I know even caught a trophy marlin with a brass door knob for a lure. When anglers here catch marlin that weigh 1,000 pounds or more, they call them "granders"; there's even a "wall of fame" in Kailua-Kona's Waterfront Row honoring 40 anglers who've nailed more than 20 tons of fighting fish. Many now tag and release so the marlin can live to fight again.

You can go down to Honokohau Harbor and walk the docks, inspect the boats, talk to captains and crew, or you can arrange a charter through **Kona Charter Skippers Association** (across from Kona Pier at 75-5663 Palani Rd., Kailua-Kona HI 96749; ☎ **808/329-3600**), which serves as a booking desk for the local boats. Most big game charter boats carry six passengers max. Half-day and full day charters are available. A half-day charter ranges from $225 to $375, and a full-day from $325 to $600, depending on the size of the boat (they range from 26–40 ft.). The price is the same no matter how you book—unless you find a captain who's hungry and hasn't been out for a while, in which case you may not want to fish with him anyway. The boats supply all equipment, bait, tackle, and lures; no license is required. You bring your own sandwiches. Sorry, no beer on board.

Many captains now tag and release marlins and keep the mahimahi for dinner— that's Island style. If you want to eat your mahi or have your trophy marlin mounted, tell the captain before you go.

OCEAN KAYAKING

Imagine sitting at sea level, eye-to-eye with a turtle, a dolphin, even a whale—it's possible in an oceangoing kayak. Anyone can kayak: Just get in, find your balance, and paddle. After a few minutes of instruction and a little practice in a calm area (like the lagoon in front of the King Kamehameha's Kona Beach Hotel), you'll be ready to explore. Beginners can practice their skills in Kailua and Kealakekua bays;

intermediates might try paddling from Honokohau Harbor to Kona Coast Beach Park; the Hamakua Coast is a challenge for experienced kayakers. You can rent one- and two-person kayaks, wave-surfing models, and more from **Kona Kai-yaks,** Gentry's Kona Marine, Honokohau Small Boat Harbor (☎ **808/326-2922**), starting at $8 an hour or $20 a day.

SAILING: SEEING THE BIG ISLAND BY SLOOP

For most folks visiting Hawaii, a day sailing means taking a Mai Tai–laced party cruise out of Waikiki and coming back 90 minutes later with a headache and a $150 bill. But there's a better way: the *Maile,* a 50-foot Gulfstar sloop, one of the most comfortable yachts under sail in the islands today. You take the helm or leave it all to Capt. Ralph Blancato, whose sea log rivals Captain Cook's. He knows his boat, he knows Hawaii, and he knows people. He even knows how to cook: line-caught mahi, ono, and wahoo are often daily specials. The *Maile* (☎ **800/726-SAIL**) sails year-round from Kawaihae Harbor. A 4-hour excursion (10am–2pm) is $145 a person and includes a light lunch and beverages. Sunset sails, also $145, last 3 hours and include dinner, wine, and spectacular ambiance. Week-long sail-and-snorkel cruises around the island ($980 a person), and 10-day interisland voyages are also available. There's a four-person minimum on all trips.

SCUBA DIVING

The Big Island's leeward coast offers some of the best diving in the world, because the water's calm (protected by the two 13,000-ft. volcanoes), warm (75–81°), and clear (visibility is 100-plus-ft. year-round).

Want to swim with fast-moving game fish? Try Ulua Cave at the north end of the Kohala Coast (Ulua is the Hawaiian name for giant trevally). How about a dramatic underwater encounter with large, feeding manta rays? Manta Ray Village, located outside Keauhou Bay off the Kona Surf Resort, is a proven spot.

There are a dozen dive operators on the west side of the Big Island, plus one in Hilo. They offer everything from scuba certification courses (you must be certified to dive, although some operators will offer an "intro" dive), to guided-boat dives. One of Kona's most popular dive operators is **Kona Coast Divers,** 74-5614 Palani Rd., Kailua-Kona (☎ **808/329-8802**; e-mail: http://konacoastdivers.com). Kona's oldest five-star PADI facility is run by Jim and Julie Robinson. You can't miss their shop, a light-house–shaped building located a half-mile from Kailua Bay, which has everything: classrooms and a pool for training, gear rental, retail sales, and charter-boat dives. Scuba-diving magazines have consistently rated Kona Coast Divers as one of the best outfitters in the world. A two-tank dive off one of their custom dive boats costs about $70; certification courses run $200 to $300.

Dive operators in the Kohala Coast area include **Red Sail Sports,** located at both the Hilton Waikoloa Village, Kohala Coast (☎ **808/885-2876**), and at The Orchid at Mauna Lani, Kohala Coast (☎ **808/885-2000**); and **Sea Adventure** at the Mauna Lani Bay Resort (☎ **808/885-7883**).

NIGHT DIVING WITH MANTA RAYS

Most people aren't going to get in the water in Hawaii after dark with a flashlight and dive into the inky black depths. No way. However, if you're into this sort of thing, here's one dive you won't want to miss: swimming with manta rays on a night dive. It's the experience of a lifetime. **Kona Coast Divers** (see above) will take you on a one-tank night dive for $55. **Jack's Diving Locker,** on Alii Drive below the

Palm Cafe, Kailua-Kona (☎ 808/329-7585) will take you on a two-tank sunset and night dive for $95, equipment and snacks included. Don't fret if you're not a certified diver; Jack's also takes snorkelers for $35.

SNORKELING

If you come to Hawaii and don't snorkel, you miss half the fun. The year-round calm waters along the Kona and Kohala coasts are home to spectacular marine life. Some of the best snorkeling areas on the Kona-Kohala Coast include Hookena, Honaunau, White Sands, Kona Coast State Park, Puako, and Spencer beach parks. **Hapuna Beach Cove,** at the foot of the Hapuna Beach Prince Resort's $5,000-a-night suite (usually occupied by gazillionaires), is a secret little cove where you can snorkel not only with schools of oama, yellow tangs, needlefish, and green sea turtles but also, once in a while, somebody rich and famous. But if you've never snorkeled in your life, **Kahaluu Beach Park** is the best place to start. Just wade in and look down at the schools of fish in the bay's black-lava tide pools, which are guarded from the open ocean by a 1,000-foot-long breakwater. But probably the best snorkeling for all levels is to be had in **Kealakekua Bay,** reachable only by boat (see below).

Beach concessions at all the resorts, tour desks, and dive shops all offer equipment rentals and lessons for beginning snorkelers. Gear rental is about $15 a week (including mask, fins, and snorkel); prices go up slightly for prescription masks and high-end snorkels. Dive shops and marine operators who rent gear include **Kona Coast Divers,** 75-5614 Palani Rd., Kailua-Kona (☎ 808/329-8802); **Snorkel Bob's,** in the parking lot of Huggo's Restaurant at 75-5831 Kahakai Rd, Kailua-Kona (☎ 808/329-0770); **Red Sail Sports,** located at the Hilton Waikoloa Village, Kohala Coast (☎ 808/885-2876), and **The Orchid** at Mauna Lani, Kohala Coast (☎ 808/885-2000); and **Sea Adventure,** Mauna Lani Bay Resort (☎ 808/885-7883).

Adventurous types can snorkel with manta rays on night dive-and-snorkel cruises; see "Night Diving with Manta Rays," above.

SNORKELING CRUISES TO KEALAKEKUA BAY

An underwater preserve rich with marine life, calm Kealakekua Bay attracts on a daily basis big bargelike dive boats that disgorge schools of black-finned, pale-faced bipeds who flail about under the water like lost frogs—from a fish's eye view, at least. So far, though, the fish still outnumber the people. Coral heads, lava tubes, and underwater caves all provide an excellent habitat for Hawaii's vast array of tropical fish, making mile-wide Kealakekua the Big Island's best accessible spot for snorkeling and diving. Without looking very hard, I always see octopuses, free-swimming Moray eels, parrot fish, and goat fish; once in a while, a pod of spinner dolphins streaks across the bay.

I'm not big on the big boats; less is more here. A solo kayak is best; for information on renting one, see "Ocean Kayaking," above. If you'd rather go in a group or put someone else in charge of steering you there, take a smaller boat, like a **Captain Zodiac** (Gentry's Marina, Honokohau Harbor; ☎ 808/329-3199). It's basically a 15-passenger inflatable rubber life raft, pioneered by Jacques Cousteau, that takes you on a 4-hour personalized adventure. It's a wild ride 14 miles down the Kona Coast to Kealakekua, where you'll spend about 1¹/₂ hours snorkeling in the bay.

Fair Wind Snorkeling and Diving Adventures (☎ 808/322-2788 or 800/677-9461) will take you on a 4¹/₂-hour sail-and-snorkel cruise from Keauhou Bay to Kealakekua on their 60-foot catamaran. The cost is $69 for adults, $38 for children ages 6 to 17.

Snorkeling Kealakekua—and Swimming to England

Flying down the Kona Coast, bow high, the sleek craft skims the water like a flying fish, its twin engines driving us so fast that the coastline goes by in a blur. We laugh in the wind as we go skipping across the big blue sea. Oh, the joy of a fast boat.

Uncle Danny Almonte, our guide, points out historic and cultural landmarks along our 11-mile voyage. Bottle-nosed dolphins surface off the bow, and we slow to smile back at them before they take off on a food run. A speed boat (one of those scarab-looking jobs) comes roaring up full of bluster to check out our boat, to see what it would do. We're neck-and-neck for a while, but soon they disappear in our wake.

We glide into Kealakekua Bay, the Big Island's best dive spot and the last place on earth seen by Capt. James Cook, who stumbled onto the islands in 1778 while looking for the Northwest Passage and claimed them for Great Britain. There it is around the bend: the white obelisk that marks the death site of the great navigator, almost hidden in mangroves on the site of Kaaawaloa, an ancient village gone to dust.

It's 9am on a fine mid-November day, and I'm already in the water, among the shiny tropical fish. The water temperature's 76°, the air 80° and climbing. Another perfect day.

From sea level, I scan the rocky red cliffs trying to imagine what it was like when Captain Cook returned to the Big Island aboard the *Resolution,* with a broken fore-mast, to meet his doom on February 14, 1779. There was no god's reception for Cook this time, as there had been a year earlier. The bay ran red with blood that day: Cook, four marines, four Hawaiian chiefs, and 13 warriors were killed. I approach Cook's monument by sea, clamber over slippery rocks, and sit down on the jetty. I look for the brass plaque that's supposed to mark the spot where he fell,

SNUBA

Big Island Snuba, 74-5660 Palani Rd., Kailua-Kona (☎ **808/326-7446**), will take you on a 45-minute Snuba dive for $50 to $55, either from the beach or aboard a boat (the cost of the boat ride is extra).

SURFING

Most surfing off the Big Island is for the experienced only, but beginners can catch a wave, too. Surfing lessons cost about $30 an hour, and board rentals are about $15 for the day. For lessons and rentals in Kona, check out **Honolulu Surf Company,** Kona Inn Shopping Village (☎ **808/329-1001**), and **Pacific Vibrations,** 75-5702 Alii Dr., (☎ **808/329-4140**). On the Kohala Coast, call **Ocean Sports,** Royal Waikoloan Hotel (☎ **808/885-5555**).

Experienced surfers should check out the waves at Pine Trees (north of Kailua-Kona), Lyman's, and Kahaluu (the shoreline along Alii Dr. in Kona) on the west side, and Hilo Bay Front Park and Keaukaha Beach Park on the east side.

WHALE-WATCHING

Hawaii's most impressive visitors—45-foot humpback whales—return to the waters off Kona every winter. Capt. Dan McSweeney, a whale researcher for more than 20 years, is always here to greet them, as well as the other whales who spend the warmer months in Hawaiian waters, like old friends. Since Captain Dan works daily with the but see only empty black rocks and bright fish. Maybe it's the hot tropic sun, but I decide to do something I've wanted to do for a long time: Take a quick visit to the United Kingdom.

No, I hadn't had too much sun. It's a feat that's possible, thanks to an 1877 land title transfer. Hawaiian Princess Miriam Likelike and her British consul husband, Archibald Scott Cleghorn, deeded a 5,682-square-foot parcel on the shore of Kealakekua to England for $1, "to keep and maintain" a monument to Capt. James Cook. Hawaii was then a kingdom, so you could go from one kingdom to the other by taking a single step over an imaginary line in the sand.

Intrigued ever since I first heard about this geographic delight, I wanted to do it—just to say I did—and now here was my chance. Nobody's looking, so I put one foot in England and left the other in Hawaii, standing between two islands like a latter-day Colossus of Rhodes. Silly, I know, but a little whimsy amuses me greatly.

While exploring the rest of this England, I notice the whitewashed monument could use a touch-up. Once a year, I'm told, tars in Her Majesty's Service, usually up from Sydney on cadet training missions, stop by to spit-shine the obelisk and its salt-tarnished plaque commemorating Captain Cook.

I step back into Hawaii, slip into the warm water, and swim through schools of fish to the starboard side, where Uncle Danny (that show-off) is playing with a *he'e* caught on a coral head, letting the little gray Hawaiian octopus grip his left arm with eight suction cup tentacles.

"Where'd you go?" Uncle Danny asks. "Just got back from England," I say. "Over there?" he says, eyebrows raised, hip to the fact there will always be an England in Hawaii.

---

whales, he has no problem finding them; he frequently drops an underwater microphone into the water so you can listen to their songs. If the whales aren't singing, he may use his underwater video camera to show you what's going on.

In humpback season—roughly December to April—**Captain Dan McSweeney's Year-Round Whale-Watching** (☎ **808/322-0028**) makes two 3¹/₂-hour trips a day; during the rest of the year, Dan schedules one morning trip daily to look for pilot, sperm, false killer, melon-headed, pygmy killer, and beaked whales. It's $39.50 for adults, $29.50 for kids under 11. Captain Dan guarantees a sighting, or he'll take you out again for free. There are no cruises from May 1 to June 30, though; that's when he goes whale watching in Alaska.

WINDSURFING

Anaehoomalu, on the Kohala Coast, is one of the best beaches for windsurfing, because there are constant 5- to 25-knot winds blowing onshore (toward the beach), so if you get in trouble, the wind brings you back to shore (instead of taking you out to sea). Learning is easy, claims Nailima Ahuna, a windsurfing instructor at **Ocean Sports,** Royal Waikoloan Hotel (☎ **808/885-5555**). He starts beginners on a land simulator to teach them how to handle the sail and come about (that means to turn around and come back). After about 15 minutes of instruction on land, you're ready to hit the water and sail away. Instruction is $35 an hour, and equipment rental is $20 an hour or $85 for 5 hours. Advanced windsurfers should head to Puako and Hilo Bay.

7 Hiking & Camping

by Rick Carroll, with Jeanette Foster

Hikers get to see a face of the Big Island that most visitors don't. Both day-hikers and backpackers can to step into the heart of a still-active volcano, experience the solitude of the tropical rain forest, and discover remote, hidden beaches.

For information on camping and hiking on the Big Island, contact **Hawaii Volcanoes National Park,** P.O. Box 52, Volcano, HI 96718 (☎ **808/967-7311**), **Puuhonua O Honaunau National Historic Park,** Honaunau, HI 96726 (☎ **808/ 328-2326**), **State Division of Forestry and Wildlife,** P.O. Box 4849, Hilo, HI 96720 (☎ **808/933-4221**), **State Division of Parks,** P.O. Box 936, Hilo, HI 96721 (☎ **808/974-6200**), or **County Department of Parks and Recreation**, 25 Aupuni St., Hilo, HI 96720 (☎ **808/961-8311**). For other information sources and general tips on hiking and camping in Hawaii, see "The Active Vacation Planner," Chapter 3.

For guided day-hikes, contact Dr. Hugh Montgomery of **Hawaiian Walkways,** P.O. Box 2193, Kamuela, HI 96743 (☎ **800/457-7759**). A lifelong resident of Hawaii, Hugh offers a variety of half-day and full-day hikes, ranging from shoreline trail hikes to explore ancient Hawaiian petroglyphs to hikes up 13,000-foot Mauna Kea to Lake Waiau, a little glacial lake that's one of the highest in the world. Half-day hikes start at $60; full-day hikes with lunch are $100.

Camping equipment is available for rent from **Pacific Rent-All,** 1080 Kilauea Ave., Hilo (☎ **808/935-2974**). It's for sale at **C&S Cycle and Surf** in Waimea (☎ **808/885-5005**); **Gaspro** in Hilo (☎ **808/935-3341**), Waimea (☎ **808/ 885-8636**), and Kona (☎ **808/329-7393**); and **The Surplus Store** in Hilo (☎ **808/ 935-6398**) and Kona (☎ **808/329-1240**).

HAWAII VOLCANOES NATIONAL PARK

Hawaii Volcanoes National Park is a wilderness wonderland. Miles of trails not only lace the lava, but also cross deserts, rain forests, beaches, and, in the winter, snow at 13,000-feet. Trail maps are sold at park headquarters and are highly recommended. Check conditions before you head out on a trail. It can be cool and rainy anytime of the year; come prepared for hot sun and cold rain and hard wind. Always wear sunscreen and bring plenty of drinking water.

KILAUEA IKI TRAIL

You'll experience the work of the volcano goddess, Pele, firsthand on this hike. The 5-mile trail begins at park headquarters, goes down thorugh a forest of ferns into still-fuming Kilauea Iki Crater, and across the crater floor past the vent where a 1959 lava blast shot a fountain of fire 1,900 feet into the air for 36 days. Allow 4 hours for the fair-to-moderate hike. Don't go if you have respiratory problems; the fumes will get you.

HALEMAUMAU TRAIL

This moderate 3¹/₂-mile hike starts at the Visitor Center and goes down 500 feet to the floor of Kilauea crater, crosses the crater, and ends at Halemaumau Overlook.

DEVASTATION TRAIL

Up on the rim of Kilauea Iki Crater, you can take a brief walk through an earthly Hades and see what Kilauea did to a once-flourishing ohia forest; the scorched earth with its ghostly tree skeletons stands in sharp contrast to the rest of the nearby lush forest that escaped the hellfire. Everyone can—and should—take this half-mile hike on a boardwalk across the eerie bed of black cinders. The trailhead is on Crater Rim Road at Puu Puai Overlook.

KIPUKA PUAULU (BIRD PARK) TRAIL

This easy 1¹/₂-mile, hour-long hike lets you see native Hawaiian flora and fauna in a *kipuka,* a little oasis of living nature in a field of lava. For some reason (gravity or rate of flow, perhaps) the once red-hot lava skirted—perhaps even surrounded—this miniforest and let it survive. At the trail head at Mauna Loa Road is a display of plants and birds you'll see on the walk. Go early in the morning or in the evening (or even better, just after a rain) to see native birds like the *apapane* and *iiwi.* The apapane is a small, bright-red bird with black wings and tail that sips the nectar of the red-blossom ohia lehua trees. The iiwi has the same colors, but is much larger and has a curved bill. Native trees along the trail include giant ohia, koa, soapberry, kolea, and mamani. Be sure to close the gate at the entrance—it's there to keep out wild pigs, the scourge of native plants.

MAUNA LOA TRAIL

Probably the most challenging hike in Hawaii, this 18-mile trail goes from the lookout to a cabin at the Red Hill at 10,035 feet, then 11.6 more miles up to the primitive Mauna Loa summit cabin at 13,250 feet, where the climate is called sub-Arctic, whiteouts are common, and overnight temperatures are below freezing year-round; there's often snow in July. This 4-day round-trip hike requires advance planning, great physical condition because of the altitude, and registration at the Visitor Center. The park rangers will want to know you're there for your own safety. Call the visitor center at **808/967-7184** for maps and details. The trailhead begins where Mauna Loa Road ends, 13¹/₂ miles north of Hi. 11.

CAMPGROUNDS & WILDERNESS CABINS

Three park campgrounds are accessible by car: **Kipuka Nene, Namakani Paio,** and **Kamoamoa.** Each has pavilions with picnic tables and fireplaces, but no wood is provided. Tent camping is free; no reservations are required. Stays are limited to 7 days per campground per year. Permits must be obtained from the park (P.O. Box 52, Volcano, HI 96718; ☎ **808/967-7311**). Backpack camping at hiker shelters and cabins is available, but you must register at park headquarters. **Kilauea Military Camp** is a rest and recreation camp for active and retired military personnel a mile from the park headquarters; facilities include 62 one- to four-bedroom cabins, a 100-bunk dorm, a cafeteria, bowling alley, a bar, general store, weight room, and tennis and basketball courts. Rates range from $25 to $73 a night; call **808/967-8334** for further details and to reserve.

The following cabins and campgrounds are the best of what the park and surrounding area has to offer:

Halape Shelter

This backcountry site, about 7 miles from the nearest road, is the place for people who want to get away from it all and enjoy their own private white-sand beach. The small, three-sided stone shelter, with a roof but no floor, can accommodate two people comfortably, but four's a crowd. You could pitch a tent inside, but if the weather is nice, you're better off setting up near the beach. There's a catchment water tank, but check with rangers on the water situation before hiking in (sometimes they don't have accurate information on the water level; bring extra water just in case). Other facilities include a small grill and a pit toilet. Go on weekdays if you're really looking to get away from it all. It's free to stay here, but you're limited to 3 nights. Permits are available at the park visitors' center on a first-come first-served basis no earlier than noon on the day before your trip. For more information, contact **Hawaii Volcanoes National Park** (☎ **808/967-7311**).

Kilauea State Recreation Area Cabin

This state park cabin in Volcano village sleeps up to six and has a kitchen, dining/ living room, two bedrooms, and a bathroom with hot shower. Utensils, blankets, bedding, and towels are all provided. You can stay up to 5 nights during a 30-day period. Fees are on a sliding scale; they begin at $10 a night for one and go down to $5 per person for six. Make reservations early—the cabin is booked months in advance. To reserve, contact the **State Division of Parks,** P.O. Box 936, Hilo, HI 96720 (☎ **808/974-6200**).

Namakani Paio Campgrounds & Cabins

Just 5 miles west of the park entrance is a tall eucalyptus forest where you can pitch a tent in an open grassy field. The trail to Kilauea Crater is just a half-mile away. No permit is needed for tent camping, but stays are limited to 7 days. Facilities include pavilions with barbecues and a fireplace, picnic tables, outdoor dishwashing area, rest rooms, and drinking water. There also are 10 cabins that accommodate up to four each. Each cabin has a covered picnic table at the entrance and a fireplace with a grill. Toilets, sinks, and hot showers are available in a separate building. Groceries and gas are available in the town of Volcano, a mile away. Make cabin reservations through **Volcano House,** P.O. Box 53, Volcano, HI 96718 (☎ **808/967-7321**). Cost is $32 per night for two, $38 for three, and $44 for four.

WAIMANU VALLEY'S MULIWAI TRAIL

This difficult 2- to 3-day hiking adventure—only for the hardy—takes you to a hidden valley some call Eden. It probably looks just as it did when Capt. James Cook "discovered" the islands: Virgin waterfalls and pools, spectacular views, and a chance to merge with the environment bring hikers back time and time again.

The trail, which goes from sea level to 1,350-feet and down to the sea again, takes more than 9 hours to hike in and more than 10 hours to hike out. Be prepared for clouds of blood-thirsty mosquitoes, and look out for wild pigs. If it's raining, forget it: You'll have 13 streams to cross before you reach the rim of Waimanu Valley, and rain means flash floods.

You must get permission to camp in Waimanu Valley from the **Division of Forestry and Wildlife,** P.O. Box 4849, Hilo, HI 96720-0849 (☎ **808/933-4221**). Permits to the nine designated campsites are assigned by number. They're free, but you're limited to a 7-day stay. Facilities are limited to two composting pit toilets. The best water in the valley is from the stream on the western wall, a 15-minute walk up a trail from the beach. Water from the Waimanu Stream drains from a swamp, so skip it. Be sure to pack out what you take in.

To get to the trail head, take Hi. 19 to the turnoff for Honokaa. From Honokaa, drive 9^1/$_2$ miles to the Waipio Valley Lookout. Unless you have four-wheel drive, this is where your hike begins. Walk down the road and wade the Wailoa Stream, cross the beach and go to the northwest wall. The trail starts here and goes up the valley floor, past a swamp, and into a forest before beginning a series of switchbacks that parallel the coastline. These switchbacks go up and down about 14 gulches. At the ninth gulch, about two-thirds of the way along the trail, is a shelter. After the shelter, the trail descends into Waimanu Valley, which looks like a smaller version of Waipio Valley, but without a sign of human intrusion.

WAIPIO VALLEY CAMPING

Camping is permitted on the east side of the Waipio Stream in lush Waipio Valley. There's a grove of ironwood trees that provides a nice shady spot. Permits, which are free but limited to 7 days, must be applied for in person at **Hamakua Sugar Company** (☎ **808/776-1104**) in Paauilo (north of Hilo), weekdays from 7am to 4pm. There are no facilities in Waipio Valley. You must dig (and cover) your own latrine. Water is available from the stream, but be sure to treat it before drinking.

8 Golf & Other Outdoor Activities

by Rick Carroll, with Jeanette Foster

BICYCLING & MOUNTAIN BIKING

For mountain-bike and cross-training bike rentals in Kona, see **Dave's Bike and Triathlon Shop** on Alii Drive (☎ **808/329-4522**). Dave rents Italian-made Fila, British-made Muddy Fox, and KHS mountain bikes for $12 a day, or $60 a week. It's a deal. He offers free advice and local weather reports (like which roads are closed by lava). He also rents bike racks for rental cars so you can drive-and-bike, as your trip dictates. On the Kohala Coast, check out the range of available bikes for rent from **Red Sail Sports,** at the Hilton Waikoloa Village (☎ **808/885-2876**) or The Orchid at Mauna Lani (☎ **808/885-2000**). Bike rentals start at $5 an hour or $15 a day.

The best place to bike on the Big Island is probably the North Kohala coast from Waimea to Hawi, over the scenic Kohala Mountains; it's one of the island's most popular rides. If you don't want to head out alone, the best outfit to ride with is **Chris' Adventures** (☎ **808/326-4600**); call for rates.

BIKING AROUND THE BIG ISLAND

When was the last time you bicycled around a tropical island? Jump on a 21-speed Italian-made mountain bike and do it here; it's a 225-mile circle island tour. A novice can do it in 6 days or less. Serious bikers do it in two.

Here's a couple of tips if you're going to try to make your way around the island: Plan your trip. Make advance reservations. Get a bike that fits. Go early in the day; just after sunrise is best. Wear lightweight bike togs and a helmet. Take two water bottles and sunscreen. Bring rain gear. Stay on the road, because razor-sharp lava and kiawe thorns cause blow-outs. Bring a patch kit, cables, and a lock. Have fun!

BIRDING

Native Hawaiian birds are few and, I'm sorry to say, dwindling. Of 77 native species, 23 are extinct, 29 are endangered, and one is threatened. Hawaii may be the endangered bird capital of the world, but it still offers extraordinary birding for anyone nimble enough to traverse tough, mucky landscape. And the best birding is on the Big Island: It's got the best habitats, the least human intrusion, widest variety of eco-climates, and the most native forest birds. Birders the world over come hoping to see three Hawaiian birds in particular: *akiapolaau,* a woodpecker wanna-be with a war club–like head; *nukupuu,* an elusive little yellow bird with a curved-beak, one of the "crown jewels" of Hawaiian birding; and *alala,* the "critically endangered" Hawaiian crow that's now almost impossible to see in the wild.

The best spots for accomplished birders to go on their own are the ohia forests of **Hawaii Volcanoes National Park,** usually at sunrise or sunset, when the little forest birds (apapane and amakihi) seem to be most active. You may also see native birds in the ohia forest at the entrance to the Thurston Lava Tube. The Hawaiian Nene goose can be spotted at the park's Kipuka Nene Campground, a favorite nesting habitat that soon may be closed to the public. Geese and pheasants sometimes appear on the Volcano Golf Course in the afternoon. The White-tailed Tropic Bird often rides the thermals caused by steam inside Halemaumau Crater.

Other Big Island spots to see native Hawaiian and other birds include:

Hakalau National Wildlife Preserve   The first national wildlife refuge established solely for forest bird management is on the eastern slope of Mauna Kea above the Hamakua Coast. It's open for birding by permit only on the last weekend of each month, and can be reached only by four-wheel drive vehicle and on foot. Contact the Refuge Manager, Hakalau Forest, 154 Wainuenue Ave., Room 219, Hilo, HI 96720 (☎ **808/933-6915**).

Hilo Ponds   Ducks, coots, herons (night and Great Blue), cattle egrets, even Canadian geese and the Snow Goose fly into this popular coastal wetlands in Hilo, near the airport. Take Kalanianaole Highway about 3 miles east, past the industrial port facilities to Loko Waka Pond and Waiakea Pond.

Saddle Road Kipukas   Of course, you're not supposed to take your rental car on the 53-mile Saddle Road (Hi. 200) from Hilo to the Kohala Coast between Mauna Kea and Mauna Loa, but it's a beautiful drive—especially at sunset—and one of the best places to see Iao, the Hawaiian hawk, as it soars over the rolling grasslands. Along the way you'll see kipukas (islands of old forest surrounded by young lava flows), which are natural preserves for the Elepaio, Omao, Akiapolaau, Hawaii Creeper, Iiwi, and Apapane. To enter a kipuka, you must pick your way across razor-sharp lava, and then sit and wait for the birds.

BIRDING TOURS IN THE PU'U O'O RAIN FOREST

If you don't know an apapane from a nukupuu, go with someone who does. Until I ventured into the Pu'u O'o rain forest with Big Island naturalist Rob Pacheco of Hawaii Forest and Trail, I thought Hawaii's native birds could only be seen stuffed under glass at the Bishop Museum. Now, even rank amateurs like me can see Hawaii's *rara avis* in the wild.

We set off with walking sticks on the Puu Oo trail, on Mauna Kea's southern slope. Our destination: a Saddle Road *kipuka*—a green island in a sea of black lava. Into the forest we step, trading bright hot sun for the cool half-light under-tree ferns, and almost immediately hear a distant symphony. Soon we begin to see native birds everywhere, like the *iiwi,* a scarlet flash of a honeycreeper with a curvy pink bill. We spy several *elepaio,* a chubby brown-and-white striped flycatcher whose voice seems tied to its flirty tail. We also hear a haunting warble of the *omao,* a solitary gray bird found only on the Big Island that's hard to spot until it sings.

Rob spots a squadron of *apapane.* He counts—five, six, seven, eight—before I see one. Binoculars at the ready, I stand at the edge the forest looking for little red birds that rocket overhead. "There they go," Rob says. I hear the whir but can't get my field glasses up in time to see apapane on the wing. They're fast little birds. Finally, I see where the whir/blur stops: in an ohia tree full of showy red blossoms that look like thistles on the town. I watch the apapane dip its curved beak deep into an ohia blossom. From now on, this little red bird will not elude me.

Hawaii Forest and Trail, P.O. Box 2975, Kailua-Kona, HI 96745 (☎ **808/ 322-8881** or 800/464-1993; e-mail: hitrail@aloha.net) offers full-day birding trips, including transportation, continental breakfast, lunch, and all gear, for $129 adults, $95 ages 13 to 17, and $65 ages 4 to 12. He offers a group rate of $1,050 for up to 10 guests, and $105 each for one or two more.

THE SEARCH FOR THE LAST HAWAIIAN CROW: MCCANDLESS RANCH

The nearly extinct *'alala,* or Hawaiian crow, has, for reasons all its own, chosen to make its last stand on earth at McCandless Ranch, a 17,000-acre working cattle ranch above Kealakekua Bay. Habitat degradation and hunters have caused their population to shrink to almost nothing; it seems almost as if the birds themselves have abandoned hope. But a wild flock of about 20 crows clings to life in the native forest between 3,000 and 6,000 feet above sea level, where ornithologists keep watch with fingers crossed and try to encourage mating.

It's impossible to spot one in the wild; even on the ranch, you'll come away lucky if you see one. One morning, I was: A mating pair soared across the sky. Bigger than hawks and owls, they have great wings with white tips and look like they could fly forever. These great birds don't look endangered, only lonely; but I could sense a distinct air of doom. If you want to see the 'alala before they disappear forever, you'd better hurry.

Contact **McCandless Ranch Ecotour,** P.O. Box 500, Honaunau, HI 96726 (☎ **808/328-9313;** fax 808/328-8671). An overnight stay at the ranch's B&B (see "Accommodations," above, for details) and guided tour (departing at 4:30am) is $400 for two.

GOLF

Most of the Big Island's golf courses are carved out of lava beds. Gigantic earth scrapers take barren, black fields of lava and turn them into spectacular fairways and manicured greens with malevolent bunkers and water hazards. All the courses below require cart rental; it's included in the greens fee.

✪ MAUNA KEA BEACH GOLF COURSE

This Robert Trent Jones, Jr. championship course is consistently rated one of the top golf courses in the United States. Located on the grounds of the Mauna Kea Beach Resort on the Kohala Coast, this par-72, 7,114-yard challenge is breathtakingly beautiful. The signature third hole is 175 yards long (and a shocking par-3), but the Pacific Ocean and shoreline cliffs stand between the tee and the green, giving every golfer, from beginner to pro, a real opportunity to improve their game. Another par-3 that confounds golfers is the 11th hole, which drops 100 feet from tee to green and plays down to the ocean, into the steady trade winds. When the trades are blowing, 181 yards might as well be 1,000 yards. Greens fees are $80 for hotel guests and $130 for nonguests. Facilities include putting greens, a driving range, lockers and showers, a pro shop, and a restaurant serving welcome cold drinks and sandwiches. For tee times or information, call **808/882-7222** or 808/882-5888. Call early, as the course is popular, especially for early weekend tee times.

✪ HAPUNA GOLF COURSE

Since its opening in 1992, this 18-hole championship course on the grounds of the Hapuna Prince Resort, next door to the Mauna Kea Beach Resort, has won numerous awards, including *Golf Magazine* awards as "most environmentally sensitive" course and one of the "top 10 new courses in the nation." The U.S. Golf Association named it "The Course of the Future." Well, the future is here, and it's a 6,027-yard, links-style course that extends from the shoreline to 700 feet above sea level, with views of the pastoral green hills of the Kohala Mountains and sweeping vistas of the Kohala coastline. Designed by Arnold Palmer and Ed Seay, the elevation changes on the course may bother some golfers (not to mention the winds at the higher elevations), but it's nothing that practice won't take care of. There are few elevated tee boxes and only 40 bunkers. Facilities for this resort course include putting green, driving range, lockers and showers, pro shop, and restaurant. Greens fees are $80 for guests and $130 for nonguests. This course gets crowded on weekends, so reserve early. For reservations and tee times, call **808/882-1111.**

✪ MAUNA LANI FRANCES I'I BROWN CHAMPIONSHIP COURSES

There are two highly regarded courses here: the **Mauna Lani South** and the **Mauna Lani North.** The South Course, a 7,029-yard, par-72, has an unforgettable ocean hole: the 221-yard 7th bordered by the sea, a salt-and-peppered sand dune, and kiawe trees. It drops downhill and—depending on the wind—can take anything from a wood to a wedge. The North Course may not have the drama of the oceanfront holes, but, because it was built on older lava flows, the more extensive indigenous vegetation gives the course a Scottish feeling. The hole that's cursed the most is the 140-yard, par-3 17th; it's spectacularly beautiful but plays right into the surrounding lava field. The PGA Seniors Tour takes place here every year. Greens fees are $70 for guests and $150 for nonguests. Twilight rates are available. Facilities include two driving ranges, a golf shop, lessons, a restaurant, and a putting green. These courses are always crowded, so call early (☎ **808/885-6655**).

WAIKOLOA GOLF COURSES

The **Waikoloa Beach Course** was designed by Robert Trent Jones, Jr., who has carried on his father's approach to design: "Hard par, easy bogey." Most golfers will remember the par-5 12th hole, at 505 yards from the back tee. An elevated tee surrounded by lava with bunkers at the corner, it plays to a sharp dogleg left. The **Waikoloa King's Course** is about 500-yards longer. Designed by Tom Weiskopf and Jay Morrish, the links-style King's Course features a double green at the 3rd and 6th holes and several carefully placed bunkers that make the most of the ever-present trade winds. Greens fees are $80 for hotel guests and $95 for nonguests. Facilities included a pro shop and showers. This is a very popular course with local residents, so book early. For information and reservations, call **808/885-6060** or 808/885-4647.

HORSEBACK RIDING

Paniolo Riding Adventure in Waimea (☎ **808/889-5354**) has a range of different ent rides to suit any riding ability. They even have mules—which offer a smoother, more surefooted ride. Rides begin at $70 for a $2^{1}/_2$-hour trip that takes in views of the Kona and Kohala coasts. Advanced riders should call **King's Trail Rides,** Hi. 11 at mile marker 111, Kealakekua (☎ **808/323-2388**). The trips, which are limited to four people, head down the mountain along Monument Trail to the Captain Cook Monument in Kealakekua Bay, where they stop for lunch and a quick dip in the bay. The $95 price tag includes snorkeling gear and lunch.

RIDING PARKER RANCH

To ride Parker Ranch is to be lost in time and space; it looks familiar and foreign all at once, stretching as it does under the volcano out west of the moon. The land, barren and rolling and dimpled by craters, looks positively lunar, especially when cows jump in the soft chiaroscuro light. You gain a scant clue to the ranch's vast grandeur on a 2-hour trail ride that begins at Mauna Kea Stables in the Old West town of Waimea. Other trail rides are "nose-to-tail," but not on the Parker Ranch—it's too big for that. Here, you can gallop to the horizon across scenic upland pastures dotted with volcanic cinder cones and strewn with bleached white cattle bones. Corrals hold Texas longhorns and lost heifers; the wide open range even offers a rare glimpse of wild Kona donkeys. Always, the final surprise is that we really are way out west—in Hawaii. **Mauna Kea Riding Stables** (☎ **808/885-4288**) offers guided trail rides for beginners to experts across Parker Ranch. You must be 8 or older, and weigh less than 210 pounds. It's $35 for a 1-hour ride, $60 for 2 hours, including instruction and trail guide.

SKIING MAUNA KEA

Weather changes fast atop Mauna Kea, 13,000 feet above sea level. All four seasons can occur in one day. Avalanches, blizzards, and whiteouts are common. Not what you expect from Hawaii, eh?

Downhill skiing in Hawaii sounds like an oxymoron, but there's a season atop Mauna Kea. Even in bad years, there's 2 months of skiing, March and April. But it can snow any month of the year up here; there's even been skiing in July and August. And when the skiing's good, it's good: The mountain has 100 square miles of virgin powder, 5-mile-long–runs, and vertical drops of 2,500 to 4,500 feet per run. **Ski Guides Hawaii** (☎ **808/885-4188**) will take you up for a full day of skiing at $180 a person, including transportation to Mauna Kea, lunch, and ski gear. However, they don't take beginners; Mauna Kea isn't the place to learn how to ski. Call any time, though—you never know when it's ski season in Hawaii.

TENNIS

You can play for free at any Hawaii County tennis court; for a detailed list of all the courts on the island, contact **Hawaii County Department of Parks and Recreation,** 25 Apuni St., Hilo, 96720 (☎ **808/961-8720**). The best courts are in Hilo at the Hoolulu Tennis Stadium, located next to the Civic Auditorium on Manono Street. In Kona, the best courts are at the Old Airport Park. Most of the resorts in the Kona-Kohala area do not allow nonguests to use their tennis facilities. However, two hotels that do offer court rentals are **King Kamehameha's Kona Beach Hotel,** 75-5660 Palani Rd. (☎ **808/329-2911**), and **Keauhou Beach Hotel,** 78-6740 Alii Dr. (☎ **808/322-4237**). Courts are $5 per person, per hour. Equipment rental and lessons are available.

9 Orientation & Adventure Tours

by Rick Carroll

Hawaii Forest & Trail. P.O. Box 2975, Kailua-Kona, HI 96745. ☎/Fax **808/322-8881** or 800/464-1993; fax 808/322-8883; e-mail: hitrail@aloha.net.

If you'd like to discover natural Hawaii off the beaten path—but don't necessarily want to sleep under a tree to do it—here's your ticket. Naturalist and educator Rob Pacheco will take you out for day trips in his plush four-wheel drive Suburban to some of the Big Island's most remote, pristine natural areas. Rob has exclusive access into private and state land holdings that harbor some of the islands' best intact ecosystems, so he can show you truly native natural areas of the Big Island that otherwise are inaccessible. Rob fully narrates his trips, offering extensive natural, geological, and cultural history interpretation (and not just a little humor). Since he only takes a maximum of seven people, his trips are highly personalized to meet the groups interests and abilities.

Rob offers day trips into the Puu Oo Ranch Rain Forest (see "Birding," above), to the Hualalai volcano (which Rob calls Hawaii's "best-kept secret"), into the Hakalau Forest National Wildlife Refuge, into Hawaii Volcanoes National Park (where he'll take you hiking through a lava tube and right up to the oozing flow after dark, when the lava is most spectacular—conditions permitting, of course), and to other south Kona private access areas. He also offers customized trips (from 1 to several days) for birders, families, and other private groups. There's about 3 to 4 hours of easy-to-moderate walking, over terrain manageable by anyone in average physical condition, on each day trip.

Full-day trips are $129 per adult, $95 for children ages 13 to 17, and $65 for children ages 4 to 12; children under three are free. Rob offers a private group rate of $1,050 for up to 10 guests, with an additional charge of $105 per person for one or two more. All prices include pickup and drop-off, continental breakfast, lunch, snacks, water and other beverages, and the use of binoculars, daypacks, walking staffs, any necessary outerwear, access charges, and tax. Charges are less for half-day trips. Call for a schedule of trips offered while you're on the Big Island. This is a Big Island adventure definitely worth the splurge—it might well be the highlight of your entire trip.

Kona Historical Society Walking Tours. ☎ 808/323-2005.

This nonprofit organization hosts two historic walking tours in the Kona region. The 90-minute **Kailua Village Walking Tour** is the best informed tour of the Kona Coast offered today. It takes you all around historic Kailua-Kona, from King Kamehameha's last seat of government to the site of Kona's unique cattle shipping, with lots of Hawaiian history and colorful lore along the way. Walks are conducted Tuesday to Saturday at 9:30am and Friday at 1pm. The cost is $10; you must call and reserve a spot in advance.

The historical society also offers a "Preservation in Progress" walking tour of historic Uchida Coffee Farm. It will eventually be an open-air living history museum; right now, you can see the fascinating restoration process in action. Call for tour times and reservations.

Hilo Sampan History Tours. ☎ 808/959-7864.

Here's an ideal way to sightsee: Catch a sampan and ride around Hilo like everyone did back in the 1930s. These open-air jitneys served as Hilo's main source of transportation between 1931 and 1940. In 1994, the Hilo Sampan Co., an independent, nonprofit group, revived the historic transit system by returning three original vintage sampans to service on two routes, which make hourly loops around the town Monday to Saturday from 8am to 4pm. The history route runs around downtown, taking in the port, the beaches, Banyan Gardens, and some lovely old residential neighborhoods. The sampans start at Hilo Shopping Center, but you can pick them up anywhere along the route; call for the location nearest you. The driver delivers an animated running commentary on Hilo's colorful history, and local passengers often contribute historic or personal anecdotes. At $2 for a daily unlimited pass, it's the Big Island's best transit bargain—cheap, friendly, and fun.

Green Sand Beach Tours. ☎ 808/929-9664.

This is a 4-hour guided tour to Green Sand Beach, the southernmost beach in the United States. This unique beach is really worth seeing but can only be reached by four-wheel drive, so this is a great way to go. The tour starts in Naalehu and includes a visit to an ancient *heiau,* nature and history commentary, and 2 hours of relaxing and boogie boarding (if conditions permit) at the beach; the cost is $30 per person.

10 Exploring the Big Island by Ca...

Realistically, plan on taking 4 days to circumnavigate ...
is a big mistake—everything'll just fly by in a blur. Here ...

Day One   Take off from Kailua-Kona for a morning div...
the afternoon at Puu Honua O Honaunau, the city of ref... ...ing south
on Hi. 11 for Naalehu, around the southern tip. You'll d... past macadamia nut
orchards on the southern flanks of Mauna Loa, which last erupted in 1984. The road
begins to climb over old lava flows as it wends past sun-bleached storefronts of the
rural Kau District. You'll pass South Point, the southernmost point in the United
States; it's worth the 24-mile side trip only if you collect geographic esoterica. Spend
the night at one of the cozy B&Bs (Carson's Volcano Cottage is my personal
favorite) in the cool up-lands of Volcano village, on the outskirts of the Big Island's
greatest attraction, Hawaii Volcanoes National Park. If you arrive early enough, head
into the park after dark; that's the best time to see the lava flow.

Day Two   Explore Hawaii Volcanoes National Park, where every day's the Fourth
of July. Drive Chain of Craters Road. Walk into otherworldy Thurston Lava Tube,
hike Devastation Trail, or ride down to the coast, where the lava meets the sea.
After you've explored the park, go wine tasting at Volcano Winery and explore the
village a bit. Later, head downhill 29 miles, past the orchid farms, to Hilo, for soft-
shell crabs and beignets at Roussel's, my favorite Hilo restaurant. Dolphin Bay
Hotel is a good choice for the night.

Day Three   Spend the morning exploring Hilo. (If you're in Hilo on a Wednesday or Saturday morning, shop Hilo Farmers Market for anthuriums and starfruit.)
In the afternoon, make a quick stop at lovely Akaka Falls, then head out along the
Hamakua Coast, past the sugar cane fields to Honokaa, gateway to Waipio Valley.
Stop at Waipio Valley Lookout, or take a walk down the slick, zig-zagging San Francisco–steep (25% grade) road to the valley floor where taro fields abound, waterfalls
spill down the cliffs, and the mile-long black-sand beach beckons. Take a plunge in
the foamy waves before heading for an overnight stay at one of the B&Bs in the area,
such as excellent Waipio Wayside (Jackie Horne's homemade pesto omelette is a five-
star treat).

Day Four   Take Hi. 19 over hill-and-dale across Parker Ranch (the world's biggest private spread) to the cowboy town of Waimea. Go horseback riding across the
ranch or just sightsee, stroll, and soak up some local color. Merriman's is a great
choice for lunch. Cruise down from misty Waimea and glide across Mauna Kea's
foothills to the leeward coast. Take Queen Kaahumanu Hwy. (Hi. 19), a smooth
black ribbon cutting a chunky 1859 lava flow, past fantasy resorts that bloom like
flowers in brimstone. Bright red, orange, and purple bougainvillea glow in slate-black
lava fields, while roadside graffiti spelled out in white rocks will let you know who
was here yesterday. If you're ready for a break, head for the Royal Waikoloan's
Petroglyph Bar for a cool drink and then stop in for a visit at the nearby Waikoloa
Petroglyph Field before getting back in the car for the last leg of your trip. Once
you're back in Kailua-Kona, celebrate your circle island tour with a sunset dinner at
the Palm Cafe while manta rays leap in the tide pools just across the street.

by Rick Carroll

THE KONA COAST
IN & AROUND KAILUA-KONA

Ellison S. Onizuka Space Center. At Keahole Airport. ☎ **808/329-3441.** Admission $2, 50¢ children 12 and under. Daily 8:30am–4:30pm.

This small museum has a real moon rock and memorabilia in honor of Big Island–born astronaut Ellison Onizuka, who died in the 1986 *Challenger* space shuttle disaster. His portrait also hangs in Imin Senior Center in Holualoa, and Mauna Kea's Visitor Center is also named in his memory (see below). The general store run by his parents in Holualoa is now closed.

Hulihee Palace. On Alii Dr., Kailua-Kona. ☎ **808/329-1877.** Admission $4 adults, $1 students, 50¢ children under 12. Mon–Fri 9am–4pm, Sat–Sun 10am–3pm. Guided tours given all day; arrive at least an hour before closing.

This two-story New England–style mansion of lava rock and coral mortar, erected in 1838 by governor of the island of Hawaii, John Adams Kuakini, overlooks the harbor at Kailua-Kona. The largest, most elegant residence on the island when it was erected in 1838, Hulihee (it means "turn and flee") was the gracious summer home of Hawaii's royalty. Now run by Daughters of Hawaii, the palace features many 19th-century mementos and furniture. You'll get lots of background and royal lore on the guided tour.

Across the street is **Mokuaikaua Church** (☎ 808/329-1589), the oldest Christian church in Hawaii. John Adams Kuakini built it 2 years before he built the palace. It's constructed of lava stones, but its architecture is New England–style all the way. The 112-foot steeple is still the tallest man-made structure in Kailua-Kona.

Kamehameha's Compound at Kamakahonu Bay. On grounds of King Kamehameha Hotel. ☎ **808/329-2911.** Free admission; self-guided tour. Daily 9am–4pm.

Out behind this concrete hotel is a compound of thatched houses that includes Ahuena Heiau, the restored temple of peace and prosperity built by Kamehameha, who lived here until his death in 1819. *Kamakahonu* means "the eye of the turtle"; this place is named for a rock here that resembles a turtle, but the rock is now buried under the cement pier. Such is progress.

Kona Pier. On the waterfront, Kailua-Kona. ☎ **808/329-7494.**

This is action central for water adventures. Fishing charters, snorkel cruises, and party boats all come and go here. Come by around 4pm, when the captains weigh in with the catch of the day, usually huge marlin and sailfish—the record-setters often come in here. It's also a great place to watch the sun set.

Kaupulehu Petroglyphs. At Kona Village Resort. ☎ **808/325-5555.** Free admission. Guided tours Mon–Fri at 11am.

Here you can see some of the finest images in the Hawaiian islands. Archaeologist Georgia Lee has counted more than 324 petroglyphs, and he's only documented half the site so far. There are many petroglyphs of sails, canoes, fish, and chiefs in headdresses, plus a burial scene with three stick figures. Kite motifs—rare in rock art—similar to those found in New Zealand are also here. To get there, turn off Hi. 19 to the gatehouse, then proceed 2.3 miles to the resort. The petroglyphs are reached via a footpath that goes past the luau grounds.

Big Island Highlights for Kids

Thurston Lava Tube, Hawaii Volcanoes National Park   It's scary, it's spooky, and it's perfect for any kid. You hike downhill through a rain forest full of little chittering native birds to enter this huge, silent black hole full of drips, cobwebs, and tree roots that stretches underground for almost a half-mile to a fork in the tunnel, which leads up a stairway to our world or—here's the best part—down an unexplored hole that probably goes all the way to China. Double dare you.

Hilton Waikoloa Village   Almost a mini-Disney World, this place is made for kids: bottle-nosed dolphins imported from Florida leap out of pools, man-made waterfalls splash into swimming pools, Italian-made boats on underwater tracks take you to your room. There's even a Japanese-style bullet train in the lobby; plenty of exotic African birds, including scarlet macaws and pink flamingoes; and a good old-fashioned American ice-cream shop under a waterfall. Oh, yeah, Hawaii's somewhere around the edges, too. See "Accommodations," above.

Submarine Rides   I think it's a rip-off, but your kids are gonna want to do it, and you're probably gonna let them. For some reason, these sub rides are one of the most popular tourist attractions in Hawaii. You go down 60 feet, see some fish and coral, and come back. No big deal; a mask, snorkel, and some fins do the trick just as well. Yet millions of people drop a small bundle on this underwater tourist ride. I was going to say "trap," but . . . it's a good way to go if the snorkel route isn't for you. **Atlantis Submarine** tours depart Kailua Pier hourly, 7 days a week; call **800/548-6262** to reserve.

Fishing out of Kona   When your kid catches a fish bigger than you, that's something to write home about. It can happen any day of the year on the Kona Coast, where huge pelagic fish migrate across the Pacific along thermal bands only a mile offshore. You'll fish with tuna to catch marlin and sailfish, and eat peanut-butter-and-jelly sandwiches. See "Hitting the Water," above.

Watching the Volcano   Any kid who doesn't get a kick out of watching a live volcano set the night on fire has been watching too much television. Take hot dogs, bottled water, and go to it—and let me know how it goes.

UP-COUNTRY KONA: HOLUALOA

On the slope of Hualalai volcano above Kailua-Kona sits the small village of Holualoa, attracting travelers weary of super resorts who are looking for a little art and culture. And shade.

This funky up-country town, centered around two-lane Mamaloha Highway, is nestled amid a lush tropical landscape where avocados grow as big as footballs. Little more than a wide spot in the road, Holualoa is a cluster of brightly painted, tin-roofed plantation shacks enjoying a reprise as B&Bs, art galleries, and quaint shops (see "Shops & Galleries," below, for details). In two blocks, it manages to pack in two first-rate galleries, a frame shop, a potter, a glassworks, a goldsmith, an old-fashioned general store, a vintage 1930s gas station, a tiny post office, a Catholic church, a

Impressions

I think the Kona coffee has a richer flavor than any other.

—Mark Twain

library that's open 2 days a week, and the **Kona Hotel,** a hot-pink clapboard structure that looks like a Western move set; you're welcome to peek in, and you should.

The cool up-slope village is welcome relief for anyone seeking escape from Kailua-Kona's constant sun. And it's the best place in Hawaii for a coffee break. That's because Holualoa is in the heart of the coffee belt, a 20-mile-long strip between 1,000 and 1,400 feet elevation where all the Kona coffee in the world is grown in rich volcanic soil of the cool uplands. Everyone's backyard seems to teem with glossy green leaves, ruby-red cherries (that's what they call coffee on the vine, because it's a fruit), and the air smells like a San Francisco espresso bar. The **Holuakoa Cafe** is a great place to get a freshly brewed cup.

To reach Holualoa, follow narrow, winding Hualalai Road up the hill from Hi. 19; it's about a 15-minute drive.

SOUTH KONA

The Painted Church. Hi. 19, Honaunau. ☎ **808/328-2227.**

Oh, those Belgian priests—what a talented lot. At the turn of the century, Father John Berchman Velghe borrowed a page from Michaelangelo and painted Biblical scenes inside St. Benedict's Catholic Church so the illiterate Hawaiians could visualize the white man's version of creation.

Puu Honua O Honaunau National Historical Park. Honaunau. ☎ **808/328-2288.** Admission $2. Visitor Center open daily 6am–5:30pm; park closes at midnight. From Kailua-Kona, take Hi. 11 to mile marker 104, turn right on Hi. 160, drive 3¹/₂ miles to park entrance.

With its fierce, haunting idols, this sacred site on the black lava Kona Coast looks forbidding. To ancient Hawaiians, however, it must have been a welcome sight, for Puu Honua O Honaunau served as a 16th-century place of refuge, providing sanctuary for defeated warriors and *kapu* (taboo) violators. A great rock wall—1,000 feet long, 10 feet high, and 17 feet thick—defines the refuge where Hawaiians found safety. On the wall's north end is Hale O Keawe Heiau, which holds the bones of 23 Hawaiian chiefs. Other archaeological finds include burial sites, old trails, and a portion of an ancient village. The National Park Service, when it took over this site in 1961, restored it to its precontact state. On a self-guided tour of the 180-acre site, you can see and learn about reconstructed thatched huts, canoes, and idols, and feel the *mana* (power) of old Hawaii.

A cultural festival, usually held in June, invites visitors to join in games, learn crafts, sample Hawaiian food, see traditional hula, and experience life in the islands before outsiders arrived in the late 1700s. Every Labor Day weekend, one of Hawaii's major outrigger canoe races starts here and ends in Kailua-Kona, 18 miles away. Call for details on both events.

Kona Historical Society Museum. On Hi. 11, between mile markers 11 and 12, Kealakekua. ☎ **808/323-3222.** Mon–Fri 8am–3pm. Admission $2.

This well-organized pocket museum tells the story of this fabled coast with artifacts and photos. It also offers history walks of Kailua Village and the historic Uchida Coffee Farm (see "Orientation & Adventure Tours," above).

THE KOHALA COAST

Kohala Coast Petroglyphs

At first glance, the huge slate of pahoehoe looks like any other smooth black slate of lava on the seacoast of the Big Island of Hawaii—until gradually, in slanting rays of the sun, a wonderful cast of characters suddenly leaps to life before your eyes. You see dancers and paddlers, fishermen and chiefs, hundreds of marchers all in a row.

North Kohala & the Kohala Coast

Everywhere, there are pictures of the tools of daily life: fish hooks, spears, poi pounders, canoes. Most common are family groups: father, mother, and child. There are post-European contact petroglyphs of ships, anchors, goats, horses, and guns.

The Hawaiian petroglyph is a great enigma of the Pacific. No one knows who made them or why, only that they're here: hard physical evidence that early Hawaiians were gifted illustrators of their life and times. Petroglyphs appear at 135 different sites on six inhabited islands, but most of them are found on the Big Island of Hawaii.

More than 3,000 petroglyphs, the largest concentration of stone symbols in the Pacific, lie within 233-acre **Puako Petroglyph Archaeological District,** near Mauna Lani Resort. Once hard to find, the enigmatic graffiti is now easily reachable, at the end of a 1.4-mile coastal walk through a keawe forest. Go in early morning or late afternoon when it's cool. Look for paddlers, sails, marchers, dancers, and family groups, as well as dog, chicken, turtle, and Lono symbols. A path at the end of Mauna Lani Resort's North Kaniku Drive leads to the petroglyphs. Take Hi. 19 to the resort turnoff, drive toward the coast on Kaniku Drive, which ends at a parking lot; the trailhead is marked by a sign and interpretive kiosk.

At the **Royal Waikoloan** (☎ **808/885-6789**) is the King's Trail, an ancient footpath by the sea that leads to a place, out by the golf course, where the black lava swirls into a flat tablet. There, early Hawaiians etched and pecked symbols that now offer faint clues to what they were thinking. The rock art of the Royal Waikoloan is especially graphic and easy to see along its handy, well-marked trail.

Puukohola Heiau National Historic Site. Hi. 270, Near Kawaihae Harbor. ☎ **808/ 882-7218.** Admission free; $1 per person for guided tour. Daily 7:30am–4pm.

This seacoast temple, called "the hill of the whale," was the last major religious struc-ture of the ancient Hawaiians, built by Kamehameha I in 1790–91. It stands 224 feet long by 100 feet wide, with three narrow terraces on the seaside and an amphithe-ater to view canoes. Kamehameha built this temple after a prophet told him he would conquer and unite the islands if he did. Four years later he fulfilled his kingly goal.

At the temple, the gods were called upon and human sacrifices were offered in hopes of rain to make crops grow on the arid Kohala Coast. The temple was attended from 1791 until 1819, a year before the American missionaries arrived in Honolulu. The 77-acre includes fishing shrines, women's shrines, and, offshore, the submerged ruins of Hale O Ka Puni, the only shrine dedicated to shark gods.

The Puukohola Visitor Center is right on Hi. 270; the heiau itself is a short walk away; but the trail's closed when it's too windy, so call ahead if you're in doubt.

NORTH KOHALA

The Original King Kamehameha Statue. Hi. 270, Kapaau.

King Kamehameha the Great stands, right arm outstretched, left arm holding a spear, as if guarding the senior citizens who have turned a century-old New England–style courthouse into an airy center for their golden years. The center is worth a stop just to meet the town elders, who are quick to point out the sites, hand you a free *Guide to Historic North Kohala,* and give you a brief tour of the courthouse, where a faded photo of FDR looms over the judge's dais and the walls are covered with the faces of innocent-looking local boys killed in World War II, Korea, and Vietnam.

But the statue's the main attraction here. There's one just like it in Honolulu, across the street from Iolani Palace, but this is the original: an 8-foot, 6-inch bronze statue by Thomas R. Gould, a Boston sculptor. It was cast in Europe in 1880, but was lost at sea in the Falkland Islands on its way to Hawaii. A sea captain eventu-ally recovered and delivered it; it was finally put here, near Kamehameha's Kohala birthplace, in 1912.

Kamehameha was born in 1750, became ruler of Hawaii in 1810, and died in Kailua-Kona in 1819. His burial site remains a mystery.

Pololu Valley Lookout. At the end of Hi. 270 in Makapala.

Glimpse the vertical jade-green cliffs of the Hamakua Coast and two islets offshore at this end-of-the-road scenic lookout, which may look familiar once you get here— it often appears on travel posters. Most people race up, jump out, take a snapshot, and turn around and drive off; but it's a beautiful scene, so linger if you can. For the more adventurous, a switchback trail leads to a secluded black-sand beach at the mouth of a wild valley once planted in taro; bring water and bug spray.

Lapakahi State Historical Park. Hi. 270, Mahukona. ☎ **808/889-5566.** Free admission. Daily 8am–4pm. Guided tours available by appointment.

This 14th-century fishing village, on a hot, dry, dusty stretch of coast, offers a glimpse into the lifestyle of the ancients. Lapakahi is the best preserved fishing village in Hawaii. Take the self-guided, mile-long loop trail past stone platforms, fish shrines, rock shelters, salt pans, and restored *hale* (houses) to a coral-sand beach and the deep blue sea. Wear good hiking shoes or tennies; it's a hearty 45-minute walk. Go early or later in the afternoon, as the sun is hot, shade is at a premium, and water is avail-able (an attendant in a thatch hut, who hands out maps, also keeps a handy cooler of ice water available in case you didn't bring your own).

Mookini Luakini. On the north shore, near Upolu Point and Airport.

On the Kohala Coast, where King Kamehameha the Great was born, stands Hawaii's oldest, largest, and most sacred religious site—the 1,500-year-old Mookini Heiau, used by kings to pray and offer human sacrifices. You need four-wheel drive to get here, as the road is rough, but it's worth the trip if you can make it. The massive three-story stone temple, dedicated to Ku, the Hawaiian god of war, was erected in A.D. 480. Each stone is said to have been passed hand-to-hand from Pololu Valley, 14 miles away, by 18,000 men who worked from sunset to sunrise. King Kamehameha, born nearby under Halley's Comet, sought spiritual guidance here before embarking on his campaign to unite Hawaii. The pre-Christian temple was designated a National Historical Landmark in 1963. Go in late afternoon when the setting sun strikes the lava rock walls and creates a primal mood.

WAIMEA (KAMUELA)

Kamuela Museum. At the junction of Hi. 19 and Hi. 250, Waimea. ☎ **808/885-4724.** Admission $5 adults, $2 children under 12. Daily 8am–5pm.

It only takes about an hour to explore tiny Kamuela Museum and its eclectic collection of stuff—including my favorites, an early Hawaiian dog-toothed death cup and a piece of rope used on the *Apollo* mission.

PARKER RANCH

Consider the numbers: 225,000 acres, 50,000 head of cattle, 700 miles of fence, 400 working horses, 27 cowboys; the ranch produces 80% of the beef marketed in Hawaii. It all began in 1809 when John Parker, a 19-year-old New England sailor, jumped ship and rounded up wild cows for King Kamehameha. The sailor put $10 down on a 2-acre site, which ultimately became the third largest ranch in America.

Since the death in 1992 of Richard Smart, the twice-married, sixth-generation heir who sought a career on Broadway (and danced with Nanette Fabray in *Bloomer Girl* at the Schubert Theater), the cowboy ranch has been managed by a corporation. Smart excluded his two sons from his will and left nearly all of his fortune to charity.

Today, a skeleton posse of 27 cowboys uses Japanese ATVs and helicopters to patrol Parker Ranch, Hawaii's biggest, where the *paniolo* (cowboy) tradition began—and lives on. There's some evidence that Hawaiian cowboys were the first to be taught by the great Spanish horsemen, the *vaqueros;* they were cowboying 40 years before their counterparts in California, Texas, and the Pacific Northwest.

The **visitor center** (Hi. 190, Waimea; ☎ **808/885-7655**); daily 9am–5pm) houses the **Parker Ranch Museum,** which has on display items that have been used throughout the ranch's 149-year history, and illustrates the 6 generations of Parker family history. A video presentation takes you inside the ranch and captures the essence of day-to-day life there.

You can also tour two historic homes on the ranch. In 1989, the late Richard Smart opened his 8,000-square-foot yellow Victorian home, **Puuopelu,** to art lovers, who discovered in the middle of this dusty cowboy ranch a French Regency gallery of 100 original works of French impressionists including Renoir, Degas, Dufy, Corot, Utrillo, and Pissarro. The collection can be seen along with Smart's other treasures, which include Venetian art, Chinese jade, and Beijing glass. Next door is **Mana Hale,** built 140 years ago, a little New England saltbox made out of koa wood.

Admission is $10 for the museum and tours of both homes; admission to the museum only is $5. If you're buying a dual ticket, the last ticket is sold at 3pm; if you're visiting the museum only, you can arrive until 4pm. Allow about 1 ¹/₂ hours to see everything. (See "Horseback Riding," above, for details on riding tours of Parker Ranch.)

MAUNA KEA

Some of us just have to be on top of things. If you do, head for the summit of Mauna Kea, the world's tallest mountain.

Mauna Kea's summit is the best place on earth for astronomical observations because its mid-Pacific site is near the equator, enjoys clear, pollution-free skies, and pitch-black nights with no urban light to interfere with the "seeing." Needless to say, the stargazing from here is fantastic, even with the naked eye. That's why Mauna Kea is home to the world's largest telescope.

Setting Out   You need four-wheel drive to make the drive to the peak, Observatory Hill, as you'll be climbing from sea level through 10 different climate zones to the alpine heights. A standard car will get you as far as the center, but check your rental agreement before you head out; some prohibit you from taking your car on the Saddle Road, which is narrow, rutted, and has a soft shoulder. For four-wheel drives, though, it's not a big deal.

Always check the weather and Mauna Kea Road conditions before you head out (☎ **808/969-3218**). Dress warmly, as the temps drop into the 30s after dark. Other tips for preparing for your drive to the summit: Drink as much liquid as possible, avoiding alcohol and coffee, in the 36 hours surrounding your trip to avoid dehydration. Don't go within 24 hours of scuba diving—you could get the bends. Avoid gas-producing food the day before like beans, cabbage, onions, soft drinks, or starches. If you smoke, take a break for 48 hours before to allow carbon monoxide in your bloodstream to dissipate—you need all the oxygen you can get. Wear dark sunglasses to avoid snow blindness and use lots of sunscreen and lip balm. Anyone under 16 is advised to stay below; the same caveat holds for anyone with a heart condition, lung ailment, or women who are pregnant.

Once you're at the top, don't overexert yourself; it's bad for your heart. I tried jogging, but had to stop after only a few steps. I felt old and feeble; every move seemed like slow motion. When I tried to change film in my camera, a simple automatic task, it took forever. There's nothing you can do about it—just know what to expect, and take it easy up there.

Access Points & Visitor Centers   Before you climb the mountain, you've got to find it. It's about an hour's drive from Hilo and Waimea. Take the Saddle Road (Hi. 200; also known as the Hawaii Belt Rd.); from Hi. 190, it's about 19 miles to Mauna Kea State Recreation Area, a good place to stop and stretch your legs. Go another 9 miles to the unmarked Summit Road turnoff, at the 28-mile marker. The higher you go, the more lightheaded you get, sometimes even dizzy; it usually sets in after the 9,600-foot marker (about 6 miles up), the last comfort zone and site of the **Onizuka Visitor Center** (☎ **808/961-2180;** open Mon 8am–noon, 1–3pm; Fri 1–5:30pm, 6:30–10:30pm; Sat–Sun 9am–10pm), named in memory of Hawaii's fallen astronaut, a native of the Big Island and a victim of the *Challenger* explosion.

Tours & Programs   If you'd rather not go it alone to the top, you can caravan up as part of a **free summit tour;** the tours, which are offered Saturday and Sunday at 2pm, start at the visitor center; you must be 16 years or older, and have a four-wheel drive vehicle. Call **808/935-3371** if you'd like to participate.

On Friday, Saturday, and Sunday nights from 6:30 to 10pm, you can do some some serious **stargazing from the Onizuka Visitor Center.** There's a free lecture at 7pm, and you'll have a chance to peer through an 11-inch telescope. Bring your own telescope or binoculars, if you've got 'em.

You can see a model of the world's largest telescope, which sits at the top of Mauna Kea, at the **Keck Control Center** in Waimea (65-1120 Mamalahoa Hwy. (Hi. 19), across from Lucy Henriques Medical Center; ☎ **808/885-7887;** Mon–Fri 8am– 4:30pm; free admission). Free brochures are available, and there's a 10-minute video explaining the Keck's mission: the search for objects in deep space.

Making the Climb   If you're heading up on your own, stop at the visitor center for about a half-hour to get acquainted with the altitude, walk around, eat a banana, drink lots of water, and take deep breaths of the crystal-clear air before you press on, upward in low gear, engine whining. It takes about 30 to 45 minutes to get to the top from there. It's a mere 6 miles, but you climb from 9,000 to 14,000 feet.

At the Summit   Up there 11 nations, including Japan, France, and Canada, have set up peerless infrared telescopes to look into deep space, searching the black holes and far-flung galaxies for signs of life. Among them sits the **Keck Telescope,** the world's largest. Developed by the UC Berkeley and CalTech, it's eight stories high, weighs 150 tons, and has 33-foot diameter mirror made of 36 perfectly attuned hexagon mirrors, like a fly's eye, instead of one conventional lens.

Also at the summit, up a narrow footpath, is a cairn of rocks; from it, you can see forever across the Pacific Ocean in a 360° view that's beyond words and pictures. When its socked in (and that can happen while you're standing there), you get a surreal look at the summits of Mauna Loa and Maui's Haleakala poking through puffy the white cumulus clouds beneath your feet.

Inside a cinder cone just below the summit is **Lake Waiau,** the only glacial lake in the mid-Pacific and the third highest lake in America (13,020 ft. above sea level). The lake never dries up even though it sits in porous lava where there are no springs and it only rains 15 inches a year. Nobody except "Ripley's Believe it Or Not" quite knows what to make of this, although scientists suspect the lake is replenished by snow melt and permafrost from submerged lava tubes. You can't see the lake from Summit Road; you must take a brief, high-altitude hike to see it, but it's an easy hike: On the final approach to the summit area, upon regaining the blacktop road, go about 200 yards to the major switchback, and make a hard right turn. Park on the shoulder of the road (which, if you brought your altimeter, is at 13,200 ft.). No sign points the way to the lake, but there's an obvious half-mile trail that goes down to it about 200 feet across the lava. Follow the base of the big cinder cone on your left; you should have the summit of Mauna Loa in view directly ahead as you walk.

THE HAMAKUA COAST
NATURAL WONDERS ALONG THE COAST

Akaka Falls. On Hi. 19, 8 miles north of Hilo. Turn left at Honomu and head 3.6 miles inland on Akaka Falls Rd. (Hi. 220).

One of Hawaii's most scenic waterfalls is an easy 1-mile paved loop through a rain forest, past bamboo and ginger and down to an observation point, where you'll have a perfect view of 442-foot Akaka and nearby Kahuna Falls, a mere 100-footer.

Hawaii Tropical Botanical Garden. Hi. 19, Onomea Bay (7 miles north of Hilo). ☎ **808/ 964-5233.** Daily 8:30am–5:30pm. Admission $15 adults, children under 16 free; includes van shuttle to and from Onomea Valley.

More than 1,800 species of tropical plants thrive in this little-known Eden-by-the-sea. The 40-acre garden, nestled between the crashing surf and a thundering waterfall, has the world's largest selection of tropical plants growing in a natural environment, including a torch ginger forest, a banyan canyon, an orchid garden, a banana grove, a bromeliad hill, and a golden bamboo grove, which rattles like a jungle drum in the trade winds. The torch gingers give new meaning to their name, towering as they do on 12-foot stalks. Each spectacular specimen is named by genus and species, and caretakers point out new or rare buds in bloom. Some endangered Hawaiian specimens, like the rare Gardenia remyi, are flourishing in this habitat.

What I like best about this place is that it's seldom crowded; you can wander around by yourself all day, taking pictures, making notes, or just soaking up the natural tranquility. It's so quiet you can almost hear the plants grow. And, no matter how often you visit, it's always different.

Laupahoehoe Beach Park. Laupahoehoe Point exit off Hi. 19.

This idyllic place holds a grim reminder of nature's fury. In 1946, a tidal wave swept across the village that once stood on this lava-leaf (that's what "laupahoehoe" means) peninsula and claimed the lives of 20 students and four teachers. A memorial recalls the tragedy in this pretty little park, where the land ends in black seastacks that remind me of tombstones. It's not a place for swimming, but the views are spectacular.

HONOKAA

Worth a visit to see the remnants of plantation life when sugar was king, Honokaa is a real place that hasn't yet been boutiqued into a shopping mall; it looks as if someone has kept it in a bell jar since 1920. There's a real barber shop, a real Filipino store, some really good shopping (see "Shops & Galleries," below), and a real hotel with creaky floorboards that serves real hearty food. It also serves as the gateway to spectacular Waipio Valley (see below).

Honokaa has no attractions, per se, but you might want to check out the **Katsu Goto Memorial,** next to the library at the Hilo end of town. Katsu Goto, one of the first indentured Japanese immigrants, arrived in Honokaa in the late 1800s to work in the sugar plantations. He learned English, quit the plantation, and aided his fellow immigrants in labor disputes with American planters. On Oct. 23, 1889, he was hanged from a lamppost in Honokaa, a victim of local-style justice. Today, a memorial recalls Goto's heroic human rights struggle.

THE END OF THE ROAD: WAIPIO VALLEY

Long ago, this lush tropical place was the valley of kings, who called it the valley of "curving water" (which is what Waipio means). From the black-sand bay at its mouth, Waipio sweeps back 6 miles between sheer, cathedral-like walls that reach almost a mile high. Here, 40,000 Hawaiians lived in a garden of Eden etched by streams and waterfalls amid evergreen taro, red bananas, and wild guavas. Only about 50 Hawaiians live in the valley today, tending taro, fishing, and soaking up the ambiance of this old Hawaiian place.

A sacred place, many of the ancient royals are buried in Wapio's hidden crevices; some believe they rise up to become Marchers of the Night, whose chants reverberate through the valley. It's here that the caskets of Hawaiian chiefs Liloa and Lono Ika Makahiki, recently stolen from Bishop Museum, are believed to have been returned by Hawaiians. The valley is steeped in myth and legend, some of which you may hear, usually after dark in the company of Hawaiian elders who sometimes tell about Nenewe the Shark Man, who lives in a pool, and the ghost of the underworld, who periodically rises to the surface through a tunnel by the sea.

To get to Waipio Valley, take Hi. 19 from Hilo to Honokaa, then Hi. 240 to ✪ **Waipio Valley Lookout,** a grassy park on the edge of Waipio Valley's sheer cliffs with splendid views of the wild oasis below. This is one of my favorite places to open

Hilo

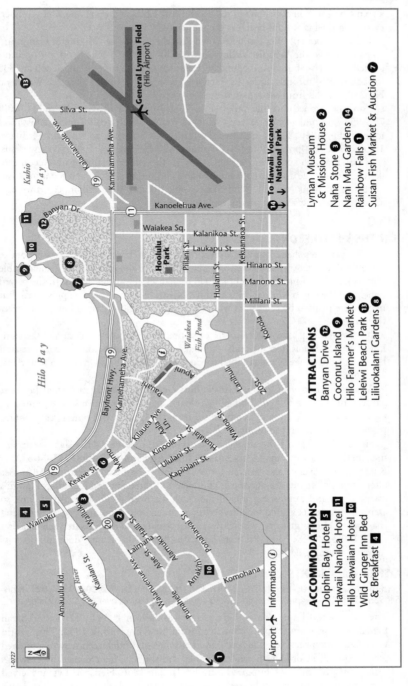

ATTRACTIONS
Banyan Drive **12**
Coconut Island **9**
Hilo Farmer's Market **6**
Leleiwi Beach Park **13**
Liliuokalani Gardens **8**

Lyman Museum
& Mission House **2**
Naha Stone **3**
Nani Mau Gardens **14**
Rainbow Falls **1**
Suisan Fish Market & Auction **7**

ACCOMMODATIONS
Dolphin Bay Hotel **5**
Hawaii Naniloa Hotel **11**
Hilo Hawaiian Hotel **10**
Wild Ginger Inn Bed
& Breakfast **4**

Airport ✈ Information ⓘ

General Lyman Field
(Hilo Airport)

To Hawaii Volcanoes
National Park

Kuhio
Bay

Hilo Bay

Silva St.

Kalanianaole Ave.

Kamehameha Ave.

Banyan Dr.

Kanoelehua Ave.

Waiakea Sq.

Kalanikoa St.

Laukapu St.

Hinano St.

Manono St.

Mililani St.

Kekuanaoa St.

Pilani St.

Hualani St.

Hoolulu
Park

Waiakea
Fish Pond

Koholo St.

Kamani

Punahoa

Bayfront Hwy.

Kamehameha Ave.

Kilauea Ave.

Aala St.

Kinoole St.

Hualalai St.

Ululani St.

Kapiolani St.

Mamo

Keawe St.

Waianuenue Ave.

Alae St.

Laimana St.

Alamuku

Punahele

Kaiulani St.

Wailuku River

Wailuku

Amauulu Rd.

Wainaku

Amakihi

Komohana

Ponahawai St.

Wainea St.

Lanihuli

Kohoalu

253

a picnic basket. You can sit at old redwood picnic tables and watch the white combers race upon the black-sand beach at the mouth of Waipio Valley.

From the lookout, you can hike down into the valley (see "Hiking & Camping," above), or take the **Waipio Valley Shuttle** (☎ 808/775-7121) on a 90-minute guided tour. The shuttle runs Monday to Saturday from 9am to 4pm; tickets are $35 for adults, $14 for kids under 11. Get your tickets at Waipio Valley Art Works on Hi. 240, 2 miles from the lookout.

You can also explore the valley on a **Waipio Valley Wagon Tour** (☎ 808/775-9518), a mule-drawn surrey that takes you on a narrated 90-minute historical tour of the valley. Tours are offered Monday to Saturday at 9:30am, 11:30am, 1:30pm, and 3:30pm; they're $40 for adults, $20 for children. Call for reservations.

If you want to spend more than a day in the valley, plan ahead: Accommodations are simple and sparse in the valley, and require advance reservations (see "Accommodations," above). While it's possible to camp (see "Hiking & Camping," above), it does put a strain on the ecology.

HILO
ON THE WATERFRONT

Old Banyan trees shade **Banyan Drive,** the lane that curves along the waterfront to the Hilo Bay hotels. Most of the trees were planted in the mid-1930s by memorable visitors like Babe Ruth (in front of Hilo Hawaiian Hotel), Leo Carrillo, Jr. (he played Pancho to the Cisco Kid), and Richard M. Nixon (before he became president), but many were planted by celebrities whose fleeting fame didn't last as long as the trees themselves.

It's worth a stop along Banyan Drive—especially if the coast is clear and the summit of Mauna Kea is free of clouds—to make the short walk across the concrete arch bridge in front of the Naniloa Hotel to **Coconut Island,** if only to gain a panoramic sense of place.

Also along Banyan Drive is **Liluokalani Gardens,** the largest formal Japanese garden this side of Tokyo. This 30-acre park, named for Hawaii's last monarch, Queen Liluokalani, is pretty as a postcard from the Orient with bonsai, carp ponds, pagodas, and a moon gate bridge.

Since 1914, Hilo fishermen have delivered the catch of the day, fresh ahi, mahimahi, and opakapaka, to **Suisan Fish Auction** (☎ 808/935-8051), at Kamehameha Avenue and Banyan Drive. The boats return to harbor just at sunrise after fishing all night; the auction is conducted in three lingoes, including Hawaii's own pidgin, and can last an hour if the catch has been good. It begins at 8am, so arrive at 7am to get a good look as the fishers unload the boats and get ready to send the fish to chefs, grocers, wholesalers, and retailers. The **Suisan Fish Market** (☎ 808/935-9349; Mon–Fri 8am–5pm, Sat 8am–4pm) is next door, if you miss the early-morning action.

OTHER HILO SIGHTS

Lyman Museum & Mission House. 276 Haili St. (at Kapiolani St.). ☎ 808/935-5021. Mon–Sat 9am–5pm, Sun 1–4pm. Admission $4.50 adults, $2.50 seniors over 60, $2.50 children.

The oldest wood-frame house on the island was built in 1839 by David and Sarah Lyman, a missionary couple who arrived from New England in 1832. This hybrid Cape Cod combined New England– and Hawaiian-style architecture with a pitched thatch roof. Built of hand-hewn koa planks and timbers, it's crowned by Hawaii's first corrugated zinc roof, imported from England in 1856. Here, the Lymans served as the spiritual center of Hilo, receiving such guests as Mark Twain, Robert Louis Stevenson, and Hawaii's own curious monarchs.

Opened as a museum in 1931, the well-preserved house is the best example of missionary life and times in Hawaii. Next door, the **Island Heritage Museum** continues the story of the islands with exhibits ranging from poi pounders to sea shells.

Naha Stone. In front of Hilo Public Library, 300 Waianuenue Ave.

This 2^1/$_2$-ton stone was used as a test of royal strength: Ancient legend says that whoever could move the stone would conquer and unite the islands; as a 14-year-old boy, King Kamehameha the Great moved the stone—and fulfilled his destiny. The **Pinao stone,** next to it, once guarded an ancient heiau.

Nani Mau Gardens. 421 Makalika St. (3 miles south of Hilo Airport on Hi. 11). ☎ **808/ 959-3541.** Daily 8am–5pm. Admission $6.50 adults, $6 seniors, $4 children 6–18. Tram tours $4 more. Reservations required for parties of 5 or more.

Just outside Hilo is Nani Mau Gardens, where Makato Nitahara, who turned a 20-acre papaya patch into a tropical garden, claims to have every flowering plant in Hawaii. That's more than 2,000 varieties, from fragile hibiscus, whose boom lasts only a day, to durable red anthuriums imported from South America.

Rainbow Falls. West on Waianuenue Ave., past Kaumana Dr.

Go early in the morning, just as the sun comes over the mango trees, to see Rainbow Falls at its best; the 80 falls spill into a big round natural pool surrounded by wild ginger. If you like legends, try this: Hina, the mother of Maui, lives in the cave behind the falls. In the old days, before liability suits and lawyers, people swam in the pool, but it's now prohibited.

ON THE ROAD TO THE VOLCANO
VOLCANO VILLAGE: GATEWAY TO HAWAII VOLCANOES NATIONAL PARK

In the 19th century, before tourism became Hawaii's middle name, the islands' singular attraction for world travelers wasn't the beach, but the volcano. From the world over, curious spectators gathered on the rim of Kilauea's Halemaumau crater to see one of the greatest wonders of the globe. Those who came to stand in awe took shelter after sundown in a large grass hut perched on the rim of Kilauea—Hawaii's first tourist hotel, which became **Volcano House** (see "Accommodations," above).

Since Kilauea and environs were officially designated Hawaii Volcanoes National Park in 1917, a village has popped up at its front door. Not even a real town, Volcano is just a wide spot in Old Volcano Road, a 10-block area with two general stores, a post office, and a new firehouse, built in 1 weekend by volunteers. Volcano has no stoplights, no school or jail, and neither church nor cemetery (but there is a winery). There's not even a baseball diamond, which is probably just as well since it rains a lot in Volcano—100 inches a year—which makes everything grow Jack-and-the-Beanstalk–style. If Volcano didn't have a real volcano in its backyard, it would probably be called Rain Forest.

Geographically speaking, Volcano isn't actually the gateway to Hawaii Volcanoes National Park; it's really a little off to the side and north. Hi. 11, the Hawaii Belt Road, which leads directly to the park, bypasses Volcano village. But if you're going to see the volcano, Volcano is a great place to spend a few days—in fact, it's the only place (see "Accommodations").

Even if you're just visiting the park for the day, it's worth turning off to stop for gas at **Volcano General Store,** on Haunani Road, where kindly clerks give directions and sell fresh orchid sprays, local poha berry jam, and bowls of chili rice, a local favorite. The dining room at **Kilauea Lodge** (see "Dining," above) is the immediate area's only restaurant; the fresh ohelo berry pies are a rare treat.

Volcano Winery, off Hi. 11 at the end of Volcano Golf Course Road (☎ **808/ 967-7479**) is worth a stop to taste the local wines, pressed from hybrid grapes from California. Lift a glass of Volcano Blush or Passion Star Chablis and toast Madame Pele at this boutique winery, founded by a big-animal vet–turned–wine maker who imported grapes developed by the University of California at Davis and planted them on the slopes of Mauna Loa. Open daily 10am to 5pm; tastings are free.

APPROACHING THE PARK FROM THE SOUTH: CROSSING THE KAU DESERT

Badland, lava land, hot, scorched, quake-shaken bubbling up new/dead land: This is the great Kau Desert, layer upon layer of lava flows, of which only those in recent history have been recorded—1790, 1880, 1920, 1926, 1950, 1969, 1971, 1974. The dates draw closer in time the farther you go across the desert, crossing the Great Crack and the Southwest Rift Zone, a major fault zone that looks like a giant groove in the earth, onward to Kilauea Volcano, which created all this desert.

After miles of sad blackness under heartbreak blue sky, there's a sign by the side of the two-lane road, on Hi. 11 between mile markers 37 and 38, that tells you matter-of-factly of the footprints out there in the lava. There's a trailhead, so you stop to crunch across old a'a and pahoehoe to see the evidence of misadventure in the desert. Almost a mile across the frozen-stiff 1790 flow, there they are: Whose? Why? How? Flashback to 1790: King Kamehameha wages war to gain control of Hawaii. Opposing forces led by Keoua attempt to cross the desert. Kilauea Volcano erupts, killing 80 warriors—dead in their tracks—as you can readily see at this ghoulish roadside attraction. Keoua, who took it as a sign from the gods, surrendered to Kamehameha and was later sacrificed at the temple. Something to think about as you continue on deeper across the great Kau Desert toward still bubbling Kilauea Volcano, which rearranges not only the landscape but the course of history.

HAWAII VOLCANOES NATIONAL PARK

I've been to Yellowstone and Yosemite and other national parks, and they're spectacular, all right; but they're all ho-hum compared to this one: Here, nothing less than the miracle of creation is the daily attraction.

But this is no Eden—instead, you'll think you've arrived in hell. All the legendary elements are here: fire and brimstone, whiffs of sulfur, eye-stinging plumes of smoke, red-hot burning lava, and miles of scorched black earth. Only the devil himself seems to be absent from this otherworldly place. At the center of the 250,000-acre park is a volcano, Kilauea, going off at this very moment, destroying whatever stands in the way of its fiery progress—and, at the same time, creating the newest land on Earth. It began erupting for the 27th time since 1920 in 1983, and it shows no sign of abating.

Founded in 1916, Hawaii Volcanoes National Park is Hawaii's premier natural attraction. Most people drive through the park (it has 45 miles of good roads, some of them often covered by lava flows) and call it a day. But it takes at least 3 days to explore the park fully, including such oddities as Halemaumau Crater, a still simmering pit of fire; the intestinal-looking Thurston Lava Tube; Devastation Trail, a short hike through hell right next to an Eden-like rain forest; and finally, the end of Chain of Craters Road, where lava regularly spills across the man-made two-lane blacktop to create its own red-hot freeway to the sea. In addition to some of the world's weirdest landscape, the park also has hiking trails, rain forests, campgrounds, a historic old hotel on a crater's rim, and a unique poetic vocabulary that describes in Hawaiian words what otherwise is impossible in English.

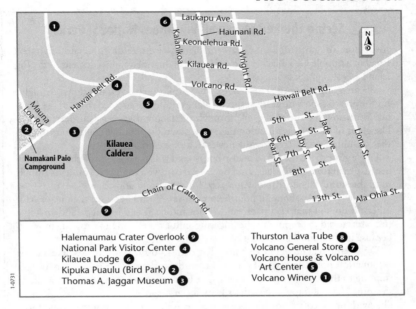

Halemaumau Crater Overlook **9**
National Park Visitor Center **4**
Kilauea Lodge **6**
Kipuka Puaulu (Bird Park) **2**
Thomas A. Jaggar Museum **3**

Thurston Lava Tube **8**
Volcano General Store **7**
Volcano House & Volcano
Art Center **5**
Volcano Winery **1**

Volcano Vocabulary   The lava that looks like swirls of chocolate cake frosting is called *pahoehoe,* which results from a slow-moving flow that curls artistically as it flows. The big, blocky, jumbled lava that looks like a chopped-up parking lot is called *a'a.* It's caused by lava that runs so fast that it overruns itself. You also may hear the words "vog" and "laze." *Vog* is volcanic smog made of volcanic gases and smoke from forests set on fire by a'a and pahoehoe. Vog stings your eyes and can cause respiratory illness; don't subject yourself to it for too long. *Laze* results when sulfuric acid hits the water and vaporizes and mixes with chlorine to become, as any chemistry major knows, hydrochloric acid. Stay upwind of laze.

In Hawaii, volcanoes aren't the violent pyroclastic killers like Mount Pinatubo in the Philippines or even Mount St. Helens in Oregon. Vulcanologists refer to Hawaii's volcanic eruptions as "quiet" eruptions, since gases escape slowly instead of building up and exploding violently all at once. What that means is slow-moving, Jell-O–like oozing lava that provides excellent, safe viewing most of the time. In Hawaii, people run to volcanoes instead of fleeing from them.

JUST THE FACTS

When to Go   The best time to go is when Kilauea is really pumping. You may be lucky and be in the park when the volcano is really active and fountaining; mostly, the lava runs like a red river downslope into the sea. If you're on another island and hear a TV news bulletin that the volcano is acting up, catch the next flight to Hilo to see the spectacle. You won't be sorry. Your favorite beach'll still be there when you get back.

Access Points   Hawaii Volcanoes National Park is 29 miles from Hilo, on Hawaii Belt Road (Hi. 11). If you're staying in Kailua-Kona, it's 100 miles, or about a 2¹/₂-hour drive, to the park. Admission is $5 per vehicle; you can come and go as often as you want for 7 days. Hikers and bicyclists pay $3; bikes are only allowed on roads and paved trails.

Seeing the Red at Hawaii Volcanoes National Park

Just before the hot tropic sun quits for the day, we race down Chain of Craters Road in a nimble Geo Tracker through fields of black lava, on a descent to the Big Island's "volcano coast."

We are gong to see the red—that's what I call the live volcano show. At night, it's the greatest show on earth: a spectacular explosion of fire; red rivers of fire flowing just below the surface, visible through the fissures between your feet; Jell-O–like globs of molten lava inching their way down the mountain and pouring into the steaming Pacific, creating the newest land on earth.

I have gone to see the red so many times—and will go again, every chance I get—because each time is different. And once you see it, you can't tear your eyes from it until the sulfur literally drives you away. It's downright addictive.

Usually I go just about an hour before sunset, always in a hurry, alone or with others, it doesn't matter. I pack sandwiches and beer, and a banana and an apple (for later, to rid my mouth of the lingering sulfur taste), plus an extra jug of water because it's hot out there on the lava, even after dark.

We see the telltale plume of smog that rises 1,000 feet in the sky, like a giant exclamation point, and speed on. As I scan downslope, I see ruby rivers of lava running to the sea. We come to a halt: The two-lane blacktop ends under a pile of steaming black plumpy stuff with a silvery sheen—hardened *pahoehoe* lava. It looks like swirls of chocolate frosting. We arrive just as the sun hits the horizon and turns this hellish landscape into God's land, with sunbeams radiating against virgin pink clouds. And the best is still to come.

Tonight, the glow on the mountain is like a distant forest fire. The first step onto the hardened lava is scary. It crunches like crushed glass under the heels of my hiking boots. I can see a red road map of molten lava glowing in the cracks and flowing in fiery rivulets about a foot below the surface. And there's still a nervous mile-long walk ahead, in pitch-black darkness, to the intersection of lava and sea—but it's a walk that I know is worth the trouble.

Silhouettes against the fire, we stand at the edge of the earth like primal natives witnessing the schizophrenic act of creation and destruction. The lave hisses and spits and crackles as it moves, snakelike, in its perpetual flow to the sea, dripping like candle wax into the wavy surf. Fire and water, the very stuff of islands: The lava still burns underwater until the ocean, the vast Pacific Ocean, finally douses the fire and transforms it into yet more black-sand beach.

At the turn of the century, folks used to singe postcards and send them home to disbelieving friends. Today, most people, I've noticed, try to douse the lava with bottled water, but it vaporizes instantly—that's what 2,500°F will do. I know a man in Hilo who drops silver dollars in the path of the lava, then retrieves them, lava and all; they cool and harden into paperweights. I like to toast ballpark franks on a long kiawe stick—smokes 'em fast, from the inside out.

Information and Visitor Centers   For information before you go, contact Hawaii Volcanoes National Park, P.O. Box 52, Hawaii National Park, HI 96718 (☎ 808/967-7184). **Kilauea Visitor Center** is at the entrance of the park, just off Hi. 11, 29 miles from Hilo. It's open daily from 7:45am to 5pm.

For the latest eruption update and information on volcanic activity in the park, call the park's 24-hour hot line: **808/967-7977.** Updates on volcanic activity are also posted daily on the bulletin board at the visitor center.

Hawaii Volcanoes National Park

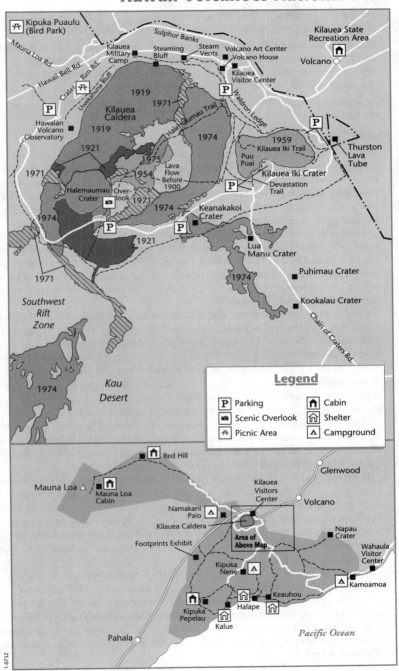

Kipuka Puaulu (Bird Park)
Mauna Loa Rd.
Hawaii Belt Rd.
Craters Rim Rd.
Uwekahuna Bluff
Sulphur Banks
Kilauea Military Camp
Steaming Bluff
Steam Vents
Volcano Art Center
Volcano House
Kilauea Visitor Center
Kilauea State Recreation Area
Volcano
1919
1971
Kilauea Caldera
1919
Hawaiian Volcano Observatory
1921
1975
1954
1971
Halemaumau Trail
1974
1959
Kilauea Iki Trail
Puu Puai
Kilauea Iki Crater
Devastation Trail
Thurston Lava Tube
Halemaumau Crater
Over-look
Lava Flow Before 1900
1971
1974
1971
1974
Keanakakoi Crater
1921
Lua Manu Crater
1974
Puhimau Crater
Kookalau Crater
1971
Southwest Rift Zone
Chain of Craters Rd.
1974
Kau Desert

Legend

P	Parking	Cabin
Scenic Overlook		Shelter
Picnic Area		Campground

Red Hill
Mauna Loa
Mauna Loa Cabin
Glenwood
Kilauea Visitors Center
Volcano
Namakani Paio
Kilauea Caldera
Area of Above Map
Napau Crater
Footprints Exhibit
Wahaula Visitor Center
Kipuka Nene
Keauhou
Kamoamoa
Kipuka Pepelau
Halape
Kalue
Pahala
Pacific Ocean

1-0732

Hiking and Camping in the Park   Hawaii Volcanoes National Park offers a wealth of hiking and camping possibilities. See "Hiking & Camping," above, for details.

Accommodations In & Around the Park   If camping isn't your thing, don't worry. In addition to historic Volcano House, on the rim of Halemaumau crater, adjacent Volcano village has plenty of comfortable and convenient places to stay; see "Accommodations," above.

Emergencies   Call **808/967-7311** around the clock if you have an emergency in the park.

SEEING THE HIGHLIGHTS

Your first stop should be **Kilauea Visitor Center,** a rustic parklike structure in a shady grove of trees just inside the entrance to the park. Here you can get up-to-the-minute reports on the volcano's activity, learn how volcanoes work, see a film showing blasts from the past, get information on hiking and camping, and pick up the obligatory postcards, taken by some great photographers who risked their lives on the lava to capture the awesome fury of a live volcano.

Filled with a new understanding of vulcanology and Madame Pele, walk across the street to **Volcano House;** go through the lobby and out the other side, where you can have a good look at **Halemaumau Crater,** a 3-mile-wide, 1,000-foot-deep pit, once known as one of "the greatest wonders of the globe." The bubbling pit of hellfire's out now, but you can see wisps of steam that could, while you're standing there, turn into something more.

Now, get out on the highway and drive by the **Sulphur Banks,** which smell like rotten eggs, and the **Steam Vents** (no big deal). Stop at the **Thomas A. Jaggar Jr. Museum** (☎ **808/967-7643;** open daily 8:30am–5pm; free admission) for a good look at Halemaumau and (maybe) Mauna Loa, 20 miles to the west. Jaggar Museum, named for the MIT scientist who founded Hawaiian Volcano Observatory in 1912, shows eruption videos, explains the Pele legend in murals, and monitors earthquakes (a precursor of eruptions) on a seismograph. For some reason, I can't keep my eyes off the seismograph, and I always get goose bumps when it twitches.

Once you've seen everything at the museum, drive around the crater to the other side, park, and take the short walk to the edge, past stinky sulphur banks and steam vents, to stand at the overlook and stare in awe at this once-fuming and bubbling old fire-pit, which still generates ferocious heat out of vestigial vents.

If feel the need to cool off now, go to the **Thurston Lava Tube,** the coolest place in the park. You'll hike down into a natural bowl in the earth, called a *kipuka*—a forest preserve the lava didn't touch—full of native birdsongs and giant tree ferns. You'll see a black hole in the earth; step in. It's all drippy and cool, with bare roots hanging down. You can either resurface into the bright daylight, or poke on deeper into the tube, which is supposed to go for another mile or so—nobody I know has even been there and back.

If you're still game for a good hike, try **Ke Iki Crater,** a hot 3-hour hike across the floor of the crater, which became a bubbling pool of lava in 1959 and sent fountains of lava 1,900 feet in the air, completely devastating a nearby ohia forest and leaving another popular hike ominously known as **Devastation Trail.** The half-mile walk is like being reduced to miniature and forced to hike across the inside of your Weber barbecue. (See pp. 234–236 in "Hiking & Camping" for details on these and other park hikes).

Now, take the rest of the day off. You can kick back wherever you're staying (see "Accommodations," above; I like Carson's historic cottage), have dinner, and, about an hour before sunset, head back into the park and 23 miles down **Chain of**

Craters Road. Get ready to see the red—that's what I call Madame Pele's nightly fireworks (see box above). It's a vivid display you'll never forget. At the barricades, hike into the current site of the lava flow. Take water and a flashlight and wear sturdy shoes.

SOUTH POINT: LAND'S END

The history of Hawaii is condensed here, at the end of 11 miles of bad road that peters out at Kaulana Bay, in the lee of a jagged black lava point—the tail end of the United States. This Plymouth Rock of Hawaii is a kind of open-faced midden, littered by layers of stuff left by successive conquerors. There are old Japanese truck farms, abandoned World War II military barracks, a deserted Pacific Missile Tracking site, a Mitsubishi wind farm (with 38 spinning propellers), rusty junk cars made in Detroit, and herds of fat cattle on leasehold land held in trust by descendants of New England missionaries. And amid the debris on this windswept point stands a reminder of the lost kingdom, a poignant sculpture of a Hawaiian man bound in chains.

No historic marker marks the spot or gives any clue as to the significance of the place. If you walk out to the very tip, beware of the big waves that lash the shore. The nearest continental landfall is Antarctica, 7,500 miles away.

It's a 2^1/$_2$-mile four-wheel drive and a hike down a cliff from South Point to the anomaly known as **Green Sand Beach** (see "Beaches," above). If you'd rather not go on your own, a tour company operating out of Naahelu will be happy to take you down; see "Orientation & Adventure Tours," above.

12 Shops & Galleries

by Jocelyn Fujii

Although the visual arts are flourishing on the Big Island, the line between shop and gallery is often too fine to define, or even to approach. Too many self-proclaimed "galleries" purvey schlock, or a mixture of art, craft, and tacky souvenirs. The result is an amalgam of items for the home, gifts to go, jewelry and accessories, interior accents, and all manner of accoutrements at various prices and levels of taste and quality. The galleries and shops below offer a broad mix in many media, but you'll find that bowls made of rare native woods such as *koa* are especially abundant on this island. This is an area in which politics and art intersect: Although reforestation efforts are underway to plant new koa trees, the decline of old-growth forests is causing many artists to turn to equally beautiful, and more environmentally correct, alternative woods.

THE KONA COAST

KAILUA-KONA

Kailua-Kona's shopping prospects pour out into the streets in a festival atmosphere of T-shirts, trinkets, and dime-a-dozen souvenirs, with Alii Drive at the center of this activity. **Kona Square,** across from **King Kamehameha's Kona Beach Hotel;** the hotel's shopping mall, with close to 2 dozen shops, including a Liberty House; and the **Kona Inn Shopping Village** on Alii Drive all include shops galore for vacationers' needs, but be forewarned: The going can be rocky for those with seriously refined tastes. In Kailua-Kona, tacky is king—so set your shopping expectations accordingly.

Just Looking

The finest art on the Kona Coast hangs, of all places, in a bank. Award-winning **First Hawaiian Bank,** 74-5593 Palani Rd. (☎ **808/329-2461**), has art lovers making special trips to view Hiroki Morinoue's mural, John Buck's prints, Chiu Leong's ceramic sculpture, Franco Salmoiraghi's photographs, Setsuko Morinoue's abstract fiber wall-piece, and other works that were incorporated as part of the bank's design, rather than added on as an afterthought. Artists Yvonne Cheng and Sharon Carter Smith, whose works are included, assembled this exhibition, which is destined to achieve immortality as a sterling example of corporate sponsorship of the arts.

Hobie Hawaii. Kona Inn Shopping Village. ☎ **808/329-1001.**

No tourist town would be complete without a Hobie Hawaii. Towels, visors, body boards, flip-flops, sunglasses, swimsuits, and everything else you need for ocean and shore action—including sunscreens of every ilk, a must in the west Hawaii sun—can be found at Hobie, a chain of formula shops devoted to sun and surf.

✪ **Hula Heaven.** Kona Inn Shopping Village. ☎ **808/329-7885.**

With its devoted islandwide following (collectors fly in from the neighbor islands to shop here), Hula Heaven is a must—the best place for men's and women's clothing and vintage Hawaiiana. Owners Gwen and Evan Olins are passionate collectors whose shop spills over with 1920s to 1950s collectibles: hula girl lamps, out-of-print books, John Kelly prints, Don Blanding dinnerware, Mundorff prints, Matson liner menus, vintage ukuleles and guitars, and aloha shirts for both the serious collector and the casual wearer. Gwen's fondness for textiles is reflected in the window displays, which often feature one-of-a-kind 1940s fabrics, and on the racks, where traditional tea-timer tops and muumuus in spirited old prints mingle with new clothing in faithfully reproduced fabrics. Hula Heaven has the island's largest and best collection of vintage aloha shirts in all price ranges, and a story to go with each. Because even the new merchandise has the vintage look, the shop exudes a sense of nostalgia and celebration of times past.

Kona Arts & Crafts Gallery. 75-5699 Alii Dr. ☎ **808/329-5590.**

If you cross Alii Drive from the seawall, you'll come across a mind-boggling selection in this tiny shop: chimes, hula implements, wood carvings, pressed seaweed under glass, hand-painted tiles, tikis, koa brushes and mirrors, and koa bowls from $30 to $200. There's junk for sure, but the prices are low and there's a big selection—all of it made by Hawaii artists. A highlight: posters and cards by renowned Kona artist Herb Kane.

Noa Noa. Kona Inn Shopping Village. ☎ **808/329-8187.** Also at King's Shops, Waikoloa. ☎ **808/885-5449.**

Many of the items are familiar, but you'll find some new and beautifully crafted things in this room of deep browns and ambers, awash in the fragrances of spices and grasses. Rattan, ikat fabrics, Lombok baskets, Balinese masks, and cheerful tropical clothing, designed by the owner and made in Bali exclusively for Noa Noa, imbue the shop with the smells and textures of a Balinese village. Bells, belts, basket handbags, masks, trays, jewelry, and artifacts from Java and Borneo make for some interesting shopping.

Te-Noe, Inc. No address; phone order only. ☎ **808/322-3579.**

Noelani Whittington's grandfather planted the coffee trees on their farm when he was 85 years old. He's well past 90 now, but the trees are yielding tasty coffee beans that Noelani and her husband, Rick, sell wholesale and retail in 2-ounce, 3-ounce, and 1-pound bags. The 100% Kona coffee is available by phone order or at various outlets in Kailua-Kona. The beans are hand-roasted only 15 pounds at a time and packed with a great deal of individual attention. Also available from the farm are the seasonally available pin-cushion and miniature king protea, and, in 1997, the dazzling Telopa protea, resembling torch gingers in all-red and all-white. Protea are sturdy, showy flowers with a long afterlife: they dry beautifully. The 2-ounce coffee bags sell for $3.60 plus shipping; the protea, a dozen for $30, can ship anywhere in the United States. Because the selection varies with the time of year, there are always surprises.

EDIBLES & EVERYDAY THINGS ALONG THE KONA COAST

Kailua-Kona

For everyday grocery needs, **KTA Stores** (Kona Coast Shopping Center, at Palani Rd. and Queen Kaahumanu Hwy.; and in Keauhou Shopping Center) is always my first choice. KTA has a way of finding top-notch local products, such as Kona smoked marlin, Hilo-grown rainbow trout, taro chips, poha jams, and *kulolo,* the decadently dense taro-coconut steamed pudding. The fresh fish department is always an adventure; if anything esoteric or rare is running, such as the flashy red *aweoweo,* it's sure to be on the counters at KTA, along with everyday necessities. A few doors away in the same shopping center, **Kona Healthways** is the only full-service health food store for miles, selling organic produce, bulk grains and cereals, vitamins, snacks, fresh fruit smoothies, and sandwiches and salads from its take-out deli. Organic greens, grown with special cachet in the South Kona area, are a small but strong feature of the produce section.

By far the best and busiest place for produce and flowers straight from the farm is the **Farmers Market** in Kaiwi Square, in Kona's old industrial area (follow the sign on Queen Kaahumanu Hwy.; open Sat 7am–4pm, Sun 7am–noon); it teems with dedicated vendors and eager shoppers. You'll find live catfish, taro, organic vine-ripened tomatoes, fresh Kamuela string beans, lettuces, potatoes, and just-picked blooms such as anthuriums and feathery, sturdy protea at friendly prices.

South Kona

Down Hi. 11 in Kainaliu, the **Kimura Store** is an old-fashioned general store, a treasure trove of everything you need and don't need, from cookware and aspirin to incense holders and endless rows of fabrics that attract longtime buyers from all corners of the island. Also in Kainaliu, **Ohana O Ka Aina Cooperative** offers wholesome sandwiches, juices, wheat-free desserts, a different soup each day, smoothies, and body care products—good stuff for health foodies.

Further south in Kealakekua, **Kamigaki Market** is a reliable source for food items, especially for specialties of the region, such as macadamia nuts and Kona coffee. In Honaunau, farther south, keep an eye out for the **Bong Brothers Store** on Hi. 11 and its eye-catching selections of fresh local fruit—from chirimoya (in season) to starfruit and white Sugarloaf pineapples. The Bongs are known for their Kona coffee and deli items, but I think their black, very hip Bong Brothers T-shirts are the find of the region and season.

UP-COUNTRY KONA: HOLUALOA

At some point, the single-laned village called Holualoa went from being a resting place for coffee workers and farmers on horseback to a village of artists who create wondrous works in ramshackle old coffee mills and gleaming studios with million-dollar views. Charming Holualoa, 1,400 feet and 10 minutes above Kailua-Kona at the top of Hualalai Road, is a place for strong espresso, leisurely gallery-hopping, and nostalgic explorations across several cultural and time zones. **Paul's Place** is Holualoa's only all-purpose general store, a time warp tucked between frame shops, galleries, and studios. Prominent Holualoa artists include jewelry maker/sculptor Sam

Rosen, who years ago set the pace for found-object art; ceramist and wood sculptor Gerald Ben; print maker Nora Yamanoha; glass artist Wilfred Yamazawa; sculptor Cal Hashimoto; and Hiroki and Setsuko Morinoue of Studio 7 gallery.

Holualoa Gallery. 76-5921 Mamalahoa Hwy. ☎ **808/322-8484.**

Owners Matthew and Mary Lovein are resident artists who have converted an old coffee mill into an art studio and showcase for regional artists. The selection includes Tai Lake koa furniture, fused glass bowls by award-winning Patricia Van Asperen-Hume, and potter Matt Lovein's raku, sculpture, and 4-foot-tall ceramic vessels on which his wife, a painter, has put the finishing touches. Large and small pieces, from furniture to sculpture and metal jewelry, make up the constantly changing collection.

Kimura Lauhala Shop. Mamalahoa Hwy. ☎ **808/324-0053.**

Tsuruyo Kimura, looking 20 years younger than her 80-odd years, presides over a labor-intensive legacy that's increasingly difficult to maintain. The shop is lined with goods, from rolled-up mats and wide-brimmed hats to coasters and coin purses, made of *lauhala,* the fragrant, resilient fiber woven from leaves of the *hala* (pandanus) tree. They're smooth to the touch, become softer with use, and often vary in color (terra-cotta to beige) according to region and growing conditions of the hala. Woven in varying widths, lauhala in its finer weaves is time-consuming and expensive. Although Kimura uses a covey of local weavers who use the renowned hala leaves of Kona, there are some South Pacific imports to bolster the supply.

Kona Arts Center. Mamalahoa Hwy.; Box 272, Holualoa, HI 96725. No telephone.

Because they've never had a phone, anyone interested in the pottery, tie-dye, weaving, painting, and other arts-and-crafts workshops of this nonprofit center, in a ramshackle tin-roofed former coffee mill, have to write or drop in. Carol Rogers is director of the program, a mainstay of the local arts community since 1965.

✪ Studio 7. Holualoa. ☎ **808/324-1335.**

Some of Hawaii's most respected artists, among them gallery owners Setsuko and Hiroki Morinoue, exhibit their works in this serenely beautiful studio. Smooth pebbles, stark woods, and a garden setting provide the backdrop for Hiroki's paintings and prints and Setsuko's pottery, paper collages, and wall pieces. The Print Gallery houses sculptural pieces, and a ceramic-pottery area toward the back showcases the works of Clayton Amemiya, Chiu Leong, Jan Bovard, and Gerald Ben, whose mixed-media sculptures of ceramic raku with wood continue to be a pleasing attraction. With the Morinoues at the helm of the newly activated, volunteer-driven **Holualoa Foundation for Culture and the Arts,** this is the hub of the Holualoa art community. Foundation activities include events by visiting artists, including performing artists, at Holualoa's Kona Imin Center.

KAINALIU-KEALAKEKUA

Blue Ginger Gallery. Hi. 11, Kainaliu. ☎ **808/322-3898.**

It's gone heavily Balinese lately (what hasn't?), but David Bever still makes striking stained-glass cabinets, and his wife, Jill Ami Meyers, still paints silks at the old wooden home they long ago transformed into a roadside gallery. Of the artists represented here, 90% are from the island; the rest of the works are Balinese imports. Black bamboo furniture from the jungles of Bali accent a room with Sachi Nifash tropical oil paintings, Thomas Stoudt koa wood boxes, Ina Koch platters and bowls (handmade, not thrown) of underwater scenes, Pat Pearlman silver jewelry. Hawi artist Kalalani paints silk hangings and silk kimonos that are in demand.

The Grass Shack. Hi. 11, Kealakekua. ☎ **808/323-2877.**

Cross your fingers that the traffic signal planned for this junction at Hi. 11 and Konawaena won't spoil the parking. The Grass Shack has been here for 25 years, offering a large selection of local wood crafts, plus Niihau shell leis, packaged coffee, hula implements, pahu drums, nose flutes, wiliwili seed leis, and lauhala (woven pandanus leaves) in every form. Bowls, boxes, and accessories of Norfolk pine, the rare kou, milo, avocado, mango, monkeypod, hau, and other local woods take up a sizable portion of the shop. Lauhala baskets, made of fiber from the region and the Hamakua Coast, are among the Shack's finest, as are the custom ukuleles and feather gourds for hula dancing.

THE KOHALA COAST

Shops on the Kohala Coast are concentrated in the resorts, most notably the **Hilton Waikoloa Village,** where the hotel and the neighboring King's Shops offer a long string of possibilities. Highly recommended is **Flamingo's** in Hilton Waikoloa's main arcade, a must for stylish men and women. Vintage purses, the fabulously successful Avanti line—whose aloha shirts, classic mandarin-style tea-timer tops, and slinky dresses in authentic 1930s to 1950s retro prints, reproduced on silk, are an international hit—slinky Betsey Johnson dresses, Cut Loose contemporary clothing, and a head-turning assortment of aloha shirts reflect the owners' discerning tastes. Next door, the **Sandal Tree** carries footwear with style and kick: Italian sandals at non-Italian prices, designer pumps, and footwear to carry you from sailing deck to dance floor.

Among my favorites at the **King's Shops** is **Noa's Ark** for children, a tot-sized space filled with tropical cottons, mini-muumuus, pint-sized aloha shirts, and even sophisticated linens and jerseys, in cradle-to-teen sizes. Its sister store for adults, **Noa Noa,** is several doors away on the mall, filled with exotic artifacts from Java and Borneo and tropical clothing for easygoing life in the Pacific Rim. **Kunah's** offers Kahala, Kamehameha, and other very hip aloha shirts, as wells as baseball caps, flipflops, swim shorts, and colorful tropical-print canvas bags. For snacks, ice, sunscreen, wine, postcards, and everyday essentials, head for the **Whalers General Store.**

Just Looking

The **Mauna Kea Beach Hotel** (62-100 Mauna Kea Beach Dr.; ☎ 808/882-7222) is home to one of the world's most impressive collections of Asian and Oceanic art, and it's all displayed unpretentiously, in public and private spaces. Laurance Rockefeller planned his resort so the art would be totally integrated into the environment: indoors, outdoors, in hallways, lounges, and alcoves. The result is a spiritually and aesthetically uplifting view in every direction. A 7th-century granite Buddha is the oldest work in a collection that includes art from China, Japan, India, Southeast Asia, Melanesia, and Polynesia, including Hawaii. The Lloyd Sexton Gallery and John Young paintings throughout the hotel reflect Rockefeller's commitment to the finest.

NORTH KOHALA

Ackerman Gallery. Two locations on Hi. 270, Kapaau: Across from the Kamehameha statue, and 3 blocks away, on the opposite side of the street; ☎ **808/889-5971** for both.

Crafts and fine arts are housed in two separate galleries a few blocks apart. In their 16 years in Kapaau, painter Gary Ackerman and his wife, Yesan, have amassed tasteful gifts and crafts and the works of award-winning Big Island artists. Ackerman's impressionistic paintings have a strong presence in the fine-arts gallery, hung among

Kelly Dunn's hand-turned Norfolk pine bowls, Jer Houston's heirloom-quality koa-and-ebony desks, and Wilfred Yamazawa's handblown glass perfume bottles and sculptures. From Volcano, Chiu Leong sends his pit-fired ceramic pieces, and Ira Ono, his masks and books of handmade paper. Primitive artifacts, Asian antiques, and Cal Hashimoto's bamboo sculpture are among the discoveries of this pleasing and attractive gallery.

Kohala Kollection. Kawaihae Shopping Center, Kawaihae. ☎ **808/882-1510.**

This two-story gallery, the biggest draw next to Cafe Pesto in this industrial harbor area, features Pegge Hopper originals and prints, North Kohala painter Harry Wishard's landscapes, Avi Kiriaty oils, and works in all media by more than 150 artists, primarily from the Big Island. The two-dimensional art is displayed upstairs, but the Cal Hashimoto sculptures and lamps (bamboo with copper, ohia with copper) and the jewelry boxes, jewelry, furniture, baskets, and bowls are tastefully arranged downstairs. The selection ranges from affordable wood accessories to water-jade jewelry and ceramics, from a few dollars on up.

WAIMEA & PARKER RANCH

Shops here range from the small roadside storefronts lining Hi. 19 and Hi. 190, which intersect in the middle of town, to complexes such as Parker Square and Waimea Center, where you'll find the trusty old **KTA Super Store,** the one-stop shop for all your basic necessities, plus a glorious profusion of interesting local foods. At **Parker Ranch Shopping Center** across the street, you'll find **Big Island Coffee Co.** and a smattering of shops and casual eateries, but all in all, the selection (except for **Viviana** boutique, which has tasteful clothing, but nothing Hawaiian) is unremarkable. The petite but satisfying **Opelo Plaza,** the historic **Spencer House,** and **Parker Square** will likely be your most diverse and rewarding stops.

Hilo's wonderful **Dan De Luz Woods** (see below) has a Waimea branch at 64-1013 Mamamlahoa Hwy., in front of the True-Value hardware store.

Bentley's Home & Garden Collection. Parker Square. ☎ **808/885-5565.**

You can almost feel the presence of Martha Stewart in this place. This is a very gardenesque shop of indulgences for people who like to raise flowers and herbs, cook with them, breathe potpourried air, take relaxing baths, and look good. You'll find a wide variety of items, from glassware, linens, and chenille throws to home fragrances, stuffed animals, and Wild West gift wrap—including the extremely luxurious Thymes gardenia soaps, $14.95 for two bars!

✪ **Cook's Discoveries.** At the Historic Spencer House, in front of Waimea Center, Hi. 190. ☎ **808/885-3633.**

It's a heady mix: Hawaii-themed wearables, fine collectibles, locally made crafts, books, Hawaiian quilts, and ranching memorabilia. You could start with Waipio poi hotcakes at **Maha's Cafe** in one part of the tiny shop; then select a lei by Alice Humbert from her veranda flower shop, **Made in a Hawaiian Garden;** and then dive into the nooks and crannies of **Cook's Discoveries.** Treasures you'll find: palaka nightshirts and napkins, the original 1929 bronze bell from the historic interisland freighter *Humu'ula,* Hawaiian collectible silver spoons, kupe'e shell necklaces by Patrick Horimoto, the rare miniature kukui nut lei, pareus by Tutuvi, lauhala baskets, T-shirts, Doug Tolentino originals and prints, and hundreds of other surprises. The rare ivory and silver Ming's jewelry has collectors hovering over the counter, while foodies throng to the Hamakua coffee, mango chutney, Manoa Farms Ginger Lime Marmalade, and the Cooks' own Triple Chocolate Chunk Cookies (as deadly as they sound). Another special touch: The flower shop sells hand creams, sea salts, and handmade potpourris Alice Humbert makes from the harvests of her own garden. The old-fashioned tea cups filled with potted narcissus and tea roses make superb gifts.

Gallery of Great Things. Parker Square, Waimea. ☎ **808/885-7706.**

Here's an eye-popping assemblage of local art and Pacific Rim artifacts. Browse under the watchful gaze of a 150-year-old Tongan war club (not for sale) and authentic rhinoceros- and deer-horn blow guns from Borneo, among the plethora of treasures from Polynesia, Micronesia, and Indonesia. You'll find jewelry, glassware, photographs, fiber baskets, and the ubiquitous koa hand-turned bowls of beautifully grained woods. The politically incorrect koa still appears abundantly here in furniture and small accessories, alongside politically correct Marian Berger's smashing, universally appealing watercolors of endangered birds. You can hand over thousands for primitive artifacts or fancy furniture, or $15 for hairsticks and pens, $3 for coconut soap, and $25 for carved boxes or the nuts-and-bolts kukui nut lei.

Imagination. Parker Square. ☎ **808/885-0430.**

A Hilo transplant, this children's shop is stacked high with upscale toys, dolls, books, games, and other upper-end diversions. The selection is strong in educational toys and European and Asian imports—sure to appeal, at least, to the parents who are buying.

Kaleonapua of Hawaii. Hi. 19. ☎ **808/885-4045.**

The name means "voice of the flower," and indeed, the flowers here sing. Owners Corinne and Matthew Weller grow and sell protea and make leis to order, everything from crown flower to maile. The luxurious cymbidium orchids, protea, anthuriums, potted plants, and flower arrangements command reasonable prices.

Kamuela Hat Company. Hi. 190, Waimea Center. ☎ **808/885-8875.**

The requisite hats of the *paniolo* life are here in spades. Choose from among Kona lauhala, Stetsons, Panamas, Italian straw, white coconut, and more. You'll also find all the other accoutrements of a life astride: Belts, macho buckles, Western jewelry, and oilskin jackets à la J. Peterman, plus cowboy boots at non-Dallas prices. A personal favorite are the slippers made of *palaka,* the two-color plaid that has come to symbolize the rugged ranching and plantation eras of Hawaii. Styled into thongs, they're a statement for the nonfashionistas.

✪ Up-Country Connection. At Mauna Kea Center, Hi. 19 and 190. ☎ **808/885-0623.**

You may not be looking for a $1,900 koa chest, but it's here, along with a large, antique koa mirror reflecting the Ed Kayton originals on the wall. This warm, gleaming gallery offers an even mix of fine art, antiques, and crafts, all of impeccable taste. Limited edition prints, ceramics, and sculptures in bronze and clay are among the discoveries. There are some one-of-a-kind finds for bountiful budgets: a $1,200 coconut-wood Polynesian drum; Hawaiian musical instruments of feathers and coconut shells; Jerry Kotz's hand-turned Norfolk pine bowls; and Erik Wold's raku-fired ceramic vases for under $100.

✪ Waimea Booksellers. Opelo Plaza, Hi. 19. ☎ **808/885-8616.**

You couldn't ask for much more from a bookstore: more than 20,000 titles, readings by local poets and authors, and window benches and chairs in which to peruse your selections. The broad selection spans children's books to literary fiction to Thomas Mann and *How to Find Your Ideal Country Home*—tailor-made for Waimea.

They accept trades, too: Bring in what you've finished reading for trade credit and spend as much time as you want deciding between *Tiffany Windows, Cleopatra's Nose* (essays on the unexpected), the out-of-print *The Lore of Ships,* and countless other tomes on and off the literary beat. This friendly store also has more than 20 book-review subscriptions for connoisseurs.

Waimea Farmers Market. Hi. 19, at 55-mile-marker on the Hamakua side of Waimea town, on the lawn in front of the Department of Hawaiian Home Lands, West Hawaii office.

Small and sublime, with only about five booths, this Farmers Market draws a loyal crowd from 7am to noon on Saturday mornings. Waimea is lei country and the island's breadbasket, so you can imagine the protea, vegetables, vine-ripened tomatoes, pansies, and tuberose stalks you can buy here, all at reasonable prices. One of the stellar attractions is Honopua Farm, selling organic vegetables such as a dozen different lettuces, fennel, three different types of kale, and many other finds you'd never encounter in a supermarket. And the flowers: freesias in season, irises, heather, star-of-Bethlehem, Australian tea, and cleome, all freshly clipped. The colors and fragrances change with the season. You'll find Marie McDonald at the booth, one of Hawaii's premier lei makers. (If you want one of her designer Waimea leis, you have to order ahead; call **808/885-4148.**) Also here is Bernice Berdon, considered the best maker of *akulikuli* leis, a Waimea signature that comes in eye-popping yellows, oranges, and fuchsia. Ask about her bat-face kika, the cigar-flower lei with bat-faced blossoms.

Waimea Design Center & Art Gallery. Opelo Plaza, Hi. 19. ☎ **808/885-6171.**

Arrive on a rainy day and you may be greeted with a sign on the door: "Too much rain. Back on Wednesday." But come in acceptable weather and you'll find a melange of local art, Asian antiques, oil paintings, gilded Buddhas, native wood bowls, and, yes, T-shirts.

Waimea General Store. Parker Square. ☎ **808/885-4479.**

This place has always offered a superb assortment of Hawaii-themed books, soaps and toiletries, cookbooks and kitchen accessories, candles and linens. It's a charming, unpretentious country store with greeting cards and dolls, Japanese hapi coats and Island teas, rare kiawe honey, preserves, and countless gift items from the practical to the whimsical. Lovers of Crabtree and Evelyn soaps, fragrances, and cookies won't be disappointed.

THE HAMAKUA COAST

Waipio Valley Artworks. Kukuihaele. ☎ **808/775-0958.**

The focus here is strictly local, with a strong emphasis on wood works. Housed in an old wooden building at the end of the road before Waipio Valley, the gallery/boutique offers one of the largest selections of local woods in the state: pheasant wood, sandalwood, hau, kamani, avocado, mango, koa, kou, and a rainbow of native and introduced woods. All the luminaries of wood-turning have works here: Jack Straka, Robert Butts, Scott Hare, Kevin Parks. Their bowls, rocking chairs, and jewelry boxes exhibit flawless craftsmanship and gleaming, richly burnished grains. More affordable are the pens and hair accessories, and the Tropical Dreams ice cream served in a corner of the gallery.

HONOKAA

Every Saturday morning from 7am, about a dozen local farmers and vendors set up their wares at the **Honokaa Farmers Market** in front of the Botelho Building. No crafts or arts here—just edibles, good and fresh. Vendors bring their home-baked breads and pastries, bananas, papayas, and bushels of freshly picked garden vegetables—and, like at the other farmers markets around the island, they're all available at unbeatable prices.

Honokaa Market Place. 45-3321 Mamane St. ☎ **808/775-8255.**

New and old, antiques and imports mingle freely in this eclectic selection of Hawaiian, Asian, and Indonesian handicrafts. Open since late 1994, the shop is gaining recognition for its old and new Hawaiiana. There's more than the usual selection of wood bowls (koa, mango, hau, kou, ohia, kamani, Norfolk pine), and the Hawaiian quilts come in several forms: wall hangings, pillows, full-sized, and the more affordable Hawaiian quilt patterns made in the Philippines. Hawaiian prints and lithographs, clothing from Bali, a few Oriental antiques, and a profusion of beads attract shoppers, collectors, and jewelry makers who can buy and string on the spot.

Honokaa Trading Company. Mamane St. ☎ **808/775-0808.**

"Rustic, tacky, rare—there's something for everyone," comments owner Grace Walker, who provides a lion's share of the town's local color. Every inch of the labyrinthine, 2,200-square-foot bazaar is occupied with antiques and collectibles, new and used goods, and countless treasures, all of it plantation memorabilia or Hawaiiana. Bark cloth fabrics from the 1940s, rhinestone jewelry and rattan furniture from the 1930s, vintage ukuleles, Depression glass, dinnerware from Honolulu's landmark Willows restaurant, koa lamps, Francis Oda airbrush paintings—it's an unbelievable conglomeration, and surprises lurk around every corner. Vigilant collectors make regular forays here to scoop up the 1950s ivory jewelry and John Kelly prints.

Kamaaina Woods. Lehua St., down the hill from the post office, Honokaa. ☎ **808/775-7722.**

The showroom is adjacent to the workshop, so visitors can watch the craftspeople at work on the other side of the glass panel. Local woods are the specialty here, with a strong emphasis on koa and milo bowls. Boxes, carvings, albums, and smaller accessories are also included in the mix, but bowl-turning is clearly the focus. Prices begin at about $10.

Seconds to Go. Mamane St. ☎ **808/775-9212.**

Elaine Carlsmith spends a lot of time collecting vintage pottery, glassware, kimonos, fabrics, and other treasures, only to let them go to eager nostalgia seekers. In her 15 years in this spot, many memories and beautiful things have passed through her doors. Current find: a three-piece koa set, over a century old, that includes desk with high-backed chair. Old maps, music sheets, rare and out-of-print books, and reams of ephemera are here for the finding, along with vintage ivory jewelry and the irrepressible Don Blanding dinnerware. The 1,500-square-foot main store is a few doors away from the warehouse, where furniture and larger pieces are displayed.

HILO

Shopping in Hilo is centered around the **Kaiko'o Hilo Mall** at 777 Kilauea Ave., near the state and county buildings; the **Prince Kuhio Shopping Plaza** at 111 E. Puainako, just off Hi. 11 on the road north to Volcano, where you'll find a supermarket, drug store, Liberty House, and other standards; and the **Bayfront** area downtown, where the hippest new businesses have taken up residence in the historic buildings lining Kamehameha Avenue. For other practical needs, there's a **KTA Super Store** at 323 Keawe St. and another at 50 E. Puainako; **Sure Save** supermarkets are at Kaiko'o Mall and 1990 Kinoole St.

For shopping that's more fun than obligatory, here are our Hilo highlights:

Basically Books. 46 Waianuenue Ave. ☎ **808/961-0144.**

This is a sanctuary for lovers of books, maps, and the environment. Get your bearings by browsing among the nautical charts, U.S. Geological Survey maps (the authoritative word in cartography), street maps, out-of-print books, atlases, compasses, and countless travel books. Specializing in Hawaii and the Pacific, the bookstore is a bountiful source of information that will enhance any visit. Even the most knowledgeable residents stop by here to keep current and conscious.

Dan De Luz Woods. 760 Kilauea Ave. ☎ **808/935-5587.**

The unstoppable Dan De Luz has been turning bowls for more than 30 years. In his workshop behind the store, he turns koa, milo, mango, kamani, kou, sandalwood, hau, and other Island woods, some very rare, into bowls, trays, and accessories of all shapes and sizes. You can find bookmarks, rice and stir-fry paddles, letter openers, and calabashes priced from $3 to $1,000.

Hana Hou. 38 Kalakaua St. ☎ **808/935-4555.**

Michele Zane-Faridi has done a superlative job of assembling, designing, and collecting things of beauty that evoke old and new Hawaii. Sumptuous fabrics from the obi of vintage kimono are sewn into cushions and one-of-a-kind vests, dresses, and shirts. From Niue in the South Pacific come lauhala hats, purses, and baskets; from Western Samoa, Tonga, and Fiji, one-of-a-kind lauhala floor mats in durable double-weave. A believer in mat maintenance, Michele instructs you in the repair and reweaving of this precious fiber, or arranges to do it herself. The collector's dream—vintage silver and ivory jewelry by Ming's—disappears quickly from the elegant, evocative selection.

The Most Irresistible Shop in Hilo. 110 Keawe St. ☎ **808/935-9644.** Also at Prince Kuhio Plaza. ☎ **808/959-6515.**

It's not really the most irresistible shop in Hilo, but there aren't many tastes or categories of gift items that are overlooked here: T-shirts, greeting cards, Tahitian and Balinese pareus, jewelry, stuffed animals, glassware, ceramic ware, candles, fine bone china, Japanese blue ceramic ware, porcelain, Hawaiian dish towels, koa cutting boards, plumeria hand lotion, incense, and countless other tchotchkes. The fragrant, creamy coconut soap from Volcano is a find at $3.50; and if you can't find fresh mangoes, at least you can smell like one, with the fruity Mango Perfume, also made in Volcano.

Plantation Memories. 179 Kilauea St. ☎ **808/935-7100.**

Owner Billy Perreira has a particular fondness for plantation memorabilia and the resourcefulness it reflects. In his shop of plantation memories, everything has a story, and he's likely to know most of them: the one-of-a-kind handmade wooden wheelbarrow, made by a man for his young son; the hand-painted wooden signs from the neighboring sugar communities: Honomu, Hakalau, Hilo; plus vintage Hawaiian clothing, toys, china, furniture, lamps, baskets, textiles, and countless other collectibles from the turn of the century through the 1950s.

✪ Sig Zane Designs. 122 Kamehameha Ave. ☎ **808/935-7077.**

Sig Zane evokes such loyalty that people make special trips from the outer islands for his culturally enlightening, inspired line of authentic Hawaiian wear. The partnership of Zane and his wife, revered hula master Nalani Kanakaole, is unrivaled in its creativity, style, and esthetic and educational value. One step in the door and you'll see: The shop is awash in gleaming woods, lauhala mats, and clothing and accessories, from handmade house slippers to aloha shirts, pareus, muumuus, dresses, T-shirts, purses, baskets, jewelry, rugs, and various made-in-Hawaii crafts. Everything is of top quality, and his fabric prints carry a cultural significance that deepens their visual beauty. New designs (the *ma'o,* Hawaiian cotton; the *'ohai* Kalae, unique to South Point; the Niulani, coconuts on the stalk, without leaves) appear constantly, yet the old favorites remain fresh and compelling: ti, *koa, kukui,* taro, the *lehua* blossoms of the ohia tree, and many others. Koa books by Jesus Sanchez and intricately carved tapa-beating implements of ohia wood are popular, but the best and the brightest are the Sig Zane bed covers, cushions, and custom-ordered upholstery, which bring the forest into your room.

A SPECIAL ARTS CENTER & GALLERY

East Hawaii Cultural Center. 141 Kalakaua St. (across from Kalakaua Park), Hilo. ☎ **808/ 961-5711.**

Part gallery, part retail store, and part consortium of the arts, the cultural center is run by volunteers in the visual and performing arts. Keep it in mind for gifts of Hawaii, or if you have any questions regarding the **Hawaii Concert Society, Hilo Community Players, Big Island Dance Council,** and **Big Island Art Guild.** The art gallery and gift shop exhibit locally made cards, jewelry, handmade books, sculpture, and wood objects, as well as museum-quality works, such as sculptures by Patrick Sarsfield and Henry Bianchini. Also of note: Kay Yokoyama watercolors, Nellie Kim paintings and sketches, Steve Irvine oils and acrylics, Tomas Belsky drawings and paintings, and many other works in all price ranges. Ceramics, fine art, prints, and affordable sketches and drawings with Hawaii themes are included in the selection. Some of the regularly changing exhibits are eagerly anticipated, such as the international **Shoebox Sculpture** show every June, in which each work has to be small enough to fit in a shoebox.

EDIBLES

Abundant Life Natural Foods. 292 Kamehameha Ave. ☎ **808/935-7411.**

Stock up here on healthy snacks, fresh organic produce, vitamins and supplements, bulk grains, baked goods, and the latest in health foods. There's a sound selection of natural remedies and herbal body, face, and hair products. The take-out deli makes fresh fruit smoothies, sprout- and nutrient-rich sandwiches, soups, salads, and daily specials, such as pasta or vegetable pie with a salad on the side. Senior citizens get a 10% discount.

Big Island Candies. 500 Kalanianaole Ave. ☎ **808/935-8890.**

Abandon all restraint as you pull in—the smell of butter mixing with chocolate is thick as honey, and shortbread cookies dipped in milk chocolate, coffee shortbread dipped in white chocolate, chocolate-dipped macadamia nuts, Hawaiian macadamia nut turtles, macadamia nut rocky road, and dozens of other dangers will make it very hard to be sensible, anyway. Allan Ikawa's vigilance about quality control demands eggs straight from a nearby farm, pure butter, Hawaiian cane sugar, no preservatives, and premium chocolate. Gift boxes are available, and they're carted interisland in staggering volumes. The "Hawaiian Da Kine" line is irrepressibly local: mochi crunch, Chinese preserved plum, fortune cookies, animal crackers, and other crunchy morsels—all dipped in chocolate, of course.

Doris' Island Delights. Hilo Shopping Center, 1221 Kilauea Ave. ☎ **808/935-7113.**

Doris' hibachi seasonings, made with Hawaiian salt, are easily transported and waiting to be paired with chicken, steak, fish, or vegetables at your welcome-home barbecue. Among the 10 flavors: Hilo-style with vinegar, chili pepper-lemon, lemon-herb, and, for those on salt-restricted diets, no-salt seasoning with chili pepper and other condiments. The lilikoi and strawberry waiwi (small guava) cream cheeses don't require refrigeration until opening, and the Stone cookies, like the sun-dried, jerkylike strips of ahi, require nothing more than strong jaws and a taste for local specialties. Cookies to love: Donna's shortbread and Hilo Kine's cornflake, chocolate chip, and macadamia nut shortbread.

✪ **Hilo Farmers Market.** Corner Kamehameha and Mamo. ☎ **808/969-9114.**

More than 60 vendors from around the island bring their flowers, produce, and baked goods to this teeming corner of Hilo every Wednesday and Saturday from sunrise to 4pm. Because many of the vendors sell out early, it's best to go as early as you can. Expect to find a dizzying assortment: fresh homegrown oyster mushrooms from Kona—three or four different colors and sizes—about $5 a pound; the creamy, sweet, queenly Indonesian fruit called rambutan; moist, warm breads, from focaccia to walnut; protea, anthuriums, gingers, hecliconias, orchids, and an array of flowers; fresh aquacultured seaweed; corn from Pahoa; Waimea strawberries; taro and taro products; foot-long, miso-flavored, and traditional Hawaiian *laulau;* and fabulous ethnic vegetables with unpronounceable names. The selection changes by the week, but it'll always be reasonable, fresh, and appealing, and a good cross-section of the island's specialties.

Paradise Gourmet. 308 Kamehameha Ave. ☎ **808/969-9146.** Also at Prince Kuhio Plaza, 111 E. Puainako. ☎ **808/959-2339.**

Hilo is the crunchy-snack capital of the world, and the snack center of Hilo is Paradise Gourmet, where fish jerky, beef jerky, Maui onion jelly, taro chip popcorn, and a sublime macadamia nut shortbread will clamor for your attention. Ohelo berry jam, from berries said to be the favorite food of the volcano goddess, is one of the big sellers, but my favorites are the silky Hot Guava Sauce, the Maui Onion Sauce, and the buttery Cornflake Cookies. You can also buy 100% Kona coffee and a variety of tropical teas, from mango to passion fruit to an apple-litchi blend.

THE PUNA REGION

Keaau Natural Foods. Keaau Shopping Center, 16-586 Old Volcano Rd. ☎ **808/966-8877.**

This recently relocated health food store is three times as big as its original location. In addition to the loose herbs, vitamins, cosmetics, and large selection of fresh organic produce, there are prepared dishes aplenty. Ginger Moon bakery brings in healthy food to go: pizzas, curries, rice-and-vegetable dishes, tofu salad, eggless dishes, and a changing roster of vegetarian specialties. Fresh juices, Kau navel oranges, Puna papayas, sandwiches, and snacks have all the makings of a topnotch picnic lunch for your explorations of east Hawaii.

Pahoa Natural Groceries. Government Main Rd., Pahoa. ☎ **808/965-8322.**

We never pass through Pahoa without stopping here for sandwiches, salads, and fresh fruit for a picnic at Lava Tree State Park or at the ponds of Kapoho. The prolific kitchen makes eight different puddings and 12 different salads and dips a day, as well as stunning sandwiches: artichoke-frittata, shrimp-and-avocado, garden burgers. Other choices for takeout include Mexican casseroles, spinach lasagna, tofu salad, and everything from pasta to buckwheat noodles. There are always fresh pies and cookies, fresh organic produce, and local specialties such as Kapoho papayas and oranges. To accompany the chips and snacks, there's beer and wine—all in a very small store.

VOLCANO

Volcano Store. At Huanani and Old Volcano Hwy. ☎ **808/967-7210.**

Walk up the wooden steps into a wonderland of flowers and Island specialties. Tangy lilikoi butter (transportable, and worth a special trip) and flamboyant sprays of cymbidiums, tuberoses, dendrobiums, anthuriums, hanging plants, mixed bouquets, and calla lilies (splendid when grown in Volcano), make a breathtaking assemblage in the enclosed front porch. Volcano residents are supremely blessed to have these blooms at such prices (Honolulu residents pay $3.50 for a single obake anthurium!). The flowers can also be shipped (orders are taken by phone); Marie and Ronald Onouye and their staff pack them meticulously. Many a recipient has gushed about the fresh, carefully wrapped treasures that arrive on time and in good shape. If mainland weather is too humid or frosty for reliable shipping, they'll let you know. Produce, stone cookies (as in hard-as-stone) from Mountain View, Hilo taro chips, Jill's Country Kitchen shortbread and white chocolate cookies, and other food and paper products round out the very pleasing selection.

GALLERY & STUDIO VISITS

✪ **Volcano Art Center.** Hawaii Volcanoes National Park. ☎ **808/967-8222.**

The Volcano Island's frontier spirit and raw, primal energy have spawned a close-knit community of artists. Although their works appear in galleries and gift shops throughout the island, the Volcano Art Center is the hub of the island's arts activity. Housed in the original 1877 Volcano House, VAC, as it's called, is a nonprofit art education center that offers exhibits and shows that change monthly, as well as workshops and retail space. Marian Berger's watercolors of endangered birds, Dietrich Varez oils and block prints, Avi Kiriaty oils, Kelly Dunn and Jack Straka woods, Brad Lewis photography, and Mike Reily furnishings are among the works you'll see as you wander around those old wooden floors. Of the 300 artists represented, 90% come from Hawaii Island. The fine crafts at VAC include baskets, jewelry, mixed media pieces, stone- and wood-carving, and the journals and wood diaries of Jesus Sanchez, a third-generation Vatican bookbinder who has turned his skills to the woods of this island.

✪ Volcano Artists Hui

Adding to the vitality of the art environment are the studio visits offered by the Volcano Artists Hui, six highly respected artists in various media who open their studios to the public by appointment. **Chiu Leong's** (☎ **808/967-7637**) airy, geometric studio and showroom is a mountain idyll that shows off splendidly his raku, pit-fire, and porcelain works, which are highly esteemed and coveted by collectors. You can visit **Pam Barton** (☎ **808/967-7247**) and see how she transforms vines, leaves, roots, bark, and tree sheddings into stunning fiber sculptures and vessels, from baskets to handmade paper and books. Photographer **Mary Walsh** (☎ **808/985-8520**), painter and sculptor **Patrick Sarsfield** (☎ **808/967-7220**), and ceramist **Zeke Israel** (☎ **808/985-8554**) also open their studios as part of the hui, as does **Ira Ono** (☎ **808/967-7261**), an artist in collage mixed-media who makes masks, water containers, fountains, paste-paper journals, garden vessels, and goddesses out of clay and found objects.

13 Luaus & Other Local Fun: The Big Island After Dark

by Jocelyn Fujii

Jokes abound about the neighbor islands and nightlife being oxymorons, but there are a few pockets of entertainment, most of it in the Kailua-Kona and Kohala Coast resorts. Your best bet is to check the local newspapers—***Honolulu Advertiser, West Hawaii Today***—for special shows, such as fund-raisers for Punana Leo or local Hawaiian and civic groups that are occasionally held at venues such as Kona Surf. Other than that, regular entertainment in the local clubs usually consists of mellow Hawaiian music at sunset, small hula groups, or jazz trios.

Some of the island's best events are usually held at **Kahilu Theatre** in Waimea (☎ **808/885-6017**), so be on the lookout for any mention of it during your stay. Hula, the top Hawaiian music groups from all over Hawaii, drama, and all aspects of the performing arts use Kahilu as a favored venue.

LOCAL NIGHTLIFE

KAILUA-KONA

King Kamehameha's Kona Beach Hotel (☎ **808/329-2911**) holds a **luau and Polynesian revue** on the beach, next to the Ahuena Heiau, on Tuesday, Wednesday, Thursday, and Sunday. The hotel also offers Hawaiian and contemporary music at its **Billfish Bar** on Wednesday and Thursday evenings and *paniolo* music on Friday, Saturday, and Sunday.

Elsewhere in Kailua-Kona, the **Jolly Roger,** on Waterfront Row (☎ **808/ 329-1344**) is the spot for live entertainment from 8pm to closing on Friday and Saturday evenings—top 40s, Hawaiian music, and dancing near the ocean. At the **Keauhou Beach Hotel's Kuakini Terrace** (☎ **808/322-3441**), there's Hawaiian entertainment Wednesday, Friday, and Saturday evenings. Nearby, at the Kona Surf, the **Polynesian Paradise Revue** (☎ **808/322-3411**) is an 18-year tradition (more sunset than after-dark) in a large room on the cliffs above Keauhou Bay; it's free to the public and very popular.

THE KOHALA COAST RESORTS

Evening entertainment here usually takes the form of a luau or indistinctive lounge music at scenic terrace bars with scintillating sunset views. The **Kona Village Resort's** luau (see below) is the best luau on the island and one of the top three in the state, worth the price of admission. Otherwise, the resort roundup includes the Hilton Waikoloa Village's **"Legends of the Pacific"** dinner show (☎ **808/885-1234**) on Fridays, the **Royal Waikoloan luau** (☎ **808/885-6789**) on Sundays and Wednesdays, the **Mauna Lani Bay Hotel's seafood buffet** (☎ **808/885-6622**) on Friday and Saturday nights, and the **Mauna Kea Beach Hotel's luau** (☎ **808/882-7222**) on Tuesdays.

If you get a chance to hear or see the **Lim Family,** don't miss them. Immensely talented in hula and song, members of the family perform in the intimate setting of the **Atrium Bar at Mauna Lani Bay Resort** (☎ **808/885-6622**) and at the **Hapuna Beach Prince Hotel** (☎ **808/880-1111**), where Nani Lim and Gary Haleamau fill the open-air **Reef Lounge** with their celestial sounds as the sun sets on Hapuna Beach below.

The hot newcomer on the Kohala Coast is the **Mauna Lani Bay's Honu Bar** (☎ **808/885-6622**), a sleek, chic place for light supper, live light jazz with dancing, gourmet desserts, fine wines, and after-dinner drinks in an intimate, convivial atmosphere marred only by the cigar smoke. (Alas, it has fallen to the trend of selling cigars along with topnotch liqueurs, wines by the glass, and Petrossian caviar by the spoonful.) Although the pool, chess, and backgammon tables contribute to the decidedly masculine feeling of the place, it's about the liveliest after-dark oasis on the coast.

HILO

Hilo's most notable events are special or annual occasions such as the **Merrie Monarch Hula Festival,** the state's largest, which continues for a week after Easter Sunday with hula competition from all over the world, demonstrations and craft fairs, and a colorful spirit of pageantry that takes over the entire town. Tickets are always hard to come by; call **808/935-9168** well ahead of time. Special concerts are also held at the **Hawaii Naniloa Hotel's Crown Room** (☎ **808/969-3333**), the Hilo venue for name performers when they fly in from Oahu and the outer islands. For dancing and live music on weekends, head for **Fiascos** (Waiakea Square; ☎ **808/935-7666**). The second floor comes alive on Friday and Saturday nights with dancing and live contemporary and Hawaiian music and, on Thursday nights, line dancing and country music. If you're a blues lover, see what's playing at **Lehua's Bay City Bar and Grill** (☎ **808/935-8055**), on Hilo's bayfront. Live blues pours out of the large windows and onto the streets twice a month, on Friday and Saturday nights.

HULA

On this and all the islands, word of mouth is your best source for finding and supporting good hula, and the place for that is usually a *halau* (hula school) fund-raiser. Check the local papers or ask your hotel concierge if any of Hilo's hula halau are having a fund-raising concert or backyard luau that's open to the public. It's these local, community-based events that offer the greatest authenticity and spirit, often with spontaneous contributions of dance and song by visiting aunts and cousins.

LUAU!

Kona Village Luau. Kona Village Resort. ☎ **808/325-5555.** Fridays at 6pm; reservations required. Part of the Full American Plan for Kona Village guests; for nonguests, $63 for adults, $35 for children 6–12, $21 for children 2–5. AE, MC, V.

The longest continuously running luau on the island is still the best, a combination of an authentically Polynesian venue with a menu that works, impressive entertainment, and the spirit of old Hawaii. The feast begins with a ceremony in a sandy kiawe grove, where the pig is unearthed after a full day of cooking in its rock-heated underground oven. In the open-air dining room, next to prehistoric lagoons and tropical gardens, you'll sample a Polynesian buffet: poissun cru, poi, laulau (butterfish, seasoned pork, and taro leaves cooked in ti leaves), lomi salmon, squid luau (cooked taro leaves with steamed octopus and coconut milk), ahi poke, opihi (fresh limpets), coconut pudding, taro chips, sweet potato, chicken long rice, steamed breadfruit, and the shredded kalua pig. The bounty and generosity are striking. The Polynesian revue, a fast-moving, mesmerizing tour of South Pacific cultures, is far from limited to ancient and modern hula, and manages, miraculously, to avoid being clichéd or corny.

7 | Maui, the Valley Isle

What is it about Maui?

It's not the biggest island, nor the most scenic; it's mostly rural, not very cosmopolitan, a vestigial Third World sugar plantation with new K-Marts and Costcos. Despite all that, this island is the one—the one that manages to fulfill the expectations of all who come to Hawaii in search of the perfect tropical paradise. It's the realization of the dream.

And everybody, it seems, knows it. Twice named "best island in the world" in the annual *Condé Nast Traveler* readers' poll, Maui is Hawaii's second most-visited island (after Oahu), welcoming 2¹/₂ million people each year to its sunny shores. Maui has really made a name for itself.

On a map, Maui doesn't look like much—a tiny apostrophe with an attitude—but it's bigger than you think. The 727.3–square-mile island has three peaks more than a mile high, thousands of waterfalls and pools, 120 miles of shoreline, more than 80 golden-sand beaches (including two more than a mile long), some great seaside hotels, and endless summer weather. But the real key to Maui's success is this: location, location, location. It's perfectly located, smack dab in the middle of the inhabited Hawaiian chain, with a clear view of five nearby islands. Many people—continental people, mainland people, people who live landlocked lives—somehow feel comforted by the presence of the other islands in plain sight. I'm not sure why; I only know that to be all alone on the vast Pacific is an isolation only solo sailors crave. In the empty ocean, even migratory whales seek out Maui.

There's more than a *sense* of place about Maui and its community of neighbor islands; some believe that Maui, Lanai, Molokai, and Kahoolawe once comprised Maui Nui, or Big Maui, an ancient geo-political entity known even today as Maui County. If sea levels fell only 300 feet, geologists say, the four islands would be joined, and the island of Maui Nui would stand again (but it would still be only half as big as the Big Island.)

One of the larger Pacific isles even on its own, Maui is the result of a marriage of two shield volcanoes, 10,023-foot-high Haleakala and 5,788-foot-high Puu Kukui, that spilled enough lava between them to create a valley—and inspire the island's nickname. Thanks to this unusual makeup, Maui has a variety of tropical delights: cloud-wreathed peaks, sparkling waterfalls, remote valleys and rain forests, golden beaches, coral reefs, and sparkling seas. Maui packs a lot of nature in and around its landscape. And its micro-climates offer distinct variations on the tropic island theme: The island's as lush as an equatorial rain forest in Hana; dry as the Arizona desert in Makena; hot as Mexico in Lahaina; and cool and misty, like Oregon, up in Kula. The shores of Hookipa are ideal for windsurfers, and channel breezes challenge golfers in Kapalua.

What really sets Maui apart from all the other islands in Hawaii and the rest of the Pacific though, is the sleepy volcano that last erupted more than 200 years ago. One of the world's great natural wonders, Haleakala (or "House of the Sun") is a red, orange, and black bowl so big and so deep that it makes its own weather, has its own mountain range, and can swallow the island of Manhattan whole. When people say they want to see the real Hawaii, I always steer them gently away from the coco palm beaches and plummy coastal resorts and send them up 38 steep miles to the hard edge of the cold summit to peer down into the very heart of the matter: Haleakala's otherworldly crater, with its raw lava and primal ferns, all here a million years ago, before we were a speck in Mother Nature's eye.

The first thing you'll notice about Maui, before you get to the natural wonders, is the giant resorts threatening to almost overtake this paradise (see box below). But they're not really what the valley isle is all about. Beyond the big resorts, Maui is a collection of cowboy ranches, dwindling sugar plantations, and new suburban tracts set around pint-sized historic sugar towns. Maui is the home of the Maui onion, juicy as an apple and sweeter than Georgia's Vidalias; its vineyards on the fertile slopes of Haleakala produce wine grapes; and now coffee, too, is growing here. Maui lacks the urban electricity of Honolulu, but it isn't as moribund as Molokai. Visitors from other small towns in America and elsewhere find it just right: warm and friendly and not too foreign, with a pastoral lifestyle perfect for relaxing.

At the same time, Maui has an energy that can nudge devout sunbathers right off the beach. People get inspired to do things they might not do otherwise, like rise before dawn to catch the sunrise over 10,000-foot Haleakala Crater, then board bicycles to coast the 38 miles back down to sea level; or head out to sea on a lonely kayak to look for wintering humpback whales; or discover a whole new world of exotic flowers and tropical fish; or fly in open–cock pit planes, or ride a horse from mauka to makai, or even go pig hunting to save a rain forest. Who knows what Maui will drive you to? Come and see.

1 Orientation

by Rick Carroll

ARRIVING

If you think Maui looks like a round person with a big head, you'll probably arrive on its neck, at **Kahului Airport.**

At press time, three airlines fly directly from the mainland to Maui: **United Airlines** (☎ **800/241-6522**), which offers one flight a day nonstop to Maui from San Francisco, and one from Los Angeles; **Hawaiian Airlines** (☎ **800/367-5320**), which has several daily flights from San Francisco and Los Angeles with a stopover in Honolulu, but no plane change; and **Delta Airlines** (☎ **800/221-1212**). The other carriers fly to Honolulu, where you'll have to pick up an interisland flight in to Maui. **Aloha Airlines** (☎ **800/367-5250**) and **Hawaiian Airlines** (☎ **800/ 367-5320**) offer jet service from Honolulu. **Mahalo Airlines** (☎ **800/462-4256**) flies twin-engine planes from Honolulu; and **Aloha Island Air** (☎ **800/323-3345**)

Maui: Here Today, Gone Tomorrow?

Parisians used to tell the joke that the best view of Paris was from the Tour Montparnasse, because it was the only place in the city from which you couldn't see the Tour Montparnasse. On Maui's Kaanapali Beach, promoted as the most beautiful in the world, the best place to sit may be on the beach facing seaward, because it's the only spot where you can't see the wall-to-wall condominium complexes, hotels, and malls. The sprawling resort developments now form an almost unbroken chain from Lahaina to the elegant Ritz-Carlton Kapalua at the island's northern tip.

Maui's economic success holds both perils and prosperity: With the island now receiving two million visitors per year, it faces the challenge of keeping its natural beauty and relaxed way of life from being trampled under those four million feet.

Maui has only 729 square miles of solid ground, much of it under cultivation. The resident population is about 100,000, so the impact of 40,000 tourists on any given day is huge. Even so, development proceeds at a breakneck pace: about half of the local news concerns zoning battles, permits, and debates over the price of economic success. But before you conclude that tourism is ruining Maui, consider that the industry also provides half the island's jobs, supports 80% of the businesses, and accounts for 40% of property taxes. Residents are understandably ambivalent. Tourism is what makes Maui run, but can it run fast enough?

Despite prices as steep as the slopes of Haleakala, thousands are rushing to get their piece of the rock before it's all gone. Building in the islands is expensive because materials have to be shipped from the mainland. The average price of a home is $300,000—and a home, in a tropical environment, doesn't need to be very elaborate. This explains the proliferation of pre-fab homes (you can order one as a kit and assemble it yourself) and the cement-block aesthetic of most condo and hotel developments. Still, business is booming: One Mauian reported, "Twenty years ago, Kihei was a sleepy little town. Only a couple of cars went by all day." Now Maui has traffic jams, and a safety task force is being organized to deal with an alarming accident rate. There's no doubt that Maui's getting crowded. When you plan your trip, you may have to adjust your expectations as well as your budget.

Maui has grown so much that development is entering a new phase. The *Maui Visitor* reports that "retail centers"—malls—are one of the up-and-coming real estate markets, and that there's "a rich inventory of just about any kind of property available to investors." Residents are not so sanguine: in the little cowboy town of Makawao, they've been fighting a proposed supermarket development since 1993. Makawao feels charming but not cloying, a real town and not a put-on. But all that could change. People habitually refer to Maui as Paradise, and we all know what happened there.

also flies small planes, but they're just as reliable, and you may be able to get lower fares.

Landing at Kahului After flying 5 hours across the Pacific, you deplane at Kahului, which once sat in the middle of a sugar cane field but is now bordered by a new 62-acre retail-industrial complex with a K-Mart that makes you wonder why you left home. Or if you did. Wait, the worst is yet to come. The airport is still so small that a single plane can cause a long wait at the baggage carousel, rental car shack, and rental car pickup—the three obstacles you must clear to get out onto the highway.

If you don't like the chaos at the big beaches and along the strips, you can always spend your vacation underwater with a snorkel on, or you can go up-country. Much of Maui is protected and will never be bulldozed for new homes and shopping centers. In addition to Haleakala National Park, there are 10 state parks, 15 county parks, 4 marine preserves, and private parks owned by groups like the Nature Conservancy.

Other areas, like the north coast traversed by the "Heavenly Road to Hana," are somewhat immune to development. This torturous 50-mile road, flanked by towering cliffs, forests, and waterfalls, is itself a major attraction (despite 617 curves and 56 single-lane bridges), but the area seems unsuitable for big resorts. Still, subdivisions are planned on this wet and rural coast, provoking opposition from natives who fear the loss of their traditional—but not legally unshakable—right to public access to the sea and shore. Remoteness and inaccessibility are relative terms, and the more rugged half of Maui can no longer be relied upon to save itself.

While the future of Maui seems to hang in the balance, a few entrepreneurs are hoping to do well by doing good. These operators raise environmental consciousness by letting you see what you'll be missing if we aren't careful. The saga of Maui's most famous endangered species, the humpback whale, is a case in point. Once hunted nearly to extinction, the Pacific population has rebounded to somewhere between 2,000 and 3,000. Globally, whale watching is now a $100 million business, but one that combines entertainment with education. Many no doubt walk away from their encounter with these awesome and mysterious mammals with a new sense of responsibility for the planet.

Ecotourism has been promoted as a way to save the environment by transforming it into an economic as well as a natural resource. But even here, there's a catch: The more people come to observe and appreciate, the more pressure there is on the environment. Even in a strictly controlled setting like a national park, degradation of the site is a serious problem. Even respectful visitors who appreciate the pricelessness of such places have feet, use bathrooms, and need somewhere to sleep. It all translates into wear and tear and what might be called collateral development.

Maui lies like a rare jewel in the vast Pacific. Public officials and community groups are trying to keep it that way, without turning you away. By all means, visit Maui—but you may want to do it sooner rather than later. Legend has it that the god Maui snared the sun from the top of Haleakala in order to prolong daylight so his mother could dry her clothes. Present-day Mauians are finding it harder to make time stand still.

—*Bruce Murphy*

The Kahului Airport bottleneck is further compounded by poor urban planning. Maui expanded its small, friendly interisland airport into a major international airport, hoping to attract free-spending Japanese on jumbo jets which never came, then built a busy retail complex at the end of the runway where three traffic-choked two-lane roads, one from greater downtown Kahului, converge, usually the minute you arrive.

After collecting your baggage from the poky, automated carousels, step out, take a deep breath, and proceed to your right to the rental car pavilion. After confirming that you do have a car, wait curbside—in the distance you can see the majestic West Maui Mountains and beautiful Iao Valley—for the appropriate shuttle van to take you a half-mile away to the rental car pickup, where there's usually another long line. This process can take as long as an hour, sometimes more. Be patient. Look for rainbows. Notice how clouds form over Iao Valley. Try whistling "Tiny Bubbles."

If possible, avoid landing on Maui between 3 and 6pm, when a major traffic jam occurs at the first intersection. Once you clear Kahului, do not ever return to this area until you have to catch your flight home.

Avoiding Kahului   You can avoid Kahului Airport altogether by taking an **Aloha Island Air** (☎ **800/323-3345**) flight to **Kapalua–West Maui Airport,** which is convenient if you're planning to stay at any of the hotels in Kapalua or at the Kaanapali resorts. If you're staying in Kapalua, it's only a 10- or 15-minute drive to your hotel; a shuttle can pick you up and take you to your hotel. It's about 20 or 25 minutes to Kaanapali (as opposed to 35 or 40 min. from Kahului).

Aloha Island Air also flies into tiny **Hana Airport,** but you have to make a connection at Kahului to get there.

VISITOR INFORMATION

The **Maui Visitors Bureau** is located at 1727 Wili Pa Loop, Wailuku, Maui, HI 96793 (☎ **808/244-3530** or 800/525-MAUI; fax 808/244-1337). To get there from the airport, go right on Hi. 36 (the Hana Hwy.) to Kaahumanu Avenue (Hi. 32). Follow it past Maui Community College and Wailuku War Memorial Park onto East Main Street in Wailuku. At North Market Street, turn right, and then right again on Mill Street; go left on Kala Street and left again onto Wili Pa Loop.

There are also a few regional tourist boards that can help you out. The **Kaanapali Beach Resort Association** is at 45 Kai Ala Dr., Kaanapali-Lahaina, HI 96761 (☎ **800/245-9299**); and the **Wailea Destination Association** is at 3750 Wailea Alanui Dr., Wailea, HI 96753 (☎ **808/879-4258**).

THE REGIONS IN BRIEF
CENTRAL MAUI

This flat, often windy, corridor between Maui's two volcanoes is where you'll most likely arrive—it's where the main airport is—but you probably won't be spending time here, except to explore Iao Valley, the region's saving grace.

Kahului   On every island, I suppose, there's got to be a practical place where you can commit retail—you know, get gas, find film, eat junk food, get fast cash at the ATM, and go to the mall. Kahului looks just like the place you came to Maui to avoid. It's got used-car lots, fast-food joints, and banks on every corner, traffic lights and traffic jams, even a 24-hour gas station. It's a good example of bad urban planning: a Costco next to a wildlife preserve, and Maui's three main roads ending in a killer intersection that puts lost tourists at direct odds with homebound locals. Unless you're a serious mall rat on holiday in the islands or need to fill up your rental car on the way to the airport, once you land, get out as quick as you can.

Wailuku   With faded wooden storefronts, Wailuku might be just another funky old Maui hill town except for a singular backyard attraction: **Iao Valley.** While most people race through Wailuku en route to see the natural beauty of the valley, this quaint little town is worth a brief visit, if only to see a real place where real people actually appear to be working at something other than a suntan. This isn't a tourist town; it's the county seat, so you'll see men in neckties and women in dressy suits on important missions in the tropical heat. The town has a spectacular view of

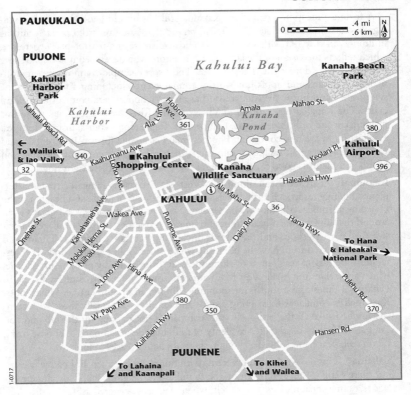

Haleakala crater, a great Mexican restaurant, a tofu factory, some interesting bungalow architecture, a Frank Lloyd Wright building on the outskirts of town, and the town's main attraction, the always endearing Bailey House Museum.

WEST MAUI

This is the fabled Maui you see on postcards. Jagged peaks, green velvet valleys, a wilderness full of native species—the majestic West Maui mountains are the epitome of earthly paradise. The beaches here are some of the islands' best. And it's no secret: This stretch of coastline along Maui's "forehead," from Kapalua to the historic port of Lahaina, is the island's most bustling resort area (with South Maui close behind).

Kapalua North beyond Kaanapali and the shopping centers of Napili and Kahana, the road starts to climb and the vista opens up to fields of silver-green pineapple and manicured golf fairways. Turn down the country lane of Pacific pines toward the sea, and you could only be in Kapalua. The windswept western foothills of Pu'u Kukui (the "hill of enlightenment"), the second wettest summit on earth, roll down to sea in a 1,500-acre patchwork of green slopes that end at five bays, once frequented by royalty, but are now the domain of two gracious hotels. They're set on one of Hawaii's best gold-sand beaches, hugging a bay that's a marine-life preserve; across the channel, the island of Molokai looms. Weather in the channel can get rugged, with gusty winds and April showers that spoil spring breaks, but generally Kapalua is most agreeable.

A former pineapple plantation, Kapalua still has an old general store and vintage Victorian church. The 23,000-acre pineapple plantation still operates, and its buildings, in tidy red with white trim, lend realism to the master-planned resort, which reflects the vision of the late Colin Cameron, who developed it and made sure that things were done right. They still are. The resort champions innovative environmental programs and holds noteworthy annual events, including a food-and-wine symposium and music festival. It also has an art school where you can learn local crafts. The Kapalua Bay Hotel and Villas and the Ritz-Carton, Kapalua, share this magnificent site with three favorite golf courses, ample tennis courts, historic features, a collection of swanky condos and homes (many available for vacation rental), and wide open spaces that include a rain forest preserve. What's good for the salvation of fish and plants is good for the human soul. I wish I were there right now.

Kaanapali   Farther south along the West Maui coast is Hawaii's first master-planned family resort. Mid-rise hotels line nearly 3 miles of gold-sand beach; they're linked by a landscaped parkway and separated by a jungle of plants. Golf greens wrap around the slope between beachfront and hillside properties. Whalers Village—a seaside mall with 48 shops and restaurants, including such fancy names as Tiffany and Co. and Louis Vuitton, plus the best little whale museum in Hawaii—and other restaurants are easy to reach on foot along the waterfront walkway or by resort shuttle, which also serves the small West Maui airport, just to the north. Shuttles also go to Lahaina, 3 miles to the south, for shopping, dining, entertainment, and boat tours. Kaanapali is popular with meeting groups and families—especially those with teenagers, who'll like all the action. If your company's not picking up the tab and you can't afford luxury digs, there are plenty of midrange deluxe condos to choose from. If you seek peace and solitude, though, there are better places to look.

Lahaina   This old whaler seaport teems with timeshare salesmen and bad whale art, but there's still lots of real history to be found amid the gimcrack. This vintage village is a tame version of its former self, when whalers swaggered ashore in search of women and grog. Now, you'll find art galleries, cute cafes, and a few old hotels, like the newly restored 1901 Pioneer Inn, on the waterfront. Don't miss a meal at Avalon, home of Caramel Miranda, the queen of desserts.

SOUTH MAUI

This is the hottest, sunniest, driest, most popular coastline on Maui for sun lovers—Arizona by the sea. Rain rarely falls and temperatures stick around 85° year-round. On former scrub land from Maalaea to Puu Olai, where cacti once grew wild and cows grazed, are now three distinctive resorts—Kihei, Wailea, and Makena—each appealing to a different crowd.

Kihei   The funky old Hawaiian fishing village of Kihei has evolved into Maui's best vacation bargain. Budget travelers swarm like sun-seeking geckos to lay out on eight sandy beaches along this scalloped, condo-packed, 7-mile stretch of coast. Kihei is neither charming nor quaint; it's a wide spot in the road that keeps spreading, a collection of condos, chain restaurants, and malls by the sea. What it lacks in aesthetics, though, it more than makes up for in sunshine and affordability.

Wailea   Only a decade ago this was dust; but now Wailea is a manicured oasis of multimillion-dollar resort hotels along 2 miles of palm-fringed gold coast—sort of Beverly Hills–by-the-sea, except California never had it so good: warm, clear water full of tropical fish, year-round golden sunshine and clear blue skies, and hedonistic pleasure palaces on 1,500 acres of black lava shore indented by five beautiful beaches. Amazing what a billion dollars can do.

Maui

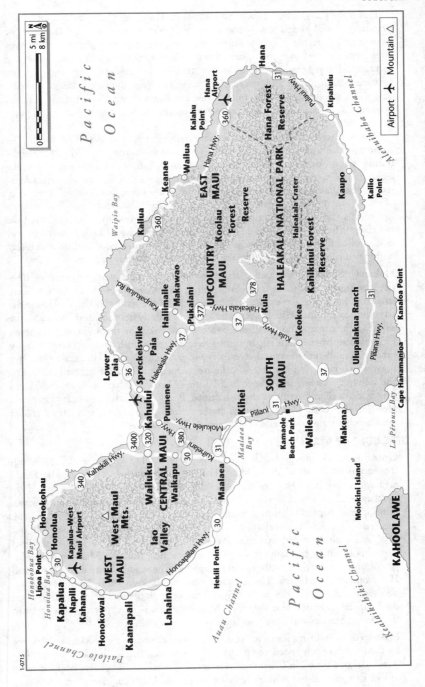

This is the playground of the stretch-limo set. The planned resort development—practically a well-heeled town—has a shopping village, three prized golf courses of its own and three more in close range, and a tennis complex. A growing number of large homes sprawl over the upper hillside. The resorts along this fantasy coast are spectacular, to say the least: Next door to the Four Seasons, the most elegant, is the Grande Wailea Resort and Spa, a public display of ego by Tokyo mogul Takeshi Sekiguchi, who dropped $600 million in 1991 to create his own minicity. There's nothing like it in Hawaii, and maybe even on the planet. It's so gauche you gotta see it.

Nice natural features include the coastal trail, a 3-mile round-trip path along the oceanfront with pleasing views everywhere you look—out to sea and to the neighboring islands, or inland to the broad lawns and gardens of the hotels. The trail's south end borders an extensive native coastal-plant garden, as well as ancient lava-rock house ruins juxtaposed with elegant oceanfront condos. But the chief attractions, of course, are those five outstanding beaches (the best is Wailea).

Yet, this 1,500-acre master plan by the sea is a little overblown and contrived for my taste; it feels as soulless as a California suburb and there's little except sun and sand that's indigenous to Hawaii. But if you want to drop out and do absolutely nothing, this is the place—perfect for a luxuriously mindless vacation.

Makena   Suddenly, the road enters raw wilderness. After Wailea's overdone density, the thorny landscape is welcome relief. One man-made object, a three-story structure that looks like a county hospital, violates the natural order. This lone oasis is the Maui Prince Hotel, erected by Japanese railway heir Yoshiaki Tsutsumi, the world's richest man, who installed a *sukoshi* bit of Tokyo on this arid coast. His stark, white ryokan-by-the sea is elegant, expensive, and, thankfully, the only one on 2,500 otherwise undisturbed coastal acres. Beyond it you'll discover Haleakala's last lava flow, which ran to the sea in 1790; the bay named for French explorer La Perouse; and a chunky, *a'a* lava trail known as the King's Highway, which leads around Maui's empty south shore past ruins and fish camps. Puu Olai stands like Maui's Diamond Head on the shore, where a sunken crater shelters tropical fish, and empty golden sand beaches stand at the end of dirt roads.

UP-COUNTRY MAUI

Once you've got enough beach time in, you'll probably take notice of the 10,000-foot mountain in the middle of Maui. The slopes of Haleakala ("House of the Sun") are home to cowboys, growers, and other country people who wave back as you drive by; they're all up here enjoying the crisp air, emerald pastures, eucalyptus, and flower farms of this tropical Olympus; there's even a misty California redwood grove. You can see a thousand tropical sunsets reflected in the windows of houses old and new, strung along a road that runs like a loose hound at 3,000 feet above sea level from Haiku, near the famous windsurfing beaches, through Makawao, an old-paniolo-turned–New Age village, and Kula, where the road leads up to the crater and **Haleakala National Park.** The rumpled two-lane blacktop of Hi. 37 turns to gravel on the other side of Tedeschi Winery, where wine grapes and wild elk flourish on the Ulupalakua Ranch, the biggest on Maui. A stay up-country is a nice contrast to the sizzling beaches and busy resorts below.

Makawao   Maybe it's me, but I've always missed the point about Makawao, except for the Fourth of July rodeo and parade, when everyone dresses up like a paniolo (see "Calendar of Events" in Chapter 3). Lovers of Hawaiiana and gallery hoppers seem to like this turn-of-the-century town, which looks like a fugitive from a Western movie set in a green sea of pastures peopled by black-and-white cows, but Makawao just reminds me of early Santa Cruz. Hui No'eau Visual Arts Center, Hawaii's premier arts society, is definitely worth a peek.

Kula   A feeling of pastoral remoteness prevails in this up-country community of old flower farms, humble cottages, and new suburban ranch houses with million dollar views that take in ocean, isthmus, the West Maui mountains, more ocean dotted with Lanai and Kahoolawe and, at night, the string of pearls that lights the gold coast from Maalaea to Puu Olai. They flourish at a cool 3,000 feet just below the cloud line along a winding road on the way up to Haleakala National Park. Everyone here grows something—Maui onions, carnations, orchids, and proteas, that strange-looking blossom that looks like a "Star Trek" prop—and B&Bs cater to guests seeking cool tropic nights, panoramic views, and a rural upland escape.

EAST MAUI

On the Road to Hana: Paia   When old sugar towns die they usually fade away in rust and red dirt. Not Paia; it looked to the wind and the sea and became the windsurfing capital of Hawaii, maybe the world. It's the island's artsy counterculture center, where a whiff of patchouli oil rides the trade winds and tie-dye outsells old-fashioned palaka. This sugar town, which just celebrated its 100th birthday, has survived fires, tidal waves, sugar barons, and dope-smoking hippies, who kept the place alive in the 1960s.

Today, nearby Sprecklesville is almost a ghost town, but plantation camps still cluster about Paia Mill, a rusty yellow contraption with smokestacks that looks like an industrial age relic from feudal England. The days of sugar on Maui, too, are drawing to a close. Although stores are empty and gas stations closed, many still stop here on the way to and from Hana, if only to poke into the Maui Crafts Guild, a cooperative owned by 40 local craftspeople; Paia Fish Market, which serves fresh local fish; or Wunderbar, a Teutonic biergarten owned by a Swiss chef who once cooked for the King of Sweden. But the main attraction is the wind that roars through the isthmus of Maui to the daily delight of windsurfers who come to Paia from around the world to fly on gossamer wings linked to surfboards.

Hana   Set between an emerald rain forest and a forever blue Pacific is a village probably best defined by what it lacks: golf courses, shopping malls, McDonald's; except for a gas station and a bank with an ATM, you'll find little of what passes for progress here. Instead, you'll discover the simple joys of fragrant tropical flowers, the sweet taste of backyard bananas and papayas, and the easy calm and unabashed small-town aloha of Old Hawaii. What saved "Heavenly" Hana from the inevitable march of progress? The 52-mile road that winds around 600 curves and crosses more than 50 one-lane bridges that separates it from Kahului. You can go to Hana for the day—it's a 3-hour drive (and a half-century away)—but 3 days are better.

2 Getting Around

by Rick Carroll

The only way to see Maui is by rental car. There's no real islandwide public transit.

CAR RENTALS

All the major rental-car agencies are on Maui and cars are usually plentiful, except on holiday weekends, which in Hawaii also means King Kamehameha Day, Prince Kuhio Day, and Admission Day (see "When to Go" in Chapter 3). The following national companies have offices on Maui, usually at both Kahului and West Maui airports: **Alamo** (☎ 800/327-9633); **Avis** (☎ 800/321-3712); **Budget** (☎ 800/527-0700); **Dollar** (☎ 800/800-4000); **Hertz** (☎ 800/654-3011); and **National** (☎ 800/227-7368).

Island Riders (☎ **808/661-9966** in Lahaina; **808/874-0311** in Kihei) has exotic cars and motorcycles for rent. It's a toy store for big boys and girls: You can rent a Rolls Royce Corniche convertible, a Ferrari Daytona 'Spyder, or a red-hot Dodge Viper; they even have Harley Davidson motorcycles, but only for licensed bikers and cops on holiday.

EASY RIDING AROUND MAUI: HARLEYS FOR HIRE

Don black denim and motorcycle boots and ride around Maui on a hog. Fatboys, DynaWide Glides, Softail Customs, and Road Kings—they're all for hire for about $100 a day at **Island Riders,** 126 Hinau St. (next to Pizza Hut) in Lahaina (☎ **808/661-9966**), and now in Kihei at 1794 S. Kihei Rd. (☎ **808/874-0311**). Forget the greasy Hell's Angels image; latter-day Wild Ones are button-down corporate types, or California Highway Patrol officers on holiday. Everybody's doing it—so get yourself a Harley for a day or more. Whether you blast up Haleakala's grand corniche or haul-ass up to Hana, it's the most fun you can have on two wheels in the islands.

DRIVING AROUND MAUI

Maui only has a handful of major roads: Two roads follow the coastline around the two volcanoes that form the island, Haleakala and Puu Kukui; one road goes up to Haleakala's summit; one road goes to Hana; one goes to Wailea, and one to Lahaina. It sounds simple, right? Well, it isn't, because the names of the few roads change en route. Study a recent map before you venture forth; the best is *Map of Maui,* 5th Edition, by James A. Bier (University of Hawaii Press; at major bookstores for $2.95).

From Kahului Airport, you'll immediately find yourself on Kuihelani Highway (Hi. 38), which leads to a dangerous Y-intersection in an industrial park that's under construction. Go straight and you intersect Honoapiilani Highway (Hi. 30), which leads to West Maui. Hi. 30 becomes dirt-and-gravel Kahekili Highway (Hi. 340) just beyond Kapalua, following the north coast and diminishing to a rugged one-lane road before returning to Wailuku, where it once again becomes Honoapiilani Highway.

From the Y-intersection, to the left is Hana Highway (Hi. 36). If you jog left, you'll be on the nameless Hi. 35, which leads to Mokulele Highway (still Hi. 35); follow it to Piilani Highway (Hi. 31) to reach Wailea and Makena. Hana Highway becomes Hi. 360 as it goes to Hana, and becomes Piilani Highway (Hi. 31) as it heads to Kipahulu. It becomes a bumpy, unpaved four-wheel drive road around the southeastern face of Haleakala, until it joins Kula Highway (Hi. 37) at Tedeschi Winery. Kula Highway intersects on the north with Haleakala Highway (Hi. 377), which goes to the summit of the crater.

Traffic Advisory   Mokulele Highway (Hi. 35) is a dangerous strip that's often the scene of head-on crashes involving intoxicated and speeding drivers; be careful. Also, be alert on the Honoapiilani Highway (Hi. 30) en route to Lahaina, since drivers who spot whales in the channel between Maui and Lanai often slam on the brakes and cause major tie-ups and accidents.

OTHER TRANSPORTATION OPTIONS

Taxis   **Alii Taxi** (☎ **808/661-3688** or 808/667-2605) offers islandwide, 24-hour service. You can also call **Kihei Taxi** (☎ **808/879-3000**), **Wailea Taxi** (☎ **808/874-5000**), and **Yellow Cab of Maui** (☎ **808/877-7000**) if you need a ride.

Shuttles   SpeediShuttle (☎ **808/875-8070**) can take you between Kahului Airport and all the major resorts from 5am to 9pm daily. Rates vary, but figure on $22 for two to Makena, and $40 for two to Kapalua. Be sure to call before your flight to arrange pickup.

Free shuttle vans operate within the resort areas of Kaanapali, Kapalua, and Wailea, and a new shopper's shuttle links Kaanapali with Kahului; if you're staying in those areas, your hotel can fill you in on the exact routes and schedules.

FAST FACTS: Maui

American Express   In South Maui, at the Grand Wailea (☎ 808/875-4526); and in West Maui at the Ritz Carlton Kapalua (☎ 808/669-6016), and the Westin Maui at Kaanapali Beach (☎ 808/661-7155).

Dentists   Emergency dental care is available at Maui Dental Center, 162 Alamaha St., Kahului (☎ 808/871-6283).

Doctors   Doctors on Call (☎ 808/667-7676) will make hotel visits; or call West Maui Healthcare Center, Whaler's Village, Suite H-7, Kaanapali (☎ 808/ 667-9721) until 10pm nightly.

Emergencies   Call 911 for police, fire, and ambulance. District stations are located in Hana (☎ 808/248-8311), and Lahaina (☎ 808/661-4441).

Hospitals   Maui Memorial Hosptial is at 221 Mahalani, Wailuku (☎808/ 244-9056); Hana Medical Center is on Hana Highway (☎808/248-8924); and Kula Hosptial is at 204 Kula Hwy., Kula (☎ 808/878-1221).

Newspapers   The *Maui News* is the island's daily paper.

Poison Control Center   In an emergency, call 800/362-3585.

Post Office   In Lahaina, there are branches at the Lahaina Civic Center, 1870 Honoapiilani Hwy. (☎ 808/667-6611); and at the Lahaina Shopping Center (☎ 808/661-0550). In Kahului, there's a branch at 138 S. Puunene Ave. (☎ 808/ 871-4710); and in Kihei, at 1254 S. Kihei Rd. (☎ 808/879-2403).

Weather Reports   For the current weather, call 808/877-5111 from 4:30pm to 8:30pm; for Haleakala National Park weather, call 808/572-7749; for surf and wave conditions, call 808/877-3477.

3 Accommodations

by Rick Carroll

The price of this earthly paradise can be steep or cheap—it's up to you. Maui has something for every budget, from $15-a-night state park cabins to a $10,000-a-night penthouse. In between, you'll find gingham-and-lace–curtained B&Bs, bunks on working ranches, a tent camp on Olowalu reef, and Mrs. Nakamura's famed Aloha Cottage, at the end of the Hana road.

The rates listed below are rack rates, but you can usually do better, particularly at the big hotels; see "Tips on Finding Accommodations" in Chapter 3. Hawaii adds 10.17% in taxes to all hotel bills. Parking is free unless otherwise noted.

CENTRAL MAUI

Maui Seaside Hotel. 100 Kaahumanu Ave., Kahului, Maui, HI 96732. ☎ **808/877-3311** or 800/367-7000. Fax 808/922-0052. 190 rooms. A/C TV TEL. $70–$100 single or double. Extra person $12. AE, MC, V.

If you've got to stay in Kahului because you have an early flight and want to be near the airport, your choices are limited. This is probably the best of the lot. The rooms are small and somewhat outdated, but they're clean, and the prices are good. Some of the rooms have kitchenettes. The restaurant serves a variety of inexpensive dishes, ranging from Asian to Italian. All in all, the Maui Seaside is a bargain, but don't bother spending more than a night in Kahului if you don't have to.

WEST MAUI

KAPALUA

✪ **Kapalua Bay Hotel & Villas.** 1 Bay Dr., Lahaina, HI 96761. ☎ **808/669-5656** or 800/367-8000. Fax 808/669-4694. 194 rms, 3 suites, 100 one- and two-bedroom condos. A/C TV MINIBAR TEL. $260–$1,260 double. AE, DC, JCB, MC, V.

If you're looking for elegant, intimate digs in a spectacular natural environment, look to this hotel at Kapalua, the old but still-functioning pineapple plantation that seems to command Maui's north shore. Few Hawaiian resorts have the luxury of open space like this one. The hotel (along with its neighbor, the Ritz-Carlton) sits seaward of 23,000 acres of green fields lined by spiky Norfolk pine windbreaks.

The 1970s-style rectilinear hotel sits down by the often windy shore, full of angles that frame stunning views of ocean, mountains, and that blue sky full of white clouds. Past the lobby is a tastefully designed maze of oversized rooms overlooking a palm-fringed gold-sand beach that's one of the best in Hawaii, as well as an excellent Ben Crenshaw golf course and all that open space. Decor is casual: sand-colored walls, bright tropical prints, rattan furniture with a touch of blue. Plantation shutter doors open onto private lanais with a view of Molokai across the channel. My favorite is Room 130, a ground-floor suite full of Philippine mahogany and old Manila rattan furniture that's only a few steps from Kapalua Beach.

This hotel is the perfect retreat for harried urban souls seeking escape in the tropics. The natural beauty of this unspoiled coast contributes to the overall sense of serenity. You'll never want to leave until it's time for the plane to take you back to reality, as woeful departees often say.

Dining/Entertainment: The most appealing dining spot is the Bay Club (see "Dining," below), in its own plantation-style building on a promontory overlooking the sea, specializing in seafood for lunch and dinner. The casual Pool Terrace serves continental breakfast and lunch. Other options are located in the rather confusing lobby building. There's entertainment in the two lounges every evening.

Services: Limited room service; twice-daily maid service; ice service (ice is delivered to your room late every afternoon and on request); resort shuttle service; complimentary airport transfer to the Kapalua West Maui Airport; lei greeting; church services; daily morning coffee, afternoon tea and snacks in the lobby; chilled pineapple juice by the pool; secretarial services; baby-sitting services on request; complimentary introductory scuba lessons. Rooms have VCRs, and there's a free video library.

Facilities: Two swimming pools, exercise facility with one-on-one fitness training (for a fee) and classes. The Kapalua resort also has a famous trio of golf courses (each with its own pro shop) and 10 Plexi-pave tennis courts for day and night play. Villa guests have access to two additional tennis courts. Children between the ages of 5 and 12 might want to take advantage of Kamp Kapalua, where they can enjoy snorkeling, surfing, tide-pool exploration, lei-making, and cookie-baking, among other activities. Adults can plan similar activities (except for the cookie-baking) through the hotel's Beach Activity Center. The Kapalua Shops are within easy walking distance.

Kapalua Villas. 500 Office Rd., Kapalua, HI 96761. ☎ **808/669-8088** or 800/545-0018. Fax 808/669-5234. 165 one- and two-bedroom condos and three-bedroom luxury homes. A/C TV TEL. Winter, $185–$365 condo; off-season $165–$345 condo; $700–$1,000 home. AE, DC, DISC, JCB, MC, V.

For golfers, they're ideal; for families, just the thing; for anyone weary of the resort scene, this is the way to go: palatial condos and townhouses along the oceanfront cliffs and fairways at Kapalua Resort that are a bargain on this idyllic coast, especially if you're traveling with a group.

These upscale dwellings have just about everything: full kitchens, laundry, and handsome furnishings. The contemporary units, most of them built in the early 1980s, are arranged in three clusters—bay, golf, and ridge. Each shares a private pool, barbecue area, and parking. They're individually owned and decorated, and the management office is staffed around the clock. My favorite villas are the two-bedroom units near Kapalua Bay Hotel; they're on a bold headland, only a short walk to Kapalua Beach, one of the best in Hawaii. They also have great Japanese-style sunken tubs for soaking.

Guests have access to all of the resort's amenities, and enjoy special golf rates, advance tee times, complimentary tennis, and shuttle service throughout Kapalua and to the nearby airport. There's maid service only twice a week, though, so you'll have to pick up after yourself.

✪ **Ritz-Carlton, Kapalua.** 1 Ritz-Carlton Dr., Kapalua, HI 96761. ☎ **808/669-6200** or 800/ 262-8440. Fax 808/669-1566. 550 rms, 48 suites. A/C TV MINIBAR TEL. $285–$2,800 double. Wedding/honeymoon and other special packages available. AE, DC, DISC, MC, V. Valet parking $10; free self-parking.

Of all the Ritz-Carltons in the world, this is probably the best. It's in the best place (Hawaii), near the best beach (Kapalua), and it's got an amazing staff (John Toner, take a bow). I love it. If you were (God forbid) a wealthy 19th-century sugar planter, you might have envisioned an estate something like this. It rises proudly on a knoll overlooking the sea at the northern end of West Maui, in a singularly spectacular setting between the rain forest and the sea. During construction, hundreds of ancient Hawaiians were discovered buried in the sand, so the hotel was moved inland to avoid disrupting the graves. The setback improved the hotel's outlook, which now has a commanding view of Molokai.

The style is fancy plantation, elegant but not imposing. The public spaces are open, airy, and graceful, with plenty of tropical foliage and landscapes by artist Sarah Supplee that recall the not-so-long-ago agrarian past. Rooms are up to the usual Ritz standard, done in beige with tropical lithographs and outfitted with marble baths, private lanais, in-room fax capability, and voice mail. Hospitality is the keynote here; you'll find the exemplary service you expect from Ritz-Carlton seasoned with good old-fashioned Hawaiian aloha.

The Ritz is a complete universe, one of those resorts where you can sit by the pool with a book for 2 weeks. The management, which realized its appeal early on, brings Maui to the hotel by cosponsoring the Kapalua Wine and Food Festival, an Easter arts and crafts festival, sports contests, and other events that involve guests directly with the local community.

Dining/Entertainment: Dining is excellent at the Anuenue Room (formerly The Grill), as well as at the new outdoor Terrace (for breakfast and dinner) and poolside (for lunch). As for the Anuenue Room's extraordinary Sunday brunch: Not even the wealthy planters had it this good. Whether you have your gourmet fare regular or macrobiotic, it'll be memorable, thanks to Executive Chef Patrick Callarec and crew. It's a small hike to the beach, so fortunately the Beach House serves daytime drinks and light fare. Cocktails are served in the Lobby Lounge, where magician/ bartender Gordon Fushikoshi can levitate a $100 bill and otherwise amuse you; it doubles as an espresso bar in the morning. A new pool bar serves drinks by the three pools.

Services: 24-hour room service, twice-daily towels, nightly turndowns; private club floors with concierge, continental breakfast, light lunch, afternoon snacks, drinks, newspapers, and a private lounge where club guests can enjoy them. Airport and golf course shuttle, secretarial services, daily kids' programs, lei greetings, special services for international guests, including multilingual employees.

Facilities: The resort boasts three top-rated golf courses. Meeting facilities and ballrooms accommodate incentives winners and groups. There's also a tennis complex, three pools, a nine-hole putting green, a croquet lawn, a beach volleyball court, a fitness center and salon, guests-only full-day guided backcountry hikes, and a historic plantation-style wedding chapel.

Kaanapali

Hyatt Regency Maui. 200 Nohea Kai Dr., Lahaina, HI 96761. ☎ **808/661-1234** or 800/ 233-1234. Fax 808/667-4497. 815 rms, 35 suites. A/C TV MINIBAR TEL. $240–$320 terrace or mountain view; $240–$380 ocean view. Regency club floors $390–$450. Packages available. AE, DC, DISC, JCB, MC, V. Valet parking $8; free self-parking.

One of several large fantasy hotels built by Christopher Hemmeter for Hyatt in the 1980s, this hotel, the southernmost of the Kaanapali Beach Resort properties, has lots of imagination without going over the edge. The grand interior is sophisticated—and exaggerated—enough to go beyond pomp and make the experience of being there fun. Asian art and exotic birds vie for attention in the lobby, an expansive atrium filled with trees and gardens. The grounds are parklike, with a dense riot of plants and flowers along the entry lane, and the swimming pools feature man-made grottos, slides, and a suspended walking bridge; there's even a man-made beach in case the adjacent public beach is just too crowded.

Only the pool, a row of palms, and a strip of lawn separates the hotel's three wings from the beach. All the rooms are pleasantly decorated in rich colors, floral prints, and Asian lamps—a welcome change from the typical beiges—and have separate sitting areas and private lanais. In-room amenities include safes, hairdryers, coffeemakers, and irons and boards.

Dining/Entertainment: Swan Court is a romantic setting for dinner; its rollaway walls open wide to let in the moonlight, and tables sit beside a waterfall pool where greedy black and white swans cruise in for a handout. Steaks and seafood are served in the open-air Lahaina Provisions Company, while Spats (formerly a disco) serves Italian fare; the Pavilion is a casual poolside choice. The "Drums of the Pacific" dinner show keeps things rolling at night. In addition to the lounges, the cool pool has a swim-up bar for cocktails.

🤸 Family-Friendly Resorts

Grand Wailea Resort Hotel and Spa (Wailea)   This is a great place for kids and families. Every time I go here the sounds of laughter of children fill the air. Water slides, fountains, funny Botero art, a kids camp—this is Disneyland by the sea.

Westin Maui (Kaanapali)   First you build a waterfall, then you add a shopping arcade that looks like a zoo full of exotic parrots, then you add hotel rooms topped by penthouses, and you do it all on the beach at Kaanapali—which appeals not just to kids, but to everyone.

Kea Lani Suites and Villas (Wailea)   It looks like Las Hadas or some Arab poobah's tent. Inside, every room's a suite, so the kids can watch laser discs on TV, check out the computer center, or hang out at their own pool.

Services: Concierge; room service; twice-daily maid service; baby-sitting available on request. Two Regency Club floors have private concierge, complimentary breakfast, sunset cocktails, and snacks. The activity desk can help you plan island sightseeing, arrange cruises, and make airline reservations. Camp Hyatt kid's program offers daytime and evening supervised activities for 3- to 12-year-olds. Special programs include "Tour of the Stars," a rooftop astronomy program.

Facilities: The hotel's Great Pool is one of the main attractions. The health club has a weight and exercise room, classes, Jacuzzi, sauna, and massage studio. There are also six hard-surface tennis courts, two nearby Kaanapali Resort golf courses, a game room, and a small lending library. Snorkeling gear, bicycles, kayaks, boogie boards, and video and underwater cameras are available for rent. *Kiele V*, the Hyatt's 55-foot catamaran, sponsors snorkel trips, whale-watching excursions, and evening cruises.

Kaanapali Alii. 50 Nohea Kai Dr., Lahaina, HI 96761. ☎ **808/667-1666** or 800/642-MAUI. Fax 808/661-1025. 264 one- and two-bedroom apts. A/C TV TEL. Winter $245–$490; mid-Apr–mid-Dec $215–$425. AE, MC, V.

Right among the beachfront luxury hotels at the southern end of the resort is this complex, which looks like just another hotel and has about the same rates and grounds—and yet it's different. Here your money gets you a spacious condo with a large lanai and plenty of breathing room for the family. The luxurious, individually owned and decorated units have full kitchens, washer and dryer, whirlpool tub, private lanai, and daily maid service. Amenities include concierge, exercise room, sauna, tennis courts, pools, Jacuzzi, barbecue grills, activities desk, and a nice stretch of golden beach. If you don't feel like fixing dinner, there are plenty of restaurants within walking distance, or you can order room service from the Maui Marriott next door. Club Alii level includes full-size rental car, fully stocked bar, plush terry robes, and grocery package (including champagne); call for rates.

Kaanapali Beach Hotel. 2525 Kaanapali Pkwy., Lahaina, HI 96761. ☎ **808/661-0011** or 800/262-8450. Fax 808/667-5978. 430 rms, 3 suites. A/C TV TEL. $145–$225 double; $190–$535 suite. AE, CB, DC, DISC, JCB, MC, V.

This old beach hotel, set in a garden by the sea, is Maui's most genuinely Hawaiian place to stay. You live aloha here.

This isn't a luxury property, but it's not bad, either. The three low-rise wings are set around a grassy parklike lawn with coco palms and a whale-shaped swimming pool. With a sweet flower lei around your neck, you'll enter a spacious room done in wicker and rattan, with framed sepia-tone photos of Hawaiians having fun on the beach that's just outside. All accommodations feature minirefrigerators and lanais that look toward the courtyard and the beach. The deluxe beachfront rooms are separated from the water only by Kaanapali's landscaped walking trail. My favorite is the oceanfront Molokai Suite, with its view of 85-foot high Kekaha Rock and Molokai and Lanai in the distance.

Old Hawaiian values and customs are close at hand. As part of the hotel's Hawaiian activities program, you can learn to cut pineapple, weave lauhala, even dance the *real* hula. There's hula and music in the open courtyard restaurant every night, an arts and crafts fair every Friday, and kids' programs. The menus at the hotel's three restaurants feature native Hawaiian dishes as well as modern Hawaiian cuisine (there's also a poolside bar). Other amenities include a United Airlines desk, baby-sitting, free scuba and snorkeling lessons, coin-op laundry, shops and beauty salon, beach equipment rentals (boogie boards, snorkeling and scuba equipment, sailboats, windsurfers, and catamarans), and access to 11 tennis courts and the Kaanapali golf courses.

It's older and less high-tech than its upscale neighbors, but the Kaanapali has an irresistible local style and real Hawaiian warmth that's absent in many other Maui hotels.

Maui Marriott Resort. 100 Nohea Kai Dr., Lahaina, HI 96761. ☎ **808/667-1200** or 800/ 228-9290. Fax 808/667-8181. 720 rooms, 19 suites. A/C TV TEL. $205–$310 double; $400– $1,000 suite. Packages available. AE, DC, DISC, JCB, MC, V. Parking $7.

In this glamorous neighborhood, a pink building seems Floridian and chintzy-looking—like plastic flamingos. Maui doesn't need that. Only Hawaii's original Pink Palace, the 1927 Royal Hawaiian on Waikiki, really pulls off that look in the islands.

But the Maui Marriott hangs in there, attracting loyal fans who care less about exterior colors and more about what they're getting for their money ('cause this place ain't cheap). It's an easygoing place with all the amenities. Fountains and waterfalls, pools and coconut groves set the mood on 15 beachfront acres. The rooms are freshly renovated in light woods and oceany blue-greens, a striking contrast to the pink exterior. They all come with a minifridge, safe, iron and board, hairdryer, and private lanai, and 9 out of 10 face the ocean.

But the 20 shops in the arcade make the hotel feel like a shopping mall by the sea. There's a total of 7 bars and restaurants, if you count the new Pizza Hut kiosk (another markdown in my book—but I don't like the Burger King at Honolulu International, either). There are lots of activities for guests though, including classes in Hawaiiana (including lei-making, hula, ukulele, quilting, and language lessons) and snorkeling, plus multiple pools for swimming and relaxing, tennis, nearby golf, and other sports. The nightly luau is rated "Best Luau" by both the *Maui News* and the *San Francisco Chronicle*, two newspapers that know a good luau when they see it.

Dining/Entertainment: The restaurants include Moana Restaurant, which offers daily breakfast buffet on a garden terrace; the Lokelani Room, a romantic supper club that serves fresh seafood and island cuisine at dinner only; and Nikko Steak House, with teppanyaki cooking at tabletop grills (also dinner only). Entertainment includes sing-along karaoke in the Lobby Bar, and the nightly Hawaiian luau.

Services: Room service from 6am to 10pm; 24-hour laundry, baby-sitting, and interpreter services; activity and car-rental desks; notary, fax, and express mail services.

Facilities: Two swimming pools, two whirlpools, children's pool, five tennis courts (three lit for night play), exercise room with Universal weights, Life-Cycles, and Stairmasters; video game room; nine-hole putting green (the three resort courses are nearby); conference facilities. Retail arcade includes beauty salon, international center, flower stand, 1-hour photo shop, massage therapist, Ocean Activities Center, and more.

Napili Kai Beach Club. 5900 Honoapiilani Rd., Lahaina, HI 96761. ☎ **808/669-6271** or 800/367-5030. Fax 808/669-5740. 162 units (studios to three-bedroom apts). TV TEL. $160– $230 double studio, $270–$320 one-bedroom (sleeps up to four), $400–$520 two-bedroom (sleeps up to six). Packages available. MC, V.

Just south of the Bay Club restaurant, several condos and small hotels border another inviting bay and beach at Napili. This comfortable complex, with direct beach access, is one of Maui's senior resorts, and it's easy to see why its fans are so devoted. The complex is a cluster of one- and two-story units with double-hipped Hawaii-style roofs that face their very own gold-sand safe-swimming beach, where the waves that roll ashore are in the low to mid-70s year-round. Many units have a view of the Pacific, with Molokai and Lanai in the distance. The best units are in the older beachfront Lahaina Building, a good deal—with ceiling fans—at $205, but the best deals are in the less expensive Honolulu Building, which is fully air-conditioned and set back from the shore around a grassy parklike lawn and pool deck.

Papakea Resort. 3543 Lower Honoapiilani Rd., Lahaina, HI 96761. ☎ **808/669-4848** or 800/367-7052. Fax 808/669-0061. 364 units (studios, one-bedroom, and two-bedroom apts). TV TEL. Winter $135–$280; early Apr–late Dec $120–$260. AE, MC, V.

Just north of Kaanapali Beach is this oceanfront, low-rise, Hawaiian-style condo complex. It's homey, breezy, and gracious, and the prices are good. Once you're on the property, more obtrusive neighbor properties vanish and you're free to focus on the 13 acres of green lawns and gardens, and the sea. There's no sandy beach here, but you won't have to walk far. The studios, one- and two-bedroom condos come with full kitchens (with microwave), washer/dryers, and daily maid service. There are two oceanfront pools and spas, putting greens, tennis and shuffleboard, barbecues, and staffed front and activities desks. Golf, shops, and restaurants are just a short drive away.

Sheraton Maui. 2605 Kaanapali Pkwy., Lahaina, HI 96761. ☎ **808/661-0031** or 800/782-9488. Fax 808/661-0458. 510 rms, 16 suites, 30 family-sized junior suites. A/C TV TEL. $270–$3,000. 15 wheelchair-accessible rms, 10 designed for the hearing impaired. Packages available. AE, CB, DC, DISC, ER, JAL, JCB, MC, V.

Still a hard-hat construction zone when I stopped by for a preview, the Sheraton Maui is due to reopen in late 1996, after a complete $150 million remake on its prime beachfront site at Black Rock. The grand dame of Kaanapali Beach, built in 1963, has been completely redesigned and will re-emerge as a virtually new hotel with six buildings of six stories or less. The lobby has been elevated to take advantage of panoramic views, and a new lagoonlike pool meanders through lush tropical landscaping. A fitness center, a game center, and laundry facilities are being added to the usual list of Kaanapali features: golf, tennis, ocean sports, shopping, and beach. The new emphasis is on family appeal, with a new class of rooms for families, summer activity programs, and other kid-friendly amenities. Irons, coffeemakers, hairdryers, and other touches in the rooms will make for easy travel, but it's anybody's guess right now as to what the rooms will look like.

Not everything is changing, thankfully. Cliff divers will still swan-dive off the torch-lighted lava rock headland in a traditional sunset ceremony. It's quite a sight to see.

Dining/Entertainment: The Discovery Room features breakfast and dinner buffets, as well as à la carte dining and panoramic views of Black Rock Promontory, the beach, and Molokai and Lanai. There are also some casual eateries and bars, one with karaoke. There's also a nightly luau (except Sun).

Services: Valet laundry; baby-sitting service; room service; Avis Rent-A-Car direct line; nondenominational poolside services on Sunday.

Facilities: 24-hour coin-op laundry; two outdoor pools; three outdoor tennis courts; conference facilities; activities desk; access to nearby Kaanapali golf courses.

Westin Maui. 2365 Kaanapali Pkwy., Lahaina, HI 96761. ☎ **808/667-2525** or 800/228-3000. Fax 808/661-5831. 761 rms, 32 suites. A/C TV MINIBAR TEL. $255–$400 standard double; $475 Royal Beach Club double, $650–$2,000 suite. Special wedding/honeymoon and other packages available. AE, DC, DISC, ENROUTE, JCB, MC, V. Valet parking $5; free self-parking.

Families and honeymooners alike love the Westin, another Christopher Hemmeter fantasy makeover of the late 1980s (à la the Hyatt Regency Maui). It's fun, open, friendly, and exotic, too: With two 11-story towers rising over five pools (one for adults only) connected by slides, grottos, and waterfalls, this beachfront fantasy hotel works because Hemmeter didn't get too carried away—although the pink fla-mingos at Sound of The Falls restaurant come real close. The grounds are estatelike and the interior public areas always busy with tropical birds shrieking, waterfalls splashing, and people strolling around the elaborate pool complex. The oversized architecture, requisite colonnade, and $2 million art collection make a pleasing back-drop for all the action.

The guest rooms were all renovated in 1995, so they have a fresh, up-to-date look. In addition to the standard features, each one comes with a safe, an iron and board, a coffeemaker, and its own lanai. Several outdoor restaurants and lounges take ad-vantage of the casual mood and balmy weather. Golf, tennis, and shopping are all at hand, and the beach walk out front is good for a morning jog or walk. Groups find the hotel convenient, with lots of indoor and outdoor meeting space. A coordinator known as the Director of Romance can help throw an unforgettable wedding.

Dining/Entertainment: The poolside Cook's at the Beach offers free evening hula shows. The Villa Terrace, Westin's other casual dining room, features Hawaiian music nightly and a popular all-you-can-eat fresh seafood buffet, a top value. Al-though Sound of the Falls, the fine dining room, was closed at the time of this writ-ing, it's well known and well liked for its elegant Sunday brunch amid flamingos and the sound of waterfalls (fake, but pretty).

Services: Nightly turndowns; twice-daily maid service; club floors with breakfast, champagne, concierge, lounge, and special amenities; multilingual staff; American Express and Hertz Rent-a-Car desks; Japanese Guest Services desk; secretarial services; nondenominational church services every Sunday. Guest Services will help you plan sightseeing and activities. Kids' program in which counselors supervise children up to 12 years old Monday through Friday on and off the property.

Facilities: Five swimming pools, Jacuzzi, aquacise classes, scuba lessons for begin-ners and refresher courses. Health club with weight training, aerobic, and exercise rooms. Golf at Kaanapali's two courses, tennis, beauty salon, 8 retail shops, business center, conference facilities.

LAHAINA

House of Fountains Bed & Breakfast. 1579 Lokia St., Lahaina, HI 96761. ☎ **808/ 667-2121.** Fax 808/667-2120. 6 rms, 2 suites. A/C TV. $85–$115 double or suite, $15 for extra person. Full breakfast included. No credit cards.

Talk about escape: A young German couple ran away to Maui for their honeymoon, fell in love with the island, bought a big house above Lahaina, and turned it into one of Lahaina's best B&Bs. Their 7,000-square-foot contemporary home, in a quiet resi-dential subdivision at the north end of town, is very popular with visitors from around the world. The oversized rooms are fresh and quiet, with ceramic tile floors, bright tropical fabrics, and wicker furnishings. The four downstairs rooms all open to flower-filled private patios. Breakfast is served in the sunny dining room. Guests share a pool, Jacuzzi, and barbecue area; you're welcome to curl up on the living room sofa with a book from the library. A stay here is like visiting old friends. The only downside is that the nearest beach is about 10 minutes away.

Lahaina Inn. 127 Lahainaluna Rd., Lahaina, HI 96761-1502. ☎ **808/661-0577** or 800/ 669-3444. Fax 808/667-9480. 12 rms. A/C TEL. $89–$129 double. Continental breakfast included. AE, DISC, JCB, MC, V. Next-door parking $5.

If the romance of historic Lahaina catches your fancy, a stay here will underscore the experience. Built in 1938 as a general store, swept by fire in the mid-1960s, and reopened as a hotel in the 1970s, this place deteriorated into a flea-bag with an eyesore bar at street level. In 1986 though, rescue came: It was saved from extinction by Rick Ralston, the Waikiki airbrush artist who became the Crazy Shirts millionaire—and a one-man historic restoration society. About a million dollars of T-shirt money has brought the place back to life as a charming, antique-filled inn right in the heart of Lahaina.

If you like old hotels that have a genuinely historic feel, you'll love this place. As it is with old hotels, some of these Victorian antique–stuffed rooms are small; if that's problem, ask for a larger one. All come with private bath and lanai. The best room in the house is no. 7 ($99), which overlooks the beach, the town, and the island of Lanai; you can watch the action below or close the door and ignore it. Downstairs is a fine and popular storefront bistro, David Paul's Lahaina Grill (see "Dining," below). No TV, no kids under 15.

Lahaina Shores Beach Resort. 475 Front St., Lahaina, HI 96761. ☎ **808/667-1666** or 800/ 642-MAUI. Fax 808/661-1025. 152 studios and one-bedrooms, 2 penthouses. A/C TV TEL. $120–$190 double, $140–$225 penthouse (sleeps up to four). AE, MC, V.

What's special about this place is the location—right on the beach, just outside the rowdy, trafficky central core of Lahaina. It's a catbird seat for watching whales and ships coming and going, day and night, from Lahaina's busy harbor. Although the beach isn't the greatest on the coast, it is the site of the only beachfront luau in these parts, so you won't have far to go for a roast-pig dinner show.

Lahaina Shores is affordable and convenient. The roomy, individually owned condo units come with full kitchens, VCRs, and ample space, plus daily maid service and a concierge; laundry facilities are available. In general the bathrooms are small, but they do the job. There's a pool and spa off the newly renovated lobby. Shops and restaurants are right next door at the 505 Front St. complex. All in all, an agreeable place.

✪ Pioneer Inn. 658 Wharf St., Lahaina, HI 96761. ☎ **808/661-3636** or 800/457-5457. Fax 808/667-5708. 35 units. A/C TEL. $90–$120 double, $155 junior suite, $225 full suite. AE, DC, MC, V. Parking $4 in lot 2 blocks away.

The first time I checked into the Pioneer Inn back in the 1970s, a room overlooking Lahaina Harbor went for $20 and included a can of Raid insect repellent. Those days are long gone (I miss them), but this venerable waterfront hotel has never looked better. With a $5 million restoration, Texas oilman Howard Lennon saved this great old Lahaina landmark (1901) from sure death from termites and worse: greedy developers with high-rise schemes. Somebody should give him a medal.

This once rowdy home-away-from-home for sailors and whalers now seems almost respectable, almost like visiting your great-grandma's house—old but nice, even charming (a word never before associated with this relic). The hotel is a two-story plantation-style structure with big verandas that overlook the streets of Lahaina and the harbor. All the rooms are all totally remodeled with vintage baths and new curtains and carpets; they even have TVs now. The quietest rooms face either the garden courtyard, devoted to refined outdoor dining accompanied by live (but quiet) music, or the block-square banyan tree next door. For my money, the best room in house is no. 47, over the banyan court, with a view of the ocean and all the harbor action. But if you want a front row seat for all the Front Street action, book no. 48, which usually overlooks the bird man who tries to get you to pose for a picture with his scarlet macaws.

Plantation Inn. 174 Lahainaluna Rd., Lahaina, HI 96761. ☎ **808/667-9225** or 800/ 433-6815. Fax 808/667-9293. 19 rms, 4 suites. A/C TV TEL. Winter $119–$170 double, $209– $219 suite; low season $104–$159 double, $185–$195 suite. Rate includes breakfast at a choice of two nearby restaurants. AE, DC, DISC, JCB, MC, V.

There's a romantic charm to this nostalgic inn. It looks like it's been here 100 years or more, but looks can be deceiving: This Victorian-style place is actually of 1990s vintage—an artful deception. The rooms are small but tastefully done with Victorian period furniture and hardwood floors; there are four-poster canopy beds and armoires in some rooms, brass beds and wicker in others. All rooms are equiped with VCRs, fridges, private baths, and lanais; the suites have kitchens.

The hotel can be hard to find; it's about a block off Lahaina's busy Front Street, and sequestered behind the inn's small, often noisy swimming pool and Gerard's, a decent French restaurant (see "Dining," below); it can be pricey, but hotel guests get a discount on dinner.

SOUTH MAUI
KIHEI

Aston Maui Lu Resort. 575 S. Kihei Rd., Kihei, HI 96753. ☎ **808/879-5881** or 800/ 92-ASTON. Fax 808/879-4627. 120 rms. A/C TV TEL. Winter $119–205; low season $99–$185. AE, DC, DISC, JCB, MC, V.

At the quiet, northern end of Kihei, the Polynesian-style Maui Lu offers a nostalgic Old Hawaii atmosphere on its 28 green acres by the sea. They don't make them like this anymore. Ask for a beach unit if you like to be right on the sand; the rest of the resort is across the road and up on a rise, around a swimming pool in the shape of the island of Maui (no kidding). The big, airy rooms, all restored in 1991 with sand-colored carpets and rattan furniture, have ceiling fans, Hawaiian art, two double beds, coffeemakers, and small refrigerators. Tennis and laundry facilities are available. A new restaurant, Ukulele Grill, has an inspired local chef and a reasonably priced continental/Hawaiian gourmet menu; it serves breakfast, dinner, and Sunday brunch.

Maui Coast Hotel. 2259 S. Kihei Rd., Kihei, HI 96753. ☎ **808/874-6284** or 800/895-6284. Fax 808/875-4731. 257 rms, 113 one- and two-bedroom suites. A/C TV TEL. $119–$139 double; $179–$300 suite. Room/car packages available. AE, DC, DISC, JCB, MC, V.

Built in 1993, this off-beach midrise stands as one of the only moderately priced new hotels in Hawaii. That's big news, especially on Maui, where luxury abounds. The chief advantage of this hotel is not only its price, but its location—about a block from Kamaole I Beach Park, one of the nicest on this condo coast; and the mid-Kihei location offers plenty of diversions within walking distance, including bars, restaurants, and shopping. Rooms are clean and simple; they remind me of college dorms, only there's lots of extras: sitting areas, coffeemakers and free coffee daily, hairdryers, whirlpool tubs, minifridges, in-room safes, ceiling fans, furnished private lanais. There's a casual restaurant, a sushi bar, and a poolside bar with nightly entertainment. Additional amenities include room service, activities desk, laundry, two pools (one for the kids), two Jacuzzis, tennis, and gift shop. This ain't the Ritz, but you'll be very comfortable here—and your wallet will thank you.

⑤ My Waii Cottage. 2128 Iliili Rd., Kihei, HI 96753. ☎ **800/225-7978.** E-mail hawaii4u@sprynet.com. One-bedroom, two-bath cottage (sleeps up to four). TV TEL. Winter $165, Apr 15–Dec 15 $135 (5-day minimum). MC, V.

You can stay a day, a week, or a month. You'll be tempted to quit your life and take up occupancy right here in this thoroughly modern sunshine-colored cottage by the sea. Sitting on one-third of an acre at Kamaole Beach 1, the cottage is very private and well appointed, with sand-colored tile floors, white walls, ceiling fans, and the ubiquitous Pegge Hopper lithos, plus two baths, a full kitchen with dishwasher, washer/dryer, VCR, an outside shower for beachgoers—and 165 feet of private oceanfront. Sorry, there's no maid service.

WAILEA

Aston Wailea Resort. 3700 Wailea Alanui Dr., Wailea, HI 96753. ☎ **808/879-1922** or 800/92-ASTON. Fax 808/875-4878. 550 rms, 50 suites. A/C TV TEL. $199–$319 double, $319–$1,350 suite. AE, DC, DISC, ER, JCB, MC, V.

Tasteful, low-rise, and user-friendly, this classic 1970s-style hotel is like a tropical garden by the sea. Airy and comfortable, with touches of Hawaiian art (and a terrific aquarium that stretches forever behind the front desk), it just feels right—like you're really in the islands at last. This open-air resort hotel full of tapa, weavings, and authentic carvings (as opposed to silly faux tikis) was the first to be built in Wailea; while it set the tone for what was to come, it remains the most Hawaiian of all.

What's truly special here is how the hotel fits its environment without overwhelming it. Eight buildings, all low-rise except for an eight-story tower, spread along 22 gracious acres of lawns and gardens spiked by coco palms, with lots of open space and a half-mile of oceanfront on a point between Wailea and Ulua beaches. It has what I call "a Hawaiian sense of space." And the big, grassy, parklike lawns are a luxury on this now-crowded coast.

All bases are covered: restaurants, lounges, pools, shops, tennis, and your choice of golf. Most rooms have ocean views and all have private lanais. Otherwise, they're simple, small, and could use refreshing, but the hotel has new management for the first time in 20 years, a new name (this used to be the Maui Inter-Continental), and many more changes just around the corner, like the high-powered scope along the coastal path—whoever spots the first whale of the day gets a free breakfast.

My favorite place in the resort is Hula Moons, a nostalgic open-air tropical bar that's a shrine to Hawaii's poet laureate Don Blanding, who wrote the 1930s book *Hula Moons* and started Hawaii's annual Lei Day celebrations. At night, under the flickering torches, it becomes a romantic seaside haunt evoking the nostalgia of old Hawaii.

Dining/Entertainment: Hula Moons is outdoor casual, serving pizza, burgers, and cool drinks at lunch, then fresh Hawaii seafood specialties at dinner; there's a free hula show nightly. The Lanai Terrace is an open-air, ocean-view restaurant that serves breakfast daily and dinner (Tues–Sat only). Kai Puka Lounge offers full cocktail service with dramatic ocean views, Hawaiian music, and seasonal *pupus* (hors d'oeuvres). Wailea's "finest" luau takes place on Tuesday, Thursday, and Friday and features two-time world-champion fire/knife dancer Efi.

Services: Lei greeting, room service, same-day laundry and valet, multilingual concierge. A comprehensive Hawaiian Culture Program offers free activities like lei making and hula lessons; there's also an activities and culture program for the kids.

Facilities: Three swimming pools, small pocket beaches nearby, gift shop, newsstand, beauty salon, barber shop. Three championship golf courses nearby. There's a terrific 34,000-square-foot open-air rooftop banquet pavilion with an unparalleled view of Haleakala and the Pacific; indoor conference facilities are equally impressive.

✪ **Four Seasons Resort Wailea.** 3900 Wailea Alanui Dr., Wailea, HI 96753. ☎ **808/874-8000** or 800/334-MAUI. Fax 808/874-6449. 380 rooms, 73 suites. A/C TV MINIBAR TEL. $295–$610 double; $515–$5,500 suite. Seasonal packages available with car, breakfast, golf, honeymoon, or other extras. Second room at $250 for families. AE, DC, JCB, MC, V.

It's hard to beat this four-time Five Diamond Award–winner. Set by the sea on Maui's endless summer coast, it's a modern version of a Hawaiian palace—sort of a contemporary Iolani Palace—with columns, fountains, reflecting pools, waterfalls, and a view of the Pacific and Haleakala. Although the hotel sits on the beach between two other hotels, the open courtyard of pools and gardens creates its own world, so you don't feel like you're in chockablock resort row. And its understated, casual luxury just makes everybody relax.

The hotel just completed a $4 million room facelift. Each one, done in seashell pastels and rattan, is big—about 600 square feet—and have furnished private lanais, nearly all with ocean views. A teak armoire hides the remote control TV and VCR. The grand bathrooms feature deep marble baths, showers for two, and lighted French makeup mirrors. Other amenities include safes, irons and boards, hairdryers, and plush terry robes.

Service is attentive, but not cloying. At the pool, guests feel pampered with special touches like iced Evian and chilled towels as they lounge in casbahlike tents. And you'll never see a housekeeping cart in the hall: The cleaning staff work in teams (one cleans, one goes for supplies, one restocks the minibar) so they're as unobtrusive as possible and in and out in minutes.

This ritzy neighborhood has great restaurants, Wailea Shopping Village, the Wailea Tennis Center (known as Wimbledon West), and six nearby golf courses. Then there's that great beach, with gentle waves and islands framing the view on either side. You can watch whales spouting and leaping from your lanai in winter and sunsets year-round.

If money's no factor, this is the place to spend it. And bring the kids.

Dining/Entertainment: The Four Seasons lured Honolulu's favorite chef, George Mavrothalassitis, from the famed Halekulani to open Seaside, a new casual spot for lunch, pupus, and dinner, featuring tables a few feet from the ocean and Hawaiian entertainment for sunset cockails nightly. Its attractive menu, ranging from the familiar to the adventurous, redefines poolside fare in the quality of preparation, execution, and ingredients. He's also notably improved the cuisine at Seasons, the hotel's signature restaurant, and at Pacific Grill (see "Dining," below).

Services: Lei greeting, 24-hour room service, twice daily maid service, voice mail, free overnight shoe-shine, same-day dry cleaning and laundry, 1-hour and overnight pressing, complimentary valet and shuttle around resort, airport limousine service, rental cars at concierge desk, 24-hour medical service. Club floor rooms have special privileges. Year-round kids' program with loads of activities and a complete children's facility, plus a teen recreation center; kids over 12 get complimentary scuba and windsurfing lessons.

Facilities: Fitness center with weight room and steam room; game room; video library; salon; putting green; shops; beach pavilion with snorkels, boogie boards, kayaks, and other water sports gear; conference facilities; on-site tennis; nearby golf.

Grand Wailea Resort & Spa. 3850 Wailea Alanui Dr., Wailea, HI 96753. ☎ **808/875-1234** or 800/888-6100. Fax 808/879-4077. 787 rms, 53 suites. A/C TV MINIBAR TEL. $370–$495 double, $1,100–$10,000 suite. Packages available. AE, DC, DISC, JCB, MC, V.

Here's where grand becomes grandiose. When it opened in 1991, this was the world's most expensive hotel project ($600 million), the pinnacle of Hawaii's brief fling with fantasy megaresorts. This monument to excess is a kid-filled amusement park by the sea, extremely popular with families, incentive groups, and conventions; it's the grand prize in Hawaii vacation contests, the dream of many honeymooners.

This hotel really is too much. It's got a zillion-dollar Japanese restaurant decorated with real rocks hewn from the slopes of Mount Fuji; 10,000 tropical plants in the lobby; an intricate pool system with not only pools, slides, waterfalls, and rapids, but also a water-powered elevator to take you up to the top; Hawaii's most elaborate spa (not even the Romans had it this good); Hawaii's most expensive hotel suite, a 5,500-square-foot pad with a 180° view of paradise (Tony Bennett was in residence the day I popped by); a restaurant in a man-made tide pool; a floating

New England–style wedding chapel; Maui's largest banquet facilities; and nothing but ocean-view rooms, outfitted with all the amenities you could ask for (including a daily fruit basket). And it's all crowned with $30 million worth of original art, much of it created expressly for the hotel by Hawaii artists and sculptors. There's also a fantastic beach in the front yard. And Maui's out there, somewhere, too.

Dining/Entertainment: Six restaurants and 12 bars range from fine dining to casual poolside snacks, serving everything from Japanese and Italian specialties to local seafood and spa cuisine; you shouldn't want for anything. A nightclub features laser light shows, a hydraulic dance floor, and 20 video monitors. There's also luau grounds for 300.

Services: Lei greeting; complimentary valet parking; 24-hour room service; twice-daily towel service; same-day laundry and dry cleaning; multilingual concierge; infant care center; art and hotel tours; Budget Rent-A-Car and American Express tour desks; 100 Napua Club rooms with attendants, complimentary continental breakfast, cocktails, and tea service.

Facilities: The 50,000-square-foot Spa Grande, Hawaii's largest, with a blend of European-, Japanese-, and American-style techniques; 2,000-foot long Action Pool, featuring a 10-minute swim/ride through mountains and grottos; complimentary dive and windsurf lessons; seaside wedding chapel; conference facilities. Kids enjoy a computer center, video game room, arts and crafts, 60-seat children's theater, and outdoor playground. Five golf courses, including two 18-hole championship courses, nearby.

⑤ Kea Lani Hotel Suites & Villas. 4100 Wailea Alanui Dr., Wailea, HI 96753. ☎ **808/ 875-4100** or 800/882-4100. Fax 808/875-1200. 413 units. A/C TV TEL. $265–$450 suite (sleeps up to four); $795 one-bedroom villa (sleeps up to four); $895–$995 two-bedroom villa (sleeps up to six); $1,094–$1,195 three-bedroom villa (sleeps up to eight). Packages available. AE, DC, DISC, JCB, MC, V.

Sure, it looks out of place: This blinding white complex of arches and turrets is anything but Hawaiian. The fanciful resort is an architectural cousin of Las Hadas, the Arabian Nights fantasy resort in Manzanillo, Mexico. But Hawaii does what Mexico can never do—for starters, you can drink the water. Inside the lobby, flowers and fountains soften the harem look, and the big blue Pacific opens up before you.

The fantasy doesn't stop at your room door. This is Hawaii's only all-suite luxury resort. Each 840-square-foot creamy-white suite comes with a microwave kitchenette, a living room with a high-tech media center and a pullout sofa (perfect if you're traveling with the kids), a marble wet bar, an oversized marble bathroom with a shower big enough for a party, and a lanai overlooking the pools, lawns, and the beach beyond. There's even a hairdryer, an iron and board, and a European coffeemaker accompanied by fresh Kona coffee beans.

No wonder Kea Lani is one of the world's top tropical resorts and—it says right here in the press kit—a favorite of Goldie Hawn, Jack Nicholson, and Joe Montana, who are regular villa guests. The villas *are* something else; some are as big as 2,200 square feet, and each comes with its own plunge pool and gourmet kitchen.

My favorite touch (besides the cookies and milk served at bedtime) is the adults-only pool, where you don't have to suffer the joyful exuberance of other people's children if you don't want to.

Dining/Entertainment: The elegant, open-air Kea Lani Restaurant features imaginative Pacific cuisine and ocean views (see "Dining," below, for review); try Caffe Ciao for authentic Italian pastas, pizza, organic salads, and home-cured meats. The adjoining patio cafe features a wood-burning brick pizza oven. There's live Hawaiian entertainment in the lobby bar.

Services: Lei greeting; CD, video and laser-disc rental; in-suite dining; complimentary valet; self-serve washer/dryer on each floor; concierge; complimentary cribs, high chairs, and year-round children's program; tour and activity desk.

Facilities: Gold-sand beach; two lagoon pools with 140-foot water slide; adult lap-pool; swim-up bar; two Jacuzzis; fitness center; outdoor wedding area; floral, gift/sundry and jewelry shops; salon; banquet and meeting facilities. Nearby is Wailea Tennis Club, plus three championship 18-hole golf courses.

MAKENA

Maui Prince Hotel. 5400 Makena Alanui, Makena, HI 96753. ☎ **808/874-1111** or 800/321-MAUI. Fax 808/879-8763. 300 rms, 13 suites. A/C TV MINIBAR TEL. $230–$395 double, $440–$840. Packages available. AE, DC, JCB, MC, V.

This is far and away my favorite little hotel on Maui. Spare, simple, and well-sited, on a great gold-sand beach just over a dune with nothing around it except immaculate gardens, ocean, and mountains, this is one of the island's great retreats. It's like a Japanese ryokan by the sea.

This lone oasis was erected by Japanese billionaire and railway heir Yoshiakai Tsutsumi, who installed a *sukoshi* bit of Tokyo on this arid coast. Few hotels in Hawaii have so much luxurious open space and such serene views and peaceful solitude as this one, which has most of the 1800-acre Makena Resort all to itself. The stark white structure looks like a county hospital stuck in the woods—from the outside. Inside, there's an atrium garden with a waterfall stream rich with koi, an ocean view from every room, and a simplicity to the furnishings that makes some people uncomfortable and others feel blissfully clutter-free. Rooms are small, but come with private lanais, minirefrigerators, and VCRs, expensive Shiseido soaps and lotions and hairdryer in the bathroom, and a cotton yukata in the closet.

The beach out front is the best in Makena, an old cattle landing district with historic sites to explore and Puu Olai, a bit of volcanic punctuation marking Maui's southernmost shore—an exceptional whale-watching or view-admiring perch.

Dining/Entertainment: Dining, in both the Hawaii Regional and Japanese restaurants, is excellent (see "Dining," below, for reviews). Casual Cafe Kiowai offers seasonal and international specialties, and the clubhouse restaurant serves lunch and snacks. The Molokini Lounge has local Hawaiian music nightly.

Services: Lei greeting, welcome goodie basket, library, complimentary early-morning coffee and tea, complimentary valet parking, multilingual concierge, same-day dry cleaning and laundry, complimentary daily kids program, early arrival and late departure services.

Facilities: Secluded beach, 36 holes of Robert Trent Jones–designed golf at North and South Courses, six Plexi-pave tennis courts (two with night play), adult and kid's pools, fitness center, six-station fitness trail, conference facilities.

UP-COUNTRY MAUI
KULA

Bloom Cottage. RR 2, Box 229, Kula Hwy., Kula, HI 96790. ☎ and fax **808/878-1425.** 1 two-bedroom cottage. TV TEL. $105 double, including breakfast fixings (2-night minimum); $15 extra person. No credit cards.

A garden of flowers inspired the name of this cozy, private English country cottage at 3,000 feet, on the way to Haleakala's summit. The cottage is cheerful and homey, with country decor, handmade quilts, a koa rocker, four-poster bed, fireplace, VCR, and lots of books. The second alcove bedroom can sleep a third person. Breakfast supplies are stocked in the full kitchen. Other special features include a lanai overlooking a garden in perpetual bloom, and views of the ocean and West Maui mountains. The hosts are lifelong residents who know Maui well and can help you enjoy the special features of Maui's up-country.

Silver Cloud Ranch. Old Thompson Road (RR 2, Box 201), Kula, HI 96790. ☎ **808/878-6101.** Fax 808/878-2132. 1 cottage, 6 rms in main house, 5 studios in bunkhouse. $75–$135 double, including full breakfast. DISC, MC, V.

Old Hawaii lives on at Silver Cloud Ranch, founded in 1902 by a sailor who jumped ship when he got to Maui. The former working cattle spread has a commanding view of four islands, the West Maui Mountains, and the valley and beaches below. The Lanai Cottage is a favorite of honeymooners, nestled in a flower garden with an ocean-view lanai, red claw-foot bathtub, full kitchen, and wood-burning stove to warm chilly nights; there's a futon available if you're traveling with a third person. The best rooms in the main house are on the second floor: the King Kamehameha Suite (with king bed) and the Queen Emma Suite (with queen bed). Each has a royal view, but some prefer Emma's. The Paniolo Bunkhouse, once used by real cowboys, is now fully restored and has five private studios with private bath, kitchenette, and views of the Pacific or Haleakala (go for the ocean view). All guests are free to use the main house and kitchen.

It's cool and peaceful at the 2,800-foot level. Bring a sweater. One-lane Thompson Road is an ideal morning walk (about 3 miles round-trip), and you can go horseback riding next door at Thompson Ranch. Silver Cloud has a TV available, if you feel visually deprived, but after a few Maui sunsets you won't remember why you bothered to ask.

MAKAWAO

Olinda Country Cottage & Inn. 536 Olinda Rd., Makawao, HI 96768. ☎ **808/572-1453.** 2 suites; 1 one-bedroom cottage (sleeps up to five). TV TEL. $85 suite, $95 cottage double, $15 per extra person. Breakfast included; 2-night minimum. No credit cards.

This place will definitely give you a different take on Maui. It's a quiet retreat at 4,000 feet, surrounded by Haleakala Ranch, towering eucalyptus groves, and a protea farm. The large, romantic cottage is filled with country antiques and has a kitchen, fireplace, washer/dryer, VCR, and views of the ocean and mountains. The beautifully resored Tudor-style home has two two-room suites with private baths and a huge living area to share.

EAST MAUI
ON THE ROAD TO HANA

Huelo Point Flower Farm. P.O. Box 1195, Paia, HI 96779. ☎ **808/572-1850.** 2 cottages, 1 main house. TV. $110 double cottages; $1,850 per week for house (sleeps up to six). Continental breakfast included. No credit cards.

Here's a little Eden by the sea, on a spectacular, remote 300-foot sea cliff near a waterfall stream: a 2-acre estate overlooking Waipio Bay with two guest cottages and a main house all available for rental. Despite its seclusion, off the crooked road to Hana, it's just a half-hour to Kahului Airport (so is just about everything else on Maui) or about 20 minutes to Paia's shops and restaurants. The studio-sized Gazebo cottage has a koa-wood captain's bed, TV, stereo, kitchenette, and a half-bath with outdoor shower. The new 900-square-foot Carriage House apartment sleeps four and has glass walls facing mountain and sea, plus kitchen, den, decks, and a loft bedroom. The two-bedroom main house has an exercise room, fireplace, cathedral ceilings, and other extras. There's a natural pool with waterfall and an oceanfront hot tub. You're welcome to pick fruit, vegetables, and flowers from the extensive garden. Homemade scones, tree-ripened papayas, and fresh-roasted coffee are available to start your day.

HANA

Hamoa Bay Bungalow. P.O. Box 773, Hana, HI 96713. ☎ **808/248-7884.** 1 studio. TV TEL. $125 double. Light breakfast included. No credit cards.

Down a country lane guarded by two Balinese statues stands a little bit of Indonesia in Hawaii, a carefully crafted bungalow overlooking Hamoa Bay. Only 2 miles beyond Hasegawa's General Store on the way to Kipahulu, this enchanting retreat sits on 4 verdant acres within walking distance of black-sand Hamoa Beach (which James Michener considered one of the most beautiful in the Pacific). The romantic, 600-square-foot Balinese-style cottage is distinctly tropical, with giant Elephant bamboo furniture from Indonesia, batik prints, a king bed, full kitchen, and screened porch with hot tub and shower. Host Jody Baldwin, a lifelong Mauian who lives on the estate, serves a tropical breakfast of fruit, yogurt, and muffins and is happy to share the secrets of the Hana Coast, including the great mountain hiking trail nearby.

Hana Plantation Houses. c/o 2957 Kalakaua Ave., Honolulu, HI 96715. ☎ **808/923-0772** or 800/228-HANA. 12 units. TV TEL. $80 studio, $100–$160 one-bedroom (sleeps two) and two-bedroom (some units sleep up to six). AE, MC, V.

Hana Plantation Houses has studios and homes throughout the Hana area. The lovely folks who run it will set you up with the accommodation that's right for you—they've got something for everyone, whether your looking for a romantic cottage or a vacation house for the family—and will do everything in their power to make your visit as pleasant as can be. Their fully equipped vacation rentals all come with kitchens; some are waterfront, others have ocean views or tropical garden settings.

The Hana Plantation Houses office is located off Hana Highway, in Hana Gardenland Botanical Gardens. You'll see a sign on your right at Kalo Road.

Heavenly Hana Inn. P.O. Box 790, Hana, HI 96713. ☎/fax **808/248-8442.** 3 suites. TV. $175 double; $30 extra per person. Continental breakfast included. No credit cards.

This Japanese-style inn is a spare, elegant hostelry often likened to a Kyoto ryokan. It's small, friendly, and neat, recently renovated by new owners who improved on the Oriental motif with new fish ponds, gardens, and dry creek beds to ponder. Each suite has a raised futon bed and a tiled private bathroom with deep soaking tub; there are wood floors and shoji screens throughout, and TV in the sitting room. Most of the woodwork and furniture was handmade by Hana craftsmen. The inn is on the ocean side of Hana Highway, close to the black-sand beach at Waianapanapa State Park.

Hotel Hana-Maui. P.O. Box 9, Hana, HI 96713. ☎ **808/248-8211** or 800/321-HANA. Fax 808/248-7202. 96 rms and suites, 47 cottages. MINIBAR. $335 double, $395–$550 suite, $450–$815 double cottage. Rates include Hana Airport transport. Packages available. AE, DC, JCB, MC, V.

It doesn't get any better than this gracious roadside inn, attracting old money, royalty (Princess Di slept here), and international celebrities, who come to soak up the end-of-the-road tropical ambiance of this naturally healing retreat. Built in 1946 on 66 acres of Hana Ranch land, the Hana-Maui entered luxury ranks in 1989, but its Old Hawaii air remains intact. This bastion of tranquility has large suitelike rooms in single-story buildings set on shady lawns; all come with private patios, bleached wood floors, Hawaiian quilts on the beds, wonderful bathrooms with large soaking tubs overlooking private gardens, fridges, and coffeemakers. Terry robes and fresh coffee beans assure a pleasant start to the day. The best accommodations are the Sea Ranch cottages, small but exquisite plantation-style cottages at water's edge with hot tubs on the lanais. A remodeled turn-of-the-century home serves as a conference center and executive retreat (Hilary Rodham Clinton slept there).

There's no swimming here, but much-celebrated Hamoa Beach, with pavilion and beach amenities for guests, is about 3 miles away via free shuttle or down a pleasant country lane. There are lots of trails, quiet starry nights, and genuine Hawaiian atmosphere. The only thing wrong, besides the food (which leaves a bit to be desired), is that you can't stay here forever.

Do note, however, that the hotel was up for sale at the time of this writing, with the potential buyers reportedly close to sealing the deal and naming a new management company. It's hard to know what this means for the future; hopefully, they'll be smart enough to keep the best of Hana-Maui in place.

Dining/Entertainment: The dining room once was home to two of the finest chefs in Hawaii (Jean-Marie Josselin and Amy Ferguson-Ota), but has since fallen into disrepute because of escalating prices and declining quality and service. The new owners will no doubt institute significant changes: a new menu, new training, and hopefully, a reinvigorated spirit for a flagging operation that's failed to maintain the high standards of its heyday. The present Sunday menu at the hotel features a $28.95 international buffet, à la carte New York steak with grilled Maui onions for $25.50, grilled catch of the day for $29, and a vegetarian lasagna for $20.50—hardly imaginative fare for what was formerly a fine dining room, and obviously a menu in dire need of some TLC. Salads, sandwiches, and soups are served for lunch. Don't miss the Friday night luau, featuring song and dance by the hotel staff and their kids.

Services: Lei greetings; nightly turndowns on request.

Facilities: Library, riding stables, hiking trails, tennis, pool, three-hole practice golf course, bicycles, beach equipment, rental cars. Also salon, wellness/health center with spa treatments and activities, shops, free beach shuttle.

🅢 **Waianapanapa State Park Cabins.** Off Hana Hwy. c/o State Parks Division, 54 S. High St., Rm. 101, Wailuku, HI 96793. ☎ **808/243-5354.** 12 cabins. $10–$30 (sleep up to six). Maximum stay 5 nights. No credit cards.

These twelve rustic cabins are the best lodging deal on Maui. The only problem is that everybody wants one, so make your reservations early—up to 6 months in advance. The cabins are warm and dry and come complete with kitchen, living room, bedroom, and bathroom with hot shower, and are furnished with bedding, linen, towels, dishes, and cooking and eating utensils. The setting is a beautiful tropical jungle scene unlike any other in the islands. The key attraction at this 120-acre state beach park is the unusual horseshoe-shaped black-sand beach on Pailoa Bay, popular for shore fishing, snorkeling, and swimming. There's a caretaker on site, along with rest rooms, showers, picnic tables, shoreline hiking trails, and historical sites. But bring mosquito protection—this *is* the jungle.

4 Dining

by Jocelyn Fujii

Luscious cuisine lurks in every wrinkle of this gorgeous island. It was here on Maui that Hawaii's chefs first became as celebrated as their glamorous clients from the mainland, who, in the 1970s, began very wisely to buy chunks of premium land as hideaways from the fast lane. In the past decade, with the ascension of Hawaii Regional Cuisine into national prominence, and with Maui an increasingly popular destination, the islands' best chefs have opened their Maui doors and turned this island into Hawaii's culinary nexus. It's a mixed bag, of course. Planet Hollywood and Hard Rock Cafe have little to do with food, yet they inevitably cause a media flurry when celebrity investors saunter down Front Street. Good food on this island means chefs like David Paul, Mark Ellman, Steve Amaral, and arrivals from outer islands: Peter Merriman (Big Island), Jean-Marie Josselin (Kauai), Roy Yamaguchi (Oahu), and George Mavrothalassitis, who turned heads when he hopped from Oahu's Halekulani to Maui's Four Seasons. You can also dine well, at moderate to high prices, at Lahaina's open-air waterfront watering holes. There are budget eateries, but not many; Maui's old-fashioned, multigeneration mom-and-pop diners are disappearing by attrition, eclipsed by the flashy newcomers, or clinging to the edge of existence in the older neighborhoods of central Maui. Although you'll have to work harder to find them, you won't have to go far to find bountiful examples of creative cuisine, pleasing style, and stellar views in up-country, south, and west Maui.

In the listings below, reservations are not necessary unless otherwise noted.

CENTRAL MAUI

Kahului has its own food court on the second floor of the **Kaahumanu Center,** the structure that looks like a white *Star Wars* umbrella in the center of town. The best news is that most of the eateries therein serve excellent food. The **Juiceland** kiosk near the top of the elevator offers vitamin-rich (and delicious!) freshly squeezed beet, celery, wheat grass, carrot, ginger, and creative combinations of vegetable and fruit juices, as well as smoothies made from the legendary fresh fruits of Maui. Busy shoppers seem more than willing to dispense with fine china and other formalities to enjoy a no-nonsense meal on Styrofoam plates that efficiently refreshes them between spurts of shopping. Among the standouts: **Maui Tacos,** one of Mark Avalon's four palate-pleasing Mexican diners sprinkled throughout Maui (see p. 307). The green burritos, painted naturally with spinach, are the best this side of the Rio Grande. **Yummy Korean B-B-Q,** part of a chain well-known on Oahu, proffers soups, sesame bean sprouts, potato salad, and many combinations of vegetables, meats, fish, and ribs infused with the assertive flavors of Korea. **Panda Cuisine** serves tasty Chinese food. One spot that's always abuzz is the Kaahumanu Center's **Coffee Store** (see p. 315), a no-nonsense java stop that serves sandwiches, salads, pasta, and nearly 2 dozen different coffee drinks for shopping-mall regenerates.

When you leave Kaahumanu Center, take a moment to gaze at the West Maui Mountains to your left from the parking lot. It's one of Maui's wonders, a kaleidoscopic show of clouds, sunlight, textured canyons, and deep greens that reflect the mystical qualities of the old mountain.

WAILUKU/KAHULUI

Hamburger Mary's. 2010 Main St., Wailuku. ☎ **808/244-7776.** Most items under $7. DISC, MC. V. Mon–Wed 10am–10pm, Thurs–Sat 10am–midnight, bar Mon–Sat 10am–1:30am. AMERICAN.

Hamburger Mary's is famous for its one-third–pound hamburgers and as a gay hangout; but it's also Wailuku's version of Cheers, a place where gays and straights are equally at home enjoying wholesome food. Among their specialties: excellent homemade soups (fish chowder, spicy black bean, lentil) and burgers on three different types of bread, heaped high with vegetables and smothered in homemade dressings. Fans rave about the veggie burgers, crowned with grilled onions and homemade Thousand Island dressing. They're made with larger, meatier garden *steaks* (as opposed to garden *burgers*), and you can pile them high with sautéed mushrooms and other toppings for a small extra charge.

⑤ Industrial Grinds. Wailuku Industrial Park, 830 Kolu St., Wailuku. ☎ **808/244-0500.** Lunches $6. No credit cards. Mon–Fri 7am–2pm. ESPRESSO BAR/DELI.

The former Cafe Kup a Kuppa, popular among Wailuku businesspeople, has been renamed Industrial Grinds in its new, larger location at the Wailuku Industrial Park. The menu has expanded, and the business now focuses on takeout, delivery, and catering; there are no tables. You can order several kinds of bento-style lunches, hot pasta, quesadillas, quiches, garden burgers, curries, sandwiches, and salads. Steaming mugs of espresso and cappuccino and frosty shakes and smoothies still sell apace. Pizza may be forthcoming; plans are afoot to install a pizza oven.

Marco's Grill & Deli. 444 Hana Hwy., Kahului. ☎ **808/877-4446.** Main courses $12.95–$19.95. AE, DC, DISC, JCB, MC, V. Mon–Fri 7am–10pm, Sat–Sun 7:30am–10pm. ITALIAN.

Located in the elbow of central Maui, where the roads to up-country, west, and south Maui converge, Marco's is popular among area residents who like the homemade Italian fare and friendly informality of the place. This is one of those comfortable neighborhood fixtures favored by all generations, who stop here for breakfast, lunch, and dinner, before and after movies, on the way to and from baseball games and concerts. The antipasto salad, vegetarian lasagna, and roasted peppers with garlic, provolone cheese, and anchovies are taste treats, but don't ignore the meatballs and Italian sausage: homemade and tasty, they're served on French bread with all the trimmings.

Ⓢ **Maui Bake Shop.** 2092 Vineyard St., Wailuku. ☎ **808/242-0064.** Most items under $5. No credit cards. Mon–Fri 7am–5:30pm, Sat 7am–3pm. BAKERY/DELI.

Sleepy Vineyard Street has seen many a mom-and-pop business come and go, so it was a pleasant surprise to see that a world-class European bakery had opened its doors to a welcoming public. Maui native Claire Fujii-Krall and her husband, baker José Krall (who was trained in the South of France and throughout Europe), are turning out buttery brioches, healthy nine-grain and two-tone rye breads, focaccia, strudels, sumptuous fresh fruit gâteaux, fruit tarts, puff pastry, mousses, and dozens of baked goods and confections. The breads are baked in one of Maui's oldest brick ovens, installed in 1935; a high-tech European diesel oven handles the rest. The front window displays the more than 100 bakery and deli items, among them salads, a popular eggplant marinara focaccia, homemade quiches, and a moist $3 calzone with a chicken/pesto/mushroom/cheese filling baked in it. Homemade soups (clam chowder, minestrone, cream of asparagus) team up nicely with sandwiches made with freshly baked bread, and they're light enough (well, almost) to justify the Ultimate Dessert: white chocolate macadamia nut cheesecake.

Ⓢ **Restaurant Matsu.** Maui Mall, Kahului. ☎ **808/871-0822.** Most items under $6. No credit cards. Mon–Thurs 9am–6pm, Fri–Sat 9am–5:30pm, Sun 10am–4pm. JAPANESE/LOCAL.

Customers have come from Hana (more than 50 miles away) for Matsu's California rolls, while regulars line up for the cold saimin, made with julienned cucumber, egg, char siu (Chinese-style sweet pork), and red ginger on noodles; and the bento plates, various assemblages of chicken, teriyaki beef, fish, and rice that make great take-out lunches for working folks and picnickers. The katsu pork and chicken, breaded and deep-fried, are another specialty of this casual Formica-style diner. We love the tempura udon and the saimin, steaming mounds of wide and fine noodles swimming in homemade broths and topped with condiments. The daily specials are a changing line-up of home-cooked classics: ox tail soup, roast pork with gravy, teriyaki ahi, miso butterfish, and breaded mahimahi.

Ⓢ **A Saigon Cafe.** 1792 Main St., Wailuku. ☎ **808/243-9560.** Main courses $6.50–$16.95. MC, V. Mon–Sat 10am–10pm, Sun 10am–9pm. VIETNAMESE.

Saigon's feisty flavors find full expression in Jennifer Nguyen's authentic Vietnamese cuisine, which has gained a sterling reputation even among picky Maui residents. The menu covers the gamut, from a dozen different soups to cold and hot noodles (including the popular beef noodle soup called *pho*) and chicken and shrimp cooked in a clay pot. Wok-cooked Vietnamese specialties—sautéed, with spicy lemongrass and sweet and sour sauces—highlight the produce of the season, and the fresh catch (ono, opakapaka) comes whole and crisp or steamed with ginger and garlic. You can create your own Vietnamese "burritos" from a platter of tofu, noodles, and vegetables that you wrap in rice paper and dip in garlic sauce. Among our favorites are the shrimp lemongrass ($8.50), piquant and refreshing, and the tofu curry ($6.75), swimming in herbs and vegetables straight from the garden. The Nhung Dam, the Vietnamese version of fondue—a hearty spread of basil, cucumber, mint, romaine, bean sprouts, pickled carrots, turnips, and vermicelli, wrapped in rice paper and dipped in a legendary sauce—is cooked at your table.

Sharktooth. Kaahumanu Shopping Center, Kahului. ☎ **808/871-6689.** Main courses $7.95–$21.95. AE, DC, DISC, MC, V. Daily 11am–10pm; bar open until midnight. AMERICAN.

Kahului's newest and hippest watering hole is also the island's first microbrewery, with a brewmaster from California who concocts such brews as Hula Girl Pale Ale, Poi Dog Wheat, Sharktooth Amber Ale, Big Kahuna Brown Ale, and Brewer's Da Kine. You can get hoppy and happy in this friendly, upbeat spot on the second floor of the spiffed-up shopping center. The long bar and prominent TV are decidedly macho, but the booths in the rest of the dining room hold their own as a fine spot for baby-back ribs (in a tangy, spicy, secret marinade), filet mignon and rib-eye steaks ($14.95–$21.85), pasta, sandwiches, chili and rice (made with Sharktooth Ale), and the obligatory sashimi and ahi poke. Local fishermen supply the fresh catch daily (ahi, striped marlin, blue marlin, opakapaka), which turns up blackened or grilled, and is very popular. The danger-zone dessert is called Chocolate Frenzy, a frenetic combo of three sensuous chocolates layered in a dense cake, topped with raspberry sauce—a killer.

Siam Thai. 123 N. Market St., Wailuku. ☎ **808/244-3817.** Reservations recommended for 4 or more. Main courses $5.95–$8.50. AE, CB, DISC, DC, JCB, MC, V. Mon–Fri 11am–2:30pm, daily 5–9pm. THAI.

This local favorite specializes in Evil Prince chicken and other coconut- and spice-infused Thai specialties that are much favored by Westerners. Expect lots of fresh basil, lemongrass, ginger, cabbage, spices, and tofu on the menu, as well as a feisty, winning Siam Chicken, a whole Cornish game hen deep-fried with garlic and soy sauce. The Thai snapper (*pla rad prik*) is deep-fried crisp and whole in a sweet-and-sour sauce and heaped with onions, red peppers, and condiments—tasty, but not for the faint-hearted.

Stanton's of Maui. Maui Mall, Kahului. ☎ **808/877-3711.** Most items under $5.95. AE, DC, DISC, MC, V. Mon–Thurs 8am–6pm, Fri 8am–9pm, Sat 8am–5:30pm, Sun 9am–4pm. COFFEE SHOP/DELI.

Everything from local Kaanapali and Kona coffee from the Big Island to Ethiopian mocha and Haitian Blue French Roast is sold here, in light, dark, decaf, and rotating flavors of the day. To accompany the high-octane libations is a small but attractive menu of soups, sandwiches, and salads (three-bean and the house salad with tuna or feta cheese are recommended). This being Maui, a growing list of vegetarian items is de rigueur, and much appreciated, particularly the tofu burger, piled high with sprouts, tomatoes, cucumbers, and a special dressing. The retail section sells an amazing array, from coffees and cigars to quality teas, incense, homemade beeswax candles, and the crowning glory: Beeman's chewing gum in Clove, Teaberry, and Black Jack flavors—a flash to the past. There are plans for live music on Fridays and jazz on Sundays, too.

WEST MAUI
KAPALUA

The Bay Club. Kapalua Bay Hotel & Villas. ☎ **808/669-5656.** Reservations recommended for dinner. Dress code at dinner: collared shirts with long slacks for men; no jeans, shorts, or T-shirts for women. Main courses $24–$38. AE, CB, JCB, MC, V. Daily 11:30am–2pm, 6–9:30pm. SEAFOOD.

The classic enjoyments—a stellar view, beatific sunsets, attentive service from bow-tied servers—are matched by a seafood menu that's simple, good, and lasting. They haven't changed The Bay Club much because there's simply no need to. At lunch, the shrimp, white cheddar, and Kula tomatoes, served on fresh Molokai bread, are a match for the Caesar, one of four elegant salads tossed tableside. With at least four types of fresh fish prepared several different ways, the signature bouillabaisse, rack of lamb, and sautéed prawns and scallops, dinner is an elegant, romantic occasion. Adding to the pleasure of the open-air dining room is the view of Molokai and Lanai, a view that changes as the sun moves south to eventually set behind Lanai in the winter months.

Grill & Bar at Kapalua. 200 Kapalua Dr., 18th hole of Kapalua Golf Course. ☎ **808/669-5653.** Reservations recommended for dinner. Main courses $7.95–$29.95. AE, DC, DISC, MC, V. Daily 11am–3pm, cafe menu 3–10:30pm, dinner 5–10pm. AMERICAN.

With the recent closure of the beloved Market Cafe in the Kapalua Shops, the Grill and Bar is the only casual eatery in the resort, perhaps the only place where you can still order an old-fashioned tuna salad or fresh-roasted turkey breast sandwich for under $7 or $8. This place is casual, nothing special, catering to the golf and sports set with everything from herb-roasted chicken and Chinatown duck to pizza, burgers, and classic sandwiches. With its recent purchase by the Jameson's restaurant chain, it'll probably eventually conform to the Jameson's steak-and-seafood formula, with hollandaise and garlic butter on everything.

Plantation House. 200 Plantation Club Dr. (right at Kapalua Plantation Golf Course), Kapalua Resort. ☎ **808/669-6299.** Reservations recommended. Main courses $18–$24. AE, MC, V. Daily 8:30am–3pm, 5:30–10pm. SEAFOOD/ISLAND REGIONAL.

With its teak tables, fireplace, and open sides, Plantation House gets high marks for ambiance: the 360° view from high among the resort's pine-studded hills takes in Molokai and Lanai (they look close enough to touch), the ocean, the rolling fairways and greens, the northwestern flanks of the West Maui Mountains, and the daily sunset spectacular. Your choices include fresh seafood prepared five ways: Mediterranean (seared), Up-country (sautéed with Maui onion and vegetable stew), Island (pan-seared in sweet sake and chili-sesame sauce), Asian Pacific (charred with Asian mushrooms and sake sauce), and Rich Forest (with roasted wild mushrooms); as well as prawns, pasta, duck in cabernet sauce, and rosemary-infused double-cut lamb chops. Definitely not cool is the $3 charge for all split menu items. Tsk tsk.

FROM KAPALUA TO KAANAPALI: KAHANA/NAPILI

Ⓢ **Maui Tacos.** Napili Plaza, 5095 Napili Hau St. ☎ **808/665-0222.** Most items under $6.95. No credit cards. Mon–Sat 11am–9pm, Sun 11am–8pm. MEXICAN.

As if he had anything more to prove, Mark Ellman of Avalon fame put gourmet Mexican on paper plates and on the island's culinary map. Barely more than a take-out counter with a few tables, this and the other three Maui Tacos on the island

(Kaahumanu Center in Kahului, Lahaina Square in Lahaina, Kamaole Beach Center in Kihei) are the rage of hungry surfers, discerning diners, burrito buffs, and Hollywood glitterati like Sharon Stone, whose picture adorns a wall or two. Regardless, the food is rave quality: excellent fresh fish tacos, chimichangas, searing salsas, and mouth-breaking compositions such as the Hookipa, a "surf burrito" of fresh fish, black beans, and salsa. The green spinach burrito contains four kinds of beans, rice, and potatoes—a knockout. It's all great, and you can schlep in wearing a tank top and swim trunks, and nobody will care.

✪ **Roy's Kahana Bar & Grill.** Kahana Gateway, 4405 Honoapiilani Hwy. ☎ **808/669-6999.** Reservations strongly suggested. Main courses $12–$25. AE, DC, DISC, MC, V. Daily 5:30–10pm. EURO-ASIAN.

It's big, noisy, busy, and important, bustling with young, hip servers impeccably trained to deliver the blackened ahi or perfectly seared lemongrass shutome (broadbill swordfish) hot to your table, in a room that sizzles with cross-cultural tastings. Roy's is known for its rack of lamb and fresh seafood (usually eight or nine choices), and for its large, open kitchen that turns out everything from pizza to sake-grilled New York steak and roasted half-chickens in garlic and orange, glistening in cardamom and cabernet sauce; it rarely fails its public. If pot-stickers are on the menu, don't resist. Large picture windows open up the room but don't quell the noise, another tireless trait long ago established by Roy's Restaurant in Honolulu, the flagship of the burgeoning empire of Roy Yamaguchi.

Sea House Restaurant. Napili Kai Beach Club, 5900 Honoapiilani Hwy. ☎ **808/367-5030.** Reservations required for dinner. Main courses $12–$24. AE, MC, V. Mon–Thurs, Sat–Sun 8–11am, noon–2pm (pupu menu 2–9pm); daily 5:30–9pm (winter); 6–9pm (summer). STEAK/ SEAFOOD.

The Sea House is neither glamorous, famous, nor hip, but it's worth mentioning for its view of Napili Bay, one of the two most gorgeous in west Maui, and because the hotel it serves, Napili Kai Beach Club, is a charming throwback to the days when hotels blended in with their surroundings, had lush tropical foliage, and were sprawling rather than vertical. Although Sea House can't compete with Kapalua's Bay Club next door, it offers a million-dollar view and a congenial, unpretentious atmosphere where $24 buys you rack of lamb, $23 buys you fresh island fish in one of seven preparations, and $19 buys you a jumbo shrimp, scallop, and mahimahi brochette. This isn't gourmet fare, but it's a value: all main courses come with chowder or Kula salad, vegetables, and rice or potato.

KAANAPALI

Very Expensive

Swan Court. Hyatt Regency Maui. ☎ **808/661-1234.** Reservations recommended for dinner. Main courses $26–$39. AE, DC, DISC, JCB, MC, V. Mon–Sat 6:30–11:30am, daily 6–10pm. CONTINENTAL.

As snobby as it can be, Swan Court is hard to resist. But come here as a splurge, or on a bottomless expense account, because it's pricey. No wonder: The combination of waterfalls, ocean view, Japanese gardens, and swans and flamingos serenely gliding by is irresistibly romantic, especially with alfresco dining and appropriately extravagant fare. There's tiered seating, but a table by the waterfalls adds an extra layer of refreshment. Hunan marinated lamb chops and the island-style bouillabaisse are perennial favorites, but the ever-changing seafood and game specials will compete for your attention. Salad lovers will be won over by the baby lettuces with orange slices, pecans, and a tangy citrus dressing.

Expensive

Hula Grill. Whaler's Village. ☎ **808/667-6636.** Reservations recommended for dinner. Main courses $12.95 and up. AE, MC, V. Daily 11am–11pm. HAWAII REGIONAL/SEAFOOD.

It was a leap for Peter Merriman, one of the originators of Hawaii Regional Cuisine, to go from his smallish, Big Island up-country enclave to a large, high-volume dining room on the beach. But he's managed to transfer, resoundingly, the successes of Merriman's (which he maintains by commuting, and with the help of his chef there, Sandy Barr) to Maui's busy western shoreline, and has redefined restaurant-chain cuisine. You'll dine in a charming setting of vintage Hawaiiana accented with kitschy hula dolls, koa walls, and authentic Hawaiian canoes. The superb menu includes his signature wok-charred ahi, firecracker mahimahi (baked in tomato, chili, and cumin aioli), scallop and lobster pot-stickers, crab and corn cakes, and six different fresh fish preparations, including his deservedly famous ahi poke rolls, lightly sautéed rare ahi wrapped in rice paper with Maui onions. From the Barefoot Bar menu, you can order gourmet appetizers and Hawaii Regional dim sum (macadamia nut/crab wonton), fresh ono fish-and-chips, pizza, and smoked turkey sandwiches—a combination of American classics and ethnic favorites spiced with fresh local ingredients. Merriman's penchant for sniffing out the best fresh produce and seafood set the standards for Hawaii Regional Cuisine and continues, untarnished, in touristy Kaanapali. Note to dessert lovers: The homemade ice cream sandwich, a tower of vanilla ice cream, mac nut brownies, raspberry puree, and whipped cream, was featured in *Bon Appetit.*

Leilani's on the Beach. Whaler's Village. ☎ **808/661-4495.** Reservations suggested for dinner. Main courses $14.95 and up. AE, DC, MC, V. Daily 11am–11pm. STEAK/SEAFOOD.

This is standard surf-and-turf for surfer appetites: prime rib for $23.95, half-pound cheeseburgers for $8.95, 14-ounce filet mignon for $25.95, and eight types of fresh island fish for under $20. You'll get an ocean view and a casual, festive atmosphere where quantity ranks higher than quality. Leilani's is part of the popular Maui restaurant chain that owns Kimo's in Lahaina and the neighboring Hula Grill.

LAHAINA

Very Expensive

✪ **Avalon.** 844 Front St. ☎ **808/667-5559.** Reservations recommended. Main courses $14.95–$36.95. AE, CB, DC, JCB, MC, V. Daily 11:30am–10pm. HAWAII REGIONAL.

Foodies have remained loyal to Avalon and chef-owner Mark Ellman's tireless commitment to fresh ingredients, healthy fare, and clean, crisp flavors. One of the original 12 chefs who established Hawaii Regional Cuisine, Ellman has remained one of Hawaii's avant-garde chefs, and Avalon his proving grounds. Walk off Front Street through a small courtyard and there it is, casual and tucked away, putting out flavors that suggest California, Indonesia, Thailand, China, Japan, and Vietnam. Looking more like dessert than salad, the colorful column called Chili Seared Salmon Tiki Style is an edible high-rise of mashed potatoes, eggplant, greens, tomato salsa, and salmon with a plum vinaigrette; it's one of the more flamboyant of his signature dishes, and every bit as good as it looks. Personal favorites: Maui onions with a zesty tamarind ketchup, Asian pasta with seafood in a tomato-ginger sauce, and Szechuan sugar-snap peas. You'll agonize over the nightly specials, from Hawaiian gumbo and fish pot-stickers to luau roasted garlic seafood. Vegetarians have satisfying choices, and many dishes can be ordered mild, medium, or spicy. The sole dessert, the Caramel Miranda, is a heroic concoction of macadamia-nut–brittle ice cream, caramel sauce, and exotic local fruit (the best of what's in season).

♻ David Paul's Lahaina Grill. 127 Lahainaluna Rd. ☎ **808/667-5117.** Reservations required. Main courses $19–$38. Prix fixe dinner $45. AE, DC, DISC, MC, V. Daily 5:30–10pm, bar until midnight. NEW AMERICAN.

Chef David Paul is a creative genius who has long transcended trendy acceptability at his chic Lahaina oasis, located in a historic building next to the faithfully restored Lahaina Hotel. A recent expansion (the second time in 3 years—a testament to his success) has created the chef's table for 10, set in the picture window looking out over Lahaina town, where nine-course menus are custom-created and personally presented by the chef. Paul has also embraced what he calls "market cuisine": The menu is determined by the availability of the best fresh ingredients, and therefore changes at least weekly, often more frequently. Expect one culinary marvel after another. Lahaina Grill is famous for its tequila shrimp with firecracker rice, but there are so many other temptations: kalua duck in reduced plum wine sauce (a must!), spicy crab cake in a sesame Dijon sauce, the pricey-but-worth-it lobster risotto in wild mushrooms and Gorgonzola cheese; the roasted pepper and Kula-corn chowder is a happy marriage of Maui and the Southwest, and the eggplant napoleon, whether or not you're vegetarian, is recommended.

Gerard's. Plantation Inn, 174 Lahainaluna Rd. ☎ **808/661-8939.** Reservations recommended. Main courses $24.50–$32.50. AE, D, JCB, DISC, MC, V. Daily 6–10pm. FRENCH.

Gerard Reversade's fans remember his bistro down the street, where people flew in from the neighbor islands for his breast of duckling a l'orange. Gerard's following and menu have grown since then. Winner of the *Wine Spectator* Award of Excellence for 1994 and 1995, Gerard's Gallic offerings still score high in this competitive culinary atmosphere. A worthy starter is the shiitake and oyster mushroom appetizer, savory and steaming in puff pastry, or the ahi tartar with taro chips, followed by the roasted Hawaiian snapper in a spicy orange and ginger butter sauce. Game lovers also have some sophisticated choices: venison with peppered sauce and poha berry compote, Ulupalakua lamb stew, and a popular rosemary rack of lamb. Note to vegetarians: Gerard's is very accommodating with vegetarian requests.

Expensive

Chart House. 1450 Front St., at Honoapiilani Hwy. (Hi. 30). ☎ **808/661-0937.** Main courses $15.95–$30. AE, CB, D, DISC, MC, V. Daily 5–10pm. AMERICAN.

Chart House restaurants have a knack for finding terrific locations with ocean views, and Lahaina has one of the best. (The other Maui locations are at 100 Wailea Ike Dr. in Wailea, and at 500 N. Puunene in Kahului.) Chart House's location is its strongest suit: Perched at the north end of Front Street, removed from congested Lahaina proper and elevated for optimal view, the restaurant offers a singular look at Lanai, Molokai, the ocean, and the sunset. Otherwise, expect the unremarkable fare that marks all other Chart Houses: prime rib, East-West Prawns and Garlic Steak, and an assortment of fresh fish in teriyaki, garlic herb, and mayonnaise sauces. Especially indulgent is the signature Mud Pie, a weighty dessert of Kona coffee ice cream, Oreo cookie crust, fudge, almonds, and whipped cream.

Longhi's. 888 Front St. ☎ **808/667-2288.** Main courses $16–$27. AE, CD, JCB, DISC, MC, V. Daily 7:30am–10pm. SEAFOOD/PASTA.

Longhi's is past its prime, and its verbal menu is irritating. It's grown like Pinocchio's nose and is impossible to remember, turning what should be the quiet perusal of dinner options into a lengthy, rapid-fire performance by the waiter and an SAT test for the poor diner that can easily spoil the experience in the open-sided, two-story dining room. The pastas and seafood (lobster tail for $50, crab cakes for $10.50) have long been the mainstays of this formerly chic restaurant, but many consider the food too rich, the service too self-important, and all in all (especially with such welcoming prospects as Avalon and David Paul's down the street), not a very cheering experience. Exceptions: It's fine for breakfast, especially for the deservedly famous vegetable frittata, and the wine list and martinis are impressive.

Moderate/Inexpensive

⑤ **Cheeseburger in Paradise.** 811 Front St. ☎ **808/661-4855.** Main courses $5.95–$9.95. AE, MC, V. Daily 11am–11pm. AMERICAN.

Wildly successful, always crowded, highly visible, and very noisy with its live music in the evenings, Cheeseburger is a shrine to the American classic. This is burger country, tropical style, with everything from tofu and garden burgers to the biggest, juiciest beef and chicken burgers, served on whole-wheat and sesame buns baked fresh daily. There are good reasons that the two-story green-and-white building next to the seawall is always packed: good value, good grinds, and a great ocean view. The Cheeseburger in Paradise, $6.95 for the hefty hunk with jack and cheddar cheeses, sautéed onions, lettuce, fresh tomatoes, and Thousand Island dressing, is a paean to the basics. You can build your own burger, too, by adding sautéed mushrooms, bacon, grilled ortega chilies, and other condiments for an extra charge. Onion rings, chili cheese fries, and a cold beer complete the carefree fantasy.

Hard Rock Cafe. 900 Front St. ☎ **808/667-7400.** Main courses $5.95–$14.95. AE, DC, MC, V. Daily 11:30am–10pm, bar until midnight. AMERICAN.

You know the formula: rock-and-roll memorabilia everywhere you look, loud music, good chili, fresh grilled fish with baked potato and salad (a bargain at $13.95), and sky-high, jaw-breaking grilled burgers weighing in at a third of a pound. With fries and salad, the grilled turkey burger is a good value (for Hawaii) at $7.25, but my favorite is the grilled ahi sandwich, smoky and satisfying with all the condiments. Vegetarians say the grilled veggie burger puts garden burgers to shame.

Kimo's. 845 Front St. ☎ **808/661-4811.** Reservations recommended. Main courses $9.95–$14.95. AE, DC, MC, V. Daily 11am–3pm, 5–10:30pm. STEAK/SEAFOOD.

Kimo's has a loyal following that keeps it from falling into the faceless morass of waterfront restaurants serving surf-and-turf with great sunset views. It's a formula restaurant (sister to Leilani's and Hula Grill) that works not only because of its oceanfront patio and upstairs dining room, but because, for the price, there are some satisfying choices. It's always crowded, especially during happy hour, with people having fun on a deck that takes in Molokai, Lanai, and Kahoolawe. The fresh catch in garlic lemon and a sweet basil glaze is a top seller, rivaling the hefty prime rib, complete with salad, carrot muffins, herb rolls, and herb rice. Keep in mind that the waistline-defying Hula Pie—macadamia-nut ice cream in a chocolate wafer crust with fudge and whipped cream—originated here.

⑤ **Lahaina Coolers.** 180 Dickensen St. ☎ **808/661-7082.** Most items under $14. AE, MC, V. Daily 7am–2am (kitchen open until midnight). AMERICAN.

A huge billfish hangs above the bar, and epic wave shots and wall sconces made of surfboard fins line the walls at this indoor/outdoor restaurant, with open windows on three sides taking advantage of the shade trees to create a cordial, cheerful ambiance. The bar is open until 2am, so you can go from the Surfer Special (a gourmet bean burrito) or fruit pancakes to their famous mango daiquiri at the end of the day. A new pasta machine promises great things for the selection—shrimp pesto linguine, smoked salmon fettuccine in dill-caper cream sauce—the nightly steak and fish specials, at $16 to $18.50, are two of Lahaina's terrific deals. The Evil Jungle Pizza, grilled chicken in a spicy Thai peanut sauce, is a novelty and one of several successful "tropic pizzas." A big plus: Everything can be prepared vegetarian upon request.

⑤ Lahaina Fish Company. 831 Front St. ☎ **808/661-3472.** Main courses $7.95–$22.95. AE, JCB, MC, V. Daily 9–10am, noon–2pm, 5–10pm. SEAFOOD.

The open-air dining room is literally over the water, with flickering torches after sunset and an affordable menu that covers the seafood-pasta basics. If you have to wait for a table—and many people do—the beach end of Hammerheads Fish Bar, with the draft from the huge refrigerator, is *not* where you want to be. Between noon and 3pm, head to an oceanside table and, for $8.95, order a hamburger, cheeseburger, chickenburger, fishburger, a generous basket of peel-and-eat shrimp, or sashimi; lingering is highly recommended. From noon to 5pm, the $2.50 happy-hour Mai Tai special keeps the crowd longer, and at sunset, a new cycle begins. Nightly specials range from island fish-and-chips for $7.95 to seven pasta dishes, standard steak-and-seafood combinations, and four types of fresh island fish prepared in Asian, American, and European styles. Keith's Cajun-style ahi is a winner.

Planet Hollywood. 744 Front St. ☎ **808/667-7877.** Main courses $7.95–$16.95. AE, DC, JCB, MC, V. Daily 11am–midnight. AMERICAN/CALIFORNIAN.

I can't believe I paid $3 for a Planet Hollywood menu; the fact that I capitulated to such hype is pure ignominy. This is Hard Rock Cafe with a Blade Runner twist, with pink vinyl tablecloths, zebra-printed booths and carpets, a bloody Arnold Schwarznegger statue in your face, and a sequined Dorothy Lamour strapless sarong on the wall (from a 1914 movie she made with Don Ho). Chrome, suspended acrylic cages, neon galore, and blaring rock music greet you as you step in off Front Street. For $6.50 you can order a basket of Cap'n Crunch–covered chicken with a Creole mustard sauce, and for a quarter more, Texas nachos. Prices have gone up recently but remain within reason: The world-famous cheeseburgers and french fries are $7.75, Thai shrimp pasta $12.95, and Caesar salad $6.95. For Front Street Lahaina, it's not highway robbery, but think twice about buying the menu, because in the end it can all add up to a big "Who cares?"

Scaroles Village Pizzeria. 505 Front St. ☎ **808/661-8112.** Main courses $6.95–$24.50. AE, DC, DISC, MC, V. Daily 11am–9:30pm. PIZZA.

With thin or thick crust, more than a dozen toppings, and the signature clam-and-garlic pizza that you can smell from around the corner, Scaroles draws a steady stream of diners to its corner cafe at the popular shopping complex called 505 Front. Appetizers, sandwiches (on homemade bread), pasta, and Scaroles' famous tiramisu make this more than a pizza joint. In addition to the walk-in traffic, this busy, cozy corner attracts loyal fans of Scaroles Ristorante on Wainee Street, an Italian-food fixture, and the newer Scaroles Ristorante Too at the Wailea Tennis Club.

SOUTHWEST MAUI
KIHEI/MAALAEA
Expensive

✪ A Pacific Cafe Maui. Azeka's Place II, 1279 S. Kihei Rd. ☎ **808/879-0069.** Reservations recommended. Main courses $21–$24. AE, DC, CB, MC, V. Daily 5:30–10pm. HAWAII REGIONAL.

This is the busiest restaurant on Maui every night of the week—so make your reservations as early as possible, because it's difficult to get in. Jean-Marie Josselin brought his singular talents from Kauai to a strip mall in Kihei and made it a cornerstone of exemplary cuisine. You'll dine on rattan chairs at hammered copper tables, under very high ceilings in a room bordered with windows (but you'll be so busy enjoying the food, you won't notice the parking lot). From the open kitchen comes a stream of unforgettables from a menu that changes daily. The warm potato salad with shrimp, mussels, calamari, and clams is infused with the delicate flavor of chervil. The tiger-eye ahi sushi tempura, a signature item, comes light and delectable, presented on curled ginger, beets, and radish sprouts. The steamed mussels in lemongrass ginger broth is a hit at $9.50, and the garlic-sesame mahimahi in lime-ginger sauce is highly recommended at $23. Josselin's brilliance soars right down to the last spoonful of ginger crème brûlée—you can't go wrong here.

Carelli's on the Beach. 2980 S. Kihei Rd. ☎ **808/875-0001.** Reservations recommended. Main courses $22–$34. AE, MC, V. Daily 6–10pm, bar until 11pm. ITALIAN/SEAFOOD.

Kihei's well-tanned, chicly attired trendetti come here for pasta, seafood, and the view. It is stupendous: With its prime on-the-sand location at Keawakapu Beach, you can view the sunset in ravishing surroundings over cioppino (the most popular item, at $30), fresh fish, ravioli, carpaccio, and other Italian favorites. The wood-burning brick oven turns out great pizzas, and the food is top-drawer, but there's something very inhospitable here. Although there's no minimum order at the 13-seat marble bar, there is a $25-per-person minimum to sit at a table on the dining floor; and if you stick to the bar, you're likely to have your back to the ocean. So there's an attitude here, definitely.

The Waterfront at Maalaea. 50 Hauoli St., Maalaea Harbor. ☎ **808/244-9028.** Reservations recommended. Main courses $18–$38. AE, DC, DISC, MC, V. Daily 5:30–8:30pm (last seating). SEAFOOD.

The Waterfront has won awards for wine excellence, service, and seafood, but its biggest boost is word of mouth. Loyal diners rave about the friendly staff and seafood, served in unfancy surroundings with a bay and harbor view. You have nine choices of preparations for the fresh fish, ranging from en papillote (baked in buttered parchment) to Southwestern (smoked chili and cilantro butter) to light cuisine (broiled or poached, then topped with steamed and fresh vegetables). The baked triple cream Danish appetizer is an excellent starter, but there are so many choices: Kula onion soup, an excellent Caesar salad, lobster chowder. Vegetarians favor the grilled eggplant layered with Maui onions, tomatoes, and spinach, served with red pepper coulis and Big Island goat cheese.

Moderate

Buzz's Wharf. Maalaea Harbor. ☎ **808/244-5426.** Reservations suggested. Main courses $10.95–$24.95. AE, CB, DC, DISC, JCB, MC, V. Daily 11am–10pm. AMERICAN.

Buzz's is another formula restaurant that offers a superb view, substantial sandwiches, meaty french fries, and surf-and-turf fare that's satisfying, but not sensational. Still, it's a fine way station for whale-watching over a cold beer and a fresh mahimahi sandwich with fries, or, if you're feeling extravagant, the house specialty, Prawns Tahitian ($16.95 at lunch, $23.95 for dinner). Buzz's prize-winning dessert—Tahitian Baked Papaya, a warm, fragrant melding of fresh papaya with vanilla and coconut—is the pride of the house. The bright, airy dining room looks out over Maalaea Harbor, Haleakala, and the ocean.

The Greek Bistro. 2511 S. Kihei Rd. ☎ **808/879-9330.** Reservations recommended. Combination and family-style dinners $17–$22 per person; family-style platter $35 for two. AE, DC, CB, JCB, MC, V. Daily 5–9:30pm. GREEK.

The banana trees, yellow ginger, and hibiscus that surround the tile-floored terrace add immeasurably to the dining experience at this indoor/outdoor bistro, especially in chaotic Kihei. Homemade pita bread, quality feta and spices, classic spanakopita (spinach pie in microthin layers of phyllo dough), and chicken and lamb souvlaki (the Greek version of shish kebab) are some of the authentic and well-received Mediterranean offerings. Popular items are the family-style combination platters, and the keiki (child's) menu of steak, shrimp, or souvlaki, all served with pasta for $8.95. Also popular is the Greek lasagna, chopped lamb and beef with cinnamon and cheeses, and the Mediterranean chicken breast, an elaborate platter of mushroom-and-wine–infused organic skinless chicken, served with linguine and vegetables.

La Pastaria. Lipoa Shopping Center, 41 E. Lipoa St. ☎ **808/879-9001.** Reservations recommended. Main courses $7–$26. AE, CB, DISC, MC, V. Mon–Fri 11am–2pm, daily 4–10pm. ITALIAN/SEAFOOD.

It's worth searching out this bistro from among the faceless strip malls of Kihei, because it offers singular entertainment to go with its menu: It's the only place around with pasta and jazz nightly, and each lives up to the other. The pasta is made fresh daily and served with marinara sauce, pesto, creamy clam, primavera, Bolognese, pomodoro, you name it. Gourmet pizzas come heaped with grilled chicken, pesto shrimp, clams, garlic sauce, vegetables, and any number of savory combinations, on thin or thick crust. Nightly specials are invariably the best-sellers: The fresh opakapaka is served in white wine and capers or in a savory pomodoro sauce of tomatoes, garlic, and fresh basil. For $8, you can tuck into a grilled asparagus-green onion salad with marinated vegetables over organic greens. The last Wednesday of each month is devoted to "dinner theater," where diners can tuck into a four-course, $45 dinner while performers take over the stage in the corner with tunes from *Phantom of the Opera* and other Broadway hits. La Pastaria is *the* jazz hot spot on weekends, when all diners seem to be music lovers or members of Maui's tight jazz and arts community. (See "Maui After Dark," below).

Stella Blues Cafe & Deli. Long's Center, 1215 S. Kihei Rd. ☎ **808/874-3779.** Main courses $9.95–$14.95. DISC, MC, V. Daily 8am–10pm. AMERICAN.

People in Kihei love coffee, bagels, and the blues, and this place has 'em all. Stella Blues gets going at breakfast and moves into the bluesy riffs of the night with the greatest of ease. You can start the day dining indoors or out over fresh-squeezed orange juice and a tofu scramble (the East Coast scramble is a hit, too—salmon, egg, and onion). Stella's Caffelatte, a steaming, bracing mug of cinnamon-mocha-orange, is the front-runner among the many coffee drinks that fuel the Kihei crowd. At lunch, a mind-boggling selection of sandwiches—nearly 2 dozen kinds, from corned beef to tempeh burger—is prepared with only the best ingredients: Jarlsberg Swiss, albacore tuna, and hormone-free, antibiotic-free Montana beef (with half the fat of chicken). After 5pm the menu expands, with something to please everyone. Among the hits: the Vegetarian Delight, spinach lasagna, Thai-style chili chicken, top sirloin steak, and homemade crab cakes in lemon chive butter. Wednesdays through Sundays, live music keeps the place jumping.

Inexpensive

Ⓢ **Alexander's Fish & Chicken & Chips.** 1913 S. Kihei Rd. ☎ **808/874-0788.** Fish-and-chips $5.95–$10.95. MC, V. Daily 11am–9pm. FISH-AND-CHIPS/SEAFOOD.

Look for the ocean mural in front, Kalama Park across the street, and a marketplace next door: This is Alexander's, a friendly neighborhood take-out stand with patio seating outside and a very busy kitchen. Fresh ono, mahimahi, and ahi, broiled or fried, fly out of the kitchen with baskets of french fries or rice, for less than $6. Equally popular are the 13-piece shrimp, chicken, oyster, calamari, rib, or fish baskets for $14.95 to $16.95. Fresh fish, Cajun chicken, teriyaki chicken, barbecued beef, and shrimp sandwiches, along with onion rings, cornbread, chicken wings, and other side orders in a light and tasty batter, make this a budget-friendly family favorite. And they use canola oil!

⑤ The Coffee Store. Azeka's Place II, 1279 Kihei Rd. ☎ **808/875-4244.** Most items under $8.50. AE, CB, DC, DISC, MC, V. Sun–Thurs 6am–10pm, Fri–Sat 6am–11pm. COFFEE HOUSE.

This simple, classic coffee house for caffeine connoisseurs serves 2 dozen different types of coffee and coffee drinks, from mochas, lattés, and frappés to cappuccino, espresso, and toddies. Breakfast items include smoothies, lox and bagels, quiches, granola, and an egg-and-mushroom breakfast quesadilla for under $6. Pizza, salads, vegetarian lasagna, veggie-and-shrimp quesadillas, and sandwiches (garden burger, tuna, turkey, or ham) also move briskly from the take-out counter. There are only a few small tables, and they fill up fast, often with musicians and artists who spent the previous evening entertaining at the Wailea and Kihei resorts. This place belongs to habitués; everyone seems to know each other here.

Kihei Caffe. 1945 S. Kihei Road. ☎ **808/879-2230.** Most items under $7. No credit cards. Daily 5am–3pm. COFFEE HOUSE.

At breakfast, you can order healthy—Meusli and papaya—or go out on a limb with the eggs, sausage, gravy, and biscuits. For lunch, the tiny indoor/outdoor cafe serves everything from couscous and tabouleh to pastrami and salami sandwiches. Until its midafternoon closing, people wander in for Kona coffee, cappuccino, and excellent fresh-baked pastries.

⑤ Shaka Sandwich & Pizza. 1295 S. Kihei Road. ☎ **808/874-0331.** Pizzas up to $25.95. Daily 10am–9pm. (Delivery hours 10:30am–9pm). PIZZA.

Award-winning pizzas share the limelight with New York–style hoagies and Philly cheese steaks, and they're all terrific. Shaka uses fresh Maui produce, long-simmering homemade sauces, and homemade Italian bread, and the scent of simmering garlic wafts through the parking lot. You can choose thin or Sicilian crust on the pizza, with gourmet toppings: Maui onions, spinach, anchovies, jalapeno peppers, and an array of other vegetables. Don't be misled by the whiteness of the white pizza; with the perfectly balanced flavors of olive oil, garlic, and cheese, you won't even miss the tomato sauce. Clam-and-garlic pizza, spinach pizza (with olive oil, spinach, garlic, and mozzarella), and the Shaka Supreme (with at least 11 toppings!), will satisfy even the most demanding pizza lovers. You can have your pie delivered, take it out, or dine in Shaka's modest new dining room.

WAILEA

Very Expensive

✪ Kea Lani Restaurant. Kea Lani Hotel, 4100 Wailea Alanui Dr. ☎ **808/875-4100.** Reservations preferred for dinner. Main courses $26–$38. AE, DC, JCB, MC, V. Daily 6:30–11am, 5:30–10pm. EURO-PACIFIC.

Executive Chef Steve Amaral's organic garden, which started as a tiny patch, is now about a half-acre and growing. He's passionate about it—it fuels his creativity. Breakfast is a bountiful buffet, a feast for eyes and palate. Diners will see cornucopian carts spilling over with lilikoi, figs, starfruit, avocado, coconut, mangoes, litchis, Surinam cherries, herbs, edible flowers, and countless other colorful things from the garden and from Ono Farms, which provides what Amaral can't grow at sea level. The dining room reopens for fine dining at dinner, when it's transformed into a Mediterranean fantasy: ocean view, candlelight flickering over tile floors, flawless service, and a brilliant, unforgettable menu that changes seasonally—but Amaral's touch is consistent. In the winter, expect wild mushroom strudel with kabocha pumpkin and a drizzle of basil oil; lobster chowder with homemade melba toast; opakapaka "hunter style," with wild mushrooms and garlic mashed potatoes; and grilled Wagyu free-range beef from the Big Island's Kahua Ranch, as tender as the lightest snapper, with a flavor somewhere between butter and smoke. Year-round, the menu celebrates the harvest of land and sea, and it's so joyfully and exquisitely executed that the dining experience becomes an exalted one.

Hana Gion. Stouffer Renaissance Wailea Beach Resort, 3550 Wailea Alanui Dr. ☎ **808/ 879-4900.** Reservations recommended. Main courses $27–$80. AE, DISC, JCB, MC, V. Mon– Wed, Fri–Sun 6–9:30pm. JAPANESE.

From food presentation to service and atmosphere, the Japanese aesthetic is gorgeously expressed here. You can sit at the sushi bar, in private rooms seating four to six, or in the intimate, narrow, stone-floored dining room with lacquer panels and bamboo. Kimono-clad servers expertly set up the pots for *yosenabe* or *shabu shabu* at your table, with the accompanying platters of beef, fresh seafood, and vegetables; as with the teppanyaki grill, another popular feature, you cook everything to your taste. Kyoto-style kaiseki dinners, the extravagant Japanese table d'hote, and the sushi bar, with its authentically and rigorously trained Japanese chefs, are other appealing features.

Raffles. Stouffer Renaissance Wailea Beach Resort, 3550 Wailea Alanui Dr. ☎ **808/879-4900.** Reservations recommended. Main courses $25–$38 for grill items; prix fixe $65 per person with wine for Hawaii Regional selections. AE, DISC, JCB, MC, V. HAWAII REGIONAL/AMERICAN GRILL.

Raffles is heading in new directions with the addition of its American grill menu, a nod to the national trend favoring choice, weighty grilled meats: 18-ounce Porterhouse steaks, 12-ounce filet mignons, 10-ounce veal chops, 8- or 16-ounce New York steaks. By also serving its Hawaii Regional menu of lighter fare, Raffles is covering both ends of the culinary spectrum, from light, fresh, and slightly ethnic to meaty American steak-and-potatoes classics. Chicken, veal, steaks, and a broiled lobster brochette make up the grill entrées; the rack of lamb and famous crisped whole fish remain Raffles staples. Among the Hawaii Regional items, the Gingered Lobster Tiki—a delicate vertical composition of rice, lomi salmon, ahi poke, lobster, and ginger aioli—is making waves. The restaurant offers limousine pickup service from other hotels in Wailea.

☉ Seasons. Four Seasons Resort Wailea. ☎ **808/874-8000.** Reservations recommended. Main courses $29–$42; Prix fixe $62–$95. AE, CB, DC, DISC, JCB, MC, V. Daily 6:30–9:30pm. HAWAII REGIONAL/PROVENÇAL.

"Sometimes I get fish in the morning, and it's still alive!" exclaims Senior Executive Chef George Mavrothalassitis, who has found his match in Maui's abundance of fresh produce and seafood. Formerly the wunderkind behind La Mer and Orchids at Halekulani in Honolulu, Mavrothalassitis is working his magic at this oceanfront, open-air temple of food, where his mastery of both Provençal and Hawaii Regional cuisines finds flawless expression. Renowned for his use of local ingredients and the most vaunted traditions of his native Provence, he still makes a bouillabaisse that reigns supreme. He has also transplanted his Hawaiian salt-crusted red snapper in *ogo* (seaweed) sauce, and the papillote of kumu (parchment-baked goat fish with shiitake mushrooms, ogo, and Maui onion). Other winners: yellowtail tuna smoked in kiawe, served with cucumber, mint, and tomato; gray snapper (*uku*) with fresh thyme; and charbroiled *opakapaka* with braised fennel. (In a lamb loin casserole, the vegetables cooked for 12 hours—in the heat of a pilot light!) Save room for dessert: You can go light with *pikake* (jasmine) sorbet, medium with lemon cappuccino, or devil-may-care with a velvety, moussey mound of Hawaiian Vintage Chocolate. My choice is the cheese tray with walnut bread—a Gallic finale like no other.

Expensive

⊙ **Joe's Bar & Grill**. Wailea Tennis Club, 131 Wailea Ike Place. ☎ **808/875-7767.** Reservations recommended. Main courses $14–$28. AE, DC, MC, V. Daily 11am–2pm, 5:30–10pm. AMERICAN REGIONAL.

Bev and Joe Gannon of Haliimaile General Store, the acclaimed Maui eatery in the middle of a cane field, didn't disappoint their waiting public when they opened their new restaurant on top of the Wailea Tennis Club Pro Shop. It became instantly chic—another banner for Bev Gannon's creative cookery. At lunch, there's a 360° view that spans golf course, tennis courts, the ocean, and Haleakala. At night, the other elements take over: the 43-foot handcrafted copper bar, theater lighting, folk dolls and ceramics on the wall, high ceilings, and plank floors. A familiar nasal voice greets you through the bathroom sound system: "Here we go! There you are! Some elegant cheese soufflé!" You can visit Julia Child in the loo anytime you can pull yourself away from the tender, succulent grilled quail, the smoked salmon quesadilla, the lobster pot pie, the grilled lamb chops in mint balsamic glaze . . . the menu is brilliant in its simplicity. Just try the mashed potatoes and gravy and see if they aren't the best you've ever had.

Pacific Grill. Four Seasons Resort Wailea, 3900 Wailea Alanui Dr. ☎ **808/874-8000.** Reservations recommended for dinner. Main courses $16–$27. AE, CB, DC, DISC, JCB, MC, V. Daily 6am–2:30pm, 5:30–9:30pm. PACIFIC RIM.

The Four Seasons' all-day dining room is like most hotels' fine dining rooms. The view alone is luxurious, and coupled with a thoughtful and imaginative menu, it's a room that shines from morning to evening. Terrace seating is recommended—the better to view the West Maui Mountains with—but beware of the wind that comes down the slopes of Haleakala and stirs things up in the afternoon. At lunch, the menu includes some low-calorie, low-cholesterol, low-fat, and low-sodium "alternative cuisine" choices, such as whole-wheat rigatoni with artichoke hearts and roasted eggplant. Heartier appetites and bolder palates may prefer the Cajun mahimahi sandwich with lemon-thyme aioli or the poached filet of salmon on wilted greens.

SeaWatch. 100 Wailea Golf Club Dr. ☎ **808/875-8080.** Reservations required for groups of 8 or more. Main courses $16 and up. AE, DC, MC, V. Daily 8am–3pm, 3–5:30pm, 5:30–10pm. ISLAND CUISINE.

SeaWatch's use of fresh Maui produce, Big Island goat cheese, and Island fish in ethnic preparations sets it apart from most other upscale clubhouse restaurants—but in the end, the restaurant is underwhelming. However, you can dine on the terrace or under high ceilings in a room with pretty views, on a menu that's earnest and skillful, and carries the tee-off-to-19th-hole crowd with ease. Pacific crab cakes, Chinese chicken salad, Vietnamese spring rolls, fresh fish tacos, and the fresh catch sandwich are some of the local favorites at lunch. At dinner, the standouts are miso-chili-glazed tiger prawns and the nightly fresh catch, which can be ordered in one of five preparations.

Inexpensive

Maui Onion. Stouffer Renaissance Wailea Beach Resort, 3550 Wailea Alanui Dr. ☎ **808/ 879-4900.** Most items under $10.75. AE, DISC, JCB, MC, V. Daily 10am–6pm. AMERICAN.

Poolside dining on patio furniture, under a canopy of white alamandra blossoms dripping from vines in the trellises, with an ocean view—that's Maui Onion. We recommend it for the carefree and bold among you who love onion rings, french fries, hamburgers, and smoothies—skip the lackluster salads. The Maui onion rings are the best in the world: thick, juicy, and crisp, cooked in a miracle batter that seals in moisture and flavor. The fries, Cajun-style and thin, are equally commendable. After these successes, a so-so sandwich would be acceptable. Thankfully, the sandwiches, particularly the mahimahi with honey mustard and the tuna melt on sourdough, are also enthusiastically recommended.

MAKENA

✪ **Hakone.** Maui Prince Hotel, 5400 Makena Alanui. ☎ **808/874-1111.** Reservations recommended. Complete dinners $28–$42; Kaiseki (24-hour advance notice) $85. AE, DISC, JCB, MC, V. Daily 6–9pm. JAPANESE.

The Prince Hotels know Japanese cuisine and spared no effort to create a slice of Kyoto here, complete with sandalwood walls and pillars that were assembled by Japanese craftsmen and imported. Hakone offers super-luxe Japanese fare, very haute-Kyoto, gorgeously presented, and pricey. Expect some difficult choices. One appealing feature is the option of ordering nine selections of sushi, a California roll, and vegetable tempura for $35; like all dinner selections, it comes with appetizer, rice, miso soup, and pickled vegetables. Sashimi, tempura, broiled fish, California roll, and dessert comprise another of the popular combination dinners, which range from lobster ($38) to steak ($29) to tempura ($28). Our advice is to strongly consider these combinations, because if you have a yen for sushi, your à la carte bill will hit you like a lead balloon. Among our à la carte favorites are the steamed clam and the chawan mushi, a melt-in-your-mouth, celestially delicate custard with morsels of chicken and shiitake mushrooms.

Prince Court. Maui Prince Hotel, 5400 Makena Alanui. ☎ **808/874-1111.** Reservations recommended. Main courses $19.95–28.95; Sun brunch $31.95. AE, DC, JCB, MC, V. Thurs–Mon 6–9pm, Sun 9:30am–1pm. HAWAII REGIONAL.

Half the Sunday Brunch experience is the fabulous view of Makena Beach, the crescent-shaped islet called Molokini, and Kahoolawe island. The other half is the lavish buffet, spread over several tables: pasta, omelets, cheeses, pastries, sashimi, crab legs, smoked salmon, fresh Maui produce, and a dazzling array of ethnic and continental foods. The Prince Court dinners continue the epicurean tradition, but former chef Roger Dikon, one of the 12 charter chefs of Hawaii Regional Cuisine, is missed. The tasting menu changes weekly to feature the best of the seafood and produce in season. The Trio of Hawaiian Fish, with its sampling of three different fresh fish prepared three different ways, is reliably good, but if you're feeling reckless, you may want to attempt the Mixed Seafood Grill, a half lobster stuffed with crab, fish, and more seafood in a lobster-brandy-basil sauce.

UP-COUNTRY MAUI

HALIIMAILE (ON THE WAY TO UP-COUNTRY MAUI)

✪ **Haliimaile General Store.** Haliimaile Rd., Haliimaile. ☎ **808/572-2666.** Reservations recommended. Main courses $16–$24. AE, DC, MC, V. Daily 11am–2:30pm, 5:30–9:30pm; sushi bar Tues–Sat; Sun brunch 10am–2:30pm. AMERICAN.

What was once an old plantation store in the middle of the cane fields is now one of Maui's most appealing eateries. You'll dine at tables set on old wood floors under high ceilings (sound ricochets fiercely here), in a peach-colored room emblazoned with massive, bold works by local artists. The food, a blend of eclectic American with ethnic touches, manages to avoid the usual pitfalls of Hawaii Regional cuisine: the same-old, same-old, I'm-bored-with-seared-ahi syndrome. Instead, you can order the spicy Rack of Lamb Hunan style, a blend of sesame-black bean flavors served with mashed potatoes—exotic yet homey. Or chef Bev Gannon's Brie and grape quesadilla, famous for good reason, or the soft flour tortilla with Chinese roasted duck, called Peking Duck Taco. The Paniolo Ribs in a tangy barbecue sauce and the Szechuan Barbecued Salmon (on a sublime wilted salad), topped with caramelized onions, garlic, orange peel, and peppercorns, are simple yet inspired.

KULA

Grandma's Coffee House. End of Hi. 37, Keokea. ☎ **808/878-2140.** Most items under $8.95. No credit cards. Sun 7am–3pm, Mon–Tues 7am–5pm, Wed–Sat 7am–8pm. COFFEE HOUSE/AMERICAN.

Alfred Franco's grandmother started what is now a five-generation coffee business back in 1918, when she was 16 years old. Today the tiny wooden coffee house he named after her, still fueled by homegrown Haleakala coffee beans, is the quintessential roadside oasis. About 6 miles before the Tedeschi Vineyard in Ulupalakua, Grandma's is a gathering place for espresso, home-baked pastries, inexpensive pasta, sandwiches (including garden burgers for carnophobes), and local plate lunch specials that change daily. Aside from Grandmother's coffee cake, muffins, cinnamon rolls, and pastries, baked fresh daily, the specials include Hawaiian beef stew, ginger chicken, saimin, chicken curry, lentil soup, and a spate of sandwiches piled high with Kula vegetables.

Kula Lodge. Haleakala Hwy. (Hi. 377). ☎ **808/878-2517.** Reservations recommended for dinner. Main courses $14–$22. AE, MC, V. Daily 6:30–11:30am, 11:45am–9pm. HAWAII REGIONAL/AMERICAN.

The good news is that the food has improved mightily at this chalet on the hill, making it as much a stop for enjoyable dining as it is for the sunrise-to-sunset view. The bad news is that if it's the chef's night off, quality can be spotty. But the million-dollar view through the large picture windows spans the flanks of Haleakala, rolling 3,200 feet down to central Maui, the ocean, and the West Maui Mountains. If possible, go for sunset cocktails and watch the colors change into deep purples and end-of-day hues. When darkness descends, a roaring fire and lodge atmosphere turn the attention to the coziness of the room. Recommended are the roasted rack of lamb in Dijon sauce, flavorful and tender, served with ratatouille; and the ginger-infused seared salmon. For breakfast, Kula Lodge is known for its tofu scramble, eggs Benedict, and French toast made with homemade cinnamon bread; for lunch, it's known for the tempeh and roast turkey sandwiches. Keep in mind that groups of ravenous bicyclists torquing downhill from sunrise at the summit may descend en masse at any time.

⑤ Kula Sandalwoods. Haleakala Hwy. (Hi. 377). ☎ **808/878-3523.** Most items under $8.75. DISC, MC, V. Mon–Sat 6:30am–2pm, Sun brunch 6:30am–noon. AMERICAN.

Chef Eleanor Loui, graduate of the Culinary Institute of America, makes hollandaise sauce every morning from fresh up-country egg yolks, sweet butter, and Myers lemons her family grows in the yard above the restaurant. This is Kula cuisine, with produce from the backyard and everything made from scratch: French toast with home-baked Portuguese sweet bread, sandwiches on home-baked French baguettes, hamburgers drenched in a special cheese sauce made with grated sharp cheddar. The Kula Sandalwoods Salad features grilled chicken breast with crimson Kula tomatoes and onions, and, when the garden allows, just-picked red oak, curly green, and red leaf lettuces. "This is very basic home cooking, but everything is fresh," says the chef, who works with her husband, sister, and brother in their parents' restaurant. The Kula Sandalwoods Omelette is an open-faced wonder with sour cream, green onions, bacon, and cheddar cheese, served with cottage potatoes—a gourmet treat for $7.25. You'll dine in one of two separate rooms, on the gazebo or the terrace, with dazzling views in all directions, including, in the spring, a yard dusted with lavender jacaranda flowers and a hillside ablaze with fields of orange akulikuli blossoms. Although the downhill bicyclists descend here for breakfast too, there's still plenty of seating.

Upcountry Cafe. Andrade Building, 7-2 Aewa Place (just off Haleakala Hwy.), Pukalani. ☎ **808/572-2395.** Most dinner items under $14.95. MC, V. Mon, Wed–Sat 6:30am–3pm, Thurs–Sat 6–9pm, Sun 6:30am–1pm. AMERICAN/LOCAL.

Pukalani's inexpensive, casual, and very popular cafe features cows everywhere: on the walls, chairs, menus, aprons, even the exterior. But the food is the draw: simple home-cooked comfort food like meat loaf, roast pork, and humongous hamburgers, plus home-baked bread, oven-fresh muffins, and local faves such as saimin and Chinese chicken salad. Soups and salads (homemade cream of mushroom, Cobb and Caesar salads) and shrimp scampi with bow-tie pasta are among the cafe's other pleasures. The signature dessert is the cow pie, a naughty pile of chocolate cream cheese with macadamia nuts in a cookie crust, shaped like you-know-what.

MAKAWAO

Casanova Italian Restaurant. 1188 Makawao Ave. ☎ **808/572-0220.** Reservations recommended for dinner. Main courses $8–$15. AE, DC, MC, V. Mon–Sat 11:30am–2pm, daily 5:30–9pm. Lounge: Daily until 12:30am or 1am. Deli: Mon–Sat 8am–6:30pm, Sun 8:30am–6:30pm. ITALIAN.

Look for the tiny veranda with a few stools, always full, in front of a deli at Makawao's busiest intersection—that's the most visible part of Casanova's restaurant and lounge. Makawao's center of nightlife consists of a stage and dance floor adjoining a cozy cafe and bar in the wing next to the deli. Pizza, gnocchi, rosemary lamb chops, and pasta in a dozen shapes, colors, and flavors appear on a menu that has made this Maui's most brightly shining Italian star. You can dine simply or lavishly, from a tomato, garlic, and four-cheese pizza ($13) to penne with lobster tail and scallops in a tomato-garlic-sherry sauce ($19). Ask about the house specialty, a whole fresh fish baked with garlic, wine, and herbs, an exquisitely flavored dish that must be ordered a half-hour in advance—it's worth every minute and dollar.

Courtyard Deli. 3620 Baldwin Ave. ☎ **808/572-3456.** Most items under $9. AE, MC, V. Sun–Thurs 7am–6pm, Fri–Sat 7am–9pm. DELI.

Located behind the Makawao Steak House, the Courtyard Deli covers most of the bases: outdoor dining under a large coral tree, an extensive selection of health-conscious salads and sandwiches, and deadly desserts. Although there are murmurings aplenty about the service, few complain about the food: gourmet pizzas and polenta lasagna, mushroom burgers and faux-bacon BLT, vegetarian burgers and home-roasted turkey, and savory salads of rice, potato, pasta, or beans. In true deli fashion, the judicious lunches lead inevitably to dessert, which the Courtyard Deli makes unsparingly: lilikoi cheesecake, carrot cake, honey apple pie, and a spate of sweets, including, on occasion, gourmet chocolates that have regulars wondering why the sweetness doesn't rub off on the service.

Kitada's Kau Kau Corner. 3617 Baldwin Ave. ☎ **808/572-7241.** Most items under $6.75. No credit cards. AMERICAN/JAPANESE.

This is saimin central, a cross between grandma's kitchen and a cowboy diner, a modest old storefront known for its paniolo-size servings and the tastiest saimin in up-country Maui. Kitada's plate lunches are legendary (the hamburger plate is adored by the reckless), and the dry mein, a heap of noodles, is a cross between saimin and

Chinese fried noodles. You'll see everyone from up-country ranch hands to expensively dressed Makawao ladies digging in. Local color and cheap eats, lots of it.

Makawao Steak House. 3612 Baldwin Ave. ☎ **808/572-8711.** Reservations recommended for dinner. Main courses $16–$25. AE, MC, V. Mon–Fri 11am–2pm, 5–9:30pm; Sat–Sun 5–10pm. STEAK/SEAFOOD.

The ho-hum menu is forgiven by the homey atmosphere (three fireplaces, rustic ambiance), and by the fact that no *paniolo* town is worth its salt without its own neighborhood steak house. This one has been here for a long time, with a menu that's unchanging but consistent in quality, if predictable and, for some items, pricey. (We think $16 is a lot to pay for chili, lean turkey or not.) In true cowboy fashion, hefty is the operative word here, as in 14-ounce prime rib ($22), 16-ounce rosemary pork chops ($18), and the famous Dickie's Blue Plate Special, a kiawe-broiled Porterhouse in a sauce of garlic, capers, and olive oil. For carnophobes, other best-sellers include the zesty Caesar salad with artichokes, the Makawao artichoke topped with Parmesan and garlic butter, and the fresh fish, broiled or sautéed in lemon butter and capers.

Polli's Mexican Restaurant. 1202 Makawao Ave. ☎ **808/572-7808.** Main courses $6–$15. DISC, MC, V. Daily 7am–10pm. MEXICAN.

This is a democratic restaurant whose extensive menu is equally considerate to health foodies, vegetarians, and carnivores. In other words, there's something for everyone, from baby back ribs and steak dinners to substitutions of tofu or vegetarian taco mix, happily accommodated on all menu items. Sizzling fajitas are the house special, featuring fish, shrimp, chicken, tofu, or steak in a dramatic entrance, on a crackling hot platter with vegetables and spices, six flour tortillas, sour cream, and guacamole—a good group endeavor. Expect the full roster of south-of-the-border favorites, from the usual tamales, tacos, and burritos to cheese-, mushroom-, and Mexi-burgers, laced with jalapenos and pepper jack cheese ($6.95). Best of all, the menu is lard free.

EAST MAUI
PAIA

Ⓢ **Charley's Restaurant.** 142 Hana Hwy. ☎ **808/579-9453.** Reservations accepted. Main courses $10–$19. AE, DISC, MC, V. Daily 7am–2:30pm, pupu bar 2:30pm–5pm, dinner 5–10pm. AMERICAN/PIZZA.

A little tavern with a big and skillful kitchen, Charley's is known as the best place for breakfast in Paia; yet it eases gracefully into dining for all hours, from lunch to midafternoon pupus to busy, social dinners over pizza and beer—and the best steamed clams in town. Any day starts splendidly with the Cajun-style eggs Benedict made with fresh ono (wahoo), or the plate-sized whole wheat, blueberry, or macadamia nut pancakes ($2.50 to $5.95). At lunch, the quarter-pound hamburgers are served on home-baked Kaiser buns, and at dinner, the pizzas, pastas, kiawe-smoked ribs, and fresh steamers steal the show. The hugely successful ribs are marinated in Charley's own honey-barbecue sauce, then smoked and charbroiled for extra sizzle. Fresh herbs, feta cheese, sun-dried tomatoes, spinach, clams, shrimp, and other condiments top the pizzas; no greasy pepperoni here. The dinner nonpareil, however, is the plump, succulent Washington clams, fresh and sweet and swimming in a lemon butter–garlic broth. For $8.95 as an appetizer and $12.50 as a main course with Caesar salad and sourdough garlic bread, the clams aren't only a value, they're among the best we've ever had—they'd hold their own in the finest restaurants on the island.

Ⓢ **Pic-nics.** 30 Baldwin Ave. ☎ **808/579-8021.** Most items under $6.95. No credit cards. Daily 7am–7pm. SANDWICHES/PICNIC LUNCHES.

If there were a nut burger Hall of Fame, Pic-nics would be a lifetime member. The spinach nut burger, an ingenious vegetarian blend topped with vegetables and ched-dar cheese, is the signature item on a long and varied menu of elegant and no-fuss picnic fare for the drive to Hana or up-country Maui. Don't be fooled by the few tables and bustling take-out counter that make it look like a health-food McDonald's; these are gourmet sandwiches (Kula vegetables, home-baked breast of turkey, Cajun chicken, Cajun fish) worthy of the finest picnic spot. The rosemary herb-roasted chicken can be ordered as a plate lunch (two scoops of rice and Haiku greens) for $6.95, or as part of the Hana Bay picnic ($19.95 for two) that includes an array of sandwiches, meats, Maui-style potato chips, and home-baked cookies and muffins. You can order old-fashioned fish-and-chips too, or shrimp-and-chips, or pastries baked fresh daily. Those needing a refueling on the way to or from Hana can try the Chocolate Rocket or the Tropical Lightning (double espresso with steamed milk), two of the several coffee drinks made with Maui blend coffee.

The Vegan. 115 Baldwin Ave. ☎ **808/579-9144.** Main courses $4.95–$8.95. MC, V. Daily 4–9pm. GOURMET VEGETARIAN/VEGAN.

Every day the chefs here prove that vegan doesn't have to mean boring. Wholesome foods with ingenious soy substitutes and satisfying flavors appear on a menu that defies deprivation. Garlic noodles, called Pad Thai noodles, are the best-selling item, cooked in a creamy coconut sauce and generously seasoned with garlic and spices. Curries, grilled polenta, pepper steak made of Seitan (a meat substitute), and organic hummus are among the items that draw vegetarians from around the island. Proving that desserts are justly deserved, Vegan offers a carob cake and coconut milk–flavored tapioca pudding that hint of Thailand and are devoid of dairy milk.

ON THE HANA ROAD

Mama's Fish House. 799 Poho Place (Hi. 36), Kuau Cove. ☎ **808/579-8488.** Reservations recommended for dinner. Main courses $23.94–$34.95. AE, DC, DISC, JCB, MC, V. Daily 11am–2:30pm, pupus 2:30–5pm, dinner 5–9:30pm. SEAFOOD.

Mama's is getting pricier and pricier since it opened its doors as Hawaii's first fresh-fish restaurant in the early 1970s, but diners still come here for the ocean view and the fact that it's a stone's throw from the world's finest windsurfing beach. Seafood, prepared 10 different ways, is the forte here, seared with herbs, grilled with wasabi butter, or pan fried with Maui onions, all served in a Polynesian setting of shells and carved woods. The ever-popular house specialty, Fish Hawaiian, is sautéed with coconut milk and lime juice, much like a cooked version of poisson cru. Served with coconut and Molokai sweet-potato fries, it has a decidedly Tahitian bent.

⑤ Pauwela Cafe. 375 W. Kuiaha Rd., Haiku. ☎ **808/575-9242.** Most items under $5.25. No credit cards. Mon–Sat 7am–3pm, Sun 8am–2pm. INTERNATIONAL.

It's a long drive from anywhere, but the kalua turkey sandwich is reason enough for the journey. Because it's located in an industrial center of sailboard and surfboard manufacturers, you may find a surf legend dining at the next table. For many rea-sons, the tiny cafe with concrete floors and six tables has a strong local following. Becky Speere, a gifted chef, and her husband, Chris, a food service instructor at Maui Community College and former sous chef at the Maui Prince Hotel, infuse every sandwich, salad, and muffin with a high degree of culinary finesse. We never dreamed we could dine so well on Styrofoam plates. The scene-stealing kalua turkey is one success layered on the other: warm, smoky and moist shredded turkey, served with cheese on home-baked French bread and covered with a green chili and cilantro sauce. It's arguably the best sandwich on the island. The black-bean chili bursts with flavor and is served over rice with sour cream, cheese, and onions—a hearty, healthy choice. The salads, too, are fresh and uncomplicated, offered with homemade dressings that make the difference. For breakfast, eggs chilaquile launches the day with layers of corn tortillas, pinto beans, chilies, cheese, and herbs, topped with egg custard and served hot with salsa and sour cream—the works, for an unbelievable $4.50.

HANA

The Cafe at Hana Gardenland. Hana Hwy. at Kalo Rd. ☎ **808/248-8975.** Most items under $8.95. MC, V. Daily 9am–5pm. HEALTHY AMERICAN CUISINE.

The light, healthy fare and foliage both indoors and out are pure, garden-style Hana; and a koi pond, art gallery, and gift shop are uplifting accessories to a menu that has won the hearts of diners with its honest simplicity: ahi salad in Hana papaya halves, mushroom and spinach quiche with organic greens, three-cheese lasagna, garlic potato salad, and generously towering sandwiches on whole-wheat Maui Crunch bread. When Hilary Rodham Clinton and her daughter, Chelsea, came to Hana, they dined on steamed eggs with salsa on Maui Crunch bread, and waffles topped with fresh mangos. Most of the produce is grown on the Gardenland property, and the Espresso Bar serves teas, Hana-blend coffee, fresh orange, carrot, and lemon juices, as well as smoothies made with freshly picked bananas and papayas.

Hana Ranch Restaurant. Hana Hwy. ☎ **808/248-8255.** Reservations recommended for dinner. Main courses $16.95–$34.95. AE, DISC, JCB, MC, V. Daily 11am–3pm, Fri–Sat 6–8:30pm; takeout daily 6:30am–6:30pm. AMERICAN.

Part of the Hotel Hana-Maui operation, the Hana Ranch Restaurant is an informal alternative to the hotel's beleaguered dining room. But the steep climb in prices, for a casual restaurant, seems exploitive given the paucity of restaurants in Hana. Here are some of your dinner choices: New York steak for $22.95, steak and lobster for $42.95, prawns and pasta for $22.95, and a few Pacific Rim options, such as spicy shrimp wontons and the predictable fresh fish poke. Aside from the weekly, warmly received Wednesday "Pizza Night," the luncheon buffet is a more affordable prospect: barbecue ribs, chicken, baked potatoes, beans, and salads for $8.95. There are indoor tables as well as two outdoor pavilions that offer stunning ocean views. At the take-out stand adjoining the restaurant, saimin, a $6.25 teriyaki plate lunch, and mahi sandwich for $4.25 are reasonable alternatives for the dine-and-dash set.

5 Beaches

by Rick Carroll, with Jeanette Foster

Maui has more than 80 accessible beaches, from newly formed black beaches to luxurious golden sands; there's even a rare red-sand beach. All are accessible to the public, as provided by Hawaii law, and most have facilities. Here are our favorites:

WEST MAUI BEACHES
✪ KAPALUA BEACH

The beach cove that fronts the Kapalua Bay Hotel and Villas is the stuff of dreams: a golden crescent bordered by two palm-studded points. The sandy bottom slopes gently to deep water at the bay mouth; the water's so clear that you can see where the gold sands turn to green, and then deep blue. Protected from strong winds and currents by the lava-rock promontories, Kapalua's calm waters are great for snorkelers

⭐ Frommer's Favorite Maui Experiences

Diving Molokini Crater. Moorish idols, trumpet fish, butterfly fish, parrot fish, rainbow wrasses—Hawaii has more than 650 species of tropical fish, and Molokini is home to nearly all of them. This sunken crater off the Wailea Coast is Maui's most popular dive spot, but the fish still outnumber the snorkelers.

Watching the Whales. The Pacific humpback whale is one of the largest creatures on earth, averaging 40 to 50 feet in length and weighing 80,000 or 90,000 pounds. The majestic mammals commute from Alaska to Maui each winter, where they're protected and celebrated as the star attraction of the annual whale-watch season.

Swimming the Seven Sacred Pools. There are more than seven of these fern-shrouded waterfall pools, and none of them are sacred, but they're all beautiful. They spill seaward at Oheo Gulch, on the rainy eastern flanks of Haleakala. Some try to swim in the pools nearest the sea; if you do, keep an eye on the sky overhead, so a sudden cloudburst doesn't send you cascading out to sea and into the waiting jaws of sharks.

Hiking Haleakala. Exploring this spectacular crater on foot is the best way to experience it. Sliding Sand Trail takes you inside the gargantuan pit, which looks so lunarlike that NASA's moon men trained here. Said to be the biggest of its kind in the world, the crater even has its own mountain range. Be on the lookout for silverswords: these outrageous spiky green plants, which look like artichokes on acid, grow like weeds in the jumble of black lava near the summit and inside the House of the Sun.

Driving the Heavenly Road to Hana. Going to Hana is all about the journey, not the destination. Go slow, top down, early in the morning—dawn isn't too early. Take your time, go with the flow. Stop at Puohokamoa Falls and take a splash, buy a pandanus hat from a Samoan weaver, nibble on some fresh apple bananas, smell the wild ginger. Spend the day at Waianapanapa Beach. Don't hurry back to civilization; stay in a romantic B&B and drive back tomorrow—or the next day.

Partying Lahaina-Style. Anytime's the right time to be in this historic port town, where a Friday-night party mood prevails any day of the week. Go gallery hopping, pub crawling, dine on a fabulous meal as the sun sets over the harbor, and end a perfect Maui day by watching the moonbeams dance on the crashing surf.

Spotting a Nene Goose. A claw-footed, flightless bird that looks like a Canadian goose with zebra stripes, the endangered Hawaiian nene lives on lava and the largesse of Hawaii (it's the official state bird). You usually can see a nene at Haleakala Park headquarters, where they often greet visitors with a high-pitched little voice—*nay-nay*—that mimics their baby-talk name.

Exploring Iao Valley. When the sun strikes Iao Valley, in the West Maui Mountains, an almost ethereal light sends rays out in all directions, like a biblical holy picture. This really may be Eden.

and swimmers of all ages and abilities, and the bay is big enough to paddle a kayak around without getting into the more challenging channel that separates Maui from Molokai. Waves come in just right for riding. Fish hang out by the rocks, as if they know that this is a marine preserve. The beach is accessible from the hotel on one end, which provides sun chairs with shades and a beach activities center for its guests,

Beaches & Outdoor Activities on Maui

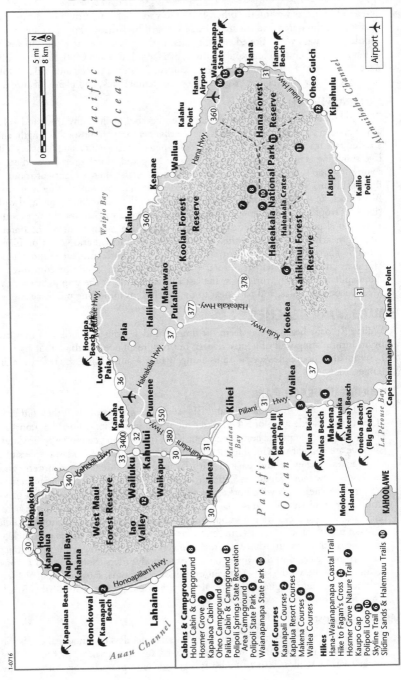

Cabins & Campgrounds
- Holua Cabin & Campground ⑧
- Hosmer Grove ⑦
- Kapalaoa Cabin ⑨
- Oheo Campground ⑥
- Paliku Cabin & Campground ⑬
- Polipoli Springs State Recreation Area Campground ⑤
- Polipoli State Park ⑤
- Waianapanapa State Park ⑯

Golf Courses
- Kaanapali Courses ②
- Kapalua Resort Courses ①
- Makena Courses ④
- Wailea Courses ③

Hikes
- Hana-Waianapanapa Coastal Trail ⑮
- Hike to Fagan's Cross ⑭
- Hosmer Grove Nature Trail ⑦
- Kaupo Gap ①
- Polipoli Loop ⑩
- Skyline Trail ⑥
- Sliding Sands & Halemauu Trails ⑩

and a public access way on the other. It isn't so wide that you burn your feet getting in or out of the water, and the inland side is edged by a shady path and cool lawns. Outdoor showers are stationed at both ends. Parking is limited to about 30 spaces in a small lot off Lower Honoapiilani Road, by Napili Kai Beach Club, so arrive early; next door is a nice, moderately priced oceanfront restaurant, Kapalua's Bay Club. Facilities include showers, rest rooms, lifeguard, rental shack, and plenty of shade.

KAANAPALI BEACH

Four-mile-long Kaanapali is one of Maui's best beaches, with grainy gold sand as far as the eye can see. The beach parallels the sea channel through most of its length, and a paved beach walk links hotels and condos, open-air restaurants, and Whalers Village shopping center. Because Kaanapali is so long and most hotels have adjacent swimming pools, the beach is crowded only in pockets—there's plenty of room to find seclusion. Summertime swimming is excellent. The best snorkeling is around Black Rock, in front of the new Sheraton; the water's clear, calm, and populated with clouds of tropical fish. Facilities include outdoor showers; you can use the rest rooms at the hotel pools. Various beach activity vendors line up in front of the hotels, offering nearly every type of water activity and equipment. Parking is a problem, though. There are two public entrances: at the south end, turn off Honoapiilani Highway into the Kaanapali Resort, and pay for parking there; or continue on Honoapiilani Highway, turn off at the last Kaanapali exit, at the stop light near the Maui Kaanapali Villas, and park next to the beach signs indicating public access.

SOUTH MAUI BEACHES

Wailea Resort's beaches may seem off-limits, hidden from plain view as they are by an intimidating wall of luxury resorts; but they're all open to the public by law. Look for the "Shoreline Access" signs along Wailea Alanui Drive, the resort's main boulevard.

KAMAOLE III BEACH PARK

Three beach parks—Kamaole I, II, and III—stand like golden jewels in the front yard of the funky seaside town of Kihei, which all of a sudden is sprawling like suburban blight. The beaches are the best thing about Kihei (if you don't count A Pacific Cafe). All three are popular with local residents and visitors because they're easily accessible. On weekends they're jam-packed with fishermen, picnickers, swimmers, and snorkelers. The most popular is Kamaole III, or Kam-3, as locals say. The biggest of the three beaches, with wide pockets of golden sand, it's the only one with a playground for children and a grassy lawn that meets the sand. Swimming is safe here, but scattered lava rocks are toe stubbers at the water line, and parents should watch to make sure their kids don't venture too far out, as the bottom slopes off quickly. Both the north and south shores are rocky fingers with a surge big enough to attract fish and snorkelers, and the winter waves attract bodysurfers. Kam-3 is also a wonderful place to watch the sunset. Facilities include rest rooms, showers, picnic tables, barbecue grills, and lifeguard. There's also plenty of parking, on South Kihei Road, across from the Maui Parkshore condos.

WAILEA BEACH

Wailea, which means "water of Lea," the Hawaiian goddess of canoe makers, is the best golden sand crescent on Maui's sun-baked southwestern coast. One of five beaches within Wailea Resort, Wailea is big, wide, and protected on both sides by

The Kapalua/ Kaanapali Coast

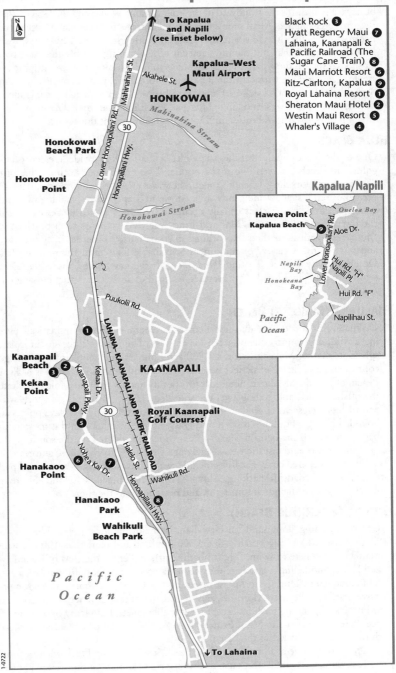

Black Rock ❸
Hyatt Regency Maui ❼
Lahaina, Kaanapali &
  Pacific Railroad (The
  Sugar Cane Train) ❽
Maui Marriott Resort ❻
Ritz-Carlton, Kapalua ❾
Royal Lahaina Resort ❶
Sheraton Maui Hotel ❷
Westin Maui Resort ❺
Whaler's Village ❹

To Kapalua
and Napili
(see inset below)

Kapalua–West
Maui Airport

Akahele St.

HONKOWAI

Mahinahina St.

Mahinahina Stream

Honokowai
Beach Park

Lower Honoapiilani Rd.

Honoapiilani Hwy.

30

Honokowai
Point

Honokowai Stream

Puukolii Rd.

Kaanapali
Beach

Kekaa
Point

Kekaa Dr.

Kaanapali Pkwy.

LAHAINA-KAANAPALI AND PACIFIC RAILROAD

KAANAPALI

30

Royal Kaanapali
Golf Courses

Hanakaoo
Point

Nohea Kai Dr.

Halelo St.

Wahikuli Rd.

Hanakaoo
Park

Honoapiilani Hwy.

Wahikuli
Beach Park

Pacific
Ocean

↓ To Lahaina

Kapalua/Napili

Hawea Point
Kapalua Beach

Oneloa Bay

Aloe Dr.

Lower Honoapiilani Rd.

Napili
Bay

Honokeana
Bay

Hui Rd. "H"
Napili Pl.

Hui Rd. "F"

Napilihau St.

Pacific
Ocean

1-0722

black lava points. It's the front yard of the Four Seasons Wailea and the Grand Wailea Resort Hotel and Spa, Maui's most elegant and outrageous beach hotels respectively. From the beach, the view out to sea is magnificent, framed by neighboring Kahoolawe and Lanai and the tiny crescent of Molokini, probably the most popular snorkel spot in these parts. The clear waters tumble to shore in waves just the right size for gentle riding, with or without a board. From shore, you can see Pacific humpback whales in season (Dec–Apr), and unreal sunsets nightly. Facilities include rest rooms, outdoor showers, and limited free parking at the blue "Shoreline Access" sign, which points toward Wailea Alanui Drive, the main drag of this resort.

ULUA BEACH

One of the most popular beaches in Wailea, Ulua is a long, wide, crescent-shaped gold-sand beach between two rocky points. When the ocean's calm, Ulua offers Wailea's best snorkeling; when it's rough, the waves are excellent for bodysurfers. The ocean bottom is shallow and gently slopes down to deeper waters, making swimming generally safe. The beach is usually occupied by guests of nearby resorts; during the high season (Christmas–Mar and June–Aug), it's carpeted with beach towels and packed with sunbathers like sardines in cocoa butter. Facilities include showers and rest rooms. A variety of equipment is available for rent at the nearby Wailea Ocean Activity Center. To find Ulua, look for the new, blue "Shoreline Access" sign on South Kihei Road, near Stouffer Wailea Beach Resort. A tiny parking lot is nearby.

MALUAKA (MAKENA) BEACH

On the southern end of Maui's resort coast, development falls off dramatically, leaving a wild, dry countryside of green kiawe trees. The Maui Prince sits in isolated splendor, sharing Makena Resort's 1,800 acres only with a couple of first-rate golf courses and a necklace of perfect beaches. The strand nearest the hotel is Maluaka Beach, often called Makena, notable for its beauty and its views of Molokini Crater, the offshore islet, and Kahoolawe, the so-called "target" island. It's a short, wide, palm-fringed crescent of golden, grainy sand set between two black lava points and bounded by big sand dunes topped by a grassy knoll. Swimming in this mostly calm bay is considered the best on Makena Bay, which is bordered on the south by Puu Olai cinder cone and historic Keawala'i Congregational Church, whose graveyard sits on its own sheltered cove. Facilities include rest rooms, showers, a landscaped park, lifeguard, and roadside parking. Along Makena Alanui, look for the "Shoreline Access" sign near the hotel, turn right, and head down to the shore.

ONELOA BEACH (BIG BEACH)

Oneloa, meaning "long sand" in Hawaiian, is one of the most popular beaches on Maui. Locals call it "Big Beach"—it's 3,300 feet long and more than 100 feet wide. Mauians come here to swim, fish, sunbathe, surf, and enjoy the view of Kahoolawe and Lanai. Snorkeling is good around the north end, at the foot of Puu Olai, a 360-foot cinder cone. During storms, however, big waves lash the shore and a strong rip current sweeps the sharp drop-off, posing a danger for inexperienced open-ocean swimmers. There's no facilities except for portable toilets, but plenty of parking. To get there, drive past the Maui Prince Hotel to the second dirt road, which leads through a kiawe thicket to the beach.

On the other side of Puu Olai is Little Beach, a small pocket beach where assorted nudists work on their all-over tans, to the chagrin of uptight authorities who take a dim view of public nudity. You can get a real nasty sunburn and a lewd conduct ticket, too.

EAST MAUI BEACHES
HOOKIPA BEACH PARK, PAIA

Two miles past Paia, on the Hana Highway, is one of the most famous windsurfing sites in the world. Due to hard constant wind and endless waves, Hookipa attracts top windsurfers and wave jumpers from around the globe. Surfers and fishermen also enjoy this small, gold-sand beach at the foot of a grassy cliff, which provides a natural amphitheater for spectators. Except when international competitions are being held, weekdays are the best time to watch the daredevils fly over the waves. When waves are flat, snorkelers and divers explore the reef. Facilities include rest rooms, showers, pavilions, picnic tables, barbecue grills, and a parking lot.

HAMOA BEACH, HANA

This half moon–shaped, gray-sand beach (a mix of coral and lava) in a truly tropical setting is a favorite of sunbathers seeking rest and refuge at Hotel Hana-Maui (which maintains the beach and tries to act like it's their private beach—it's not, so just march down the lava rock steps and grab a spot on the sand). James Michener said of Hamoa: "Paradoxically, the only beach I have ever seen that looks like the South Pacific was in the North Pacific—Hamoa Beach . . . a beach so perfectly formed that I wonder at its comparative obscurity." The 100-foot wide beach is three football fields long and sits below 30-foot black lava sea cliffs. An unprotected beach open to the ocean, Hamoa is often swept by power rip currents. Surf breaks offshore and rolls ashore, making it a popular surfing and bodysurfing area. The calm left side is best for snorkeling in the summer. The hotel has numerous facilities for guests; there's an outdoor shower and rest rooms for nonguests. Parking is limited. Look for the Hamoa Beach turn-off from Hana Highway.

WAIANAPANAPA STATE PARK

Four miles before Hana, off the Hana Highway, is this beach park, which takes its name from the legend of the Waianapanapa Cave, where Chief Kaakea, a jealous and cruel man, suspected his wife, Popoalaea, of having an affair. Popoalaea left her husband and hid herself in a chamber of the Waianapanapa Cave. She and her attendant ventured out only at night, for food. Nevertheless, a few days later, Kaakea was passing by the area and saw the shadow of the servant. Knowing he had found his wife's hiding place, Kaakea entered the cave and killed her. During certain times of the year, the water in the tide pool turns red as a tribute to Popoalaea, commemorating her death. Scientists claim, however, that the water turns red due to the presence of small red shrimp.

Waianapanapa State Park's 120-acres have 12 cabins, a caretaker's residence, a beach park, picnic tables, barbecue grills, rest rooms, showers, a parking lot, a shoreline hiking trail, and a black-sand beach (it's actually small black pebbles). This is a wonderful area for shoreline hikes (bring insect repellent, as the mosquitoes are plentiful) and picnicking. Swimming is generally unsafe, though, due to strong waves breaking offshore, which roll into the beach unchecked, and strong rip currents. Because Waianapanapa is crowded on weekends with local residents and their families as well as tourists, weekdays are generally a better bet.

6 Hitting the Water

by Rick Carroll, with Jeanette Foster

Maui's big blue sea is full of fun year-round. Underwater, the world teems with exotic marine life, and offshore winds provide perfect conditions for sailing.

BODY BOARDING (BOOGIE BOARDING) & BODYSURFING

You can rent boogie boards and fins from **Snorkel Bob's** at three different locations: 34 Keala Place, Kihei (☎ **808/879-7449**); Napili Village Hotel, 5425 Lower Honoapiilani Rd., Napili (☎ **808/669-9603**); and 161 Lahainaluna Rd., Lahaina (☎ **808/661-4421**) for $29 a week. All locations are open 8am to 5pm daily.

In winter, Maui's best bodysurfing spot is Mokuleia Beach, known locally as Slaughterhouse because of the cattle slaughterhouse that once stood here, not because of the waves—although these waves are for expert bodysurfers only. To get to Mokuleia, take Honoapiilani Highway just past Kapalua Bay Resort; various hiking trails will take you down to the pocket beach.

Storms from the south bring fair bodysurfing conditions and great boogie boarding to the lee side of Maui: Oneloa (or Big Beach), Ulua, Kamaole III, and Kapalua beaches are all good choices.

DEEP-SEA FISHING

Marlin, tuna, ono, and mahimahi await the baited hook in Maui's coastal and channel waters. No license is required; just book a sportfishing vessel out of Lahaina or Maalaea harbors. Most charter boats that troll for big game fish carry six passengers max. You can walk the docks, inspecting boats and talking to captains and crew, or book through an activities desk or one of the outfits recommended below.

If you want to fish out of Maalaea, I recommend **Rhythm and Blues Sportfishing** (☎ **808/879-7098**); Capt. Mike Crawford is an experienced fishermen with top-flight gear and a comfortable 36-foot Pacifica sportfishing boat. Or try the **Maalaea Activities** desk at the harbor (☎ **808/242-6982**).

At Lahaina Harbor, go for **Hinatea Sportfishing,** slip 27 (☎ **808/667-7548**); **Ace Sportfishing** (☎ **808/667-7548**), which represents 11 sportfishing boats offering both trolling and bottom fishing; or check with **West Maui Charter** (☎ **808/ 326-7324**), offering everything from light- to heavy-tackle fishing.

Shop around. Prices vary widely according to the boat, the crowd, and the captain. A shared boat for a half-day of fishing starts at $75. A full-day exclusive boat can range from $450 to $900. Also, many boat captains tag and release marlin, or keep the fish for themselves (sorry, that's Hawaii style). If you want to eat your mahimahi for dinner or have your marlin mounted, tell the captain before you go.

OCEAN KAYAKING

Gliding silently over the water, propelled by a paddle, seeing Maui from the sea the way the early Hawaiians did—that's what ocean kayaking is all about. One of Maui's best kayak routes is along the Kihei Coast, where there's easy access to calm water. Mornings are always best, as the wind comes up around 11am, making seas choppy and paddling difficult.

For the uninitiated, Michael and Melissa McCoy of **South Pacific Kayaks,** at 2439 S. Kihei Rd., Kihei (☎ **808/875-4848**), and 505 Front St., Lahaina (☎ **808/ 661-8400**) offer kayak tours (with snorkeling) that include lessons and a guided tour. Tours run from 2 1/2 to 5 hours, and range in price from $39 to $125. The McCoys also offer kayak rentals starting at $20 a day.

Ron Bass of **Maui Sea Kayaking** (☎ **808/572-6299**), a former ski instructor who traded in his poles for paddles, leads safe, well-informed, personally guided kayak tours off the Wailea Coast and on custom-designed sea expeditions to remote island shores by special arrangement.

SAILING

Trade winds off the Lahaina Coast and the hard wind that rips through Maui's isthmus make sailing around the island exciting. Many different boats, from a three-masted schooner to spacious trimarans, offer day cruises from Maui. Avoid dinner cruises, however, if you like to eat even more than you like to sail; the entrees are usually less palatable than airplane food.

You can experience the thrill of competition sailing with **Alihilani Yacht Charters,** 107 Kahului Heliport, Kahului (☎ 808/667-7733). There's nothing like it, especially when all you have to do is hold on and cheer. *First Class* and *World Class,* two 65-foot custom yachts designed for Maui waters, take 24 passengers each for a 90-minute sail every day at 2pm. Be prepared to get wet: The captains and crews of these two equally matched, cutter-rigged, high-tech yachts are serious about winning their regatta. One vessel picks up passengers at Lahaina Harbor and sails north to meet the second boat, which departs from Kaanapali Beach. They meet in the middle off west Maui's coast for the daily duel in the wind. This exciting ride is $35 for adults, $25 children 12 and under.

For details on day cruises to Lanai, see "Lanai for the Day: Cruises from Maui" in Chapter 9. **Trilogy Excursions** (☎ 808/661-4743), which offers sail-and-snorkel tours on their custom-built, multihull sailboats, is my favorite.

SCUBA DIVING

Everyone dives Molokini, a marine-life park and one of Hawaii's top dive spots. This crescent-shaped crater has three tiers of diving: a 35-foot plateau inside the crater basin (used by beginning divers and snorkelers), a wall sloping to 70 feet just beyond the inside plateau, and a sheer wall on the outside and backside of the crater that plunges 350 feet. This underwater park is very popular thanks to calm, clear, protected waters and an abundance of marine life, from manta rays to clouds of yellow butterfly fish.

For personalized diving, **Ed Robinson's Diving Adventures** (☎ 808/879-3584) is the best on Maui, maybe all of Hawaii. This widely published underwater photographer offers specialized charters for small groups. Most of his business is repeat customers. Ed offers two-tank dives for $85; his dive boats depart from Kihei Boat ramp. In Lahaina, call **Lahaina Divers,** 143 Dickenson St. (☎ 808/667-7496), one of Maui's few Five Star PADI-IDC facilities, offering every sort of diving service and instruction you could possibly need. Maui's largest diving retailer, with everything from rentals to scuba diving instruction to dive boat charters, is **Maui Dive Shop,** which can be found all over the island: in Kihei at Azeka Place II Shopping Center (☎ 808/879-3388), Kamaole Shopping Center (☎ 808/879-1533), and Kihei Town Center (☎ 808/879-1919); in Lahaina at Lahaina Cannery Mall (☎ 808/661-5388) and 626 Front St. (☎ 808/667-0722). Other locations include Wailea Shopping Village (☎ 808/879-3166), Whalers Shopping Village, Kaanapali (☎ 808/661-5117), Kahana Gateway, Kahana (☎ 808/669-3800), and 444 Hana Hwy., Kahului (☎ 808/871-2111).

SNORKELING

Snorkel Bob's can rent everything you need at their three Maui locations: 34 Keala Place, Kihei (☎ 808/879-7449); Napili Village Hotel, 5425 Lower Honoapiilani Rd., Napili (☎ 808/669-9603); and 161 Lahainaluna Rd., Lahaina (☎ 808/661-4421).

An Expert Shares His Secrets: Maui's Best Dives

Ed Robinson, of Ed Robinson's Diving Adventures (see above), knows what makes a great dive. Here are five of his favorites on Maui; he'll be happy to take you to any or all of them:

Hawaiian Reef   This area off the Kihei-Wailea coast is so named because it hosts a good cross-section of topography and marine life typical of Hawaiian waters. Diving to depths of 85 feet, you'll see everything from lava formations and coral reef to sand and rubble, plus a diverse range of both shallow and deep-water creatures. You'll see for yourself why this area was so popular with ancient Hawaiian fishermen: large helmet shells, a healthy garden of large antler coral heads, and large schools of snapper are common.

Third Tank   Located off Makena Beach at 80 feet, this World War II tank is one of the most picturesque artificial reefs you're likely to see around Maui. It acts like a fish magnet: Because it's the only large solid object in the area, any fish or invertebrate looking for a safe home comes here. Surrounding the tank is a cloak of schooling snapper and goat fish just waiting for a photographer with a wide-angle lens. For it's small size, the Third Tank has more animal life per square inch than any other site we dive.

Molokini Crater   The backside is always done as a live boat drift dive. The vertical wall plummets from over 150 feet above sea level to around 250 feet below. Looking down to unseen depths gives you a feeling for the vastness of the open ocean. Pelagic fish and sharks are often sighted, and living coral perches on the wall, which is home to lobster, crabs, and a number of photogenic black coral trees at 50 feet.

Enenue Side   Named after common chub or rudder fish, Enenue Side gently slopes from the surface to about 60 feet, then drops rapidly to deeper waters. The shallower area is an easy dive, with lots of tame butterfly fish. It's also the home of Morgan Bentjaw, one of our friendliest moray eels. Enenue Side is often done as a live boat drift dive to extend the range of the tour. Diving depths vary. We usually do a 50-foot dive, but on occasion will invite advanced divers to drop to the 130-foot level to visit the rare boar fish and the shark condos.

Reef's End   Almost every kind of fish found in Hawaii can be seen in these crystalline waters. Reef's End is an extension of the rim of Haleakala crater, which runs for about 200 yards underwater, barely breaking the surface. Reef's End is shallow enough for novice snorkelers and exciting enough for experienced divers. The end and outside of this shoal drop off in dramatic terraces to beyond diving range. In deeper waters there are shark ledges at varying depths, and dozens of eels, some of which are tame, including moray, dragon, snowflake, and garden eels. The shallower inner side is home to Garbanzo, one of the largest and first eels to be tamed. The reef is covered with cauliflower coral; in bright sunlight it's one of the most dramatic underwater scenes in Hawaii.

La Perouse Pinnacle   In the middle of scenic La Perouse Bay, site of Haleakala's most recent lava flow, is a pinnacle rising from the 60-foot bottom to about 10 feet below the surface. Getting to the dive site is half the fun: the scenery above water is as exciting as that below the surface. Underwater, you'll enjoy a very diversified dive. Clouds of damsel and trigger fish will greet you on the surface. Divers can approach even the timid bird wrasse. We find more porcupine puffers here than anywhere else, as well as schools of goat fish and fields of healthy finger coral. La Perouse is good for snorkeling and those long, shallow second dives.

Snorkeling on Maui is easy because there are so many great spots that you can just wade in the water with a face mask and look down to see the tropical fish. Mornings are best, because local winds don't kick in until around noon. Maui's best snorkeling beaches include Kapalua; Black Rock, at Kaanapali; along the Kihei coastline, especially at Kamaole III; and along the Wailea coastline, particularly at Ulua Beach.

Two truly terrific places are worth the effort to get to, because they're home to Hawaii's tropical marine life at its best:

Molokini   Like a crescent moon fallen from the sky, this sunken crater sits almost midway between Maui and the uninhabited island of Kahoolawe. Tilted so that only the thin rim of its southern side shows above water in a perfect semicircle, Molokini stands like a scoop against the tide and serves, on its concave side, like a natural sanctuary for tropical fish and snorkelers, who commute daily in a fleet of dive boats to this marine-life preserve. See "Taking a Snorkel Cruise," below, for details on getting there.

Ahihi-Kinau Natural Preserve   You can't miss in Ahihi Bay, a 2,000-acre State Natural Area Reserve in the lee of Cape Kinau, on Maui's rugged south coast, where Haleakala spilled red-hot lava that ran to the sea in 1790. Fishing is strictly *kapu* here, and the fish know it; they're everywhere in this series of rocky coves and black-lava tide pools. It's just far enough off the tourist trail to qualify for what I call the "real Hawaii." The black, barren, lunarlike land stands in stark contrast to the green-blue water, which covers a sparkling mosaic of tropical fish who thrive in this marine preserve, making for excellent snorkeling. Après-snork, check out La Perouse Bay on the south side of Cape Kinau, where the French admiral La Perouse became the first European to set foot on Maui. A lava rock pyramid known as Perouse Monument marks the spot. To get there, drive south of Makena past Puu Olai to Ahihi Bay, where the road turns to gravel and sometimes seems like it'll disappear under the waves. At Cape Kinau, there are three four-wheel-drive trails that lead across the lava flow; take the shortest one, nearest La Perouse Bay.

TAKING A SNORKEL CRUISE

If you'd like take a snorkel boat to Molokini, check with the **Ocean Activities Center,** 1847 S. Kihei Rd., Kihei (☎ 808/879-4485), which also operates out of a number of hotels and condos; or you can call **Maui Classic Charters** (☎ 808/879-8188) direct. Snorkeling cruises usually run about $50. If you'd like to combine your snorkeling adventure with some whale watching, see "Whale-Watching Cruises," below. If heading over Lanai for a pristine day of snorkeling sounds like a good idea, see "Lanai for the Day: Cruises from Maui" in Chapter 9; of those trips, **Trilogy Excursions** (☎ 808/661-4743 or 800/874-1119) offers my favorite snorkel-and-sail trip in the islands.

SNUBA

Maui Classic Charters (☎ 808/879-8188) offers Snuba for an extra $50 on their charters to Molokini.

SURFING

Even if you've never seen a surfboard before, Andrea Thomas claims she can teach you the art of riding the waves. She's instructed thousands at **Maui Surfing School** (☎ 808/875-0625). She has taken students as young as three and as "chronologically gifted" as 70. She backs her classes with a guarantee that she'll get you surfing or you'll get 110% of your money back. Two-hour lessons are $55, available by appointment only.

Expert surfers visit Maui in winter when the surf's really up. The best surfing beaches include: Honolua Bay; Lahaina Harbor (in the summer, there'll be waves just off the channel entrance with a south swell); Maalaea (a clean, world-class left); and Hookipa (watch out for the sailboards when the wind is up). Surfboards can be rented from **Hunt Hawaii Surf and Sail** in Paia (☎ **808/575-2300**), starting at $20 a day.

WHALE WATCHING

Every winter, pods of Pacific Humpback Whales make the 3,000-mile swim from the chilly waters of Alaska to bask in Maui's summery shallows, fluking, spy hopping, spouting, and having an all-around swell time.

The humpback whale, protected as Hawaii's official state mammal, is a cottage industry here. No creature on earth is celebrated in so many ways as the whale: there are whale posters, whale pins, whale T-shirts, whale jewelry, whale art, and whale murals—some of it quite awful. Don't waste your money on whale stuff; go see the real thing. You can—the humpback is the star of the annual whale-watch season, which usually begins in December and lasts, sometimes, until May. If you're here in season and haven't seen a whale, you haven't seen Maui.

Humpbacks are one of the world's oldest, most impressive inhabitants: Adults grow to be about 45 feet long and weigh a hefty 40 tons; when they splash, it looks as if a 747's hit the drink. Humpbacks are officially an endangered species; in 1992, the Hawaiian Islands were designated as a Humpback Whale National Marine Sanctuary for their protection. Despite the world's newfound ecological awareness, humpbacks and their habitats and food resources are still under threat from whalers and pollution.

Only about 600 to 800 humpback whales appear in Hawaii waters each year. Oahu used to be the place for whale watching, until Pearl Harbor; since then, they've traditionally headed to the waters off Maui. From my Oahu beach house, I watch them parade there every December or so. Some are moving up the island chain to less populated islands like Kauai, but last winter was a banner whale-watching year for Maui. After 5 or 6 months there, they pass by me again on their way back to Alaska.

WHALE WATCHING FROM SHORE

The best time to whale-watch is between January and April. Just look out to sea. There's no best time of day for whale watching, but I've noticed that when the sea is glassy and there's no wind, I always see more. A Scripps Institute marine biologist once told me it's because whales are the only mammals without hair and they don't like wind on their body when they leap out of the water. Once you see one, keep watching in the same vicinity; they may stay down 30 minutes. Bring a book. And binoculars, if you can.

Some good whale-watching points on Maui are:

McGregor Point   On the way to Lahaina, there's a Scenic Lookout at mile marker 9 (just before you get to the Lahaina Tunnel); it's a good viewpoint to scan both the Au'au and the Alalakeiki channels for whales.

Maui Aston Wailea Resort   On the Wailea coastal walk, stop at this resort (formerly the Maui Inter-Continental) to look for whales through the telescope installed by the Hawaii Island Humpback Whale National Marine Sanctuary as a public service.

Olowalu Reef Along the straight part of Honoapiilani Highway, between McGregor Point and Olowalu, you'll see whales leap out of the water—I think they tickle their bellies on the shallow reef. Sometimes, their appearance brings traffic to a screeching halt: People abandon their cars and run down to the sea to watch, causing a major traffic jam. If you stop, pull off the road so others may pass.

Puu Olai It's a tough climb up this coastal landmark near the Maui Prince Hotel, but you're likely to be well rewarded: This is the island's best spot for offshore whale watching. On the 360-foot cinder cone overlooking Makena Beach, you'll be at the right elevation to see Pacific Humpbacks as they dodge Molokini and cruise up Alalakeiki Channel between Maui and Kahoolawe. If you don't see one, you'll at least have a whale of a view.

WHALE WATCHING CRUISES

For a closer look, take a whale-watching cruise. Go by sail and you'll see more; whales seem to like sailboats best, probably because they're quiet and don't smell like oil spills.

The **Pacific Whale Foundation** (☎ 808/879-8811) is a nonprofit foundation in Kihei the helps whales instead of just gawking at them. The organization supports their whale research by offering cruises and snorkel tours, some to Molokini and Lanai. They operate a 53-foot motor vessel called *Whale I,* and a 50-foot sailing ketch called *Whale II,* and their rates for a 3-hour whale-watch cruise would make Moby Dick smile: It's $30 for adults, $15 for kids. Cruises are offered December through May.

The *Kai Nani,* a sleek 46-foot catamaran, sails at 7:30am daily from Makena Beach in front of the Maui Prince Hotel. The *Kai Nani* is the first boat to drop anchor at Molokini, so you arrive before the snorkeling hordes from Maalaea and Lahaina. The 5-hour excursion costs $65 for adults and $40 for kids 12 and under. Call the **Ocean Activities Desk** at **808/874-1111** to reserve. Bring a towel and your swimsuit; everything else, fins, mask, snorkel, continental breakfast, and usually whales, are provided.

You can also call nonprofit **Whales Alive International** (☎ 808/874-6855) to book a tour with marine mammal expert Stan Butler aboard a 60-foot catamaran out of Maalaea Harbor.

If you want to combine ocean activities, a snorkel or dive cruise to Molokini, the sunken crater off Maui's south coast, may be just the ticket. I once saw 20 whales on the way there, at no extra charge. See "Scuba Diving" and "Taking a Snorkel Cruise," above.

WHALE WATCHING BY KAYAK

Seeing a humpback whale from an ocean kayak is awesome. The expert guides at **South Pacific Kayaks** (☎ 808/875-4848 in Kihei; **808/661-8400** in Lahaina; or 800/776-2326) lead small groups on 3-hour excursions into the calm waters off Makena and Lahaina to see behemoths at sea level. The cost is $55.

WINDSURFING

Except for Oahu's Kailua Bay, Maui has Hawaii's best windsurfing beaches. Hookipa, known all over the globe for its brisk winds and excellent waves, is the site of several world championship contests. Kanaha also has dependable winds; when conditions are right, it's packed with colorful butterflylike sails. During the winter, the town of Paia becomes windsurfing central, with windsurfers from around the world flocking there to check out the wind, the waves, and those who ride them.

Complete equipment rental (board, sail, rig harness, and roof rack) is available from $35 to $45 a day, and $200 to $250 a week. Lessons, from beginning to advanced, range in price from $60 to $75 for a 2- or 3-hour lesson. **Hawaiian Island Windsurfing,** 415 Dairy Rd., Kahului (☎ **808/871-4981**), offers lessons, rentals, and repairs. Other shops featuring rentals and lessons are **Hawaiian Sailboarding Techniques,** 444 Hana Hwy., Kahului (☎ **808/871-5423**); **Maui Windsurf Co.,** 520 Keolani Place, Kahului (☎ **808/877-4696**); and **Second Wind Windsurfing,** 111 Hana Hwy., Kahului, (☎ **808/877-7467**).

For daily reports on wind and surf conditions, call the **Wind and Surf Report** at **808/877-3611.**

7 Hiking & Camping

by Rick Carroll, with Jeanette Foster

In the past decade, Maui has grown from a rural island to a fast-paced resort destination, but its natural beauty remains largely inviolate; there are still many places that can be explored only on foot. Those interested in seeing the backcountry—complete with virgin waterfalls, remote wilderness trails, and quiet meditative settings—should head for Haleakala's up-country or the tropical Hana coast.

Camping on Maui can be extreme (inside a volcanic crater) or benign (by the sea in Hana). It can be wet, cold and rainy, or hot, dry and windy, often all on the same day. If you're heading for Haleakala, remember that U.S. astronauts trained for the moon inside the crater; bring survival gear. Don't forget both your swimsuit and rain gear if you're bound for Waianapanapa, and bring your own equipment, as there's no place to rent gear on Maui yet. If you need to buy equipment, check out **Gaspro,** 365 Hanakai, Kahului (☎ **808/877-0056**); **Maui Expedition,** Kihei Commercial Center, (☎ **808/878-7470**); or **Maui Sporting Goods,** 92 N. Market, Wailuku (☎ **808/244-0011**).

For more information on Maui camping hiking-trails and to obtain free maps, contact **Haleakala National Park,** P.O. Box 369, Makawao, HI 96768 (☎ **808/ 572-9306**), and the **State Division of Forestry and Wildlife,** 52 S. High Street, Wailuku, HI 96793 (☎ **808/984-8100**). For information on trails, hikes, camping, and permits for state parks, contact the **Hawaii State Department of Land and Natural Resources,** State Parks Division, P.O. Box 1049, Wailuku, HI 96793 (☎ **808/984-8109**).

Backcountry Guides   Naturalist Ken Schmidt at **Hike Maui,** Kahului (☎ **808/ 879-5270**) has lived on Maui for 17 years and knows its backcountry well. He's an excellent guide, historian, botanist, geologist, and storyteller of ancient legends. He offers more than 50 different kinds of trips for small groups, ranging in price from $75 per person for a half-day tropical valley hike to $110 for the trip of a lifetime into Haleakala.

A new all-day hike to the lush rain forests and waterfall pools of the West Maui Mountains is offered exclusively by **Kapalua Nature Society** (☎ **808/669-0244** or 800/KAPALUA). Groups of up to nine hikers can go on guided hiking tours, which include a picnic lunch and transportation to and from the trails. Two exclusive hikes are offered: the easy, 2-mile Mauna Lei Arboretum/Puu Kaeo Nature Walk, which starts at 1,000 feet above sea level and goes to the 1,635-foot summit of Puu Kaeo; and the breathtaking 3-mile Manienie Ridge Hike, a more strenuous hike with moderate slope, some uneven footing, and close vegetation. Kapalua Nature Society is a not-for-profit organization dedicated to preserving the island's natural and cultural heritage. Proceeds go toward the education and preservation of Pu'u Kukui rain forest. Each hike goes from 8am to 1:30pm Friday and Saturday; the cost is $80 adults, $50 ages 12 to 18.

HALEAKALA NATIONAL PARK

For complete coverage of the national park, see "Exploring the Island," below.

INTO THE CRATER: SLIDING SANDS & HALEMAUU TRAILS

Hiking into Maui's dormant volcano is really the way to see it. One of the largest volcanic craters in the world, with terrain that ranges from burnt-red cinder cones to ebony-black lava tubes, it's simply spectacular. The crater has some 32-miles of hiking trails, two camping sites, and three cabins.

Of the national park's 36 miles of trails, the best route takes in two of them: into the crater along **Sliding Sands Trail,** which begins on the rim at 9,800 feet and descends into the belly of the beast, to the crater floor at 6,600 feet; and back out along **Halemauu Trail.** You'll need 2 days for this difficult hike. Only the hardiest hikers should consider making the 11.3-mile one-way descent, which takes 9 hours, and the equally as long returning ascent in 1 day. The descending and ascending trails aren't loops; the trailheads are miles (and several thousand feet in elevation) apart, so you'll need to make transportation arrangements in advance. So arrange to stay at least 1 night in the park; two or three will allow you more time to actually explore the fascinating interior of the volcano. See below for details on the cabins and campgrounds in the crater.

Before you set out, stop at park headquarters to get camping and hiking updates. Day hikers must register for the hike down Sliding Sands Trail at the box near the Visitor Center.

A word of warning about the weather: The weather at nearly 10,000 feet can change suddenly and without warning. Come prepared for cold, high winds, rain, even snow in the winter. Temperatures range from 77° down to 26° (they're even lower with the wind-chill factor), and high winds are frequent. Rainfall varies from 20 inches a year on the west end of the crater to more than 200 inches on the eastern side. Bring boots, waterproof wear, warm clothes, extra layers, and lots of sunscreen—the sun shines very brightly up here.

The trailhead to Sliding Sands is well-marked and the trail easy to follow switchback over ash and cinders. As you descend, look around: The view of the entire crater is breathtaking. In the afternoon, waves of clouds flow into the Kaupo and Koolau gaps. Vegetation is spare to nonexistent at the top, but the closer you get to the crater floor, the more vegetation you'll see: bracken ferns, pili grass, shrubs, even flowers. On the crater floor, the trail travels through flat, ash-covered flows of basalt and cinder-covered cones, passing by rare silversword plants, volcanic vents, and multicolored cinder cones.

The Halemauu Trail goes over red and black lava and past vegetation like evening primrose as it begins its ascent up the crater wall. Occasionally, riders on horseback use this trail as an entry and exit from the park. The proper etiquette is to step aside and stand quietly next to the trail as the horses pass.

Some Shorter & Easier Options   Hiking into it is the best way to experience this curious crater. Take a one-quarter–mile walk down the **Hosmer Grove Nature Trail** or start down **Sliding Sands Trail** for a mile or two to get a hint of what lies ahead. Even this short hike is exhausting at the high altitude. A good day hike is **Halemauu Trail** to Holua Cabin and back, an 8-mile, half-day trip.

STAYING IN THE CRATER

Most people stay at one of three tent campgrounds, unless they get lucky and win the lottery—the lottery for one of the crater's three wilderness cabins. For more information and reservations, contact Haleakala National Park, P.O. Box 369, Makawao, HI 96768 (☎ **808/572-9306**).

The Cabins   It can get really cold and windy down in the crater (see above), so try for a cabin. They're warm, protected from the elements, and reasonably priced. Each has bunks with mattresses (but no bedding; bring your own), table, chairs, cooking utensils, and a wood-burning stove with firewood (you may also have a few cockroaches). The cabins are spaced throughout the crater, so each one is an easy walk from the other: Holua cabin is on the Halemauu Trail, Kapalaoa cabin on Sliding Sands Trail, and Paliku cabin on the western end by the Kaupo Gap. The rates start at $19 a night for one person, $23 a night per person for two, and $9 per person per night for 3 to 12 people.

The cabins are so popular that the National Parks Service has a lottery system for reservations. Requests for cabins must be made 3 months in advance (be sure to request alternate dates). You can request all three cabins at once; you're limited to no more than 2 nights in one cabin and no more than 3 nights within the crater per month.

The Campgrounds   If you don't win the cabin lottery, all isn't lost, as there are three tent camping sites that can accommodate you: two inside the crater, and one just outside at Hosmer Grove.

Hosmer Grove is the park's best camping area, in or out of the crater. Located at 6,800 feet, it's a small, open grassy area surrounded by a forest. Trees protect campers from the winds, but nights still get real cold. Hard to believe, I know, but sometimes there's ice on the ground up here. This is the best place to spend the night in a tent if you want to see the Haleakala sunrise. Come up the day before, enjoy the park, take a day hike, then turn in early. The enclosed, glass visitor center at the summit opens at sunrise for those who come to greet the dawn—a welcome windbreak. Facilities include a covered pavilion with picnic tables and grills, chemical toilets, and drinking water. Food and gas is 50 miles away. No permits are needed at Hosmer Grove, and there's no charge; but you can only stay for 3 nights in 30 days.

The two tent camping areas inside the crater are **Holua,** just off Sliding Sands Trail at 7,250 feet; and **Paliku,** just before the Kaupo Gap at the western end of the crater, at 6,380 feet. Facilities at both campgrounds are limited to pit toilets and catchment water. Water at Holua is limited, especially in summer. No open fires are allowed in the crater, so bring a stove if you plan to cook. Tent camping is restricted to the rocky campsite or the horse stable near the cabin; the inviting grassy lawn is *kapu.* Camping is free, but limited to 2 consecutive nights, and no more than 3 nights a month inside the crater. Permits are issued daily at Park Headquarters on a first-come, first-served basis. Occupancy is limited to 25 people.

HIKING & CAMPING AT KIPAHULU

You can set up at **Oheo Campground,** a first-come, first-served drive-in campground with tent sites for 100 near the ocean, and Oheo Gulch (Seven Sacred Pools) with a few tables, barbecue grills, and chemical toilets. No permit is required, but there's a 3-night limit. No food or drinking water is available, so bring your own. Bring a tent, because it rains 60 inches a year here. Contact **Kipahulu Ranger Station,** Haleakala National Park, HI 96713 (☎ **808/248-7375**).

Hiking from the Crater   If you hike from the crater rim down **Kaupo Gap** to the ocean in Kipahulu, more than 20 miles away, you'll pass through climate zones ranging from Arctic to tropical. On a clear day, you can see every island except Kauai on the trip down. Out past the "Baby Pigs Crossing," you'll find Oheo Campground.

Approaching Kipahulu from Hana   If you drive to Kipahulu, you'll have to approach it from the Hana Highway, as it's not accessible from the crater. From the ranger station, it's a short hike past the famous **Oheo Gulch** (also known as the Seven Sacred Pools) to two spectacular waterfalls. The first, **Makahiku Falls,** is easily reached from the central parking area: Cross the bridge between the fourth and fifth pools, go 100 yards to a gate on the right-hand side, and follow the pasture trail up the left side of pools for a half-mile to the overlook. If you hike another $1^1/_2$ miles up the pasture trail and through a bamboo forest, you reach **Waimoku Falls.** It's a good uphill hike, but press on to avoid the pool's crowd. Don't go in hard rain, as it swells the streams.

SKYLINE TRAIL, POLIPOLI SPRINGS STATE RECREATION AREA

This is some hike—strenuous but worth every step if you like to see the big picture. It's 8 miles, all downhill, with a dazzling 100-mile view of the islands dotting the blue Pacific, plus the West Maui Mountains, which seem like a separate island.

   The trail is located just outside Haleakala National Park at Polipoli Springs National Recreation Area; however, you access the trail by going through the national park to the summit. The Skyline Trail starts just beyond the Puu Ulaula summit building on the south side of Science City, and follows the southwest rift zone of Haleakala from its lunarlike cinder cones to a cool redwood grove. The trail drops 3,800 feet on a 4-hour hike to the recreation area, in the 12,000-acre Kahikinui Forest Reserve.

   There is a **campground** at the recreation area, at 6,300 feet. There's no fee or reservations required, but your stay must be limited to 5 nights. One 10-bunk cabin is available for $50 a night; it has no electricity, a cold shower, and a gas stove. To reserve, call **808/984-8109** between 8am and 4pm weekdays.

POLIPOLI STATE PARK

One of the most unusual hiking experiences in the state can be found at Polipoli State Park, part of the 21,000-acre Kula and Kahikinui Forest Reserve on the slope of Haleakala. At Polipoli, it's hard to believe that you're in Hawaii: First of all, it's cold, even in the summer, since the loop's at 5300 to 6200 feet; second, this former forest of native koa, ohia, and mamane trees, which was overlogged in the 1800s, was reforested in the 1930s with introduced species: pine, Monterey cypress, ash, sugi, red adler, redwood, and several varieties of eucalyptus. The result is a cool area, with muted sunlight filtered by towering trees.

   The **Polipoli Loop** is an easy, 5-mile hike that takes about 3 hours; dress warmly for it. To get there, take the Haleakala Highway (Hi. 37) to Keokea and turn right onto Hi. 337; after less than a half-mile, turn on Waipoli Road, which climbs swiftly. After 10 miles, Waipoli Road ends at the Polipoli State Park campgrounds. The well-marked trailhead is next to the parking lot, near a stand of Monterey cypress; the tree-lined trail offers the best view of the island.

   Polipoli Loop is really a network of three trails: Haleakala Ridge, Plum Trail, and Redwood Trail. After a half-mile of meandering through groves of eucalyptus, blackwood, swamp mahogany, and hybrid cypress, you'll join the Haleakala Ridge Trail, which, about a mile into the trail, joins with the Plum Trail (named for the plums that ripen in June and July). It passes through massive redwoods and by an old Conservation Corps bunkhouse and a rundown cabin before joining up with the Redwood Trail, which climbs through Mexican pine, tropical ash, Port Orford cedar, and—of course—redwood.

Camping is allowed in the park with a permit from the **Division of State Parks,** P.O. Box 1049, Wailuku, HI 96793 (☎ **808/984-8109**). There's one cabin, available by reservation.

WAIANAPANAPA STATE PARK
HANA-WAIANAPANAPA COAST TRAIL

This is an easy 6-mile hike that takes you back in time. Allow four hours to walk along this relatively flat trail, which parallels the sea, along lava cliffs and a forest of hala tress. The best time to take the hike is either in the early morning or late evening, when the light on the lava and surf makes for great photos. Midday is the worst time; not only is it hot (lava intensifies the heat), but no shade or potable water is available.

There's no formal trailhead; join the route at any point along the Waianapanapa Campground and go in either direction. Along the trail, you'll see remains of an ancient *heiau* (temple), stands of lauhala trees, caves, a blowhole, and a remarkable plant, *naupaka,* that flourishes along the beach. Upon close inspection, you'll see that the naupaka have only half-blossoms; according to Hawaiian legend, a similar plant living in the mountains has the other half of the blossoms. One ancient explanation is that the two plants represent never-to-be reunited lovers: as the story goes, the two lovers bickered so much that the gods, fed up with their incessant quarreling, banished one lover to the mountain and the other to the sea.

CAMPING AT WAIANAPANAPA

Tucked in a tropical jungle, on the outskirts of the little coastal town of Hana, is Waianapanapa State Park, a black-sand beach set in an emerald forest. Waianapanapa has 12 cabins and a tent campground. Go for the cabins (see "Accommodations," above), as it rains torrentially here, sometimes turning the campground into a mud-wrestling arena. If you opt to tent-camp, it's free, but limited to 5 nights in a 30-day period. Permits are available from the **State Parks Division,** P.O. Box 1049 Wailuku, HI 96793 (☎ **808/984-8109**). Facilities include rest rooms, outdoor showers, drinking water, and picnic tables.

HANA: THE HIKE TO FAGAN'S CROSS

This 3-mile hike to the cross erected in the memory of Hana Ranch and Hotel Hana-Maui founder Paul Fagan offers spectacular views of the Hana coast, particularly at sunset. The uphill trail starts across Hana Highway from the Hotel Hana-Maui. Enter the pastures at your own risk; they're often occupied by glaring bulls with sharp horns and cows with new calves so beware the bulls, avoid the nursing cows; don't wear red. Watch your step as you ascend this steep hill on a jeep trail across open pastures to the cross and the breathtaking view.

8 Golf & Other Outdoor Activities

by Rick Carroll, with Jeanette Foster

BICYCLING

It's not even close to dawn, but here you are, rubbing your eyes awake, riding in a van up the long, dark road to the top of Maui's sleeping volcano. It's colder than you ever thought possible for a tropical island. The air is thin. You stomp your chilly feet while you wait, sipping hot coffee. Then comes the sun, exploding over the yawning Haleakala Crater, big enough to swallow Manhattan—a mystic moment you won't soon forget, imprinted on a palette of dawn colors. Now you know why Hawaiians named it the House of the Sun. But there's no time to linger. Decked out in your screaming yellow parka, you mount your special steed and test its most important feature, the brakes—because you're about to coast 38 miles down a 10,000-foot volcano.

Cruising down Haleakala, from the lunarlike landscape at the top, past flower farms, pineapple fields, and eucalyptus groves, is quite an experience—and just about anybody can do it. This is a safe, comfortable, no-strain bicycle trip for everyone, from the kids to grandma. The trip usually costs around $120 and includes hotel pickup, transport to the top, bicycle and safety equipment, and meals. Call **Maui Downhill** in Kahului (☎ 808/871-2155); **Aloha Bicycle Tours** in Kula (☎ 808/249-0911; e-mail: http://www.maui.net/~bikemaui); **Maui Mountain Chasers** in Makawao (☎ 808/871-6014 or 800/231-6284); and **Mountain Riders Bike Tours** in Kahului (☎ 808/242-9739).

GOLF

Maui's challenging and beautiful courses offer a range of golfing opportunities for everyone, from duffer to professional. All the courses listed below include the required cart rental in the greens fee; most offer twilight rates. Be sure to book your tee times early.

✪ KAPALUA RESORT COURSES

The views from these three championship courses at Kapalua Resort are worth the greens fees alone. The first to open was the **Bay Course,** a par-72, 6,761-yard course inaugurated in 1975. Designed by Arnold Palmer and Ed Seay, this course is a bit forgiving with its wide fairways; the greens, however, are difficult to read. The well-photographed 5th overlooks a small ocean cove; even the pros have trouble with this rocky par-3, 205-yard hole.

The **Village Course,** another Palmer/Seay design, is a par-71, 6,632-yard course. It's the most scenic of the three courses; the hole with the best vista definitely is the 6th, which overlooks a lake with the ocean in the distance. But don't get distracted by the view—the tee is between two rows of Cook pines.

The **Plantation Course,** scene of the Lincoln/Mercury Kapalua International and the Kirin Cup World Championship of Golf, is Ben Crenshaw/Bill Coore–designed. A 6,547-yard, par-73 course on a rolling hillside of the West Maui Mountains, this one is excellent for developing your low shots and precise chipping. Facilities for the three courses include locker rooms, driving range, and an excellent restaurant. Greens fees at the Village Course and the Bay Course are $110, and fees at the Plantation are $120. Fifty-four holes gives you a better chance at getting a tee time; weekdays are best. Call **808/669-8044.**

KAANAPALI COURSES

From high handicappers to near-pros, both Kaanapali courses offer a challenge. The **North Course** (originally called the Royal Lahaina Golf Course) is a true Robert Trent Jones design: an abundance of wide bunkers, several long, stretched-out tees, and the largest, most contoured greens on Maui. The par-72, 6,305-yard course has a tricky 18th hole (par 4, 435 yd.) with a water hazard on the approach to the green.

The **South Course,** a par-72, 6,250-yard course, is an Arthur Jack Snyder design; although shorter than the North Course, it does require more accuracy on the narrow, hilly fairways. Just like its sister course, it has a water hazard on its final hole, so don't tally up your score card until the final putt is sunk.

Options include driving range, putting course, and lunch at the clubhouse. Greens fees are $120; weekday tee times are best. Call **808/661-3691.**

✪ WAILEA COURSES

There are three courses to choose from at Wailea. The **Blue Course,** a par-72, 6,700-yard flat, open course designed by Arthur Jack Snyder and dotted with bunkers and water hazards, is a golf course for duffers and pros alike. The wide fairways appeal to beginners, and the undulating terrain make it a course everyone can enjoy. A little more difficult is the par-72, 7,073-yard championship **Gold Course,** with narrow fairways, several tricky dogleg holes, and the classic Robert Trent Jones, Jr. challenges: natural hazards, like lava rock walls, and native Hawaiian grasses. The **Orange Course,** originally an Arthur Jack Snyder design, was renovated by Robert Trent Jones, Jr. to a more challenging course.

With 54 holes to play, getting a tee time is slightly easier on weekends than at other resorts, but weekdays are best (the Gold Course is usually the toughest to book). Facilities include a pro shop, restaurant, locker rooms, and a complete golf training facility. Greens fees are $130. Call **808/879-2966** or 808/875-5111.

MAKENA COURSES

Here you'll find 36 holes of "Mr. Hawaii Golf"—Robert Trent Jones, Jr.—at its best. Add to that spectacular views: Molokini islet looms in the background, humpback whales gambol offshore in the winter, and the tropical sunsets are spectacular. This is golf not to be missed; the par-72, 6,876-yard **South Course** has a couple of holes you'll never forget. The view from the par-4 15th hole, which shoots from an elevated tee 183 yards downhill to the Pacific, is magnificent. The 16th hole has a two-tiered green that's blind from the tee 383 yards away (that is, if you make it past the gully off the fairway). The par-72, 6,823-yard **North Course** is more difficult and more spectacular. The 13th hole, located partway up the mountain, has a view that makes most golfers stop and stare. The next hole is even more memorable: a 200-foot drop between tee and green. Facilities include clubhouse, driving range, two putting greens, pro shop, lockers, and lessons. Beware of crowded conditions on weekends. Greens fees are $80 for Makena Resort guests and $110 for nonguests. Call **808/879-3344.**

HORSEBACK RIDING

Maui offers spectacular adventure rides through rugged ranch lands, into tropical forests, and to remote swimming holes. For a day-long tour on horseback—complete with swimming and lunch—call **Adventure on Horseback,** Makawao (☎ **808/ 242-7445** or 808/572-6211); the cost is $130 per person. Or ride from sea level to the cool pastures of up-country Maui for a personal tour of Tedeschi Winery with **Makena Stables,** 7299 S. Makena Rd. (☎ **808/879-0244**), for $145. If you are out in Hana, **Oheo Stables,** Hana Hwy., Kipahulu (☎ **808/667-2222**), has relaxed rides through the mountains above Oheo Gulch (Seven Pools) for $95.

If you enjoy your ride, kiss your horse and tip your guide.

HALEAKALA ON HORSEBACK

If you'd like to ride down into Haleakala's crater, contact **Pony Express Tours** in Kula (☎ **808/667-2200** or 808/878-6698); they offer half-day rides down to the crater floor and back up, lunch included, for $120 per person. A full-day ride, at $150 per person, explores the crater floor extensively. Gentler 1- and 2-hour rides are also offered at Haleakala Ranch, located on the beautiful lower slopes of the volcano, for $35 and $60. Pony Express provides well-trained horses and experienced guides, and all riding levels are accommodated. In order to ride, you must be at least 10 years old, weigh no more than 230 pounds, and wear long pants and closed-toe shoes. Charley Aki of **Charley's Trail Rides and Pack Trips** (☎ **808/248-8209**) leads guided overnight horseback rides into the crater for groups of two or more; rates start at $300 a person per night, including meals, tent, and sleeping bag.

WAY OUT WEST ON MAUI: RANCH RIDES

Mendes Ranch & Trail Rides. On Kahekili Hwy., 4 miles past Wailuku. ☎ **808/871-5222.**

The 300-acre Mendes Ranch is a real-life working cowboy ranch in West Maui that has the essential elements of an earthly paradise—rainbows, waterfalls, palm trees, coral-sand beaches, lagoons, tide pools, a rain forest, and its own more than mile-high volcanic peak. Allan Mendes, a third-generation wrangler, raises 300 head of beef cattle, Brahmas, Texas Longhorns, and painted ponies. Just last year, he opened the ranch to trail rides.

Allan will take you from the edge of the rain forest and out to the sea. On the way, you'll cross tree-studded meadows where Texas longhorns sit in the shade like surreal lawn statues, and past a dusty corral where Allan's father, Ernest, a champion roper, is at the day's task breaking in a wild horse. All the while, Allan keeps close watch, turning often in his saddle on his pinto, Pride, to make sure everyone is happy. He points out flora and fauna and fields questions, but generally just lets you soak up Maui's natural splendor in golden silence. The 4-hour ride costs $130, and ends with a high-noon barbecue back at the corral, complete with ribs, baked beans, and potato salad—the perfect ranch-style lunch after a full morning in the saddle.

Ulupalakua Ranch Trail Rides. Makena Stables, 7299 Makena Rd. ☎ **808/879-0244.**

Our horses look like rugby players in leather ankle-guards as they pick their way over sharp black lava on a ride through a hellish landscape out of Dante's Inferno.

The earth stopped burning here 200 years ago (which, in volcano time, is only yesterday). The scorched landscape reflects the sun's heat like an asphalt parking lot in August; I'm glad I have a bottle of water in my saddlebag. My companions are a young couple from Philadelphia who've never seen land like this. Lunarlike, he says. A desert, she offers. Neither description does the place justice.

We lean far forward in our saddles as we ride straight uphill on Maui's Ulupalakua Ranch, a multitiered spread that stretches from Perouse Bay almost to the summit of Haleakala. Our goal on this 3-hour ride is the very vent that spilled all this mess. Our horses nimbly make their way there, under thickets of kiawe with stilettolike thorns that can puncture a leather boot, past old lava tubes holding bleached-white bones (likely those of cows who strayed, but who knows?). Nothing stirs in this dead zone, except suffocating trail dust kicked up by our horses. I pull a red bandana across my face like a bandit as we ride on deeper into this devil land.

Ahead stands the source of this insane landscape: a crater with a telltale tongue of lava spilling out its downhill lip. I hike up to the edge and look in at the dead ashes of this long-silent fire-pit, and then downslope at the wide ribbon of destruction that layers the earth from here to the ocean—a good 5 miles—and hope it'll be a long time before it roars again.

Enough of this hell: Down we go, following a dusty jeep trail past cinder cones to Perouse Bay, spooking Axis deer from China as we ride slowly down to the ever blue sea.

Ulupalakua Ranch offers a selection of guided rides: A 2-hour ride is $99; a 3-hour ride $115, and a 3-hour sunset ride $130. Call to reserve.

TENNIS

Maui County has excellent tennis courts located all over the island. All are free and available from daylight to sunset; a few even have night lights, allowing play to continue until 10pm. The courts are available on a first-come, first-served basis. When someone's waiting for a court, please limit your play to no more than 45 minutes. For a complete list of all public tennis courts, contact **Maui County of Parks and Recreation,** 200 S. High St., Wailuku, 96793 (☎ **808/243-7232**).

Private tennis courts are available at most resorts and hotels on the island. The **Kapalua Tennis Garden and Village Tennis Center,** Kapalua Resort (☎ **808/ 669-5677**), is home to the Kapalua Open, featuring the largest purse in the state, on Labor Day weekend, and the Kapalua Betsy N. Aglesen Tennis Invitational Pro-Am in November. Court rentals are $10 an hour for resort guests and $12 an hour for nonguests. In Wailea, the **Wailea Tennis Club,** 131 Wailea Iki Place (☎ **808/ 879-1958**), has both grass and Plexi-pave courts. Per-day court rentals are $10 for paved courts and $20 for grass courts for resort guests, $15 for paved courts and $25 for grass courts for nonguests.

9 High-Flying Adventure Tours

by Rick Carroll

BARNSTORMING MAUI

Upside-down over Maui, I'm struck with amazing clarity: To really understand the big picture, you've got to see it from the sky. Up here, you can really see the Hawaiian Islands for what they are—just a few volcanic peaks piercing the vast Pacific.

"Here we go," the pilot warned as the plane suddenly fell out of the sky like a dead leaf. Maui spun crazily as we corkscrewed, laughing, screaming, free-falling through the sky/sea continuum in a fire-engine red, open-cockpit 1935 Waco biplane. Only a shoulder harness kept me from all that wild blue yonder.

The red dirt islands of Kahoolawe, Lanai, and Molokai float on the misty horizon; Oahu gleams like a diamond to the north; and the Big Island's Mauna Kea peaks above the clouds. At 2,500 feet—our cruising altitude—Maui shows like a topographic map of itself. Even the colors are correct: gray volcanic peaks, golden uplands dotted with green trees, ice-blue waterfalls, green sugar cane fields, golden beaches, emerald lagoons, the whole thing skirted by white-capped waves and the deep blue ocean. The colors of the Pacific—lime green, cobalt blue, deep purple—will astound you; on some days, it's punctuated with wheezy whale exclamations. And the architecture of the clouds . . .

Too soon, the Waco biplane touches down back at Kahului's airport. The only problem now is that the rest of the day looms ahead, dull and flat as the runway.

To take a biplane ride, contact **Biplane Barnstormers,** in the light green hangars on the east side of Kahului Airport, near the control tower (☎ **808/878-2860**). Flights are offered between 9am and 3pm daily; aerobatics flights are best in morning, sightseeing is best at midday. It's $99 for a 20-minute flight for two; a 100-minute full-island flight is $450 for one or two; a 30-minute aerobatics flight is $175. Reserve all flights a day or two in advance.

A SPECTACULAR COPTER RIDE TO THE WALL OF TEARS

Pablo Picasso once said that the three greatest inventions of the 20th century were the blues, cubism, and Polish vodka. Had he ever visited Hawaii, he might have added the helicopter.

There's a *huhu* over helicopters in Hawaii—too many are flying too low, sometimes taking too many risks—but only a helicopter can bring you face-to-face with volcanoes, waterfalls, and remote places like Maui's little-known Wall of Tears, up near the summit of Puu Kukui in the West Maui Mountains.

This isn't a wild ride; it's a gentle gee-whiz zip into a seldom-seen Eden, and one of Maui's most popular honeymoon flights. On this day, I find myself in the company of kissy-face newlyweds from Chicago who can't keep their hands off each other, even up here.

Puu Kukui is Hawaiian for "candlenut hill," although that tag's too small for something that pokes 5,788 feet out of the Pacific. It only looks like a hill because its neighbor, Haleakala, is nearly twice as tall.

Up the steep northeastern slope we rise, until the pilot finds a "keyhole" slot in the velvet green ramparts so narrow it seems no helicopter could pass. We hold our breath and enter the caldera of this old defunct volcano, where we find an almost mythical place, soft and moist and cool and green. Waterfalls, too many to count, spill from pool to pool and streak the sheer cliffs of the canyon; 1,100-foot-high Honokohau Falls roars in a 600-foot cascade to a pool, then falls another 500 feet to another pool, like a spectacular Slinky. Ahead, deep, narrow valleys, untouched since the day they exploded out of the Pacific 10 million years ago, glisten with silver streams that run to the sea. Everything's larger than life in this rain forest (which is otherwise off-limits to all except scientists, botanists, and water conservationists): Hapuu tree ferns, normally 10 feet tall, grow to 20 feet and more, forming a leafy canopy that shades 18 Hawaiian plants found nowhere else in the world, including rare Hawaiian daisies, wild orchids, and the endangered silversword. This place is like nothing I've ever seen before. The Vs etched in the cliffs by centuries of falling water begin to look erotic, like Georgia O'Keeffe still lifes (an observation not lost on the honeymooners). We all shiver at the natural spectacle.

The first chopper pilots in Hawaii were good ol' boys on the way back from *Veetnam*—hard-flying, hard-drinking cowboys who cared more about the ride than the scenery en route. Not anymore: The Sunshine Helicopter pilots are a cross between a disc jockey, tour guide, and Disneyland "A" ride operator—except this fantasyland is real.

"Want that shot, Rick?" the pilot asked, holding the chopper steady while I zoomed in on hundreds of tiny waterfalls that turned the mossy cliffs into a "wall of tears." I put my camera down to stare in awe at the primal splendor. No camera or words can ever do this place justice.

Sunshine Helicopters (107 Kahului Heliport, Kahului; ☎ **808/871-0722**) will take you on a 30-minute, narrated helicopter flight over West Maui and Puu Kukui. The cost is $89 for adults, and includes a keepsake videotape of the flight. It's the most fun you can have in 30 minutes—even for honeymooners.

10 Making the Most of Your Trip to Maui: A Suggested Itinerary

by Rick Carroll

There's enough to see and do on Maui to keep you busy for years—so squeezing it all into a week can be a real trial. But it's doable. You can even do it in less, if you have to. If you only have 3 days to spend on Maui, stay in the old whaling capital of Lahaina to gain a sense of history, then make day trips by car.

Day One   Drive up to the summit of Haleakala. It's an awesome sight any time of day, so even if you can't manage dawn, don't miss the mountain. It has everything to do with Maui. Getting there will take you through the lumpy volcanic landscape and past the farms and ranches of Up-country, a bucolic haven from the resort development and steamy winds below. After the park, you'll end up at Kula, around the 3,000-foot level, where gardens feature the weird pincushion and feather-duster blooms known as protea (a South African original, living comfortably on Hawaii's slopes). Turn left and keep on going around the high shoulder of the mountain until you reach Tedeschi Vineyards; stop for a taste of Maui wine and a picnic at the tables under the giant wild avocado trees. Or turn right and spend the afternoon poking around the shops of Makawao. Either way, you'll be reminded that Maui's more than just a tropical beach.

Day Two   Head for Hana—but go early in the morning before the crooked road becomes crowded with traffic. Wear your swimsuit and plan to stop at roadside waterfall parks for a swim. Go slow and really enjoy the natural surroundings. Get out and walk by the taro patch in the botanical gardens, enjoy the peaceful vista of the Keanae Peninsula and the other sights—it's all part of the Hana road experience. Plan an overnight stay in Hana in a B&B or vacation rental as a reasonable alternative to the wonderful but expensive Hotel Hana-Maui. Some friends and I pitched tents at Oheo Gulch, bathing in the pools at dusk and then falling asleep to the sound of the rain overhead.

Day Three   Spend the morning in Hana, then take a hike up to Fagan's Cross or down to the famous Red Sand Beach before heading back down the Hana Highway. You may want to check out the funky shops in Paia, then head for Wailuku. After lunch there, head up to Iao Valley State Park. Tour buses roll into the valley in the misty hills behind quaint Wailuku town for a quick photo-op: the Iao Needle rock formation. But head out on your own if you can, as there's much more here to see. Go for a hike, or spend time at the park's collection of miniature houses that represent Maui's plantation cultures from an architectural perspective. Bloody ancient battles occurred in this neighborhood; you can still feel the presence of the spirits, and may even experience what folks in Hawaii call "chicken skin."

On the way back down from the valley, visit the Bailey House Museum in Wailuku for all the historic details. Then take the rest of the day off and hit the beach at Kaanapali, where you can wiggle your bare feet in the sand and watch the sunset.

Day Four   Now it's time to sail, splash, and snorkel. Take Trilogy's snorkel cruise to Lanai (see "Lanai for the Day," Chapter 9), a two-for-one island experience. You board in Lahaina Harbor and admire Maui from offshore, then get off at Lanai and see a glimpse of life on that nearly private plantation-turned-luxury-enclave. Snorkeling occurs in Lanai's clear waters, famed as a divers' favorite for the undersea lava caverns.

Day Five   Explore Makena, the natural part of Maui's south coast resort cluster, where you can catch a catamaran to Molokini islet for a day of snorkeling or a whale watch in season. Or bump down a dusty road to La Perouse Bay for some extraordinary snorkeling in green pools set amid lava fingers left over from when Haleakala last exploded and sent lava running to the sea in 1790. Equestrians will mount up at Makena Stables and head out for a day of rough riding across the lava flows on the Ulupalakua Ranch.

Day Six   Collapse at your favorite beach—probably Kapalua, one of the finest gold-sand beaches in Hawaii—and work on your tan. (You don't want people back home

Adventures for Kids—and Kids at Heart

A Submarine Ride   A real sub takes you and the kids down into the shallow coastal waters off Lahaina, where you'll see plenty of fish, who come around to be fed by chumming divers—you may even see a shark. They love it, and you stay dry the entire time. When the biz began in Hawaii a few years ago, it was quite a novelty, and quite expensive; now several outfits are competing for your submarine dollar, so the price is getting down around where it should be. But it's still cheaper to rent a snorkel and fins. Easy for me to say—I like to get wet. Tours leave on the hour from 8am to 2pm daily from Lahaina Harbor; tickets are $69 or $79, depending on the tour you choose. Call **Atlantis Submarines** at **808/667-2224** or 800/548-6262 to reserve.

The Sugar Cane Train   Small kids love this ride, as do train buffs of all ages. A steam engine pulls open passenger cars of the Lahaina/Kaanapali and Pacific Railroad on a 30-minute, 12-mile round-trip through sugar cane fields between Lahaina and Kaanapali while the conductor sings and calls out the landmarks. Along the way, you can see Molokai, Lanai, and the backside of Kaanapali. Tickets are $13 for grown-ups, $6.50 for kids; call **808/661-0089.**

Incredible Journeys!   Just because you won't go up in a helicopter doesn't mean you can't see Maui from the air. You can—without leaving the Hyatt Regency Maui's lobby—in a virtual reality flight trainer that replicates a seven-passenger helicopter. Said to be first of its kind in the world, the chopper simulator "lifts off" with vibrations and sounds, then shows off Maui on a wraparound dome-shaped theater screen before "touching down" in the Hyatt's lobby. It takes you flying over the island's craters, rain forests, waterfalls, beaches, and valleys without leaving terra firma. It's virtually amazing—anyone with a fear of flying should see Maui like this. Everyone else, please follow me to Kahului Heliport for the real thing. **Hyatt Regency Maui** (200 Nohea Kai Dr., Kaanapali Beach; ☎ **808/661-0092**) runs 40-minute shows daily 9am to 9pm.

Star Searches   After sunset, the stars over Kaanapali shine big and bright because the tropical sky is almost pollutant-free, and no big-city lights interfere with the cosmic view. Amateur astronomers can probe the Milky Way, see the rings of Saturn and Jupiter's moons, and scan the Sea of Tranquillity in a 90-minute star search on the world's first recreational computer-driven telescope. Not just for kids, this $10 cosmic adventure on the rooftop of the **Hyatt Regency Maui** (200 Nohea Kai Dr., Kaanapali Beach; ☎ **808/661-1234**) is for anyone who's starry-eyed.

to think you didn't hit the beach.) Eat lunch at the open-air Bay Club, perched on a black lava point with the island of Molokai in the distance. Then go back to the beach.

Day Seven   Head around the wild side of Maui on the narrow coastal highway beyond Kapalua. Your destination is Mendes Ranch, where you can spend the day riding from mauka to makai (mountain to the sea) on the best-looking working cowboy ranch this side of Pecos. Or take a kayak cruise around Kapalua Bay and look for endangered sea turtles among the tropical fish. End your perfect week on Maui with a splurge—a sunset dinner at Avalon. I make it a policy to never leave Maui until I eat there.

11 Exploring the Island

by Rick Carroll

CENTRAL MAUI

Central Maui isn't exactly tourist central; this is where real people live. Most likely, you'll land here and head directly to the beach. However, there are a few sights worth checking out if you feel like a respite from the sun 'n' surf.

KAHULUI

Under the airport flight path, next to Maui's busiest intersection and across from Costco and K-Mart in Kahului's new business park, is the most unlikely place: **Kanaha Wildlife Sanctuary,** Hi. 386 at Hi. 38 (☎ **808/984-8100**). Look for a parking area off Haleakala Highway (behind the new mall) and you'll find a 1.8-mile trail that meanders along the shore to a shade shelter and lookout. Rub your eyes, there it is, complete with a sign proclaiming it to be the permanent home of the endangered black-neck Hawaiian stilt, whose population is now down to about 1,000. Small wonder. Naturalists say this is the best place to see endangered Hawaiian Koloa ducks, stilts, coots, and other migrating shorebirds. If I were an endangered black-neck Hawaiian stilt or Koloa duck, I'd split for the more natural-looking Kealia Pond National Wildlife Preserve in Kihei (see below).

IN NEARBY WAIKAPU

Waikapu has two attractions that are worth a peek, especially if you're trying to kill time before your flight out.

Relive Maui's past by taking a 30-minute narrated tram ride around fields of pineapple, sugar cane, and papaya trees at **Maui Tropical Plantation** (1670 Honoapiilani Hwy.; ☎ **808/244-7643**). A shop sells fresh and dried fruit. The working plantation is open daily from 9am to 5pm. Admission is free; the tour is $8.50 for adults and $3.50 for kids 5 to 12.

Marilyn Monroe and Frank Lloyd Wright meet for dinner every night at **Waikapu Golf and Country Club,** 2500 Honoapiilani Hwy. (☎ **808/244-2011**), one of Maui's most unusual buildings. Neither actually came to Maui in real life, but these icons of architecture and glamour who traded on the curvilinear live on in this paradise setting. Wright designed this place for a Pennsylvania family in 1949, but it never happened. In 1957, Marilyn and husband Arthur Miller wanted it built for them in Connecticut, but they separated the following year. When Tokyo billionaire Takeshi Sekiguchi went shopping at Taliesen West for a signature building to adorn his 18-hole golf course, he found the blueprints, and had Marilyn's Wright House cleverly redesigned as a clubhouse. A horizontal in a vertical landscape, it doesn't quite fit the setting, but it's still the best-looking building on Maui today. You can walk in and look around at FLW's architecture and the portraits of MM in Monroe's, the restaurant.

WAILUKU

This historic gateway to Iao Valley (see below) is worth a visit, if only for a brief stop at **Bailey House Museum** (2375-A Main St.; ☎ **808/244-3326**). Missionary and sugar planter Edward Bailey's 1833 home is a treasure trove of Hawaiiana. The house is an architectural hybrid of stones laid by Hawaiian craftsmen and timbers joined in a display of Yankee ingenuity. Inside, you'll discover an eclectic collection, from precontact artifacts like scary temple images, dog-tooth necklaces, and a rare lei made of tree snail shells, as well as latter-day relics like Duke Kahanamoku's 1919 redwood surfboard and a koa wood table given to President Ulysses S. Grant, who had to refuse it because he couldn't accept gifts from foreign countries. Every time I come here, I see something new. Last time, it was a Maui O'o, an extinct bird last seen on Molokai in 1904, which I'd somehow overlooked before. Yet here it was, in a glass case, a black bird with bright yellow wing feathers, its little feet crossed as if it had just dropped out of the sky. There's also a gallery devoted to a few of Bailey's landscapes, painted from 1866 to 1896, which capture on canvas a Maui we only imagine today.

The museum is open daily from 10am to 4:30pm. Admission is $4 adults, $3.50 seniors, and $1 children 6–12.

A DAY TRIP TO IAO VALLEY

Only 5 miles from Kahului, above the funky hill town of Wailuku, past the Bailey House museum where the little plantation houses stop and the road climbs ever higher, Maui's true nature begins to reveal itself. The transition between suburban sprawl and raw nature is so quick that most people who drive up into the valley don't realize that they're suddenly in a rain forest. Walls of the canyon begin to close around them, and a 2,250-foot needle pricks gray clouds scudding across the blue sky. After the hot tropic sun, the air is moist and cool, and the shade a welcome comfort. This is Iao Valley, a 6.2-acre state park that's a place of great nature, history, and beauty, enjoyed by millions of people from around the world for more than a century.

Iao (literally "Supreme Light") Valley, 10 miles long and 4,000 acres in size, is the eroded volcanic caldera of the West Maui Mountains. The head of the Iao Valley is a broad circular amphitheater where four major streams—the Nakalaloa, the Poohoahoa, the Kinihipai, and the Ae—converge into Iao Stream. At the back of the amphitheater is rain-drenched Puu Kukui, the West Maui Mountains' highest point. No other Hawaiian valley lets you to go from seacoast to rain forest so easily. This peaceful valley, full of tropical plants, rainbows and waterfalls, swimming holes, and hiking trails, is a place of solitude, reflection, and escape for residents and visitors alike.

JUST THE FACTS

When to Go   The park is open daily from 7am to 7pm year-round. Go early in the morning or late in the afternoon, when the sun's rays slant into the valley and create a mystical mood. You can bring a picnic and spend the day, but be prepared at any time for a tropical cloudburst, which often soaks the valley and swells both waterfalls and streams.

Access Points   There's only one way in and one way out. From Wailuku, take Hi. 32 3.6 miles to the entrance to the state park.

Information and Visitor Centers   For information, contact **Iao Valley State Park,** 54 High St., Wailuku (☎ **808/984-8109**). The **Hawaii Nature Center,** 875 Iao Valley Rd., (☎ **808/244-6500**) is an important stopping point for all who want to explore Iao Valley on their own or on guided trips.

Hiking   The **Hawaii Nature Center** offers 90-minute guided hikes of the valley's dark, cool rain forest every day at 2pm, and at 9am and 10:45am on Wednesday. It's $12.50 per person; you must be over 8 years old.

SEEING THE HIGHLIGHTS

You're invited to follow two paved walkways that loop into the massive green amphitheater, across the bridge of Iao Valley Stream, and along the stream itself. The one-third–mile loop on a paved trail is Maui's easiest hike—you can take your grand-mother on this one. The leisurely walk will allow you to enjoy lovely views of the Iao Needle and the lush vegetation. Others often proceed beyond the state park border and take two trails deeper into the valley, but the trails enter private land, and "No Trespassing" signs are posted.

The feature known as **Iao Needle** is an erosional remnant comprised of basalt dikes. The phallic rock juts an impressive 2,250 feet above sea level. There's also supposed to be a rock formation that some people think resembles the profile of John F. Kennedy, but I've never seen it.

Youngsters play in **Iao Stream,** a peaceful brook that belies its bloody history. In 1790, King Kamehameha and his men engaged in the bloody battle of Iao Valley to gain control of Maui. When the battle ended, so many bodies blocked Iao Stream that the battle site was named Kepaniwai, or "damning of the waters." An architectural heritage park of Hawaiian, Japanese, Chinese, Filipino, and New England–style houses stands in harmony by Iao Stream at **Kepaniwai Heritage Garden.** This is a good picnic spot, as there are plenty of picnic tables and benches. You can see ferns, banana trees, and other native and exotic plants in the **Iao Valley Botanic Garden** along the stream.

THE SCENIC ROUTE TO WEST MAUI: KAHEKILI HIGHWAY

On this road named for savage King Kahekili, who built houses out of the skulls of his enemies (a practice Maui planners perhaps should've adopted to slow the island's growth), the true wild nature of Maui is on full display. Narrow and winding Kahekili Highway (Hi. 340) weaves for 20 miles along an ancient Hawaiian coastal footpath from Wailuku to Honokohau Bay, at the island's northernmost tip, past blowholes, sea stacks, sea-bird rookeries, and the imposing 636-foot Kahakaloa headland. On the land side, you'll pass high cliffs, deep valleys dotted with plantation houses, cattle grazing on green plateaus, old wooden churches, taro fields, and houses hung with fishing nets. It's slow going—you can only drive about 10 miles an hour along the dirt-and-gravel road—but it's probably the most beautiful drive in Maui. Your rental car company might try to deter you, but it's not really a hard drive, and the views are spectacular. If you lose your heart on Maui, it'll probably be somewhere along this coastal highway.

At Honokohau, you can pick up Hi. 30 and continue on to the West Maui resorts.

WEST MAUI
A WHALE OF A PLACE IN KAANAPALI

If you haven't seen a real whale yet, go to **Whalers Village** (2435 Kaanapali Pkwy.), a shopping center that has adopted the whale as its mascot. You can't miss it: A huge, almost life-size metal sculpture of a mother whale and two nursing whalelets greets you. A few more steps, and you're met by the looming, bleached-white bony skeleton of a 40-foot sperm whale; it's pretty impressive.

On the second floor of the mall is the **Whale Center of the Pacific** (☎ 808/661-5992), a museum celebrating the "Golden Era of Whaling" (1825–60) from the whaler's point of view: Harpoons and scrimshaw are on display; the museum has even recreated the cramped quarters of a whaler's seagoing vessel.

Across the way you'll find the **Hale Kohola** (House of the Whale), which tells the story from the whale's point of view, as it were. Here's where you can learn about the evolution of the whale: The museum houses exhibits on 70 species of whales and more whale lore than you could hope to absorb during your entire 2-week vacation in Hawaii. I like to look in on the Bone Room, where volunteers scrape and identify the bones of marine mammals that wash ashore in Hawaiian waters to use in future exhibits. You can also sit and watch movies about whales, buy any number of whale souvenirs, and get a free *Whale Watch Guide* that points you out the door and toward the ocean now that you more or less know what whales look like.

Both museums are open during mall hours, daily from 9:30am to 10pm. Admission to the museums is free.

Sightseeing in Historic Lahaina

When "there was no God west of the Horn," Lahaina was the capital of Hawaii and the Pacific's wildest port. Today, it's a mild, mallified version of its old self—mostly a hustle-bustle of whale art, time shares, and "Just Got Leid" T-shirts. I'm not sure the rowdy whalers would be pleased. But, if you look hard, you'll still find the historic port town they loved, filled with the kind of history that inspired James Michener to write his best-selling epic novel, *Hawaii*.

At the headquarters of the **Lahaina Restoration Foundation,** at the Baldwin Home, 96 Front St. (at Dickenson St.; ☎ 808/661-3262), you can pick up a self-guided walking tour map, which will take you to Lahaina's most historic sites—from the Royal Taro Patch and the ruins of King Kamehameha's Brick Palace to the Seamen's Cemetery and old jail yard, where the most drunk and disorderly sailors were thrown for a day of drying out—where you'll learn the stories of those who lived Lahaina's colorful past, from the missionary doctor who single-handedly kept a cholera epidemic from killing Maui's people to the boy king who lived on his very own island.

Below are my favorite places to rediscover historic Lahaina:

Baldwin Home Museum. 96 Front St. (at Dickenson St.). ☎ **808/661-3262.** Admission $3 adults, $2.50 seniors, $1 children. Daily 10am–4:30pm

The oldest house in Lahaina, this coral-and-rock structure was built in 1834 by Rev. Dwight Baldwin, a doctor with the fourth company of American missionaries to sail round the Horn to Hawaii. Like many missionaries, he came to Hawaii to do good—and did very well. After 17 years of service, Baldwin was granted 2,600 acres for farming and grazing in Kapalua. His ranch manager experimented with what Hawaiians called *hala-kahiki,* or pineapple, on a 4-acre plot; the rest is history. Open for guided tours, the house looks as if Baldwin just stepped out for a minute to tend a sick neighbor down the street.

Next door is the **Master's Reading Room,** Maui's oldest building. This became visiting sea captains' favorite hangout once the missionaries closed down all of Lahaina's grog shops and banned prostitution; but by 1844, once hotels and bars started reopening, it lost its appeal. It's now the headquarters of the plucky band of historians who try to keep this town alive and antique at the same time.

Banyan Tree. At the Courthouse Building, 649 Wharf St.

Of all the banyan trees in Hawaii, this is the biggest, most sheltering of all—it's so big that you can't get it in your camera's viewfinder. It was only 8 feet tall when it was planted in 1873 by Maui Sheriff William O. Smith to mark the 50th anniversary of Lahaina's first Christian mission; the big old banyan from India is now more than 50 feet tall, has 12 major trunks, and shades two-thirds of an acre in Lahaina's courthouse square.

The Brig *Carthaginian II.* Lahaina Harbor. ☎ **808/661-8527.** Admission $3. Daily 10am–4:30pm.

Lahaina

Baldwin Home Museum **5**
Banyan Tree **8**
The Brig *Carthanigan II* **7**
505 Front Street Shops & Restaurants **11**
Lahaina Cannery Mall **1**
Lahaina Harbor **10**
Lahaina Inn **3**

Lahaina Restoration Foundation **5**
Lahaina Whaling Museum **4**
Master's Reading Room **6**
Maluuluolele Park **12**
Pioneer Inn **9**
The Sugar Cane Train (Lahaina-
     Kaanapali & Pacific Railroad) **2**

This authentically restored square-rigged brigantine is an authentic replica of a 19th-century whaling ship, the kind that brought the first missionaries to Hawaii. This floating museum features exhibits on whales and 19th-century whaling life. You won't believe how cramped the living quarters were—they make today's cruise ship cabins look downright roomy.

Lahaina Whaling Museum. 865 Front St. ☎ **808/661-4775.** Daily 9:30am–9pm. Free admission.

Yankee whalers came to Lahaina to reprovision ships' stores, get drunk, and raise hell with "the girls of old Mowee." Everything was fine and dandy until 1819, when Congregational missionaries arrived and declared the port town "one of the breathing holes of hell." They tried to curb drinking and prostitution, but failed; Lahaina grew ever lawless until the whaling era came to an end with the discovery of oil in Pennsylvania and the birth of the petroleum industry. That rambunctious era is recalled in this small museum full of art and relics from Lahaina's glory days.

Maluuluolele Park. Front St.

At first glance, this Front Street park appears to be only a hot, dry, dusty softball field. But under home plate is one of my favorite historical sites in Lahaina: it's the edge of Mokuula, a tiny island now buried under tons of red dirt and sand, where a royal compound once stood more than 100 years ago. Here, Prince Kauikeaoulu, who ascended the throne as King Kamehameha III when he was only 10, lived with the love of his life, his sister Princess Nahienaena. Missionaries took a dim view of incest, which was acceptable to Hawaiian nobles in order to preserve the royal bloodline. Torn between love for her brother and the new Christian morality, Nahienaena grew despondent and died at the age of 21. King Kamehameha III, who reigned for 29 years—longer than any other Hawaiian monarch—presided over Hawaii as it went from kingdom to constitutional monarchy, and absolute power over the islands began to transfer from island nobles to missionaries, merchants, and sugar planters. Kamehameha died in 1854; he was 39. In 1918, his royal island, containing a mausoleum and artifacts of the kingdom, was demolished and covered with dirt to make a public park. The baseball team from Lahainaluna School, the first American school founded by missionaries west of the Rockies, now plays games on the site of this royal place, still considered sacred to many Hawaiians.

SOUTH MAUI

The South Maui resorts aren't about sightseeing; this hot, dry, sunny coast is where you come for fun in the sun. Still, there's a little worthwhile exploring to do:

KIHEI

Capt. George Vancouver discovered Kihei in 1778, when it was only a collection of fisherman's grass shacks on the hot, dry, dusty coast (hard to believe, eh?). A **totem pole** stands today where he's believed to have landed, across from Aston Maui Lu Resort (575 S. Kihei Rd.). Vancouver sailed on to discover British Columbia, where a great international city and harbor now bears his name.

West of the junction of Hi. 31 and Hi. 350 is **Kealia Pond National Wildlife Preserve** (☎ 808/875-1582), a 500-acre U.S. Fish and Wildlife wetland preserve where endangered Hawaiian stilts, coots, and ducks hang out and splash. These ponds work two ways: as bird preserves and as dikes that keep the coral reefs from silting from runoff. You can take a self-guided tour along a boardwalk dotted with interpretive signs and shade shelters, through sand dunes and around ponds to Maalaea Harbor. The boardwalk starts at the outlet of Kealia Pond on the ocean side of N. Kihei Road (look for the dirt parking area at beach access).

WAILEA

The best way to explore this golden resort coast is to rise with the sun and head for Wailea's 1 1/2-mile **coastal nature trail,** stretching between the Kea Lani Hotel and the keawe thicket just beyond the Renaissance Wailea. It's my favorite morning walk on Maui, a serpentine path that meanders uphill and down past native plants, old Hawaiian habitats, and a billion dollars worth of luxury hotels. You can pick up the trail at any of the resorts or from clearly marked Shoreline Access points along the coast. The best time to go is when you first wake up; by midmorning, the coastal trail is too often clogged with pushy joggers (somebody should tell them that this is a scenic nature walk, not a fitness loop), and it gets crowded with beachgoers as the day wears on. As the path crosses several bold black lava points, it affords new vistas of islands and ocean; there are benches so you can pause to contemplate the view across Alalakeiki Channel, which jumps with whales in season. Sunset is another good time

The South Maui Coast

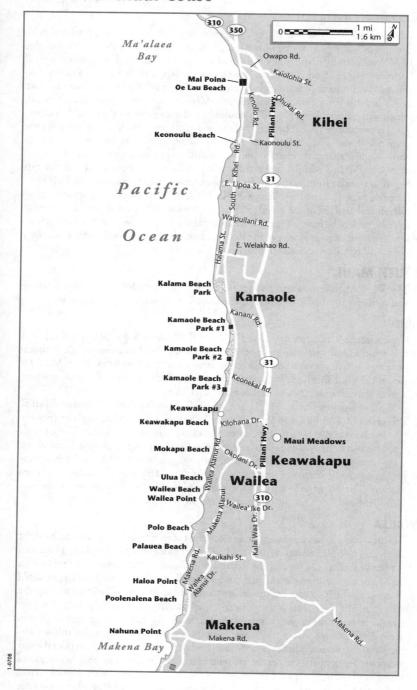

310
350

Ma'alaea Bay

Owapo Rd.
Kaiolohia St.

Mai Poina
Oe Lau Beach

Kenolio Rd.

Piilani Hwy.

Ohukai Rd.

Kihei

Keonoulu Beach

S. Kihei Rd.

Kaonoulu St.

Pacific

E. Lipoa St.

31

South Kihei Rd.

Waipuilani Rd.

Ocean

Halama St.

E. Welakhao Rd.

Kalama Beach
Park

Kamaole

Kamaole Beach
Park #1

Kanani Rd.

Kamaole Beach
Park #2

Kamaole Beach
Park #3

31

Keonekai Rd.

Keawakapu
Keawakapu Beach

Kilohana Dr.

● Maui Meadows

Mokapu Beach

Okolani Dr.

Wailea Alanui Rd.

Piilani Hwy.

Keawakapu

Ulua Beach
Wailea Beach
Wailea Point

Wailea

310

Polo Beach

Makena Alanui

Wailea 'Ike Dr.

Kalai Waa Dr.

Palauea Beach

Makena Rd.

Kaukahi St.

Haloa Point

Wailea
Alanui Dr.

Poolenalena Beach

Makena

Makena Rd.

Nahuna Point

Makena Bay

Makena Rd.

0   1 mi
     1.6 km

N

1-0708

to hit the trail; many come down here to watch the glorious end of yet another perfect day in paradise.

MAKENA

A few miles south of Wailea, the manicured coast turns to wilderness; now you're in Makena.

Once cattle were driven down the slope from upland ranches, lashed to rafts, and sent into the water to swim to boats that waited to take them to market. Now, **Makena Landing** is the best place to launch kayaks bound for Perouse Bay and Ahihi-Kinau preserve. From the landing, go south on Makena Road; on the right is **Keawali Congregational Church** (☎ 808/879-5557). Surrounded by Ti leaf, which by Hawaiian custom provides protection, and built of coral block cut from the reef in 1831, this Protestant church sits on its own cove with a gold-sand beach and always attracts a Sunday crowd for its Hawaiian language service.

A little farther south on the coast is **La Perouse Monument,** a pyramid of lava rocks that marks the spot where French explorer Admiral Compte de la Perouse set foot on Maui in 1786. The first Westerner to "discover" the island, he described the "burning climate" of the leeward coast, observed several fishing villages near Kihei, and sailed on into oblivion, never to be seen again; some believe he may have been eaten by cannibals in what now is New Hebrides. To get there, drive south past Puu Olai to Ahihi Bay, where the road turns to gravel. Go another 2 miles along the coast to La Perouse Bay; the monument sits amid a clearing in black lava at the end of the dirt road.

HOUSE OF THE SUN: HALEAKALA NATIONAL PARK

At once forbidding and compelling, Haleakala National Park (The "House of the Sun") is Maui's main natural attraction. More than 1.3 million people a year go up the 10,023-foot-high mountain to peer down into the crater of the world's largest dormant volcano. (Haleakala is officially considered to be only dormant, not extinct, although it hasn't rumbled and spewed lava since 1790.) That hole would hold Manhattan.

But there's more to do than just stare in a big black hole. Just going up the mountain is an experience. Nowhere else on the planet can you climb from sea level to 10,000 feet in 45 minutes and never leave the ground. The snaky road passes through big puffy cumulus clouds to offer magnificent views of the isthmus of Maui, the West Maui Mountains, and the calm blue Pacific Ocean.

Many drive up to the summit in predawn darkness to watch the sunrise over Haleakala; others take a trail ride inside the bleak lunar landscape of the crater (see "Horseback Riding," p. 342), or coast down the 38-mile road from the summit on a bicycle with special breaks (see "Bicycling," p. 340). Hardy adventurers hike and camp inside the crater (see "Hiking & Camping," p. 336). Those bound for the interior bring their survival gear, for the terrain is raw, rugged, and punishing. Not unlike the moon. However you choose to experience Haleakala National Park, it will prove memorable—guaranteed.

JUST THE FACTS

Haleakala National Park extends from the summit of Mount Haleakala down the volcano's southeast flank to Maui's eastern coast, beyond Hana. There are actually two separate and distinct destinations within the park: **Haleakala Crater** and the **Kipahulu** coast. The crater gets all the publicity, but Kipahulu draws crowds too,

Impression

There are few enough places in the world that belong entirely to themselves. The human passion to carry all things everywhere, so that every place is home, seems well on its way to homogenizing our planet, save for the odd unreachable corner. Haleakala crater is one of those corners.

—Barbara Kingsolver, the *New York Times*

because it's lush, green, and tropical, and home to Oheo Gulch, also known as Seven Sacred Pools. No road links the crater and the coast; you've got to approach each separately, and you need at least a day to see each place.

When to Go   At the 10,023-foot summit, weather changes fast. Summer is dry and warm, winter's wet, windy, and cold. Always call the park for current weather conditions before you go (☎ 808/572-7749), or the **National Weather Service** for a recorded forecast at **808/877-5111.**

From sunrise to noon the light is weak, but the crater is usually free of clouds. The best time for photos is in the afternoon, when the sun lights the crater and clouds are few. Go on full-moon nights for spectacular viewing. Expect showers on the Kipahulu coast.

Access Points   **Haleakala Crater** is 38 miles, or about a 90-minute drive, from Kahului. To get there, take Hi. 37 to Hi. 377 to Hi. 378. For details on the drive, see "The Drive to the Summit," below. Pukalani is the last town for water, food, gas.

Kipahulu, on Maui's east end near Hana, is 60 miles from Kahului on Hi. 36 (the Hana Hwy.). Due to traffic and rough road conditions, plan on the drive taking 4 hours, one-way. (see "The Road to Hana," below). Hana (see below) is the only nearby town for services, water, gas, food, and overnight lodging; some facilities may not be open after dark.

Information, Visitor Centers & Ranger Programs   For information before you go, contact **Haleakala National Park,** Box 369, Makawao, HI 96768 (☎ 808/572-7749).

Haleakala National Park Headquarters   One mile from the park entrance, at 9,745 feet, is the park headquarters (☎ 808/572-9306), open daily from sunrise to 3pm. Here you can pick up information and publications, sign up for guided hikes, get camping permits and, occasionally, see a Hawaiian nene goose; one or more are often here to greet visitors. Rest rooms and drinking water are available.

Park rangers lead free **crater rim walks** in summer, starting at park headquarters and varying from 30 minutes to 2 hours. Check current schedules and sign up at headquarters. Rangers also offer excellent, informative free **guided hikes into the crater** at 9:30, 10:30, and 11:30am daily from the summit visitor center.

Free 3-hour guided hikes are offered to **Waikomoi Preserve.** The hikes leave from Hosmer Grove on Monday, Thursday, and Friday at 9am and take you into a cloud forest full of native plants, birds, and insects that live nowhere else on earth. Wear sturdy shoes and carry rain gear.

Haleakala Visitor Center   The crater visitor center is near the summit of Mount Haleakala, 11 miles from the park entrance. It offers a panoramic view of the crater, with photos identifying the various features, and exhibits that explain the

Haleakala National Park

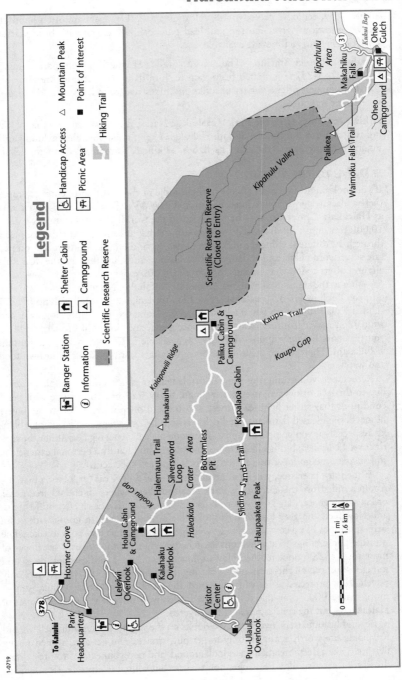

Legend

⛾ Ranger Station	⛺ Shelter Cabin	♿ Handicap Access	△ Mountain Peak
ⓘ Information	▲ Campground	🪑 Picnic Area	■ Point of Interest
	Scientific Research Reserve		⌇ Hiking Trail

To Kahului

Park Headquarters

Hosmer Grove

Leleiwi Overlook

Holua Cabin & Campground

Kalahaku Overlook

Koolau Gap

Halemauu Trail

Silversword Loop

Haleakala Crater Area

Bottomless Pit

△ Hanakauhi

Kalapawili Ridge

Visitor Center

Sliding Sands Trail

Puu-Ulaula Overlook

△ Haupaakea Peak

Kapalaoa Cabin

Paliku Cabin & Campground

Kaupo Trail

Kaupo Gap

Scientific Research Reserve (Closed to Entry)

Kipahulu Valley

Palikea △

Kipahulu Area

Makahiku Falls

Kaloni Bay

Oheo Gulch

Oheo Campground

Waimoku Falls Trail

31

378

N

0 1 mi
   1.6 km

1-0719

archaeology, ecology, geology, and vulcanology. Park rangers are often handy to answer questions, give lectures, and lead guided hikes; check with headquarters for schedule. No facilities are available.

Kipahulu Ranger Station   The ranger station near the Kipahulu park entrance (☎ 808/248-7375) is staffed from 9am to 5pm daily. No facilities are available. Kipahulu rangers offer a variety of walks and hikes year-round; check at the station for current activities.

Hiking & Camping in the Park   Haleakala National Park offers a number of hiking and camping possibilities at both Haleakala Crater and Kipahulu, including cabins and campgrounds in the crater itself. See "Hiking & Camping," above, for details.

THE DRIVE TO THE SUMMIT

If you look on a Maui map almost in the middle of the part that resembles a torso, there a black wiggly line that looks like this: WWWWW. That's **Hi. 378,** also known as **Haleakala Crater Road**—the only road in the world that goes from sea level to 10,000 feet in just 38 miles. This grand corniche has at least 33 switchbacks; passes through 12 different climate zones; goes under, in, and out of clouds; takes you past rare silversword plants and endangered Hawaiian geese sailing through the clear, thin air; and offers a view that extends for more than 100 miles.

Going to the summit takes about 2 hours from Kahului. No matter where you start out, you'll follow Hi. 37 (Haleakala Hwy.) to Pukalani, where you'll pick up Hi. 377 (Upper Kula Rd.), which you'll take to Hi. 378. Along the way, expect fog, rain, and wind. You may encounter stray cattle, loose geese, and downhill bicyclists. Fill up your gas tank before you go—the only gas available is 17 miles below the summit at Pukalani. There are no facilities beyond the ranger stations. Bring your own food and water.

Remember, you're entering a high altitude wilderness area. Some people get dizzy due to the lack of oxygen; pregnant women, heavy smokers, and people with heart conditions may suffer lightheadedness, shortness of breath, nausea or worse: severe headaches, increased flatulence, and dehydration. Bring water and a jacket or a blanket, especially if you go up for sunrise. Everyone makes such a big deal about the sunrise over Haleakala; but it's likely to be cold, damp, and hardly a personal experience, so I suggest you go for sunset instead, which is no less spectacular.

At the **park entrance,** you'll pay an entrance fee of $4 per car (or $2 for a bicycle). About a mile from the entrance is **Park Headquarters,** where an endangered **nene,** or Hawaiian goose, may greet you with its unique call. With a black face, buff cheeks, and claw feet, the gray-brown bird looks like a small Canadian goose with zebra stripes; it moos like a cow, doesn't like to migrate, and prefers lava beds to lakes. The unusual goose clings to a precarious existence on these alpine slopes. Vast flocks of more than 25,000 once roamed Hawaii, but hunters, pigs, feral cats and dogs, and mongoose preyed on the nene, nearly causing its extinction. By 1951, there were only 30 left. Now protected as Hawaii's state bird, the number of wild nene is increasing—more than 1,000, some raised in captive flocks, now inhabit the upland slopes of Haleakala—but the species remains endangered.

Beyond headquarters, two scenic overlooks on the way to the summit, Leleiwi and Kalahaku, are worth a stop, if only to get out, stretch, and get accustomed to the heights. Take a deep breath, a good look around, and pop your ears. If you feel dizzy, drowsy, or get a sudden headache, don't worry—it's just the altitude. (Remember, private pilots carry oxygen above 9,000 feet.)

Leleiwi Overlook is just beyond mile marker 17. From the parking area, a short trail leads you to a panoramic view of the lunarlike crater. When the clouds are low and the sun is in the right place, usually around sunset, you may experience a phenomenon known as the "Specter of the Brocken"—you can see a reflection of your shadow, ringed by a rainbow, in the clouds below. It's an optical illusion caused by a rare combination of sun, shadow, and fog that occurs on only three places on the planet: Haleakala, Scotland, and Germany.

Two miles farther along is **Kalahaku Overlook,** the best place to see a rare **silversword.** The silversword is the punker of the plant world, its silvery bayonets displaying tiny purple bouquets—like a spacey artichoke with an attitude. This botanical wonder proved irresistible to humans, who gathered them in gunnysacks for Chinese potions, British specimen collections, Rose Bowl parade floats, and just for the sheer thrill of having something so rare. Silverswords grow only in Hawaii, take from 4 to 20 years to bloom, then, usually between May and October, send up a 1- to 9-foot stalk with a purple bouquet of sunflowerlike blooms. They're now endangered, so don't even think about taking one home.

Continue on, and you'll quickly reach **Haleakala Visitor Center,** which offers spectacular views. You'll feel as if you're at the edge of the earth. But don't turn around here; the actual summit's a little farther on, at **Puu Ulaula Overlook** (also known as Red Hill), the volcano's highest point, where you'll find a mysterious cluster of buildings known as **Science City** (see box below). If you do go up for sunrise, **Puu Ulaula Observatory,** a triangle of glass that serves as a wind break, is the best viewing spot. After the daily miracle of sunrise—the sun seems to rise out of the vast crater (hence the name, "the House of the Sun")—you can see all the way across Alenuihaha Channel to the often snowcapped summit of Mauna Kea on the Big Island.

Making your Descent Put your car in low gear; that way, you won't suddenly see smoke coming from your engine, and you won't destroy your brakes by riding them the whole way down.

Haleakala National Park's Very Own "X-File": Science City

Once you're atop otherworldly Haleakala, you may wonder what exactly goes on in those seven mysterious silver domes up there. I know I did. Here's all I've been able to learn through official channels:

Although maps call it Science City, this cluster of domes is actually known as the "Haleakala High Altitude Observatory." Reportedly, in 1951 scientists began studying radio waves from space and the glow of the night sky from the research site. Now they do such little things as observe the sun, bounce lasers off the moon, and take detailed pictures of our spacecraft—and maybe theirs.

The Mees Solar Observatory is the one that studies the sun (How appropriate for the House of the Sun, eh?); while the Lunar Ranging Experiment (LURE) Observatory claims to measure the motions of the Pacific Basin by bouncing laser beams off reflectors left on the moon by Apollo astronauts.

The U.S. Air Force admits that it maintains the Maui Space Surveillance Site and keeps a 3.7-meter Advanced Electro-Optical System Telescope trained on our spacecraft and satellites—but we all know what everyone's really looking for up there.

Visitors from Earth, I'm sorry to report, are cordially *not* welcome at this research facility. Hmmm. This may require a Fox and Scully–style investigation. Because, as we all know, the truth is out there.

TROPICAL HALEAKALA: KIPAHULU'S OHEO GULCH (THE SEVEN SACRED POOLS)

If you're thinking about heading out to the so-called Seven Sacred Pools, out past Hana at the Kipahulu end of Haleakala National Park, let's clear this up right now: There are more than seven pools—about 22, actually—and none of them are sacred. It's all a PR scam that has spun out of control into contemporary myth. Folks here call it by its rightful name, Oheo Gulch, others call it Kipahulu; but by any name, it's beautiful—a series of 200-, 300-, and 400-foot waterfall pools cascading into the sea. This dazzling series of pools and cataracts is so popular that it now has its own roadside parking lot. Head out along Hi. 31 past Hana. The Hi. 31 bridge passes between the fourth and the fifth pools from the ocean; the others, plus magnificent 400-foot Waimoku falls, are uphill, via an often-muddy but rewarding hour-long hike (see "Hiking & Camping," above). Check with the Haleakala Park ranger at the **Kipahulu Ranger Station** (☎ 808/248-7367 or 808/248-7375) before hiking up to or swimming in the pools, and always keep one eye on the sky; you'd be surprised how many people get blown out to sea by cloudbursts.

SIGHTSEEING IN UP-COUNTRY MAUI

Come up-country and discover a different side of Maui: On the slopes of Haleakala, cowboys, planters, and other country people make their homes in serene, neighborly communities like Makawao and Kula that are a world away from the bustling beach resorts. Even if you can't spare a day or two in the cool up-country air, there are some sights that are worth a look on your way to or from the crater. Shoppers and gallery hoppers might really want to make the effort; see "Shops & Galleries," below.

On Hi. 377, about seven-tenths of a mile from where it joins up with Hi. 37 south of Haleakala Crater Road (Hi. 378) is **Kula Botanical Garden** (☎ 808/878-1715), where you can take a self-guided, informative, leisurely stroll through more than 700 native and exotic plants. The 5-acre garden offers a good overview of Hawaii's exotic flora in one small, cool place. It's open daily from 9am to 4pm; admission is $4 adults, $1 children 6 to 12.

On the southern shoulder of Haleakala, off Hi. 37 (Kula Hwy.), is **Ulupalakua Ranch,** a 20,000-acre spread once owned by legendary sea captain James Makee, celebrated in the Hawaiian song and dance *Hula O Makee.* Wounded in a Honolulu waterfront brawl in 1843, Captain Makee moved to Maui and bought Ulupalakua. He renamed it Rose Ranch and planted sugar as a cash crop. He grew rich and toasted life until his death in 1879. Still in operation, the ranch is now home to **Tedeschi Vineyards and Winery** (☎ 808/878-6058) established in 1974 by Napa vintner Emil Tedeschi, who began growing California and European grapes here and producing serious still and sparkling wines, plus a silly wine made of pineapple juice. The rustic grounds of Maui's only winery are the perfect place for a picnic. Pack a basket before you go, but don't BYOB: There's plenty of great wine to enjoy at Tedeschi's free wine tasting. Spread your picnic lunch under the sprawling camphor tree, pop the cork on a Blanc du Blanc, and toast your good fortune in being here. Winery tours are offered daily from 9:30am to 2:30pm.

EAST MAUI & HEAVENLY HANA

Hana is Paradise on Earth—or just about as close as you can get to it, anyway. In and around Hana you'll find a lush tropical rain forest dotted with cascading waterfalls and sparkling blue pools, skirted by red- and black-sand beaches. This is probably what you came to Maui looking for.

THE ROAD TO HANA

Top down, sunscreen on, radio tuned to KMVI for a little Hawaiian music on a Maui morning. We're heading for Hana along the Hana Highway (Hi. 36), a wiggle of a road that runs along Maui's northeastern shore. The drive takes at least 3 hours—but take all day. Going to Hana is about the journey, not the destination.

There are wilder roads and steeper roads and even more dangerous roads, but in all of Hawaii no road is more celebrated than this one. It winds for 50 miles past taro patches, magnificent seascapes, waterfall pools, botanical gardens, and verdant rain forests, and ends at one of Hawaii's most beautiful tropical places.

The outside world discovered the little village of Hana in 1926, when the narrow coastal road, carved by pick-ax wielding convicts, opened with 56 bridges and 600 hairpin switchbacks. The mud and gravel road, often subject to landslides and wash-outs, was paved in 1962, when tourist traffic began to increase; it now exceeds 400 cars and 12 vans a day, according to storekeeper Harry Hasegawa. That figures out to be about 500,000 people a year on this road, which is way too many. Go at the wrong time, and you'll be stuck in a bumper-to-bumper rental car parade—peak traffic time is midmorning and midafternoon year-round, especially on weekends.

In the rush to "do" Hana in a day, most visitors spin around town in 10 minutes flat and wonder what all the fuss is about. It takes time to take in Hana (like a week or two), to play in the waterfalls, sniff the tropical flowers, hike to bamboo forests, and take in the spectacular scenery. I once spent a summer in Hana, and that wasn't long enough.

If you really must "do" the Hana Highway in a day, go just before sunrise and re-turn after sunset: On a full-moon night, you'll believe in magic when the sea and the waterfalls glow in soft white light and mysterious shadows appear in the jungle. And you'll have the road almost to yourself on the way back. Better yet, splurge on a Sea Ranch cottage at Hotel Hana-Maui, spend the night in a B&B, or pitch a tent at Kipahulu (see "Accommodations" and "Hiking & Camping," above) and come home, with a smile, in a day or two.

Akamai tips: Forget your mainland road manners. Practice aloha, give way at the one-lane bridges, wave at oncoming motorists, let the big guys in four-by-fours with pig-hunting dogs in the back have the right-of-way—it's just common sense, brah. If the guy behind you blinks his lights, let him pass. Oh, yeah, and don't honk your horn—in Hawaii, it's considered rude.

A Great Plunge Along the Way

A plunge in a waterfall pool is everybody's tropical island fantasy. Trouble is, most waterfalls are usually out of sight at the end of a muddy trail in some distant mos-quito-choked valley. Except for **Puohokamoa Falls.** The 30-foot falls spills into an idyllic pool in a fern-filled amphitheater. Naturalist Ken Schmidt of Hike Maui, who leads hikes deeper into Puohokamoa Valley (see "Hiking & Camping," above), says its name, loosely translated, means "valley of the chickens bursting into flight"—which is what hot, sweaty hikers look like as they take the plunge.

I park the mandatory red Mustang convertible at mile marker 11 on Hana High-way, clamber over river rocks, scramble up a Tarzan trail through dense jungle and—bingo—plunge into the ice-cold pool of upper Puohokamoa Falls. Elapsed time, car to pool: 6 minutes. My kind of hike. My kind of falls.

Keanae Peninsula & Arboretum

Farther along the winding road, about 26^1/$_2$ miles past Paia at mile marker 17, the old Hawaiian village of **Keanae** stands out against the Pacific like a place time forgot. Here, on an old lava flow graced by an 1860 stone church and swaying palms, is one of the last coastal enclaves of native Hawaiians. They still grow taro in patches and pound it into poi, the staple of the old Hawaiian diet; they still pluck *opihi* (shellfish) from tide pools along the jagged coast and cast throw-nets at schools of fish. At nearby **Keanae Arboretum,** Hawaii's botanical world is divided into three parts: native forest; introduced forest; and traditional Hawaiian plants, food, and medicine. You can swim in pools of Piinaau Stream, or press on along a mile-long trail into Keanae Valley, where a lovely tropical rain forest waits at the end.

Waianapanapa State Park

At mile marker 51, shiny black-sand Waianapanapa Beach appears like a vivid dream, with bright green jungle foliage on three sides and cobalt blue water lapping at its feet. Waianapanapa is Hawaiian for "glistening water," which you can see for yourself on a day trip to this great beach on the outskirts of Hana. The 120-acre park on an ancient 'a'a lava flow includes sea cliffs, lava tubes, arches, and the black-sand beach—plus a dozen rustic beach cabins. For information, contact the **Department of Land and Natural Resources,** 54 S. High St., #1010, Wailuku, HI 96793 (☎ 808/984-8109); or see "Accommodations" above. Also see "Beaches" and "Hiking & Camping," above.

HANA

Green, tropical, almost Tahiti-like **Hana,** which some call heavenly, is a destination all its own, a small coastal village in a rain forest inhabited by 2,500 people, many part Hawaiian. But Hana is even more than a destination—it's a memory, a state of mind, one of those magic places that people think about when they daydream as an escape from the humdrum world.

Beautiful Hana enjoys more than 90 inches of rain a year—more than enough to keep the scenery lush. Banyans, bamboo, breadfruit trees—everything seems larger than life in this small town. Especially the flowers, like wild ginger and plumeria. Several roadside stands offer exotic blooms for $1 a bunch. Just "put money in box." It's the Hana honor system.

The last unspoiled Hawaiian town on Maui is, oddly enough, the home of Maui's first resort, which opened in 1946. Paul Fagan, owner of the San Francisco Seals baseball team, bought an old inn and turned it into the **Hotel Hana-Maui** (see "Accommodations," above), which gave Hana its first, and as it turns out, last, taste of tourism. Others have tried to open hotels and golf courses and more resorts, but Hana, which is interested in remaining Hana, always politely refuses.

In a wood frame 1871 building that served as the old Hana District Police Station is the history of the place in artifacts, memorabilia, and photographs. **Hana Museum Cultural Center** (Uakea Rd.; ☎ **808/248-8622**) has some real treasures, so take a few minutes to see it. You'll also want to stop in **Hasegawa General Store,** a Maui institution (see "Shops & Galleries," below).

On the green hills above Hana stands a 30-foot-high white cross made of lava rock. The cross was erected by citizens in memory of Paul Fagan, who founded the Hana Ranch as well as the hotel, and helped keep the town alive. The 3-mile hike up to **Fagan's Cross** provides a gorgeous view of the Hana coast, especially at sunset, when Fagan himself liked to climb this hill. See "Hiking & Camping," above, for details.

Most day-trippers to Hana miss the most unusual natural attraction of all: **Red Sand Beach.** Officially named Kaihalulu Beach, which means "roaring sea," everyone here calls it Red Sand Beach. It's easy to see why: The beach is as red as a Ferrari at a five alarm fire. It's really something to see. The beach is on the ocean side of Kauiki Hill, just south of Hana Bay, in a wild, natural setting on a pocket cove.

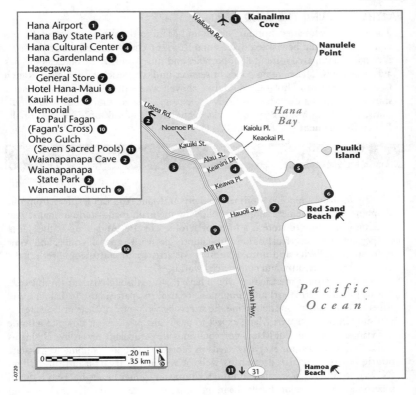

Hana Airport ❶
Hana Bay State Park ❺
Hana Cultural Center ❹
Hana Gardenland ❸
Hasegawa
  General Store ❼
Hotel Hana-Maui ❽
Kauiki Head ❻
Memorial
  to Paul Fagan
  (Fagan's Cross) ❿
Oheo Gulch
  (Seven Sacred Pools) ⓫
Waianapanapa Cave ❷
Waianapanapa
  State Park ❷
Wananalua Church ❾

Kauiki, a 390-foot-high volcanic cinder cone, lost its seaward wall to erosion and spilled red cinders everywhere to create the red sands. The only other red sand beach in the world is supposed to be in Iceland. Moah bettah you see Maui's.

To get there, walk south on Uakea Road, past the Hotel Hana-Maui to the end of the parking lot for Sea Ranch Cottages. Turn left, cross an open field, past an old Japanese cemetery, and follow a well-worn footpath a short distance down a narrow cliff trail. Or if you're staying at the Hana-Maui, walk to the very last cluster of Sea Ranch Cottages, turn left, and follow the coastal trail around Kauiki Head. In this private, romantic setting, some beachgoers shed their clothes, so try not to be offended.

JUST BEYOND HANA

About 10 miles past Hana is the Kipahulu section of **Haleakala National Park,** home to **Oheo Gulch,** also known as the Seven Sacred Pools. For details on this region of the park, see "Haleakala National Park" and "Hiking & Camping," above.

A mile past Oheo Gulch on the ocean side of the road is **Lindbergh's Grave.** First to fly across the Atlantic Ocean, Charles A. Lindbergh (1902–74) found peace in the Pacific; he settled in Hana, where he died of cancer in 1974. The famous aviator is buried under river stones in a seaside graveyard behind the 1857 **Palapala Hoomau Congregational Church,** where his tombstone is engraved with his own words: "If I take the wings of the morning and dwell in the uttermost parts of the sea . . . "

FARTHER AROUND THE BEND

Those of you who are continuing on around Maui to the fishing village of **Kaupo** and beyond should be warned that Kaupo Road, or Old Piilani Highway (Hi. 31), is rough and unpaved, often full of potholes and ruts. You may encounter wild pigs and stray cows. There are no goods or services until you reach **Ulupalakua Ranch** (see "Sightseeing in Up-Country Maui," above), where there's a winery, a general store and a gas station, which is likely to be closed. Ask around about road conditions, or call the **Maui Public Works Department** (☎ **808/248-8254**) or the **Police Department** (☎ **808/248-8311**).

12 Shops & Galleries

by Jocelyn Fujii

It's easy to make shopping a primary activity on Maui. You can leapfrog from one shopping mall to the next simply by following the main road—and rationalize that walking from store to store is a form of aerobic exercise. And Maui is the queen of specialty products: Kula onions, up-country protea, Kaanapali coffee, and some 4 dozen art galleries and untold numbers of artists and craftspeople reflect the island's thriving creative and commercial worlds.

As with any tourist destination, you'll have to wade through bad art (in this case, oceans of trite marine art) and mountains of trinkets, particularly in Lahaina and Kihei, where touristy boutiques line the streets between rare pockets of treasures. If you shop in south or west Maui, expect to pay resort prices, clear down to a bottle of Evian or sunscreen. But Maui's gorgeous finds are particularly rewarding. Residents work, live, and shop for everyday needs in central Maui and it's home to first-rate boutiques for specialized tastes as well: Wailuku has its own antiques alleys (N. Market and Main streets), and the Kaahumanu Center in neighboring Kahului is becoming more fashionable by the month. Also in Kahului is the $28 million Maui Arts and Cultural Center, a dream venue for the performing and visual arts, with two theaters and a 3,500 square-foot gallery. Up-country, Makawao's boutiques are worth seeking out.

A Creative Way to Spend the Day: The Art School at Kapalua

Make a bowl from clay or paint a premade one, then fire it and take it home. Or paint a picture, or learn ballet, or learn to sketch like the masters. West Maui's only art school, featuring local and visiting instructors, is open daily for people of all ages and skill levels. Classes in using your camera, sketching, painting on silk, throwing at the potter's wheel, and in the performing arts (ballet, creative dramatics, yoga, and the Pilates stretch for muscular development) are offered in a charming 1920s plantation building that was part of an old cannery operation in the heart of the Kapalua Resort. Costs range from $5 a class for nonmembers ($8 with supplies) for a children's creative-movement class to $325 for nonmembers for a twice-weekly, 4-week class in potting on the wheel and hand-building ceramics. Contact the **Art School at Kapalua,** Kapalua Resort (☎ **808/665-0007**).

CENTRAL MAUI

KAHULUI

Kahului's best shopping is concentrated in three places. Almost all of the shops listed below are at one of these centers:

Kaahumanu Center (Kaahumanu Ave.; ☎ **808/877-3369**) is a commercial hub only 5 minutes from the Kahului Airport. More manageable than Honolulu's Ala

Moana, with a thoughtful selection of food and retail shops, Kaahumanu covers all the bases, from the finest arts and crafts to a Foodland Supermarket, with everything in between: a thriving food court; the island's best beauty supply; mall standards like Sunglass Hut, The Gap, Radio Shack, Local Motion (surf and beach wear, including the current fad, women's board shorts, a combination of hot pants and men's surf trunks), and Tiger Lily (a women's boutique for fashionistas); department stores J.C. Penney, Liberty House, and Shirokiya; Penthouse, the beloved discount outlet for Liberty House; and Honsport, offering a large selection of sporting goods at low prices. Open Monday to Friday 9:30am to 9pm, Saturday 9:30am to 7pm, and Sunday 10am to 5pm.

Rough around the edges and dramatically eclipsed by the Kaahumanu Center down the street, **Maui Mall** (70 E. Kaahumanu Ave.; ☎ **808/877-7559**) is still a place of everyday good things, from Longs Drugs, which anchors the modest mall, to 60-minute photo processing and a Star Market.

Dining and upscale shopping seem to have sprouted up overnight in **Dairy Center** (385 Dairy Rd.), a commercial center on the way to the Kahului Airport. Who would've thought that Dairy Road would harbor chic boutiques and Maui's ultimate bathing-suit shop? Word is out that this part of Kahului is going from wallflower to swan with shops like Summerhill, recently moved from Paia; Kyras, with bathing suits from size 2 to 28 and an owner aiming to make it Maui's most complete bathing-suit line; Baby's Choice, for those too young to buy; and Shibui and Milagros, with carpets, gift items, ethnic interiors, and furniture—antique and new—imported from South America.

Caswell-Massey. Kaahumanu Center. ☎ 808/877-7761.

As America's oldest perfume company, established in 1752, Caswell-Massey triple-mills all its soaps (so they last three times longer), scents them with natural oils, and uses old-fashioned, tried-and-true methods and ingredients. Most notable for visitors is the impressive line of made-on-Maui perfumes, eight scents made of botanical (not synthetic) ingredients, ranging from Ginger and Plumeria to Victorian Vanilla. They prepare handsome, custom-designed baskets for no extra charge. You can hand-pick your selection from hundreds of specialty products, from the decadent Earth Treasures (bath salts with 23k gold flakes and gems, $30 to $70) to Damask rose shampoo and bath gels, eye creams, body lotions, old Swedish soaps, freesia bath gel, sachets, candles, perfume bottles, potpourris, room mists, oil lamps, and a dizzying array of pamperings.

Cost Less Imports. Maui Mall. ☎ 808/877-0300.

Natural fibers are everywhere in this tiny corner of the mall. Lauhala, sea-grass mats, bamboo blinds, grassy floor and window coverings, shoji-style lamps, burlap yardage, baskets, tactile Balinese cushions. Asian, Indonesian, and Polynesian imports, as well as top-of-the-line, made-on-Maui soaps and the Japanese cloth hangings called *noreng* attract buyers who love the clean simplicity, textures, and fragrances of Asia and the Pacific.

Lightning Bolt Maui Inc. 55 Kaahumanu Ave. ☎ 808/877-3484.

There's an excellent selection of women's board shorts, aloha shirts, swimwear, sandals and shoes, beach towels, and everything else needed for fun in the sun. Quality labels such as Patagonia and high-tech, state-of-the-art outdoor gear like Polartec sweaters and moccasins attract adventurers heading for the chilly hinterlands as well as the sun-drenched shores.

Lisa's Beauty Supply & Salon. Kaahumanu Center. ☎ **808/877-6463.**

Cosmetics are just the beginning: This shop is a sensory overload, with every conceivable item for a well-groomed life—every product you've seen or heard advertised, and many you've never heard of. These are professional products of high quality, at often lower-than-drugstore prices. If you've lost your emery boards or hairdryer, or have broken a nail or forgotten your favorite shampoo, Lisa's is a must. Browse among the shelves of Matrix, Paul Mitchell, Aveda, Joico, $2 eye crayons that are as good or better than name brands, hairbrushes and accessories, Sorme lipsticks, Jordana blush, Cici lip colors, aromatherapy oils, soaps, cosmetics cases, and countless other items that promise fragrant and impeccably groomed days ahead.

✪ **Maui Hands.** Kaahumanu Center. ☎ **808/877-0368.**

Maui hands have made most of the items in this tiny store. The assortment of arts and crafts includes paintings, prints, and fine art to toe rings and glow-in-the dark tops made of glass marbles (a tchotchke handsomer than it sounds) for $4. Of the 170 artists represented, 98% come from Maui, so this is an ideal stop for made-on-Maui products of decent quality. The koa ukulele by the Maui Ukulele Company is a treasure, but those with lesser budgets have plenty of choices: original watercolors, handcrafted jewelry of semiprecious stones (the fiery Sri Lankan moonstones are a find!), ipus (gourds for chanting and hula), raku pieces, fish rubbings, bamboo tongue drums ($30), hand-painted silk scarves, and, on the posh end, ultrasleek, meticulously crafted Norfolk pine bowls. For $20 you can buy a seashell picture frame, kitschy but not tacky, to frame your Maui memories.

The original Maui Hands remains in Makawao at The Courtyard, 3620 Baldwin Avenue (☎ **808/572-5194**).

✪ **Maui Swap Meet.** South Puunene Ave., next to Kahului Post Office. ☎ **808/877-3100.**

At Christmas, some 200 vendors line the fairgrounds; the rest of the year there are 100 to 150 booths, which still means it's a large and popular swap meet. Every Saturday from 7am to noon, they gather with their baked goods, local fruits and vegetables, crafts, resale goods, household items, and a plethora of homemade ethnic foods. "Maui people love to eat," says the event's coordinator, and you'll see what she means: Hawaiian apple strudel, banana bread, Filipino cascaron (coconut doughnuts), and, if the women from the local Hongwanji are there, Japanese pastries and manju galore. The Swap Meet is ablaze with fresh tropical flowers at friendly prices: gingers, heliconia, roses, orchids, protea, haku lei, and the full range of blooms in season. Admission is 50¢, and if you go before 7am while the vendors are setting up, no one will turn you away.

Serendipity. Kaahumanu Center. ☎ **808/871-1116.**

Container loads of Balinese crafts are streaming into Maui to appear in shops like this. Serendipity is well endowed in the natural fibers, warm tones, and the admirable workmanship of Bali, but don't expect Bali prices. A hand-carved wooden Buddha goes for under $2,000, an antique bench for $1,100, handsome leather and fiber bags, dowry chests, jewelry, urns, sarongs, rayon garments, and painted-wood, cat-shaped benches that can double as narrow tables, for $69.

Summerhouse. Dairy Center. ☎ **808/871-1320.**

We all knew that things were happening at Dairy Center when Paia's beloved Summerhouse, a longtime favorite of fashion slaves, moved there recently, bringing its cadre of customers with it. The move to Kahului, where residents live and work, brought a stronger focus on career dressing, but the casual, comfortable lines that made it a staple remain: wash-and-wear, silky rayons by Russell Berens, cool linens by Flax, fluttery rayons by URU, and name brands such as Nicole Miller, Avanti Silks, and Cafe shirts for men. A new line called Zingaro is already a hit, and Summerhouse's costume jewelry is already enlivening the Kahului office scene.

Tiger Lily. Kaahumanu Center. ☎ **808/871-2465.**

The boutique for well-dressed, well-heeled women has become much more mainstream in its tastes since it moved to this shopping center from a charming old building across the street. Who shops here? Women who go to parties, polo, gallery openings, four-star restaurants, and, yes, the office. Wrinkle-prone linens, wrinkleless cotton cashmeres, party dresses, sweaters, handbags, and worry-free garments for travel and leisure are well represented.

✪ **Ukulele Clothing Company.** Kaahumanu Center. ☎ **808/871-7290.**

Even with its limited selection, Ukulele remains one of Maui's most stylish sources of aloha wear. The Ukulele label of aloha shirts and dresses comes in rayons and cottons, in Hawaiian fabric prints, long- and short-sleeves, and strong statements such as the long-sleeved palaka shirt reminiscent of plantation life. Other labels, such as the ubiquitous (for good reason) Kahala, are judiciously selected and displayed.

WAILUKU

Just as they love to dine out, Mauians love to shop, and Wailuku, the old part of town, makes it easy for them to indulge their passion. Wailuku is the center of antiquing on Maui, and arguably all of Hawaii. Stroll along Main and Market streets and enter a varied world of nostalgia, kitsch, posh antiquities, humor, and collectible fervor. Some of the shops in Wailuku have classic antiques sharing space with light-hearted, borderline ephemera, or whimsical 1950s ashtrays in the shadow of priceless, centuries-old armoires.

Bird of Paradise Unique Antiques. 56 N. Market St., Wailuku. ☎ **808/242-7699.**

Owner Joe Myhand loves furniture, old Matson liner menus, blue willow china, kimonos for children, and anything nostalgic that happens to be Hawaiian. The furniture in the strongly Hawaiian collection ranges from 1940s rattan to wicker and old koa—those items tailor-made for kamaaina living and leisurely moments on the lanai. Myhand also collects bottles and mails his license plates all over the world. The collection ebbs and flows with his finds, keeping buyers waiting in the wings for his Depression glass, California pottery from the 1930s and 1940s (Bauer, Metlox, Vernon, Friscan ware, the occasional precious Roseville), old dinnerware, and occasionally, that vintage aloha shirt you can't live without.

✪ **Brown-Kobayashi.** 160-A N. Market St., Wailuku. ☎ **808/242-0804.**

This is an exquisite shop that exudes a sense of graceful living. Prices range from $2 to $7,000 in this 750-square-foot treasure trove. Asian antiques mingle quietly with old and new French, European, and Hawaiian objects, expressing an eclectic, yet cohesive, esthetic. Marc Kobayashi and Ronald Brown opened the shop in 1995 and word spread swiftly about their treasures: carved bamboo teapots, made by an aging master; the 1890s red lacquer Chinese bridal cabinet with large brass medallions and calligraphy pole; antique crystal, Peking glass, or rock coral jewelry; Matson liner menus; armoires, tables, desks, and one-of-a-kind furnishings for indoor-outdoor beachfront living or up-country chalets. One scholar's cabinet was inlaid with blackwood, the rare Chinese wood called hung-mu; others, of old koa, have flown out of the shop.

✪ **Jovian Gallery.** 7 N. Market St., Wailuku. ☎ **808/244-3660.**

Jovian is a dream gallery: It's as if owner Marcia Godinez teleported a sleek design atelier from Manhattan into the quaint streets of Wailuku. It's filled with Godinez's favorite things—and, thankfully for the rest of us, she has a remarkable sense of design. "I never bring anything in based on whether it's going to sell," she says. "If I really like it, we'll do okay with it." She loves courageous, iconoclastic artists like Deb Aoki, a brilliant and tender-hearted satirist who works in all media; painter Diana Lehr's lush landscapes; Fernando Elvira from Spain; Deybra, with her child-like renditions of cats and dogs; and designers of T-shirts, jewelry, ceramics, sculpture, and assorted gift items from all over the country—and, of course, Maui. Powerful pieces of handblown glass, voluptuous ceramic teapots, mesh knapsacks, provocative journals, and serious two-dimensional art express Godinez's hearty salute to the creative process.

Memory Lane. 130 N. Market St., Wailuku. ☎ **808/244-4196.**

The 1,500-square-foot showroom is filled with fine art, Hawaiian collectibles, Oriental antiques, kitsch, vintage textiles and aloha shirts, English crystal from the 1700s, Depression glass, antique silver, and furniture "from the very old to the 1950s and Federal," says the owner. Like all shop owners in Wailuku, Joe Ransberger, a painter, finds that old koa furniture is a rarity that flies out of the store to collectors, who must lie in wait. Some things he can't part with, such as the curly koa chest made in the 1800s, and some of the one-of-a-kind wood-pulp rayon textiles. Prices range from $1 to $30,000, with many pieces over $1,000. It's a treasure hunt from the moment you enter: One elderly man, searching for a needle for his antiquated 78 r.p.m. phonograph, miraculously found one here.

Traders of the Lost Art. 62 N. Market St., Wailuku. ☎ **808/242-7753.**

You'll have to wade through a dense landscape of collectibles and kitsch to ferret out that 100-year-old mahogany box made in Paris, or Matchbox cars from the 1970s, or trade-bead bracelets from Africa. Carpets from Katmandu, Hawaiian carvings, nautical Oceanic art, and a koa and mango loveseat with pheasant wood arms ($2,900) have been some of Traders' finds. You can also find postcards, expensive and inexpensive aloha shirts, and an occasional teak treasure in the musty recesses of this store.

CENTRAL MAUI EDIBLES

Star Market in the Maui Mall, **Foodland** in the Kaahumanu Center, and **Safeway** at 170 E. Kamehameha Ave. will satisfy your ordinary grocery needs. On Saturdays, you may want to check out the **Maui Swap Meet** (see above). A few sources of local specialties, flowers, health foods, and other mighty morsels are worth checking out:

The service isn't always the friendliest at **Down to Earth Natural Foods** (1910 Vineyard St.; ☎ **808/242-6821**), but no one can complain about the merchandise. Fresh organic Maui produce, a bountiful salad bar, sandwiches and smoothies, vitamins and supplements, freshly baked goods, chips and snacks, whole grains, and several packed aisles of vegetarian and health foods have made Down to Earth a health-food staple for many years.

Established in 1941, **Ooka Super Market** (1870 Main St., Wailuku.; ☎ **808/ 244-3931**), Maui's ultimate homegrown supermarket, is a mom-and-pop business that has grown by leaps and bounds but still manages to keep its neighborhood flavor. Ooka sells inexpensive produce (fresh Maui mushrooms for a song), Maui specialties such as manju and mochi, and a rainbow of potted and freshly cut flowers at the best prices in town. Protea cut the same day, freesias in season, hydrangeas, fresh lei, torch gingers from Hana, up-country calla lilies in season, and multicolored anthuriums comprise what is one of Maui's finest and most affordable retail flower selections. Prepared foods are also a hit: Bentos and plate lunches, roast chicken and laulau, and specialties from all the Islands abound. The fresh fish is always fresh, and the seaweed, poi, Hilo fern shoots, Kula persimmons, and dried marlin from Kona are among the local delicacies that make Ooka a favorite among residents and visitors.

Most of the space at **Shirokiya** (Kaahumanu Center; ☎ 808/877-5551) is devoted to food, with a well-stocked prepared-foods section, but check out the fresh produce (bananas, papayas), juices, health-food supplements, and home appliances and audio-video equipment as well. Dee Lite Bakery has a small corner, with its famous haupia cakes and other white-and-bright pastries, but most of the other foods are local or Japanese plate-lunch fare, offered in neatly packaged bento boxes or hot from the counter. Specialties such as Maui manju and Maui mochi are also available.

Located in the northern section of Wailuku, **Takamiya Market** (359 N. Market St., Wailuku; ☎ 808/244-3404) is much loved by local folks and visitors, who often drive all the way from Kihei to stock up on picnic fare and mouthwatering ethnic foods for sunset gatherings and beach parties. This is a highly recommended stop for all those with adventurous palates. Unpretentious home-cooked foods from East and West are prepared daily and served on Styrofoam plates from an ethnic smorgasbord. From the chilled-fish counter come fresh sashimi and poke, and in the renowned assortment of prepared foods are mounds of shoyu chicken, tender fried squid, roast pork, kalua pork, laulau, Chinese noodles, fiddlehead ferns, and Western comfort foods such as corn bread and potato salad. Fresh produce and paper products are also available, but it's the prepared foods that have made Takamiya's a household name in central Maui.

WEST MAUI
KAPALUA

Honolua Store. 502 Office Rd., next door to the Ritz-Carlton Kapalua. ☎ **808/669-6128.**

Walk on the old wood floors peppered with holes from golf shoes and find your everyday essentials: stationery, soft drinks, paper products, wines, snacks, fresh fruit and produce, and a take-out stand with sandwiches, plate lunches, and deli items. The corner Plantation Gallery carries aloha shirts and Hawaii-themed items like quilt-patterned wrapping paper, Maui onion mustard and pickled onions, and other made-on-Maui products.

Kapalua Shops. Kapalua Bay Hotel and Villas, Kapalua Resort. ☎ **808/669-1029.**

Shops have come and gone in this small, exclusive, and once chic shopping center, now much quieter than in days past. Tiny **Mandalay** still sells East-West luxe with its silk clothing and handful of interior accents. Kapalua old-timer **South Seas Trading Post** brims with exotic artifacts such as Balinese beads, tribal masks, jewelry, and stunning coconut-shell bowls with mother-of-pearl inlay. Proudly displayed recently was a lizard-skin wood drum, called kundu, sealed with "ceremonial pig's blood," for $825. Around the corner is **San Luigi,** where skins are for shoes. Mostly, though, the Italian shoetique has a small and not overwhelmingly expensive selection of Italian footwear in all grades of leather, fiber, and even futuristic plastic. In one of its many Maui locations, the sleek **Lahaina Galleries** occupies a corner of the mall with art works by Guy Buffet, Macedo, Andrea Smith, and others.

Village Galleries. 1 Ritz-Carlton Dr., Ritz-Carlton Kapalua. ☎ **808/669-1800.**

Village Galleries' recent 25th-anniversary celebration was an event worth noting in the fickle world of Maui art. Maui's finest exhibit their works here and in the other two Village Galleries in Lahaina. Take heart, art lovers: There's no clichéd marine art here. Translucent, delicately turned bowls of Norfolk pine gleam in the light, and George Allan, Betty Hay Freeland, Joyce Clark, Diana Lehr, and Pamela Andelin are among the pantheon of respected artists represented in the tiny gallery. Watercolors, oils, sculpture, handblown glass, Niihau shell lei, jewelry, and all media are represented. The Ritz-Carlton's monthly Artist-in-Residence program features Village Gallery artists in demonstrations and special workshops.

FROM KAPALUA TO KAANAPALI

Kahana Gateway is an unimpressive mall built to serve the condominium community that has sprawled along the coastline north of Kaanapali, before Kapalua. If you need a women's swimsuit, however, **Rainbow Beach Swimwear** is a find, boldly situated near the waistline-challenging dining mecca, Roy's Kahana Bar and Grill. At Rainbow, you'll find a wide selection of suits for all shapes, at lower-than-resort prices, slashed even further during their frequent (and welcome) sales.

KAANAPALI

Rhonda's Quilts. Hyatt Regency Maui. ☎ **808/667-7660.**

Dolls, children's clothing, locally made tiles in Hawaiian quilt patterns, books, stuffed animals, and an occasional antique kimono from Japan are scattered throughout this cheerful, cutesy store. The eclectic assortment includes a small selection of women's clothing among the antique quilts and Americana. The "Hawaiian" quilts, however, are a misnomer; they're actually made in the Philippines and sell at a fraction of what the real thing would cost; the quilt pillows ($80–$150) are made locally.

✪ **Sandal Tree.** Westin Maui. ☎ **808/667-5330.** Also at Hyatt Regency Maui. ☎ **808/661-3495.**

It's unusual for a resort shop to draw local customers on a regular basis (add time and parking costs to that pair of sandals); but Sandal Tree has a flock of footwear fanatics who come here from throughout the Islands for their chic kicks. Three of the six Sandal Tree resort shops throughout Hawaii are on Maui. (The third is at the Grand Wailea Resort.) They sell rubber thongs and topsiders, sandals and dressy pumps, athletic shoes and hats. Accessories range from fashionable knapsacks to indulgences such as a very undowdy octagonal handbag. Prices are realistic, too.

Whalers Village. 2435 Kaanapali Pkwy. ☎ **808/661-4567.**

Whalers Village has gone shockingly upscale. Once you've stood under the authentic whale skeleton or squeezed the plastic whale blubber at the **Whale Center of the Pacific** (see "Exploring the Island," above), you can blow a bundle at **Tiffany, Chanel, Gucci, Louis Vuitton, Coach, Sharper Image,** or any of the 70 shops and restaurants that have sprouted up in this beachfront shopping center. The posh Euro trend doesn't bode well; there's next to nothing here that's Hawaiian. Some of the village's mainstream possibilities: the **Body Shop** for the best and most globally conscious products for bath and home; **Hobie Hawaii** for swim and surf things; **Paradise Clothing** for Speedos and bathing suits; and **Canoe** for crisp, tasteful aloha shirts. **The Eyecatcher** has one of the most extensive selections of sunglasses on the island, located just across from the busiest **ABC** store in the state. The most comforting stop of all is the **Maui Yogurt Company,** where Maui-made Roselani ice cream is sold in mouthwatering flavors, including a bracing mint chocolate chip. The Village is open daily from 9:30am to 10pm.

LAHAINA

Lahaina's merchants and art galleries go all out on Friday night, when **Art Night,** from 6:30 to 9pm, evokes an extra measure of hospitality and community spirit. The Art Night openings are usually marked with live entertainment and refreshments and a livelier-than-usual street scene.

If you're in Lahaina on the second or last Thursday of each month, stroll by the front lawn of the **Baldwin Home,** corner of Front and Dickenson streets, for a splendid look at lei-making and an opportunity to meet the gregarious senior citizens of Lahaina. In a program sponsored by the American Association of Retired Persons, they gather from 10am to 4pm to demonstrate lei-making, sell their floral creations, and, equally important, to socialize.

Shopping Centers   Any day of the week, the waterfront shopping/dining complex at the southern end of Lahaina simply known as **505 Front Street** (☎ 808/ 667-0727) is a place to tuck into pizza (**Scaroles**), shop (**Foreign Intrigue Imports** and **Maui To Go**), attend Maui's best luau (the **Old Lahaina Luau;** see "Maui After Dark," below), have a sunset drink (**Old Lahaina Cafe**), buy art deco posters or rock-star paintings (**New York–Paris**), and ease into Avanti's popular retro-silk aloha shirts. It's not a large complex, and it gets mixed reviews, but surprises lurk in some corners.

What was formerly a big belching pineapple cannery is now a maze of shops and restaurants at the northern end of Lahaina town known as **Lahaina Cannery Mall** (1221 Honoapiilani Hwy.; ☎ 808/661-5304). Find your way through the T-shirt and sportswear shops to **Lahaina Printsellers,** home of rare maps, antique originals, prints, paintings, and wonderful 18th-to-20th century cartography representing the largest collection of engravings and antique maps in Hawaii. The scent of coffee will lead you to **Sir Wilfred's Coffee House** a few doors away, where you can unwind with espresso and croissants, or you can head for **Compadres Bar and Grill,** where the margaritas flow freely and the Mexican food is tasty. Artist **Guy Buffet** has his gallery here. For film, water, notebooks, aspirin, groceries, sunscreen, and other things you can't live without, nothing beats **Longs Drugs** and **Safeway,** two old standbys that anchor the Cannery.

Lahaina Center (900 Front St.; ☎ 808/667-9216) is north of Lahaina's most congested strip. Across the street from the center, the seawall is a much-sought-after front-row seat to the sunset. The shops reflect the nouveau bent of the center: **Banana Republic, Bebe Sport, Liberty House,** the **Hilo Hattie Fashion Center** (for inexpensive aloha wear), an **ABC Discount Store,** the **Blue Tropix** nightclub, and about a dozen other recreational, entertainment, and shopping prospects.

Foreign Intrigue Imports. 505 Front St. ☎ **808/667-4004.**

The large selection of interior accents puts a new spin on the often tired world of Balinese imports. Gorgeous hand-painted wooden trays, gilded Buddhas, oversize umbrellas, cat benches, chests and armoires of all sizes, and sturdy hemp pouches and accessories make the collection an intriguing one. Furniture, textiles, wood carvings, wall hangings, and hundreds of functional and nonfunctional accessories line the shop and reflect the mastery of detail that Balinese villagers possess. Shops like this, however, are best enjoyed by those who haven't been to Bali and thus won't compare prices between here and there.

✪ **Gallery Ltd.** 716 Front St. ☎ **808/661-0696.**

One of the beauties of Lahaina, the Gallery is easy to miss among the bright windows of Front Street. You'll need a good chunk of browsing time here; the jade and pearls alone could account for the better part of an afternoon. The Gallery is awash in gorgeous antiquities, from snuff bottles and netsuke to lacquer ware, jade carvings, Buddhas, scrolls, screens, and precious jewelry, most of it Chinese and Japanese. Antiques make up half of the impressive selection.

Martin Lawrence Galleries. Lahaina Market Place, 126 Lahainaluna Rd. ☎ **808/661-1788.**

The front is garish, with pop art, kinetic sculpture, and bright, carnivalesque glass objects. Toward the back of the gallery, however, there's a sizable inventory of two-dimensional art and some plausible choices for collectors of Keith Haring, Andy Warhol, and other controversial artists. The focus is on pop art and national and international artists; only one artist represented here is from Maui.

Maui to Go. 505 Front St. ☎ **808/667-2292.**

Shop here for high-quality, made-on-Maui products: plump sun-dried macadamia nuts (with no cholesterol), up-country jams in several flavors, Maui coffee, Maui teas and potpourris, Maui onion mustards and condiments, cookies, chocolates, and many other island delectables. Owners Colleen Noah-Marti and her husband, Gerard, make sure their shop is stocked with Maui's finest specialty products, but the selection isn't only for foodies. Other items from far-flung islands include fiber handbags, place mats, books, lauhala mats from the South Pacific, and other accessories for the home.

Lahaina Arts Society. 649 Wharf St. ☎ **808/661-0111.**

Not many people know that Lahaina's old harborside courthouse, in the shade of the block-sized banyan tree on Front Street, is the home of the 30-year-old Lahaina Arts Society, one of only two art societies on this art-drenched island. (The other, Hui No'eau, is located in up-country Makawao.) With its Banyan Tree Gallery upstairs and its Old Jail Gallery downstairs in the 1860s building, the LAS is a great place to view the works of Maui artists on a regular basis. The galleries are open daily, the exhibits change monthly. On weekends and holidays, artists who are members of the nonprofit organization spread out their works under the banyan tree. Their works, there and in the galleries, range from two- and three-dimensional art to jewelry and crafts, from $6 to $30,000. This isn't an exclusive organization, so the work is mixed. The 300-plus member artists range from beginners to Maui's luminaries (Betty Hay Freeland, George Allan), whose efforts help fund scholarships for high school students, benefits for the homeless, and many other good causes, including nine programs throughout Maui that teach art to children at risk.

Pebbles on the Beach. 867 Front St. ☎ **808/661-9002.**

There are more earrings than elbow room in this narrow boutique—but what fun to browse! This is one of the smallest and brightest windows on action-packed Front Street. Glittery costume jewelry and less flamboyant designs with gemstones and silver line the counters. There's a little Venice and a lot of Venice Beach in the boldness of the adornments, but even the most conservative shoppers admit that Pebbles will put a smile on your face.

✪ **Village Galleries in Lahaina.** 120 Dickenson St. ☎ **808/661-4402**; also at 180 Dickenson St. ☎ **808/661-5559.**

Twenty-five-year-old Village Galleries is the oldest continuously running gallery on Maui, and it's highly esteemed as one of the few galleries with consistently high standards. The selection of mostly original two- and three-dimensional art offers a good look at the quality of work emanating from the island. Collectors know Village Galleries as a respectable showcase for regional artists. (There's another location at the Ritz-Carlton; see p. 289.)

SOUTH MAUI
KIHEI

Kihei is one long strip of strip malls. Most of the shopping to be done here is concentrated in **Azeka Place** and **Azeka Place II** (more often called Azeka I and Azeka II), a stone's throw from each other on South Kihei Road. Fast foods abound at Azeka I—Blimpie Subs, Taco Bell, Pizza Hut, Baskin Robbins—as do tourist-oriented clothing shops like Crazy Shirts and the overly tropical Tropical Tantrum. Azeka II, the newer and glossier of the two, houses several noteworthy attractions, including the popular restaurant called A Pacific Cafe, the Liberty House department store, Penthouse (the beloved discount outlet for Liberty House), General Nutrition Center, and a cluster of specialty shops with everything from children's clothes to shoes, sunglasses, and swimwear. Also on South Kihei Road is the **Kukui Mall** with its movie theaters, Waldenbooks, Subway, Whaler's General Store, and Bernunzio's Bakery.

Some of the worthy shopping stops in Kihei:

Aloha Books. Kamaole Beach Center, 2411 S. Kihei Rd. ☎ **808/874-8070.**

Owner Tom Holland has been a collector and dealer in Hawaiian antiques, collectibles, and art, and his new bookstore reflects his passion. The shelves are stocked with books on and about Hawaii, particularly vintage Hawaiiana, and the walls are draped with vintage Hawaiian and Polynesian art. There are new, used, and rare books, and, although this isn't a big bookstore, the titles cover a range of tastes: *The National Lifeguard Manual, The Executive Diet, Impact of a Saint, Alfred Stieglitz,* guidebooks in Japanese, Jack London's *Tales of Hawaii,* and the usual best-selling Crichton paperbacks and Dick Francis whodunits. If there's an out-of-print Don Blanding or 1940s music sheet to be found in the neighborhood, it's likely to be here.

✪ **Hawaiian Moons Natural Foods.** 2411 S. Kihei Rd. ☎ **808/875-4356.**

Don't think of Hawaiian Moons as a place for only health foodies. It's a mini-supermarket with one of the best selections of made-on-Maui products I've encountered on the island, and is recommended for anyone who loves wholesome, unadulterated food that isn't boring. The Mexican Tortillas are made on Maui (and good!), and much of the produce here, such as organic vine-ripened tomatoes and organic onions, is grown in the fertile up-country soil of Kula. There's Ono Farms Organic Coffee grown in Hana, and a spate of Maui Teas by the Hawaiian Tea Company in Wailuku. Chocolate-covered macadamia nuts from Captain Cook are aptly named Tropical Temptations, and there are Tropical Gourmet Salsas to follow the Dave's 100% Natural muffins and cakes. Big Island tempeh (a sensible soybean meat substitute), eggs from up-country, Watler's Tofu and Volcano Spices (spicy garlic-lemon powdered seasonings) made on Maui, Maui bagels, Maui shiitake mushrooms, organic lemongrass and okra, Maui Crunch bread, free range Big Island turkeys and chickens (no antibiotics or artificial nasties), fresh Maui juices are some of the reasons for coming here. The deli dispenses tasty soups, hot specials, and salads, including the Thai tofu salad and a roasted potato salad. Cosmetics are also top-of-the-line: sunblocks, fragrant floral oils, healthy kukui-nut oil from Waialaua on Oahu, and the Island Essence made-on-Maui mango-coconut and vanilla-papaya skin lotions, the ultimate in body pampering.

Maui Sports & Cycle. Dolphin Plaza, 2395 S. Kihei Rd. ☎ **808/875-2882;** also at Longs Center, 1215 S. Kihei Rd. ☎ **808/875-8448.**

South Maui's new water-sports retail and rental shop is a hit among beachgoers and water-sports enthusiasts. A friendly, knowledgeable staff helps you choose from among the mind-boggling selection of snorkel gear, boogie boards, kayaks, beach umbrellas, coolers, and view boards for "snorkeling lying down." The snorkel gear is of high quality, and with a selection so extensive you can tailor your choice to your budget as well as your fit. Prescription masks are available, as are underwater cameras, sunscreens and lotions, jewelry, T-shirts, postcards, and a huge selection of hats, and visors by the bushel.

Old Daze. Azeka I, 1280 S. Kihei Rd. ☎ **808/875-7566.**

Up-country interior decorators have discovered Kihei's new attraction, a colorful shop of Hawaiian collectibles and American antiques. If the Hawaiian silver collectible spoons don't strike you, perhaps the rag dolls or carved tiki-god ashtrays will. The collection features a modest furniture selection, Hawaiian pictures, 1960s ashtrays, Depression glass, old washboards, souvenir plates from county fairs, and an eclectic assortment of items for table and home. Choices range from hokey to rustic to pleasantly nostalgic, with many items for the kitchen.

WAILEA

Shopping in Wailea is limited to upscale resort shops that sell specialty items to carry you from breakfast to sailing to a super-luxe dinner. **Sandal Tree** (see Kaanapali, above), with its affordable-and-up designer wear, raises the footwear banner at the Grand Wailea Resort, while stores like **Mandalay,** in Grand Wailea Shops and the Four Seasons Resort Maui, specialize in sumptuous Thai silks and Asian imports, from resort wear to the very dressy. More Wailea highlights:

Coast Gallery Wailea. Aston Wailea Resort, 3700 Wailea Alanui Dr. ☎ **808/879-2301.**

From its inception in the mid-1980s, Coast has maintained a high profile and level of esteem for its well-balanced mix of local, national, and international artists. Wood carvings, feather art, oil paintings, jewelry, bronze sculpture, prints, ceramics, and tasteful marinescapes reflect the discriminating tastes of the gallery owners, who include old masters and new talent in the selected works. This is a powerful and attractive venue for Island artists, who are well represented in the collection.

Grand Wailea Shops. Grand Wailea Resort, 3850 Wailea Alanui Dr. ☎ **808/875-1234.**

The gargantuan Grand Wailea Resort has always been known for its long arcade of shops and galleries tailored to hefty pocketbooks. **Cartier, Lahaina Printsellers** (the premier store for old maps and prints), **Dolphin Gallery, Mandalay, Sandal Tree,** the blindingly white resort shop called **Cruise,** and the **Napua Gallery,** which houses the private collection of the resort owner, are some of the shops that line the arcade.

✪ **Mango Club.** Kea Lani Hotel, 4100 Wailea Alanui Dr. ☎ **808/874-1885.**

Shop here for the hip retro look; there are treasures on those racks of aloha shirts, vintage muumuus, 1940s tea-timer tops, and contemporary silk aloha shirts in authentic fabric prints from the 1920s to 1940s. Draped on the walls are collectible treasures with collectible prices, such as aloha shirts and Chinese-collared muumuus from the 1940s in vintage rayon. A dress or aloha shirt in good shape could carry a price tag in the hundreds of dollars, but the Avanti modern retros offer the same look in silk crepe at a fraction the price. Bali cloth shoes, picture frames, Baik Baik Balinese men's shirts, and the popular Pau Hana line of vintage-looking dresses have customers scrambling for their credit cards.

Wailea Shopping Village. 3750 Wailea Alanui Dr.

Wailea's only shopping complex is a mediocre assemblage of usually empty boutiques, a couple of galleries and gift shops, and the ubiquitous **Whalers General Store,** where people shop for macadamia nuts, newspapers, postcards, ice, sunscreen, Hawaiian teas, and wines at inflated prices. Otherwise, the center is filled with the likes of **Su-Su's Boutique** (resort wear); **Lahaina Galleries,** which has three other locations on the island; **For Your Eyes Only,** a sunglass boutique; and **Mephisto Maui** for high-priced, quality French footwear for scaling Haleakala and the back trails of the island. Two bright spots in this complex are **The Elephant Walk** gift shop, where you can find quilted palaka house slippers, Lilikoi Gold Passion Fruit Butter, and gorgeous coconut lidded bowls; and the tiny **Wailea Espresso,** a kiosk near the parking lot where cappuccino and cinnamon rolls move briskly.

UP-COUNTRY MAUI: MAKAWAO

Besides being a shopper's paradise, Makawao is the home of the island's most prominent arts society, **Hui No'eau Visual Arts Center** (2841 Baldwin Ave.; ☎ **808/572-6560**). Designed in 1917 by C. W. Dickey, one of Hawaii's most prominent architects, the two-story, Mediterranean-style stucco home that houses the center is located on a sprawling, manicured 9-acre estate. A tree-lined driveway leading there features Maui's two tallest Cook Island pines. Also a part of the estate is a former sugar mill that was at one time run by mule power. A legacy of Maui's prominent kamaaina, Harry and Ethel Baldwin, the estate became an art center in 1976 and remains a complete esthetic experience. Visiting artists offer lectures, classes, and demonstrations, all at reasonable prices, in basketry, jewelry-casting, glass blowing, clay, woodblocks, painting, and all conceivable media. Hui No'eau is in a class by itself in Hawaii; Maui artists long to exhibit here, considering it the most prestigious of venues.

Hurricane. 3639 Baldwin Ave. ☎ **808/572-5076.**

Makawao's newest attraction is a small, split-level boutique with gleaming knotty-pine floors and a cache of finds with intriguing labels. Hemp skirts by Two Star Dog, handmade cloth coasters by Two Fish, earrings by Stick It In Your Ear, and fabulous two-color pareu-print shirts for women by Toes on the Nose are a few of the items that make browsing here a form of entertainment. Lining the entrance are Kahala aloha shirts and dresses by Avi Kiriaty, best-selling fine artist whose block prints (also carried in the store) are brilliantly translated into fabric. Felt and fiber hats, chenille throws, Sigrid Olsen dresses and T-shirts (a pricey $41 for a T-shirt!), and a head-turning assortment of books, bamboo vases, art deco clocks, and hemp-and-leather knapsacks are a few of our favorite things.

✪ **The Mercantile.** 3673 Baldwin Ave. ☎ **808/572-1407.**

A Makawao must, Mercantile carries the most seductive selection in town for men and women who pamper their homes as much as themselves. You'll find the most sumptuous soaps in Hawaii (vetiver, honey, and lavender from Provence), Chinese needlepoint rugs, all-cotton down sofas, and breathtaking Tiffany-style table and floor lamps in opihi shells and stained glass. Mercantile is also the only showcase in Hawaii for the pure and good bath products of Kiehl's Pharmacy in Manhattan. There's casual, easy-care clothing, linens, Italian lamps, an 1800s wooden chest, and less expensive choices such as koa hair sticks, silk eye pillows filled with flax seeds, scented neck pillows, and an eye-catching section of Bopla dinnerware, decorated by different designers and made of durable hotel porcelain. Flatware, Finnish crystal,

Maui teas and candies, and organically grown Ono Farms coffee from Kipahulu, Maui, also salute the good life. Don't forget the counter near the entrance, with its French pens of marvelous heft and extravagant Laguiole pocket knives.

✪ **Ola's.** Paniolo Bldg., 1156 Makawao Ave. ☎ **808/573-1334.**

Doug Britt's scintillating paintings and the photographs by his wife, Sharon, line the walls of Makawao's new attraction. The Britts own Ola's on Kauai and helped set up Makawao's version, under different ownership (sisters Cindy Heacock and Shari O'Brien) but designed around the same concept of handmade American-made art by more than 100 artists, including Hawaii's best. Ola's is a bright, crisp, uncluttered, and thoughtfully designed space with a beach-glass counter, concrete floors, and objects that look great, feel good, and have varying degrees of utility. There's the koa-maple checkerboard, a masterpiece of detail; the melodious thumb pianos, called strumsticks; elegant Lundberg studio glass, including a celestial lamp; cards; jewelry; and exquisite porcelain vases, with Picassoesque anatomical features, by Donna Polseno. Chopsticks, silks, glass, wood, ceramics, bath products . . . You'd think chocolate would be over the top—but this is the sole purveyor of Bella's at Ola's, a line of fourth-generation, handmade chocolates from Brooklyn, offered in 12 varieties in milk and semisweet: vanilla Italian cream, Champagne truffles, half-dipped glazed Australian apricots, chocolate-covered candied ginger, and others, at $18.50 a pound.

Home Collections. 3669 Baldwin Ave. ☎ **808/572-8507.**

Up-country women have a penchant for home decorating, and this is the one place they find fresh Kula flowers, garden implements, furniture, glassware, candles, and a large selection of woven area rugs. "Hawaiian" quilts made in the Philippines (less expensive than those made in Hawaii) reflect an unfortunate trend of sacrificing authenticity for affordability, but the owners are candid about the trade-off, and the quality is acceptable. Candles, Body Time beauty products, coconut implements, glassware, dinnerware, and other unique gifts for self and home reflect the buyer's enthusiasm for bringing the rest of the world to Makawao.

Viewpoints Gallery. 3620 Baldwin Ave. ☎ **808/572-5979.**

Maui's only fine arts cooperative showcases the work of dozens of Maui artists in an airy, attractive gallery located in a restored theater with a courtyard, glass-blowing studio, and restaurants. Viewpoints features two-dimensional art, jewelry, fiber art, stained glass, papermaking, sculpture, and other media.

UP-COUNTRY EDIBLES

Working folks in Makawao who long to eat in arrive at **Rodeo General Store** (3661 Baldwin Ave.; ☎ **808/572-7841**) to pick up their spaghetti and lasagna, sandwiches, salads, and changing specials from the deli. Even in their plastic-wrapped paper trays, the pastas are tasty, as if they came from a neighborhood trattoria in Little Italy. You can pick up all the necessary accompaniments here, from fresh produce, wine, and soft drinks to paper products and fabulous baked goods.

Down to Earth Natural Foods (1169 Makawao Ave.; ☎ **808/572-1488**) always has fresh salads and sandwiches at the salad bar, a full section of organic produce (Kula onions, strawberry papayas, mangos and litchis in season), bulk grains, vitamins and supplements, beauty aids, herbs, juices, snacks, condiments, tofu, seaweed, soy products, and aisles of vegetarian and health foods—canned, packaged, prepared, and fresh. Whether it's a smoothie, Ginger Blast, or burrito, you'll find it here.

Untold numbers have creaked over the wooden floors to pick up Komoda's famous cream puffs in the more than 6 decades that **T. Komoda Store and Bakery** (3674 Baldwin Ave.; ☎ 808/572-7261) has spent in this spot. Oldtimers know to come early, or the cream puffs will be sold out. Then the cinnamon rolls, doughnuts, pies, chocolate cake, and assorted edibles take over, keeping the aromas of fresh baking wafting through the old store. Pastries aren't all; Maui potato chips, poi, candies, and small bunches of local fruit in season keep the customers coming.

FRESH FLOWERS IN KULA

Like anthuriums on the Big Island, proteas are a Maui trademark and an abundant crop on Haleakala's rich volcanic slopes. They also travel well, dry beautifully, and can be shipped worldwide with ease. Among Maui's most prominent sources are **Sunrise Protea** (☎ 808/876-0200) in Kula. It has a walk-through garden and gift shops and provides friendly service and a larger-than-usual selection. If you want the freshly cut flowers, they arrive from the fields on Tuesday and Friday afternoons. **Proteas of Hawaii** (☎ 808/878-2533) is another reliable source that offers regular walking tours of the University of Hawaii Extension Service gardens across the street in Kula. **Clouds Rest Protea** (☎ 808/878-2544) has a garden and extensive selection, and will ship anywhere in the United States.

For flower shopping from other parts of Maui, **Ooka Super Market** (see p. 368) and the Saturday morning **Maui Swap Meet** (see p. 366) are the best and least expensive places for tropical flowers of every stripe.

EAST MAUI

ON THE HANA ROAD: PAIA

Hula Girl Antiques. 71 Baldwin Ave., Paia. ☎ 808/579-8700.

The name captures the spirit of this shop. Vintage Hawaiiana is the owners' passion; they've scoured estate sales and private collections for aloha shirts, muumuus, 1950s tablecloths, out-of-print books, Hawaiian sheet music, old maps and ephemera, four-strand rattan furniture, and every conceivable piece of nostalgia relating to Hawaii. Dolls are big here: Raggedy Anns, old storybook dolls, Oriental dolls, pincushion dolls. Old hats, estate jewelry and rhinestones, collectible silver spoons, and antique obis also have a presence in the sizable shop, but it's the salt-and-pepper shakers that stand out. There are sea shells, animals, Hawaiian floral kitsch from the 1950s, and an array of colorful, humorous sets that creative up-country folks have built theme dinners around.

Katie's Place Gifts & Collectibles. At Baldwin Ave. and Hana Hwy., Paia. ☎ 808/579-8660.

More hula dolls! Find the wiggling collectibles here for $65 to $150 to go with the Don Blanding dinnerware (popular and hard to find), Depression glass, salt-and-pepper shakers, Matson liner menus, music sheets, vintage 1940s bark cloth curtains, tablecloths and linens, and countless other snippets of the past. Ephemera and textiles galore, with prices ranging from $10.95 to $60. As with all collectibles shops, there are things for both serious and whimsical collectors, and the selection changes constantly.

Maui Crafts Guild. 43 Hana Hwy., Paia. ☎ 808/579-9697.

The old wooden storefront at the gateway to Paia houses local crafts of high quality and in all price ranges, from pit-fired raku to bowls of Norfolk pine and other Maui woods fashioned by Maui hands. Weavings, basketry, scarves, jewelry, bamboo flutes, koa accessories, prints, paintings, pressed flowers, and hundreds of items are displayed in the rustic two-story gift gallery. This is a recommended stop for unique gifts to go; they ship anywhere, and all artists are selectively screened.

Nuage Bleu. 76 Hana Hwy., Paia. ☎ **808/579-9792.**

Casual to dressy women's clothing, French bath products, ceramics, glassware, children's clothing, accessories and handbags, and an eclectic blend of indulgences make up the offerings of this longtime Paia fixture. Although it's a trendy store with a focus that changes with prevailing tastes, there's always a level of style here.

EDIBLES ON THE ROAD TO HANA

A golden retriever named Mahi holds court with his growing public at **Maui Grown Market** (914 Hana Hwy., Paia; ☎ **808/572-1693**). As much of an attraction as the Maui produce sold here, Mahi has a gregarious nature that prompts some dog-sick visitors to take her to Hana for the day. But the friendly country-store holds its own, with avocado trees, a white picket fence, and picnic tables on a deck. Maui produce abounds: fresh bananas, papayas, starfruit, chirimoyas, pineapples, tomatoes, onions, mangoes in season, lettuces, and whatever can be harvested from all corners of the island. Jams made in Makawao and Maui onion mustards are big sellers, as well as the sandwiches drenched in homemade dressings. There are many options for the 54-mile Hana drive, among them the Hana box lunches in coolers loaned for the day for a returnable $5 deposit.

Homegrown aloha is what you'll find at the roadside oasis known as **Uncle Harry's Hawaiian Crafts and Fresh Fruits** (on the Hana Hwy., Keanae; ☎ **808/248-7019**) about halfway to Hana. Local papayas, bananas, lilikoi, coconut, and other produce from the region are sold at this Keanae landmark, a legacy of the late Uncle Harry Mitchell, a local legend and respected Hawaiian elder who devoted his life to the Hawaiian-rights and nuclear-free movements. You can browse among the wood carvings and Hawaiian crafts and stock up on smoothies, chips, and snacks for the road.

HANA

✪ **The Hana Coast Gallery.** Hotel Hana-Maui. ☎ **808/248-8636.**

Tucked away in the lush folds of this posh hideaway hotel, the gallery is known for its high level of curatorship and commitment to the cultural art of Hawaii. One section of the 3,000-square-foot gallery is called The Library, containing works of Rembrandt, Renoir, and other old masters, but the rest is a paean to original Island art and the master crafts of Hawaii. Fifty-three well-established Hawaii artists display their sculptures, paintings, prints, feather work, stone work, carvings, and three-dimensional works in displays that are so natural they could well exist in someone's home. The strong presence of native Hawaiian artists lends cultural weight to the aesthetic statement. We recommend that you make this gallery one of your reasons for going to Hana; it's an esthetic and cultural experience that informs while it enlightens.

Hasegawa General Store. Hana Hwy. ☎ **808/248-8231.**

Established in 1910, immortalized in song since 1961, burned to the ground in 1990, and back in business in 1991, this legendary store is indefatigable and more colorful than ever in its third generation in business. The aisles are choked with a maze of merchandise that includes Hana-blend coffee specially roasted and blended for the store, Ono Farms organic dried fruit, fishing equipment, every tape and CD that mentions Hana, the best books on Hana to be found, Maui potato chips, T-shirts, beach and garden essentials, mugs, baseball caps, film, baby food, napkins, and a tangle of marvelous miscellany.

13   Maui After Dark

by Jocelyn Fujii

The island's most prestigious entertainment venue is the $28-million **Maui Arts and Cultural Center** in Kahului (☎ 808/242-7469), a long-awaited, first-class center for the visual and performing arts. Don't laugh, but it's as precious to Maui as the Met is to New York, with a visual arts gallery, an outdoor amphitheater, offices, rehearsal space, a 300-seat theater for experimental performances, and a 1,200-seat main theater. Since its 1994 opening, the state-of-the-art facilities have attracted first-rate performers and sold-out shows, from Tony Bennett to Hawaii's premier cultural event of the decade, the Halau o Kekuhi's riveting five-act saga of Pele's migration, called "Holo Mai Pele." The Maui Symphony Orchestra, the Hawaii International Film Festival's Maui venue, and the Maui Academy of Performing Arts are among the cultural entities housed at the center. Whether it's hula, the Iona Pear Dance Company, Willie Nelson, or Hawaiian music icon Keali`i Reichel, only the best will appear at the Maui Arts and Cultural Center. The center's activities are well-publicized locally, so check the *Maui News* or ask the hotel concierge what's going on at the center during your visit.

Hawaiian Music

With a few exceptions (Makawao's **Casanova** and **Wunderbar** in Paia), your other nightlife options for live entertainment are pretty much limited to the resort areas, where the major hotels generally have lobby lounges offering regular Hawaiian music, soft jazz, or hula shows beginning at sunset. If the duo called Hapa or the soloist called Keali'i Reichel are playing anywhere on their native island, don't miss them; they're a Hawaiian music bonanza, among the finest Hawaiian musicians around today.

Jazz & Blues

To find out what's happening in blues or jazz, look in at **La Pastaria** in Kihei. They seem to be the nightlife nexus for this genre, with quality music and overflow crowds that linger into the wee hours. The thriving blues scene throughout Hawaii can be credited to the efforts of Louie Wolfenson and the **Maui Blues Association,** which books sold-out events at clubs throughout the state. Check the papers to see what's on while you're on Maui. Their annual Memorial Day blues festival on Maui grows by the year and is worth tracking down.

Movies

Film buffs can check the local newspapers to see what's playing at the few theaters around town: **Kaahumanu Theatres** in Kaahumanu Center (☎ 808/873-3133); **Maui Theatre** in Kahului Shopping Center (☎ 808/877-3560); **Kukui Mall Theater** at 1819 S. Kihei Rd. (☎ 808/875-4533); and **Wallace Theatres** in Lahaina (☎ 808/661-3347), at Wharf Cinema Center, 658 Front St., and the new Front Street Theatres at the Lahaina Center, 900 Front St.

CENTRAL MAUI: KAHULUI

It's awfully quiet in these parts, but when last we checked, **Stanton's** (☎ 808/877-3711) in the Maui Mall was gearing up to fill central Maui's late-night void with live entertainment—jazz, blues, rock—on Friday and Saturday nights and Sunday afternoon jam sessions.

WEST MAUI: LAHAINA

In west Maui, the only real after-dark action is at **Blue Tropix Nightclub** (☎ 808/667-5309), located upstairs and past the pool hall at the Lahaina Center (900 Front St.). What used to be Lahaina's biggest dance floor is now the town's only dance floor, a scene that pulses with heavy metal, retro relapses, and 1960s, 1970s, and 1980s music—live and disco—on various theme nights. "Polyester Playground," "Disco Inferno," "Live rock-and-roll with The Missionaries," and reggae parties are some of the witty themes and groups featured at this Lahaina hot spot. It's open from 8pm to 2am Thursday through Monday; Tuesday and Wednesday are for special events and private parties. Expect a $5 cover charge nightly after 9pm and half-price drinks after 10pm, except for special evenings. No tank tops or rubber slippers.

Longhi's (☎ 808/667-2288) in Lahaina recently discontinued its Friday and Saturday night live jazz, but an occasional special gig can be expected if ultracool rock-and-rollers or jazz musicians who are friends of the owner happen to be passing through. It wouldn't hurt to ask what's happening there.

You won't have to ask what's happening at **Cheeseburger in Paradise** (☎ 808/661-4855), the two-story green-and-white building at the corner of Front and Lahainaluna streets. Just go outside and you'll hear it: loud, live, and lively tropical rock blasting into the streets and out to sea daily from 4:30 to 11pm.

SOUTH MAUI: WAILEA & KIHEI

The Grand Wailea Resort's **Tsunami** (☎ 808/875-1234), Maui's most high-tech club, happens to be south Maui's only nightspot for dancing. But what a club: 10,000 square feet, marble, with a state-of-the-art hydraulic dance floor pulsing with laser lights, huge video screens, futuristic decor, and well-dressed revelers. It's all disco, no live music, and is closed on Monday and Tuesday. From Wednesday through Sunday, the DJ plays everything from 1980s hits to top-40 on weekends. Thursday is ladies' night: no cover charge for women, drink specials, and a flower or other memento for the wily females who turn out to "dress and impress." Otherwise, the cover charge is $5 on Friday and $10 on Saturday. Open Friday and Saturday 9pm to 4am, Wednesday until 1am.

Our favorite in Wailea is the **lobby bar at the Kea Lani Hotel** (☎ 808/875-4100), an intimate, sophisticated, open-air lounge that has established itself as an ideal spot for meeting friends and relaxing over fine libations and music. If Passion and Grace are playing, don't miss them; they're a mainland group with strong Maui ties who attract family and friends from all over the island for stellar light jazz with a Latin beat. The lounge is open Thursday and Sunday from 5:30 to 10:30pm, and Friday and Saturday until 11pm. Everything from mellow pianists to world-renowned guitarists have filled this cozy corner with music.

Kihei is Maui's blues pulse, and since Stella Blues discontinued its live music altogether, **La Pastaria** (☎ 808/879-9001) is the only game in town. And what a venue it is. The cozy trattoria offers pasta and jazz nightly and remains a magnet for the arts and music cognoscente, who gather for Broadway dinner theater, jazz, blues, Hawaiian music, and surprise guests. The music emanating from the corner stage is first-rate, and the feeling of informality and intimacy prompts high-energy improvisation and family-style jamming on those nights when visiting bands are featured. There are several levels to the music scene here: piano bar, light jazz, and classics, nightly 6:30 to 9:30pm; late-night entertainment Monday to Thursday 9:30pm to 12:30am; and dinner theater the last Wednesday of every month, which could be anything from *Broadway à la Carte* to *Phantom of the Opera* and other musical revues, from 6:30 to 9:30pm. La Pastaria is also one of Kihei's most popular

An Intimate Affair: Luau, Maui Style

Most of the larger hotels in Maui's major resorts offer luau and Polynesian entertainment on a regular basis. You'll pay about $55 or more to attend one, and to protect yourself from disappointment, don't expect it to be a homegrown affair prepared in the traditional Hawaiian way. The labor-intensive nature of this traditional Hawaiian feast makes it an impossible endeavor for large-scale commercial operations offered on a regular basis. There are, however, commercial luaus that capture the romance and spirit of the affair with quality food and entertainment in outdoor settings:

Maui's best luau is indisputably the nightly **Old Lahaina Luau,** on the beach side of 505 Front St. in Lahaina (☎ **808/667-1998**). This is the consummate luau, with a healthy balance of entertainment, showmanship, good food, educational value, and sheer romantic beauty. It begins at sunset, on a grassy lawn with a view of Kahoolawe, Molokai, and Lanai, and features Tahitian and Hawaiian entertainment, including ancient hula and an intelligent narrative on its rocky course of survival into modern times. The entertainment is riveting, even for jaded locals, and the Hawaiian maiden who emerges from the darkness in a torch-lit canoe heading for shore elicits sighs of admiration. A local Hawaiian family caters the food: imu-roasted kalua pig, lomi salmon, poi, dried fish, poke, breadfruit, sweet potato, and, for the more cautious, teriyaki steak, barbecued chicken, and mahimahi. Cost is $57 plus tax; they're often booked a week in advance, so call ahead. By some standards, the size of the luau—250 maximum—is considered small.

In Hana, the **Hotel Hana-Maui** (☎ **808/248-8211**) hosts a Tuesday night luau that's even more intimate, with usually about 40 to 50 guests. Guests ride to Hamoa Beach in a shuttle from the hotel and spend the evening with casual, family-style entertainment with special touches that can only occur in a remote rural setting like Hana. The food is authentically Hawaiian, and when the kalua pig is unearthed (with bare hands!), guests can get close to the smoking pit. Cost is $55.09.

For other resort luaus, check with your concierge to see what's recommended and close to you. In west Maui, other resort luaus include those at the Royal Lahaina Resort, the Maui Marriott, and the Hyatt Regency Maui. South Maui's Wailea features a luau or some kind of Polynesian entertainment at the Aston Wailea Resort, Grand Wailea Resort, and Renaissance Wailea Beach Resort.

If you'd like to be prepared for your luau, head over to **Wailea Shopping Village** (3750 Wailea Alanui Dr.), where free hula lessons are offered every Wednesday; there's also Polynesian entertainment every Tuesday.

restaurants for lunch and dinner (see "Dining," above), so it's a good bet in more ways than one. Popular local musician Willie K., the Eric Gilliom Project (a funk band), and Passion and Grace from San Francisco and Maui are among the headliners who have made this spot an after-dark mecca.

ON THE HANA HIGHWAY: PAIA

In Paia, on the Hana Highway only 15 minutes from Kahului, the **Wunderbar** (☎ **808/579-8808**) jumps with live music and dancing Thursday, Friday, and Saturday after 10pm, and Sunday from 3 to 6pm. Reggae, rock, and the blues riffs of local and visiting musicians fill the courtyard and the streets of Paia. This European-style restaurant also offers live piano music during weekend dinner hours.

UP-COUNTRY MAUI: MAKAWAO

Up-country in Makawao, the partying never ends at **Casanova** (☎ **808/572-0220**), the popular Italian ristorante (see "Dining," above) where the good times roll with the pasta. If a big-name mainland band is resting up on Maui following a sold-out concert on Oahu, you may find its members setting up for an impromptu night here. On Maui, word spreads quickly. DJs take over on Wednesday (ladies' night) and Thursday nights. Every other Thursday is a fund-raiser for the Maui Aids Society, and Friday and Saturdays, live entertainment draws fun-lovers from even the most remote reaches of the island. Entertainment starts at 9:45pm and continues to 12:30 or 1am. Expect good blues, rock-and-roll, reggae, jazz, Hawaiian, and the top names in local and visiting entertainment. Elvin Bishop, the local duo Hapa, Los Lobos, and many others have filled Casanova's stage and limelight.

Molokai, the Most Hawaiian Isle

8

Molokai is often called the last *real* Hawaiian place. That idea may conjure up romantic visions of bare-breasted hula dancers, fierce golden-skinned warriors, and endless nights of torch-lit luaus, but think again: The reality is something else entirely.

Formed by two volcanoes, the long, narrow island is the result of a merger that didn't quite work out—one side is hot, dry, and flat, like Mexico; the other is lush, green, and steepled, like Tahiti. It's a schizophrenic island that's always described in negatives: Molokai has no Disneyesque fantasy resorts, no fancy restaurants, no stoplights or movie theaters, no air conditioners or Golden Arches, and no buildings taller than a coconut tree. And that's all to the good, for less is more on Molokai, Hawaii's last raw outpost (if you don't count Niihau or Kahoolawe—and I don't).

The cradle of Hawaiian dance, aquaculture, and sacred rites, Molokai lives on its reputation as the most Hawaiian place chiefly through its lineage; there are, in fact, more people here of Hawaiian blood than on any other island. The residents cling to an old-style life of subsistence, taking fish from the sea and hunting wild pigs and Axis deer on the range. Some folks still catch reef fish in throw nets and troll the reef for squid, a traditional Hawaiian delicacy.

The simple life of the people and the absence of contemporary landmarks is what attracts those in search of the "real" Hawaii. But what makes them stand in awe is this little island's diverse natural wonders: Hawaii's highest waterfall and greatest collection of fishponds; the world's tallest sea cliffs; plus sand dunes, coral reefs, rain forests, hidden coves—and empty, gloriously empty beaches.

Exploring the "Real" Hawaii   A long, thin island only 38 miles tip-to-tip and 10 miles wide, Molokai stands like a big green wedge in the blue Pacific. It has an east side, a west side, a backside, and a topside. It also has one of the sorriest-looking settlements in all of Hawaii—and it's not the old leper colony of Kalaupapa, whose shy residents keep a clean house.

The few tourists are separated from the adventurers at Hoolehua, Molokai's tin-roofed, lava rock airport. Those who deplane in boots—hiking or cowboy—are going one place, and those in tasseled loafers or white tennies are heading for quite another. Most everyone ends up barefoot on the beach, but the transition is toughest on city slickers.

On the red dirt southern plain, where most of the island's 6,000 residents live, the funky village of Kaunakakai looks like a Hollywood film set of a ghost town. With sun-faded clapboard structures on a three-block grid, this decrepit island capital has gone beyond the limits of rustic charm: Old houses are propped up with car jacks, junk cars rust in front yards, and horses stand tethered in tall grass by the side of the road. At mile marker zero, in the center of town, the island is divided into East and West so dramatically that an arid cactus desert lies on one side, and a lush coco-palm jungle on the other.

Eastbound, along the coastal highway named for King Kamehameha V, are Gauguin-like, palm-shaded cottages, set on small coves or near fishponds; spectacular vistas that take in Maui, Lanai, and Kahoolawe; and a fringing coral reef visible through the crystal-clear waves.

Out on the sun-scorched west end is the island's lone destination resort, Kaluakoi, overlooking a gold-sand beach too big to fit on a postcard with water usually too rough to swim. A few old-timers inhabit the old hilltop plantation town of Maunaloa, now being remade into an upscale version of itself. Cowboys ride the range on Molokai Ranch, a 53,000-acre spread. At the foot of the dry, rolling hills is a savannalike Safari Park, with a zoo's who of giraffes, wildebeest, and other exotics, all blissfully unaware that they're *way* out of Africa.

Elsewhere around the island, in hamlets like Kualapuu, old farmhouses with pickup trucks in the yards and sleepy dogs under the shade trees stand amid row crops of papaya, coffee, and corn—just like farm towns in Anywhere, USA.

But that's not all there is. The "backside" of Molokai is a rugged wilderness of spectacular beauty. On the outskirts of Kaunakakai, the land rises gradually from sea-level fishponds to cool uplands and the Molokai Forest, long ago stripped of sandalwood for the China trade. All that remains is an indentation in the earth that natives shaped like a ship's hull, a crude matrix that gave them a rough idea of when they'd cut enough sandalwood to fill a ship (It's identified on good maps as Luanamokuiliahi, or Sandalwood Boat).

The land inclines sharply to the lofty mountains and the nearly mile-high summit of Mount Kamakou, then ends abruptly with emerald green cliffs, which plunge into a lurid aquamarine sea dotted with tiny deserted islets. These breathtaking 3,500-foot sea cliffs, the highest in the world, stretch 14 majestic miles along Molokai's north shore, laced by waterfalls and creased by five Eden-like valleys—Halawa, Papalaua, Wailau, Pelekunu, and Waikolu—once occupied by early Hawaiians who built stone terraces and used waterfalls to irrigate taro patches.

Long after the sea cliffs were formed, a tiny volcano erupted out of the sea at their feet and spread lava into a flat, leaflike peninsula called Kalaupapa—the infamous leper exile where Father Damien de Veuster of Belgium gave his life caring for the afflicted in the 1860s. A few people remain in the remote colony by choice, keeping it tidy for the daily company that arrives on mules and small planes.

What a Visit to Molokai is *Really* Like   Centuries ago, I suspect, Molokai was a more vibrant place than it is today. It is, after all, where the hula dance was born and where, at one of the largest *heiau* in the Pacific (a four-tier stack of sacred rocks longer than a football field), ancient wizards called *kahunas* practiced dark rituals of human sacrifice and set taboos that still send shivers down the spines of those who believe in the ways of old.

But today, with no industries but farming and tourism, Molokai is peaceful and quiet. It's the ideal place to do nothing except take in the fresh air, listen to the silence, and stare out to the sea in what Robert Louis Stevenson called "a fine state of haze." Each day passes under the hot tropic sun much like the one before it.

Molokai

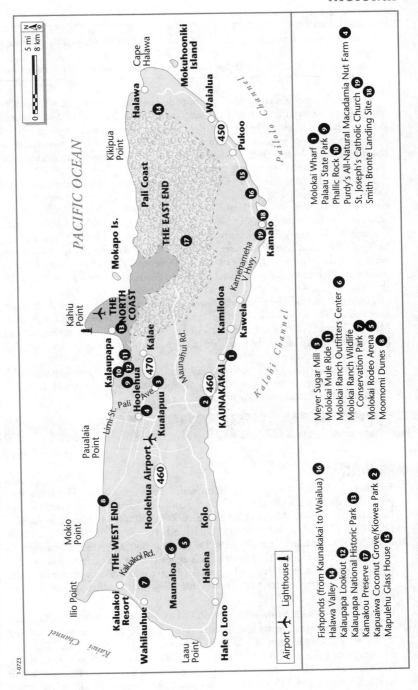

Airport ✈   Lighthouse ⬧

Molokai Wharf **1**
Palaau State Park **9**
Phallic Rock **10**
Purdy's All-Natural Macadamia Nut Farm **4**
St. Joseph's Catholic Church **19**
Smith Bronte Landing Site **18**

Meyer Sugar Mill **3**
Molokai Mule Ride **11**
Molokai Ranch Outfitters Center **6**
Molokai Ranch Wildlife Conservation Park **7**
Molokai Rodeo Arena **5**
Moomomi Dunes **8**

Fishponds (from Kaunakakai to Waialua) **16**
Halawa Valley **14**
Kalaupapa Lookout **12**
Kalaupapa National Historic Park **13**
Kamakou Preserve **17**
Kapuaiwa Coconut Grove/Kiowea Park **2**
Mapulehu Glass House **15**

1-0723

385

Impressions

Molokai is a sacred land . . . a spiritual island where the land is meant for a spiritual purpose.

—John Kaimikawa, Molokai *kumu hula* (hula teacher)

There's plenty of aloha on Molokai, but the so-called "friendly island" remains ambivalent about tourists. One of the least visited Hawaiian islands, Molokai welcomes visitors on its own take-it-or-leave-it terms and makes few concessions beyond that of gracious host; it never wants to attract too big of a crowd, anyway. A sign at the airport offers the first clue: "Slow down, you on Molokai now"—a caveat to heed on this island, where life proceeds at its own pace.

Rugged, red dirt Molokai isn't for everyone, but anyone who likes to explore remote places and seek their own adventures should love it. The best of the island can only be seen on foot, mule, or horse, or via kayak or sailboat. The sea cliffs are only accessible by sea in the summer, when the Pacific is calm, or via a 10-mile trek through the Wailau Valley—an adventure only a handful of hardy hikers attempt each year. The great Kamakou Preserve is open just once a month, by special arrangement with the Nature Conservancy. Even Moomomi, which holds bony relics of prehistoric flightless birds and other Lost World creatures, needs a guide to divulge the secrets of the dunes.

Those in search of nightlife have come to the wrong place; Molokai shuts down after sunset. The only public diversion, except for softball games under the lights of Mitchell Pauole Field, is at Pau Hana Inn on Friday and Saturday nights, when a local band steps up under the giant banyan tree and rocks the open-air seaside bar with amplified pop tunes.

The "friendly" island may captivate you—on the other hand, you may leave with your head shaking, never to return. It all depends on how you approach Molokai. Boots or loafers. Either way, take it slow.

1 Orientation

by Rick Carroll

ARRIVING

By Plane   Molokai has two airports, but you'll fly into the one at **Hoolehua Airport,** on a dusty plain about 6 miles from Kaunakakai town, which everyone calls "the Molokai Airport." **Molokai Air Shuttle** (☎ 808/545-4988), **Hawaiian Airlines** (☎ 808/567-6510 or 808/553-3644), **Island Air** (☎ 808/567-6115 or 800/652-6541), and **Mahalo Air** (☎ 808/567-6515 or 800/277-8333) all have direct daily flights from Honolulu to Molokai; it's about a 25-minute trip. If you're arriving from any island other than Oahu, you'll still need to connect through Honolulu. Hawaiian is the only airline that flies jets into Molokai; the other airlines fly twin-engine planes in.

By Boat   The *Maui Princess* (☎ **808/667-6165,** or 808/553-5736 from Molokai) arrives at Kaunakakai Harbor at a concrete pier that looks like something the Army Corps of Engineers built in World War II; everyone calls it "the wharf." The 118-foot ferry sails twice a day to and from Lahaina, Maui. The ferry departs Kaunakakai at 5:45am and 3:55pm, in case you can't take Molokai's lassitude. Round-trip fare is $50 for adults and $25 for kids, and includes continental breakfast and a free island map.

VISITOR INFORMATION

Look for a sun-faded yellow building on the main drag, Kamehameha Highway (Hi. 460), on the right just past the town's first stop sign, at the zero-mile marker; it's the **Molokai Visitors Association,** P.O. Box 960 Kaunakakai, Hawaii 96748 (☎ **808/553-3876;** interisland 800/553-0404; from the U.S. and Canada, 800/ 800-6367). They can give you all the information you need on what to see and do while you're on the friendly isle.

If you want to pick up information on Molokai while you're in Honolulu, stop by the **Hawaii Visitors and Convention Bureau** at 2270 Kalakaua Ave., Suite 801, Honolulu (☎ **808/923-1811**); brochures, maps, and guides are available for free.

Information is also available via the Internet. **Molokai's Home Page** is at **http:/ molokai.com/.** You also might want to visit the **Hawaii Visitors and Convention Bureau** at **http://www.visit.hawaii.org.**

THE REGIONS IN BRIEF

KAUNAKAKAI

Dusty cars are parked diagonally along Ala Malama Street. Kids ride around in the back of pickups. It could be any small town USA, except it's Kaunakakai, Molokai, 96748, where Friendly Isle Realty and Friendly Isle Travel offer islanders dream homes and impossible vacations, Rabang's Filipino Food posts bad checks in the window, antlered deer-head trophies guard the grocery aisles at Misaki's Market, and Kanemitsu's, the town's legendary bakery, churns out fresh loaves of onion cheese bread daily.

Molokai's main settlement is Hawaii's prime candiate for urban renewal. Once an ancient canoe landing, Kaunakakai was the royal summer place of King Kamehameha V. The port town bustled when pineapple and sugar were king, but those days, too, are gone. With Old West–style store fronts laid out in a three-block grid on a flat dusty plain, Kaunakakai is seedy and rundown, on the edge of becoming a ghost town. Even Kalaupapa, the place of exile, is in better shape. But as long as benign neglect can be sold as rustic charm, this plantation town will survive. There's a general store, a gas station, and two markets with sparse, overpriced goods.

THE NORTH COAST

Upland from Kaunakakai, the land tilts skyward and turns green with scented plumeria in yards and glossy coffee trees all in a row until it blooms into a true forest—then abruptly ends at a great precipice, falling 3,000 feet to the sea. The green cliffs are creased with five V-shaped cliffs so deep that light in the crevices is seldom seen (to paraphrase a Hawaii poet).

The north coast is the wild coast, a remote, forbidding place with a solitary peninsula—**Kalaupapa**—for exiled lepers (it's now a national historical park). Easy on the eyes, difficult to visit.

THE WEST END

This end of the island, as dry as Arizona and as bleak as Mexico, is home to **Molokai Ranch and Wildlife Park.** The rugged rolling terrain slopes down to Molokai's only destination resort, **Kaluakoi,** a cul-de-sac of condos clustered around a 20-year-old seafront hotel near 3-mile-long Papohaku, the island's biggest beach. On the way to Kaluakoi—where everyone shows up at least once, if only to wait in line to eat dinner at Ohia Lodge—you'll find **Maunaloa,** a 1920s-era pineapple plantation town that, in Molokai's first and only urban renewal project, is in the midst of being transformed into a master-planned community, Maunaloa Village.

THE EAST END

The area east of Kaunakakai becomes lush, green, and tropical, with golden pocket beaches and a handful of cottages and condos that are popular with thrifty travelers. Beyond Kaunakakai, the two-lane road curves along the coast past piggeries, palm groves, and a 20-mile string of fishponds as well as an ancient *heiau,* Damien-built churches, and a few contemporary condos by the sea. It ends in the earthly paradise of **Halawa Valley,** one of the Hawaii's most beautiful valleys.

2 Getting Around

by Rick Carroll

Getting around Molokai isn't easy if you don't have a rental car, and rental cars are often hard to find on Molokai. On holiday weekends—and remember, Hawaii celebrates different holidays than the rest of the United States (see "When to Go" in Chapter 3)—rental car agencies simply run out of cars. Book before you go. The best way to get a car is to book it through the hotel at which you're staying. And be sure to bring your confirmation documents; if you don't, you may be out of luck, or competing with others for a car. There's no municipal transit or shuttle service, but a 24-hour taxi service is available.

Rental Car Agencies Rental cars are available from **Budget** (☎ **808/567-6877**) and **Dollar** (☎ **808/567-6156**); both agencies are located at the Molokai Airport.

Taxi & Tour Services **Molokai Off-Road Tours & Taxi** (☎ **808/553-3369**) offers regular taxi service as well as island tours. **Kukui Tours & Limousines** (☎ **808/ 553-5133**) has air-conditioned limos available for tours, airport shuttle, and 24-hour taxi service.

FAST FACTS: Molokai

Molokai, like Lanai, is part of Maui County. For **local emergencies**, call 808/ 553-5355 for police, 808/553-5601 for fire, 808/553-5911 for an ambulance, and 808/553-5331 for **Molokai General Hospital,** in Kaunakakai. Downtown Kaunakakai also has a **post office** (☎ 808/567-6144) and several banks, including the **Bank of Hawaii** (☎ 808/553-3273), which has a 24-hour ATM.

Rawlins Chevron Service (zero-mile marker, Kaunakakai; ☎ 808/553-3214) is the "last stop to the airport from Kaunakakai"—where you'll rush to fill up your rental car with 87-octane at the self-serve pump. Or wish you had. It's open Monday through Thursday from 6:30am to 8:30pm, Friday and Saturday until 9pm, and on Sunday from 7am to 6pm.

3 Accommodations

by Rick Carroll

An island that had no hotels for the longest time, Molokai has only one real beachfront hotel, built in the 1970s, and it's in marginal shape. But five resort condos by the sea and a growing collection of unique B&Bs have swelled the rental pool to a record high of 700 units—about the size of one midsize Waikiki hotel.

Of all the islands, Molokai is the most affordable, although accommodations are more Motel 6 than Ritz-Carlton—and some are just plain funky. Overall, condos are your best bet. Most are well-furnished and tenderly cared for; some are in need of renovations. Gardens are always lush and trim. Most have pools. Since Molokai restaurants and supermarkets are few and limited, the kitchens that are in many of the units will come in handy. Bed-and-breakfast or vacation rentals offer more options. **Destination Molokai Association** (☎ **800/800-6367;** fax 808/553-5288) lists several in addition to those below.

Please note that taxes of 10.17% are added to every hotel bill. Parking is free unless otherwise noted.

KAUNAKAKAI

Hotel Molokai. Kamehameha V Hwy. (P.O. Box 546), Kaunakakai, HI 96748. ☎ **808/ 553-5347** or 800/423-6656. Fax 808/553-5047. 51 rms. $59 standard double, $75 poolside double, $110 oceanfront double, $125 family unit. AE, MC, V.

These old swayback Polynesian chefs' huts are vintage roadside landmarks that suggest the South Seas and look mighty inviting. A cluster of 55 steepled two-story cottages with lanais, the modified A-frames are nestled under coco palms along a gray-sand beach with a view of Lanai. Billed as an oceanfront hotel, it's actually on Molokai's fishpond coast; but waves do break on the reef a quarter-mile offshore. The rustic 30-year-old hotel is nice and friendly; it's a favorite of Canadian snowbirds and budget travelers. The restaurant is closed for renovations, the rooms could use a little more than the daily maid service, and the cottages are hot in the afternoon; but, hey, this is laid-back Hawaii—and it won't cost you a fortune to stay here.

Molokai Shores Suites. Kamehameha V Hwy. (P.O. Box 1037), Kaunakakai, HI 96748. ☎ **808/553-5954** or 800/535-0085. Fax 800/633-5085. 100 oceanfront apts. TV. $125 one-bedroom apt (sleeps up to four); $159 two-bedroom apt (sleeps up to six). Discounted rates for weekly and extended stays; corporate, military, and seniors as well. Special condo/car packages. AE, MC, V.

Bright, clean, basic units with kitchens and large lanais face a small gold-sand beach and the ocean beyond in this quiet complex of three-story Polynesian-style buildings, less than a mile from Kaunakakai. Alas, the beach is mostly for show (offshore, it's shallow mud flats underfoot), fishing, or launching kayaks, but the swimming pool comes with an ocean view. Well-tended gardens, spreading lawns, and palms frame a restful view of fishponds, offshore reefs, and neighbor islands. The central location can be a plus, minimizing driving time from the airport or town, and it's convenient to the mule ride and ferry dock as well as the lush East End countryside.

Pau Hana Inn. Kamehameha V Hwy. (P.O. Box 860), Kaunakakai, HI 96748. ☎ **808/ 553-5342** or 800/423-6656. Fax 808/553-5047. 40 units. $45 double; 6 oceanfront units $90 double; 3 poolside studios with full kitchens $90 (sleeps up to four). AE, DISC, MC, V.

This is an old and funky seaside hotel that's living on its laurels. The owner of the no-frills cottage-style complex has had the place on the market for years now. So the Pau Hana, last remodeled a decade ago, is on the slide; it's really in need of some serious TLC. However, Pau Hana's white knight may have arrived—at press time, it had just been taken over by new owners. The individual cottages are small and spartan; still, those by the ocean and pool are quite nice, the grounds are tropically lush, and the pool's always crystal clear. There's a restaurant (yes, they still serve mahiburgers—see "Dining," below), and the open-air bar attracts a crowd, especially on Friday nights.

THE WEST END

Colony's Kaluakoi Hotel & Golf Club. Kaluakoi Resort (P.O. Box 1977), Kepuhi Beach, HI 96770. ☎ **808/552-2555** or 800/777-1700. Fax 808/552-2821. 177 units. TV TEL.

$135–$145 studio; $160–$170 one-bedroom apt; $190 one-bedroom cottage. AE, DISC, JCB, MC, V.

Since it's the only resort hotel on the island, this place manages to draw a crowd— not just tourists but locals, too, who come for sunset drinks and leisurely dinners (often protracted due to a shortage of waitstaff) in an old Polynesian-style setting that enjoys a faultless location, overlooking gold-sand Kepuhi Beach.

The hotel, a funky lava-rock Sheraton with deer tracks imprinted on the walkways, was built in 1977, but later sold to Japanese speculators who have since lost interest, apparently—the Kaluakoi is in sore need of a major overhaul. It's a shame that this jewel is in decline. The setting is terrific, especially when the big winter surf comes thundering straight at you as you safely lounge poolside over Mai Tais. The open setting is appropriate to the environment: a series of lava-walled paths connects the lobby, stores, and the great hall, which holds restaurant and lounge; it's all fronted by a pool overlooking the sea and a championship Ted Robinson–designed 18-hole golf course.

Sadly, all this isn't enough to justify the rates, unless you're a golfer. Even if you get a deal on a cottage, you're hostage to the hotel's lone restaurant, which will test both patience and palate; there are often glacial delays. Book a condo with a kitchen to survive.

Kaluakoi Villas. Kaluakoi Resort, 1131 Kaluakoi Rd., Maunaloa, HI 96770. ☎ **808/552-2721** or 800/525-1470. Fax 800/477-2329. 77 units available in a 148-unit complex. TV. $120–$145 studio; $145–$195 one-bedroom apt; $195 one-bedroom cottage. AE, MC, V.

These old-fashioned two-story Polynesian-style cottages by the sea aren't fancy, but they're airy, comfortable, and affordable. Set around an old coconut grove that lends grace to this tired old resort, the best units are in the handful of detached duplex "cottages" that edge the oceanfront golf greens; they have soaring Polynesian roofs, showers with floor-to-ceiling windows overlooking private tropical gardens, and ground-level lanais. The kitchenettes are minimalist, but they work. Screened wood jalousies open to let breezes flow through, the furnishings are fresh, and everything's close: the Ohia Restaurant and Lounge as well as the pool, tennis courts, and golf course. The tradeoff is privacy: Many people walk by on their way to Kepuhi Beach, the golf course, and the Colony hotel.

Ke Nani Kai Resort. Kaluakoi Resort (P.O. Box 289), Maunaloa, HI 96770. ☎ **808/552-2761** or 800/888-2791. Fax 808/552-0045. 120 apts. TV TEL. $95–$115 one-bedroom apt (sleeps up to four); $125–$135 two-bedroom apt (sleeps up to four; $10 extra each for up to two more). 2-night minimum; 4-night minimum Dec 15–Jan 4. AE, MC, V.

A home away from home, especially for families who'll like the space and quiet. These large apartments are set up for full-time living with real kitchens, washer/dryers, VCRs, attractive furnishings, and breezy lanais. There's a huge pool, a volleyball court, tennis courts, and golf on the neighboring Kaluakoi course. These condos are the farthest from the sea of those at Kaluakoi Resort, but it's just a brief walk down to the hotel facilities and the beach beyond. The two-story buildings are surrounded by parking and garden areas.

✪ Paniolo Hale. Kaluakoi Resort, Lio Place (P.O. Box 190), Maunaloa, HI 96770. ☎**808/552-2731** or 800/367-2984. Fax 808/552-2288. 77 units. TV. $99–135 studio (1–2 persons); $115–$160 one-bedroom apt (sleeps up to four); $45–$195 two-bedroom apt (sleeps up to four; $10 per person extra for one or two more). 3-night minimum; 1-week minimum Dec. 20–Jan. 5. Discount on weekly rates. Special condo/car packages available. AE, MC, V.

This is far and away Molokai's most charming lodging, and probably its best value. Paniolo Hale's two-story Old Hawaii ranch-house design is airy and homey, with oak floors and walls of folding glass doors that open to huge screened verandas, doubling your living space. The one- and two-bedrooms come with two baths, so they accommodate three or four easily. Some have hot tubs on the lanai. Units are spacious and well equipped, with full kitchens and washer/dryers. They're comfortably furnished by the owners, who run their own rental operation.

The whole place overlooks the Kaluakoi Golf Course, a green barrier that separates these condos from the rest of Kaluakoi Resort. Hotel shops, a restaurant, and a lounge are just across the fairway, as is Kepuhi Beach (these are the closest units to the beach); it's a scenic place to walk and beachcomb, but the seas are too hazardous for most swimmers. There's a pool, paddle tennis, and barbecue facilities on the property, which adjoins open grassland countryside.

THE EAST END

Dunbar's Beachfront Cottages. Kamehameha V Hwy. (HC01, Box 901), Kaunakakai, HI 96748. ☎ **808/558-8362** or 800/225-7978. Fax 206/391-9121. 2 cottages. TV TEL. $100 two-bedroom cottage (sleeps up to four); $600 per week. Free parking. No credit cards.

Five-star cottages by the sea—two appealing, newly built (the paint was drying when I stopped by) green-and-white plantation-style cottages, each on its own secluded stretch of swimmable beach with only fishponds for neighbors; you'll feel like you're on your own island. Pu'unana Cottage has a king bed and two twins, while Pauwalu Cottage has a queen, a double, and sofa bed; it could accommodate more than four. Both have full kitchens, VCRs, washer/dryers, ceiling fans, and comfortable tropical decor. Your hosts, friendly local banker Kip Dunbar and wife Leslie, live nearby. The remote setting, some 18 miles from Kaunakakai, is peaceful, with views of nearby Maui, Lanai, and Kahoolawe.

Honomuni House. Kamehameha V Hwy. HC01, Box 700, Kaunakakai, HI 96748. ☎ **808/558-8383.** 1 one-bedroom cottage (sleeps up to four). TV. $80 double; $510 per week. $10 for each extra adult, $5 per extra child. No credit cards.

Old stonework taro terraces and house foundations testify that Honomuni Valley was popular with ancient people, whose groves of breadfruit, coconut, fruit, ginger, and coffee still flourish in the wilderness. Modern folks can sample this mini-Eden at a remote cottage—17.5 miles from Kaunakakai, a mile or more from the nearest public beach area—set in the forest along the foot of the East End upslope. Freshwater prawns and native fish hide out in the stream that carved the valley. Experienced hikers will enjoy exploring upstream, where they'll find pools for swimming and watching (or catching) prawns, and, farther up, a waterfall of their very own. Guests are welcome to enjoy the tropical fruits grown by hosts Jan and Keaho Newhouse, whose home is on the site.

✪ **Kamalo Plantation Bed & Breakfast.** Kamehameha V Hwy. (HC 1, Box 300), Kaunakakai, HI 96748. ☎/fax **808/558-8236.** 1 cottage, 2 rms in main house. $75 cottage (sleeps up to four); $65 double with private bath, $55 double with shared bath. Continental breakfast included. No credit cards.

Glenn and Akiko Foster's 5-acre spread includes an ancient *heiau* ruin in the front yard, plus leafy tropical gardens and a lime orchard. The genial Fosters have lived and sailed in the islands for many years, and are full of island lore. Their place is easy to find: It's right across the East End road from Father Damien's historic St. Joseph church. The cottage is on its own, tucked under some trees. The rooms in the home each have a small lanai and facilities for making coffee or tea. Guests are provided with beach mats and towels. A breakfast of fruit and fresh baked bread is served every morning.

Puu O Hoku Ranch. Kamehameha V Hwy. (HC-01, Box 900) Kaunakakai, HI 96748 ☎ **808/ 558-8109.** I cottage, 1 hunting lodge. Cottage $80 double (sleeps up to six; $10 extra per person); hunting lodge $825 (sleeps up to 20). No credit cards.

Escape to a working cattle ranch! *Puu o Hoku,* or Star Hill Ranch, spreads across the East End of Molokai. Ranch manager Jack Spruance welcomes visitors to the two-bedroom cottage, and larger groups at the rustic nine-bedroom lodge. The ranch, at mile marker 25, is the last place to stay before Halawa Valley. If you stay here, you'll be blessed with lovely pastoral and ocean views—and, as the name suggests, lots of stars at night.

Wavecrest Resort. Kamehameha V Hwy. (P. O. Box 1037), Kaunakakai, HI 96748. ☎ **808/ 558-8103** or 800/535-0085. Fax 800/633-5085. 126 units. TV. $109–$139 one-bedroom apt (sleeps up to four); $149–$169 two-bedroom apt (sleeps up to six). Discounted rates for weekly and extended stays; corporate, military, and senior discounts available. Special condo/car packages. AE, DISC, MC, V.

When you want to get away and pull up the drawbridge, this is a suitable place to go. The condos—some of them newly remodeled—are in three-story tropical structures surrounded by lawns, palms, mountainous inland slopes, and the solitude of the island's lush East End. The units, individually decorated by the owners, come with full kitchens, large lanais, and either garden or ocean views. It's more remote than Molokai Shores—it's about a dozen miles of leisurely driving to Kaunakakai, seven more to the airport, and a substantial drive to West End activities—but more appropriately tropical than West End properties. Fortunately, there's a small store on the property for snacks or drinks and video rentals, as well as two lighted tennis courts and a swimming pool. The haunting views of the three neighboring islands really provide a unique sense of place, but the shoreline here isn't Molokai's best for swimming.

4 Dining

by Jocelyn Fujii

Molokai's claim to fame is that it's Hawaii's refuge for those who want to "get away from it all." As such, it's a package deal: Accompanying the absence of elevators and traffic lights is an unmistakable earthiness, a rough-hewn appeal that really works for some travelers—but not all. Sybarites, foodies, and pampered oenophiles had best lower their expectations upon arrival, or turn around and leave the island's natural beauty to nature lovers.

Personally, I like the unpretentiousness of the island; it's an oasis in a state where plastic aloha abounds. Most Molokai residents possess an innate warmth that translates into a deep integrity in their style of life. They hunt, fish, collect seaweed, grow potatoes and tomatoes, and prepare for the back-yard luau. And if you happen to be walking past on the beach (as I was on my first trip to the island many years ago), they may invite you in with a broad, generous wave of the arm, hollering (as they did to me, a stranger), "Come eat, come eat! Got plenty food."

Unlike Lanai, which is small and rural but offers some of the finest dining in the islands, Molokai—although more than double Lanai's population—provides no such mix of innocence and sophistication. You must meet this island on its own terms. Molokai doesn't pretend to be anything more than an island of old ways and an informal lifestyle, a lifestyle closer to the land than a chef's toque. Although some of the best produce in Hawaii is grown on this island, you're not likely to find much of it served in its restaurants, other than in the beleaguered dining room of Colony's

Kaluakoi Hotel, in the take-out items at Outpost Natural Foods, or at the Molokai Pizza Cafe, which I found to be one of the most pleasing eateries on the island.

The rest of the time, content yourself with ethnic or diner fare, the local color at Pau Hana Inn, or by cooking for yourself. The many visitors who stay in condos find that it doesn't take long to sniff out the best sources of produce, groceries, and fresh fish to fire up at home when the island's other dining options are exhausted.

Since there are so few restaurants on Molokai, I've eschewed price categories. And I've listed just the town rather than the street address, because, as you'll see, street addresses are as meaningless on this island as fancy cars and sequins.

Reservations are not accepted unless otherwise noted.

KAUNAKAKAI

Kanemitsu's Bakery & Restaurant. 79 Ala Malama St., Kaunakakai. ☎ **808/553-5855.** Most items under $5.50. No credit cards. Mon, Wed–Sun 5:30am–2pm; Wed–Thurs 5–8pm; Fri–Sun 5–8:30pm. Bakery: Mon, Wed, Thurs 5:30am–8pm; Fri–Sun 5:30am–9pm. BAKERY/DELI.

From early morning to late night, this local legend fills the Kaunakakai air with the sweet smells of baking—first the irresistible scent of cinnamon in the early morning air, then bread, and more bread. Here since 1942, this third-generation restaurant-bakery has expanded its repertoire from baking to coffee shop to deli fare: mahi burgers, egg salad sandwiches, honey-dipped fried chicken. Kanemitsu's Molokai bread, developed in 1935 in a cast-iron, *kiawe*-fired oven, is an island signature, served at the Pau Hana Inn and the Kaluakoi Resort's restaurants, and in just about every local home. Flavors range from apricot-pineapple to mango (in season) to raisin sweet-bread, but the classics remain the regular white and wheat breads.

Not many people know about Kanemitsu's other life as a late-night institution for die-hard bread lovers. Those in the know follow the baking aromas and line up at the bakery's back door at about 10:30 at night, when the bread is whisked hot out of the oven and into waiting hands. You can order your fresh bread with butter, jelly, cinnamon, cream cheese, "whatever," say the bakers, and they'll cut the hot loaves down the middle and slather on the works so it melts in the bread. The loaves go for $2.50 to $3.50, and the back-door business goes on until the baking's done in the wee hours.

Molokai Drive-Inn. Kaunakakai. ☎ **808/553-5655.** Most items under $6. No credit cards. Mon–Thurs, Sun 6am–10pm; Fri–Sat 6 am–10:30pm. AMERICAN.

It's just a greasy spoon, and the $6 plate-lunch prices are a bit steep, but this is one of the rare drive-up places with fresh *akule* (mackerel) when available ($6 with rice and cole slaw), and fried saimin for $2.75. The honey-dipped fried chicken is a favorite among residents, who also come here for the floats, shakes, pot-stickers, and other health-defying choices. But don't expect much in terms of ambiance: This is a fast-food take-out counter with the smells of frying in the surrounding air—and no pretensions otherwise or ambitions to be anything else.

✪ **Molokai Pizza Cafe.** Kahua Center, on the old Wharf Rd. ☎ **808/553-3288.** Pizzas $8.65–$21.45. No credit cards. PIZZA.

This place was the talk of the town when it opened—"Molokai has pizza now," locals announced proudly—and its excellent pizzas and sandwiches have made it a Kaunakakai staple. There are seven different pizzas, each named after a Hawaiian island. (Niihau has yet to arrive in the Kaunakakai pizza pantheon.) The Mexican food, one of the most popular of the regularly rotating specials, is as noteworthy as the best-selling pizzas: the Molokai (pepperoni and cheese), the Big Island (pepperoni, ham, mushroom, Italian sausage, bacon, and vegetables), and the Molokini, simple individual pizza-with-cheese slices. Coin-operated cars and a toy airplane follow the children's theme, but adults should feel equally at home with the very popular $11 baby-back barbecue rib plate or the oven-roasted chicken dinner. Children's art and letters in the tiled dining room are an entertaining and charming touch. "Dear Uncle Sam," reads one of them. "Thank you from the bottom of our tummies."

☼ Outpost Natural Foods. 70 Makaena, Kaunakakai. ☎ **808/553-3377.** Most items under $5. No credit cards. Sun–Fri 10am–3pm. VEGETARIAN.

The healthiest and freshest food on the island is served at the lunch counter of this health-food store, around the corner from the main drag on the makai side of Kaunakakai town. The tiny store abounds with dewey-fresh Molokai potatoes, herbs, corn, watermelon, and other produce complementing its selection of vitamins, cosmetics, and health aids. But the real star is the closet-sized lunch counter. The salads, burritos, tempeh sandwich, taco salad, tofu-spinach lasagna special, and mock chicken, turkey, lamb, and meat loaf (made from oats, sprouts, seeds, and seasonings) will likely dispel the notion most folks have about vegetarian food being boring. Not so! Outpost serves stellar, hearty lunches using no animal products and a cornucopia of creativity. The Eastern taco salad, for example, contains brown rice topped with lentil stew and a cashew-pimento cheese poured over the works. Greens, sprouts, and a soy sour cream crown this marvel—invented, like all items on the menu, by the loving hands that prepare it.

Pau Hana Inn. Oceanfront, Kaunakakai. ☎ **808/553-5342.** Most items under $15. MC, V. Mon–Fri 6:30–10:30am, 11am–2pm, 6–9pm; Sat–Sun 6:30am–noon, 6–9pm. LOCAL.

You'll jump right into the heart of the localfest at this Molokai institution. With its orange booths, Formica tables, and open-sided dining room adjoining a banyan-shaded concrete terrace, Pau Hana Inn is the island's focal point for nightlife. Affectionately regarded more for its character and value than for its culinary excellence, "the Inn" features a tasty tostada salad as its lunchtime star; teriyaki short ribs, prime rib, and roast pork are the dominant dinner entrees. The saimin is an inexpensive option any time of the day. Much appreciated by value-conscious diners is the Chinese platter, an occasional special.

Rabang's. Kaunakakai. ☎ **808/553-5841.** Most items under $4.50; combination plate $5.50. Daily 7am–8pm. No credit cards. FILIPINO.

Sweet-sour turkey tail prepared Ilocano-style (as opposed to Tagalog) and a Filipino dish called *pinat bet* are the Rabang's specialties. As one habitué says, "Rabang's is *known* for its pinat bet"—a mixture of eggplant, string beans, pumpkin, lima beans, and other vegetables, with a smidgen of pork. The diner is a bit more in the thick of things and a cut above in presentation than seedy Oviedo's down the street. It's still extremely casual, though, and very cozy, with only a few tables (which are always full at lunchtime).

EN ROUTE TO THE NORTH COAST

Kualapuu Cook House. Kualapuu. ☎ **808/567-6185.** Main courses $7.50–$17.95. No credit cards. Mon–Fri 7am–8pm, Sat 7am–2pm. AMERICAN.

The rusting wagon frame in front of the old shingled plantation house marks the island's most popular diner and breakfast spot. Local farmers and cowboys love to chitchat over a cup of coffee and one of the renowned omelets (humongous) or steak-and-eggs (more humongous!), or "Aka's Specialty," a fresh-fish-and-eggs extravaganza named after a famous Molokai cowboy. Local food, or American food with a local twist, is the dominant genre here. At lunch and dinner, gourmet burgers, chili, and

⊛ Frommer's Favorite Molokai Experiences

A Mule Ride to Kalaupapa. If you do only one thing on Molokai, this should be it. The journey to Kalaupapa is Hawaii's most awesome trail ride. You can sit back and let the mule do the walking on the precipitous path—down 26 switchbacks and past cliffs taller than 300-story skyscrapers—to Molokai's historic leper colony.

Horsing Around in the Malihini Rodeo. Billy Crystal would love it—a rodeo for city slickers. Veteran cowboy Jimmy Duvauchelle, Jr., coaches would-be rodeo stars on basic horsemanship, then turns them loose with a herd of cattle in an arena. It's the most fun you can have on a horse in Hawaii.

Watching the Sunset from Kaluakoi. Grab a wicker chair on the seaside lanai of Ohia Lounge, order a Mai Tai, and get set for another dazzling Pacific sunset. Molokai's tropical sunsets—often red, sometimes orange, always different—are an everyday miracle that stop people in their tracks.

Celebrating the Ancient Hula. Hula is the heartbeat of Hawaiian culture, and Molokai is the birthplace of the hula. While most visitors to Hawaii never get to see the real thing, it's possible to see it here—once a year, on the third Saturday in May, when Molokai celebrates the birth of the hula at its Ka Hula Piko Festival. The day-long festival at Papohaku Beach Park includes dance, music, food, and crafts.

a rich steak-and-shrimp plate keep the cooks in nonstop action. Accompanied by rice, baked potato, vegetables, and salad, the Cook House dinners are a deal, especially when the fishermen have just dropped off some fresh mahi or ahi. You can dine indoors or out. Unsolicited advice: Save room for the chocolate–macadamia-nut pie.

THE WEST END

We're sorry to report that JoJo's Cafe in Maunaloa, one of Molokai's finest eateries, closed its doors in the summer of 1996. A new restaurant is scheduled to open on the location in late 1996; look for it while you're in Maunaloa.

Ohia Lodge. Colony's Kaluakoi Hotel and Golf Club. Maunaloa. ☎ **808/552-2555.** Reservations recommended at dinner. Main courses $10.95–$22.75. AE, DISC, MC, V. CONTINENTAL/HAWAII REGIONAL.

A promising new chef and a new menu augur well for this beleaguered dining room, but they've still got the sluggish service and decor to overcome. Long lines at the entrance are just one sign of the problem; diners sometimes must stand in line to pay the cashier upon leaving, too. The high-ceilinged, split-level room has a flowered carpet, brown tile floor, and medievalish lanterns that hang in clusters. The room, however, with its stunning view of the Kepuhi Beach, is well positioned for spectacular sunsets and close enough to hear the waves. On a clear day, diners are treated to a view of the Makapuu Lighthouse on Oahu, and whales are in full view during the height of the winter whale season. At the time of this writing, renovations are planned that will add a *paniolo* (cowboy) theme to the room, with water-sports memorabilia that will remind diners of the canoe races that take off yearly from Kepuhi Beach.

Because Ohia is the closest thing to fine dining Molokai has to offer and the only full-service restaurant serving the hotel and the neighboring condos, diners expect more than so far has been delivered. Let's hope that changes. The new menu includes a fresh catch that's broiled, sauteed, or wok-seared, served with sauteed Indonesian vegetables; steaks and veal chops; and barbecued baby-back ribs that are growing in popularity.

5 Beaches

by Rick Carroll, with Jeanette Foster

With imposing sea cliffs on one side and lazy fishponds on the other, Molokai has little room for beaches along its 106-mile coast. Still, a big gold-sand beach flourishes on the West End, and you'll find tiny pocket beaches on the East End. The emptiness of Molokai's beaches are both a blessing and a curse: The welcome seclusion means no lifeguards, and nobody to rely upon except yourself.

KAUNAKAKAI'S BEACH
ONE ALII BEACH PARK
This thin strip of sand, once reserved for the *ali'i* (chiefs), is the oldest public beach park on Molokai. You'll find One Ali'i Beach Park (pronounced *onay*, not *won*) by a coconut grove on the outskirts of Kaunakakai. Safe for swimmers of all ages and abilities, it's often crowded with splashy families on weekends, but it can be all yours on weekdays. Facilities include outdoor showers, rest rooms, and free parking.

WEST END BEACHES
PAPOHAKU BEACH
Nearly 3 miles long and 100 yards wide, gold-sand Papohaku Beach is one of the biggest in Hawaii (17-mile-long Polihale Beach on Kauai is the biggest). The big surf and riptides make swimming risky except in summer, when it's calm waters make it hospitable. It's great for walking, beachcombing, picnics, and sunset watching year-round. Go early in the day when the tropic sun isn't so fierce, and the wind is calm. The beach is so big that you may never see another soul except at sunset, when a few people gather on the shore to watch the sun sink into the Pacific in hopes of seeing the elusive green flash, a daily natural wonder when the horizon is cloud-free. Facilities include outdoor showers, rest rooms, picnic grounds, and free parking.

KEPUHI BEACH
Duffers see this picturesque golden strand in front of the Kaluakoi Resort and Golf Course as just another sand trap, but sunbathers like the semiprivate grassy dunes; they're seldom, if ever, crowded. Beachcombers often find what they're looking for here, but swimmers won't: They'll have to dodge lava rocks and risk riptides to survive. Oh, yes—and look out for errant golf balls. There are no facilities or lifeguard, but cold drinks and rest rooms are handy at the resort.

EAST END BEACHES
SANDY BEACH
Molokai's most popular swimming beach—ideal for families with small kids—is a roadside pocket of gold sand protected by a reef with a great view of Maui and Lanai. You'll find it at Hi. 450 at mile marker 20. There are no facilities, but nearby Wavecrest Condo has a general store.

HALAWA BEACH PARK
At the foot of scenic Halawa Valley is this beautiful black-sand beach with a palm-fringed lagoon, a wave-lashed island offshore, and a distant view of the West Maui mountains across the Paililo Channel. The swimming is safe in the shallows close to shore, but where the waterfall stream meets the sea, the ocean is often murky and unnerving; I like to see who's in the water with me. A winter swell creases the

Molokai Beaches & Outdoor Activities

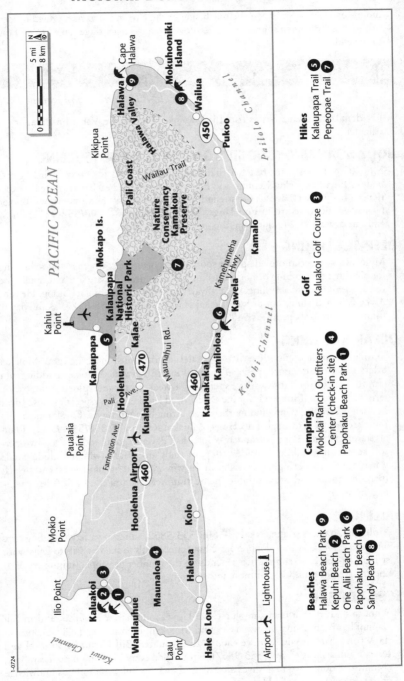

Beaches
Halawa Beach Park 9
Kepuhi Beach 2
One Alii Beach Park 6
Papohaku Beach 1
Sandy Beach 8

Camping
Molokai Ranch Outfitters Center (check-in site) 4
Papohaku Beach Park 1

Golf
Kaluakoi Golf Course 3

Hikes
Kalaupapa Trail 5
Pepeopae Trail 7

Airport ✈   Lighthouse 🗼

1-0724

mouth of Halawa Valley on the north side of the bay and attracts a crowd of local surfers. Facilities are minimal; bring your own water. To get there, take Hi. 450 east to the end.

6 Hitting the Water

by Rick Carroll, with Jeanette Foster

For details on the activities listed below, see "The Active Vacation Planner" in Chapter 3.

BODY BOARDING (BOOGIE BOARDING) & BODYSURFING

Molokai only has three beaches that offer ridable waves for body boarding and bodysurfing: Papohaku, Kepuhi, and Halawa. Even these beaches are only for experienced bodysurfers, due to the strength of the rip currents and undertows. Boogie boards can be rented from **Fun Hogs**, Kaluakoi Resort (☎ **808/552-2242**) for $5 an hour or $20 for 24 hours (fins are included in the price).

DEEP-SEA FISHING

Molokai's waters can provide prime sporting opportunities, whether you're looking for big game sportfishing or bottom fishing. When customers are scarce, Captain Joe Reich goes commercial fishing, so he always knows where the fish are biting. He runs **Alyce C Sportfishing** out of Kaunakakai Harbor (☎ **808/558-8377**). A full day of fishing for up to six people is $400.

OCEAN KAYAKING

During the summer months, when the waters on the north shore are calm, Molokai offers some of the most spectacular kayaking in Hawaii. You can paddle from remote valley to remote valley, spending a week or more exploring the exotic terrain. However, Molokai is for the experienced kayaker only, especially those adept in open ocean swells and guiding the kayak through rough waves. Kayak rentals and tours are available through **Fun Hogs**, Kaluakoi Resort (☎ **808/552-2242**). Rentals start at $25 for a one-person kayak for a half day and go up to $45 for a two-person kayak for a full day. Guided tours of the south shore (which include whale watching and snorkeling) are available in the winter, and tours of the west end (which include snorkeling) are available in the summer, each at a cost $40 for the 2- to 3-hour tour.

SAILING

Molokai Charters, Kaunakakai (☎ **808/553-5852**), offers a variety of sailing trips on *Satan's Doll,* a 42-foot sloop, from 2-hour sunset sails to full day sails to Lanai with swimming and snorkeling. Price depends on the number of people (minimum of 4) and the type of tour. Call for more information.

SCUBA DIVING

Want to see turtles or manta rays up close? How about sharks? Molokai resident Bill Kapuni has been diving the waters around Molokai his entire life; he'll be happy to show you whatever you're brave enough to encounter. **Bill Kapuni's Snorkel and Dive,** Kaunakakai (☎ **808/553-9867**), can provide everything you need: gear, boat, even instruction. Two tank dives are $85 and include Bill's voluminous knowledge of the legends and lore of Hawaii.

Molokai's Best Snorkeling Spots

Most Molokai beaches are too dangerous to snorkel in winter, when big waves and strong currents are generated by storms that sweep down from Alaska. Stick to the Kumimi Beach on the East End in winter. In summer, roughly May to mid-September, when the Pacific Ocean takes a holiday and turns into a flat lake, the whole west coast of Molokai opens up for snorkeling. "Fun Hog" Mike Holmes's favorite snorkel spots are:

- **West End: Kawaikiunui, Ilio Point,** and **Pohaku Moiliili** are all special places seldom seen by even those who live on Molokai. You can reach Kawaikikunui and Pohaku Moiliili on foot after a long, hot, dusty ride in a four-wheel–drive vehicle, but it's much easier and quicker to go by sea. Expert sailor/diver/kayaker Holmes takes you on his new 28-foot catamaran *Nanea* on snorkel tours to all three places, so you can dive secluded coves full of fish on the coast of Molokai's West End.

- **Dixie Maru,** on the West End. This is a good, gold-sand family beach, because the cove is well protected and the reef is close and shallow. To get there, take Kaluakoi Road to the end of the pavement, and then take the footpath 100 yards to the beach.

- **Kumimi Beach,** on the East End, at mile marker 20–21 off Kamehameha V Highway. The reef is easily reachable, and the waters are calm year-round.

SNORKELING

When the waters are calm, Molokai offers excellent snorkeling; you'll see a wide range of butterfly fish, tangs, and angelfish. Good snorkeling can be found—when conditions are right—at many of Molokai's beaches (see box). Snorkeling gear can be rented for $8 a day from **Molokai Fish & Dive Corp.** in Kaunakakai (☎ 808/553-5926), or from **Fun Hogs,** Kaluakoi Resort (☎ 808/552-2242), for $7.50 a day. Both places will point out that day's best snorkeling spots. Snorkeling tours are available for $45 from **Bill Kapuni's Snorkel & Dive** (☎ 808/553-9867) or from **Fun Hogs** (☎ 808/567-9292) for $40 (see "Kayaking," above).

WHALE WATCHING

The humpback whales that frequent the waters around Molokai from mid-December through mid-March can be seen up-close-and-personal with **Molokai Charters,** Kaunakakai (☎ 808/553-5852), which has a 42-foot sloop, *Satan's Doll.*

7 Hiking & Camping

by Rick Carroll, with Jeanette Foster

HIKING MOLOKAI'S PEPEOPAE TRAIL

Molokai's most awesome hike is the **Pepeopae Trail;** it takes you back a few million years to a time before any human or creature set foot on the island. On the cloud-draped trail (actually a boardwalk across the bog), you'll see mosses, sedges, native violets, knee-high ancient ohias, and lichens that evolved in total isolation over eons. Eerie intermittent mists blowing in and out will to give you an idea of this island at its creation.

The narrow boardwalk, built by volunteers, protects the bog and keeps you out of the primal ooze. Don't get off it; you could damage this fragile environment, or get lost. The 1¹/₂-mile round-trip takes about 90 minutes to hike—after you drive about 20 miles deep into the Molokai Forest Preserve on a four-wheel–drive road. Plan a full day for this outing. Better yet, go on a guided nature hike with The Nature Conservancy, which guards this unusual ecosystem. For information, write The **Nature Conservancy of Hawaii,** 1116 Smith St., Suite 201, Honolulu, HI 96817. No permit is required for this easy hike. You should call ahead (☎ **808/537-4508,** ext. 252; or 808/553-4236 on Molokai), to check on the condition of the ungraded four-wheel–drive red-dirt road that leads to the trailhead.

To get there, take Hi. 460 west from Kaunakakai for 3¹/₂-miles and turn right on the Molokai Forest Reserve Road. After about 5 miles, you'll reach the boundary to the Forest Reserve. At the Waikolu Lookout and picnic area, just over 9 miles on the Molokai Forest Reserve Road, sign in at the box near the entrance. Continue on the road for nearly 11 miles. Be on the lookout for the turnoff sign saying Puu Kolekole; this fork will lead to the clearly marked trailhead.

HIKING TO KALAUPAPA

This hike is like going down a switchback staircase with what seems like a million steps. You don't always see the breathtaking view because you're too busy watching your step. It's easier going down—you go from 3,000 feet to sea level in 2 miles—which takes about an hour, and sometimes takes twice as long on the way up. The trailhead starts on the mauka side of Hi. 470, just past the Mule Barn (you can't miss it). Check in there at 8am, get a permit, and go before the mule train departs. You must be 16 or older (it's an old state law that kept kids out of the leper colony) and should be in good shape. Wear good hiking boots or tennies; you won't make it past the first turn in zoris.

CAMPING

One of the best year-round places to camp on Molokai is Papohaku Beach Park on the island's west end, a drive-up seaside site that's a great getaway. The island's largest beach is ideal for rest and relaxation. Facilities include rest rooms, drinking water, outdoor showers, barbecue grills, and picnic tables. Groceries and gas are available in Maunaloa, 6 miles away. Kaluakoi Resort is a mile away. Obtain camping permits by contacting **Maui County Parks Department,** P.O. Box 526, Kaunakakai, HI 96748 (☎ **808/553-3204**). Camping is limited to 3 days, but if nobody's applied, they waive the time limit. Cost is $3 a person per night.

Molokai Ranch Outfitters Center (☎ **800/254-8871**) offers three new camps—two at the beach, one on a high plateau—just opened in the summer of 1996, providing visitors with a new eco-adventure. "The concept," says boss Billy Whitford, "is to check in at the Outfitter's Center and leave your car at the door; in order to get to camps you have to hike, bike, or horse ride." Beach camps on coastal ranch lands are only accessible by kayak. Call to arrange a camping adventure.

8 Other Outdoor Activities: Bicycling, Golf & Tennis

by Rick Carroll, with Jeanette Foster

BICYCLING

Only those who have ridden Molokai know it's probably the best Hawaiian island for bicycling. There are few cars and lots of wide open roads—including the mostly flat coastal highway, plus more than 50 miles of mountain-bike roads on the west end alone. Mike Holmes at **Fun Hogs** (Kaluakoi Hotel & Golf Club Beach Activities Center, Maunaloa; ☎ **808/552-2242**), has 21-speed bikes for rent, cheap ($6 an hour or $15 a day). He's also happy to dispense advice on where to go. **Molokai Ranch Outfitters Center** also rents mountain bikes for $75 for a full day of riding on 50 miles of ranch roads, including drop off at one of three trails, lunch, and shuttle back to the center.

GOLF

Golf is one of Molokai's best-kept secrets; it's challenging and fun, tee times are open, and the rates are lower than your score will be. Most popular is the par-72, 6,564-yard **Kaluakoi Golf Course,** which designer Ted Robinson calls "the most spectacular and unusual course in the islands." The course meanders along the ocean (six holes are along the shoreline) and through the woods (pheasants, Axis deer, and wild turkeys freely roam the fairways); it offers hilly, wooded fairways bisected by ravines, and a grand finish, beginning at the par-3, 16th hole. Called "The Gorge," the 16th plays 190 yards over a deep ravine to a two-tiered green. When you finish that, both the 17th and 18 holes are very long par-4s, with greens blind from the tee. Facilities include driving range, putting green, pro shop, and restaurant. It's rarely crowded; greens fees are $55 for Kaluakoi Resort guests and $75 for nonguests. Call **808/552-2739.**

TENNIS

Maui County only has two tennis courts on Molokai. Both are located at the **Mitchell Pauole Center** in Kaunakakai (☎ **808/553-5141**). Both courts have night lights and are available on a first-come, first-served basis.

9 From Mule Rides to Ocean Kayaks: Outfitters & Adventure Tour Operators

OUTFITTERS & TOUR GUIDES

Molokai Fish & Dive (☎ **808/553-5926**) in Kaunakakai is a mind-boggling store filled with outdoor gear. You can rent snorkeling gear, fishing gear, and even ice chests here. This is also the hot spot for fishing news and tips on what's running where.

Fun Hogs (Kaluakoi Hotel & Golf Club Beach Activities Center, Maunaloa; ☎ **808/552-2555**) is the place to go if you need advice on how best to enjoy Molokai's great outdoors, on land or in the water, and the gear to do it. Mike Holmes—resident sailor, kayaker, diver, biker, and hiker—calls himself a "fun hog" because he's done almost everything on Molokai. He shares his adventures, dispenses good local advice on where to go, and rents everything you need—including boogie boards, kayaks, mountain bikes, and snorkel gear—from his Kepuhi Beach shack.

Molokai ranch headquarters, a big old barn in Maunaloa called **Molokai Ranch Outfitters Center** (☎ **808/552-2681;** daily 9am–5pm) is where you go to sign up for horseback trail rides, the Malihini Rodeo (see box below), the Molokai Ranch Wildlife Park (see "Seeing the Sights," above), Molokai Ranch hunting expeditions (see below); or to rent mountain bikes (see above)—there's more than 50 miles of old "cane haul" roads to ride—and kayaks.

If it's action you're looking for, call **Molokai Action Adventures** (☎ **808/ 558-8184**). Island guide Walter Naki will take you skin diving, reef trolling, kayaking, hunting for Axis deer or wild boar or Spanish goats, or "whatevah" on custom four-wheel–drive tours into Molokai's remote, hidden valleys. His rate is $50 for 4 hours, but the price drops if more people join in the fun.

✪ MULE RIDES TO KALAUPAPA

The first turn's a gasp, and it's all downhill from there. You can close their eyes and hold on for dear life, or slip the reins over the pommel and sit back, letting the mule do the walking down the precipitous path to Kalaupapa National Historic Park, Molokai's famous leper colony.

Even if you have only 1 day to spend on Molokai, spend it on a mule. It's a once-in-a-lifetime ride for most—the cliffs are taller than a 300-story skyscraper—but Buzzy Sproat's mules go up and down the narrow 2.9-mile trail daily, rain or shine, without ever losing a rider or mount on 26 switchbacks. From 1,600 feet on the nearly perpendicular ridge, the sure-footed mules step down the muddy trail, pausing often on switchbacks to calculate their next move—and always, it seems to me, veering a little too close to the edge. Each switchback is numbered; by the time you get to number 4, you'll catch your breath, put the mule on cruise control, and begin to enjoy Hawaii's most awesome trail ride.

The mule tours are offered once daily starting at 7:50am, and they last until about 3:30pm. It's $120 per person for the all-day adventure, and includes the round-trip mule ride, a guided tour of the settlement, a visit to Father Damien's Church and grave, lunch at Kalawao, and souvenirs. To go, you must be 16 years or older, and physically fit. Contact **Molokai Mule Ride,** 25 Mule Barn Pkwy. (on Hi. 470, 6 miles north of Hi. 460). Call **808/567-6088** or 800/567-7550; advance reservations are required.

MOLOKAI RANCH TROPHY HUNT

When wildlife manager Pilipo Solotario—sort of the Noah of Molokai—set up Molokai's wildlife park, he introduced two giraffes to the island, along with other various exotic African imports like oryx, eland, Auodad, and blackbuck. At the time, the goal was to preserve endangered African wildlife and let folks see them in the wild, in a setting that resembled their natural habitat as closely as possible. Little did Solotario suspect that the animals would go forth and multiply in such numbers that the game preserve itself was in danger of being nibbled down to sand.

Islands are fragile ecosystems, and Molokai is always teetering on the edge; the animal population explosion was threatening the island itself. To deal with it, a land conservation program has been instituted on 2,400 acres of former game-preserve land. It involves something called "thinning"—a euphemism for hunting formerly endangered exotic animals before island residents themselves become an endangered species.

If you're opposed to this sort of thing, skip ahead. If you're still here, this is the deal: You can hunt year-round with rifle or bow and arrow for oryx, Indian blackbuck, Greater Kudu, and Barbary sheep with an experienced guide. Contact **Molokai Ranch Outfitters Center** (☎ 800/254-8871). The cost is $400 a day, plus $1,000 or more for bagged trophy. It costs about $1,250 to bag a trophy eland, but Molokai's a lot closer than Kenya.

AN ADVENTURE FOR EVERYONE: A WAGON RIDE TO ILI'ILI'OPAE HEIAU

In a wagon drawn by two horses, I bump along a dirt trail through an incredible mango grove, bound for an ancient temple of human sacrifice. The temple of doom—right out of *Indiana Jones*—is Ili'ili'opae, a huge rectangle of stone made of 90 million rocks, overlooking the once important village of Mapulehu and four ancient fishponds. The wagon glides under the perfumed mangos, then heads uphill through a kiawe forest filled with Java plums to the heiau, which stands across a dry stream bed under cloud-spiked Kaunolu, the 4,970-foot island summit.

Hawaii's most powerful *heiau* attracted kahunas from all over the islands, who came to learn the rules of human sacrifice at this university of sacred rites. Contrary to Hollywood's version, historians say the victims here were always men, not young virgins, and they were strangled, not thrown into a volcano, while priests sat on lauhala mats watching silently. Spooky, eh?

This is the biggest, oldest, and most famous heiau on Molokai. It's a massive 22-foot-high stone altar, dedicated to Lono, the Hawaiian god of fertility. The heiau resonates with *mana* (power) strong enough to lean on. Legend says Ili'ili'opae was built in a single night by a thousand men, who passed rocks hand over hand through the Wailau Valley from the other side of the island; each received a shrimp ('*opae*) in exchange for the rock (*ili'ili*). Others say it was built by menehunes, the mythic elves who accomplished Herculean feats.

After the visit the awesome temple, the horse-drawn wagon takes you back to the mango grove for a beachside lunch and an old-fashioned backyard ukulele songfest. Popular with families, this little adventure may sound too down-home for some, but the search for the "real" Molokai begins here.

Contact **Molokai Wagon Rides,** King Kamehameha V Highway (Hi. 450), at the 15-mile marker (☎ **808/558-8380**). The adventure is $35 per person; it begins daily at 10:30am and is done when *pau.*

10   Seeing the Sights

by Rick Carroll

KAUNAKAKAI

Molokai Wharf. At the end of Wharf Rd., Kaunakakai.

Even if you're not shipping out to Lahaina on the *Maui Princess,* you may want to head down to the wharf. It's a semipicturesque place to fish, photograph, and hang out.

Post-A-Nut. Hoolehua Post Office. Puu Peelua Ave., near Maunaloa Hwy. ☎ **808/567-6144.** Mon–Fri 7:30–11:30am, 12:30–4:30pm.

Postmaster Margaret Keahi-Leary will help you say "Aloha" with a dried Molokai coconut: Write a message on the coconut with a felt pen, and she'll send it via U.S. mail over the sea. Coconuts are free, but postage is $3 for a mainland-bound 2-pound coconut.

Kapuaiwa Coconut Grove/Kiowea Park. Along Hi. 450, 2 miles west of Kaunakakai.

This royal grove—a thousand coconut trees on 10 acres planted in 1863 by the island's high chief Kapua'iwa (later King Kamehameha V)—is a major roadside attraction in Molokai. The shoreline park, 2 miles west of Kaunakakai, is a favorite subject of sunset photographers and visitors who delight in a hand-lettered sign that warns, DANGER: FALLING COCONUTS. In its backyard, across Kamehameha V Highway, stands "Church Row": seven churches, each a different denomination, stark evidence of the missionary impact on Hawaii.

THE NORTH COAST

Most people never get a chance to see Hawaii's most dramatic coast in total; but nobody should miss the opportunity to glimpse it from the Kalaupapa Lookout at Palaau State Park. On the way, there are a few diversions (arranged here in geographical order).

EN ROUTE TO THE NORTH COAST

The only reason to visit the defunct Del Monte pineapple town of **Kualapuu** is not to see the new coffee plantation or the world's largest rubber-lined reservoir (even if it does hold 1.4 billion gallons of water), but to visit Kualapuu Cook House (see "Dining," above).

Meyer Sugar Mill. Hi. 470, 2 miles below Kalaupapa Overlook. ☎ **808/567-6436.** Admission $2.50 adults, $1 students. Mon–Sat 10am–2pm.

En route to the California Gold Rush in 1849, Rudolph W. Meyer, a German professor, came to Molokai, married the high chiefess Kalama, and, after planting corn, wheat, and potatoes, began to operate a small sugar plantation near his home. Now on the National Register of Historic Places, the restored 1878 sugar mill, with its century old steam engine, mule-driven cane crusher, copper clarifiers, and redwood evaporating pans—all in working order—is the last of its kind in Hawaii. The mill also houses a museum that traces the history of sugar growing on Molokai and features special events such as wine tastings every 2 months, taro festivals, an annual music festival, and occasional classes in ukulele-making, loom-weaving, and sewing; call for schedule.

Palaau State Park. On Hi. 470, just off Hi. 460.

This 234-acre piney woods park 8 miles out of Kaunakakai is a sleeper. It doesn't look like much until you get out of the car and take a hike, which literally puts you between a rock and a hard place: Go right and you end up on the edge of Molokai's magnificent sea cliffs, with its panoramic view of the infamous Kalaupapa leper colony; go left, and you come face to face with a stone phallus.

If you have no plans to scale the cliffs on mule or foot (see "From Mule Rides to Ocean Kayaks" and "Hiking and Camping," above), the ✪ **Kalaupapa Lookout** is the only place from which to see the former place of exile. The trail is marked and there are historic photos and interpretive signs to explain what you're seeing. It's airy and cool in the ironwood forest, which many claim is the island's best campground. You can camp free here, but hardly anybody does, probably because of the legend associated with the Phallic Rock.

Six feet high, pointed at an angle that means business, Molokai's famous **Phallic Rock** is a legendary fertility tool that appears to be working today. According to Hawaiian legend, a woman who wishes to become pregnant only need rub the rock with reverence during an overnight stay and . . . Voila! It's probably just a coincidence, of course, but the rock shows recent evidence of rubbing and Molokai does have a growing population of young, pregnant women. If you want to avoid an unwanted pregnancy, it might be wise to avoid camping in the rock's vicinity.

Phallic Rock is at the end of a well-worn uphill path, through an ironwood grove past other rocks that vaguely resemble sexual body parts. No mistaking the big guy, though—it's definitely a giant erect male penis. Supposedly, it belonged to Nanahoa, a demigod who quarreled with his wife, Kawahuna, over a pretty girl. In the tussle, Kawahuna was thrown over the cliff, and both husband and wife were turned to stone.

Of all the phallic rocks in Hawaii and the Pacific, this is the one to see. It's so famous, it's featured on a postcard with a tiny, awe-struck Japanese woman standing next to it.

THE LEGACY OF FATHER DAMIEN: KALAUPAPA NATIONAL HISTORIC PARK

An old tongue of lava that sticks out to form a peninsula, Kalaupapa became infamous because of man's inhumanity to victims of a formerly incurable contagious disease.

King Kamehameha V sent the first lepers—nine men and three women—into exile on this lonely shore, at the base of ramparts that rise like temples against the unbroken Pacific, on January 6, 1866. More than 11,000 lepers arrived between 1865 and 1874, dispatched to disfigure and die in one of the world's most beautiful—and lonely—places. They called Kalaupapa "The Place of the Living Dead."

One of the world's least contagious diseases, leprosy is caused by a germ, *Mycobacterium leprae,* that attacks the nerves, skin, and eyes. It's transmitted by direct, repetitive person-to-person contact over a long period of time. American scientists found a cure for the disease, sulfone, in the 1940s.

Before science intervened, there was only Father Damien. Born to wealth in Belgium, Joseph de Veuster traded a life of excess for exile among lepers; he gave his life caring for the afflicted at Kalaupapa. Father Damien, as he became known, volunteered to go out to the Pacific in place of his ailing brother when he was 33. Horrified at the conditions in the leper colony, Father Damien worked at Kalaupapa for 11 years, building houses, schools, and churches, and giving patients hope of redemption. He died on April 15, 1889, in Kalaupapa, of leprosy. He was 49.

A hero nominated for Catholic sainthood, Father Damien is buried not in his tomb next to St. Philomena Church, but in his native Belgium. His hand was recently returned to Molokai, however, and was re-interred at Kalaupapa as a relic of his martyrdom.

This small peninsula is probably the final resting place of more than 11,000 souls. The sand dunes are littered with grave markers, sorted by the religious affiliation—Catholic, Protestant, Lutheran, Buddhist—of those who died here. But so many are buried in unmarked graves that no census of the dead is believed to be either accurate or complete.

Kalaupapa is now a National Historic Park and one of Hawaii's richest archaeological preserves, with sites that date to A.D. 1000. About 60 former patients choose to remain in the tidy village of whitewashed houses with tombstones on the coast and statues of angels in their yards. The original name for their former affliction, "leprosy," was officially banned in Hawaii by the State Legislature in 1981. The politically correct name now is "Hansen's Disease," for Dr. Gerhard Hansen of Norway, who discovered the germ in 1873. The few residents of Kalaupapa I've met say they prefer to call their disease leprosy, although none are too keen on being called lepers.

Impressions

In the chronicle of man there is perhaps no more melancholy landing than this. . . .
—Robert Louis Stevenson, on Kalaupapa

Smile. It No Broke Your Face.

—sign at Kalaupapa

I Wanna Be a Cowboy

The big brown cow regarded me suspiciously as I approached the herd, like an old cowpoke with a crooked grin. Little did that cow know: This was my first time in a rodeo arena. Only the saddle kept my knees from knocking as I gave my horse a kick and rode into the herd. I was supposed to separate the big brown cow from the rest of the herd.

What am I doing here? I wondered. The day before, after surviving the mule ride up and down the world's highest sea cliffs, in my euphoria I accepted an invitation to the Malihini Rodeo, Hawaii's newest adventure for rodeo wannabes. Malihini (Hawaiian for "newcomer") is the rodeo for people who never dreamed they'd be in a rodeo. It puts city slickers like me on the back of a real cowboy horse and sends them into Molokai's new rodeo arena to compete in four actual events.

I was having trouble picturing myself aboard a Brahma bull. "Don't worry," said Uncle Billy at the Molokai Ranch Outfitters Center, "Just sign this liability waiver, and we can get going." I signed up, jumped in a van full of other Malihini Rodeo stars, and we rode out on the high plains of Maunaloa to the Molokai Rodeo Arena.

My colleagues included a guy who looked like Fabio with a hangover; a sophisticated blonde New Yorker who said she was an equestrienne and only rode English style; her 17-year-old daughter, Katy, a budding ballerina who fell off the last horse she rode; a German couple who spoke little English but nodded agreeably at everything; and Malia, a skinny young woman in tight blue jeans with a string of Indian feathers tattooed on her upper left arm. She said she was an elephant trainer at the Honolulu Zoo.

Outside, the whole world smelled like cow manure. It was going to be a long day. As we entered the arena, we met a real cowboy.

Most people don't associate cowboys with Hawaii. But you'll find some mighty big ranches on the Big Island, Maui, and Molokai—places where the Hawaiian *paniolo* lifestyle never died. The Molokai Ranch is one of those places. "This is the last Hawaii," says Jimmy Duvauchelle, Sr., 52, a hulking fourth-generation cowboy. When Duvauchelle's not riding the Ranch, a 53,000-acre spread that takes in

Kalaupapa welcomes visitors who arrive on foot, by mule (see "Mule Rides to Kalaupapa," p. 396), or by small plane. You can visit Father Damien's St. Philomena church, built in 1872. Once off-limits, the quiet village is now open to visitors, who can see it from a yellow school bus driven by resident tour guide Richard Marks, an ex-seaman and sheriff who survived the disease. You won't be able to roam freely, and you'll only be allowed to enter the museum, the craft shop, and the church.

Father Damien Tours (☎ **808/567-6171**) takes you into the valley on a 10-minute flight from Hoolehua Airport; the cost is $60 per person. The tour includes a slow pass by shoreline tombstones, a spin around 400-foot Kauhako crater topped by a white cross donated by Great Britain and, often, a glimpse of the rumps of departing Axis deer. The crater (the last of three to erupt on Molokai and form the flat peninsula) is interesting because of a little-explored "bottomless" lake in its caldera. Lunch is a sandwich and soda under the ironwood trees at Judd Park, a peaceful green seaside perch with an unforgettable view of the velvet cliffs and "the painful shores" of Kalaupapa.

a third of the island and is home to 6,000 head of cattle, he "baby-sits" the Malihini Rodeo. "We are very cultural, very traditional here," he says. "We like to do things we did when we were young—ride horses, round up cattle. This is our lifestyle, and we want to share it with you."

After greeting everyone personally, he showed us how to approach a horse—look him straight in the eye, and give him pat on the neck—how to get on, make the horse go, and turn left and right and stop. Now it was time to mount up.

"Who's experienced with horses?" he asked. "Do mules count?" I asked. "Sure, Rick," he said. That's how I ended up on a big red horse named Maikai (Hawaiian for *good*). In the next hour I would ride around barrels at breakneck speed, weave around poles, and somehow manage with my "A" team to move a herd of cattle from one end of the arena to the other and hold them, trembling, against the wall for 5 long seconds. We did this several times, with varying degrees of success—and often hilarious results.

Now I had to separate a single cow from the herd and send it to the other end of the arena without spooking its pals. It's called "cutting." Slowly, I approached the herd, trying to make eye contact with the cow I hoped to cut; then some unseen communication flashed like e-mail between my horse and the cow, and it moved. It actually left its companions and trotted off while the rest of the herd stood fast— kinda like the climactic scene in *Babe*. Nothing to it.

My victorious "A" team cheered. "It was nothing," I said, giving my horse named Good a big pat on the neck. Nothing like a good smart horse.

Riding in the Malihini Rodeo is the most fun you can have on a horse in Hawaii. Your adventure begins at the **Molokai Outfitters Center** (☎ **808/552-2681**) in Maunaloa. The cost is $75 per person. The rodeo is held Wednesday, Thursday, and Friday; it lasts from 9am to 12:30pm. No experience is necessary, but you must be at least 16 years old and weigh no more than 250 pounds. It's a good idea to wear closed-toe shoes and long pants, preferably jeans, so you don't get roughed up while riding. They rent cowboy boots, if you need 'em, dude.

THE WEST END
MAUNALOA

"Eleven hundred feet above the ocean in the rolling hills of west Molokai, something wonderful is happening," the real estate prospectus says. "A classic island town is becoming new again."

In the first and only urban renewal on Molokai, the 1920s-era pineapple plantation town of Maunaloa is coming down. The termite-filled houses built by Libby, McNeil, and Libby are being scraped by bulldozers; in their place is rising a new tract of $125,000 houses. Streets are being widened and paved, curbs and sidewalks are going in. Historic Maunaloa is being transformed into Maunaloa Village.

All this gentrification is unsettling to longtime residents, who resisted the change— and the end of an era of cheap rents. Across the street, the Maunaloa General Store faces an uncertain future. Only Jonathan Socher's Big Wind Kite Factory (see "Shops & Galleries," below), the town's main attraction, remains in place for now, his kites and books wrapped in cellophane against constant clouds of red dust raised by construction crews. Even the Cooke Island pines of Maunaloa need a bath.

Maunaloa's too noisy to visit now, but when it's all put back together, the only master planned village in Hawaii will have a museum, a bed-and-breakfast, a town park, and tidy new plantation-style houses with steel rafters, solar water heaters, low-flow fixtures and toilets, and underground utilities—uptown stuff for Molokai. And with the newly opened Molokai Outfitters Center (see "Outfitters & Tour Guides," above) and Molokai Rodeo Arena (see box above), the old plantation town is moving up in the world as a destination for cowboys.

✪ **Molokai Ranch Wildlife Conservation Park.** Molokai Oufitters Center, Maunaloa. ☎ **808/552-2681.** $35 adults, $15 ages 13–18, $5 ages 3–12, children under 3 free. Tues–Sat 10am–1pm.

If you've never had lunch with a giraffe or looked a Greater Kudu square in the eye, then a visit to this African safari game preserve is for you. The Molokai Ranch Wild-life Park is probably the best of its kind anywhere, because 100 exotic wild animals freely roam 350 acres of west Molokai, which look all the world like Africa's savanna. I'm no big fan of zoos—even the best seem unnatural to me—but this variation seems to work for animals and humans alike.

You ride slowly through the game preserve in a van with a guide in a safari suit (natch); the van stops periodically so you can peer and photograph antelope, oryx, Indian black buck, Greater Kudu, Barbary sheep, and other creatures. Then, in the middle of nowhere, the van stops, you alight a little nervously (there's no lions around here, are there?) and hurry inside a chain-link cage to wait for a pair of curious giraffes to come and stare at you. Sometimes, they crane their necks over the fence to eat alfalfa pellets (supplied by your trusty guide) right out of your hand. Kids love it, and so will you.

What I like most about the Molokai Ranch Wildlife Park is that the world's most dangerous animals—people—are in the cage. If giraffes could point fingers and laugh, I know they would. A must for every family.

KALUAKOI

The only redeeming elements out here are a couple of spectacular beaches, an oasis pool around a forlorn resort hotel—Molokai's only one, the Kaluakoi Hotel and Golf Club—and a cluster of seacoast condos that hug an 18-hole, par-72 golf course.

"Kaluakoi" is Hawaiian for "adz quarry;" many have been found on the barren rocky west end, probably the area first seen by Capt. James Cook in 1789, who was in search of freshwater. On nearby 110-foot Puu o Kaiaka, a crumbly cinder cone that separates Kepuhi and Papohaku beaches, San Francisco hotelier Ben Swig once planned to build a Fairmount Hotel, but his plans were defeated by islanders; so the coast is clear, like it was more than 200 years ago.

ON THE NORTHWEST SHORE

Moomomi Dunes

Undisturbed for centuries, the Moomomi Dunes, on Molokai's northwest shore, are a unique treasure chest of great scientific value. It may look just like a pile of sand to you as you fly over on final approach to Hoolehua Airport, but Mo'omomi Dunes are much more than that. Archaeologists have found adz quarries, burial sites, and shelter caves; botanists have identified five endangered plant species; and marine biologists are finding evidence that endangered green sea turtles are hauling out from the waters once again to lay eggs here. The greatest discovery, however, belongs to Smithsonian Institute ornithologists, who have found bones of prehistoric birds—some of them flightless—that existed nowhere else on earth. The shifting dunes were also burial sites for ancient Hawaiians.

Accessible by jeep trails that thread downhill to the shore, this wild coast is buffeted by strong afternoon breezes. It's hot, dry, and windy, so take water, sunscreen, and a windbreaker. I have read accounts of those who found human skeletons suddenly exposed in the dunes by the hard wind that rakes this north coast of Molokai. At Kawaaloa Bay, a 20-minute walk to the west, there's a broad golden beach that you can have all to yourself. Stay on the trails, out of the water, and along the beach.

This 920-acre preserve is open to guided nature tours once a month, led by **The Nature Conservancy of Hawaii.** Call **808/553-5236** or 808/524-0779 for exact schedule and details.

To get to Moomomi Dunes, take Route 470 (Maunaloa Hwy.) from Kaunakakai, turn northwest at Kualapuu on Route 482, then west on Route 480 through Hoolehua Village; it's 3 miles to the bay.

THE EAST END

The east end is a great green place that's cool and inviting and worth a drive to the end of the road (Hi. 450), even if one of the island's greatest natural attractions, Halawa Valley, is now essentially off-limits.

KAMAKOU PRESERVE

It's hard to believe, but close to the nearly mile high summit it rains more than 80 inches a year—enough to qualify as a rain forest. The Molokai Forest, as it was historically known, is the source of 60% of Molokai's water. Nearly 3,000 acres from the summit to the lowland forests of eucalyptus and pine is now held in preserve by the Nature Conservancy, which has identified 219 Hawaiian plants that grow here exclusively. The preserve is also the last stand of the endangered Molokai Thrush (*oloma'o*), and Molokai Creeper (*kawawahie*).

To get to this Nature Conservancy preserve, take the Forest Reserve jeep road from Kaunakakai. It's a 45-minute, four-wheel drive on a dirt trail to Waikolu Lookout Campground; from there, you can venture into the wilderness preserve on foot across a boardwalk on a 2-hour hike (see "Hiking Molokai's Pepeopae Trail," above). For more information, contact **The Nature Conservancy** at **808/553-5236.**

EN ROUTE TO HALAWA VALLEY

No visit to Molokai is complete without at least a passing glance at the island's ancient **fishponds,** a singular achievement in Pacific aquaculture. With a hunger for fresh fish and a lack of ice or refrigeration, Hawaiians perfected aquaculture in 1400. They built gated, U-shaped stone and coral walls on the shore to catch fish on the incoming tide; they would then raise them in captivity. The result: A constant ready supply of fresh fish.

The ponds stretch for 15 miles along Molokai's south shore and are visible from Kamehameha V Highway (Hi. 450). Molokai's fishponds offer a clue to the island's ancient population, since I once read somewhere that it took about a thousand people to tend a fishpond; more than 60 ponds once existed on this coast. All the fishponds are named. A few are privately owned. Some are silted in by red dirt runoff from south coast gulches. Others have been revived by folks who raise fish and seaweed.

The largest, 54-acre **Keawanui Pond,** is surrounded by a 3-foot-high, 2,000-foot-long stone wall. **Alii Fishpond,** reserved for kings, is visible through the coconut groves at One Alii Beach Park (see "Beaches," above). You can see **Kalokoeli Pond,** 2 miles east of Kaunakakai on the highway, from the road.

Our Lady of Sorrows Catholic Church, one of five built by Father Damien on Molokai and the first outside Kalaupapa, sits across the highway from a fishpond. Park in church lot (except on Sunday) for a closer look.

St. Joseph's Catholic Church. King Kamehameha V Hwy. (Hi. 450), at mile marker 9¹/₂.

The afternoon sun strikes St. Joseph's Church with such a bold ray of light that it's as if God is about to perform a miracle. The stunning brightness compels you to stop and visit the little 1876 wood-frame church, one of four Father Damien built "topside" on Molokai. Restored in 1971, the church stands beside a seaside cemetery, where feral cats play under the gaze of a Damien statue amid gravestones decorated with flower leis.

Smith Bronte Landing Site. King Kamehameha V Hwy. (Hi. 450), at mile marker 11, on the makai (ocean) side.

In 1927, Charles Lindbergh soloed the Atlantic Ocean in a plane called *The Spirit of St. Louis* and became America's hero. That same year, Ernie Smith and Emory B. Bronte took off from Oakland, California on July 14 in a single-engine Travelair air-craft named *The City of Oakland* and set out 2,397 miles across the Pacific Ocean for Honolulu. The next day, after running out of fuel, they crash-landed upside-down in a kiawe thicket on Molokai, but emerged unhurt to become the first civilians to fly to Hawaii from the U.S. mainland. The 25-hour-and-2-minute flight landed Smith and Bronte a place in aviation history—and on a roadside marker on Molokai.

Mapulehu Glass House. King Kamehameha V Hwy. (Hi. 450), at mile marker 15. ☎ **808/558-8160.** Mon–Fri 7am–noon, or by appointment. Free guided tour at 10:30am.

This 1920s-era glass house, the biggest in Hawaii, stands in a garden that in itself is worth a visit, to see the exotic tropicals that Ellen Osborne ships to the mainland (see "Shops & Galleries," below). The tour takes in both the house and the 9-acre cut-flower farm.

HALAWA VALLEY

Of the five great valleys of Molokai, only Halawa, with its two waterfalls, golden beach, sleepy lagoon, great surf, and offshore island, is easily accessible. But now, even that's changed.

No longer can you take Molokai's most popular hike, to 250-foot Moaula Falls, or enjoy this serene wilderness, a fertile valley that was inhabited for centuries. In a kind of 20th-century kapu, the private landowner, worried about slip-and-fall law-suits, has, on the advice of lawyers, closed the trail to the falls. NO TRESPASSING signs are posted, and folks have been turned away by security guards. *No aloha, here, brah.*

Once the agricultural center of Molokai, the valley was planted in taro as far as the eye could see as recently as the 19th century. A visitor noted in 1877 that "It is a very fertile valley with wild fruits, mountain shrimps, and much water in the streams, most of the land is covered with taro. . . . They totaled a thousand and 32 patches." In 1946, a tidal wave scoured the valley and turned the "velvet taro in sweet mud"—salty ponds of brittle leaf. A second tsunami doomed agriculture there in 1957, and the valley became a natural garden of earthly delights, including escaped mango, papaya, and bananas, all of which attract clouds of dreaded medflies.

The beach is still open for swimming and picnicking (see "Beaches," above), but the falls and the magnificent valley, with its 11 heiau ruins and fish shrines dating from A.D. 500, are off-limits. Offshore, the turtle-shaped island of Mokuhooniki, used by the U.S. Navy for target practice during World War II, is once again a seabird preserve.

While you're on Molokai, check with the Visitors Bureau to see if the trail has opened again. If the *kapu* is lifted and you're permitted to take the hike to Halawa Valley, forget your white tennies and shorts. Beautiful from a distance for its vari-ety of shades of green (there's a scenic lookout on the highway), the valley up close is a fecund jungle of primal ooze; it's like being in a heady perfumed steam bath full of voracious mosquitoes. The trail is always wet and often sloppy; sometimes you may be in waist-deep muck, but the reward for the tough 2-hour slog is an icy cold 40-foot-wide pool refreshed by the splashy tail of Moaula Falls.

To get to Halawa Valley, drive north from Kaunakakai on Hi. 450 for 30 miles along the coast to the end of the road, which descends into the valley past Jersalema Hou Church, where the trail begins. If you'd just like a glimpse of the valley on your way to the beach, there's a scenic overlook along the road: After Puuo Hoku Ranch at mile marker 25, the narrow two-lane road widens at a hairpin curve, and you'll find the overlook on your right; it's 2 miles more to the valley floor.

11 Shops & Galleries

by Jocelyn Fujii

Since many visitors to Molokai stay in condominiums, knowing where the grocery stores are on this island is especially important. Other than that, serious shoppers will be disappointed, unless they love kites or native wood vessels.

KAUNAKAKAI

Friendly Market Center. ☎ 808/553-5595.

You can't miss this salmon-colored wooden storefront with the blue-and-beige trim on the main drag of "downtown" Kaunakakai, where multigeneration stores are the norm rather than the exception. It is friendly! I like all of Kaunakakai's old mom-and-pop stores, but my informal survey revealed that, except for Outpost Natural Foods, Friendly has the town's best selection of produce and healthy foods. Blue corn tortilla chips, soy milk, and Kumu Farms macadamia-nut pesto, the island's stellar gourmet food, are among the items that surpass standard grocery-store fare. The meats are fresh and of good quality, and the selection is democratic, encompassing everything from prime cuts to pig blood with salt and vinegar.

Imamura Store. ☎ 808/553-5615.

Wilfred Imamura, whose mother founded the store (she died in 1992 at age 97), recalls the old railroad track that stretched from the pier to a spot across the street. "We brought our household things from the pier on a hand-pumped vehicle," he recalls. His store, appropriately, is a leap into the past, a marvelous amalgam of precious old-fashioned things. Rubber boots, Hawaiian-print tablecloths, Japanese tea plates, ukulele cases, plastic slippers, and even coconut bikini tops line the shelves. You'll walk on an ancient green linoleum floor down aisles of T-shirts, clothing, tea pots, bedspreads, dish towels, electric woks, and rice cookers. But it's not all nostalgia. The Molokai T-shirts, jeans, and palaka shorts are of good quality, and inexpensive. Less than $5 a yard, the pareu fabrics are a find.

Lorenzo's Gallery of Fine Art & Molokai Treasures. Kahua Center, on the old Wharf Rd. ☎ 808/553-3748.

Working in media ranging from sculpture to oils to watercolors and prints, nine local artists have found a home for their works in this airy gallery. The proprietor, a painter and framer who goes by the name of Lorenzo, has made a sincere effort to create a forum for local art. Noted Molokai sculptor Alapai Hanapi has some weighty wooden works here; a few feet away is a 1,600-pound koa-root coffee table, which required six people to carry it and is haunting in its complexity.

Misaki's Grocery and Dry Goods. ☎ 808/553-5505.

Established in 1922, this third-generation local legend is one of Kaunakakai's two grocery stores, as essential as the Molokai air. Some surprises lurk on the shelves, such as chopped garlic from Gilroy, California (the garlic capital of the world), but the stock mostly consists of meats, produce, baking products, and a humongous array of soft drinks. Liquor, stationery, candies, and paper products round out the selection.

Molokai Drugs. Kamo'i Professional Center. ☎ 808/553-5313.

The island's only pharmacy and full-service drug store recently moved to this new location. David Mikami, whose father-in-law founded the pharmacy in 1935, has made his drugstore more than a drugstore. It's a gleaming, friendly stop full of life's basic necessities, with generous amenities such as a phone and rest room for pass-ersby(!). You'll find the best selection of guidebooks, books about Molokai, and maps here, as well as greeting cards, paperbacks, party favors, candles, cassette players, rubber flip-flops, sunscreens, and every imaginable essential.

When Mikami's daughter, Kelly, became a pharmacist in 1995, she was the fourth in the family. The Mikamis are a household name on the island not only because of their pharmacy, but because the family has shown exceptional kindness to the often economically strapped Molokaians.

Molokai Fish & Dive. ☎ 808/553-5926.

The island's largest selection of T-shirts and souvenirs shares space with fishing, snorkeling, and outdoor gear for rent and sale. Wend your way among the fishnets, boogie boards, diving equipment, bamboo rakes, juices and soft drinks, disposable cameras, visors, beach towels, Frisbees, and the other miscellany of this chockablock store. One entire wall is lined with T-shirts. At the other end of the aesthetic spectrum are intricate feather leis, ranging from $15 to $500. By the way—the eerie sounds at the back of the store aren't some ghost, but a parrot hidden in the wings.

Molokai Ice House. At the end of Kaunakakai Wharf Rd. ☎ 808/553-3054.

A fishermen's co-op established in 1988 opened its retail doors as a fish market in 1994, and it is a find. Gathered daily from the fishing boats at the wharf, the seafood comes in all forms—sashimi, poke (the seasoned raw fish), *lomi* (mixed, seasoned, and worked with the fingers) salmon and squid, oysters, seaweed, teriyaki snapper fillets. It can't come any fresher, and it's all skillfully seasoned and reasonably priced. A growing cadre of local residents come here for their fresh aku, ahi, au, mahimahi, opakapaka, and 'opelu, whole or in fillets. The lomi 'o'io, at $2.50 a pound, and the lomi *ahi* (yellowfin tuna) may look like mashed raw fish to the uninitiated, but with perfectly balanced seasonings of green onions, a pungent type of seaweed (*limukohu*), and roasted kukui nut (*inamona*), they're delicacies sought by Molokaians and neighbor islanders. Best of all, the Molokai prices are kind and unchanging, even during the winter, when fresh fish prices notoriously skyrocket. The prepared foods are perfect for no-fuss cooking or a quiet lunch at the wharf. This fish market is a find for visitors staying and cooking in condos, in terms of quality, freshness, pricing, and heart.

Molokai Wines & Spirits. ☎ 808/553-5009.

This is your best bet on the island for a good, maybe not great, bottle of wine. The mostly domestic selection includes Heitz 1990 Cabernet Sauvignon, Au Bon Climat 1993 Pinot Noir, and the progressive Vin du Mistral 1992, by the iconoclastic Bonnie Doon winery. *Wine Spectator* reviews are tacked to some of the selections, which always helps, and the snack selection shows at least one glimmer of mercy:

Cambozola gourmet cheeses. Otherwise, it's frozen burritos, canned tuna, chips, and pre-packaged nibbles.

Take's Variety Store. ☎ 808/553-5442.

If you need luggage tags, buzz saws, toys, candy, cloth dolls, canned goods, canteens, camping equipment, hardware, pipe fittings, fishing supplies, paints—whew!—and other products for work and play, this 48-year-old variety store may be your answer. You may suffer from claustrophobia in the crowded, dusty aisles, but Take's carries everything—if you can find it. If you can't, the staff is friendly and helpful.

EN ROUTE TO THE NORTH COAST

Coffees of Hawaii Plantation Store. Kualapuu. ☎ 808/567-9023.

This is the new kid on the Kualapuu block, a combination coffee bar, store, and gallery for more than 30 Molokai artists and craftspeople. Sold here are the Malulani Estate and Muleskinner coffees, grown, processed, and packed on the 450-acre plantation surrounding the shop. (A tour of the plantation is offered weekdays at 10am and 1pm, and Saturday at 10am; it's $14 for adults and $7 for children.) You may find better prices on coffee at other retail outlets, but the crafts are worth a look. Among them: Marguerite Pennington fiber baskets of ti, coco rosettes, fern shell ginger leaves, and spider lily leaves; pikake and plumeria soaps from Kauai; perfumes and pure beeswax candles from Maui; and Molokai Maggie's tropical fruit vinegars. Koa bookmarks and hair sticks, as well as a wonderful koa pen for $18—shaped and weighted like a Montblanc—are affordable finds.

Kualapuu Market. Kualapuu. ☎ 808/567-6243.

This market, in its third generation, is a stone's throw from the new Coffees of Hawaii Store. It's a scaled-down one-stop shop with wine, food, and necessities—and a surprisingly presentable, albeit small, assortment of produce, from Ka'u Gold navel oranges to Molokai produce. The shelves are filled with canned goods, propane, rope, hoses, paper products, candies, and baking goods, reflecting an uncomplicated, rural lifestyle that makes shopping here a nostalgic experience.

Molokai Museum Gift Shop. At the old R. W. Meyer Sugar Mill, Kalae. ☎ 808/567-6436.

The restored 1878 sugar mill sits at 1,500 feet, above the town of Kualapuu (see "Seeing the Sights," above). It's a drive from town, definitely, but a good cause for those who'd like to support the museum and the handful of local artisans who sell their dolls, dishtowels, cook books, quilt sets, and other gift items in its tiny gift-gallery. A modest selection of cards, Molokai Maggie's vinegars, T-shirts, coloring books, hand-jointed bears, doll furniture, and, at Christmas, handmade ornaments of lauhala and koa are sprinkled throughout the shop. A noteworthy item is the sugar mill's raw sugar barbecue seasoning, sold in a charming pouch of *palaka*, a two-colored cotton plaid, a plantation signature. The seasoning took the grand championship at the local State Fair, and, like the wonderful Sugar Mill Cookbook—a steal for $6—is a local institution.

Purdy's All-Natural Macadamia Nut Farm. Lihipali St., Hoolehua. ☎ 808/567-6601.

The Purdys have made macadamia nut–buying an entertainment event, offering tours of the acre-and-a-half homestead and lively demonstrations of nutshell-cracking in the shade of their towering, shade-giving trees. The tour of the 70-year-old nut farm explains the growth, bearing, harvesting, and shelling processes, so that by the time you crunch into the luxurious macadamia nut, you'll have more than a passing knowledge of its entire life cycle.

Tuddie Purdy has invented a rubber holding device that has conquered the otherwise slippery (and hazardous) shelling process. The nuts aren't cheap, but they're fresh and sumptuous. Because he lacks the processing equipment (there are only 50 trees on the farm), the packaged nuts come from the Big Island, but they come so fresh that no one's complaining. You can taste them here raw and roasted, see the Purdys' Hawaiian flower and fruit trees, and sample and buy macadamia nut honey. Best of all, the Purdys have a warm personal touch that visitors remember.

The farm is generally open Monday to Saturday 9am to 1pm, Sunday by appointment. Call ahead for tour times and directions.

THE WEST END

Big Wind Kite Factory & the Plantation Gallery. Maunaloa. ☎ **808/552-2634.**

Jonathan and Daphne Socher, kite designers and inveterate Bali-philes, have combined their interests in a kite factory/import shop that dominates the commercial landscape of otherwise sleepy Maunaloa. Maunaloa's naturally windy conditions make it ideal for kite-flying classes, which are offered free when conditions are right. On one side of the old wooden structure are the kites, everything from wind socks to the Sochers' signature hula girl (it dances in the wind) and Happy Dragon. Behind the store is the kite factory, where free factory tours are offered daily.

The adjoining Plantation Gallery features local handicrafts such as milo wood bowls, locally-made T-shirts, Hawaii-themed sandblasted glassware, baskets of lauhala and other fibers, and Hawaiian-music CDs. Balinese handicrafts abound as well. Especially notable is the terrific selection of children's books and books on Molokai. And particularly exotic are the carvings of Molokai deer-horn and tagua nut, crafted in Bali, and the Himalayan pendants and snuff bottles.

Maunaloa General Store. Maunaloa. ☎ **808/552-2868.**

Walk up the old wooden steps to this old plantation store, where you can find everything from knee socks and batteries to local avocados and Snapple. Oenophiles will find an unlikely (and dusty) selection of expensive red wines, the owner's hobby. It's a small selection, but very noticeable in this small town of simple, homespun tastes.

THE EAST END

Mapulehu Glass House & Cut-Flower Farm. On King Kamehameha V Hwy. (Hi. 450), at mile marker 15. ☎ **808/558-8160.**

Gingers, lobster claw heliconias, and hardy exotic flowers color a mauka patch of Mapulehu, where owner Ellen Osborne gives daily garden tours and takes orders for shipping and airport pickup or drop-off. Gift boxes, flower bouquets (for Molokai only), and the free guided farm tours (see "Seeing the Sights," above) make this a convenient source for flower lovers. An added feature: Osborne will also drop off your order in downtown Kaunakakai, at the centrally located Molokai Visitors Association office.

Wavecrest Store. Kamehameha V Hwy. (Hi. 450), Ualapue. ☎ **808/558-8335.**

As you wend your way east toward Halawa Valley, the last stop for food and provisions is the store at the Wavecrest, an oceanside condo development. I only mention it because its selection is surprisingly good for its ilk, and also because, as "the last store on the east end," it's worth knowing about. No gourmet cheeses or wines, of course, but decent cauliflower, cabbage, and other produce; Molokai poi; Maui cookies and potato chips; plus olive oil and other culinary necessities. Video rentals, on this nightlife-challenged island, are an added attraction.

12 Molokai After Dark

by Jocelyn Fujii

Molokai nightlife is an oxymoron. Aside from the **Ohia Lodge** at the Kaluakoi Resort (see "Dining," above), which features live entertainment on Friday and Saturday nights, the only other spot for after-dark socializing is the **Pau Hana Inn** (☎ **808/553-5342**) in Kaunakakai. From 9pm to 1am on Friday and Saturday nights, the Inn's outdoor Banyan Courtyard jumps with the music of FIBRE (Friendly Isle Band Rhythmic Experience), a group that has played there for at least a decade and is well known to Molokai folks. The band plays everything from Hawaiian to contemporary to Latin to rock, and when they play, the shoes come off and the dancing starts. It's a festival of local color—in blue jeans rather than hula skirts—and the presence of the 100-year-old Bengalese banyan under which it all happens adds to the evening's pleasure.

9

Lanai, a Different Kind of Paradise

From the air, the little island looks like nothing more than a wrinkled red kidney bean floating in a big blue sea. The raw earth is slashed with deeply eroded gorges that stretch to the water's edge from the misty pine-covered summit.

As the DeHavilland Twin Otter that's brought us here departs, its tell-tale drone diminishing to nothing, a great silence falls over Lanai. The first-timers look puzzled, as they always do. Some wonder, often out loud, why they came so far across the Pacific to see an abandoned plantation with a dead yellow tractor in the field, a tin-roofed 1920s-era village that dares to call itself Lanai City, and, as far as the eye can see, disorderly rows of gray-green pineapple stalks invaded by alien cacti and weeds.

Lanai hardly meets anyone's expectations of the idyllic tropical island—no palm trees, tropical flowers, or even hula girls in grass skirts. Instead there are pine trees, mud-spattered pickup trucks, and Filipino girls in blue jeans and cowboy boots. Arrive during hunting season, and you'll see trophy deer strapped to car fenders. It's almost like stepping off a plane in Kansas in Indian summer. Big blue sky meets red dirt island in a real life Magritte painting. Hands of total strangers wave from pickup trucks. Wild turkeys stand in the middle of the road.

I hear the soft speech of local people—their pidgin patois sounds like an exotic foreign language—catch the scent of tangy salt air mingled with pine trees, and shiver a little in the cool tropical air. While others react with honest surprise, I smile as our immaculate white shuttle van rushes through the broken fields to one of the island's two hotels, for I know Lanai reveals itself slowly. There's more here than meets the eye.

Hawaii's sixth largest island (141 sq. miles) and the nation's biggest defunct pineapple patch, Lanai (pronounced *lah nigh ee*) now claims to be one of the world's top tropical destinations. It's a bold claim, since so little is here: no stop lights, barely 30 miles of paved road, no ATMs, no fast-food joints, no strip malls, no taxis— in short, none of what you usually find in a tourist destination. Instead, what you have here is something quite rare: an almost virgin island, unspoiled by what passes for progress, except for a little hard-scrabble plantation town—and, of course, its fancy new neighbors, two first-class luxury hotels where a decent room starts at $300 a night.

Lanai is aloof and alien, almost a foreign place, even though it's only 10 miles off Maui's glittery Kaanapali coast. It sits at the heart of the Hawaiian chain, but seems isolated. On a clear day, you can see almost all the other islands from Lanai's 3,370-foot high razorback summit; yet you feel removed, not just by distance but in time. It feels like the late 1930s on Lanai, or what I imagine the 1930s were like in America—agrarian and uncertain, with a great gap between rich and poor.

When people leave Lanai after spending only a few days, they say it seems like they've been gone for weeks. This time-expanding nature may be Lanai's most compelling virtue, the reason that it's such a great escape.

A BRIEF LOOK AT AN UNUSUAL PAST
THE PINEAPPLE ISLAND

This old shield volcano in the rain shadow of Maui has a history of resisting change in a big way. Early Polynesians, fierce Hawaiian kings, European explorers, 20th-century farmers—it has seen them all and sent most of them packing, empty-handed and broken. The ancient Hawaiians believed the island was haunted by spirits so wily and vicious that no human could survive there. The "cannibal spirits" were finally driven off around A.D. 1400, and people settled in.

But they never really went away, it seems. In 1778, just before Captain Cook "discovered" Hawaii, the King of the Big Island invaded Lanai in what was called "the war of loose bowels." His men slaughtered every warrior, cut down trees, and set fire to all that was left except a bitter fern whose roots gave them all dysentery.

In 1802, Wu Tsin made the first attempt to harvest on the island, but ultimately abandoned his cane fields and went away. Charles Gay acquired 600 acres at public auction to experiment with pineapple as a crop, but a 3-year drought left him bankrupt. Others tried in vain to grow cotton, sisal, and sugar beets; they started a dairy, a piggery, and raised sheep for wool; but all enterprises failed, mostly for lack of water.

Harry Baldwin, a missionary's grandson and Massachusetts Institute of Technology grad was the first to do okay for himself. He bought Lanai for $588,000 in 1917, developed a 20-mile water pipeline between Koele and Manele, and sold the island 5 years later to Jim Dole for $1.1 million.

Dole planted and irrigated 18,000 acres of pineapple, built Lanai City, blasted out a harbor, and turned the island into a fancy fruit plantation. For a half-century, he enjoyed great success. Even Dole was ultimately vanquished, however; cheaper pineapple production in Asia brought an end to Lanai's heyday.

The island still resembles old photographs taken in the glory days of Dole. Any minute now, you half expect to look up and see old Jim Dole himself rattling up the road in a Model-T truck with a load of fresh-picked pineapples. Only now, there's a new lord of the manor, and his name is David Murdock.

A NEW KING—AND A REINVENTED ISLAND

Of all who've looked at Lanai with a gleam in their eye, nobody has succeeded quite like David Murdock, a self-made billionaire who acquired Hawaii's sixth largest island in a merger more than a decade ago. About 97% of it is now his private holding.

After declaring Lanai's plantation era over, he spent $400 million to build two swell hotels on the gritty island: The Lodge at Koele, which resembles a rich English uncle's country retreat, and the Manele Bay Hotel, a green tile–roofed Mediterranean palazzo by the sea. Murdock recycled the former field hands into waitpersons, even summoning a London butler to school the natives in the fine art of service, and carved a pair of daunting golf courses out of the island's interior and along the wave-lashed coast. He then set out to attract tourists by touting Lanai as "the private island."

He's now trying to make all this pay for itself by selling vacation condos next door to The Lodge at Koele. Hardly Thoreau's cabin in the woods, Murdock's condos go for around $500,000, but as the prospectus says, you get more than just a home . . . you will acquire a sense of place. Just which place Murdock is referring to, however, is unclear, since he imported a Los Angeles architect, stones from North Carolina, and art from Asia for the Lodge, and Spanish antiques for Manele. (At this writing, only one condo has been sold, to a cash customer—no doubt some economically advantaged person like Kenny Rogers, who once served as national spokesman for Murdock's pineapple juice, a big seller.)

The redevelopment of this tiny rock should have been a pushover for the big-time tycoon, but island-style politics have continually thwarted his schemes. "Go Slow," a sun-faded sign at Dole's old maintenance shed once said. Murdock might have heeded the warning, because his grandiose plans are taking twice as long to accomplish as he planned. Every permit he's sought has stuck in the tropic heat like a damp cotton shirt. Lanai is under the political thumb of many who believe that the island's precious water supply shouldn't all be diverted to championship golf courses and Jacuzzis; and there remains opposition from Lanaians For Sensible Growth, who advocate affordable housing, alternative water systems, and civic improvements that benefit residents.

Yet, despite the challenges, in a single decade Murdock has managed to turn a plain red-dirt pineapple patch into one of Hawaii's most unusual fantasy destinations. They cultivate rich tourists here now, not pineapples.

1 Orientation

by Rick Carroll

ARRIVING

By Plane   It's easy to get to Lanai. Just catch a small plane from Honolulu International Airport for a 25-minute flight to Lanai's new $4 million airport. If you're heading to Lanai from an island other than Oahu, you'll still have to make a connection in Honolulu. Jet service is now available to Lanai, but only on **Hawaiian Airlines** (☎ 808/567-6510), which offers one flight a day. Twin-engine planes take longer and are sometimes bumpier, but offer great views since they fly lower. **Aloha IslandAir** (☎ 808/567-6115) offers nine flights a day. **Aloha Airlines** (☎ 800/367-5250) and **Mahalo Air** (☎ 808/567-6515) also fly daily from Honolulu.

Prop or jet, you'll touch down in Puuwai Basin, once the world's largest pineapple plantation; it's about 10 minutes by car to Lanai City and 20 minutes to Manele Bay. A free airport shuttle runs between the Lodge, Hotel Lanai, and Manele every 30 minutes between 7am and 11pm.

By Boat   **Expeditions Lahaina/Lanai Passenger Ferry** (☎ 808/661-3756) will take you between Maui and Lanai for about $50 round-trip. The ferry service runs five times a day, 365 days a year, between Lahaina and Lanai's Manele Bay harbor. The 9-mile channel crossing takes 45 minutes to an hour, depending on sea conditions. Reservations are recommended.

VISITOR INFORMATION

Destination Lanai (☎ 808/565-7600; fax 808/565-9316) and the **Hawaii Visitors and Convention Bureau** (☎ 808/923-1811) will both provide you with brochures,

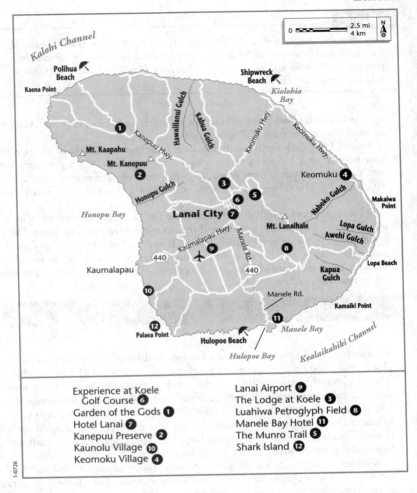

Lanai

0 ⟞⟞⟞⟞⟞ 2.5 mi	
0 ⟞⟞⟞⟞⟞ 4 km	N

Experience at Koele
Golf Course 6
Garden of the Gods 1
Hotel Lanai 7
Kanepuu Preserve 2
Kaunolu Village 10
Keomoku Village 4

Lanai Airport 9
The Lodge at Koele 3
Luahiwa Petroglyph Field 8
Manele Bay Hotel 11
The Munro Trail 5
Shark Island 12

1-0726

maps, and island guides. For a free *Road and Site Map* of hikes, archaeological sites, and other sights, contact the **Island of Lanai,** 680 Iwilei Rd., Suite 540, Honolulu, HI, 96817 (☎ **800/321-4666**).

THE ISLAND IN BRIEF

Inhabited Lanai is divided into three parts—Lanai City, Koele, and Manele—and two distinct climate zones: hot and dry, and cool and misty.

Lanai City (population 2,800) sits at the heart of the island at 1,645 feet above sea level. This is the only place on the island where you'll find services. Built in 1924, this plantation village is a tidy grid of quaint tin-roofed cottages in bright pastels, with roosters penned in tropical gardens of bananas, lilikoi, and papaya. Many of the residents are Filipino immigrants who worked the pineapple fields and imported the art, culture, language, food, and lifestyle of the Philippines. Their clapboard homes, now worth $250,000 or more, are an excellent example of historic preservation; the whole

---

Factoid

Gay Street in Lanai City is named for Charles Gay, the first person to own Lanai. He paid $200,000 in the late 1800s for the island but lost it in a drought. He was the grandson of Eliza Sinclair, who bought Niihau from King Kalakaua for $10,000 in gold and her grand piano.

---

town looks like it's been preserved under a bell jar. It looks like a Guy Buffet painting of an upscale Southern Philippines barangay.

Around Dole Park Square, old plantation buildings house general stores with basic necessities: a U.S. post office, a bank (but no ATM), and a police station with a jail that consists of three bright, blue-and-white wooden outhouse-sized cells with padlocks. The village square is lined with towering Norfolk and Cook Island pines.

In the nearby cool upland district of **Koele** is The Lodge at Koele, standing by itself on a knoll overlooking pastures and the sea at the edge of a pine forest, like a grand European manor or a British colonial hill station. The other bastion of indulgence, the Manele Bay Hotel, is on the sunny southwestern tip of the island at **Manele.** You'll get more of what you expect from Hawaii here—beaches, swaying palms, Mai Tais, and the like.

2 Getting Around

by Rick Carroll

With so few paved roads, you'll need a four-wheel–drive vehicle if you plan on exploring the island's remote shores, its interior, or the summit of Mount Lanaihale. There's a limited number of them on the island, so reserve ahead of time. A small fleet of rental vehicles are available through the hotels and at **Lanai City Service** (10-36 Lanai Ave.; ☎ **808/244-9538** or 808/565-7227), the only gas station. It's wise to reserve a car or Jeep early if you want one. You'll be able to get around if you don't, though: the airport, the two resort hotels, Lanai City, the village, Hulopoe Beach, and both golf courses are served by free shuttle vans.

Whether or not you rent a car, sooner or later you'll find yourself at Lanai City Service, the glorified name for the only gas station in town. The all-in-one grocery store, coffee bar, rental car agency, and souvenir shop serves as the island's Grand Central Station; you can pick up information, directions, maps, and all the local gossip.

FAST FACTS: Lanai

Dentists   Emergency dental care is available at Dr. Nick's Family Dentistry (☎ 808/565-7801).

Doctors   Call Straub Clinic & Hospital at 808/565-6423.

Emergencies   Call 911 for police, fire, and ambulance. For nonemergencies, call the Lanai police at 808/565-7474.

Poison Control Center   In an emergency, call 800/362-3585.

Weather Reports   Call the National Weather Service at 808/565-6033.

3 Accommodations

by Rick Carroll

The rates listed below are rack rates; you may be able to do better when you call. Hawaii adds 10.17% in taxes to all hotel bills. Parking is free, and a free guest shuttle links all three hotels, the beach park, village, and airport.

VERY EXPENSIVE

✪ **The Lodge at Koele.** P.O. Box 310, Lanai City, HI 96793. ☎ **808/565-7300** or 800/321-4666. 102 rms, 5 suites. A/C TV MINIBAR TEL. $295–$450 double, $600–$1,100 suite. AE, MC, V.

The first new building on Lanai in 50 years, The Lodge, as folks here call it, stands in a cool, often misty 21-acre grove of Norfolk Island pine trees at 1,700 feet above sea level, 8 miles inland from any beach—a locus that flies in the face of conventional wisdom, which dictated for more than a century that the beach was the only place for a Hawaii vacation hotel.

Described by its publicists as a "worldly plantation owner's residence," the 102-room resort looks like a misplaced English hunting lodge, or perhaps a British hill station in the days of the Raj. Curiously, with its grand lobby outfitted in early 19th-century Spanish Colonial furnishings and rooms done à la Laura Ashley, The Lodge has come to be a legend in its own time among its harshest critics: rich Honolulu folks who, in a brief plane ride, could escape Oahu's humidity and breathe crisp mountain air, wear wool sweaters, and sit romantically by the roaring fireplace on chilly (for Hawaii) 50° nights.

With giant stone fireplaces, stuffed furniture, and lavishly chintzed rooms, the decor is a bit arrogant for this red dirt pineapple island, but appealing nonetheless to big spenders seeking absolute seclusion. My favorite public room is The Library, which, unlike the faux libraries of Hawaii resorts, actually contains real books, some of them by local authors, and several days-old editions of mainland newspapers, in case you have a need to know. The Tea Room is a fair replica of an English pub, but don't expect a Guinness Stout; try the Lanai Daiquiri instead, made with rum-soaked Tahitian vanilla beans.

Not your typical Hawaii experience, the Lodge recently was voted "top-ranked tropical resort in the world," according to the readers of *Conde Nast Traveler*—although that tells you as much about the readers as the resort.

Dining/Entertainment: There's a formal dining room for dinner (see review in "Dining," below), and a less formal interior terrace open all day. Both specialize in local island ingredients. Entertainment is limited to quiet live music and hula and periodic guest appearances by celebrities who chat informally in a drawing room setting about their work (see box, "Talk Story with the Greats," below).

Services: Butlers available for some rooms; otherwise, typical luxury treatment with twice-daily maid service, turndowns.

Facilities: Golf at the 18-hole championship Greg Norman/Ted Robinson–designed course, the Experience at Koele; croquet lawns, stables, tennis, rental jeeps, executive putting green, pool, up-country hiking trails, extensive lawns, and garden walks. Guests have access to the Manele Bay facilities as well.

Manele Bay Hotel. P.O. Box L, Lanai City, HI 96793. ☎ **808/565-7700** or 800/321-4666. 250 rms. A/C TV MINIBAR TEL. $250–$495 double, $700–$2,000 suite. AE, MC, V.

If you want to stay at the beach, come to this sunwashed southern bluff overlooking Hulopoe Beach, one of Hawaii's best stretches of golden sand. The U-shaped hotel steps down the hillside to the pool and that great beach, then fans out in beachfront wings separated by gardens lush with Hawaiian, Chinese, and Japanese flora, man-made waterfalls, lotus ponds, and streams (coursing, hopefully, with recycled water). Bordered on the other side by golf greens on a hillside of dry land scrub, the hotel is a real oasis against the dry Arizona-like heat of Lanai's arid south coast.

This is a traditional luxury beachfront hotel: open, airy, and situated so that every room has a peek of the big blue Pacific. The lobby, called the "House of Gentle Breezes," is filled with murals depicting scenes from Hawaiian history, sea charts, potted palms, and soft camel-hued club chairs over handwoven kilim rugs. The oversized rooms, in keeping with the public spaces, are understated, done in sunny yellow with Audobon prints, mahogany armoires, huge, double-sinked marble baths with glassed-in shower and tub, and semiprivate lanais.

While its occupancy rate may be nothing to write home about, Manele Bay is the dream destination for Hawaii honeymooners, including America's richest man, Bill (Microsoft) Gates, who took over the whole island for his wedding, and vacationing celebs like Oprah Winfrey, who occupied three $2,000-a-night suites for a week and brought her personal trainer and hairdresser, even though Lanai City does have a beauty salon.

Dining/Entertainment: Hulopoe Court features innovative Hawaii Regional Cuisine and ocean views; Ihilani is the specialty dining room, with a French/Mediterranean menu (see reviews in "Dining," below). Entertainment is limited to quiet live music and hula and periodic guest lecture appearances by celebrities.

Services: Twice-daily maid service, turndown; 13 butlered suites.

Facilities: Full-service spa offers beauty and health treatments. Jack Nicklaus–designed Challenge at Manele adds 18 more holes to play, a seaside layout in nice contrast to the upland Experience (see The Lodge at Koele, above). Water sports at the neighboring beach; plus pool, library, tennis, bicycling, historic tours, and jeep tours. Guests can also enjoy the amenities at The Lodge at Koele.

MODERATE

✪ **Hotel Lanai.** 828 Lanai Ave. (P.O. Box A-119), Lanai City, HI 96763. ☎ **808/565-7211** or 800/321-4666. 11 rms. $95 single or double. AE, MC, V.

Just a few years ago, if you didn't know somebody who lived on the island, the only place to stay and eat was the 10-room Hotel Lanai, on a rise overlooking Lanai City. Built in the 1920s for VIP plantation guests, this clapboard plantation-era relic has retained its quaint character, and lives on as a country lodge. It's the cheapest hotel on the island, catering to families and local folks who can't afford $450 a night for a room. The one-story wooden building is bordered with green lawn and bright flowers under a stalwart stand of pines. The rooms are small, clean, and recently redecorated. The enclosed veranda and wood-paneled dining room attract people from around the world and the island who come in for dinner, usually fresh local ahi tuna and two scoops of rice.

The hotel serves as a down-home crossroads where total strangers meet local folks on the lanai to drink iced beer and "talk story" or play the ukulele and sing into the dark tropic night. Often, a curious visitor in search of an authentic experience will join the party and discover Lanai's very Hawaiian heart.

4 Dining

by Jocelyn Fujii

Dining on Lanai is uncomplicated and extreme. On this island of three hotels, five stores, and fewer than 3,000 residents, you can go from a greasy-spoon breakfast to a five-star dinner in less than a mile and a few hundred feet in altitude. When The Lodge at Koele and The Manele Bay Hotel opened their doors in 1990 and 1991, Lanai went from "Pineapple Island" to luxury resort—and it did so with a vengeance, quickly transforming its agricultural renown into a fine-dining cachet that immediately won top placement in the diner-rated Zagat Hawaii Restaurant Survey.

You can dine like a sultan on this island, but be prepared for high prices. The tony hotel restaurants require deep pockets (or bottomless expense accounts), and there are only a handful of other options. In addition to what's listed below, a newly opened deli and take-out counter (still unnamed at the time of this writing) next to Lanai City Service and Dollar Rent-a-Car offers a few picnic tables out front as well as sandwiches, chili plates, and extremely popular $1 shave ices.

Because there are so few eateries on this island, they're simply listed alphabetically rather than in categories or by price range.

Blue Ginger Cafe. 409 Seventh St., Lanai City. ☎ **808/565-7016.** Most items under $12. No credit cards. Daily 6am–9pm. COFFEE SHOP.

Fifty years ago, a tailor shop and laundry occupied this tiny building, followed by Dahang's pastry shop; now it's home to Blue Ginger, a very local, very casual, and moderately priced alternative to Lanai's fancy hotel restaurants. The four tables on the front porch face the cool Norfolk pines of Dole Park and are always filled with Lanai residents who "talk story" from morning to night. The tiny cafe, for big and unfussy eaters, is often jammed from 6 to 7am with construction workers on their way to work. The offerings are solid, no-nonsense everyday fare: fried saimin (no MSG, a plus), their very popular hamburgers on homemade buns, and the mahimahi with capers in a white-wine sauce. Blue Ginger also serves a tasty $1.75 French toast of homemade bread, a vegetable lumpia (Filipino version of a spring roll), and a homemade omelet for less than $5 that's reportedly luring Lodge guests away from their $20 breakfasts up the hill.

✪ **Formal Dining Room.** The Lodge at Koele. ☎ **808/565-4580.** Reservations required. Jackets required. Main courses $27–$39. AE, D, JCB, MC, V. Daily 6–9:30pm. AMERICAN.

Chef Edwin Goto's menu is a stroke of genius in this grand atmosphere of soaring ceilings, splendid fireplaces, and cheek-reddening up-country chill. What else but American classics would suffice in a hotel with game rooms, pigskin chairs, and the elusive scent of pipe smoke wafting across wide verandas and wainscoted rooms? The octagonally shaped dining room is elegant yet intimate, with a menu that has earned its rightful place in Hawaii's culinary hierarchy.

Lanai venison tops the list for game lovers, either in a fine carpaccio or roasted, with fried sweet potatoes in a bed of mashed potato purée. The simple pleasures of pan-fried oysters, chunky tomato soup (spicy, with herbed croutons and a drizzle of basil oil), and pan-roasted chicken, served with wild rice cornbread and maple sauce, become paeans to the good life. The Dining Room is known for its use of fresh herbs, vegetables, and fruit grown on the island, harvested just minutes away. Although pricey, for most visitors it remains an unavoidable indulgence. The menu changes seasonally, and always features a fresh seafood selection.

Hotel Lanai. 828 Lanai Ave., Lanai City. ☎ **808/565-4700.** Main courses $13–$17.50. AE, D, JCB, MC, V. Daily 5:30–9pm. AMERICAN.

What used to be quite the local hangout for hearty, country-style breakfasts is now a dinner-only spot where Lanai residents take their dates for cocktails and home-style meals that are simple and satisfying, though nothing to write home about. Fish sandwiches, burgers, salads, pastas, and the popular tomato-braised lamb shanks and herb-marinated grilled chicken breast populate a menu that occupies the middle ground between luxe and diner. If there's a fresh fish special, it was likely delivered that day by a local fisherman.

Guests at this charming lodge are the only ones elegible for its $3 continental breakfast; but dinner in the intimate, wood-floored dining room with two fireplaces is open to all.

Hulopoe Court. Manele Bay Hotel. ☎ **808/565-7700.** Reservations recommended. Main courses $24–$33. AE, D, JCB, MC, V. Daily 6–9:30am, 7–11pm. HAWAII REGIONAL.

Hulopoe is casual compared to the hotel's fine dining room, Ihilani, but formal compared to the Pool Grille, the lunchtime oasis for Manele Bay guests. The 17th-century palanquin in the adjoining lower lobby, the Asian accents, the tropical murals by gifted Lanai artists, and the high vaulted ceilings add up to an eclectic but very elegant ambiance, with the view of Hulopoe Bay the crowning glory. Hulopoe's salads, pastas, stir-frys, and grilled items include a double-cut lamb chop with a seaweed-rice cracker crust, a seared salmon that's smoked in-house, and several varieties of fresh fish (served seared, grilled, wok-fried, or steamed). Although most of the ingredients are fresh and local (de rigueur in Hawaii Regional cuisine), Hulopoe Court is underwhelming, eclipsed by the restaurants at The Lodge at Koele in terms of imagination and execution. Could it be that in this land of rampant Hawaii Regional cuisine, The Lodge's American comfort food is the exotic genre?

Ihilani. The Manele Bay Hotel. ☎ **808/565-2290.** Reservations required. Jackets recommended. Main courses $32–$45; set menu $85 or $95. AE, D, JCB, MC, V. Daily 6–9:30pm. FRENCH-MEDITERRANEAN.

The Manele Bay's formal dining room sits across the lobby from Hulopoe Court; its lower ceilings (beautifully painted with bird-of-paradise murals) and pleasing design permits an ocean view and a clubby, darker, more intimate ambiance. There are three sections to the split-level dining room: the terrace, overlooking the ocean and pool; the indoor middle area next to the terrace; and the elevated dining area with banquettes and private niches. The inner area, with its rich, warm ambers and mauves and luscious teak gong and Queen Anne console, suits the Mediterranean fare best.

Executive chef Philippe Padovani, formerly of The Halekulani in Honolulu and the Ritz-Carlton Mauna Lani, clearly has a deft hand with the very haute traditions of his native France. One of the dozen members of the Hawaii Regional Cuisine chefs' group—the Valhalla of contemporary Hawaii cuisine—Padovani has won a following with his Maine lobster, swimming in a delicate broth of shiitake mushrooms, which arrives in lemongrass-scented wisps of steam; and his signature mahimahi, with fiddlehead ferns, tomatoes, and capers. This simple dish has brilliantly balanced flavors that sing.

One of the best features of Ihilani is the cart of sumptuous cheeses, served with walnut bread; it's a perfect finale, but by no means should displace the Hawaiian Vintage Chocolate desserts that Padovani prepares in various mousses, cakes, and confections. He has played a significant role in getting the word out about this very luxe chocolate, made from cacao beans grown on Hawaii island lava.

Pool Grille. Manele Bay Hotel. ☎ **808/565-7700.** Main courses $9–$17. AE, D, JCB, MC, V. Daily 11am–5pm. ECLECTIC.

If this is the only restaurant in the hotel open for lunch (which it is), or you've just staggered in dusty, decrepit, and starving after an 8-mile hike from Lanai City (as I did), if you're lounging at the pool, on your way to the beach, or just really have to dine poolside—there could be a fate worse than the Pool Grille. But the attitude required for Ihilani—that the $45 lobster entree is part and parcel of the sybarite's world you've agreed to enter—applies here as well; you'll dine on $12 hamburgers (homemade bun, of course) and $12 salads under beach umbrellas, in weather that can be sweltering during the summer and fall months. The food is good, but at these prices, it had better be. You may be wearing a pareu and suntan oil as you tuck into a lunch that may cost the price of one-way airfare to the island, but this isn't hotel-chain food; in fact, I enjoyed the tuna pita sandwich, served with homemade taro chips, as much as others seemed to savor the grilled shrimp on soba noodles. Beware of the nonbiting but extremely pesky pineapple flies, which proliferate during certain seasons.

S.T. Properties. 419 Seventh St., Lanai City. ☎ **808/565-6537.** Reservations not accepted. Main courses under $7. No credit cards. Sun–Tues, Thurs–Sat 6:30am–1pm. HAMBURGERS.

The real-estate sign in front has been a landmark since the 1920s, when the tiny storefront sold canned goods and cigarettes; the 10 tables, hamburgers, and Filipino food came later. Jerry Tanigawa has kept his hole-in-the-wall a local institution, whose homemade hamburgers and bento lunches (rice with meat or fish, a plantation legacy) have fed two generations of Lanai residents. The fare—saimin, pork teriyaki, beef stew, and omelets—is a nod to sentiment, more greasy spoon than gourmet, and friendlier to pocketbook than to palate.

The Terrace. The Lodge at Koele. ☎ **808/565-4580.** Reservations recommended. Main courses $13–$21.50. AE, D, JCB, MC, V. Daily 6am–9:30pm. AMERICAN.

Located next to the Formal Dining Room, between the 35-foot-high Great Hall and a wall of glass looking out over prim English gardens, The Terrace is far from your typical hotel dining room. The food is fancy for comfort food, but it does, indeed, comfort. Hearty breakfasts of wild rice waffles and bread pudding, lunch of seared chicken breast–and-potato sandwich with red-onion gravy, and oven-braised lamb shank with polenta are among the signature items that have been known to keep guests in the hotel from morning to night. And because no restaurant can claim to be American without potatoes and corn, The Terrace puts a lot of heart into its grilled steak with creamed corn, mashed potatoes, and spicy chili sauce. They're also big on braising, particularly during the winter, and have elevated pineapple cider, made from the island's signature fruit, into a fine nectar.

5 Beaches

by Rick Carroll, with Jeanette Foster

If you like big, wide, empty golden sands and crystal clear, cobalt blue water full of bright tropical fish—who doesn't?—go to Lanai. With 18 miles of sandy shoreline, Lanai has some of Hawaii's least crowded and most interesting beaches. One, in particular, is perfect for swimming, snorkeling, and watching spinner dolphins play: That's Hulopoe Beach, Lanai's best.

Frommer's Favorite Lanai Experiences

Snorkeling Hulopoe Beach. Crystal-clear water teems with brilliant tropical fish off a postcard-perfect beach that's one of Hawaii's best. There are tide pools to explore, waves to play in, and other surprises—like a pod of spinner dolphins that often makes a splashy entrance.

Exploring the Garden of the Gods. Eroded by wind, rain, and time, this geologic badlands is worth visiting at sunrise or sunset, when the low light plays tricks on the land—and your mind.

Hiking the Munro Trail. The 11-mile Munro Trail is a lofty, rigorous hike along the rim of an old volcano, across a razorback ridge through a cloud forest, that offers big views of the nearby islands. Some hike the ridge to see the rain forest, others take a four-wheel drive to spend more time on top of the island to, maybe, catch a rare five-island view.

Four-Wheeling. Four-wheeling is a way of life on Lanai, since there's only 30 miles of pavement. Plenty of rugged trails lead to deserted beaches, abandoned villages, and wild game–filled valleys. No other island offers off-road adventures like this one.

○ HULOPOE BEACH

The bay at the foot of the Manele Bay Hotel is a protected marine preserve, and the schools of colorful fish know it. So do the spinner dolphins who come here to play, and Pacific Humpback whales who cruise by in winter (that's when the mercury drops below 80°). This palm-fringed, gold-sand beach is bordered by black lava fingers that protect swimmers from the serious ocean currents that sweep around Lanai. In summer, Hulopoe is perfect for swimming, snorkeling, or just lolling about; the water temperature is usually in the mid-70s. The protected bay is usually safe, except when swells kick up in the winter. Hulopoe is also Lanai's premier beach park, with a grassy lawn, picnic tables, barbecue grills, rest rooms, showers, and ample parking.

Hulopoe's Tide Pools   Some of the best lava-rock tide pools in Hawaii are found along the south shore of Hulopoe Bay. These miniature Sea Worlds are full of strange creatures: asteroids (sea stars), and holothurians (sea cucumbers), not to mention spaghetti worms, Barber Pole shrimp, and Hawaii's favorite local delicacy, the opihi, a tasty morsel also known as the limpet. Youngsters enjoy swimming in the enlarged tide pool at the eastern edge of the bay.

When you explore tide pools, do it at low tide. Never turn your back on the waves. Wear tennis shoes or reef walkers, as wet rocks are slippery. There's a *kapu* against collecting specimens in this marine preserve, so don't take any souvenirs home.

SHIPWRECK BEACH

This 8-mile-long windswept strand from Polihua Beach to Kahokunui—named for the rusty ship, *Liberty,* stuck on the coral reef—is a sailor's nightmare and a beachcomber's dream. The strong currents yield all sorts of flotsam, from Japanese hand-blown glass fish floats and rare pelagic paper Nautilus shells to lots of junk. This is also a great place to spot whales from December to April, when the Pacific Humpbacks cruise in from Alaska to winter in the calm offshore waters. The road to the beach is paved most of the way, but you really need four-wheel drive to get down here.

POLIHUA BEACH

So many sea turtles once hauled themselves out of the water to lay their eggs in the sunbaked sand on Lanai's northwestern shore that Hawaiians named the beach there Polihua, or "egg nest." Although Hawaii's endangered green sea turtles are making a comeback, they're seldom seen here now. You're more likely to see an offshore whale (in season), or the perennial litter that washes up onto this deserted north shore beach, at the end of Polihua Road, a 4-mile jeep trail. There are no facilities, except fishermen's huts and driftwood shelters. Bring water and sunscreen. Beware the strong currents, which make the water unsafe for swimming. This strand's really ideal for beachcombing (those little green glass Japanese fishing-net floats often show up here), fishing, or just being alone.

6 Hitting the Water

by Rick Carroll, with Jeanette Foster

You'd think that an island, any island, would be a terrific water playground but, with a few exceptions, that's not necessarily true about Lanai. Lanai actually has Hawaii's best water clarity, because it lacks major development, has low rainfall and runoff, and its coast is washed clean daily by the sea current known as "The Way to Tahiti." But the strong sea currents pose a threat to swimmers, and there are few good surf breaks. Most of the aquatic adventures—swimming, snorkeling, scuba diving—are centered on the somewhat protected south shore, around Manele Bay.

For details on the activities listed below, see "The Active Vacation Planner" in Chapter 3.

BODY BOARDING (BOOGIE BOARDING), BODYSURFING & BOARD SURFING

When the surf's up on Lanai, it's a real treat. Under the right conditions, Hulopoe and Polihua are both great for catching waves. You've got to bring your own board, though—none are available for rent.

DEEP-SEA FISHING

The 28-foot *Spinning Dolphin* will take you out on 4-hour charters, at a cost of $400 per person. Contact the **Manele Bay Hotel** (☎ **808/565-7700**) to reserve.

SCUBA DIVING

Two of Hawaii's best-known dive spots are found in Lanai's clear waters, just off the south shore: Cathedrals I and II, so named because the sun lights up the underwater grotto like a magnificent church. The **Manele Bay Hotel** (☎ **808/565-7700**) offers a variety of classes and dives, from an introductory dive in the pool (free to hotel guests) to boat dives (introductory dive $125, one-tank dive $120, two-tank dive $140).

SNORKELING

Hulopoe is Lanai's best snorkeling spot. Fish are abundant and friendly in the marine life conservation area. Try the lava rock points at either end of the beach and around the lava pools. Snorkel gear is free to guests of the two resorts. No snorkel rentals are available, so bring your own if you're not staying at one of the big two resorts.

Contact the **Manele Bay Hotel** (☎ 808/565-7700) to arrange for a sail-and-snorkel tour off the coast of Lanai with Trilogy Excursions. Continental breakfast and lunch is included for $85.

7 Hiking & Four-Wheeling

by Rick Carroll, with Jeanette Foster

A GOOD MORNING HIKE

Tucked in the corner of every closet at The Lodge at Koele is a hand-carved 4-foot-long hickory walking stick. It's there not only to admire, but to take on a hike, or an upland stroll, as they say here. The **Koele Nature Hike** is a leisurely 3-hour hike that starts by the reflecting pool in the backyard of the Lodge and takes you on a 5-mile loop trail through a cathedral of Norfolk Island pines, into Hulopoe Valley past wild ginger, and up to Koloiki Ridge, with its panoramic view of Maunalei Valley and Molokai and Maui in the distance. The trailhead isn't obvious—just keep going mauka toward the trees—and the path isn't clearly marked, but the concierge will give you a free map.

☉ FIVE ISLANDS AT A SINGLE GLANCE: HIKING & FOUR-WHEELING THE MUNRO TRAIL

In the first golden rays of dawn, a lone owl swooped low over abandoned pineapple fields as our Jeep turned left off the two-lane blacktop toward Mt. Lanaihale, the 3,370-foot summit of Lanai. Overnight, a tropical rainstorm had tattooed the tin-roofed houses. But that was all over now; the sun was up and the road ahead bone dry, a blank slate tracked only by wandering deer. With no wind, a few scattered clouds, and unlimited visibility, it was a fine morning to set out for the **Munro Trail,** the narrow winding ridge trail that runs across Lanai's razorback spine to the summit. From there, we hoped to see a rare Hawaii treat: five islands at once. On a clear day, you can see all the main islands in the Hawaiian chain, except Kauai.

Lanai's chief arboreal feature isn't the palm tree, the usual tropical icon of Hawaii, but two other interesting Pacific trees: the Norfolk Island and the Cook Island pines, so symmetrical that they look like artificial silk trees made in China. They're everywhere, on ridge lines, in the town square, and on the summit, where they do more than look picturesque: Moisture-laden clouds get snagged on the sharp boughs of the summit trees and shed welcome rain on the island, which receives a precious 37 inches a year. (Oahu's Manoa Valley, by comparison, gets 158 inches a year.) New Zealander George Campbell Munro, who came to Hawaii in 1909 to collect birds, was first to figure out this rainmaking technique, which involves hydraulics far too complex to be explained fully here. He planted the pines on horseback, dropping seeds wherever he went to both promote rain and check erosion. The summit trail is named in his memory.

When it rains, the Munro Trail becomes slick and boggy with major washouts. Rainy-day excursions often end with a rental Jeep on the hook of the island's lone tow truck—and a $150 tow charge. You could even slide off into a major gulch and never be found, so don't try it. But in late August and September, when trade winds stop and the air over the islands stalls in what is called a kona condition, Mt. Lanaihale's suddenly visible peak becomes an irresistible attraction.

When you're Lanai, look to the summit. If it's clear in the morning, get a four-wheel–drive vehicle and take the Munro Trail to the top. Look for a red dirt road off Manele Road (Hi. 440), about 5 miles south of Lanai City; turn left and head up the ridge line. No sign marks the peak. Nothing says, "Summit 3,370 feet," so you have to keep an eye out. Look for a wide spot in the road and a clearing that falls sharply to the sea. I remember some wind-bent ohia trees, a lot of ferns, and some little red flowers that looked like begonias.

The islands stand in order on the flat blue sea, just like a real-life topographic map: Kahoolawe. Maui. The Big Island of Hawaii. Even Molokini's tiny crescent. Even the summits show. You can see the silver domes of Space City on Haleakala; Puu Moaulanui, the tongue-twisting summit of Kahoolawe; and, looming like the mighty sea mountain it is, Mauna Kea peering above the clouds. At another clearing further along the thickly forested ridge, all of Molokai, including the 4,961-foot summit of Kamakou, and, more than 30 miles across the sea, the faint outline of Oahu are visible. You actually can't see all five in a single glance anymore, because George Munro's thriving pine forest blocks the view. The old forester would have been delighted.

Taking the Hike   This tough, 11-mile (round-trip) uphill climb through the groves of Norfolk pines is a lung buster, but you'll get a bonus if you reach the top: that breathtaking view of Molokai, Maui, Kahoolawe, the peaks of the Big Island, and—on a really clear day—Oahu in the distance. Figure on 7 hours. The trail begins at Lanai Cemetery along Keomoku Road (Hi. 44) and follows Lanai's ancient caldera rim, ending up at the island's highest point, Lanaihale. Go in the morning for the best visibility. After 4 miles, you'll get a view of Lanai City. The weary retrace their steps from there, while those determine to see "the view" go the last 1.3 miles to the top. Diehards go down Lanai's steep south crater rim to join the highway to Manele Bay.

8 Golf & Other Outdoor Activities

by Rick Carroll, with Jeanette Foster

BICYCLING

Mountain bikes are available free to Lodge and Manele Bay guests. Sorry, bikes are not rented to nonguests. Call **The Lodge at Koele** at **808/565-7300,** ext. 4553, for reservations.

GOLF

Golfers find the ✪ **Experience at Koele** challenging and the views outstanding. In Hawaii, it's quite an experience to play golf at 2,500 feet, on a course frequently shrouded in fog and mist. An 18-hole, par-72 championship course designed by Greg Norman, with Ted Robinson as the architect, this dramatic mountain course can only be described as a series of plunges into tropical canyons. The 8th-hole will remain in your memory forever: The view from the top of the tee is of a beautiful valley blanketed with mist, verdant with vegetation, and an azure lagoon in the distance. This 444-yard, par-4 is a double-tiered green with a 250-foot drop from tee to flagstick; there's the water plus some serious bunkers to your right and the jungle to your left. After that, the back nine would seem almost easy if the trade winds would just stop. It appears as if all the wind in the world comes sweeping across the wide fairways to give golfers a challenge that will draw them back again.

Facilities include pro shop, driving range, restaurant, and putting greens. It's fairly easy to get tee times; weekdays are best. Greens fees are $99 for guests of The Lodge at Koele and Manele Bay Hotel, $140 for nonguests. Cart rental is included. Nine-hole twilight rates are available. Call **808/565-GOLF.**

HORSEBACK RIDING

Wide-open vistas full of wild game are the joys of a Lanai trail ride. Fine steeds are available for 1- to 3-hour rides from the stables at **The Lodge at Koele** (☎ **808/565-7300**). Private and picnic rides are also available. Long pants and shoes are required; mandatory safety helmets are provided. Carry a jacket, as the weather is chilly and it rains frequently. The cost begins at $35 per person.

HUNTING

Out on the western plains of Lanai, bumping along in a GeoTracker with the local butcher's wife (who can fill a freezer with a few well placed rounds), I watched, fascinated, as a herd of Axis deer leaped together in a grand ballet. It's as if the whole earth moves, a phenomenon I've seen often underwater while snorkeling, when thousands of fish move as one.

The herds on Lanai are so great that deer—and pheasants, wild turkeys, quail, and francolins—outnumber people, some say 100 to one. Press on to the interior and you'll see biblical-looking mouflon rams posing stoically in deep ravines that crease the island. We are shopping today, taking aim with Nikon zoom lenses instead of high powered rifle scopes. The hunting season is still weeks away, and the deer know it—which is why we see them now so readily and plentiful. Come season, they vanish in the canyons and gulches or dodge birch arrows and silver bullets to survive. Hunting keeps these herbivores from gnawing the island clean to the surf, they say. Which is why you often hear distant gunfire on certain weekends and notice antlers, ram horns, and marlin tails—small, important triumphs of man over nature—on Lanai City trophy walls.

Axis deer hunts are limited to nine consecutive weekends, beginning with the weekend prior to the last Sunday in April. Mouflon sheep hunting season is the third and fourth Sunday in August by public lottery. Bird season is limited to weekends and holidays, beginning with the first Saturday in November through the third Sunday in January.

Most of the hunting areas on Lanai are private property, so in addition to a state hunting license (see "The Active Vacation Planner" in Chapter 3 for details on obtaining one), you must also get a permit from the Lanai Company (most of the hunting grounds are on their property). Permits are $275 a day; the bag limit is three deer (one buck and two does) a day for hunting with a rifle. For archery hunting, the permit is $50 a day and there are no bag limits. **The Lanai Company,** P.O. Box L, Lanai, HI 95763 (☎ **808/565-8200**), also offers a guide service for $750 per person, per day. The one-on-one service includes transportation, lunch, and processing of the deer (deboning, butchering the meat into 5-pound bags and freezing, and removing the trophy horns and slating the hides). Guns and ammunition are $30 extra per day.

TENNIS

Public courts, lit for night play as well as day, are available in Lanai City at no charge; call **808/565-6979** for reservations. The **Lodge at Koele** (☎ **808/565-7300**) and **Manele Bay Tennis Club** (☎ **808/565-2222**), offer instruction, clinics, workouts, and court rentals.

9 Seeing the Sights

by Rick Carroll

GARDEN OF THE GODS

The so-called Garden of the Gods, out on Lanai's north shore, has little to do with gods, Hawaiian or otherwise. It is, however, the ultimate rock garden: a rugged, barren, beautiful place full of rocks strewn by volcanic forces and shaped by the elements into an infinite variety of shapes and colors: brilliant reds, oranges, ochres, yellows.

When words fail those who witness this grand display of nature, they tend to ascribe something supernatural to what is admittedly an extraordinary bit of erosion in a unexpected place. One writer called it a "scattered assembly of huge rocks (with) every indication of having dropped in from nowhere." Another said the rocks "had the look of altars and temple ruins." Neither, of course, is true. The rocks are what geologists call an "ongoing posterosional event" or a "plain and simple badlands," as the *New Yorker's* John McPhee, author of such geologic gems as *Assembling California* and *Basin and Range* described it to me.

Each time I set foot on Lanai, I find myself inexplicably drawn to this desolate, windswept place, so maybe there is something beyond the natural forces of geology at work here after all. The bizarre landscape of basaltic pinnacles is great place to camp or photograph, especially at sunrise or sunset, when sunlight casts eerie shadows on the helter-skelter rocks. If Jeep ever needs a new location for its TV commercials, this is it.

Go by four-wheel drive west from the Lodge on Polihua Road; in about 2 miles, you'll see a hand-painted sign that'll point you in the right direction, left down a one-lane, red dirt road through a kiawe forest and past sisal and scrub to the site.

LUAHIWA PETROGLYPH FIELD

Most people, in a rush to get to the beach, I suppose, drive right by without a glance. But I brake for Hawaiian petroglyphs, believing that they're mysterious, fascinating characters in search of a plot.

With more than 450 known petrogylphs at 23 sites, Lanai is second only to the Big Island in its wealth of prehistoric rock art, but you'll have to search a little to find them. Some of the best are on the outskirts of Lanai City, on a hillside site known as Luahiwa Petroglyph Field. The characters you'll see incised on 13 boulders in this grassy 3-acre knoll include a running man, a deer, a turtle, a bird, a goat, and even a rare, curly-tailed Polynesian dog (some latter-day wag has put a leash on him—some joke).

How to find Luahiwa: On the road to Hulopoe Beach, about 2 miles out of Lanai City, look to the left, up on the slopes of the crater, for a cluster of reddish-tan boulders (which ancients believed formed a rain heiau, or shrine, where people called up gods Ku and Hina to nourish their crops). A cluster of spiky century plants marks the spot. Take any dirt road that veers across the abandoned pineapple fields to the boulders. Go between 3pm and sunset for ideal viewing and photo ops.

The first time I visited Luahiwa it rained so hard we couldn't see out the windshield and never saw the petroglyphs. We left a ti leaf offering and prayed for the rain to stop. We returned the next day in brilliant sunshine.

KAUNOLU VILLAGE

Out on Lanai's nearly vertical Gibraltar-like sea cliffs is an old royal compound and fishing village. Now a national historic landmark and one of Hawaii's most treasured ruins, it's believed to have been inhabited by King Kamehameha the Great and hundreds of his closest followers about 200 years ago.

Ruins of 86 house platforms and 35 stone shelters have been identified on both sides of Kaunolu Gulch. The residential complex also includes the Halulu Heiau temple, named after a mythical man-eating bird. His Majesty's royal retreat is thought to have stood on the eastern edge of Kaunolu Gulch, overlooking the rocky shore facing Kahekili's Leap, a 62-foot high bluff named for the mighty Maui chief who leaped off cliffs as a show of bravado. Nearby are burial caves, a fishing shrine, a lookout tower, and many warriorlike stick figures carved on boulders. Just offshore stands the tell-tale fin of little Shark Island, a popular dive spot that teems with bright tropical fish and, frequently, sharks.

Excavations are underway to discover more about how ancient Hawaiians live, worked, and worshipped on Lanai's leeward coast. Who knows? The royal fishing village may yet yield the bones of King Kamehameha. His burial site, according to legend, is known only to the moon and the stars.

It's a hot, dry, dusty, slow-going 3-mile Jeep drive from Lanai City to Kaunolu, but the miniexpedition is worth it. Take plenty of water, a hat to protect against the sun, and wear sturdy shoes.

KANEPUU PRESERVE

Don't expect giant sequoias big enough to drive a car through; this ancient forest on the island's western plateau is so fragile you can only visit once a month. Kanepuu, which has 48 species of plants unique to Hawaii, including the endangered Hawaiian gardenia and the once-plentiful sandalwood, survives under the Nature Conservancy's protective wing. The 590-acre forest is, botanists say, the last dry lowland forest in Hawaii; the others have all vanished, trashed by herds, agriculture, or "progress."

Due to the forest's fragile nature, guided hikes are led only 12 times a year, on a monthly, reservations-only basis. Contact the **Nature Conservancy Oahu Land Preserve** manager at 1116 Smith St., Suite 201, Honolulu 96817 (☎ **808/537-4508**) to reserve.

OFF THE TOURIST TRAIL: KEOMOKU VILLAGE

If you have absolutely nothing better to do, are sunburnt lobster red, have read all the books you brought, and are starting to get island fever, take a little drive to Keomoku Village, on Lanai's east coast.

You're really off the tourist trail now. All that's in Keomoku, a ghost town since the mid-1950s, is a 1903 clapboard church in disrepair, an overgrown graveyard, an excellent view across the 9-mile Auau Channel to Maui's crowded Kaanapali Beach, and some real empty beaches that are perfect for a picnic or a snorkel. This former ranching and fishing village of 2,000 was the first non-Hawaiian settlement on Lanai, but it dried up after the Maunalei Sugar Company failed in a drought. The village, such as it is, is a great little escape from Lanai City. Follow Keomoku Road for 8 miles to the coast, turn right on the sandy road, and keep going for 5.7 miles.

10 Shops & Galleries

by Jocelyn Fujii

If you expect Lanai to be a shopper's dream, think again. Like Molokai, Lanai is at the opposite end of the galaxy from Rodeo Drive, or even Ala Moana Center. Laid-back is the operative term here; except for dining and recreation, it'll be difficult to keep your credit card warm. Exceptions are the gift shops at The Lodge at Koele and The Manele Bay Hotel, where you can find luxury soaps, logo items, jewelry, Indonesian batiks, dresses, straw hats, and even Nicole Miller neckties. Otherwise, the stores in Lanai City are basically purveyors of necessities.

One Lanai resident told me that when Lanaians say they're going to "the city," they mean Lanai City, and when they say "town," they mean Honolulu, where they're all likely to bump into each other at Costco, Waikele, or Longs Drugs or Liberty House in Ala Moana Center. If you hear that there's a terrific back-to-school sale "in town," you might have to head for the airport instead of Dole Park.

Akamai Trading. 408 Eighth St., Lanai City. ☎ **808/565-6587.**

Located between Richard's and Pine Isle on Dole Park, Akamai sells furniture, appliances, locally made greeting cards and jewelry, hand-tooled Hawaii island leather, and bric-a-brac ranging from the predictable koa jewelry to picture frames and Norfolk pine bowls. Like just about everything else on Dole Park, this place served the plantation community in its heyday.

Heart of Lanai Gallery. 363 Seventh St., Lanai City.

Lanai artists, as well as immortals such as John Young and Maui painters Pam Andelin and Macario Pascual, have their works displayed in this otherwise unremarkable gallery. The selection includes some museum-quality crafts, such as Todd Campbell's immense Norfolk-pine bowls (not from the island's forests), plus handmade wooden accessories, baskets, and Island specialties such as one-of-a-kind plantation dolls. Lanai has more than its share of talented artists, many of whom painted the murals and walls at The Lodge at Koele and The Manele Bay Hotel; if you're lucky, you'll see some of their other work here.

International Food & Clothing. 833 Ilima Ave., Lanai City.

Old-timers still call it the "Dela Cruz" store, after the family that opened it in 1952. Again, the basics: groceries, a few housewares, T-shirts, hunting and fishing supplies, over-the-counter drugs, paper goods, and hardware.

Lanai Marketplace. Dole Square.

Everyone on Lanai, it seems, is a backyard farmer; from 8am to noon Saturday, they all throng to the square to sell their dewey-fresh produce, home-baked breads, plate lunches, and handicrafts. This is Lanai's version of the green market: petite in scale, like the island, but charming and unpretentious, especially in the shade of the sky-high pine trees that line the park.

Dolores Fabrao's jams and jellies, under the Fabrao House label (☎ **808/565-6134,** if you want to special-order) are a big seller at the market and at the resort gift shops where they're sold. The seven exotic flavors include pineapple-coconut, pineapple-mango, papaya, guaivi (strawberry guava), poha (gooseberry) in season, passion fruit, surinam cherry, and the very tart karamay jelly. All fruits are grown on the island; gift packs and bags are available.

Pele's Garden Health Food Store. 811 Houston St., Lanai City.

Lanai residents have embraced Beverly Zigmond's 500-square-foot store with open arms. Tucked around the corner from Dole Park, it opened in July 1995 with an assortment of bulk grains, vitamins, herbs, weight management products, fat-free and low-sugar snacks, and a variety of health and beauty aids. There are even natural pet foods and herbal shampoos for Fido; for their owners, fresh high-fiber bread and low-sugar cookies are flown in every week.

Pine Isle Market. 356 Eighth St., Lanai City.

A two-generation local landmark, Pine Isle specializes in locally caught fresh fish when it's available. Akule (big-eyed scad), opelu (mackerel scad), onaga (ruby snapper), opakapaka (pink snapper), mahimahi (dolphin fish), ahi (tuna), and other fish from local waters make their way to the seafood counter soon after being caught. You can also shop here for fresh herbs and spices from Pete Felipe's famous garden, fishing gear, canned goods, electronic games, and the basic essentials of work and play.

Richard's Shopping Center. 434 Eighth St., Lanai City.

The Tamashiros' family business has been on the square since 1946, and except for the merchandise, not much has changed. The "shopping center" is in fact a general store that sells groceries, paper products, ethnic foods, meats (mostly frozen), a few pieces of clothing, liquor, film, sunscreens and other recreational needs, and sundries. Until recently you could still unearth some pre-World War II items in the far niches (I still treasure my wooden ginger grater found there years ago), but these days the merchandise reflects the wants and needs of the island's modern mix: more and more visitors and construction workers, and a declining number of plantation workers.

11 Lanai After Dark

by Jocelyn Fujii, with Rick Carroll

Once, when I inquired about nightlife on Lanai, an island woman I had just met raised her eyebrows in mock umbrage. "Oh," she said, "that's personal."

Except for special programs such as the annual **Pineapple Festival** in May, when some of Hawaii's best musicians arrive to show their support for Lanai (see "Calendar of Events" in Chapter 3), the only regular nightlife venues are the **Lanai Theatre,** at the corner of Seventh and Lanai avenues, and the **Hotel Lanai.** The theater, commonly called the Lanai Playhouse, is a historic 1920s building that has received awards for its renovations. When it opened in 1993, the 150-seat theater stunned residents by offering first-run movies with Dolby sound—quite contemporary for anachronistic Lanai. It's open from Friday to Tuesday evenings, and Wednesdays during the summer months.

Across the park, the twice-monthly engagements of local artists take place in the rear section of the cozy dining room of the Hotel Lanai. On the selected Friday nights, from about 8 to 11pm, mellow guitar and contemporary Hawaiian music fills the lodge, wafting out onto the veranda and into the crisp night air.

Other than that, what happens after dark is really up to you. Dinner becomes leisurely extended entertainment. You can repair to your room with that book you've been meaning to read. Visiting artists sometimes call at The Lodge (see box

"Talk Story" with the Greats: Lanai's Visiting Artists Program

Not so very long ago, before CNN, e-mail, faxes, and modems, the word spread in person, on the lips of those who chanced by these remote islands, the most distant populated place on earth. Visitors were always welcome, especially if they had a good story to tell. The *tusitala,* or storyteller, was always held in high regard; Hawaii's kings invited them to the grass palace to discuss topics of contemporary life. Maybe you've seen the pictures in history books: King Kalakaua and Robert Louis Stevenson sitting on the beach at Waikiki, the famous author regaling His Majesty with bon mots. Or jaunty Jack London describing the voyage of his *Snark* to Queen Liliuokalani. In Hawaiian pidgin, it's called "talk story."

Hawaii grew up with this grand tradition of welcoming performing artists from every corner of the globe. Sooner or later, everyone from Kwame Ture to Tab Hunter seems to wash ashore like a note in a bottle. It's amazing, really. You never know who's going to drop in on Hawaii. Islanders may live apart from the continental drift of history, but these brief intense visits illumine the lives of these insular folks. Joan Didion once remarked that Honolulu without visitors "would be Racine, Wisconsin, Saturday night," a fate presumably worse than death.

It doesn't just happen in Honolulu. When The Lodge at Koele opened, David Murdock invited a few pals—who happened to be the late Henry Mancini, Sidney Sheldon, and Michael York—over, and they all had a good time in the Great Hall, singing, playing the piano, and reciting poetry. Kurt Matsumoto, general manager at The Lodge, liked what he saw and scheduled more informal gatherings of creative people. "We never had anything like this on this island before," said Matsumoto, born and reared on Lanai, where the only "live" entertainment in plantation days was chicken fights.

Now, in its third year, this small gathering has grown to become the year-long Lanai Visiting Artists Program. To this former black hole of art and culture comes the literati of America in a new version of "talk story." On any given weekend, you may find yourself in the company of poets, musicians, writers, actors, chefs, and other creative types. You can plan your vacation with, say, classical guitarist Carlos Barbosa-Lima, playwright Arthur Miller, humorist Calvin Trillin, author John McPhee, or who knows which Pulitzer Prize or Academy Award winner, each sharing their talent and insights in a casual living-room atmosphere.

Now, with the Lanai Visiting Artists Program, even this little island is no Racine.

Call **The Lodge at Koele** at **808/565-7300** to see who's visiting while you're on Lanai.

below), you can find an after-dinner crowd in the Tea Room at Koele or a game of billiards at Manele, the local folks out on the veranda of the Hotel Lanai will be happy to welcome you, and there's always a TV set somewhere to remind you of the great world beyond.

But one of Lanai's greatest simple pleasures after dark involves nothing more than the naked eye. Just go outside and look up. You'll find yourself enveloped by total darkness—until you notice the stars, constellations, and galaxies that make up the night sky. Since you're in the middle of the Pacific, with no distracting city lights or smog, the "seeing," as astronomers call it, is perfect. You'll see stuff you'll never see at home. Guaranteed.

12 Lanai for the Day: Cruises from Maui

by Rick Carroll

If you have only 1 day to spare but you still want to experience the essence of Lanai, there are several ways to see it in a single day:

Trilogy Excursions (☎ **808/661-4743** or 800/874-2666)   You can take a 50-foot catamaran on a 90-mile sail to Lanai for a day of sailing, snorkeling, swimming, and whale watching. Lunch is included. This is the only cruise that has access to Hulopoe Bay beach park and offers a ground tour of Lanai. If you wish, you can spend the night on Lanai and pick up a returning boat the next day. It's $149 for adults, $75.40 for children 3 to 12.

Club Lanai (☎ **808/871-1144**)   A day's outing consists of a trimaran cruise from Lahaina, Maui to Lanai's eastern shore, where you spend the day snorkeling, kayaking, and bicycling at this 8-acre beachfront estate. A light breakfast, lunch, iced tea, and juice are included. The cost is $79 adults, $59 ages 13 to 20, $29 ages 4 to 12, 3 and under free.

Ocean Riders (☎ **808/661-3586**)   Catch an inflatable black rubber Zodiac (the boats Jacques Cousteau made famous) on a trip to Lanai for a day of snorkeling. On the way, Ocean Riders takes you reef exploring past shipwrecks and coves on a wet and often wild cruise around the Pineapple island. The cost is $130 for adults and $95 for children 6 to 13, including continental breakfast, lunch, soft drinks, and all gear.

Navatek II (☎ **808/661-8787** or 800/852-4183)   The new and unusual 82-foot SWATH (Small Waterplane Area Twin Hull) vessel is designed to operate in heavy seas without spilling your Mai Tai. The ship's superstructure (the part you ride on) rests on twin torpedolike hulls that slash the water, creating a remarkably smooth ride. For all of you who go down to the sea with patches stuck behind your ears, this boat's for you; you couldn't get sick if you tried. A trip on the *Navatek II*, which glides across the 9-mile Auau Channel from Maalaea, Maui to Lanai, includes a 90-minute snorkel off Lanai's rugged west coast, a waffle breakfast, lunch, a complete sail around Lanai, and whale watching in season. It's $135 for adults, $67.50 for children.

Kauai, the Garden Isle 10

Aloof and beautiful, Kauai is the realization of the dream—a tropical island paradise come to life. All the elements are here: moody rain forests, majestic cliffs, jagged peaks, emerald valleys, palm trees swaying in the breeze, daily rainbows, and some of the most spectacular gold-sand beaches you'll find anywhere. Soft tropical air, sunrise birdsong, essence of ginger and plumeria, golden sunsets, too many waterfalls to count, Kauai touches you in ways few other islands do. You don't just go to Kauai, you absorb it with every sense. On any list of the world's most wonderful islands, Kauai is right up there with Bora Bora, Huahine, Rarotonga, and Vavau—and it's much easier to visit.

Kauai's great natural beauty derives from its inevitable decline. So much natural beauty is condensed on this small island because it's older than most—at least 10 million years old—geologically complex, and shaped by wind and rain and epic hurricanes. The last hurricane, 4 years ago, eroded the island by a century in a single day. Kauai's fabled Na Pali Coast is said to be the fastest eroding land on earth. Born at the beginning of the archipelago, Kauai is enjoying its last days in the sun—"days," I hasten to add, that will last at least a million years or more. Still, the very best time to enjoy Kauai is right now—and nearly 1 million people do each year.

Essentially a single large shield volcano that rises 3 miles above the sea floor, Kauai lies 90 miles across open ocean from Oahu, but it seems at least a half-century removed in time. The oldest and most remote of the main islands, it's often called "the separate kingdom" because it stood alone and resisted King Kamehameha's effort to unite Hawaii. It took a royal kidnap to take the Garden Isle: After King Kamehameha the Great died, his son, Liholiho, ascended the throne. He gained control of Kauai by luring Kauai's king, Kaumualii, aboard the royal yacht and sailing to Oahu; once there, Kaumualii was forced to marry Kaahumanu, Kamehameha's widow, thereby uniting the islands.

Today, the independent spirit lives on in Kauai, which refuses to surrender its island to wholesale tourism, preferring instead to take care of residents first and visitors second, which it does very well. A Kauai rule of thumb holds that no building may exceed the height of a coconut tree, between three and four stories. That restriction keeps Kauai from becoming another South Florida or Waikiki. As a result, the island, not its palatial beach hotels, is still the attention grabber. Even at Princeville, an opulent marble-and-glass luxury hotel is reduced to framing the natural glory of Hanalei's spectacular 4,000-foot-high Namolokama mountain range.

Kauai's beauty has won a best supporting role in more than 40 Hollywood films, from *South Pacific* and *Blue Hawaii* to *Jurassic Park*. But it's not just another pretty face: The island's raw wilderness is daunting, its seas challenging, its canyons forbidding; two-thirds of this island is impenetrable. This great green place remains a sanctuary for native birds and plants and fish and, in a larger sense, even humans. It's a fantasy island, all right, but it's real as a rainbow.

1 Orientation

by Rick Carroll

ARRIVING

No carriers fly direct from the mainland to Kauai; you'll have to land at Honolulu and pick up an interisland flight there. (Even if you're coming from another Hawaiian island, you'll still have to connect through Honolulu.) It's a 20-minute flight to Kauai's new Lihue Airport, on the island's eastern shore. **Aloha Airlines** (☎ 800/367-5250) and **Hawaiian Airlines** (☎ 800/367-5320) offer jet service; the flights generally cost about $78 each way. **Mahalo Air** (☎ 800/462-4256) flies twin engines into Lihue; the one-way fares are about $49 weekdays and $54 on weekends. The final approach is dramatic, and passengers on the left side of the aircraft are treated to a sneak preview of the island, with an excellent view of the Hauupu Ridge, Nawiliwili Bay, and Kilohana Crater.

Mahalo, Hawaiian, and **Aloha Island Air** (☎ 800/323-3345) also fly commuter prop planes from Honolulu to Princeville Airport, which serves Kauai's north shore.

Rental cars are available at both airports. For details, see "Getting Around," below.

VISITOR INFORMATION

The Kauai chapter of the **Hawaii Visitors and Convention Bureau** is located on the second floor of Lihue Plaza at 3016 Umi St., Lihue (☎ **808/245-3971**). For a free official *Kauai Vacation Planner,* call **800/AH-KAUAI;** for other information, call **800/262-1400** from 6am to 6pm Monday to Friday, 6am to 2pm Saturday and Sunday.

THE REGIONS IN BRIEF

Kauai's three main resort areas are quite disparate in climate, price, architecture, and accommodations; but it's a wide, wonderful range. On the south shore, dry and sunny **Poipu** is anchored by an architecturally keen Hyatt Regency and surrounded by low-rise condos, time shares, and three great beaches. The **Coconut Coast,** on the east coast of Kauai, has the most condos, shops, and traffic—it's where all the action is—but there are few safe beaches. Up on Kauai's **North Shore,** Hanalei is rainy, lush, and quiet, with spectacular beaches, deep wilderness, and only one small resort right on the sand—although up on the suburban cliffs, the glitzy Princeville Resort more than makes up for any perceived room deficiency.

LIHUE & ENVIRONS

Lihue is where most visitors first set foot on the island. This red-dirt farm town, the county seat, was founded by sugar planters and populated by descendants of Filipino and Japanese cane cutters. It's a plain and simple place with a sugar mill, used

Kauai

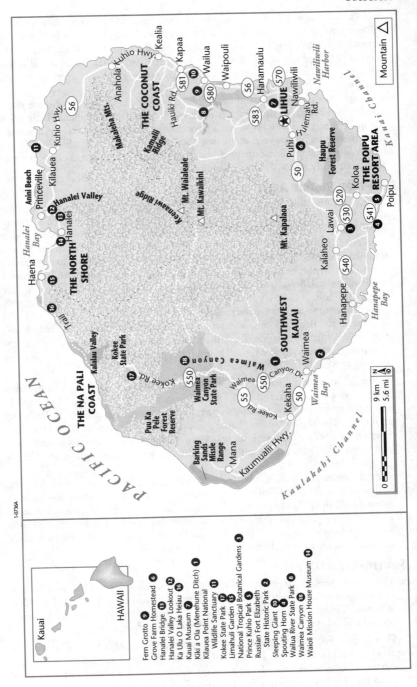

Mountain △

PACIFIC OCEAN

THE NA PALI COAST

THE NORTH SHORE

Haena
Hanalei Bay
Hanalei Valley
Hanalei
Princeville
Anini Beach
Kilauea
Kuhio Hwy 56

Makaleha Mts.
THE COCONUT COAST
Kamalii Ridge
Keeaauli Ridge

Anahola
Kuhio Hwy
Kealia
Kapaa
Wailua
Waipouli
Hanamaulu
Nawiliwili Harbor

Hauiki Rd.
581
580
56
570
583
LIHUE
Nawiliwili
Puhi
Huleemani Rd.
Haupu Forest Reserve

△ Mt. Waialeale
△ Mt. Kawaikini
△ Mt. Kapalaoa

Kalalau Valley
Kokee State Park
Kokee Rd.

Puu Ka Pele Forest Reserve

Waimea Canyon State Park
550
55
Kokee Rd.

SOUTHWEST KAUAI
Waimea Canyon
Waimea
Kekaha
Canyon Dr.

THE POIPU RESORT AREA
Koloa
520
530
541
Poipu
Lawai
Kalaheo
540
Hanapepe
Hanapepe Bay

Barking Sands Missle Range
Mana
Kaumualii Hwy.
Waimea Bay

Kaulakahi Channel

Kauai Channel

N
9 km
5.6 mi
0

HAWAII

Kauai

Fern Grotto ❾
Grove Farm Homestead ❻
Hanalei Bridge ⓭
Hanalei Valley Lookout ⓬
Ka Ulu O Laka Heiau ⓰
Kauai Museum ❼
Kiki a Ola (Menehune Ditch) ❶
Kilauea Point National Wildlife Sanctuary ⓫
Kokee State Park ⓱
Limahuli Garden ⓯
National Tropical Botanical Gardens ❸
Prince Kuhio Park ❺
Russian Fort Elizabeth State Historic Park ❷
Sleeping Giant ❿
Spouting Horn ❹
Wailua River State Park ❽
Waimea Canyon ⓲
Waioli Mission House Museum ⓮

1-0736A

439

car lots, and mom-and-pop shops, some of them boarded up and out of business. If Lihue looks like it's on the edge of bankruptcy, it is; 1992's hurricane Iniki not only reduced Kauai to a pile of kindling, it also broke the bank after Washington, D.C. ran out of federal disaster relief funds. More than 4 years later, Kauai is still scrambling to make up mounting deficits. The only thriving business in Lihue today is tourism.

There's not much to see and do in Lihue itself; it's basically one of those places you hurry through on the way to a more wonderful place, like Hanalei. Beautiful Kalapaki Beach, however, is worth a day, and the small Kauai Museum deserves a look. Better yet, book a suite at the new hotel—they'll make you a deal.

These may be the worst of times in Lihue, so be gentle with folks here and pass through quickly after spending some money. Every dollar helps.

THE POIPU RESORT AREA

On Kauai's sun-soaked south shore, sunny Poipu Beach is a pleasant resort destination of low-rise hotels set on gold-sand pocket beaches fringed by coco palms. Until Hurricane Iniki hit, Poipu was Kauai's most popular resort, with the widest variety of accommodations, from the luxury Hyatt Regency to cozy beach condos and time-share retreats. Still not all back together—two hotels are in ruins, and the sand's not back at Brennecke Beach—this otherwise wonderful place will, when legal hassles are finally solved, become a noisy construction zone for at least the next year, maybe longer. Too bad, because it's a well-done, master-planned resort with 36 holes of golf, 38 tennis courts, and two outstanding restaurants—a branch of Roy's (of Oahu fame), and the Beach House, now under the culinary thumb of celebrated Hawaii Regional chef Jean-Marie Josselin. Still, if you avoid the area around the ruins of the Sheraton and Waiohai hotels, you should find peace and quiet and be able to enjoy the best of what Poipu has to offer.

Koloa   This tiny old town of gaily painted sugar shacks just inland from Poipu Beach is where the Hawaiian sugar industry was born 161 years ago, when Ladd & Co. built a sugar mill and started raising cane. They closed the mill and walked away in July of 1996, thereby ending Kauai's plantation era. But this showcase little plantation town lives on as a tourist attraction with delightful shops, an old general store, and a vintage Texaco gas station with a 1930s Model A truck in place, just like the good old days.

At the crossroads park in Koloa, almost hidden from plain view, stands a bronze sculpture of a muscled Filipino field worker with a machete, next to two Japanese women holding stalks of cut cane. This lifelike Jan Gordon Fisher sculpture remains a powerful monument to all the immigrants from Asia, the Pacific, Europe, and Latin America whose blood and sweat made sugar Hawaii's chief industry and then stayed on in the islands to make Hawaii a cosmopolitan place.

SOUTHWEST KAUAI

This region, west of Poipu, is more remote than its eastern neighbor, and lacks its terrific beaches. But it is home to one of Hawaii's most spectacular natural wonders, **Waimea Canyon** (known as the "Grand Canyon of the Pacific"), and, farther upland and inland, one of its best parks, **Kokee State Park.**

Hanapepe   For a quick side-trip back in time, on your way out to Waimea, turn off Hi. 50 at Hanapepe, once one of Kauai's biggest towns. Founded by Chinese rice farmers who harvested the Hanapepe River valley, today it's such a picturesque old town that Hollywood used it as a backdrop in the Australian epic *The Thornbirds.* A good rest stop on the way to or from Waimea Canyon, Hanapepe has galleries selling antiques as well as art and crafts by local artists, including Georgio's surfboard art and coconut-grams.

Nearby, at Salt Pond Beach, Hawaiians since the 17th century have dried a reddish sea salt, called *alae,* in shallow red clay pans; Hawaiian alae salt is iron rich and commonly used for medicinal purposes.

Waimea   So much happened in Waimea a century or two ago that this little coastal town, the original capital of Kauai, seems to have exhausted itself and quit the march of time. Dogs sleep in the street while old pickups rust in yards, on their way to becoming planter boxes. The ambiance is definitely laid back.

On his search for the Northwest Passage in 1778, British explorer Capt. James Cook dropped anchor at Waimea on the southwest coast of Kauai, where he dis-covered a small, sleepy village of grass shacks on the island's shore. In 1815, the Russians arrived and built a fort here (it's now a National Historic Landmark), but they didn't last long: Scoundrel Georg Anton Scheffer tried to claim Kauai for Russia, but he was exposed as an impostor and expelled by King Kamehameha I.

Today, even Waimea's historic relics are spare and simple: a statue of Captain Cook alongside a bas relief of Cook's ships, *Resolution* and *Discovery,* in the town center; the rubble foundation of the first Russian fort in Hawaii; and the remains of an ancient aqueduct unlike any other in the Pacific. Except for an overabundance of churches for a town this size, there's no sign that Waimea was selected as the first landing site of missionaries in 1820. (To see the historic sites, stop at the Waimea Library, at 23-mile marker, for a self-guided tour map.)

Waimea serves today not only as the gateway to the Waimea Canyon, but the point of departure for the "forbidden" island of **Niihau.** At a small, gray barracks-looking office under a hand-lettered sign that says NIIHAU HELICOPTERS, you can buy a big-ticket ride to the last true Hawaiian island, where 200 people still live without cars, paved roads, telephones, electricity, and TV by choice. Once you're there, there's absolutely nothing to do except beachcomb, snorkel, or sit and listen to the wind and waves and watch whales frolicking offshore. (See "A Real Adventure in Paradise: Visiting 'Forbidden' Niihau," below.)

THE COCONUT COAST

The eastern shore of Kauai north of Lihue is a jumble of commerce and condos strung along the coast road named for Prince Kuhio, with several small beaches beyond. Almost anything you need, and a lot of stuff you can live without, may be found along this condo coast, known for its hundreds of coconut trees waving in the breeze. It's popular with budget travelers (particularly Canadians), who seek a place in the sun away from the big, expensive resorts.

Kapaa   The center of east coast commerce and capital of the Coconut Coast condo district, this restored plantation town by the sea looks just like an antique. False-front wooden stores line both sides of the highway; it seems as if they've been there forever—until you notice the fresh paint and new roofs and realize that everything has been rebuilt since Hurricane Iniki smacked it flat in 1992. Kapaa has made an amazing comeback without losing its funky charm, but there's still work to be done.

THE NORTH SHORE

Kauai's north shore may be the most beautiful place in Hawaii. Exotic seabirds, a half-moon bay, Bali Hai–like mountains, and mighty wilderness lie around the bend from the Coconut Coast, just beyond a series of one-lane bridges traversing the tail ends of waterfalls. This is the land of double rainbows, waterfalls, verdant taro patches, and lush valleys. There's only one road in and out, and two towns, Hanalei and Kilauea—

the former by the sea, the latter on a lighthouse cliff that's home to a bird preserve. Sun seekers may fret about all the rainy days, but Princeville Resort offers elegant shelter and two golf courses where duffers play through rainbows.

Kilauea   The village of Kilauea is home to an antique lighthouse, tropical fruit stands, little stone houses, and Kilauea Point National Wildlife Sanctuary, a wonderful seabird preserve. The rolling hills and sea cliffs are hideaways for the rich and famous, including Bette Midler and Sylvester Stallone. And the town itself has its charms: the 1892 Kong Lung Company, Kauai's oldest general store, now sells antiques, art, and crafts; you can order a jazzy Billie Holiday Pizza to go at Kilauea Bakery and Pau Hana Pizza, and fuel up at a gas station that's also a souvenir shop.

Anini Beach   This little-known residential district on a 2-mile reef (the biggest on Kauai) offers the safest swimming and snorkeling on the island. A great beach park is open to campers and day-trippers, and there's a boat ramp where locals launch sampans to fish for tuna. On Sundays, there's polo in the park and the sizzle of barbecue on the green. Several residents host guests in nearby B&Bs.

Princeville   A little overwhelming for Kauai's natural, wild North Shore, Princeville Resort is Kauai's biggest project, an 11,000-acre planned unit development set on a high plain overlooking Hanalei Bay. This residential resort community includes a luxury Sheraton hotel with a 180° view of Hanalei Bay, 10 condo complexes, new time-share units around two championship golf courses, and cliffside access to pocket beaches.

Hanalei   Picture-postcard Hanalei is the laid-back center of North Shore life and an escapist's dream; it's also the gateway to the wild Na Pali Coast (see below). Hanalei is the last great place on Kauai yet to face the developer's blade of progress; the one-lane bridges that lead to it keep the wolves at bay, and residents regularly veto schemes for marinas, resorts, and time-share condos.

Steepled Bali Hai ridges form the backdrop to half-moon Hanalei Bay, where sloops anchor and surfers play year-round. The half-moon, 2-mile-long beach, the biggest indentation on Kauai's coast, sits under towering pinnacles etched by a score of sparkling waterfalls; it's ideal for kids of all ages during the summer months, when the wild winter surf turns placid.

The first time I saw Hanalei, a dog was asleep on Weke Road, the beachfront road named for a fish. Today, that dog wouldn't stand a chance. Hanalei still retains the essence of its original sleepy, end-of-the-road charm, but there are a lot more cars and people now. Smacked flat by Hurricane Iniki, the plucky little town put itself back together again faster than Poipu; it's back on line and looking better than before. On both sides of two-lane Kuhio Highway, you'll find just enough shops and restaurants to sustain you for a week's visit—unless you're a hiker, healer, surfer, sailor, or have some other preoccupation that just might keep you here the rest of your life.

Haena   Haena isn't a town or a beach but an ancient Hawaiian district, a place of exceptional natural beauty and the gateway to Na Pali Coast. Emerald green Haena is the dream come true, just far enough from real life to keep you in an altered state of relaxation. It's the perfect tropical place, and everybody knows it: Old house foundations, terraces, and *heiau,* now covered by jungle, lie in the shadow of the new $1 million beachfront homes (some on stilts to avoid flood) of movie stars and musicians like Jeff Bridges and Graham Nash. This idyllic 4-mile coast has lagoons, bays, great beaches, great snorkeling (the coral reef is spectacular), great vistas, a new botanical garden, and the only North Shore resort that's right on the sand, Hanalei Colony Resort, one of my favorite places to stay in all of Hawaii.

THE NA PALI COAST

The road comes to an end, and now it begins: the Hawaii you've been dreaming about. The wild north shore of Kauai rises like a turreted emerald castle. Kauai's Na Pali Coast (*na pali* means "the cliffs" in Hawaiian) is one of Hawaii's greatest natural treasures, a place of extreme beauty and Hawaii's last true wilderness. Its majestic splendor will forever remain unspoiled because no road will ever traverse it. You can only enter this state park on foot or by sea. Most hike the ancient 11-mile-long trail down the forbidding coast to Kalalau Valley, an almost mythical place (see "Hiking & Camping," below). As you hike into this Eden, civilization becomes a distant memory. The lone, thin trail that creases these cliffs isn't for the faint of heart or anyone afraid of heights, like me. Those of us who aren't up to it can explore the wild coast in an inflatable rubber Zodiac, which takes you for the ride of your life (see "Helicopter Rides, Zodiac Cruises & Guided Eco-Adventures," below).

2 Getting Around

by Rick Carroll

You need a car to see and do everything on Kauai.

DRIVING AROUND KAUAI

All major rental car agencies have cars available for rent on Kauai. **Alamo** (☎ 800/327-9633); **Avis** (☎ 800/321-3712), **Budget** (☎ 800/527-0700); **Dollar** (☎ 800/800-4000); **Hertz** (☎ 800/654-3011); and **National** (☎ 800/227-7368) all operate out of Lihue Airport, with rental desks across the street from the airport (but you must go by van to collect your car). Hertz and Avis also offer rentals at Princeville Airport.

Even though no road goes completely around the island, driving on Kauai is easy. There are only two major highways, each beginning in Lihue. From Lihue Airport, turn right and you'll be on **Kuhio Hwy. (Hi. 56)**, which will take you to the Coconut Coast and the North Shore. It passes through the plantation town of Kapaa and follows the shoreline to Kilauea, Princeville, Hanalei, and Haena, dead-ending at Kee Beach, where the Na Pali Coast begins.

If you turn left from Lihue Airport, you'll be on **Kaumualii Hwy. (Hi. 50)**, which will take you to the south and southwest sections of the island. It doesn't follow the coast, however, so if you're heading to Poipu (and most people are), take **Maluhia Road (Hi. 520)** south to the coast.

Kaumualii Highway continues throught Eleele, Hanapepe, and Waimea, where Captain Cook dropped anchor and "discovered" Kauai; it then dwindles to a secondary road and leads to Polihale State Park, where it dead-ends and the Na Pali Coast begins.

From Waimea, you can take either **Waimea Canyon Road (Hi. 550)**, which follows the western rim of the canyon and affords spectacular views of it, or **Kokee Road (Hi. 55)** up through Waimea Canyon and to Kokee State Park, at more than 4,000 feet; the roads join up about halfway.

OTHER TRANSPORTATION OPTIONS

Buses   Kauai Bus (☎ 808/241-6410) operates a fleet of 15 buses that serve the entire island. It may be practical for day trips if you know your way around the island, but you can't take anything larger than a shopping bag aboard and it doesn't stop at any of the resort areas—but it does serve more than a dozen coastal towns between Kekaha on the southwest shore to Hanalei. Buses run more or less hourly from 5:30am to 6pm. The fare is $1; 50¢ for seniors, students, and disabled passengers.

Taxis   Taxi, limousine, and airport shuttle service are available from **Al's VIP Limo Taxicab** (☎ **808/742-1390**) and **Kauai Cab Service** (☎ **808/246-9554**).

FAST FACTS: Kauai

American Express   The local office is at the Hyatt Regency Poipu, 1571 Poipu Rd. (☎ 808/742-2323).

Dentists   Emergency dental care is available from Dr. Mark A. Baird, 4-9768 Kuhio Hwy., Kapaa (☎ 808/822-9393), and Dr. Michael Furgeson, 4347 Rice St., Lihue (☎ 808/246-6960).

Doctors   Kauai Medical Group accepts walk-ins at their office at 3420-B Kuhio Hwy., Suite B, Lihue (☎ 808/245-1500) and at the North Shore Clinic, Kilauea and Oka roads, Kilauea (☎ 808/828-1418). You can contact Physicians on Call 24 hours a day at 808/245-1831.

Emergencies   Dial 911 for police, fire, and ambulance.

Hospitals   Wilcox Memorial Hospital, 3420 Kuhio Hwy., Lihue (☎ 808/ 245-1100) has emergency services available around the clock.

Newspapers   The local papers are *The Garden Island* and *Kauai Times*.

Police   Dial 911 for emergencies, 808/245-9711 for other matters.

Poison Control Center   In an emergency, call 800/362-3585.

Post Office   The main post office is at 4441 Rice St., Lihue (☎ 808/245-4994); there are also satellite post offices all around the island.

Time   Call 808/245-0212.

Weather Information   For current weather, call 808/245-6001; for the forecast, call 808/241-6789. For marine conditions, call 808/245-3564; for the surf report, 808/335-3611.

Other Useful Numbers   State Commission on Persons with Disabilities is at 808/ 245-4308; Helpline Kauai is at 808/245-3411; YWCA Sexual Assault Services is at 808/245-4144; OnCall, a free 24-hour service offering news, weather, sports, and community information, is at 808/246-1441.

3 Accommodations

by Rick Carroll

Kauai offers a wide range of accommodations in all price ranges, from New Age retreats to luxury beachfront resorts—with condos, bed-and-breakfasts, and a few other options in between. However, do note that three hurricane-damaged hotels—the fabled Coco Palms, the Waiohai, and the Sheraton Poipu—have yet to be rebuilt.

The rates listed below are rack rates, but you can usually do better, particularly at the big hotels; see "Tips on Finding Accommodations" in Chapter 3. Hawaii adds 10.17% in taxes to all hotel bills. Parking is free unless otherwise noted.

LIHUE & ENVIRONS

Aston Kauai Beach Villas. 4330 Kauai Beach Dr., Lihue, HI 96766. ☎ **808/245-7711** or 800/92-ASTON. Fax 808/245-5550. 118 one-bedroom (with one or two baths; sleep up to four) and two-bedroom apts (sleep up to six). A/C TV TEL. $119–$295. AE, DC, DISC, JCB, MC, V.

These beachfront condos are a good option for families and others seeking more space and privacy than they'd get at the neighboring Outrigger or another hotel. All units come with light tropical decor and bamboo-style furniture, fully equipped kitchens, laundry facilities, and a lanai off the living room; the two-bedroom units have a lanai off each bedroom, too. Pools, spa, tennis, barbecue areas, and volleyball court are all available to guests, not to mention the Wailua Municipal golf course next door.

Kauai Marriott Resort & Beach Club. Kalapaki Beach, Lihue, HI 96766. ☎ **808/245-5050** or 800/228-9290. Fax 808/245-5049. 355 rms, 11 suites. A/C TV MINIBAR TEL. $225–$375 double, from $575 suite. AE, DC, DISC, JCB, MC, V.

This place's glitzy megafantasy resort days (as the former Westin Kauai) are history. Its 5-acre swimming pool (reputed to be Hawaii's biggest), ostentatious architecture, oversized Asian art, and abundance of columns were hallmarks of developer Christopher Hemmeter's outrageous fantasy resorts of the 1980s. A hurricane and new owners toned it down, to the extent of filling in the 2-acre reflecting pool by the lobby and replacing its ersatz plaster horse fountains à la Versailles with a faux-rock waterfall and a jungle of tropical plants. The result is grand enough to be fun, while still grounded in reality—it looks like a Hawaii hotel now instead of a European palace.

The more down-to-earth version still faces gold-sand Kalapaki Beach, one of Kauai's best beaches, and the hotel's perch at the mouth of Nawiliwili Harbor makes for interesting scenes as cruise ships and other interisland vessels pass by. The Marriott's location provides a ready supply of great golf and allows for easy arrival and departure, since Lihue Airport is only a mile away.

Dining/Entertainment: Kukui's Restaurant is a pleasant outdoor dining spot by the pool, serving tasty American and Hawaiian Regional Cuisine at dinner, as well as breakfast and lunch. The poolside Kalapaki Grill and beachfront bar/restaurant, Duke's Canoe Club, keep you fed and entertained. All options are casual and low key. Other eateries, lounges, and shops are located a short walk away at the opposite end of Kalapaki Beach.

Services: Valet and laundry, activities desk, lei greetings.

Facilities: Huge pool with waterfalls, ballrooms and meeting facilities, boutiques, 36-hole highly ranked Jack Nicklaus golf course, extensive water sports, horseback riding, health club, hair salon.

Outrigger Kauai Beach Hotel. 4331 Kauai Beach Dr., Lihue, HI 96766. ☎ **808/245-1955** or 800/688-7444. Fax 808/246-9085. 356 rms and suites. Package rates available. A/C TV TEL. $120–$165 double, from $380 suite. AE, DC, DISC, JCB, MC, V.

Out in the cane fields 4 miles north of Lihue Airport, the Outrigger (formerly the Kauai Hilton) commands a beachfront setting next door to a top-ranked municipal golf course. A fantasy pool with a grotto will keep the kids happy, and the property is home to tennis courts, restaurants, lounges, and shops. The location is a good one, about equidistant from both north and south shore activities, and also close to Wailua River and its kayaking, waterskiing, Waimea river tours, historic sites, and drive-by waterfalls. The setting and location are the draws here, not the accommodations; they're basic plain-Jane hotel rooms, not large but adequate, recently redecorated in blues. Conference facilities are available.

THE POIPU RESORT AREA

Embassy Vacation Resort at Poipu Point. 1613 Pe'e Rd., Koloa, HI 96756. ☎ 808/742-1888 or 800/92-ASTON. Fax 808/742-1924. 219 one- and two-bedroom apts. A/C TV TEL. $250–$390 one-bedroom apt (sleeps up to four), $300–$500 two-bedroom apt (sleeps up to six); $1,000 three-bedroom suite. Rate includes continental breakfast. AE, DC, DISC, JCB, MC, V.

Done in an architectural style that echoes the nearby Hyatt's retro look, this tasteful four-story condo complex, nestled in the sand dunes on the Poipu coast and overlooking a rocky shore, is Kauai's newest. And it's got a new twist: it's a part timeshare, part condo/hotel operation.

This is a great family spot, filled with mostly happy kids splashing in the lagoonstyle pool and poking around the sea cliffs. The spacious, nicely furnished luxury apartments come with large lanais, full kitchens, and laundry facilities. The best units are the two-bedroom corner suites with views of the Haupu Mountain range, Shipwreck Beach, and the Hyatt. Amenities include daily maid service, bell desk, concierge, front desk, fitness center with sauna and steam room, a lagoon pool bordered with man-made sand beaches, and access to a coastal footpath that takes you to Makawehi Point and the cliffs overlooking Keoniloa Bay to see sea turtles, whales, and the occasional endangered monk seal.

✪ **Hyatt Regency Kauai Resort & Spa.** 1571 Poipu Rd., Koloa, HI 96756. ☎ 808/742-1234 or 800/233-1234. Fax 808/742-1557. 600 rms, 41 suites. A/C TV MINIBAR TEL. $275–$485 double, from $425 suite. Packages available. AE, CB, DC, DISC, EURO, JCB, MC, V.

This is one of Hawaii's best luxury hotels, more environmentally attuned than most and with more Hawaiian influences apparent in its opulence. Spreading over 50 oceanfront acres overlooking Shipwreck Beach at the end of the road in Poipu, this $250-million Hyatt utilizes the island style of the mid-1920s to recapture the old Hawaii of the "blue blazer" Matson Line steamship era.

The art deco lobby reflects the glory days of architect Charles W. Dickey, the father of Hawaii's regional architecture. But the rest of the three-story hotel, spread out over a rolling coastal bluff, has the steep thatched roofs of Hawaii's early vernacular, or grass shack, architecture. Other features of this climate-wise style include wide eaves, high open windows, lush gardens, and seascape vistas framed by earth-tone archways and massive walls.

The most distant quarters are a good 5-minute hike from the lobby—but upon arrival, you'll find oversized rooms (nearly 600 sq. ft.) elegantly outfitted with rattan and earth tones. All have marble baths with double sinks and spacious private lanais; most have ocean views.

Since Shipwreck Beach is too rough for most, an elaborate freshwater fantasy pool complex is a welcome attraction, with "river canyons" to speed swimmers from one pool to another. If you want the real thing, family-friendly Poipu Beach is just down the street.

Dining/Entertainment: Romantic spots like Tidepools Restaurant add to the Hyatt's honeymoon appeal. Stevenson's Library is a book-lined, partially open-air watering hole where you can relax and enjoy tropical drinks like a Tai Chi (the rum-and-juice house special) while admiring the ocean view or perusing the news. Kuhio's ups the energy level with dancing on Thursday, Friday, and Saturday nights.

Services: Luxury treatment with twice-daily towel changes and turndowns; club floors with concierge and lounge serving continental breakfast, drinks, and snacks to club guests; Camp Hyatt kids' program; lei greetings. The guest activity programs offer lots of ways to learn something about Hawaii's ecology as well as its cultural

⭐ Family-Friendly Resorts

Kauai is a family-oriented place. Nearly all of Kauai's hotels have special kids' programs, special rates for families, year-round camps, and lots of of kid-oriented activities. These three are the best of a great bunch:

Kauai Marriott Resort & Beach Club (near Lihue)   Hawaii's largest swimming pool—26,000 square feet—is the main attraction, but that's just the beginning. It's all a bit like Alice's Wonderland: freshwater lagoons with six islands that serve as a minizoo, with kangaroos, monkeys, llamas, flamingoes, and other exotic creatures; draft horses leading carriages through the tropical gardens; and a high-energy beach beside Nawiliwili Harbor, Kauai's port o' call. All around, a kid kind of place.

Hyatt Regency Kauai Resort & Spa (Poipu)   It's the collection of swimming pools—freshwater and salt, with slides, waterfalls, and secret lagoons—that make this oceanfront Hyatt a real kids' paradise. Camp Hyatt offers arts and crafts, scavenger hunts, and other special activities; and baby-sitting services and kids' activities on weekend evenings from 6 to 10pm give Mom and Dad some much-needed free time.

Embassy Vacation Resort at Poipu Point   There's not a kid in the world who wouldn't be happy at this fun place, perched on the ocean overlooking coves full of sea turtles and monk seals, with whales gliding offshore in season. There's a big, sandy-bottom pool and lots of fun kid things to do, like horseback riding, sailing, and snorkeling. Suites are family-sized and so big that a kid might get lucky and have a private room with an ocean view.

history; opportunities include dune walks with a naturalist, horse rides in Waimea Canyon, and free evening performances of Hawaiian music and hula.

Facilities: Full service spa with outdoor spa, shower garden, and lap pool; elegant indoor and outdoor meeting space (which makes the resort popular with incentive meeting groups); tennis courts; bicycles; a fantasy pool and slide complex, plus two pools and 5 acres of saltwater swimming lagoons with islands and a man-made beach; golf at Poipu Bay Resort Course; water sports, horseback riding nearby.

Ⓢ **Kiahuna Plantation Resort.** 2253 Poipu Rd., Koloa, HI 96756. ☎ **808/742-6411** or 800/688-7444. Fax 808/742-7233. 333 one- and two-bedroom apts. TV. $155–$390 one-bedroom apt (sleeps up to four); $290–$450 two-bedroom apt (sleeps up to six). AE, CB, DC, DISC, JCB, MC, V.

Like a 1950s-style garden-apartment complex, this cluster of condos sits on a gold-sand beach with gentle surf at the heart of the Poipu Beach Resort. And it's all brand new: reduced to kindling by Hurricane Iniki, Kiahuna reopened this year to raves. Its unfortunate neighbors, the Sheraton and the Waiohai, remain in ruins, so things could get noisy here when reconstruction starts. In the meantime . . .

These gracious two-story white plantation-style buildings, loaded with Hawaii style and spirit, are sprinkled throughout a garden setting with lagoons, green lawns, and a beach. All condo units come with full kitchens, daily maid service, and lanais; there's also a big swimming pool, and a sundeck with lounges.

The new Plantation Gardens restaurant is housed in an old plantation home that also serves as the office. Tennis, golf, shopping, and other restaurants are within easy walking distance.

✪ **Poipu Kapili Resort.** 2221 Kapili Rd., Koloa, HI 96756. ☎ **808/742-6449** or 800/443-7714. Fax 808/742-9162. 60 one- and two-bedroom apts; 2 two-bedroom penthouses. TV. $150–$244 one-bedroom apt (sleeps up to four); $200–$375 two-bedroom apt (sleeps up to six). Three-night minimum. Discounts for longer stays; package rates available. MC, V.

This quiet, upscale oceanfront cluster of condos is outstanding in every area but one: The nearest beach is a block away. Otherwise, the good-looking Pacific Ocean is easy to behold, right out your window. I like the home-away-from-home amenities and comforts of Poipu Kapili, and its special touches: There's a video library, a book lending library, a spacious pool, several barbecues, tennis courts lit for night play, even an herb garden that you're welcome to take samples from when you cook. All units have fully equipped kitchens, tropical furnishings, ceiling fans, private lanais, and free continental breakfast by the pool on Fridays. The oceanfront two-story townhouses are my favorite because they catch the trade winds—a plus on this hot western side of the island. If Poipu's your kind of resort, this is a wise and comfortable choice.

WAIMEA

✪ **Waimea Plantation Cottages.** P.O. Box 367, Waimea, HI 96796. ☎ **808/338-1625** or 800/9-WAIMEA. Fax 808/338-1619. 48 one- to five-bedroom cottages (sleep up to nine). TV. $135–$480 winter; $115–$450 off-season. AE, DC, DISC, JCB, MC, V.

This beachfront vacation retreat is like no other in the islands: among groves of towering coco palms are clusters of restored sugar plantation cottages, dating from the 1880s to the 1930s and bearing the names of their original plantation-worker dwellers. The lovely cottages have been transformed into cozy, comfortable guest units with period rattan and wicker furniture and fabrics from the 1930s, sugar's heyday on Kauai; each has a furnished porch lanai and a fully equipped modern kitchen and bath. Some units are oceanfront. The larger homes include the Manager's Estate, a five-bedroom home built in 1900 with an ocean view, large living and dining areas, and a lanai—perfect digs for a small family reunion. There's a good restaurant, an oceanfront pool, tennis courts, and laundry facilities. The only downsides are the black-sand beach, which is lovely but not conducive to swimming (the water is often murky at the Waimea River mouth), and the location; its remoteness, at the foot of Waimea Canyon Drive, can be very appealing, but the North Shore is an hour away. Still, a fabulous retro retreat—and a perfect place to get away from it all.

⑤ **Kokee Lodge Cabins.** P.O. Box 819, Waimea, Kauai, HI 96796. ☎ **808/335-6061.** 12 cabins (sleep up to six). $35 dormitory-style one-room cabins, $45 two-bedroom cabins. Five-night limit. No credit cards accepted for cabin reservations; send personal check for full amount.

These are an excellent choice, especially for those who plan on spending some time hiking Waimea Canyon and Kokee State Park. There are two types of cabins: the older ones have dormitory-style sleeping accommodations; the new cabins have two bedrooms. Both styles sleep six and come with cooking and eating utensils, bedding, and linens. Firewood for the stove can be purchased at Kokee Lodge, where there's also a restaurant, open for continental breakfast and lunch every day (see "Dining," below). There's also a cocktail lounge, a general store, and a gift shop.

This great deal doesn't go unnoticed: the cabins are booked year-round at almost 100%. Write far in advance for reservations—at least 4 to 6 months (holidays are booked a year ahead)—to the address listed above. But call anyway if you're in the neighborhood; there's often a vacancy due to a last-minute cancellation.

THE NORTH SHORE

⑤ **Hale Luana.** P.O. Box 1015, Hanalei, Kauai, HI 96714. ☎/fax **808/826-6931;** e-mail: sarahb@aloha.net. 1 two-bedroom cottage (sleeps up to three). $100; $650 weekly. No credit cards.

Sarah Berntson's Hale Luana ("House of Comfort") is a two-bedroom honeymoon guest home steps away from world-famous Hanalei Bay. It's like a two-story New York artist's loft in paradise, with an open-beamed cathedral ceiling, vintage rattan furniture, ceiling fan, original art, and wonderful views of the mountains, waterfalls, and the bay. Amenities include a well-equipped kitchen, private phone, cable TV and VCR, barbecue, washer and dryer, and indoor/outdoor shower.

⑤ Hanalei Bay Resort & Suites. P.O. Box 220, Hanalei, HI 96714. ☎ **808/826-6522** or 800/477-2329. Fax 808/826-6680. 161 rooms, 75 studios and one- to three-bedroom suites. A/C TV TEL. $140–$230 double, $155–$240 studio, $260–$500 one-bedroom suite, $360–$750 two-bedroom suite, from $650 three-bedroom suite. AE, DISC, DC, MC, V.

This 22-acre resort is right next door to the the ritzy Princeville Hotel (see below), overlooking the fabled Bali Hai cliffs and Hanalei Bay; it has the same majestic view, but for as little as half the price. The Hanalei Bay took a hit in Hurricane Iniki, but is now fully recovered after a $10 million renovation that recaptured the spirit of old Hawaii, especially in the three-story stucco units that step down the hill to the gold-sand, palm-fringed beach it shares with its neighbor. Rooms are decorated in island style, in blues and greens with rattan furnishings, with lanais overlooking Hanalei Bay, the lush grounds, and the distant mountains.

Inspired by Michener's *Tales of the South Pacific* (which became the play and film *South Pacific*), the Happy Talk Lounge is one of my favorite places on Kauai to sip a sunset cocktail. While the open-air restaurant may not serve memorable food, it delivers an unforgettable view (nobody goes to Princeville for the food, anyway).

✪ Hanalei Colony Resort. P.O. Box 206, Hanalei, HI 96714-9985. ☎ **808/826-6235** or 800/628-3004. Fax 808/826-9893. 52 two-bedroom apts. $100–$210 per day (sleeps up to four). Seventh night free; condo/car packages from $123 per day. Five-night minimum stay during Christmas season. AE, MC, V.

If you love the wild beauty of Kauai's remote North Shore, you'll love this condo complex: It's directly on the sand at Haena. The waves crash right out front, the haunting mountains are just out back, and there's end-of-the-road solitude all around. Roughly 35 miles from Lihue Airport, this is the last outpost beyond Hanalei—quiet, comfortable, unpretentious, scrupulously tended, and affordable. Built in the late 1960s and redone in 1992, the two-bedroom units have full kitchens and shutters to separate the bedrooms from the main living area. This little gem prides itself on being a peaceful getaway for sensitive people; to that end, there are no phones, TVs, or radios in the rooms, so you can soak up the sound of the wind, the roar of the surf, and the ubiquitous call of the wild mynah bird. I once recommended this place to Herbie Mann, the great New York jazz flute player, who was so taken by the ambiance that he delivered daily impromptu concerts to the delight of guests. Amenities include a pool, spa, and barbecue and laundry facilities.

Hanalei North Shore Properties. P.O. Box 607, Hanalei, HI 96714. ☎ **808/826-9622.** 90 vacation rental homes, cottages, condo units, and one- to four-bedroom apts throughout North Shore area. TV TEL. From $700 per week. No credit cards.

Want to rent a rock star's tree house? How about coochy-coochy entertainer Charo's beachfront estate? North Shore Properties handles all kinds of weekly rentals—from beachfront cottages and condos to romantic hideaways and ranch houses—all along the North Shore. Renting a home is a great way to enjoy the area's awesome nature, especially for travelers who like to get away from resorts and fend for themselves. Shopping, restaurants, and nightlife are abundant in nearby Hanalei; several of the rentals are even located around its scenic bay.

Princeville Hotel. P.O. Box 3069, 5520 Kahaku Rd., Princeville, HI 96722-3069. ☎ **808/ 826-9644** or 800/826-4400. Fax 808/826-1166. 252 rms, 52 suites. A/C TV MINIBAR TEL. $290–$525 double, from $925 suite. Package rates available. AE, DC, DISC, JCB, MC, V.

This jewel in the Sheraton crown enjoys one of the world's finest settings, between Hanalei Bay and Kauai's steepled, Bali Hai–like mountains, which cup this palace of marble and chandeliers like a treasure.

Full of the drama, theatrics, and European-inspired touches that recall Hawaii's decadent monarchy period, this grand hotel steppes down a cliff, so the porte cochere where you arrive is actually on the ninth floor; you take elevators down to your room and the beach which, by necessity, is on the first floor. Terracing kept this massive, institutional-looking structure from violating the skyline, but some contend—and I am among them—that the marble, trompe l'oeil paintings, spouting fountains, brass door-chimes, butler service, and silver trays of chocolate-dipped strawberries are all a bit too much for this otherwise down-to-earth corner of the world. But then, so were the monarchy years, when Hawaii's kings nearly bankrupted the kingdom in wild pursuit of imported goo-gaw. Prince Albert, the namesake for Princeville, probably would have loved this gilded lily.

The hotel does present a very civilized contrast to the majestic wilderness just down the road and will appeal to people who like to come in from a typical Kauai red-dirt day to luxuriate in an oasis that needs only small improvements in food and service to live up to its exalted pose. One nice plus is the small airport nearby, which allows you the choice of flying to Princeville directly (see "Arriving," above) rather than flying to Lihue, renting a car, and driving 30-odd miles to get here.

Each opulent room has such over-the-top extras as a door chime, dimmer switches, lighted closets, bedside control panels, safes, original oil paintings, and a "magic" bathroom window: a liquid crystal shower window that you can switch in an instant from clear to opaque. There are no lanais, but oversized windows allow you to admire the awesome view from your bed.

This resort is Kauai's most popular setting for weddings; more than 300 a year are performed outdoors by the pool. Honeymooners delight in oversized bathtubs, Italian and Pacific Rim dining, and a five-star health club and spa with whirlpools, 25-meter lap pool, and steam baths (an unneeded amenity in usually humid Hanalei), plus your choice of a seaweed wrap or Hawaiian salt glow (where you're packed in salt until cured).

Dining/Entertainment: In all of Hawaii, there's no more romantic place to dine at sunset than Cafe Hanalei, on a stone terrace overlooking Hanalei Bay. If only the overpriced food and lackadaisical service could match the view.

Services: 24-hour room service, twice-daily towels, turndowns on request, lei greetings, free daily newspapers, and complimentary resort shuttle.

Facilities: There's top-ranked golf on two Robert Trent Jones, Jr.–designed courses (the Prince Course is rated 75th among America's greatest golf courses by *Golf Digest*), tennis on 25 courts, a pool and three outdoor spas (including one really palatial one), shopping center, business center, riding stables, and in-house cinema. Famous surfing and windsurfing areas, as well as a near-shore reef to snorkel, are nearby on Princeville's side of Hanalei Bay.

Tassa Hanalei. 5121 Wainiha Powerhouse Rd. (P.O. Box 856), Hanalei, HI 96714. ☎ /fax **808/826-7298.** 3 units. $85–$105 double; $150 for six persons in largest suite. No credit cards.

Deep in a green river valley, on the banks of the babbling Wainiha, this New Age retreat is a little piece of Hawaii that many call paradise. This serene and rustic place is the perfect place to tune into nature. Sometimes I think everyone who comes to

Hawaii should be quarantined for 3 days in a place just like this so they can relax, get into the island groove, and fully enjoy their visit. Three days here would make any urban soul a civilized person.

The largest unit is a woodsy cottage, ideal for honeymooners, that looks out on a jungle of plants, including banana groves and taro, planted in an attempt to recapture Hawaii's agrarian past. Round boulders dam the river to form a cool pool that's ideal for daily plunges. Healing treatments, such as massage and colonic therapy, are available on request. An intensive week-long program is offered during the last week of each month.

4 Dining

by Jocelyn Fujii

Renowned chef Jean-Marie Josselin went against common wisdom when he selected Kapaa, on Kauai's Coconut Coast, as the site for his first restaurant in Hawaii. "People urged me to open in Poipu, where there would be a steady stream of visitors," he said to me years ago. "But I was committed to Kapaa, where local people would be able to find me too." The original A Pacific Cafe has proven to be so successful that, at last count, Josselin had opened three more of them throughout Hawaii: one on Maui, one in Poipu, after all (called the Beach House), and the recently opened A Pacific Cafe Oahu.

Josselin's two Kauai eateries remain the hottest dining tickets on the island. Fans from other islands have been known to change their departure plans just so they could dine at A Pacific Cafe—an enviable phenomenon on an island that still struggles to regain its composure more than 4 years after Hurricane Iniki. Most of Kauai's tried-and-true restaurants have reopened, however, some of them showing improvement with new chefs, decor, and a renewed determination that's bound, ultimately, to prevail.

LIHUE & ENVIRONS

Barbecue Inn. 2982 Kress St. (near Rice St.), Lihue. ☎ **808/245-2921.** Main courses $8.95–$26.95. No credit cards. Mon–Sat 7:30–10:30am, 11am–1:30pm; Mon–Thurs 5–8:30pm, Fri–Sat 4:30–8:45pm. AMERICAN/JAPANESE.

Watch for the specials at this nearly 60-year-old family restaurant, located on a small side street, where everything from soup to dessert is made in the Sasakis's kitchen. "The chocolate pie is not even chocolate pudding," they declare proudly. "It's real chocolate." Sandwiches come on homemade bread, the tuna salad is made with fresh ahi, and several-course dinner combinations of Japanese and American favorites draw long lines of diners. This modest eatery is loved by locals; settle into the small booths and tables and notice how everyone knows the people at the next table. The daily specials are considered a family value, despite a recent increase in prices.

Cafe Portofino. Pacific Ocean Plaza, 3501 Rice St., Lihue. ☎ **808/245-2121.** Reservations recommended. Main courses $12.50–$18.75. AE, CB, DC, DISC, JCB, MC, V. Mon–Fri 11am–2pm, daily 5–10pm. NORTHERN ITALIAN.

Fans come to the stylish Portofino for the authentic cuisine and romantic ambiance, two features that distinguish it as a regional favorite in the heavily competitive Nawiliwili dining scene. Draws include alfresco dining, candlelit tables with views of Kalapaki Bay and Nawiliwili Harbor, and a varied and realistically priced menu that covers sweetbreads to scampi, vegetable lasagna to bistecca (New York steak), as well as an osso bucco in orange sauce that's decidedly courageous.

Dani's Restaurant. 4201 Rice St., Lihue. ☎ **808/245-4991.** Main courses $4.95–$6. No credit cards. Mon–Sat 5–11am, Mon–Fri 11am–1:30pm, Sat 11am–1pm. AMERICAN/HAWAIIAN.

Formica all the way, and always full for breakfast, Dani's is the pancake palace of Lihue: banana, pineapple, papaya, and buttermilk, plus sweet-bread French toast and kalua-pig omelets. Regulars know that fried rice is offered on Thursdays only, and that the papaya hotcakes are a deal at $3.85. At lunch, Hawaiian specials—lau lau, kalua pig, lomi salmon, and beef stew in various combinations—dominate the otherwise standard American menu of fried foods (pork chops, liver, scallops, chicken, and more) and sandwiches. Anti-gourmet to the end.

Gaylord's. Kilohana Square, 3-2087 Kaumualii Hwy., Lihue. ☎ **808/245-9593.** Reservations recommended. Main courses $15.95–$29.95. AE, DISC, JCB, MC, V. Mon–Sat 11am–3pm, 5–8:30pm, Sun brunch 9:30am–3pm, dinner 5–9pm. CONTINENTAL/PACIFIC RIM.

One of Kauai's most splendid examples of kamaaina architecture, Gaylord's is the anchor of a 1930s plantation manager's estate on a 1,700-acre sugar plantation. You'll drive past horse-drawn carriages and enter a complex of shops, galleries, and a living room of Hawaiian artifacts and period furniture. The private dining room has a lavish table, always elegantly set, as if Queen Liliuokalani were expected any minute. Next door, winding around a flagstone courtyard overlooking rolling lawns and purple mountains, the dining room serves American classics (rack of lamb, filet mignon, prime rib) along with a few pasta dishes, fresh seafood, and a winner, free-range Cornish game hen stuffed with wild rice and basted with Grand Marnier sauce. The ambiance, historic surroundings, and soothing views from the terrace make Gaylord's a special spot for lunch, when salads, soups, fish-and-chips, Oliver Shagnasty's signature baby-back ribs, burgers, sandwiches, and lighter fare predominate, and are friendlier to your pocketbook.

Ⓢ Hamura's Saimin Stand. 2956 Kress St., Lihue. ☎ **808/245-3271.** Most items under $4.50. No credit cards. Mon–Thurs 10am–midnight, Fri–Sat 10am–1am, Sun 10am–10pm. SAIMIN.

This world-renowned saimin stand is literally just a few U-shaped counters; but Hamura's saimin and teriyaki barbecue sticks attract an all-day, late-night, pre- and post-movie crowd that acknowledges saimin as the prevailing cultural ritual, the burgers-and-fries of Hawaii. Hamura's long lines of fans wait their turn under a sign that exhorts them not to stick gum under the counters as wisps of steam curl from the kitchen, where mounds of homemade noodles are heaped with vegetables, wonton, hard-boiled egg, sweetened pork, vegetables, and several condiment combinations.

Hanamaulu Restaurant. 3-4291 Kuhio Hwy., Hanamaulu. ☎ **808/245-2511.** Reservations recommended. Main courses $5.50–$15. MC, V. Tues–Fri 9am–1pm, Tues–Sun 4:30–8:30pm. CHINESE/JAPANESE.

In passing this place, you'd never know that serene Japanese gardens with stone pathways and tatami-floored teahouses are hidden within. You can dine at the sushi bar, American-style, or in the teahouses for lunch or dinner, but you must call ahead for teahouse dining. At lunch, enter a world of chop suey, wonton, teriyaki chicken, and sukiyaki (less verve than value), with many other choices in Japanese and Chinese plate lunches, $5.75 to $6.50. Special Japanese and Chinese menus can be planned ahead for groups of up to 60 people, who can dine at low tables on tatami floors in a Japanese garden setting. Old-timers love this place, and those who came here in diapers are now stopping in for after-golf pupus and beer.

JJ's Broiler. 3416 Rice St., Nawiliwili. ☎ **808/246-4422.** Reservations recommended for dinner. Main courses $12–$20. DISC, MC, V. Daily 11am–9:30pm. AMERICAN.

Famous for its Slavonic steak (tenderloin in butter, wine, and garlic), herb-crusted ahi, and the lazy Susan of salad greens they bring to your table, JJ's is the liveliest spot on Kalapaki Bay, with open-air dining and a menu that covers more than the usual surf-and-turf with a few ethnic touches: the madly successful Chinese fajita platter, coconut shrimp, and broiled scallops with crisp string taro, a deft touch. The nautically designed room and ocean view are inviting day or night, whether you're noshing on lunchtime salads, sandwiches, and burgers ($6.95–$7.75), or the fancier dinner fare. Either way, JJ's has stalwart appeal: options for everyone, an upbeat atmosphere, and service with a smile.

Kauai Chop Suey. Pacific Ocean Plaza, 3501 Rice St., Nawiliwili. ☎ **808/245-8989.** Most items under $8. No credit cards. Tues–Sat 11am–2pm, Sun–Sat 4:30–9pm. CANTONESE.

The large, unremarkable dining room and so-so service can mean that the legions of loyal diners are coming for only one thing: good food at low prices. Local folks who work in the area come for lunch, and those who don't work nearby bring their families in the evenings. The huge menu has something for everyone. Chow mein, Cantonese shrimp, roast duck, lemon chicken, and hundreds of choices of Cantonese noodles, soups, sweet-sours, foo-yongs, and stir-frys stream across the dining room to the chopsticks of expectant diners.

Restaurant Kiibo. 299 Umi St., Lihue. ☎ **808/245-2650.** Main courses $5–$19. JCB, MC, V. Daily 11am–1:30pm, 5:30–9pm. JAPANESE.

Neither a sleek sushi bar nor a plate-lunch canteen, Kiibo is what we love: a neighborhood staple with inexpensive, unpretentious, tasty, homestyle Japanese food served in a pleasant room accented with Japanese folk art. At a tiny counter or at tables, dine on sushi, ramen, sukiyaki, tempura, teriyaki, and the steamed egg-rice-vegetable marvel called *oyako donburi*. For $6, you'll get a satsifying lunch special; $15.95 will buy a combination plate with dessert, more than satisfying and more elegant than the folksy surroundings.

Tokyo Lobby. Pacific Ocean Plaza, 3501 Rice St., Nawiliwili. ☎ **808/245-8989.** Main courses $9.95–$19.95. AE, MC, V. Mon–Sat 11am–2pm, daily 5–9:30pm. JAPANESE.

The combination plates here are a hit: for $14.95, you can get chicken, tempura, and shu mai (pork dumplings, a Hong Kong delicacy), beef teriyaki, and sushi, plus a number of other combinations, all served with soup, rice, and pickled vegetables. Chawan mushi, the light-as-air steamed custard with shiitake mushrooms, shrimp, and green onions, is a must-try appetizer, and the shrimp and vegetable tempura, with soup, rice, and pickled vegetables for $11.95, is a good bet for dinner. But what really sets Tokyo Lobby apart is the Tokyo Lobby Love Boat, a Shogunesque wooden boat rocking with a splendid cargo of sushi, tempura, and other morsels; $19.95 and a two-person minimum.

THE POIPU RESORT AREA

✪ **The Beach House.** 5022 Lawai Road, Poipu. ☎ **808/742-1424.** Reservations recommended. Main courses $20–$24. AE, DC, DISC, MC, V. Daily 5:30–9:30pm. HAWAII REGIONAL/MEDITERRANEAN.

Ever the discerning businessman, Jean-Marie Josselin has chosen the best view on the south shore for his new temple of taste. Walk through an alcove of paintings by local artists into a large room on the ocean accented with oversize floral bouquets and sliding glass doors that open or close the room, but never the view. This is a setting worthy of Josselin's cuisine.

Menus are printed daily, but look for Josselin's signature touches: wok-charred mahimahi, sizzling clams, tiger-eye ahi sushi tempura, tenderloin steak, and a host of premium poultry and fresh-fish fantasies. Potatoes in any form (warm potato salad, au gratin, mashed, in warm seafood salad, in saffron-fennel potato broth) catapult the spud to new levels of respect. With or without the sunset, this is one of the top culinary experiences on Kauai.

Brennecke's Beach Broiler. 2100 Hoone Rd., across from Poipu Beach Park. ☎ **808/ 742-7588.** Main courses $6.95–$29.95. DC, DISC, MC, V. Daily 11am–10pm. AMERICAN/ SEAFOOD.

Window boxes and views of Poipu Beach are pleasing touches at this seafood-burger house, a longtime favorite. Of course, it helps that the best hamburgers on the south shore are served here, as well as vegetarian versions that are converting even hard-surfing, party-hearty carnivores. It's so casual that you can drop in before or after the beach and dine sublimely on nachos and peppers, a wonton/egg roll pupu platter, fresh fish sandwiches, kiawe-grilled meats and kebabs, salads, and pastas, as well as the build-your-own gourmet burgers. Dinner quality can be spotty, but not so at lunch, when efficient service, consistent fare, more-than-adequate choices, and the ocean view are worth the price of admission. Brennecke's notorious mixed drinks are as famous for their names as for their kick: the Poipu Fin (with Finlandia, of course), the original Brown Nipple (bananas and cream with vodka), and others, as well as a host of witty nonalcoholic mocktails.

Dondero's. Hyatt Regency Kauai Resort & Spa, 1571 Poipu Rd. ☎ **808/742-1234.** Reservations required. Main courses $24.95–$28.30. AE, MC, V. Daily 6–10pm. ITALIAN.

The new menu is supposedly healthier and friendlier than the old one, but as the fine-dining room for the Hyatt Kauai, there's still a certain stiffness here, despite the gorgeous ocean view and open-air seating. There are few complaints about the food, however. Diners come for the flavors—including apple-walnut-Gorgonzola salad ($6) and swordfish with crabmeat ratatouille over saffron fettucine ($25)—as well as the pampering and the stellar ambiance. If price is a factor, look the other way: the penne with wild mushrooms is $16.50, fresh-vegetable linguine is $17.50, and ricotta and spinach cannelloni, $19.

Keoki's Paradise. Poipu Shopping Village, 2360 Kiahuna Plantation Dr. ☎ **808/742-7534.** Reservations recommended. Main courses $10.95–$28.95. AE, DC, MC, V. Daily 11am–10pm, bar open until midnight. STEAK/SEAFOOD.

It's large, lively, and predictable, what one could call a good value seafood restaurant rather than a do-or-die rave, but definitely a cut above Sizzler. The offerings: fresh catch for $18 to $20, usually six to eight varieties prepared baked in lemon or orange-ginger, sautéed in a citrus-shoyu sauce, grilled in teriyaki sauce, or broiled butterless, with a fresh Kauai onion. For dessert, the original Hula Pie from Kimo's in Lahaina is something to be reckoned with. The bar serves lighter fare from 4:30pm, and there's live Hawaiian music during weekend dinner hours.

Koloa Broiler. 5412 Old Koloa Rd., Koloa. ☎ **808/742-9122.** Reservations accepted only for six or more. Main courses $6.50–$14.95. AE, DC, JCB, MC, V. Daily noon–10pm. STEAK/ SEAFOOD.

Wood is the visual theme here: creaky steps on a wooden deck in Koloa town, leading up to the rustic dining room with ceiling fans and wooden trellises—a lot like the set for *Gunsmoke*, minus the swinging doors. The food, as well, is aimed at cowboy tastes rather than epicures. This is broil-your-own dining: top sirloin, mahimahi, baby-back pork ribs, beef kabobs, barbecue chicken, and more. Salad, rice, and baked beans are included in this deal, which makes it an extremely budget-friendly way to go.

La Griglia. Poipu Shopping Village, 2360 Kiahuna Plantation Dr. ☎ **808/742-2147.** Main courses $10.95–$11.95. MC, V. Daily 7am–10pm. ITALIAN.

The bakery here provides the homemade bread with which the popular panini—sandwiches heaped with meats, vegetables, cheeses, and condiments—are made. But don't get your hopes up about the pasta; at lunch, they serve it in 10 minutes or it's free, but my order was tasteless and overdone. Still, it's nice to have an informal outdoor cafe in this sterile shopping plaza, where you can drop in for espresso and a generously liqueured tiramisu, served under umbrellas in a small courtyard. The menu also features burgers (Cajun blackened, meatball, eggplant-parmigiana, and other choices) and $12.95 dinner entrees of chicken parmigiana, spinach lasagna, and eggplant parmigiana. The biggest hit of all is the sundae topped with homemade, espresso-laced hot fudge—wow.

✪ **Roy's Poipu Bar & Grill.** Poipu Shopping Village, 2360 Kiahuna Plantation Dr. ☎ **808/742-5000.** Reservations recommended. Main courses $14.95–$26.95. AE, CB, DC, DISC, JCB, MC, V. Daily 5:30–9:30pm. EURO-ASIAN.

Look for the torches outside and find your way to the loud, lively room with ceiling fans, marble tables, art by local artists, and a menu for food fetishists. Roy Yamaguchi's (of Roy's restaurants on Oahu, Maui, Tokyo, and Guam) signature touches are present in abundance: an excellent, progressive, and affordable wine selection; fresh local ingredients prepared with a nod to Europe, Asia, and the Pacific; and service so efficient it can be overbearing, as when the server intrudes, after every course, with, "And how are we doing?" Never mind, the food is terrific. You could dine all evening on the appetizers alone: nori-seared ahi with black-bean sauce, spinach-shiitake ravioli; seafood pot-stickers in Thai coconut-milk sauce. The clever Yamaguchi figured that diners would have to return to try the temptations they couldn't squeeze in, so the menu is achingly seductive: blackened sea scallops with sweet chili-butter, garlic mustard short ribs, kiawe-grilled hibachi-style salmon, and legendary Northern Chinese–style roasted duck. Creative and well executed all the way through, the menu soars with the final notes: a dark chocolate soufflé and other seductions, including our personal favorite, the pumpkin cheesecake with maple-coconut drizzle. The menu changes daily, but some staples are always there.

Tomkats Grille. 5404 Old Koloa Rd., Koloa. ☎ **808/742-8887.** Main courses $5.75–$16.95. DC, MC, V. Daily 11am–10pm, bar until midnight. AMERICAN GRILL.

Fried appetizers, fish-and-chips, inexpensive New York steak ($14.95), rotisserie chicken ($8.50 for a half), seafood salad with fresh catch ($8.50), and sandwiches and burgers for all tastes are among the offerings at the Grille, in a serene garden setting in Old Koloa Town. Old-fashioned, un-microbrewed beer is big here—everything from Watney's to Samuel Adams to Guiness Stout plus 2 dozen others, all the better to wash down the spicy jalapenos stuffed with cream cheese. For the reckless: the Cats' Combo, a basket of jumbo onion rings, mozzarella sticks, zucchini, and mushrooms, all crisply fried.

SOUTHWEST KAUAI

Brick Oven Pizza. 2-2555 Kaumualii Hwy., Kalaheo. ☎ **808/332-8561.** Sandwiches less than $6.50, pizzas $8.35–$25.60. Tues–Sun 11am–10pm. PIZZA.

The pizza in this cozy, family-run restaurant is cooked directly on the brick hearth and brushed with garlic butter. Real, not low-fat, mozzarella is used; and you have your choice of whole wheat or white crust, plus 16 toppings: Italian sausage, Portuguese sausage, bay shrimp, vegetarian, anchovies, smoked ham, and several weighty combinations. The result is a very popular pizza. Vegetarian, hot sausage, roast beef, and the stellar seafood-style pizza bread sandwiches are big at lunch.

Green Garden. Hi. 50, Hanapepe. ☎ **808/335-5422.** Reservations recommended for dinner. Most items under $13. AE, MC, V. Mon–Fri 8:30am–2pm, 5–9pm; Sat 8am–2pm, 5–9pm, Sun 7:30am–2pm, 5–9pm. AMERICAN/ISLAND.

This Hanapepe landmark continues a decades-old tradition of offering local fare in a charming, quirky setting, with layers of foliage inside and out. Green Garden has lodged a niche in the hearts of local diners and the waves of visitors who sometimes, alas, descend in large groups from tour buses. It's particularly known for its fresh fish and pies; favorites include the fresh ono sandwich, smoky and wonderful; kiawe-grilled fresh-fish dinner specials that come with soup and salad; and owner Sue Hamabata's miraculous homemade lilikoi pie.

✪ Hanapepe Bookstore Cafe & Espresso Bar. 3830 Hanapepe Rd. ☎ **808/335-5011.** Reservations recommended for dinner. Main courses $15.95–$18.95. Tues–Sat 8am–2pm, Thurs–Sat 6–10pm. GOURMET VEGETARIAN.

Expect to find postcards, magazines, jewelry, excellent slack-key music on the sound system, and delectable food in a casual, winning ambiance. Don't expect books, though—they've been phased out. But no one has really noticed because the low-fat or no-fat vegan specials and creative gourmet vegetarian cuisine have taken over re-soundingly, and to great applause. The espresso, pancakes (multigrain with bananas, multigrain with apple-spice, etc.), and homemade sourdough French toast served with fresh bananas and real maple syrup ($4.25) are a major morning attraction, as are the Hanapepe-grown taro home fries—sliced and sautéed with garlic and fresh herbs, the taro is a creative coup. Pasta, a zesty Caesar salad with homemade croutons, and the best grilled-vegetable sandwich in Hawaii are served at the U-shaped tile bar or at Formica tables under high ceilings. The seven varieties of garden burger elevate this modest staple to gourmet status. At dinner, don't resist the mushroom–wild rice–garlic bread stuffing in puff pastry, a $7 appetizer. Main courses (spinach and Gorgonzola potatoes, sautéed Portobellos with Hanapepe taro relish and saffron butter sauce, seared artichoke hearts, and more) are priced from $15.95 to $18.95, but appetizer portions are available for less. From Thursday to Saturday evenings, you can savor all this *and* listen to the finest guitarists on the island play live. All in all, a sublime experience.

Kokee Lodge. Kokee State Park. ☎ **808/335-6061.** Most items under $7. AE, CB, DC, DISC, MC, V. Daily 9am–4pm. AMERICAN.

Don't count on lounging by the fire, sipping cognac after dinner, because the Lodge, still feeling the effects of Hurricane Iniki, opens only for breakfast and lunch these days. Some consolation is offered in the cornbread and lilikoi pie, both memorable still, and the hearty sandwiches and Portuguese bean soup, the perfect tonic after a morning of hiking the hills of Kokee.

Sinaloa. Hi. 50, Hanapepe. ☎ **808/335-0006.** Reservations suggested. Main courses $10.95–$15.95. MC, V. Daily 11am–4:30pm, 5:30–10pm. MEXICAN.

Fueled by time-tested family recipes from Mazatlán, chilis imported from Mexico, fresh local ingredients, and homestyle cooking, Sinaloa is without peer as a Mexican eatery on Kauai. Several types of salsa, hearty soups, fajitas, chili rellenos, and excellent homemade tortillas are among the many features diners love at this colorful wayside taqueria. Frothy, generous margaritas and a stalwart Mexican beer selection are worthy accompaniments to the menu.

Toi's Thai Kitchen. Eleele Shopping Center, Eleele. ☎ **808/335-3111.** Main courses $8.95–$15.95. MC, V. Daily 10am–2:30pm, 5:30–9:30pm. THAI/AMERICAN.

Toi's is a sensible dining choice—informal, affordable, and authentic, using fresh herbs and local ingredients. The house specialty, Toi's Temptation (homegrown herbs, coconut milk, lemongrass, and your choice of seafood, meat, or tofu), has a following, but so do the vegetable curries, shrimp sate, and ginger sauce *nua:* your choice of seafood, meat, or tofu in a piquant stir-fry of fresh ginger. Most of the rice, noodle, soup, curry, and main course selections allow you to choose from among pork, chicken, seafood, beef, vegetarian, and tofu as the main ingredient. Buttered garlic nua, peanut-rich sates, and stir-fried Basil Delight are among Toi's many tasty preparations. All dishes come with green papaya salad, dessert, and a choice of jasmine, sticky, or brown rice.

Wrangler's Steakhouse. 9852 Kaumualii Hwy., Waimea. ☎ **808/338-1218.** Main courses $9.95–$19. AE, MC, V. Mon–Thurs 11am–8:30pm, Fri 11am–9pm, Sat 11:30am–9pm. STEAKS.

Waimea's most popular eatery serves sizzling, pepper and garlic steak at affordable prices, with good service and pleasant veranda seating in front and in the rear courtyard. Spiffed up since Hurricane Iniki, with Western touches (an iron wagon in the loft, log-framed booths with gas lanterns), Wrangler's is the quintessential local steak house, a combination of cowboy, plantation, and island traditions. That means shrimp tempura with sashimi and beef teriyaki, imu-style roast pork with cabbage, and excellent french fries and grilled mahimahi sandwiches, smoky and tender. The star, however, remains the 16-ounce New York–cut steak with mushrooms, served on a sizzling platter. Families love Wrangler's because they know it offers multicourse seafood or steak dinners at prices that won't break the bank.

Yumi's. 9691 Kaumualii Hwy., Waimea. ☎ **808/338-1731.** Most items under $5.75. No credit cards. Mon–Fri 5:30am–3pm, Sat 6am–3pm. LOCAL/PLATE LUNCH.

Yumi's serves hearty egg, sausage, and bacon breakfasts for $3, rolled sushi that flies out the door, and coconut and apple turnovers that are the rage of west Kauai. Flaky, buttery, and substantial without being weighty, the turnovers ($1.75 each) are straight out of grandmother's kitchen, extraordinary in their lightness and flavor. They're the biggest hit at this classic rural diner, local-style all the way, with Formica tables, plate lunches, and no-nonsense servers.

THE COCONUT COAST

✪ **A Pacific Cafe Kauai.** Kauai Shopping Village, 4-831 Kuhio Hwy., Kapaa. ☎ **808/822-0013.** Reservations recommended. Main courses $20–$24. DC, DISC, AE, MC, V. Open daily 5:30–9:30pm. HAWAII REGIONAL/MEDITERRANEAN.

Jean-Marie Josselin's wizardry with island ingredients and creative, cross-cultural preparations has kept A Pacific Cafe at the top of Hawaii's culinary world and on the A-list of national food critics, who continue to heap accolades upon the unstoppable chef-owner. The first of what are now four Pacific Cafes throughout Hawaii, A Pacific Cafe Kauai will win you over, too. Who can resist the light-as-air, deep-fried tiger-eye sushi with wasabi beurre blanc; the seared scallops with taro hash lumpia; any of the fresh grilled fishes in sauces of coriander, fennel seeds, white truffle, and peppercorns; or Thai coconut-lobster curry? Signature dishes—herb-crusted opakapaka with black rice, Chinese roast duck, blackened ono with papaya basil sauce, and clams in any form—are the mainstays of a menu that changes by the day and is relentlessly creative without being cloying. This is the hub of dining on the island, a casually chic spot that's always crowded and buzzing with creativity, bounty, and respect for local agriculture.

Aloha Diner. 971 Kuhio Hwy., Waipouli. ☎ **808/822-3851.** Most items under $10.75. No credit cards. Mon 10:30am–3pm, Tues–Sat 10:30am–3pm, 5:30–9pm. HAWAIIAN.

Saimin, authentic Hawaiian plates, and local fare are served at this tiny diner with electric fans and Formica tables. A little funky for the uninitiated, perhaps, but manna for lovers of Hawaiian food, who come here for the fried whole *akule* (big-eyed scad), lau lau, lomi salmon, kalua pig, squid luau (octopus and taro greens in coconut milk), and other homegrown favorites.

ⓢ Bubba's Burgers. 1384 Kuhio Hwy., Kapaa. ☎ **808/823-0069.** Most items less than $5.75. MC, V. Mon–Sat 10:30am–8pm. AMERICAN.

They dish out irreverence, great T-shirts, and authentic, old-fashioned, $2.50 hamburgers at this tiny stand in the middle of Kapaa town. The freshly ground Kauai beef is 88% fat-free and served on a toasted bun with the appropriate condiments and diced onions; you can order it open-faced (the Slopper), as the half-pound Big Bubba (three patties), the Hubba Bubba (with rice, hot dog, and chili—a Bubba's plate lunch), and in other versions. Chicken burgers, fish-and-chips, vegetarian tempeh burgers, Bubba's famous Budweiser chili, and other American standards are served up in this house of Bubba—where burger is king, attitude reigns, and lettuce and tomato cost 75¢ extra.

The Bull Shed. 796 Kuhio Ave., Waipouli. ☎ **808/822-3791.** Reservations recommended for six or more. Main courses $10.95–$28.50. AE, DC, MC, V. Daily 5:30–10pm. STEAK/SEAFOOD.

The informality and oceanfront location are a big plus, but only part of the package: This time-tested steak house on a hidden beach in Waipouli serves steaks and chops—prime rib, Australian rack of lamb, a garlic tenderloin—that've been pleasing meat lovers for years. The fresh catch, grilled to order, is part of a respectable seafood selection that includes broiled shrimp, Alaskan king crab, and Parmesan-drenched scallops. Main courses include rice and salad bar, and combination dinners aim for the ambivalent with chicken, steak, seafood, and lobster pairings.

Kapaa Fish & Chowder House. 4-1639 Kuhio Hwy., Kapaa. ☎ **808/822-7488.** Reservations recommended. Main courses $9.95–$21.95. AE, DISC, MC. V. Daily 5:30–8:30pm. AMERICAN.

Were it not for the passion-fruit margaritas (pioneered and perfected here), the garden setting, and the crisp, moist coconut shrimp served with passion-coconut sauce, one could complain that this, the last restaurant at the north end of Kapaa town, is yet another in the string of faceless surf-and-turf eateries on Kauai. But it's not. There aren't many places where you can hunker down with a simple pot of unshelled, steamed Pacific shrimp and a cold beer or margarita at an outdoor table, or order a genuine fish-and-chips plate. More conventional choices: fresh catch with papaya salsa, sautéed calamari, ginger chicken, and a crackly, spicy New York pepper steak. It's lamentable they're not open for lunch anymore, but it's worth considering for dinner.

Kountry Kitchen. 1485 Kuhio Hwy., Kapaa. ☎ **808/822-3511.** Most items under $6. MC, V. Daily 6:30am–2:30pm and 5–9pm. AMERICAN.

This place isn't for modest appetites or calorie counters. Heavy, buttery omelets are the Kountry Kitchen trademark, and you can choose your own fillings from among the mix-and-match possibilities. The kimchee (garlicky, spicy Korean pickles) omelet with cream cheese appeals to fiery palates, but the more cautious have vegetables, meats (Portuguese sausage is popular), and cheeses to choose from. Sandwiches and American dinners (steak, fish, and chicken) are standard coffeehouse fare, but we like the sky-high cornbread, sweet and defiantly rich. Caveat: Sit as far away from the grill as possible because the smell of grease travels—and clings.

Mema Thai Cuisine. Wailua Shopping Plaza, 4-361 Kuhio Hwy., Wailua. ☎ **808/823-0899.** Main courses $6.25–$16.95. AE, DC, DISC, MC, V. Mon–Fri 11am–2pm, daily 5–9:30pm. THAI.

A relative newcomer to Kauai, Thai cookery has introduced a conspiracy of curry to the island, and Mema is one of the instigators. From soup (spicy lemongrass, Thai ginger-coconut) to cool papaya salads and hot curries with complex flavors, Mema's menu appeals to many tastes, including vegetarians. Shrimp rolls, a Thai staple, come with an extra touch: black mushrooms and water chestnuts, rolled up tight among the long rice and fresh mint and cucumber. The Pad Thai is a toothsome, satisfying classic. The multicolored curries come mild, medium, or hot, and with your choice of meat, chicken, or seafood. Mema's Curry, with kaffir lime leaves, lemongrass, garlic, coconut milk, and other rich flavorings, is a house specialty, as is the panang-style Siam curry.

Norberto's El Cafe. 4-1373 Kuhio Hwy., Kapaa. ☎ **808/822-3362.** Reservations recommended for six or more. Main courses $2.95–$8.50; complete dinners $11.50–$14.95. MC, V. Mon–Sat 5:30–9pm. MEXICAN.

The lard-free, home-style Mexican fare here includes top-notch chili rellenos with homemade everything, vegetarian selections by request, and, if you're lucky, fresh fish enchiladas on those days when the chef's brother has snared his share of ahi, aku, or ono. All the sauces are made from scratch (enchiladas and chili relleno are especially popular), and the salsa comes red-hot with homegrown chili peppers fresh from the chef's garden. Norberto's signature is the spinachy Hawaiian taro-leaf enchiladas, a Mexican version of lau lau, served with cheese and taro, or with chicken. At $12.95 with beans, rice, and soup, it's a deal.

Ono Family Restaurant. 4-1292 Kuhio Hwy., Kapaa. ☎ **808/822-1710.** Most items under $11. AE, DC, DISC, MC, V. Daily 7am–3pm. AMERICAN.

The Garden Patch, a dollop of fried rice topped with fresh steamed vegetables, scrambled eggs, and hollandaise sauce, is reason enough to find Ono. Breakfast is a big deal here, with eggs Florentine leading the pack (two poached eggs, blanched spinach, hollandaise sauce), and eggs Canterbury (much like eggs Benedict, but with more ingredients) following close behind. Steak and eggs; banana, coconut, and macadamia-nut pancakes; and dozens of omelet choices attract throngs of loyalists to Ono for the first stop of the day. Lunch is no slouch either, with scads of fish, veggie, steak, tuna, and turkey sandwiches to choose from, and Ono beef or buffalo burgers with various toppings (chili, mushroom, bacon, onion rings) highlighting the menu.

Restaurant Kintaro. 4-370 Kuhio Hwy., Wailua. ☎ **808/822-3341.** Reservations recommended. Main courses $10.95–$28.95. AE, DC, JCB, MC, V. Mon–Sat 5:30–9:30pm. JAPANESE.

The sizzling grills of traditional teppanyaki dining and a well-known sushi bar are the specialties of Kintaro, a lavishly decorated Japanese dining room. You'll dine among touches of marble, Japanese antiques, shoji screens, stunning kimonos, and elegant blond woods, on choices that range from *zaru soba* (buckwheat noodles) and tempura combinations to sukiyaki dinners, *nabemono* (cook-your-own vegetables and seafood in earthenware pots), teppanyaki, and steak and seafood. Although limited budgets will require vigilance at the sushi bar, there are other pleasing options, such as the tempura combination dinners, $13.95, and the broiled salmon dinner, $14.95. Like the chicken yakitori dinner, they come with buckwheat noodles, miso soup, Japanese pickles, and rice. For $10.95, you can also order an earthenware pot of *nabeyaki* noodles: udon noodles garnished with shrimp, mushrooms, and vegetables.

Wailua Marina Restaurant. 5971 Kuhio Hwy., Wailua. ☎ **808/822-4311.** Reservations recommended. Main courses $9–$28. AE, JCB, MC, V. Tues–Sun 10:30am–4pm, 5–8:30pm. AMERICAN.

We recommend the open-air seating along the Wailua River, where you can watch the riverboats heading for the Fern Grotto over sandwiches (mahimahi is a favorite) and salads. The interior is cavernous, with a high ceiling and stuffed fish adorning the upper walls—unremarkable bordering on weird, but we love Marina anyway. Marina's famous baked stuffed pork chop, hot lobster salad, steamed mullet, stuffed prawns, teriyaki spareribs, and some 40 other items are served from a menu that doesn't pretend to be haute, and isn't. The down-home fare, unapologetic in its use of brown gravy, tartar sauce, garlic butter, and mayonnaise, also includes prime rib, filet mignon, boneless teriyaki chicken breast, and, on the lighter side, a Chinese oxtail soup with fresh ginger and mustard cabbage, a deal at $9. Except for lobster and a few steaks in the $18 to $26 range, most of the dinners are $10 to $17, including a fresh catch for $15.50 (salad and mashed potatoes included). This is a strange but lovable place, anti-nouvelle to the end. Try the onion- and mayo-laden hot lobster salad, and see for yourself.

THE NORTH SHORE

✪ **Casa di Amici.** 2484 Keneke St., Kilauea. ☎ **808/828-1555.** Reservations recommended. Main courses $12–$24. MC, V. Daily 11:30am–2:30pm, 6–9pm. ITALIAN/MEDITERRANEAN.

Veranda seating, trellises, and greenery everywhere you look, including large vases dripping with heliconias and banana stalks, are part of the cordial, comfortable atmosphere in which chef Randall Yates presents his brawny Italian cuisine. At night, the trees bordering the restaurant glitter with fairy lights, and seductive aromas of garlic and basil emanate from a room warmed by the riffs of Puccini and Verdi. Expect excellent Italian fare: perfectly cooked risotto awash in mushrooms, tarragon, and cracked pepper; a tower of polenta with Gorgonzola, Molokai sweet potato, and a drizzle of tomato sauce; duck breast in a spicy mango sauce; pesto linguine with homemade Italian sausage; and the best linguine Alfredo in the state—light, garlicky, and perfectly balanced in flavor and texture. Yates has made this Italian eatery a major Kauai attraction, bolstered with live piano music on Thursday through Saturday nights.

Chuck's Steak House. Princeville Center, Princeville. ☎ **808/826-6211.** Reservations recommended for dinner. Main courses $15.75–$26. AE, CB, DC, DISC, MC, V. Mon–Fri 11:30am–2:30pm, daily 6–10pm. AMERICAN.

Chuck's is yet another surf-and-turf spot in the long chain of unremarkable steak houses that circles the island, but the ho-hum formula appears to be succeeding in this convenient Princeville location. Booths, low lighting, and a macho ambiance confer a tropical-paniolo feeling. The offerings: sandwiches and salads for lunch and prime rib, fresh catch, top sirloin, lobster, barbecue ribs, and the usual steak house offerings for dinner. Enlivening the scene are some hefty tropical drinks and a legendary dessert: mud pie.

Hanalei Dolphin Restaurant & Fish Market. 5-5016 Kuhio Hwy., Hanalei. ☎ **808/ 826-6113.** Reservations not accepted. Main courses $10 and up; lobster dinner $75 for two. MC, V. Fish market open daily 11am–6pm, restaurant daily 5:30–10pm. SEAFOOD.

Hidden behind a gallery called Ola's on the Hanalei River are this fish market, where you can stock up for your barbecue on fresh fish and fresh mainland beef cut to order, and adjoining restaurant, which features a seafood menu with a few obligatory butcher's block items. Most appealing (besides the river view) are the appetizers: artichokes steamed simply; buttery stuffed mushrooms; ceviche fresh from the fish market. Otherwise, choose from among soy-and-ginger Hawaiian chicken ($15), scallops baked in wine and mozzarella ($17), tenderloin or New York steak, broccoli casserole, and fresh catch.

Hanalei Gourmet. Old Hanalei Schoolhouse, 5-5161 Kuhio Hwy., Hanalei. ☎ **808/ 826-2524.** Main courses $10.95–$14.95. DISC, MC, V. Open Mon–Thurs 10:30am–10:30pm, Fri 10:30am–11:30pm, Sat 8:30am–11:30pm, Sun 8:30am–10pm. AMERICAN.

The wood floors, wooden benches, and blackboards of the old Hanalei School, built in 1926, are now a haven for Hanalei hipsters noshing on the Hawaiian seafood sampler (highly recommended smoked fish and secret dip, $8.95), Tu Tu Tuna (far-from-prosaic tuna salad with green beans, potatoes, Nicoise olives, and hard boiled eggs, $6.75), roasted eggplant sandwich (a personal favorite, with red peppers, onions, cheese, and other goodies, $6.95), chicken salad boat (tarragon-laced in papaya or avocado, sans mayonnaise, $7.95 or $8.95), and more sandwiches, salads, and other winning selections. Pastries and Huevos Santa Cruz (eggs, chilis, salsa baked on a flour tortilla, with nachos-like condiments, $7.50) are breakfast headliners, but there's plenty to carry you through the rest of the day. The TV set over the bar competes with the breathtaking view of the Hanalei mountains and waterfalls, and the wooden floors keep the noise level high; but when you relax with a crusty baguette and a serving of unpeeled shrimp in Old Bay broth, all the interference fades, and Hanalei Gourmet is king.

Hanalei Wake-Up Cafe. 148 Aku Rd., at Kuhio Hwy. ☎ **808/826-5551.** Most items under $7.95. No credit cards. Daily 6am–3pm. AMERICAN.

What began as a surfers' pre-cowabunga breakfast call has turned into a morning-to-evening center of plate-lunch chic and enchilada heaven. Dawn patrol begins with pancakes, omelets, quesadillas, killer fresh fruit smoothies, the Hang Ten special (eggs and toast with bacon or Portuguese sausage), veggie tofu sauté, and the legendary Over the Falls, a custardy French toast topped with pineapple, coconut, and whipped cream—worth every penny. The informal cafe is lined with historic photos of the town from the 1900s, and the crowd is decidedly laid-back and briny. Ahi and veggie burgers; plate lunch specials (teriyaki chicken, ahi steak); the ever-popular kiawe-smoked chicken, served with Spanish rice and organic salad; and ahi tacos, enchiladas, burritos, and other Mexican favorites are a few of the afternoon and evening attractions.

✪ Kilauea Bakery & Pau Hana Pizza. Kong Lung Center (on the way to Kilauea Lighthouse). ☎ **808/828-2020.** Pizzas $10.95–$25.75. No credit cards. Mon–Sat 6:30am–9pm. PIZZA/ BAKERY.

When owner, baker, and avid diver Tom Pickett spears an ono and smokes it himself, his catch will appear on the Billie Holiday pizza, guaranteed to obliterate the blues with its brilliant notes of Swiss chard, roasted onions, Gorgonzola-rosemary sauce, and mozzarella cheese. It's amazing what pours out of this 500-square-foot bakery: basil-pesto Provençale; the Great Gonzo (with roasted eggplant, red onion, goat cheese, and roasted garlic); the classic scampi with tiger prawns, capers, lemon, cheese, and roasted garlic; and other pizzas, all made with organically grown olive oil, whole-milk mozzarella, whole-wheat or traditional crust, and homemade, long-simmering sauces. The ingredients are all from on high: chipotle pepper, roasted onion and garlic, kalamata olive, roasted red pepper, basil pesto, and a dozen other far-from-traditional toppings. The bakery breads are also noteworthy: guava sourdough, Gorgonzola-rosemary, bagels, sweet bread, and award-winning chocolate chip cookies. Many of the breads and bagels are made from sourdough starters that were named, saved, and fed in coolers in the months when the island was without electricity following Hurricane Iniki. Hint: The lunch specials and breadsticks are best-sellers, too—for good reason.

✪ **La Cascata.** Princeville Hotel, 6547 Ka Haku Rd. ☎ **808/826-2761.** Reservations recommended. Main courses $20–$30, prix fixe $48.05 per person. AE, DC, DISC, JCB, MC, V. Daily 6–9:30pm. MEDITERRANEAN/SOUTHERN ITALIAN.

The North Shore's special-occasion restaurant is sumptuous, expensive, and worth it. If you're there before dark, the view of Bali Hai and the waterfalls of Waialeale is as rewarding as the slow-roasted duck with orange-cherry chutney. Click your heels on the terra-cotta floors, train your eyes through the concertina windows, and pretend you're being served on a terrazzo in Sicily. This restaurant is worthy of adoration: lobster bisque, white-bean soup with sliced asiago cheese, grilled ahi with roasted-garlic polenta and mushrooms, and especially the grilled lamb chops with fennel and coriander—a marvel. Seafood lovers can choose the garlic–bread-crumb Island snapper in saffron beurre blanc or the cappellini with clams and white wine. While more sensible tastes go for the penne primavera with roasted peppers and seasonal vegetables, we opted for the grilled tiger-prawn risotto with asparagus, roasted peppers, and basil pesto—a culinary feat worth every penny, and every calorie. Inarguably, Hanalei's finest—and most thrilling—restaurant.

✪ **Postcards.** In the old Hanalei Museum, Kuhio Hwy., at the entrance to Hanalei town. ☎ **808/826-1191.** Reservations recommended for dinner. Main courses $6.95–$13.95. AE, DC, MC, V. Daily 6:30am–2:30pm, 5:30–9:30pm. GOURMET VEGETARIAN/SEAFOOD.

This place is really making waves. Inside what used to be the quaint Hanalei Museum, excellent gourmet vegetarian fare (plus fresh fish) is prepared fresh with locally grown organic herbs and produce, taro grown next door, Big Island tempeh (a moist soybean meat substitute), and other low-fat, no-cholesterol, high-protein ingredients, and presented in an impressive, wide-ranging menu that roams the planet like postcards. For starters: taro fritters with papaya salsa, Thai spring rolls with peanut sauce, polenta with warm goat cheese. Main dishes include shredded lobster tacos; vegetable curry in phyllo pastry; and a light, comforting medley of soup, organic local salad, and warm corn bread. Fans rave about the Thai coconut curry, served over rice with tempeh kabob and peanut sauce, and the Mexican selection of quesadillas, enchiladas, and the "Almost Famous Fish Tacos" lightly crisped in a secret beer batter. Sandwiches on freshly baked focaccia steal the lunchtime limelight, with everything from grilled vegetables and fresh catch to taro burgers and tempeh—wholesome, creative, and something to write home about. Just as you reach Hanalei, look for the immense, mossy, hollowed-out stone that serves as a freestanding lily pond outside a historic wooden building with a narrow veranda.

Tahiti Nui. Kuhio Hwy., Hanalei. ☎ **808/826-6277.** Reservations recommended. Main courses $13.95–$21.95. DC, MC, V. Daily 7am–midnight. ISLAND/SEAFOOD.

Gastronomically, this funky old-timer has long been eclipsed by the newer, hipper, and more conscientious eateries in the region. Tahiti Nui has always been more of a nostalgic choice than a culinary one, and that's truer than ever now. The so-called Hawaiian food luau on Wednesday and Friday evenings is actually held indoors, with friends and family performing in a confined room for those willing to pay resort prices ($40) for a buffet dinner and a cocktail. The bar evokes the smoky bonhomie of a

Papeete pub, but the seafood, pasta, and Island-style menu can't compete with the sincerely creative efforts of some of Tahiti Nui's neighbors.

5 Beaches

by Rick Carroll, with Jeanette Foster

Ancient Kauai is what geologists call "posterosional"—which means eons of wind and rain have created a geological masterpiece with some fabulous beaches, like Hanalei, Kee, and Kalapaki. All are accessible to the public, as provided by Hawaii law, and many have facilities. Here are our favorites:

LIHUE'S BEST BEACH
KALAPAKI BEACH

Any town would pay a fortune to have a beach like Kalapaki, one of Kauai's best, in its backyard. But little Lihue turns its back on Kalapaki; there's not even a sign pointing the way through the trafficky labyrinth to this graceful half-moon of golden sand at the foot of the new Marriott Resort & Beach Club. Fifty yards wide and a quarter-mile long, Kalapaki is protected by a jetty and patrolled by life guards, making it very safe for swimmers. The waves are good for surfing when there's a winter swell, and the view from the sand—of the steepled 2,200-foot high peaks of the majestic Ha'upu Ridge that shield Nawiliwili Bay—is awesome. Kalapaki is the best beach not only in Lihue, but the whole east coast. From Lihue Airport, go south on Kapule Highway (Hi. 51) to Rice Street, turn left, and go to the entrance of the Marriott; go past the hotel's porte cochere, turn right at the SHORELINE ACCESS sign. Facilities include lifeguards, free parking, rest rooms, and showers; food and drink are available nearby at JJ's Broiler.

THE POIPU RESORT AREA
✪ MAHAULEPU BEACH

Mahaulepu is the best-looking unspoiled beach on Kauai, and possibly the whole state. Its 2 miles of reddish-gold, grainy sand line the southeastern shore at the foot of 1,500-foot-high Haupu Ridge, just beyond the Hyatt Regency Poipu and McBryde sugarcane fields, which end in sand dunes and a forest of casuarina trees. Almost untouched by modern life—two Hawaiian boys were casting fishnets the last time I was there—Mahaulepu is a great escape from the real world. It's ideal for beachcombing, shell hunting, or just watching endless waves. Swimming can be risky, except in the reef-sheltered shallows 200 yards west of the sandy parking lot. There's no lifeguard, no facilities—just great natural beauty everywhere you look. (This beach is where George C. Scott portrayed Ernest Hemingway in the movie *Islands in the Stream*.) While you're here, see if you can find the Hawaiian petroglyph of a voyaging canoe carved in the beach rock.

To get to Mahaulepu, drive past the Hyatt Regency Poipu 3 miles east on a red dirt road, past the golf course and the stables. Turn right at the T intersection, stop and register at the security guard hut, drive 1 mile to the big sand dune, turn left, and drive a half-mile to a small lot under the trees.

POIPU BEACH PARK

Beaten up by Hurricane Iniki and not yet fully restored (two wrecked hotels still front this beach), big, wide Poipu Beach is slowly making a comeback on the sunny south shore. Much of its sand was blown out to sea in 1992; it was restored by a parade of dump trucks hauling sand from Polihale.

⭐ **Frommer's Favorite Kauai Experiences**

Snorkeling Ke'e Lagoon. Face down, floating like a leaf on a pond, watching little yellow fish dart here and there across coral in water clear as day. Face up, staring at green velvet cathedral cliffs, under a hopelessly blue sky with long-tailed tropical birds riding the trade winds. Palms rustle, a wave breaks. You can only smile and think, if this isn't paradise, what is?

Catching a Poipu Wave. Vividly turquoise, curling and totally tubular, big enough to hang ten yet small enough to bodysurf, the waves at Poipu are endless in their attraction and timeless in their hold on all who take them on. Grab a boogie board, or just jump in and go with the flow.

Hiking Waimea Canyon, the Grand Canyon of the Pacific. Ansel Adams would have loved this ageless desert canyon, carved by an ancient river. Sunlight plays against its rustic red cliffs, burnt-orange pinnacles, and blue-green valleys. There's nothing else like it in the islands.

Taking a Helicopter Ride over the Na Pali Coast. Streaking low over razor-thin cliffs, fluttering past sparkling waterfalls and down into the canyons and valleys of the fabled Na Pali Coast—it's like flying in your dreams, except there's too much beauty to absorb and it all goes by in a rush. You'll never want to stop flying over this spectacular, surreal landscape.

Hanging Out in Hanalei. While away some time in lush, fabled Hanalei. Spend the night in a historic Buddhist temple. Shop for vintage aloha shirts at Yellowfish Trading Company. Listen to the waterfalls sing behind Waioli Mission House. Order a gourmet Hubba Bubba burger at Bubba's Burgers. Or just grab a rattan chair on the veranda of Tahiti Nui and watch the cars go by. End your day with a moonlit walk along beautiful Hanalei Bay.

Dining at A Pacific Cafe. If you only have one special dinner on Kauai, have it at A Pacific Cafe. Chef/owner Jean-Marie Josselin's wizardry with fresh local ingredients and creative, cross-cultural preparations has put Kauai on the culinary map—and his casually chic restaurant on the A-list of food critics around the world. This is Hawaii Regional Cuisine at its best.

Poipu is actually two beaches in one; it's divided by a sandbar, called a *tombolo*. On the left, a lava-rock jetty protects a sandy-bottom pool that's perfect for small children; on the right, the open bay attracts swimmers, snorkelers, and surfers. And everyone likes to picnic on the grassy lawn graced by coconut trees. The swimming is excellent, with small tide pools for exploring and great reefs for snorkeling and diving, good fishing, nice waves for surfers, and a steady wind for windsurfers. Poipu attracts a daily crowd of visitors and local residents, but the density seldom approaches Waikiki levels, except on holidays. There are bathrooms, showers, picnic facilities, a nearby restaurant and snack bar, and plenty of free parking in the red dirt lot. To get to Poipu, turn on Poipu Beach Road, then right at Hoowili Road.

SOUTHWEST KAUAI
SALT POND BEACH PARK

Hawaii's only salt ponds still in production are at Salt Pond Beach, just outside Hanapepe. Generations of locals have come here to swim, fish, and collect salt crystals from the sea that are dried in sun beds. The tangy salt is used to cure fish,

Beaches & Outdoor Activities on Kauai

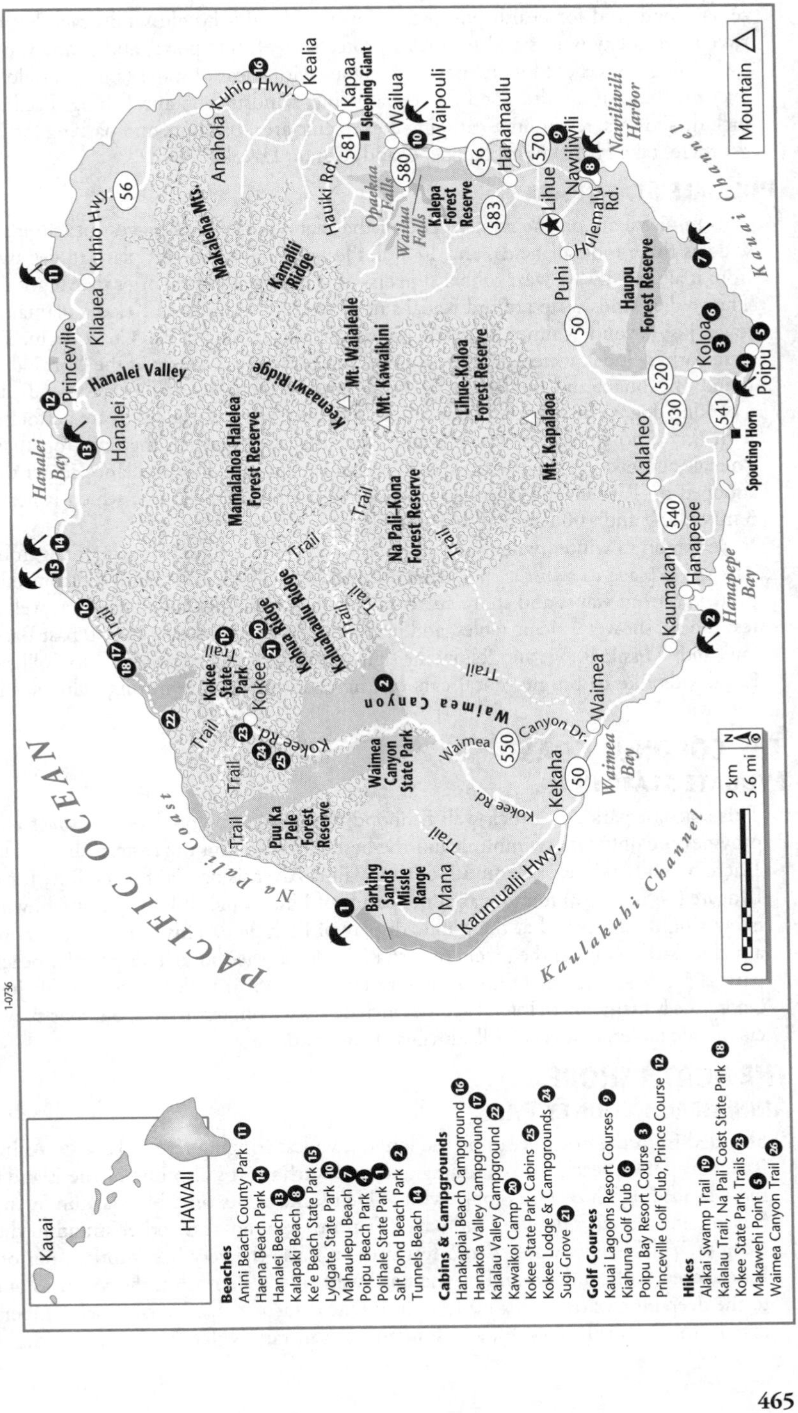
PACIFIC OCEAN
Na Pali Coast
Kaulakahi Channel
Kauai Channel
Hanalei Bay
Waimea Bay
Hanapepe Bay
Nawiliwili Harbor
Mountain
0
9 km
5.6 mi
Kauai
HAWAII
Princeville
Kilauea
Kuhio Hwy.
Anahola
Kealia
Kapaa
Sleeping Giant
Wailua
Waipouli
Hanamaulu
Lihue
Nawiliwili
Hulemalu Rd.
Puhi
Koloa
Poipu
Spouting Horn
Kalaheo
Hanapepe
Kaumakani
Waimea
Kekaha
Mana
Kaumualii Hwy.
Kokee
Hanalei
Hanalei Valley
Makaleha Mts.
Kamalii Ridge
Hauiki Rd.
Opaekaa Falls
Wailua Falls
Kalepa Forest Reserve
Mt. Waialeale
Mt. Kawaikini
Keenaawi Ridge
Mamalahoa Halelea Forest Reserve
Lihue-Koloa Forest Reserve
Haupu Forest Reserve
Mt. Kapalaoa
Na Pali-Kona Forest Reserve
Kokee State Park
Kohua Ridge
Kaluahaulu Ridge
Waimea Canyon
Waimea Canyon State Park
Waimea Canyon Dr.
Kokee Rd.
Puu Ka Pele Forest Reserve
Barking Sands Missle Range
Trail
1-0736
Beaches
Anini Beach County Park 11
Haena Beach Park 14
Hanalei Beach 13
Kalapaki Beach 8
Ke'e Beach State Park 15
Lydgate State Park 10
Mahaulepu Beach 7
Poipu Beach Park 4
Polihale State Park 1
Salt Pond Beach Park 2
Tunnels Beach 14
Cabins & Campgrounds
Hanakapiai Beach Campground 16
Hanakoa Valley Campground 17
Kalalau Valley Campground 22
Kawaikoi Camp 20
Kokee State Park Cabins 25
Kokee Lodge & Campgrounds 24
Sugi Grove 21
Golf Courses
Kauai Lagoons Resort Courses 9
Kiahuna Golf Club 6
Poipu Bay Resort Course 3
Princeville Golf Club, Prince Course 12
Hikes
Alakai Swamp Trail 19
Kalalau Trail, Na Pali Coast State Park 18
Kokee State Park Trails 23
Makawehi Point 5
Waimea Canyon Trail 26

season food, and for health purposes. The curved reddish-gold sand beach lies between two rocky points and features a protected reef, tide pools, and gentle waves. Swimming is excellent for children and anyone with a fear of water (a lifeguard looks over this beach); it's also good for scuba diving, windsurfing, and fishing. Facilities include showers, rest rooms, camping area, picnic area, pavilion, and parking lot. To get there, take Hi. 50 past Hanapepe, and turn on Lokokai Road.

POLIHALE STATE PARK

This mini-Sahara on the western end of the island is Hawaii's biggest beach; it's as wide as three football fields, and 17 miles long. It's a wonderful place to get away from it all; but always wear rubber slippers—the midday sand is hotter than a griddle. The golden sands wrap around Kauai's northwestern shore from Kekaha plantation town, just beyond Waimea, to where the ridge-backs of the Na Pali Coast begin. The state park includes ancient Hawaiian *heiau* and burial sites, a view of the "forbidden" island of Niihau, and the famed **Barking Sands Beach,** where footfall sounds like a barking dog. (The scientific explanation is simple: The grains of sand are perforated with tiny echo chambers, which emit a "barking" sound when they rub together.) Polihale also takes in the Pacific Missile Range Facility, a U.S. surveillance center that snooped on Russian subs during the Cold War, and Nohili Dune, which is nearly 3 miles long and 100 feet high in some places.

Be careful in winter, when high surf and rip currents make swimming dangerous. The safest place to swim is in **Queen's Pond,** a small, shallow sandy-bottom inlet protected from waves and shore currents. There are facilities for camping as well as rest rooms, showers, picnic tables, and pavilions. To get there, take Hi. 50 past Barking Sands Missile Range and follow the signs through the sugarcane fields to Polihale. Local kids like to burgle rental cars out here, so leave no tempting valuables in your car.

THE COCONUT COAST
LYDGATE STATE PARK

This seacoast park has a rock-wall fishpond that blunts the open ocean waves and provides the only safe swimming and the best snorkeling on the eastern shore. The 1-acre beach park, near the mouth of the Wailua River, is named for the Rev. J. M. Lydgate (1854–1922) founder and first pastor of Lihue English Union Church, who likely would be shocked at the public display of flesh here. This is a great place for a picnic, kite-flying on the green, or just a lazy day at the shore. This popular beach park is 5 miles north of Lihue on Kuhio Hwy. (Hi. 56); look for the turnoff just before the Kauai Resort Hotel. Facilities include a pavilion, rest rooms, outdoor showers, picnic tables, barbecue grills, lifeguard, and parking.

THE NORTH SHORE
ANINI BEACH COUNTY PARK

Shielded from the open ocean by the longest, widest fringing reef in Hawaii, Anini is Kauai's safest beach for swimming and windsurfing. It's also one of the island's most beautiful: Three miles long, with golden sand, it sits on a blue lagoon at the foot of emerald cliffs, looking more like Tahiti than almost any other strand in the islands. With shallow water 4 to 5 feet deep, it's also the very best snorkel spot on Kauai, even for beginners; and on the northwest side, a channel in the reef runs out to the deep blue water with a 60-foot drop that attracts scuba divers. Beachcombers love it, too: seashells, cowries, and sometimes even rare Niihau shells can be found on this great beach. Anini has a park, campground, picnic and barbecue facilities, and a boat launch ramp; several B&Bs and vacation rentals are right nearby (see "Accommodations," above). Follow Kuhio Hwy. (Hi. 56) to Kilauea; take the second exit called Kalihiwai Road (the first dead-ends at Kalihiwai Beach), and drive a half-mile toward the sea; turn left on Anini Beach Road.

HANALEI BEACH

Gentle waves roll across the face of half-moon Hanalei Bay, running up to the wide, golden sand; sheer volcanic ridges laced by waterfalls rise to 4,000 feet on the other side, 3 miles inland. Is there a beach anywhere better sited than Hanalei? Celebrated in song and hula and featured on travel posters, this beach owes its natural beauty to its age—it's an ancient sunken valley with posterosional cliffs. Hanalei Bay indents the coast a full 1 mile inland and runs 2 miles point to point, with coral reefs on either side and a patch of coral in the middle—plus a sunken ship that belonged to a king, so divers love it. Swimming is excellent year-round, especially in summer, when Hanalei Bay becomes a big, placid lake. The aquamarine water's also great for body boarding, surfing, fishing, windsurfing, canoe paddling, kayaking, and boating (there's a boat ramp on the west bank of the Hanalei River). Facilities include a pavilion, rest rooms, picnic tables, and parking. This beach is always packed with both local residents and visitors, but you can usually find your own place in the sun by strolling down the shore; the bay is big enough for everyone to enjoy. To get there, make a right turn on Aku Road just after Tahiti Nui in Hanalei, then turn right again on Weke Road; the easiest beach access is on your left.

✪ TUNNELS BEACH & HAENA BEACH PARK

Postcard-perfect, gold-sand Tunnels Beach is one of Hawaii's most beautiful. When the sun sinks into the Pacific along the fabled peaks of Bali Hai, there's no better-looking beach in the islands: You're bathed in golden rays that butter-up the blue sky, bounce off the steepled ridges, and tint the pale clouds hot pink. Catch the sunset from the pebbly sand beach or while swimming in the emerald green waters, but do catch it. Tunnels is excellent for swimming nearly year-round, and safe for snorkeling since it's protected by a fringing coral reef (the waters can get rough in the winter, though). The long, curvy beach is sheltered by a forest of ironwoods, which provide welcome shade from the tropic heat.

Around the corner is Haena Beach Park, which offers grainy, golden sand and excellent swimming in summer, with great snorkeling in crystal-clear waters amid clouds of tropical fish. These North Shore waters get fierce in winter, when big waves pose a danger. An excellent place to relax, the beach park has picnic tables, rest rooms, showers, a grassy park for camping, and free parking, but no lifeguard.

Take Hi. 56 to both beaches; they're about 5 miles past Hanalei. Tunnels has no facilities, but Haena has rest rooms, outdoor showers, barbecue grills, picnic tables, and parking.

KE'E BEACH STATE PARK

Where the road ends on the North Shore, you'll find a dandy little reddish-gold sand beach almost too beautiful to be real. Don't be surprised if it looks familiar; it was featured in *The Thornbirds*. It's on a reef-protected cove at the foot of fluted volcanic cliffs. Swimming and snorkeling are safe inside the reef, but dangerous outside; those North Shore waves and currents can be killers. The beach park has rest rooms, showers, and parking, but no lifeguard; he just lost his job thanks to budget cuts.

6 Hitting the Water

by Rick Carroll, with Jeanette Foster

Kayak Kauai Outfitters, 1 mile past Hanalei Bridge on Hi. 560 in Hanalei (☎ **808/ 826-9844** or 800/437-3507) is *the* outfitters' center in Hanalei. Now in its second decade, it's staffed by local experts who keep track of weather forecasts, sea and trail conditions, and other pertinent data that hikers, kayakers, sailors, and other back-country adventurers need to know. They also rent all the necessary equipment for independent expeditions, and lead a variety of guided activities.

For more on the activities listed below, see "The Active Vacation Planner" in Chapter 3.

BODY BOARDING (BOOGIE BOARDING) & BODYSURFING

The best beaches for bodysurfing and boogie boarding are Kalapaki Beach and Poipu Beach. You can rent boogie boards and fins for as little as $29 a week from **Snorkel Bob's Kauai, Inc.,** 4480 Ahukini Rd., Lihue (☎ **808/245-9433**), or on Poipu Road, just south of Poipu Shopping Village, in Poipu (☎ **808/742-8322**). In Kapaa, boogie boards are available at **Kauai Water Ski & Surf Co.,** Kinipopo Shopping Village, 4-356 Kuhio Hwy. (☎ **808/822-3574**).

BOATING

Kauai has many areas accessible only by boat, including the Fern Grotto, Wailua State Park, Huleia and Hanalei National Wildlife refuges, Menehune Fish Pond, and numerous waterfalls. If you want to strike out on your own, **Paradise River Boat Rentals,** at the Kilohana Plantation (☎ **808/245-9580**), rents boats ranging from a Porta-Bote (for three people) for $95 a day to a Boston Whaler (six-person capacity) for $245 a day. Included are all the amenities, such as safety equipment, coolers, dry bags (for cameras, wallet, towels, etc.), and a comprehensive orientation on where to go. They also rent a range of water toys, from snorkel equipment to boogie boards.

For Zodiac cruises along the Na Pali Coast, tours of the Fern Grotto, and other group boating activities, see "Helicopter Rides, Zodiac Cruises & Guided Eco-Adventures," below.

DEEP-SEA FISHING

Kauai's fishing fleet is smaller and less well-recognized than others in the islands, which means your chances of landing a big game fish are better—they try harder here. All you need to bring is your lunch and your luck. Charter boats start at $90 a person for a half-day, in which you share the boat with other anglers, and goes up to $850 for a full-day exclusive charter. Call **Gent-Lee Fishing,** out of Nawiliwili Harbor (☎ **808/245-7504**), or **Sport Fishing Kauai** (☎ **808/742-7013**).

FLY-FISHING FOR RAINBOW TROUT

Rainbow trout are just waiting to be hooked with a fly at Kokee State Park. The season's short—it starts on the first Saturday in August and lasts just 16 days, sometimes continuing weekends in September—and fish are $12 each (if you can catch one), but for the 1,500 fly fishermen who visit Kokee each year hoping to land a trophy rainbow trout, it's a deal. Each year, the state stocks 35,000 rainbow trout fingerlings in Puu Loa Reservoir and five Kokee streams. You can pick up a freshwater fishing license (they're $7.50 for visitors) at **Kokee Lodge** (☎ **808/241-3400**) or by calling the **State Department of Fish & Game** (☎ 808/274-3344). You'll need to bring your own gear.

KAYAKING

Kauai is made for kayaking. You can take the Huleia River into Huleia National Wildlife Refuge, the last stand of Kauai's endangered birds—it's the only way the nature refuge can be explored (for more details, see "Helicopter Rides, Zodiac Cruises & Guided Eco-Adventures," below). For the adventurous, there's the Na Pali coast, featuring majestic cliffs, empty beaches, open-ocean conditions, and monster waves. Or, you can just go out and paddle around Hanalei Bay.

    Kayak Kauai Outfitters, 1 mile past Hanalei Bridge on Hi. 560 in Hanalei (☎ 808/826-9844 or 800/437-3507) has a range of tours for independent souls. The shop's experts will be happy to tell you where to go on your own, or take you on a guided kayaking trip. Equipment rental for a two-person kayak is around $50 a day. Kayak lessons and tours (some including snacks) range from $39 to $125. They also lead a multiday hike/paddle tour of the Na Pali Coast; see "Helicopter Rides, Zodiac Cruises & Guided Eco-Adventures," below.

SAILING

Picture yourself cruising the rugged Na Pali coastline in a big 42-foot ketch-rigged yacht under full sail, watching the sunset as you enjoy a tropical cocktail, or speeding through the aquamarine water in a 40-foot trimaran as porpoises play off the bow. Call **Bluewater Sailing,** in Kilauea (☎ 808/828-1142). Prices vary from $75 for a sail-snorkel cruise to $45 for a sunset cruise.

SCUBA DIVING

Diving on Kauai is dictated by the weather. During the winter, when heavy swells and high winds hit the island, it's generally limited to the more protected south shore. Probably the best-known site along the south shore is Caverns. Located off the Poipu Beach resort area, this dive site consists of a series of lava tubes interconnected by a chain of archways. A constant parade of fish stream by (even shy lion fish are often spotted lurking in crevices), brightly hued Hawaiian lobsters hide in the lava's tiny holes, and occasionally turtles soar by.

    In summer, when the north Pacific storms subside, the magnificent North Shore opens up and you can take a dive locally known as the Oceanarium, northwest of Hanalei Bay, where you'll find a kaleidoscopic marine world in this horseshoe-shaped cove. From the rare (long-handed spiny lobsters) to the more common (taape, conger eels, and nudibranchs), the resident population is one of the more diverse on the island. The topography (pinnacles, ridges, and archways) is covered with cup corals, black coral trees, and nooks and crannies enough for a dozen dives.

    Since the best dives on Kauai are offshore, book a two-tank dive off a dive boat for the best experience. **Bubbles Below Scuba Charters,** Kapaa (☎ 808/822-3483) offers two-tank boat dives for $75 and night dives for $60. On the south side, call **Fathom Five Adventures,** Koloa (☎ 808/742-6991).

DIVING THE "FORBIDDEN" ISLAND OF NIIHAU

Manta rays, tiger sharks, and Hawaiian monk seals and tuna loom about Lehua, the little crescent island that's been off-limits for more than a century—but not anymore. It's just 90 minutes by boat from Kauai, off the north coast of the privately owned island of Niihau, and it's the hottest new dive spot in Hawaii.

    You can dive there now, but only in summer and only with Bubbles Below, the dive charter run by captains Ken and Linda Bail. They scoot across the often choppy

---

Ready, Set, Splash! Water Adventures for Kids of All Ages

Surfing with an Expert   If seven-time world champ Margo Oberg, a member of the Surfing Hall of Fame, can't get your kid—or you—up on a surfboard riding a wave, nobody can. She promises same-day results even for a klutz. See "Surfing," above.

Taking a Zodiac Down the Na Pali Coast   Go flying down Kauai's most spectacular coast on a 23-foot rubber life raft. Captain Zodiac has been taking kids of all ages exploring the Na Pali's jagged cliffs, remote beaches, and hidden sea caves for more than a decade. This is Jacques Cousteau–style adventuring at its best. See "Helicopter Rides, Zodiac Cruises & Guided Eco-Adventures," below, for details.

Paddling up the Huleia River   Indiana Jones ran for his life up this river to his seaplane in *Raiders of the Lost Ark*. Now, you and the kids can venture down it yourself, in a 12-foot-long, virtually unsinkable canoe-shaped pirogue. The picturesque Huleia (which also appeared in the remake of *King Kong*) winds through tropically lush Huleia National Wildlife Refuge, where endangered species like great blue herons and Hawaiian gallinules take wing. Ideal for everyone. See "Helicopter Rides, Zodiac Cruises & Guided Eco-Adventures," below, for details.

Racing Along in a South Seas Thunder Boat   This 38-foot Fountain race boat takes you roaring past Kauai's Na Pali coast fast. The six-passenger craft is fitted with a monster V-8 engine that turns a prop and throws a wake big enough to surf. This is no wimpy eco-kayak—it's Thunder Road at sea. Rides depart daily from Kalapaki Beach. It's $55 for a 1-hour ride, $130 for 4¹/₂ hours. Call **South Sea Thunder Boat Ride** (☎ **808/245-2222** or 808/241-3444).

---

channel to Niihau in a 35-foot cuddy cabin motorboat for some world-class diving. The three-tank trip is for experienced divers only. Divers should be comfortable on vertical drop offs, in huge underwater caverns, in possible choppy surface conditions, and in significant currents. They should also be willing to share water space with the resident sharks.

The all-day trip departs at 7:30am usually from Kikiaola Harbor in Waimea, and returns around 4:30pm. The $200 cost includes tanks, weights, computer, lunch, drinks, and a marine guide. Contact **Bubbles Below** (☎ **808/822-3483**). For a preview of the experience, check out http://aloha.net/~kaimanu.

SNORKELING

Kauai has lots of inshore reefs to make snorkelers happy. You can rent gear at **Snorkel Bob's Kauai, Inc.,** 4480 Ahukini Rd., Lihue (☎ **808/245-9433**) or in Poipu (☎ **808/742-8322**) for $15 a week. For great offshore snorkeling, try Ke'e Beach, Haena State Park, Anini Beach, Poipu Beach Park, and Salt Pond Beach Park.

Sail-snorkeling cruises run about $65 to $75; check out **Captain Andy's Sailing Adventures** in Koloa (☎ **808/822-7833**), **Captain Sundown's Catamaran Sailing** in Hanalei (☎ **808/245-6117**), or **Bluewater Sailing** in Kilauea (☎ **808/828-1142**).

SNUBA

Snuba Tours of Kauai, Kapaa (☎ **808/823-8912**), offers snuba to anyone over the age of eight. The 1¹/₂-hour guided tours are $49 per person.

SURFING

Hanalei Bay's winter surf is the most popular on the island, but it's for experts only. Poipu is an excellent spot to learn how to surf; the waves are small and—best of all—nobody laughs at you when you wipe out. Check with the local surf shops or phone **KAUAI Surfline** (☎ **808/245-3564**) to find out where surf's up.

Surf lessons are available at $50 an hour (which includes all-day equipment rental) from **Windsurf Kauai** in Hanalei (☎ **808/828-6838**). Poipu is also the site of numerous surfing schools; the oldest and best is probably **Margo Oberg's School of Surfing,** Kiahuna Plantation Resort (☎ **808/742-1750**); you can also sign up at **Nuku Moi Surf Shop,** across from Brennecke's Beach (☎ **808/742-8019**). Margo charges $45 for 90 minutes of instruction (offered daily at 11am and 2pm), which includes surfboard, boots, and leash; she guarantees that by the end of the lesson you'll be standing and catching a wave.

Equipment is available for rent (ranging from $12 a day to $65 a week) from **Hanalei Surf Co.,** 5-5161 Kuhio Hwy., Hanalei (☎ **808/826-9000**), and **Pedal & Paddle,** Ching Young Village Shopping Center, Hanalei (☎ **808/826-9069**).

WATERSKIING

Hawaii's only freshwater waterskiing is on the Wailua River. Ski boats launch from the boat ramp in Wailua River State Park, directly across the marina. **Kauai Water Ski & Surf Co.,** Kinipopo Shopping Village, 4-356 Kuhio Hwy., Kapaa (☎ **808/822-3574**) rents equipment and offers lessons and guided tours; it's $45 for a half-hour trip and $85 for an hour.

WINDSURFING

Anini Beach is one of the safest beaches for beginners to learn windsurfing. Lessons and equipment rental are available at **Windsurf Kauai** in Hanalei (☎ **808/828-6838**). It's $60 for a 3-hour lesson, including equipment; rentals are $50 a day. Serious windsurfers should head to Hanalei Bay or Tunnels.

WHALE WATCHING

When the Pacific humpback whales make their annual visit to Hawaii from Alaska from December to March, they swim right by Kauai. **Liko Kauai Cruises,** in Waimea (☎ **808/338-0333**), offers not your typical whale-watching cruise; instead, it's a $4\frac{1}{2}$-hour combination Na Pali coast tour–deep-sea fishing–historical lecture–whale-watching extravaganza, with lunch. It all happens on a 37-foot cabin cruiser that departs from Kekaha; occupancy is limited to 20 people. The cost is $85 for adults and $65 for kids 4 to 14.

Captain Zodiac also combines whale watching with their tours of the Na Pali Coast in the winter months; see "Helicopter Rides, Zodiac Cruises & Guided Eco-Adventures," below.

7 Hiking & Camping

by Rick Carroll, with Jeanette Foster

Kauai is an adventurer's delight. Its very nature calls to those who eschew resort life and head for the great outdoors. The island's greatest tropical beauty isn't easily reachable; you've got to head out on foot and find it.

You can set out on your own, or join a guided hike with the **Sierra Club Hawaii Chapter,** which schedules public hikes throughout the year (☎ **808/538-6616**). For more information on Kauai's hiking trails, contact the **State Division of Parks,** P.O. Box 1671, Lihue, HI 96766 (☎ **808/274-3446**); the **State Division of Forestry and Wildlife,** P.O. Box 1671, Lihue, HI 96766 (☎ **808/245-4444**); **Kauai County Parks and Recreation,** 4193 Hardy St., Lihue, HI 96766 (☎ **808/241-6660** or 808/245-1881); and the **Kokee Lodge Manager,** P.O. Box 819, Waimea, HI 96796 (☎ **808/335-6061**).

Despite its name, **Kayak Kauai Outfitters,** 1 mile past Hanalei Bridge on Hi. 560 in Hanalei (☎ **808/826-9844** or 800/437-3507) is the premier all-around outfitters' center on the island. It's staffed by local experts who keep track of weather forecasts, sea and trail conditions, and other pertinent information that hikers, campers, and other back-country adventurers need to know. If you don't plan to bring your own gear, you can rent it there, or at **Pedal & Paddle** in Hanalei (☎ **808/826-9069**). If you want to buy camping equipment on Kaui, the best selection is at **Gaspro,** 3990-C Rice Street, Lihue (☎ **808/245-6766**).

A Few Words of Warning about Flash Floods: When it rains on Kauai, the waterfalls rage and rivers and streams overflow and cause flash floods on roads and trails. If you're hiking, avoid dry stream beds, which flood quickly and wash out to sea. Check the weather forecast (☎ **808/245-6001** or 808/241-6789) before going hiking, camping, or sailing, especially during rainy season, November to March.

THE POIPU RESORT AREA
✪ A Good Morning Hike: Makawehi Point

Bold as a ship's prow, Makawehi Point juts out to sea on the east side of Keoneloa Beach, the beach in front of the Hyatt Regency Poipu, known locally as Shipwreck Beach because of an old marine mishap. This 50-foot-high sand dune bluff attracts a variety of people: pole fishers, whale watchers, people who just like the panoramic views of the Pacific, and daredevils who test their courage by leaping off the cliff into the waves that wrap the point (don't try it).

The trailhead begins on the east end of Shipwreck Beach, past the Hyatt. It's an easy 10-minute walk up to Makawehi Point; after you take in the big picture from there, keep going uphill along the ridge of the sand dunes (said to contain ancient Hawaiian burial sites), past the coves frequented by green sea turtles and endangered Hawaiian Monk seals, through the coastal pine forest, and past World War II coastal bunkers to the very top. Now you can see Hauupu Ridge and its 2,297-foot peak, the famously craggy ridgeline that eerily resembles Queen Victoria's profile, and in the distance, Mahaulepu Beach, one of the best looking in Hawaii. Inland, three red craters dimple the green fields; the one in the middle, the biggest one, Pu'u Huni Huni, is said to have been the last to erupt on Kauai—but it was so long ago that nobody here can remember when.

SOUTHWEST KAUAI
Waimea Canyon Trails

On a wet island like Kauai, a dry hike is hard to find; but in the desert-dry gulch of Waimea Canyon, known as the Grand Canyon of the Pacific (once you get there, you'll see why—it's pretty spectacular), you're not likely to slip and slide in the muck as you go.

Canyon Trail   You want to hike Hawaii's Grand Canyon, but you only have so much time. Well, then, take the Canyon Trail to the east rim for a breathtaking view into the 3,000-foot-deep canyon. The trailhead is near the 14-mile marker at the Kokee State Park road sign, about a mile down from the museum. Park on the side of the road and walk down the not-very-clearly marked trail on the 3.6-mile round-trip, which takes about 3 hours and leads to Waipoo Falls (as does the hike below) and back.

✪ **Hike to Waipoo Falls**   The 3-hour round-trip family hike to Waipoo Falls is one of Kauai's best hikes; the two-tiered, 800-foot waterfall that splashes into a natural pool is worth every step it takes to get there. To get to the trail, drive up Kokee Road (Hi. 550) to the Puu Hina Hina Outlook; a quarter-mile past the lookout, near a NASA satellite tracking station on the right, a two-lane dirt road leads to the Waipoo Falls trailhead. From there, the trail winds gently through a green jungle dotted with wild yellow orchids and flame-red torch ginger before it leads you out on a descending ridgeback that juts deep into the canyon. At the end of the promontory, take a left and push on through the jungle to the falls; once you're there, reward yourself with a refreshing splash in the pool.

KOKEE STATE PARK

At the end of Hi. 550, which leads you through Waimea Canyon and to its summit, lies a 4,640-acre state park of high mountain forest wilderness (3,600 to 4,000 ft. above sea level). Rain forest, bogs, and breathtaking views of the Na Pali coastline and Waimea Canyon are the draw at Kokee. This is *the* place for hiking—among the 45 miles of maintained trails are some of the best hikes in Hawaii. We've described our favorites in detail below. Official trail maps of all of the park's trails are for sale for 50¢ at the **Kokee Natural History Museum** (☎ 808/335-9975).

The **Sierra Club** offers guided hikes of the park, usually on weekends. For a schedule, write the club at P.O. Box 3412, Lihue, HI 96766, or call Micco Godinez at Kauai Outfitters Center (☎ 808/826-9844).

A few words about hiking Kokee: Always check current trail conditions; up-to-date trail information is available on a bulletin board at the Kokee Natural History Museum. Stay on established trails; it's easy to get lost here. Get off the trail well before dark. Carry water and rain gear—even if it's perfectly sunny when you set out—and wear sunscreen.

Hiking Kokee

Awaawapuhi Trail   This 3¼-mile hike (6½ miles round-trip) takes about 3 hours and is considered strenuous by most, but offers a million-dollar view. Look for the trailhead at the left of the parking lot, at the 17-mile marker between the museum and the Kalalau Lookout. The well-marked and maintained trail now sports quarter-mile markers, and you can pick up a free plant guide for it at the museum. The trail drops about 1,600 feet through native forests to a thin precipice right at the very edge of the Na Pali cliffs for a dramatic and dizzying view of the tropical valleys and blue Pacific 2,500 feet below. Not recommended to anyone with vertigo (although a railing will keep you from a major slip and fall). Go early, before clouds obscure the view, or late in the day; the chiaroscuro sunsets are something to behold.

This trail connects to the **Nualolo Trail** (3¾ miles), which provides awesome views and loops back almost to park headquarters, if you've got the time.

Halemanu-Kokee Trail   This trail takes you on a pleasant, easy-to-moderate 2.4-mile round-trip walk through a native koa and ohia forest inhabited by native birds. The trailhead is near the 15-mile marker; pick up the Faye Trail, which leads to this one. The trail links Kokee Valley to Halemanu Valley (hence the name); along the way, you'll see a plum orchard, valleys, and ridges.

Pihea Trail   This is the park's flattest trail, but it's still a pretty strenuous 7.4-mile round-trip hike. A new boardwalk on a third of the trail makes it easier, especially when it's wet. The trail begins at the end of Hi. 550 at Puu o Kila Lookout, which overlooks Kalalau Valley; it goes down at first, then flattens out as it traces the back ridge of the valley. Once it enters the rain forest, you'll see native plants and trees such as maile, ohia lehua, mokihana, and tree ferns. It intersects with the **Alakai Swamp Trail** (see below), which is now an easy stroll, mostly on a boardwalk through a fragile bog. If you combine both trails, figure on about 4 hours in and out.

Alakai Swamp Trail   This strenuous, 7-mile hike isn't for everyone; it takes 5 hours to slosh through the bog, with mud up to your knees, and it'll probably rain the whole time. But, if you want to see the "real" Hawaii, this is it—a big swamp in the heart of Kauai that's home to rare birds and plants. The trail allows a rare glimpse into a wet, cloud-covered wilderness preserve where 460 inches of rain a year is common. Come prepared for the worst, and you might get a ray of sunshine. (The only silver lining is that there are no mosquitoes above 3,000 feet).

The trailhead is just off Mohihi (Camp 10) Road, just beyond the Forest Reserve entrance sign and the Alakai Shelter picnic area. From the parking lot, the trail follows an old World War II four-wheel–drive road. Carry a compass and stick to the trail; the Division of Forestry has brown and white trail mile-markers (they also are building a boardwalk). At the end of the $3^1/2$-mile slog, if you're lucky and the clouds part, you'll have a lovely view of Wainiha Valley and Hanalei from Kilohana Lookout.

Staying at Kokee

Camping facilities include state campgrounds (one next to Kokee Lodge, and four more primitive back-country sites), one private tent area, and the Kokee Lodge, which has 12 cabins for rent at very reasonable rates (see p. 448 in "Accommodations" for details on renting a cabin). At 4,000 feet, the nights are cold, particularly in the winter; since no open fires are permitted at Kokee, the best deal is the cabins.

The **state campground at Kokee Lodge** allows tent camping only. Permits for this site can be obtained from a state parks office on any island; on Kauai, it's at 3060 Eiwa St., Lihue (☎ 808/274-3444). The permits are free, and the time limit is 5 nights in a single 30-day period. The facilities include showers, drinking water, picnic tables, a pavilion with tables, rest rooms, barbecue, sinks for dishwashing, and electric lights.

The more primitive back-country campgrounds include **Sugi Grove** and **Kawaikoi,** located about 4 miles from the park headquarters on a four-wheel–drive road. The only facilities are pit toilets, picnic tables, and water from a stream. Two-and-a-half-miles from that camping area is **Camp 10,** with a picnic area only—no rest rooms. Water is available from a stream a short distance away. Camp 10 is mainly an overnight stop for hikers and hunters. Six miles past Camp 10 is the **Waialae Cabin.** Although no one can stay at the locked cabin (it's used only by forestry personnel), camping around the cabin is permitted. There are no facilities; you can get water from a nearby stream. Permits for Sugi Grove, Kawaikoi, Camp 10, and Waialae Cabin are available from the **State Forestry and Wildlife Division,** 3060 Eiwa St., Lihue (☎ **808/274-3433**). There's no fee for the permits, but camping is limited to 3 nights.

Tent camping at **Camp Slogget,** owned by the Kauai YWCA (3094 Elua St., Lihue, HI 96766; ☎ **808/245-5959**), is available for $7.50 per adult per night, and $5 per child.

The **Kokee Lodge Restaurant** is open from 9am to 3:30pm, for continental breakfast and lunch, every day (for details, see "Dining," above). Groceries and gas aren't available in Kokee, so stock up in advance, or you'll have to make the long trip down the mountain.

NA PALI COAST STATE PARK

Simply put, the Na Pali Coast is the most beautiful part of the Hawaiian Islands. Hanging valleys open like green velvet accordions and waterfalls tumble to the sea from the 4,120-foot-high cliffs; the spatial experience is exhilarating and humbling. Whether you hike in, fly over, or take a Zodiac cruise past (see "Helicopter Rides, Zodiac Cruises & Guided Eco-Adventures," below), be sure to see this park.

Established in 1984, Na Pali Coast State Park takes in a 22-mile stretch of fluted cliffs that wrap around the northwest shore of Kauai between Ke'e Beach and Polihale State Park. Volcanic in origin, carved by wind and sea, the cliffs ("Na Pali" in Hawaiian), which heaved out of the ocean floor 200 million years ago, stand as constant reminders of majesty and endurance. Five major valleys—Kalalau, Honopu, Awaawapuhi, Nualolo, and Milolii—crease the cliffs.

Unless you fly or boat in, the park is only accessible on foot—and it's not easy. An ancient footpath, the Kalalau Trail, winds through this remote, spectacular 6,500-acre park, ultimately leading to Kalalau Valley. Of all the green valleys in Hawaii, and there are many, only Kalalau Valley is a true wilderness, probably the last wild valley in the islands. No road goes there, and none ever will. The remote valley is home to long-plumed Tropic birds, Golden Monarch butterflies, and 60 of Kauai's 120 rare and endangered species of plants. The hike into the Kalalau Valley is grueling, and takes most people 6 to 8 hours one way.

Despite its inaccessibility, this journey into Hawaii's wilderness has become increasingly popular since the 1970s. Overrun with hikers, helicopters, and boaters, the Kalalau Valley was in grave danger of being loved to death—until Hurricane Iniki came along, calling "time out" in the Kalalau Valley.

The Hawaii State Department of Land and Natural Resources closed the park for 6 months in 1996, due to unsafe, hazardous conditions as a result of the hurricane. Since then, strict rules about access were adopted. The park is only open to hikers and campers on a limited basis in summer, and you must have a permit (you can hike the first 2 miles, to Hanakapiai Beach, without a permit). Permits are free, and issued in person at the **Kauai State Parks Office**, 3060 Eiwa St., Lihue, HI 96766 (☎ **808/274-3445** or 3346). You can also request one by writing Wayne Souza, Kauai District Parks Supt., **Kauai Division of State Parks,** at the address listed above.

For more information, contact Mike Wilson, Director, **Hawaii State Department of Land and Natural Resources,** 1151 Punchbowl St., Room 130, Honolulu, HI 96813 (☎ **808/587-0320**).

HIKING THE KALALAU TRAIL

The trailhead is at at Ke'e Beach, at end of Kuhio Highway (Hi. 56). Even if you only go as far as Hanakapiai, bring water.

The First 2 Miles: To Hanakapiai Beach It's only 2 miles in to Hanakapiai Beach, but the first mile's all uphill. The tough trail takes about 2 hours one way and dissuades many, but everyone should attempt the first half-mile. It gives a good hint of the startling beauty that lies ahead. Day hikers love this initial stretch, so it's usually crowded. The islands of Niihau and Lehua are often visible on the horizon. At the 1-mile marker, you'll have climbed from sea level to 400 feet; now it's all downhill to Hanakapiai Beach. Sandy in summer, the beach becomes bouldery when winter waves scour the coast. There are strong currents and no lifeguards, so swim at your own risk. You can also hike another 2 miles inland from the beach to **Hanakapiai Falls,** a 120-foot cascade. Allow 3 hours for that stretch.

The Rest of the Way Hiking the Kalalau is the most difficult and challenging hike in Hawaii, and one you'll never forget. Even the Sierra Club rates the 22-mile round-trip into Kalalau Valley and back as "strenuous." Follow the footsteps of ancient Hawaiians along a cliffside path that's a mere 10 inches wide in some places, with sheer 1,000-foot drops to the sea. One misstep, and it's *limu* time (that's seaweed in Hawaiian). Only fear, I'm told, keeps you on the precipice. I wouldn't know—I only go down Na Pali coast in kayaks, Zodiacs, or choppers. Even the hardy and fit should allow at least 2 days to hike in and out (see below for camping information). Although the trail is usually in good shape, go in summer when it's dry; parts of the trail vanish in winter. When it rains, the trail's super-slippery, and flash floods can sweep you away.

A park ranger is now on site full time at **Kalalau Beach** to greet visitors, provide information, oversee campsites, and keep trails and campgrounds in order.

CAMPING IN KALALAU VALLEY & ALONG THE NA PALI COAST

You must obtain a camping permit; see above for details on obtaining one. The camping season runs roughly from May or June to September (depending on the site). All campsites are booked almost a year in advance, so call or write well ahead of time. Stays are limited to 5 nights.

Camping areas along the Kalalau Trail include **Hanakapiai Beach** (facilities are pit toilets and water is from the stream), **Hanakoa Valley** (no facilities, water from the stream), **Milolii** (no facilities, water from the stream), and **Kalalau Valley** (composting toilets, several pit toilets, and water from the stream). Keep your camping permit with you at all times.

8 Other Outdoor Pursuits: Golf, Birding, Riding & More

by Rick Carroll, with Jeanette Foster

BIRDING

Kauai provides some of Hawaii's last sanctuaries for endangered native birds and oceanic birds, such as the albatross.

At **Kokee State Park,** a 4,345-acre wilderness forest at the end of Hi. 550 in Southwest Kauai, you have an excellent chance of seeing some of Hawaii's endangered native birds. You may spot the 'Apapane, a red bird with black wings and a curved black bill; and the Iwi, a red bird with black wings, orange legs, and a salmon-colored bill. Other frequently seen native birds are honeycreepers, who sing like canaries: the 'Amakihi, a plain olive green bird with a long straight bill; and the 'Anianiau, a tiny yellow bird with a thin, slightly curved bill. Also often visible here is the 'Elepaio, a small, active gray flycatcher with an orange breast that perches with its tail up. The most common native bird at Kokee is the Moa, or red jungle fowl, brought as domestic stock by ancient Polynesians. Ordinarily shy, they're actually quite tame in this environment.

✪ **Kilauea Point National Wildlife Sanctuary,** 1 mile north of Kilauea (☎ **808/828-1413**), is a 31-acre headland habitat that juts 200 feet above the surf and includes cliffs, two rocky wave-lashed bays, and a tiny islet that serves as a jumping-off spot for sea birds. Here, you can easily snoop on Red-footed Boobies, who nest in trees, and Wedge-tailed Shearwaters, who burrow in nests along the cliffs. You may also see the great Frigate Bird, the Laysan albatross, and the White-tailed Tropic Bird, especially along the Ke'e cliffs and Na Pali coast, and two nesting pairs of

Hawaiian nene geese are now at home in Kilauea's cliffs. The sanctuary is open from 10am to 4pm daily; admission is $2 per family.

Peaceful Hanalei Valley is home to Hawaii's endangered Koloa duck, gallinule, coot, and Stilt. Here, **Hanalei National Wildlife Refuge** (☎ **808/828-1413**) also provides a safe habitat for migratory shorebirds and waterfowl. It's not open to the public, but an interpretive overlook along the highway affords a spectacular view. Along Ohiki Road, which begins at the west end of the Hanalei River Bridge, you'll often see white Cattle Egrets hunting crayfish in streams.

Also, see "Paddling into Huleia National Wildlife Refuge" in "Helicopter Rides, Zodiac Cruises & Guided Eco-Adventures," below.

GOLF

Kauai is a golfer's paradise; Robert Trent Jones, Jr. calls it "the best island for golf there is." From high handicapper to pro, Kauai's courses will challenge every golfer. Carts are required at all golf courses; the cost is included in the greens fees.

KAUAI LAGOONS RESORT COURSES

Choose from the Lagoons Course, with 18 holes for the recreational golfer, or the Kauai Kiele Championship Course for the low handicapper. Both were designed by Jack Nicklaus. The **Lagoons Course** is a links-style course with a bunker that's a little less severe than Kiele. Emphasis on this 6,942-yard, par-72 course is the shore game. The **Kiele Championship Course** is a mixture of tournament-quality challenge and high-traffic playability; it winds up with one of Hawaii's most difficult holes, a 431-yard, par-4 played straightaway to an island green. Amenities include airport transportation (you can jet in just for the day), practice facility, and spa. Greens fees are $100 at the Lagoon Course and $145 at the Kiele Course. Call **808/241-6000.**

KIAHUNA GOLF CLUB

Located in Koloa, this resort golf course is adjacent to the Poipu Beach Resort. This par-70, 6,353-yard Robert Trent Jones, Jr.–designed course plays around four large archaeological sites, ranging from an ancient Hawaiian temple to the remains of a Portuguese home and crypt built in the early 1800s. The Scottish-style links course has rolling terrain, undulating greens, 70 sand bunkers, and near-constant winds. The third hole, par-3, 185-yard goes over Waikomo Stream. At any given time, just about half the players on the course are Kauai residents, the other half visitors. With greens fees at $45, this is probably the best choice for the budget-conscious golfer. Facilities include driving range, practice greens, snack bar, and twilight rates. Call **808/ 742-9595.**

✪ POIPU BAY RESORT GOLF COURSE

This Poipu Bay 6,959-yard, par-72 course with a links-style layout was designed by Robert Trent Jones, Jr. This course may be easier when the trees mature and slow the constant wind that comes pouring off the ocean; when the wind is at full force, 180-yard drives are standard. Fairways and greens are undulating and water hazards are located on eight holes. The par-4, 16th-hole must have been designed after Pebble Beach. The 501-yard hole has the coastline weaving along the entire left side. You can take the safe route to the right and maybe make par (but more than likely bogey) or you can try to take it tight against the ocean and possibly make it in two. The most striking (and most insensitive to Hawaiian culture) hole is the 201-yard, par-3 on the 17th, which has a tee built *on* an ancient Hawaiian stone formation. Facilities include restaurant, locker room, pro shop, driving range, and putting greens. Greens fees are $125. This course can be crowded with resort guests, so call early for tee times (☎ **808/742-8711**).

✪ PRINCEVILLE GOLF CLUB, PRINCE COURSE

This Robert Trent Jones, Jr.–designed devil of a course sits on 390 acres molded to create ocean views from every hole. Some holes have a waterfall backdrop to the greens, others shoot into the hillside, and the famous par-4, 12th-hole has a long tee shot off a cliff to a narrow, jungle-lined fairway, 100 feet below. This is the most challenging course on Kauai; accuracy is the goal here. Being off the fairway here means your ball's in the drink. "The average vacation golfer may find the Prince Course intimidating, but they don't mind, because it's so beautiful," Jones says. "You get the grandeur, the majesty of Kauai." Facilities include a restaurant, health club and spa, locker, clubhouse, golf shop, and driving range. Greens fees are $140. Tees are always booked—everyone wants a crack at this course—so call now (☎ **808/826-5000**).

HORSEBACK RIDING

CJM Country Stables, 1731 Kelaukia St., Koloa (☎ **808/742-6096**), offers a 3-hour escorted Hidden Valley beach ride. You'll ride along the Hauupu Ridge, across sugarcane fields, and along Mahaulepu Beach (one of my all-time favorites); it's worth your time and money just to get out to this seldom seen part of Kauai. The ride is $70, and includes breakfast.

Only in Kauai can you ride a horse across the wide-open pastures of a working ranch under volcanic peaks and rein up near a waterfall pool. No wonder Kauai's *paniolos* smile and sing so much. **Princeville Ranch Stables** in Hanalei (☎ **808/826-7473**) will take you along on this 4-hour outing for $95, which includes a saddle-bag lunch. Riders must be in good physical shape. Don't forget to put your swimsuit on under your jeans, a splash in that waterfall pool feels real good.

RIDING A HORSE ALONG WAIMEA CANYON RIM

Kauai *paniolo* Les Milnes leads you on a cliffhanger of a ride along Waimea Canyon's rim trails, which offer breathtaking views of the "Grand Canyon of the Pacific." You depart from the stables at 4pm, and return down the western slope of the canyon as the sun sets behing Niihau in the distance. Only two riders at a time can go on horses specially trained to ride this cliffside trail. The 4-mile, 2-hour ride is $135 per person. Reserve at least a day in advance with **Garden Island Ranch Stables** (☎ **808/338-0052** or 808/822-3392).

HANG GLIDING

What steers like a shopping cart, soars like an eagle, and comes with a rocket-launched parachute? It's the Airborne Edge Ultralight (AEU), reputedly one of the most reliable, stable, quiet, and fun ultralight aircrafts in the world. On days when the air is still, pilot Gerry Charlebois can take you up into the wild blue yonder in his tandem power glider for a bird's-eye view of Kauai. You can hang out with this veteran airman on a low-speed reconnaissance flight at 2,000 feet above the island's flute cliffs and valleys. A boom-mounted camera records you in flight as you swoop over the rain forest and soar by jagged volcanic peaks. Chicken hearts will be glad to know this bird comes with a rocket-launched parachute—just in case. Rides start at $40. Call **Birds in Paradise** (☎ **808/822-5309**).

TENNIS

The **Kauai County Parks and Recreation Department,** 4193 Hardy, Lihue, HI 96766 (☎ **808/241-6670**), has a list of county tennis courts around the island, all of which are free and open to the public. The **Princeville Tennis Club,** Princeville Hotel (☎ **808/826-9823**), has courts available for rent for $10 per person per hour; however, book early, as they are always in demand.

9 Helicopter Rides, Zodiac Cruises & Guided Eco-Adventures

by Rick Carroll

EXPLORING THE NA PALI COAST BY WATER

✪ **Captain Zodiac Raft Expeditions.** P.O. Box 456, Hanalei, HI 96714. ☎ **808/826-9371.**

For an up-close-and-personal tour of the Na Pali Coast, book with Captain Zodiac. Clancy Greff, otherwise known as Captain Zodiac, was the first person to initiate the now-famous sea tours of the Na Pali coastline. The tours take place on 23-foot inflatable boats (Zodiacs) that allow you to get close to the incredible shoreline because they have a very shallow draft. You're just inches from the water in the quick-moving rubber craft, which gives you a feeling of intimacy with the marine world below.

The tours, always dependent on the weather and sea conditions, consist of a 3-hour sunrise snorkel tour, 4-hour morning and afternoon snorkel tours, a 2-hour sunset cruise (no snorkeling), and a 5-hour tour that includes landing on the normally inaccessible Nualolo Kai Beach for snorkeling, hiking, and lunch. Prices, depending on the trip, range from $55 to $115 for adults, $45 to $95 for kids. From May 15 to September 15, they're authorized by the State Parks Department as a backpacker and hiker shuttle service, which means that they can drop you off at one of the Na Pali Coast's remote beaches and and pick you up again at a later, prearranged time.

The best time of year to take a Zodiac cruise is during the summer months, when the ocean is calmer and the captain can maneuver the boat into caves and up to hidden waterfalls. From October to March, the weather can be rough, and trips may be cancelled; but if the weather's good in these months, you might get the added bonus of seeing whales. If you're on a trip that features snorkeling, bring your own gear if you have it; your gear will fit you better than that provided by the boat. (Nothing is worse than a leaky mask while you're snorkeling.) And bring your camera; they provide a sealing plastic bag to protect it from salt spray and water.

Once on board, try to get a seat on the starboard side (the right side as you face the front of the boat). Most of the sightseeing is on the way out; you'll have a perfect view.

A word of caution: Captain Zodiac recommends that pregnant women and small children skip this trip; neither may be comfortable in the shadeless, bouncing boat (it's sort of like riding on Jell-O).

Kayak Kauai Outfitters. Hi. 560 (1 mile past Hanalei Bridge), Hanalei, Kauai HI 96714. ☎ **808/826-9844** or 800/437-3507.

Kayak Kauai Outfitters is *the* outfitters' center on Kauai. Now in its second decade, it's staffed by local experts who keep track of weather forecasts, sea and trail conditions, and other pertinent data that Na Pali hikers, campers, sailors, and all-around adventurers need to know. They provide the necessary equipment for personal

A Real Adventure in Paradise: Visiting "Forbidden" Niihau

It all sounds wonderfully arcane, the stuff of English shipwreck novels: A 6-by-18–mile island in the middle of the sea owned now by a man named Robinson, bought for $10,000 in gold 128 years ago and inhabited since then only by a "lost" tribe of 200 Hawaiians, who have eschewed all outside interference and chosen a pure and simple life over one with 20th-century trappings. It's the last true Hawaiian enclave, where people still speak the native tongue and pay little heed to the great world beyond. However, in their modest way, these simple people have joined the so-called family business—tourism. Now, with the help of a little outfit called Niihau Helicopters, you can go visit them.

The 20-minute flight takes you back a century or more to a museum-piece island right out of the pages of Captain Cook's journal. It's eerie and wonderful all at once. I've been to Niihau on two separate occasions, and each time it proved to be a different experience, although it always seems like a mythic place.

On my first visit, 5 years ago, the island revealed itself as a brown, lifeless desert that reminded me of Mexico; there was nothing, it seemed, beyond empty spaces filled with Georgia O'Keeffe–like skeletons of sheep. The only living creatures I saw were a few wild pigs and a skittish ram. I walked Niihau's empty beaches, plucked silver-dollar–size opihis from virgin tide pools, found a green glass ball lost from a Japanese fishnet, and left without ever meeting another soul, which made me sad; not much aloha to be had here.

Now, Niihau has changed. The island, fresh with recent rain, showed itself like an emerald in the blue sea. As we touched down on the black lava bed, on the beach, next to a new tin-roofed pavilion, a small welcoming party awaited our arrival. I knew immediately that my second visit would be different.

Several women, two little girls, and a paniolo, all residents of Niihau's lone village of Puuwai, had come to say aloha, play the ukulele, and talk story. They were very shy at first and spoke English very softly; when they spoke Hawaiian, which they did to each other, it sounded like music.

Soon, I felt myself an object of great scrutiny. The hard looks came from Momi, an island girl of 10 who had never left the island, who had never seen such a strange person up close. "You are a good man," she said. I laughed at her quick study and profound insight, and we became pals. I felt a kinship with all the sailors who ever jumped ship in the days of Captain Cook.

expeditions and, best of all, lead guided kayaking treks into Na Pali—not something you do willy-nilly. Only possible between May and September, the **Na Pali Quest** is a challenging 6-day guided paddle, camp, and hiking expedition from Hanalei to Polihale, an unforgettable 28-mile (more or less) trip. The trip costs $175 per person, per day and includes transportation to and from Princeville Airport, communal gear like sleeping bags, tents, and mess kits, and a well-appointed menu. You must be able to kayak 4 to 6 miles a day. This sea trek, limited to a dozen voyagers, is so popular that you must reserve a year in advance.

FOR A BIRD'S-EYE VIEW OF WAIMEA CANYON & THE NA PALI COAST

✪ **Will Squyres Helicopter Tours.** 3222 Kuhio Hwy. (P.O. Box 1770), Lihue, HI 96766. ☎ **808/245-8881** or 808/245-7541.

"Come, let's look for shells," Momi said. So we went in search of those precious little red and white and yellow shells that comprise the rare and precious Niihau shell leis, once worn by Hawaii's queens as necklaces. "Go when the tide is low, look real hard." That's what Momi told me, and she knows. I couldn't see them at first, which made Momi laugh out loud because it was so easy for her; in no time at all, dozens of shells spilled out of her open hand.

After you find 1,000 or more shells, you dig the grains of sand out of them, then pierce each shell with a needle, and string them all together into a beautiful necklace. All this is much easier said then done (which is why Niihau shell leis are outrageously expensive to buy; they range well into the thousands of dollars in shops all across the islands). I only found five or six shells, so Momi gave me some of hers.

When we tired of looking for shells, we went snorkeling off Nanina Beach at Puu Kole, which has to be the best place in all of Hawaii to snorkel. The water is crystal-clear because there's no freshwater runoff into the lagoons. The abundant fish are big and friendly, probably because they're not used to seeing humans close-up. And there are no crowds—just you and your buddy.

As we snorkeled, the deep blue water began to boil a few hundred yards offshore. We lifted our masks to look out to sea. Whales. Spy-hopping, tail-slapping whales, jumping straight out of the water. The most whales I had ever seen in Hawaiian waters. This great performance lasted more than an hour, and ended as suddenly as it began. We applauded. We didn't know what else to do.

After lunch, I hiked a gold-sand beach that seemed to stretch forever, past Japanese glass-ball floats and seashells and driftwood, and soon found myself completely out of sight of the others. A great silence fell over the entire place. I felt very distant from the world, standing there all alone on Niihau. It felt good to return to the company of the others.

When we lifted off in the helicopter, I thought Momi would wave her arm off as we flew away, back to Kauai and the rest of our lives. I still have the shells we found that day.

The 3-hour, once-in-a-lifetime adventure costs $235 and includes two landings, one at Nanina Beach at Puu Kole Point, the other at Keanahaki Bay, where Captain Cook first anchored, plus a close-up look at the white-tipped sharks in Shark's Cove. Call **Niihau Helicopters** (☎ **808/335-3500**).

I am holding on for dear life on a white-knuckle thrill ride up and over the Kalalau Valley on Kauai's wild north shore, and into a 5,200-foot vertical temple of Mount Waialeale, the most sacred place on the island and the wettest spot on earth. This death-defying ride is spectacular—and Will Squyres will be happy to take you on it, too.

The 1-hour flight starts in Lihue and takes you through Waimea Canyon, along the Na Pali Coast, and over Waialeale Crater and the two sets of waterfalls that appeared in *Fantasy Island*. Will flies Bell206B four-passenger helicopters because they have the best safety record—the first priority in choosing a copter tour company; Will also maintains a meticulous maintenance record in the salty environs of an island where rust never sleeps. He just took delivery of a new A-star 6-passenger copter with side-by-side seats (nobody sits backwards and everybody gets a window seat) and enlarged windows. A veteran pilot, Squyres has flown several thousand hours over Kauai since 1984, and knows the island, its ever-changing weather conditions, and his copters. Other good outfits operate on Kauai, and I've flown on most of them, but Will is the one. And Kauai's the island you need to see from a helicopter. A ticket is $159, but look for special discounts; book at least a day ahead.

Ohana Helicopter Tours. 3416 Rice St., Lihue. ☎ **808/245-3996** or 800/222-6989.

Hawaiian-born pilot Bogart Kealoha delights in showing his island his way: aboard one of his three A-Star helicopters. He takes you swooping over and through 12-mile-long Waimea Canyon on a memorable sightseeing flight that also includes the valleys and waterfalls of the Na Pali Coast. The 1-hour flight is $168 per person.

ECO-TOURS AROUND THE ISLAND
Hawaiian Wildlife Tours. P.O. Box 769, Kilauea, HI 96754. ☎ **808/639-2968.**

This is environmental education in action. Biologist Dr. Carl Berg will take you and up to three other friends out into the woods and down to the shoreline to see Kauai's native and vanishing species, from forest birds and flora to hoary bats, monk seals, and green sea turtles. His personalized tours last from 2 hours to a week, and are tailored to meet the season and weather, your physical abilities, and what you want to see. He leads tours to Hanalei taro fields to see wetland birds, Crater Hill to see nene geese, Mahaulepu to see wildflowers in the sand dunes, Kilauea Lighthouse to see oceanic birds, and much more. Tours are $45 per couple for the first hour, $25 for each additional hour.

PADDLING INTO HULEIA NATIONAL WILDLIFE REFUGE
Island Adventures. ☎ **808/245-9662.**

Ride the Huleia River through Kauai's 240-acre Huleia National Wildlife Refuge, the last stand of Kauai's endangered birds, in a 12-foot-long, virtually unsinkable canoe-shaped pirogue. You paddle up the picturesque Huleia (which appeared in *Raiders of the Lost Ark* and the remake of *King Kong*) under sheer pinnacles that open into valleys full of lush tropical plants, bright flowers, and hanging vines, where great blue herons and Hawaiian gallinules take wing. The 3-hour voyage, which starts at Nawiliwili Harbor, is ideal for all—especially movie buffs, birders, and great adventurers under 12. It costs $37, which includes lunch afloat. Wear a swimsuit, T-shirt, and boat shoes.

10 Seeing the Sights

by Rick Carroll

IN & AROUND LIHUE
Grove Farm Homestead. Nawiliwili Rd. (Hi. 58), 2 miles from Waapa Rd., Lihue. ☎ **808/245-3202.** Admission $3. Tours offered at 10am and 1pm Mon, Wed, Thur. Reserve a week in advance.

You can experience a day in the life of an 1860s sugar planter on a visit to Grove Farm Homestead, which shows how good life was (for some, anyway) when sugar was king. This is Hawaii's best remaining example of a sugar plantation homestead. Founded in 1864 by George N. Wilcox, a Hanalei missionary's son, Grove Farm was one of the earliest of Hawaii's 86 sugar plantations. A self-made millionaire, Wilcox died a bachelor in 1933 at age 94. His estate looks much like it did when he lived there, complete with period furniture, plantation artifacts, and Hawaiiana.

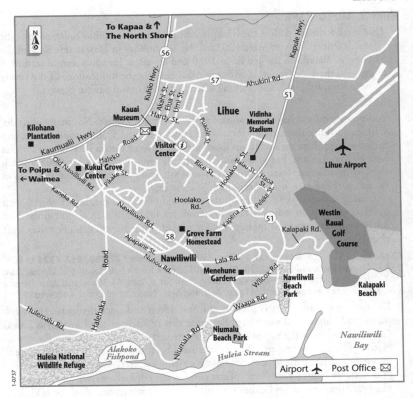

⭐ **Kauai Museum.** 4428 Rice St., Lihue. ☎ **808/245-6931.** Admission $5, seniors $4; kids under 17 free. Mon–Fri 9am–4:30pm, Sat 9am–1pm.

The history of Kauai is kept safe in an imposing Greco-Roman building that once served as the town library. This great little museum—it's the best in the outer islands—is worth a stop before you set out to explore Kauai. It contains a wealth of historical artifacts and information tracing the island's history from the beginning of time through "contact" (when Capt. James Cook "discovered" Kauai in 1778), the monarchy period, the plantation era, and to the present. You'll hear tales of the menehune (the mythical elflike people that built massive stone works in a single night) and see old poi pounders and idols, relics of sugar planters and paniolos, a nice sea-shell collection, old Hawaiian quilts, feather leis, a replica of a plantation worker's home, and much more—even a model of Cook's ship, the *HMS Resolution,* riding anchor in Waimea Bay. Vintage photographs by W. J. Senda, a Japanese immigrant of 1906, show old Kauai, while a contemporary video, shot from a helicopter, captures the island's natural beauty.

THE POIPU RESORT AREA

No Hawaii resort has a better entry: On Maluhia Road, eucalyptus trees planted in 1911 as a wind break for sugarcane fields now form a monumental tree tunnel. The leafy green and cool tunnel starts at Kaumualii Highway; you'll emerge at the beach, golden-red with perfect aquamarine waves rolling ashore.

PRINCE KUHIO PARK

This small roadside park is the birthplace of Prince Jonah Kuhio Kalanianaole, the "People's Prince," whose March 26 birthday is a holiday in Hawaii. He opened the beaches of Waikiki to the public in 1918 and served as Hawaii's second territorial delegate to the U.S. Congress. What remains here are the foundations of the family home, a royal fishpond, and a shrine where tributes are still paid in flowers.

Spouting Horn

You probably don't have a blowhole in your backyard. I don't. Not many of us do. Offhand, I think there are maybe two in Hawaii: one on Oahu's south shore, and the other right here on Kauai, on Kukuiula Bay beyond Kuhio Park (about 2 miles west of Maluhia and Poipu roads). It's quite a sight—big waves hit Kauai's south shore with sufficient force to send a spout of salt water about 10 feet or more up in the air; in the winter, it can get as high as six stories.

Usually souvenir vendors set up shop around here. You can buy T-shirts, shell necklaces, and postcards; my favorite shows Spouting Horn in its full glory. You might want to keep your money in your pocket, though; you can get better stuff elsewhere.

✪ **National Tropical Botanical Gardens.** Hailima Rd., Lawai. ☎ **808/332-7324** or 808/332-7361; reservations 808/742-2623. Admission $25 (one fee for both Lawai and Allerton Gardens). 2½-hour guided tours by reservation only, Tues–Sat at 9am, 11:30am, and 2pm. Reserve a week in advance in peak months of July, Aug, and Sept. No children under 4 allowed.

Discover an extraordinary collection of tropical fruit and spice trees, rare Hawaiian plants, and hundreds of varieties of flowers at this 186-acre preserve known as **Lawai Gardens,** said to be the largest collection of rare and endangered plants in the world. Native plants once written off as extinct have been discovered by botanists Steve Perlman and Kenneth Wood, who use rock climbing techniques to scale Kauai's impenetrable cliffs, where "lost" plants cling to the edge of survival. Back here, the plants are propagated, and either flourish here or are reintroduced to the wild. The results of this precedent-setting search-and-rescue mission may be seen at the gardens on guided 3-hour tours.

Nearby **Allerton Gardens,** a royal home site of Queen Emma in the 1860s, is known for its formal gardens in the tropics, a delicious kind of colonial decadence. It's set amidst fountains, streams, waterfalls, and European statuary where endangered green sea turtles are finally making a big comeback after Iniki.

Also see **Limahuli Garden,** which also falls under the National Tropical Botanical Gardens, in "Paradise Found: The North Shore," below.

SOUTHWEST KAUAI: WAIMEA CANYON & KOKEE STATE PARK
WAIMEA TOWN

Russian Fort Elizabeth State Historical Park

To the list of all who tried to conquer Hawaii, add the Russians. It didn't work out, though, despite a brief occupation. In 1815, a German doctor tried to claim Kauai for Russia, and supervised the construction of a fort in Waimea; but he and his handful of Russian compatriots were expelled by Kamehameha I a couple of years later.

Now a State Historic Landmark, the Russian Fort Elizabeth (named for the wife of Russia's Czar Alexander I) is on the eastern headlands overlooking the harbor, across from Lucy Kapahu Aukai Wright Beach Park. The fort, built Hawaiian-style with stacked lava rocks in the shape of a star, once bristled with cannons; it's now mostly in ruins. You can take a free, self-guided tour of the site, which affords a keen view of the west bank of the Waimea River, where Captain Cook landed, and the island of Niihau across the channel.

Kiki a Ola (Menehune Ditch)

Hawaiians were expert rock builders. They formed long lines and passed small stones hand over hand, and lifted stones weighing tons with ropes made from native plants; elaborate edifices were built using no mortar. Their mythic feats gave rise to fantastic tales of "menehunes," elflike people retained by Hawaiian kings to create massive stone works in a single night—reputedly for a payment of a single shrimp. An excellent example is Kiki a Ola, the so-called Menehune Ditch, with cut and dressed stones that form an ancient aqueduct that still directs water to irrigate taro ponds. Historians credit the work to ancient Hawaiian engineers, who applied their knowledge of hydraulics to accomplish flood control and irrigation. From Hi. 50, go *mauka* on Menehune Road; a plaque marks the spot about 1 1/2 miles up. Only a 2-foot-high portion of the wall can be seen today; the rest of the marvelous stone work is buried under the road bed.

THE GRAND CANYON OF THE PACIFIC: WAIMEA CANYON

The great gaping gulch known as Waimea Canyon is quite a sight; no other island has anything else like it. This valley, known for its reddish lava beds, reminds everyone who sees it of Arizona's Grand Canyon. Kauai's version is bursting with ever-changing color, just like its namesake. But it's smaller—only a mile wide, 3,567 feet deep, and 12 miles long.

All this grandeur was caused by a massive earthquake, which sent all the streams flowing into a single river, which then carved this picturesque canyon—quite an astonishing bit of erosion. Today, the Waimea River, a silver thread of water in the gorge, sometimes a trickle, often a torrent, but always there, cuts the canyon deeper, makes it wider, and nobody knows or can say what the final result will be 100 million years from now.

You can stop by the road and look at it, hike down in it, ride a horse along the rim, or swoop through it in a helicopter. For information on hiking through the canyon, see "Hiking & Camping," above; also see "Horseback Riding" and "Helicopter Rides, Zodiac Cruises & Guided Eco-Adventures," above.

The Drive Through Waimea Canyon & Up to Kokee

There are two ways to visit Waimea Canyon and reach Kokee State Park, 20 miles up from Waimea, by car: From the coastal road (Hi. 50), you can turn up Waimea Canyon Drive (Hi. 550) at Waimea town; or you can pass through Waimea and turn up Kokee Road (Hi. 55) at Kekaha. The climb is very steep from Kekaha, but Waimea Canyon Drive, the rim road, is narrower and rougher. A few miles up, the roads merge into Kokee Road.

The first good vantage point is **Waimea Canyon Lookout.** Take a peek at this gem and see why Mark Twain took one look and coined it the "Grand Canyon of the Pacific." From here, it's another 8 miles to Kokee. There are a few more lookout points along the way that offer spectacular views, such **Puu Hina Hina Lookout,** at 3,336 feet; be sure to pull over and spend a few minutes pondering this natural wonder. (The giant white object that looks like a golf ball and defaces the natural landscape is a radar station left over from the Cold War when we snooped on the Soviets.)

KOKEE STATE PARK

It's only 20 miles from Waimea to Kokee, but it's a whole different world, for the park is 4,345 acres of rain forest. You enter a new climate zone, where the breeze has a bite and trees look quite continental. You're in a cloud forest on the edge of an upland bog known as the Alakai Swamp, the largest bog in Hawaii, on the summit plateau of Kauai. Days are cool, wet, and mild with intermittent bright sunshine, not unlike Seattle on a good day. You'll be glad you brought your sweater, and be sure you know how to light a fire if you're staying over; overnight lows dip into the 40s. Such is the tropical paradox of Kauai.

The forest is full of native plants, such as Maile vine, mokihana berry, the ohia lehua tree, the iliau (similar to Maui's silversword), and imports like Australia's eucalyptus and even California's redwood. Pigs, goats, and black-tailed deer thrive in the forest, but the *moa*, or Polynesian jungle fowl (*Gallus gallus*), is the cock of the walk.

There's lots to see and do up here: Anglers fly-fish for rainbow trout (see "Hitting the Water," above), and hikers tackle the 45 trails that lace the Alakai Swamp. That's a lot of ground to cover, so you might want to plan on staying over. If pitching a tent is a little too rustic for you, there are some wonderful rustic cabins set in a grove of California redwoods; they're one of the best accommodations bargains in the islands (see "Accommodations," above for details). There's also a restaurant at **Kokee Lodge** that's open for continental breakfast and lunch every day (for details, see "Dining," above).

Just the Facts

When to Go   The park is open daily year-round. The best time to go is early in the morning, to see the panoramic view of Kalalau Valley from the lookout at 4,000 feet, before clouds obscure the valley and peaks.

Access Points   See "The Drive Through Waimea Canyon & Up to Kokee," above.
Information & Visitor Center   For information, contact the **State Division of Parks,** P.O. Box 1671, Lihue, HI 96766 (☎ **808/274-3446**); and the **Kokee Lodge Manager,** P.O. Box 819, Waimea, HI 96796 (☎ **808/335-6061**).

Right next to Kokee Lodge is the ✪ **Kokee Natural History Museum** (☎ **808/335-9975;** open daily 10am–4pm; free admission). This small, vital museum is the best place to learn about the forest and Alakai swamp before you set off hiking in the wild. The museum shop has great trail information, and local books and maps, including the official park trail map (50¢).

Seeing the Highlights

A **nature walk** with 35 native plants and trees is the best mini-intro to this rain forest; it starts behind the museum at the rare Hawaiian koa tree (which, you'll learn, has hard red wood, lemon-yellow flowers, and only lives on the Hawaiian Islands and in Australia). This easy, self-guided walk of about one-tenth of a mile takes about 20 minutes if you stop and look at all the plants; they're all identified along the way.

For details on hiking Kokee's 45 miles of trails on your own or on a guided hike with the Sierra Club, see "Hiking & Camping," above.

Four miles above Kokee Lodge is ✪ **Kalalau Lookout,** the spectacular climax of your drive through Waimea Canyon and Kokee. When you stand at the lookout, below you is a work in progress that began at least 5 million years ago. It's hard to stop looking; the view is breathtaking, especially when light and cloud shadows play across the red and orange cliffs.

THE COCONUT COAST
Fern Grotto

This is one of Kauai's oldest ("since 1947") and most popular tourist attractions. Ten times a day, every day, **Smith's Motor Boats** (☎ **808/821-6892**), and **Waialeale Boat Tours** (☎ **808/822-4908**) take 150 people up and down the river on motorized barges on a 90-minute, 2¹/₂-mile river trip capped by a visit to a moldy crevice in the volcanic crust of Kauai that's overwhelmed by maiden hair ferns. For some reason, this drippy green place up the river inspires otherwise clear-headed males of the species to propose marriage; some even get married here, and others renew their vows here. Go figure. However, if you've ever been in a fern bar, or even cruised up and down a river for more than 2 miles, you might want to skip this one. The large motor launches leave from Wailua Marina, at the mouth of the Wailea River, on hourly cruises from 9am to 4pm daily. Tickets are $10 adults, $5 kids; reservations are recommended.

WAILUA RIVER STATE PARK

Ancients called the Wailua River "the river of the great sacred spirit." Seven sacred temples once stood along this 20-mile river, fed by 5,148-foot Mount Waialeale, the wettest spot on earth—it gets 40 feet of rain a year and is the source of Kauai's waterfalls, rivers, and lush tropical look.

You can go up Hawaii's biggest navigable river by boat or kayak (see "Boating" and "Kayaking" in "Hitting the Water," above), or drive Kuamoo Road (Hi. 580), sometimes called the King's Highway, which goes inland along the north side river from Kuhio Highway (Hi. 56)—from the northbound lane, turn left at the stoplight just before the ruins of Coco Palms Resort—and past the heiau and historical sites to Opaekaa Falls and Keahua Arboretum, a State Division of Forestry attempt to reforest the watershed with native plants.

The entire district from the river mouth to the summit of Waialeale was once royal land. This sacred, historical site was believed to be founded by Puna, a Tahitian priest who, according to legend, arrived in one of the first double-hulled voyaging canoes to arrive in Hawaii, established a beachhead, declared Kauai his kingdom, and put everything in his sight under a kapu. All of Kauai's *ali'i* (royalty) are believed to be descended from Puna. Here in this royal settlement are remains of the seven temples, including a sacrificial *heiau,* a planetarium (a simple array of rocks in a celestial pattern), the royal birthing stones, and a stone bell to announce a royal birth. (You can still ring the bell—many people have—but make sure you have an announcement to make when it stops ringing.)

One-and-a-half miles up Hi. 580, the park has a nice overlook view of 40-foot Opaekaa Falls, probably the best-looking drive-up waterfalls on Kauai. With the scenic peaks of Makaleha mountains in the background and a restored Hawaiian village on the river banks, this waterfall (named, "rolling shrimp") is what the tourist bureau folks call an "eye-popping" photo op.

Near Opaekaa Falls overlook is **Poliahu Heiau,** the large black lava-rock temple of Kauai's last king, Kaumualii, who died on Oahu in 1824, after being abducted by King Kamehameha II. If you stop here, you'll notice two signs: One, an official 1928 bronze Territorial Plaque, which says that the royal heiau was built by menehunes, which it explains parenthetically as "Hawaiian dwarves or brownies." A more recent hand-painted sign warns visitors not to climb on the rocks, which are sacred to the Hawaiian people.

SLEEPING GIANT

If you squint your eyes just so when you're passing the 1,241-foot-high Nounou Ridge, which forms a dramatic backdrop to the coastal villages of Wailue and Waipouli, you may see the fabled Sleeping Giant. On Kuhio Hwy. just past the Waipouli Complex, a mile-long minimall, look *mauka* and you may see what appears to be the legendary giant named Puni, who, as the story goes, fell asleep after a great

The Coconut Coast

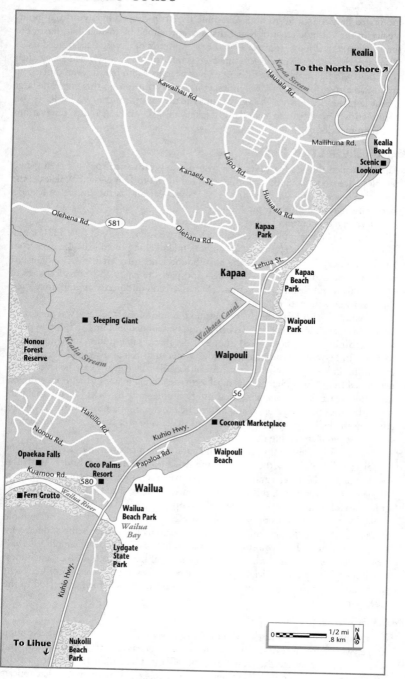

Kealia

To the North Shore ↗

Kapaa Stream

Hauaala Rd.

Kawaihau Rd.

Mailihuna Rd.

Kealia Beach

Laipo Rd.

Scenic Lookout ■

Kanaela St.

Hauaala Rd.

Olehena Rd.

581

Olehana Rd.

Kapaa Park

Lehua St.

Kapaa

Kapaa Beach Park

Sleeping Giant ■

Waikaea Canal

Waipouli Park

Nonou Forest Reserve

Kealia Stream

Waipouli

56

Haleilio Rd.

Coconut Marketplace ■

Kuhio Hwy.

Nonou Rd.

Papaloa Rd.

Waipouli Beach

Opaekaa Falls ■

Coco Palms Resort ■

Kuamoo Rd.

580

Wailua

Fern Grotto ■

Wailua River

Wailua Beach Park

Wailua Bay

Lydgate State Park

Kuhio Hwy.

0 ▬▬▬ 1/2 mi
.8 km

N

To Lihue ↓

Nukolii Beach Park

Hollywood Loves Kauai

More than 50 major Hollywood productions have been shot on Kauai ever since Hollywood discovered the island's spectacular natural beauty. Here are just a few:

- Manawaiopu Falls, Mount Waialeale, and other scenic areas around the island doubled for *Jurassic Park.*
- Kauai's lush rain forests formed a fantastic backdrop for Harrison Ford in both *Raiders of the Lost Ark* and *Indiana Jones and the Temple of Doom.*
- Mitzi Gaynor sang "I'm Gonna Wash That Man Right Outta My Hair" on Lumahai Beach in *South Pacific.*
- Ricky Nelson and Jack Lemmon sailed *The Wackiest Ship in the Army* (1960) up the Wailua River.
- Jessica Lange, Jeff Bridges, and Charles Grodin tangled with Hollywood's most famous gorilla in Honopu Valley in their remake of *King Kong* (1976).
- Elvis Presley married costar Joan Blackman near the Wailua River in *Blue Hawaii* (1961).
- Kauai's lush jungle doubled as a Vietnam war zone in the 1983 film *Uncommon Valor,* starring Gene Hackman.
- Beautiful Ke'e Beach, on the North Shore, masqueraded as Australia in the landmark miniseries *The Thornbirds,* starring Richard Chamberlain.
- Dustin Hoffman starred in *Outbreak,* the 1994 thriller filmed on Kauai about the spread of a deadly virus on a remote tropical island. He also appeared with Robin Williams and Julia Roberts in *Hook* (1991), in which Kauai appeared as Never Never Land.
- James Caan, Nicholas Cage, Sarah Jessica Parker, and Pat Morita shared laughs on Kauai (which appeared as itself) in *Honeymoon in Vegas.*

feast. If you don't see it at first, visualize it this way: His head is Wailua and his feet are Kapaa.

PARADISE FOUND: THE NORTH SHORE
ON THE ROAD TO HANALEI

The first place everyone should go on Kauai is Hanalei. The drive along **Kuhio Highway** (**Hi. 56**) displays Kauai's grandeur at its absolute best. Just before Kilauea, the air and the sea change, the light falls in a different way, and the last signs of development are behind you. Now there are roadside fruit stands, a little stone church in Kilauea, two roadside waterfalls, and the long stiltlike bridge over the Kalihiwai Stream and its green river valley that somehow always reminds me of Southeast Asia.

If you don't know a guava from a mango, stop off in Kilauea for a break at the cool, shady **Guava Kai Plantation** (at the end of Kuawa Rd.; ☎ **808/828-6121;** open daily 9am–5pm) for a refreshing free treat. After you take a walk through the orchards and see what a guava looks like on the tree, you can sample the juice of this exotic pink tropical fruit (which also makes a great jam or jelly—sold here, too).

Birders might want to stop off at **Kilauea Point National Wildlife Sanctuary,** 1 mile north of Kilauea, and the **Hanalei National Wildlife Refuge,** along Ohiki Road, at the west end of the Hanalei River Bridge. (For details, see "Birding," above.)

In the Hanalei Refuge, along a dirt road on a levee, you can see the **Hariguchi Rice Mill,** now a historic treasure.

Now the coastal highway heads due west and the showy ridge lines of Mount Namahana create a grand amphitheater. The two-lane coastal highway rolls over pastures of grazing cattle, past a tiny airport where helicopters buzz in and out, and the luxurious Princeville Hotel.

Six-and-a-half miles past Kilauea, just past the Princeville Shopping Center, is **Hanalei Valley Lookout.** Big enough for a dozen cars, this lookout attracts crowds of people, who peer over the edge into the 917-acre Hanalei River Valley. Green, green, green, so many shades of green: rice green, taro green, green streams, lace a patchwork of green ponds that back up to green velvet Bali Hai cliffs. Pause to catch the first sight of taro growing in irrigated ponds and maybe see an endangered Hawaiian black-necked stilt. Don't be put off by the crowds; this is definitely worth a look.

Farther along, a hairpin turn offers another scenic look at Hanalei town; then you cross the **Hanalei Bridge.** The Pratt truss steel bridge, prefabbed in New York City, was erected in 1912; it's now on the National Registry of Historic Landmarks. If it ever goes out, the nature of Hanalei will change forever; currently, this rusty, one-lane bridge (which must violate all kinds of Department of Transportation safety regulations) isn't big enough for a tour bus to cross.

You'll drive slowly past the Hanalei River banks and Bill Mowry's **Hanalei Buffalo Ranch,** where 200 American bison roam in the tropic sun; you may even see buffaloes grazing the pastures on your right. The herd is often thinned to make all-beef buffalo patties. (You wondered why there was a Buffalo Burger on the Ono Family Cafe menu, didn't you?)

Just past **Tahiti Nui** (see "Dining," above), turn right on Aku Road before Ching Young Village, then take a right on Weke Road; **Hanalei Beach Park** is a half-block ahead on your left (for details, see "Beaches," above).

If this exquisite 2-mile-long beach doesn't meet your expectations, head down the highway, where the next 9 miles of coast yield some of Kauai's other spectacular beaches, including **Lumahai Beach** (of *South Pacific* movie fame), **Tunnels,** where the 1960s puka-shell necklace craze began, and **Haena Beach Park** (see "Beaches," above). Once you've found your Bali Hai beach, stick around until sundown, then head back to one of the North Shore's restaurants for a Mai Tai and a fresh seafood dinner (see "Dining," above). Another perfect day in paradise, pal.

ATTRACTIONS ALONG THE WAY

Waioli Mission House Museum. Kuhio Hwy. (Hi. 56), Hanalei. ☎ **808/245-3202.** Free admission (donations gratefully accepted). Tues, Thurs, Sat 9am–3pm. Guided tours available at no charge.

If you're lucky, and time your visit just right, you can visit this 150-year-old mission house, which serves today as a living museum. It's a real treasure. Others in Honolulu are easier to see, but the Waioli Mission House retains its sense of place and most of its furnishings, so you can really get a clear picture of what life was like for the New England missionaries who came to Kauai to convert the heathens to Christianity.

Most mission houses are small, dark Boston cottages that violate the tropical sense of place. This two-story wood frame house, built in 1836 by Abner and Lucy Wilcox of New Bedford, Massachusetts, is an excellent example of how heathens converted the Christians, at least architecturally. The house features a lanai on both stories, with

The North Shore: Princeville & Hanalei

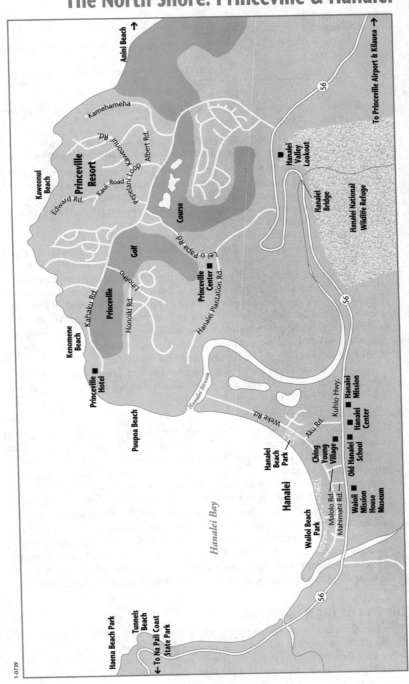

Anini Beach

To Princeville Airport & Kilauea

56

Kamehameha

Kaweonui Rd.

Albert Rd.

Princeville Resort

Kaweonui Beach

Edward Rd.

Kauf Road

Pepelani Loop

Hanalei Valley Lookout

Hanalei Bridge

Hanalei National Wildlife Refuge

Course

Lei o Papa Rd.

Golf

Kahaku Rd.

Liholino

Princeville

Honoiki Rd.

Princeville Center

Hanalei Plantation Rd.

56

Kenomene Beach

Princeville Hotel

Puupoa Beach

Hanalei Stream

Weke Rd.

Aku Rd.

Kuhio Hwy.

Hanalei Mission

Hanalei Center

Hanalei Beach Park

Ching Young Village

Old Hanalei School

Hanalei Bay

Hanalei

Malolo Rd.

Mahimahi Rd.

Waioli Mission House Museum

Waioli Beach Park

Haena Beach Park

Tunnels Beach

← To Na Pali Coast State Park

56

1-0739

491

Puff, the Magic Dragon lived by the sea, and frolicked in the autumn mist in a place called Hanalei . . .

—Peter, Paul, and Mary, "Puff, the Magic Dragon"

a cookhouse in a separate building. It has a lava-rock chimney, ohia-wood floors, and Hawaiian koa furniture.

✪ **Limahuli Garden.** Kuhio Hwy. (Hi. 56), Haena. ☎ **808/826-1053.** Admission $10 self-guided, $15 guided. Two-hour tours Tues–Fri, Sun. Advance reservations required for tours.

Out on Kauai's far North Shore, beyond Hanalei and the last wooden bridge, there's a mighty cleft in the coastal range where ancestral Hawaiians lived in what can only be called paradise: carved by a waterfall stream known as Limahuli, the valley is a lush tropical Eden at the foot of steepled cliffs Hollywood portrayed as Bali Hai in the film classic *South Pacific.*

That such a place still exists in a Hawaii so full of progress is a wonder. The 17-acre garden is at the heart of a 1,000-acre preserve begun in 1967 when gardener Juliet Rice Wichman drove out wild cattle, fenced in plants, and set out to save Kauai's endangered species in the remnant native forest. She and her grandson donated the property to the National Tropical Botanical Garden (see above), where botanists hope to save Kauai's endangered native plants. (And Limahuli's stream is sanctuary to the last five species of Hawaiian freshwater fish.) Plants are identified in Hawaiian, English, and by genus and species, family and origin. From taro to sugarcane, the mostly Polynesian imports tell the story of the people who cultivated the plants for food, medicine, clothing, shelter, and decoration.

This small, almost secret garden is ecotourism at its best. It appeals not just to green thumbs, but to all who love Hawaii's great outdoors. I didn't want to leave Limahuli; most likely, neither will you.

Ka Ulu O Laka Heiau

On a knoll above the boulders of Ke'e Beach (see "Beaches," above) stands a sacred altar of rocks, often draped with flower leis and ti leaf offerings, dedicated to Laka, the goddess of hula. It may seem like a primal relic from the days of idols, but it's very much in use today. Often, dancers (men and women) of Hawaii's hula *halau* (schools) climb the cliff, bearing small gifts of flowers. In Hawaiian myths, Lohiau, a handsome chief, danced here before the fire goddess Pele; their passion became *Haena,* which means the heat. Sometimes, in a revival of the old Hawaiian ways (once banned by missionaries), a mother of a newborn will deposit the umbilical cord of her infant at this sacred shrine. The site is filled with what Hawaiians call *mana,* or power. If you climb the cliff to visit this altar, you'll discover that you don't have to be Hawaiian to experience *mana.* To get there, from the west side of the beach, take the footpath across the big rocks almost to the point, then climb up the steep grassy hill.

THE END OF THE ROAD

To me, the real Hawaii always begins where the road stops. While this axiom isn't fail-safe, it's especially true on Kauai—for at the end of Hi. 56 the spectacular **Na Pali Coast** begins. To explore it, you've got to set out on foot or by boat or helicopter. For details on exploring this region, see "Hiking & Camping" and "Helicopter Rides, Zodiac Cruises & Guided Eco-Adventures," above.

11 Shops & Galleries

by Jocelyn Fujii

Selective, carefully targeted shopping can yield some surprises, but in general, it's safe to say that your credit cards will probably remain cooler here than on any other island except for Molokai. What's here? A few art galleries and boutiques and some languishing shopping centers—not much to distract you from afternoon hiking or snorkeling. The few gift items and treasures you'll find in Kilauea and Hanalei, however, may be among your best Hawaiian finds.

KAUAI ARTISTS TO WATCH FOR

✪ **Robert Hamada** works in a camphor-scented studio on the slopes of the mountain known as Sleeping Giant, turning out hand-turned bowls from trees he selects and prepares himself. He's well into his 70s now, but strong enough to log wood, wise enough to judge the growing conditions that create unique grain, and so skilled that his bowls are the finest in the state. The hau, kauila, camphor, kou, milo, and koa bowls are museum-quality and luminously grained, coveted among collectors nationwide. Rather than in galleries, you'll find Hamada's work spilling out of his living room and studio in his home deep in the mountains, and at selected Hawaii art shows. Call to see his Wailua studio (☎ **808/822-3229**).

Hamada is the only one of Kauai's many fine artists who keep a low profile: **Carol Bennett, Margaret Ezekiel, Laka Morton,** and **Doug Britt** are among Kauai's esteemed painters, turning out award-winning works that are widely applauded, yet which only occasionally appear in galleries. But the works of these artists are more than worth the pursuit. Britt displays and sells his paintings and handmade collectible furniture among the remarkable American arts and crafts at his gift shop, Ola's in Hanalei (see below). **David Boynton** is known for his nature photography; venues with his works for sale include the Kokee Museum and Kauai Museum. In Hanapepe, well-known impressionistic painter **James Hoyle** has relocated his gallery to the **Shimonishi Orchids** building on Hanapepe Road (see below).

GREEN MARKETS & FRUIT STANDS

The County of Kauai sponsors regular weekly **Sunshine Markets** throughout the island, featuring fresh Kauai Sunrise papayas, herbs and vegetables used in ethnic cuisines, and exotic fruit such as rambutan and atemoya, and the most exciting development in pineapple agriculture, low-acid white pineapple. Featuring grown-on-Kauai products, these Sunshine Markets, selling the full range of fresh produce and flowers at rock-bottom prices, present the perfect opportunity to see what's best and what's in season. Farmers sell their bounty from the backs of trucks or at tables set up under tarps. Mangoes during the summer, lettuces all year, fleshy bananas and juicy papayas, the full range of Filipino vegetables (wing beans, long beans, exotic squashes and melons), and an ever-changing rainbow of edibles are sold at this movable market. The biggest market features about 50 vendors at the **Kapaa New Town Park** in the middle of Kapaa town, Wednesdays at 3pm. Lihue's Sunshine Market, held Fridays at 3pm at the **Vidhina Stadium Parking Lot,** is close in size and extremely popular. The schedule for the other markets: **Koloa Ball Park,** Mondays at noon; **Kalaheo Neighborhood Center,** Tuesdays at 3:30pm; **Kilauea Neighborhood Center,** Thursdays at 4:30pm; **Kekaha Neighborhood Center,** Saturdays at 9am. For more information on the Sunshine Markets, call **808/241-6300** or 808/241-6390.

Those who miss the Sunshine Markets can shop instead at the privately run **Sunny Side Farmers Market** in the middle of Kapaa, open daily 8am to 8pm. Most people do a double-take when they pass the vivid stands of local flowers and produce, but be forewarned that they charge regular supermarket or tourist prices, not local farmers market prices. You'll find several varieties of papayas, mangoes in season, passion fruit, Hawaiian sugarloaf, low-acid white pineapples grown on Kauai, an exceptionally sweet Maui hybrid pineapple, locally grown organic lettuces, Maui onions, purple Molokai sweet potatoes, Molokai watermelons, and exotic fruits such as soursop and rambutan in season. Fruit preserves, gourmet breads, Taro Ko chips, and Kauai macadamia-nut cookies are among the made-on-Kauai products.

In other parts of the island, privately sponsored farmers markets provide additional venues for local agriculture. Like the county-sponsored Sunshine Markets, these local green markets offer the freshest, least expensive Kauai produce, picked hours or moments before the market. The **North Shore Farmers Market** at noon Saturdays, Kilauea Town Center, brings out the region's prominent organic farmers with their extraordinary lettuces and baby greens, papayas, and fruits in season.

The breadbasket of the island, Kilauea is also home to two of our favorite fruit stands on Kauai: **Mango Mama's** and **Banana Joe's,** both prominently signed along Highway 56. Both offer splendid selections of fresh fruit smoothies and local produce, along with Kauai specialties such as gourmet honey and nonperishable food items. Banana Joe's, an old favorite, offers dried fruit and macadamia nuts as well.

Also on the north shore, about a quarter-mile past Hanalei in an area called Waipa, the **Hawaiian Farmers of Hanalei,** anywhere from a dozen to 25 farmers, gather along the main road with their budget-friendly, just-picked produce. The farmers market is held every Tuesday at 2pm. You'll find unbelievably priced papayas (in some seasons, several for a dollar, ready to eat), organic vegetables, inexpensive tropical flowers, avocados and mangoes in season, and when possible, fresh seafood.

In Hanapepe town in west Kauai, the whistle goes off Thursdays at 3:30pm, causing a feeding frenzy among shoppers as they descend upon the avocadoes, papayas, mangoes, coconuts, beans, melons, eggplants, guavas, passion fruits, tomatoes, and whatever lines the road at the **Farmers Market in Hanapepe,** sponsored by the Hanapepe United Church of Christ. The market is so popular with local people, who make it a part of their weekly shopping ritual, that the produce is often sold out in 45 minutes. The market is across from the Hanapepe Post Office, at Kona Street and Hi. 50.

SHOPPING AROUND THE ISLAND
LIHUE & ENVIRONS

Downtown Lihue   In downtown Lihue, the gift shop of the **Kauai Museum** is your best bet for made-on-Kauai arts and crafts, from Niihau shell leis to books, woodworks, lauhala products, and more.

Kukui Grove Center, at Kaumualii Highway (Hi. 50) and Old Nawiliwili Road, alas, is another story. At one time the commercial center of the island, it staggers under the weight of change. There are many empty spaces, and traffic is far from what it used to be. But **Liberty House** is as department-storish as ever; its ever-economic **Penthouse** discount store, two doors away, draws budget-conscious shoppers to its serviceable selection of footwear, aloha shirts, women's wear, china, and housewares, all at severely discounted prices. The nearby **Longs Drugs** provides for basic needs, and affordable **Dan's Sports Shop** meets just about all sporting needs. At the **Indo-Pacific Trading Company,** you'll find Indonesian imports and artifacts—jewelry, textiles, carvings, temple bells, pareus, accessories. Not to be missed is the **Kauai**

Products Store, a respectable showcase of made-on-the-island products, from soaps to paintings to clothing, Kauai coffee, Kukui guava jams, fabrics, and Niihau shell leis. (For a list of Kauai products available, call **808/246-3939.**) Across the mall is the **Deli and Bread Connection,** selling soups, sandwiches, and deli items among the pots, china, coffeemakers, and hundreds of kitchen gadgets that crowd the aisles of this popular shop.

In Nearby Nawiliwili   Down the road from Lihue in Nawiliwili, on the road between Nawiliwili and Kukui Grove, at a complex called **Anchor Cove** on Kalapaki Bay, **The Amber Door,** at 3416 Rice St., is chockablock with salt and pepper shakers, Depression glass, collectible linens, and assorted vintage treasures from Hawaii and the rest of America. Timing and luck may bring you face-to-face with an antique wooden wagon-carried cradle ($425), a set of must-have 1900s china, or a mid-19th-century watercolor looking for a new home.

Across the street, at the **Pacific Ocean Plaza,** fashion slaves make a beeline for **Bamboo Lace,** an ultrachic boutique where luxury bath products, casual wear, inexpensive shoes, and one-of-a-kind gifts (not to mention a bountiful sale rack) are sold in a stylish, airy corner.

Kilohana Plantation   Kilohana, the 35-acre Tudor-style estate that sprawls across the landscape in Puhi, on Hi. 50 between Lihue and Poipu, is an architectural marvel that houses a sprinkling of galleries and shops around the popular Gaylord's restaurant (see "Dining," above). Since the Stones Gallery closed, however, there's little that's extraordinary or recommendable. Try the **Country Store** on the ground level, where you'll find Island and American crafts of decent quality, such as Jennifer Pontz–blasted glassware, koa music boxes, bark cloth cushions, chenille throws, hats, pottery, posh picnic baskets, designer wood chopsticks, and Hawaiian-themed porcelain tiles. On the other side of Gaylord's, the **Kilohana and Kahn galleries** offer a mix of crafts and two-dimensional art, from originals to affordable prints, at all levels of taste. Some works to watch for: wildlife artist Joy Shannon's photographically precise drawings of Kauai hula dancers; David Warren's monotypes; and Patrice Pendarvis's vivid watercolors.

THE POIPU RESORT AREA

Expect mostly touristy shops in Poipu, the island's resort mecca; you'll find T-shirts, souvenirs, black pearls, jewelry, and the usual quota of tired Wyland marine art and trite hand-painted silks. A quick stroll through the characterless **Poipu Shopping Village** (2360 Kiahuna Plantation Dr.), as well as the dependably overpriced resort gift shops, will give you an idea of what's available.

In neighboring Old Koloa Town, you'll find everything from **Lappert's Ice Cream** to **Crazy Shirts** T-shirts and the **Kahn Gallery,** one of the island's more reliable showcases for fine art by local artists. Look for **Kauai Fine Arts** if you have a taste for antique maps and prints, and for the **Sueoka Store** on Koloa's main drag, Koloa Road, for groceries and everyday necessities.

A few doors down from Sueoka's is the **Koloa Fish Market** (☎ **808/742-6199**), a tiny corner stand with plate lunches, prepared foods, and two stools on a closet-size veranda. It's gaining an islandwide following with its excellent fresh fish poke (several kinds), $5.95 Hawaiian-food specials, and seared ahi to go, peppered, perfectly seared, and sliced. It's as good as anything you'd find in the most reputable Hawaii restaurants, and makes a great addition to a picnic.

On Poipu Road between Koloa and Poipu, the **Kukuiula Store** is a waystop for everything from produce and sushi to go, paper products, sunscreen, beverages, and groceries.

SOUTHWEST KAUAI

Hanapepe This west Kauai hamlet is becoming a haven for artists, but finding them requires some vigilance. The center of town is off of Hi. 50; turn right on Hanapepe Road just after Eleele if you're driving from Lihue. First you'll smell the **Taro Ko** chips cooking in a tiny, modest kitchen at the east end of town, where these sumptuous lavender chips, dusted with nothing more than garlic salt, are handmade by the farmers who grow the taro in a nearby valley. Past Taro Ko chips (which make great gifts to go, by the way), Hanapepe Road is lined with gift shops and galleries, among them the cherubic **Aloha Angels,** where everything is angel-themed or angel-related; it may be too saccharine for many, but the charming owner has amassed a small and fascinating book selection. Across the street, the **Kauai Village Gallery,** housed in a building that was a set on the original *Thornbirds,* offers ho-hum Kauai art. A standout on this strip is **Kauai Fine Arts,** an odd mix that works: antique maps and prints of Hawaii, authentic Polynesian tapa, rare wiliwili seed lei, old Matson liner menus, and a few pieces of contemporary island-art. Down the street, in the **Shimonishi Orchids** building—a recommended stop for orchid lovers—the well-known impressionistic painter, James Hoyle, has set up his new gallery, surrounded by flowers and the colors that inspire him.

If you do take the turnoff into Hanapepe from Hi. 50 to reach these galleries (and the widely touted Hanapepe Bookstore Cafe and Espresso Bar; see "Dining," above), you'll miss the island's most popular purveyor of lilikoi cream pie, Jackson Wong's **Omoide Deli,** an easy-to-miss, sterile cafeteria-deli right on the highway. Stop in before or after lunch, coming or going from the west side; the lilikoi cream pie, sold whole or in individual slices, is highly recommended.

Also on Hi. 50, at Kona Street across from the Hanapepe Fire Station, the Hanapepe United Church of Christ opens its **Kokua Thrift Shop** Mondays from 9am to noon. Secondhand shoppers, take note: Many an inveterate thrift shopper has walked away with a prized aloha shirt, muumuu, kukui-nut lei, or other vintage collectible, all at rock-bottom prices. The "local-kine" booty is a matter of luck and timing, but this thrift shop is the pride and joy of the Hanapepe congregation, and rife with possibilities.

Waimea Neighboring Waimea town is filled more with edibles than art, with Kauai's favorite native supermarket, **Big Save,** serving as the one-stop shop for area residents and passersby heading for the uplands of Kokee State Park, some 4,000 feet above this sea-level village. A cheerful distraction for lovers of Hawaiian collectibles is **Collectibles and Fine Junque** on Hi. 50, where you'll discover what it's like to be the proverbial bull in a china shop (even a knapsack makes it hard to get through the aisles). Heaps of vintage linens, racks of choice aloha shirts and muumuus, rare glassware (and junque, too), books, ceramics, authentic 1950s cotton chenille bedspreads, and a back room full of bargain-priced secondhand goodies always capture my attention. This is my favorite stop in Waimea.

THE COCONUT COAST

Kapaa As you make your way to the North Shore, you'll wind through Kapaa, where all the stops are along the main thoroughfare, Hi. 56. Don't get your hopes up; quality goods are slim in this neck of the woods. The **Coconut Marketplace** features the ubiquitous **Elephant Walk** gift shop, **Gifts of Kauai,** and various other underwhelming souvenir and clothing shops sprinkled among the ice cream, noodle, and sunglass huts. One of the more attractive stops is the burnished, amber-washed **Indo-Pacific Trading Company,** sister store to the one in Kukui Grove.

Shops & Galleries 497

Nearby, set back from the main road across from Foodland, **Marta's Boat** is one of the island's more appealing boutiques for children and women. The shop is a tangle of accessories, toys, chic clothing with out-of-the-ordinary labels, and unusual gift items. Next door, **Ambrose's Kapuna Natural Foods** sells fresh Kauai fruit, nut butters, vitamins, and a small selection of healthy foods.

On the opposite side of the main highway, the green-and-white wooden storefronts of **Kauai Village,** put on the map by A Pacific Cafe (see "Dining," above), house everything from marine art (**Wyland Galleries**) to yin chiao Chinese cold pills and organic produce at **Papayas Natural Foods.** Although overpriced in some areas, Papayas carries the full range of health food products and is your best bet in the area for vitamins, hot, prepared health foods to go, health-conscious cosmetics, and bulk food items. **Longs Drugs** and **Safeway** are the familiar anchors for groceries and staples.

Less than a mile away on the main road, the **Waipouli Variety Store** is Kapaa's version of Maui's fabled Hasegawa General Store—a tangle of fishing supplies, T-shirts and thongs, beach towels and souvenirs. Fishermen love this store as much as cookie lovers swear by nearby **Popo's Cookies,** the ne plus ultra of store-bought cookies on the island. Popo's chocolate chip, macadamia nut, and other varieties of butter-rich cookies are among the most sought-after food items to leave the island.

Across the street a few feet away, in what is the old Wailua golf clubhouse, **Kia Gallery** is a must-see for Island craft lovers. Affordable lauhala mats, Sig Zane aloha wear, native wood calabashes, jewelry, and interior and household accessories with a distinctively Hawaiian flavor fill this corner treasure trove.

In Kapaa town, **Earth Beads,** on the main drag (Hi. 56), sells beads, jewelry, gemstones, and crafts materials along with a small selection of accessories for self and home. Across the street is the town's stellar newcomer, Island Hemp & Cotton, where Hawaii's most stylish selection of this miracle fabric is sold: gorgeous silk-hemp dresses, linen-hemp sportswear, and cheap, comfortable clothing and accessories that have shed the hippie image.

THE NORTH SHORE

Like Haleiwa on Oahu, Kauai's North Shore has emerged as the premier shopping destination on the island. Chic galleries and sophisticated shops, such as ✪ **Kong Lung** in Kilauea, off Hi. 56 on Kilauea Road (in a 1942 stone building, the last to be built in Kilauea Plantation), and **Ola's** and **Yellowfish Trading Company** in Hanalei (see below), have launched these former hippie villages as must-stop shopping spots. Although Hanalei is toward the end of the road for those coming from Poipu and west Kauai, my advice is to save time, energy, and some discretionary funds for this end of the island, because the few shops that are here speak volumes about quality over quantity. Kong Lung, for example, a tad snobby as it has become, nevertheless is a showcase of design, style, and quality items, from top-of-the-line bath products to aloha shirts, jewelry, ceramics, women's wear, china, stationery, and personal and home accessories. It's pricey, but there's no other store like it on the island.

In Hanalei, at ✪ **Ola's** by the Hanalei River on Kuhio Highway (Hi. 560) after the bridge (before the main part of Hanalei town), Sharon and Doug Britt have amassed a head-turning assortment of American and Island crafts, including Doug Britt's paintings and the one-of-a-kind furniture that he makes out of found objects, driftwood, and previously used materials. Britt's works—armoires, desks, tables, lamps (one had a Hawaiian thatched hale with a family inside it that lit up), bookshelves—often serve as the display surfaces for others' work, so look carefully. Lundberg Studio handblown glass, exquisite jewelry, hand-painted glass candlesticks, intricately wrought pewter switchplates, and many other fine works fill this tasteful, seductive shop.

Next door to Ola's, **Kai Kane** is a good source of aloha wear for men and women. Briny, brawny wave riders head straight for the second floor, where surfboards made by the up-and-coming North Shore shapers are sold to hard-core Hanalei Bay habitués. On the ground floor, Avanti shirts and dresses, Flax linen separates, Cut Loose dresses, hats, and an ample selection of casual wear offer great choices for the island lifestyle.

From health foods to groceries to bakelite jewelry, the **Ching Young Village Shopping Center** in the heart of Hanalei covers a lot of bases. People are never in a rush here, and there are always clusters of people lingering at the few tables outdoors, where tables of Kauai papayas beckon from the entrance of the **Hanalei Health and Natural Foods** store. Next door, **Hot Rocket** is ablaze with Cafe shirts, Jams sportswear, flamingo china, and, for collectors, the finest array of bakelite accessories on the island.

Across the street in the **Hanalei Center,** the standout boutique is ✪ **Yellowfish Trading Company,** where owner Gritt Benton's impeccable eye and zeal for collecting are reflected in the 1940s vases, bark-cloth upholstery, hand-painted silk lampshades, unusual books, must-have vintage textiles, and the occasional whimsical treasure such as an old Hopalong Cassidy lunch box.

12 Kauai After Dark

by Jocelyn Fujii

Suffice it to say that one does not come to Kauai to trip the night fantastic. For that you go to Maui or Oahu, but not Kauai. This is the island for winding down—from New York, Houston, even the hiking trails of Kokee or the Na Pali Coast.

There are two dance clubs on the island: **Gilligan's Disco** at the Outrigger Kauai Beach Hotel (4331 Kauai Beach Dr., Lihue; ☎ **808/245-1955**), and **Kuhio's** at the Hyatt Regency Kauai Resort & Spa (1571 Poipu Rd.; ☎ **808/742-1234;** see below). Gilligan's is open Fridays and Saturdays from 9:30pm to 2am, with a $5 cover charge. In the Outrigger's **Mele Lounge,** dancer Pua Kaholokula and her husband, gifted musician Robbie Kaholokula, blend their talents in Hawaiian music and dance on Mondays, Thursdays, Fridays, and Saturdays from 7:30 to 10pm. The Outrigger's **Jasmine Ballroom** is the scene for Leilani's Luau on Tuesday evenings, an all-Hawaiian buffet dinner show produced by the Kaholokulas for the hotel.

On the other side of the island, chic Kuhio's (see above) is the entertainment and dance center of the south shore, open 9pm to 1:30am Fridays and Saturdays. The art nouveau room features state-of-the-art technology (14 television monitors, sleek dance floor) to highlight its contemporary top-40s music selection. The $5 cover charge is waived for hotel guests. The Hyatt's **Stevenson's Library** revs up with live jazz from 9pm to 1:30am Friday through Monday evenings.

Index

ACCOMMODATIONS

FROMMER'S COMPLETE TRAVEL GUIDES

*(Comprehensive guides to destinations around the world, with
selections in all price ranges—from deluxe to budget)*

Acapulco/Ixtapa/Taxco
Alaska
Amsterdam
Arizona
Atlanta
Australia
Austria
Bahamas
Bangkok
Barcelona, Madrid & Seville
Belgium, Holland & Luxembourg
Berlin
Bermuda
Boston
Budapest & the Best of Hungary
California
Canada
Cancún, Cozumel & the Yucatán
Caribbean
Caribbean Cruises & Ports of Call
Caribbean Ports of Call
Carolinas & Georgia
Chicago
Colorado
Costa Rica
Denver, Boulder & Colorado Springs
Dublin
England
Florida
France
Germany
Greece
Hawaii
Hong Kong
Honolulu/Waikiki/Oahu
Ireland
Italy
Jamaica/Barbados
Japan
Las Vegas
London
Los Angeles
Maryland & Delaware
Maui

Mexico
Mexico City
Miami & the Keys
Montana & Wyoming
Montréal & Québec City
Munich & the Bavarian Alps
Nashville & Memphis
Nepal
New England
New Mexico
New Orleans
New York City
Northern New England
Nova Scotia, New Brunswick & Prince
    Edward Island
Paris
Philadelphia & the Amish Country
Portugal
Prague & the Best of the Czech Republic
Puerto Rico
Puerto Vallarta, Manzanillo & Guadalajara
Rome
San Antonio & Austin
San Diego
San Francisco
Santa Fe, Taos & Albuquerque
Scandinavia
Scotland
Seattle & Portland
South Pacific
Spain
Switzerland
Thailand
Tokyo
Toronto
U.S.A.
Utah
Vancouver & Victoria
Vienna
Virgin Islands
Virginia
Walt Disney World & Orlando
Washington, D.C.
Washington & Oregon

FROMMER'S FRUGAL TRAVELER'S GUIDES
(The grown-up guides to budget travel, offering dream vacations at down-to-earth prices)

Australia from $45 a Day
Berlin from $50 a Day
California from $60 a Day
Caribbean from $60 a Day
Costa Rica & Belize from $35 a Day
Eastern Europe from $30 a Day
England from $50 a Day
Europe from $50 a Day
Florida from $50 a Day
Greece from $45 a Day
Hawaii from $60 a Day

India from $40 a Day
Ireland from $45 a Day
Italy from $50 a Day
Israel from $45 a Day
London from $60 a Day
Mexico from $35 a Day
New York from $70 a Day
New Zealand from $45 a Day
Paris from $65 a Day
Washington, D.C. from $50 a Day

FROMMER'S PORTABLE GUIDES
(Pocket-size guides for travelers who want everything in a nutshell)

Charleston & Savannah
Las Vegas

New Orleans
San Francisco

FROMMER'S IRREVERENT GUIDES
(Wickedly honest guides for sophisticated travelers)

Amsterdam
Chicago
London
Manhattan

Miami
New Orleans
Paris
San Francisco

Santa Fe
U.S. Virgin Islands
Walt Disney World
Washington, D.C.

FROMMER'S AMERICA ON WHEELS
(Everything you need for a successful road trip, including full-color road maps and ratings for every hotel)

California & Nevada
Florida
Mid-Atlantic
Midwest & the Great Lakes
New England & New York

Northwest & Great Plains
South Central &Texas
Southeast
Southwest

FROMMER'S BY NIGHT GUIDES
(The series for those who know that life begins after dark)

Amsterdam
Chicago
Las Vegas
London

Los Angeles
Miami
New Orleans

New York
Paris
San Francisco